The Forties in America

The
Forties
in America

Volume III

Sad Sack—Zoot suits

Appendixes

Indexes

Editor

Thomas Tandy Lewis
St. Cloud State University

SALEM PRESS
Pasadena, California
Hackensack, New Jersey

Editor in Chief: Dawn P. Dawson

Editorial Director: Christina J. Moose

Project and Development Editor: R. Kent Rasmussen

Manuscript Editors: Tim Tiernan, A. J. Sobczak, Christopher Rager, Rebecca Kuzins

Acquisitions Editor: Mark Rehn

Editorial Assistant: Brett Weisberg

Research Supervisor: Jeffry Jensen

Photo Editor: Cynthia Breslin Beres

Indexer: R. Kent Rasmussen

Production Editor: Joyce I. Buchea

Graphics and Design: James Hutson

Layout: Mary Overell

Title page photo: *Jackie Robinson shaking hands with the Brooklyn Dodgers batboy while crossing home plate after hitting a home run that scored Dodger teammates Duke Snider (4) and Gene Hermanski (22). Carl Furillo (6) awaits his turn at bat. After breaking the color line in Major League Baseball in 1947, Robinson went on to a sensational career that included rookie of the year honors, several World Series titles, and several National League most valuable player awards.* (Bettmann/CORBIS)

Cover images: (pictured clockwise, from top left): Hiroshima atom bomb blast, 1945 (The Granger Collection, New York); Joe DiMaggio, 1947 (Time & Life Pictures/Getty Images); Betty Grable, pin up girl, 1942 (The Granger Collection, New York); U.S. bombers formation, 1942 (The Granger Collection, New York)

Library of Congress Cataloging-in-Publication Data

The forties in America / editor, Thomas Tandy Lewis.
    p. cm.
Includes bibliographical references and index.
    ISBN 978-1-58765-659-0 (set : alk. paper) — ISBN 978-1-58765-660-6 (vol. 1 : alk. paper) — ISBN 978-1-58765-661-3 (vol. 2 : alk. paper) — ISBN 978-1-58765-662-0 (vol. 3 : alk. paper)
    1. United States—Civilization—1945—Encyclopedias. 2. United States—Civilization—1918-1945—Encyclopedias. 3. Canada—Civilization—1945—Encyclopedias. 4. United States—History—1933-1945—Encyclopedias. 5. United States—History—1945-1953—Encyclopedias. 6. Canada—History—1945—Encyclopedias. 7. Canada—History—1914-1945—Encyclopedias. 8. Nineteen forties—Encyclopedias. I. Lewis, Thomas T. (Thomas Tandy)
    E169.12.F676 2011
    973.91—dc22
2010028115

■ Table of Contents

xlv

■ Complete List of Contents

Volume I

Volume II

Volume III

S

Sabotage. *See* **Wartime sabotage**

■ *Sad Sack*

Identification   Military-themed comic strip begun during World War II
Creator   George Baker (1915-1975)
Dates   Syndicated 1942-1960

Sergeant George Baker's wordless comic strip about a hapless enlisted man in the U.S. Army helped boost morale for American soldiers, who identified with the lowly victim of the many absurdities, bureaucracies, ironies, hardships, and humiliations of Army life.

Although Baker's cartoon creation *Sad Sack* continued as a newspaper strip until 1960, and as a children's comic book until 1982, the strip's most important period was from June of 1942 until the end of World War II three years later. It appeared in *Yank*, a weekly Army magazine for military personnel.

The strip featured a dumpy, nondescript American soldier in a series of wordless depictions of the life of the enlisted man during the 1940's. Each weekly entry was a series of eight to ten unframed panels, in which the Sad Sack always came out on the bottom of the heap. The Sad Sack's name came from scatological Army slang for a loser, a "sad sack of s——t," and the character immediately became the average enlisted man's self-image. An instant hit, the strip was first collected in book form in 1944.

Impact   Near the end of the war, Baker was discharged, and he took his Sad Sack character into civilian life, syndicating *Sad Sack* as a newspaper strip. In 1946, Sad Sack appeared in a short-lived radio show starring Herb Vigran. Three years later, it was turned into a comic book. In 1957, the character was used as a film vehicle for actor Jerry Lewis, though his portrayal was more madcap than Baker's depiction of the cartoon version of the character.

John R. Holmes

Further Reading
Arnold, Mark. *Fun Ideas Productions Presents the Best of the Harveyville Fun Times!* Saratoga, Calif.: Fun Ideas, 2006.
Hargrove, Marion. *George Baker, The Sad Sack.* New York: Simon & Schuster, 1944.
Strickler, Dave. *Syndicated Comic Strips and Artists, 1924-1995: The Complete Index.* Cambria, Calif.: Comics Access, 1995.

See also   Army, U.S.; Comic books; Comic strips; Newspapers; World War II.

■ St. Laurent, Louis

Identification   Prime minister of Canada, 1948-1957
Born   February 1, 1882; Compton, Quebec, Canada
Died   July 25, 1973; Quebec City, Quebec, Canada

Canadian minister of foreign affairs and prime minister during the 1940's, St. Laurent helped forge a greater unity in domestic politics, an increased federal role in the economy, and a new role for Canada in foreign affairs.

When Canada entered World War II, the chief task facing Canada's longest-serving prime minister, William Lyon Mackenzie King, was to maintain national unity. French Canadians were less eager to follow Great Britain's lead in the war effort and were opposed to the prospect of conscription, which was seemingly necessary for Canada's war mobilization. In December, 1941, King made a surprising move: He appointed a fifty-nine-year-old Quebec lawyer with little previous political experience—Louis St. Laurent—to join his cabinet as minister of justice.

Cabinet Minister   The appointment of St. Laurent paid off. St. Laurent was of French-English ancestry and completely bilingual. His support of King's decision in 1944 to institute a draft for soldiers to fight

Canadian prime minister Louis St. Laurent. (National Archives)

overseas helped win acceptance from Quebecers. It also enhanced St. Laurent's reputation as a mature, forward-looking leader with appeal to both English and French Canadians. At war's end, King sent St. Laurent as the Canadian delegate to the founding conference for the new United Nations in San Francisco, reflecting St. Laurent's desire to help shape Canada's foreign affairs. In 1946, St. Laurent was appointed secretary of state for external affairs. As secretary, he undertook to advance the collective security of the Western nations in the face of the Cold War. Overcoming King's reluctance, St. Laurent arranged for Canada to participate in U.N. efforts in 1947 to stabilize the Korean peninsula.

Prime Minister In 1948, King retired from political life. St. Laurent was elected his successor as leader of the Canadian Liberal Party. On November 15, 1948, St. Laurent was sworn in as Canada's twelfth prime minister. He was reelected overwhelmingly a short time afterward, on June 27, 1949. St. Laurent's career as prime minister reflected his vision of a mod-

ern, postwar Canada, as can be seen in four areas: increased unity at home, increased economic leadership by the federal government, increased sovereignty and independence from Great Britain, and increased influence in world affairs.

St. Laurent himself symbolized the unity of the English and French cultures that made up Canada. He sought to bind Canada's vast spaces, as modern engineering and a prosperous economy enabled the knitting together of Canada's far-flung provinces. In 1948, Canada began building the Trans-Canada Highway to connect all of Canada. In 1949, he secured the entry of Newfoundland into the confederation as Canada's tenth province. St. Laurent promoted direct federal assistance to citizens through Canada's social insurance and universal pension systems.

As to sovereignty, St. Laurent sought to formalize Canada's independence from Great Britain. For example, in 1949, he elevated the status of the Supreme Court of Canada as the court of last resort by disallowing appeals to the Judicial Committee of the British Privy Council. Likewise, in the British North America Act of 1949, Canada gained limited powers to amend its own constitution, without securing the consent of the British parliament. A more sovereign Canada also looked for greater independence from Great Britain in foreign policy. With the advent of the Cold War, St. Laurent looked less to Great Britain for leadership in international affairs and more to the United States. In this period, Canada's military forces and defenses began integrated operations with those of the United States. Canada was an enthusiastic founding signatory of the North Atlantic Treaty Organization (NATO) in April, 1949, and contributed actively to the U.N. operations when the Korean War broke out in June, 1950. St. Laurent also foresaw the unique role Canada could play as a multiethnic, prosperous former colony of Great Britain. His support for the April 28, 1949, London Declaration was crucial in helping to adapt the Commonwealth of Nations to allow inclusion for fully independent, non-English nations such as India. In Canada, full citizenship was extended for the first time to Asian Canadians.

St. Laurent is often portrayed as Canada's first modern campaigner, as he became affectionately known as "Uncle Louis" through his many appearances. St. Laurent continued to serve as prime minister until 1957. While campaigning, he would often say, "In Canada's century, the best is yet to come." An assessment of St. Laurent as prime minister depends on what one believes about the direction the Liberal Party took the nation, but there can be little doubt that during the late 1940's St. Laurent was the leader in taking steps toward a modernized confederation.

Impact The 1940's, marked in the first half by World War II and in the second half by the Cold War, was a pivotal decade for Canada, as it was for most nations. Canada entered the decade as a largely insular confederation, obedient to Great Britain in foreign policy, and divided among English and French cultures in domestic affairs. It emerged from the decade more unified as a nation, more independent from Great Britain, and more active on the global stage. The federal government began to see itself as responsible for the Canadian economy and undertook massive infrastructure projects and increased social insurance programs. It would be too much to say that this was solely the work of St. Laurent, but perhaps it is not too much to see him as the symbol of a more confident and internationalist Dominion.

Howard Bromberg

Further Reading

Bothwell, Robert. *The New Penguin History of Canada.* Toronto: Penguin Books, 2008. Broad-ranging history of Canada, focusing on political events and foreign affairs.

Brown, Craig, ed. *The Illustrated History of Canada.* Toronto: Key Porter Books, 2002. Collection of essays on the course of Canadian history by six Canadian historians. Lavishly illustrated.

Pickersgill, J. W. *My Years with Louis St. Laurent: A Political Memoir.* Toronto: University of Toronto Press, 1975. An inside and favorable look at St. Laurent's administration by a former Liberal Party minister and St. Laurent's closest political ally.

Thomson, Dale. *Louis St. Laurent: Canadian.* New York: St. Martin's Press, 1968. By St. Laurent's private secretary, a comprehensive biography based on two hundred interviews, archival research, and personal reminiscences.

Whitaker, Reg, and Steve Hewitt. *Canada and the Cold War.* Toronto: James Lorimer, 2003. Includes an account of how St. Laurent helped shift Canada to new postwar realities.

See also Canada and Great Britain; Canadian minority communities; Canadian participation in World War II; Canadian regionalism; Elections in Canada; Foreign policy of Canada; Military conscription in Canada; Newfoundland; North Atlantic Treaty Organization.

Salvage drives. *See* **Wartime salvage drives**

■ *A Sand County Almanac*

Identification Book about nature and ethics
Author Aldo Leopold (1887-1948)
Date First published in 1949

Often credited with initiating the environmental movement, A Sand County Almanac *was one of the first works to value nature based on scientific, as well as aesthetic or spiritual, principles. The science of ecology underlay an ethical system that viewed humans as part of an interdependent natural community.*

Aldo Leopold's *A Sand County Almanac* falls into three interconnected sections. The "Almanac" records monthly observations inspired by Leopold's Wisconsin farm. "Sketches Here and There" extends Leopold's explorations to other American locations with an emphasis on species that have been lost and lands that have been despoiled by humans. "The Upshot" considers conservation policy, outdoor recreation practices, and ethics. Decrying economics' dominance in human affairs and the long-term hazards of humans' intervention in nature, Leopold called for a change in human consciousness that could be fostered by a heightened aesthetic appreciation of nature. Drawing upon and reinforcing World War II nationalism, he promoted the wilderness because it had formed the American character. According to his "land ethic," citizens would subordinate their self-interests to the rights of nature just as they sacrifice their individual—and economic—rights to community assets such as roads, schools, and baseball fields.

Impact *A Sand County Almanac* has shaped environmental policies and legislation, especially those extending the definition of conservationism to include the preservation of nature. Leopold's arguments against a utilitarian and anthropocentric view

A Land Ethic

In A Sand County Almanac *(1949), Aldo Leopold calls for an ethic of the land, one that embraces both the individual and the community to maintain a symbiotic relationship for the good of all life on the planet.*

All ethics so far evolved rest upon a single premise: that the individual is a member of a community of interdependent parts. His instincts prompt him to compete for his place in that community, but his ethics prompt him also to co-operate (perhaps in order that there may be a place to compete for).

The land ethic simply enlarges the boundaries of the community to include soils, waters, plants, and animals, or collectively: the land.

This sounds simple: do we not already sing our love for and obligation to the land of the free and the home of the brave? Yes, but just what and whom do we love? Certainly not the soil, which we are sending helter-skelter downriver. Certainly not the waters, which we assume have no function except to turn turbines, float barges, and carry off sewage. Certainly not the plants, of which we exterminate whole communities without batting an eye. Certainly not the animals, of which we have already extirpated many of the largest and most beautiful species. . . .

In short, a land ethic changes the role of Homo sapiens from conqueror of the land-community to plain member and citizen of it. It implies respect for his fellow-members, and also respect for the community as such.

of nature have influenced radical environmentalists and ethical holists. Others argue that his views of the wilderness have led to a false—indeed, artificial—idealization of the wilderness.

Laura Cowan

Further Reading

Callicott, J. Baird, and Clare Palmer, eds. *Environmental Philosophy: Critical Concepts in the Environment.* New York: Routledge, 2005.

Meine, Curt. *Correction Lines: Essays on Land, Leopold and Conservation.* Washington, D.C.: Island Press, 2004.

See also Agriculture in Canada; Agriculture in the United States; *Our Plundered Planet.*

◾ Sarnoff, David

Identification Jewish American business executive
Born February 27, 1891; Uzlian, near Minsk, Russian Empire (now Belarus)
Died December 12, 1971; New York, New York

As head of the Radio Corporation of America (RCA), Sarnoff created the modern broadcast radio industry and was instrumental in turning television from a laboratory curiosity into an entertainment medium.

David Sarnoff was born to a poor Russian Jewish family, who immigrated to Albany, New York, in 1900 and then settled in New York City. Hard work on his pronounciation erased all but a trace of his Yiddish accent, to the point that most casual acquaintences would take him for a native New Yorker. After a fortuitous accident brought him to the offices of American Marconi (the precursor of RCA), he steadily rose in the ranks from code operator to senior executive. However, he never lost his skill with Morse code, and he kept a working telegraph key in his desk to send messages to fellow old-timers.

Sarnoff kept an eye on events in Europe, particularly the anti-Semitic Nazi regime in Germany. In 1940, he informed the U.S. government that RCA stood ready to shift its entire radio manufacturing capacity to wartime production. After the Japanese attack on Pearl Harbor in December, 1941, brought the United States into World War II, Sarnoff personally offered his own radio expertise to improve military communications. He was critical in organizing the radio communications for the 1944 D-day invasion of Normandy, and in recognition of his contributions he was given the honorary rank of brigadier general. As a result, he was thereafter referred to as "the General" by many in RCA.

After the war, Sarnoff shifted his focus back to television, which had been shelved during the war after being delayed during the 1930's as a result of legal battles with television inventor Philo T. Farnsworth. During the 1920's, Sarnoff had created the National

David Sarnoff. (AP/Wide World Photos)

Broadcasting Company (NBC) to facilitate the distribution of national radio programming to affiliate stations across the country through a pair of networks, the Red and the Blue. He now leveraged his existing NBC assets to create a parallel network for television, so that viewers would have an ample supply of quality programming. Under Sarnoff's direction, RCA began to manufacture color sets, and the NBC network often transmitted broadcasts in color. By the 1960's, color television had become standard.

Impact   Sarnoff transformed radio and television into the mass media that dominated subsequent decades and that have continued to play an important role in the twenty-first century in spite of incursions by the Internet. He was also critical in defining the American media's position during the early Cold War.

Leigh Husband Kimmel

Further Reading

Lipartito, Kenneth, and David B. Sicilia, eds. *Constructing Corporate America: History, Politics, Culture.* New York: Oxford University Press, 2004.

Lyons, Eugene. *David Sarnoff.* New York: Harper & Row, 1966.

Stashower, Daniel. *The Boy Genius and the Mogul: The Untold Story of Television.* New York: Broadway Books, 2002.

See also   Jews in the United States; Radio in the United States; Television.

■ Saturday Evening Post

Identification   Weekly general-interest magazine

The oldest magazine in the United States, the Saturday Evening Post *served as a familiar voice of patriotism during World War II and an icon of a growing American middle class in the years following the war.*

Founded by Benjamin Franklin in 1728, the *Saturday Evening Post* experienced alternating periods of success and decline prior to the twentieth century. One of the most popular periodicals in the United States during the early nineteenth century, the *Post* faltered after the Civil War and was nearly defunct by the end of the century. The magazine was revived during the early twentieth century under publisher Cyrus H. K. Curtis and editor George Horace Latimer, achieving a circulation of more than three million issues by 1937 despite the effects of the Great Depression. During this period, the *Post* cultivated a moderate-conservative image that avoided controversy and emphasized patriotism and tradition. The cover illustrations of artist Norman Rockwell became the most prominent symbol of the magazine's middle-American image during the prewar years.

The outbreak of World War II and the wave of patriotism that accompanied the American war effort proved a boon to the popularity of the *Post* during the early 1940's. Faced with the uncertainty of war and fueled by nationalism, many Americans turned to the familiar scenes and symbols that had revived the reputation of the *Post* in prior decades. Rockwell continued to play a critical role in the magazine's popularity; his "Four Freedoms" series of paintings based on the speech by President Franklin D. Roosevelt and published in the *Post* in 1943 became one of the most famous symbols of World War II-era culture in the United States.

Despite the popularity of the *Post* during the war,

the magazine continued to struggle financially, its profitability hindered by production costs resulting from its characteristically large size and abundance of photographs and illustrations. Unable to operate the magazine on circulation revenue alone, the publishers of the *Post* relied increasingly upon advertising money during the postwar years. Colorful advertisements for automobiles, home appliances, clothing, and other consumer goods appeared prominently in the pages of the magazine just as a postwar economic boom swelled the ranks of the middle class and fueled demand for these goods. The *Post* thus became both a reflection of and a prominent participant in the boom, fulfilling the desires for familiarity, normality, and material comfort that permeated an American public whose lives had been disrupted by war and economic depression.

Impact The advertising-laden format and middle-American editorial policy that the *Saturday Evening Post* adopted during the 1940's mirrored the collective national spirit of the Eisenhower era, ensuring the magazine's popularity through the 1950's. Other magazines mimicked the format of the *Post* with varying success, and the colorful advertisements published in the magazine became icons of 1950's culture, attracting the interest of scholars and collectors in subsequent decades and influencing popular culture and art, most notably in the work of Andy Warhol. The *Post* would later fall upon hard times, as the increasing popularity of television lessened general interest in magazines and the quaint Americana that the *Post* espoused assumed a diminished role in the national culture. The magazine folded in 1969 and was revived in a modified format in 1971, remaining in publication into the twenty-first century as a bimonthly magazine emphasizing health and lifestyle issues.

Michael H. Burchett

Further Reading

Cohn, Jan. *Creating America: George Horace Lorimer and the "Saturday Evening Post."* Pittsburgh: University of Pittsburgh Press, 1989.

Kawai, Ken, ed. *The "Saturday Evening Post" Magazine Covers from 1945 to 1962: An Untroubled Season—Ordinary Life in Mid-Century America.* Translated by Setsuko Ohchi. Los Angeles: Books Nippan, 1995.

See also Advertising in the United States; "Four Freedoms" speech; Home appliances; *Life*; Literature in the United States; *Look*; *Maclean's*; Magazines; Rockwell, Norman; Television; Wartime propaganda in the United States.

■ Science and technology

The Allied victory in World War II was attributed in large part to the development and use of atomic power, along with other technological innovations, leading to increased recognition and support for scientific endeavors. Many inventions and innovations had both wartime and postwar applications, including jet engines; radar; computers; medical developments such as antibiotics, vaccines, and pesticides; and television.

Many scientific and technological advancements of the 1940's were the results of meeting military needs, such as creating weapons that could be used in attacks and counterattacks on Axis forces, finding secure methods of communication that would support intelligence work and research, and the need for medicines to effectively treat military and civilian warfare victims. The United States also was aware of the need to remain scientifically and technologically competitive after World War II ended. The necessity of accurately reporting and documenting events in a world at war can be connected to other notable advancements, especially in radio and television.

Ultimate Weapon and a New Source of Power Scientific developments during the decade of the 1930's had revealed immense potential in atomic energy and power. During the early 1940's, researchers realized that this new power could be used in warfare. Scientists warned the governments of Great Britain and the United States of the devastating possibility of Axis development and use of nuclear power. After the Japanese bombing of the Pacific fleet at Pearl Harbor in December, 1941, the federal government approved the Manhattan Project for development of the atomic bomb. The chief ingredients of the bomb were fissionable uranium and plutonium. The quest for ever more powerful weapons would later lead to development of the hydrogen bomb.

Ongoing concerns surfaced about the proliferation of destructive weapons that not only exploded but started huge fires, melted or vaporized materials, left radioactive residue that endangered survivors, and caused mutations that endangered descendants of survivors. At the end of World War II, however, the Cold War between the United States and the Soviet Union led to the desire to maintain at least a balance of power that would discourage any attack, and the two superpowers built up stocks of nuclear missiles.

Scientists hoped that nuclear energy could be useful in peacetime. To make it useful, the energy had to be released in a controlled manner. In a nuclear chain reaction, neutrons produced by fission reactions cause new fission reactions. By absorbing these neutrons with a substance called a moderator, it was possible to slow down and stabilize the chain reaction. The first nuclear reactors built during the 1940's, mainly in France and Great Britain, used uranium as fuel and graphite as a moderator; they were cooled by carbon dioxide gas. In the United States, the first reactors to produce plutonium were constructed at Hanford, Washington, to take advantage of the constant flow of cold water from the Columbia River for cooling reactors. Small amounts of plutonium were later collected from the first production reactor, tested in the nuclear explosion at Alamagordo, New Mexico, and used to make the atomic bomb. The United States subsequently developed pressurized water reactors. During the following decade, the developing technology yielded nuclear power plants and nuclear-powered submarines.

Nuclear-powered submarines would run for extended periods without refueling or resurfacing. In the United States, work on a nuclear airplane began but was abandoned. No airplane could incorporate the heavy nuclear shield needed to protect human crews against radiation from the reactor. Ideas for a nuclear rocket engine also were abandoned because of the atmospheric pollution such an engine would produce.

Warcraft and Peaceful Applications Notable advances were made in tanks, aircraft, and missiles. Scientific experimentation with warcraft plastics and metal alloys later proved valuable in the manufacture of consumer goods. Although radar was first developed for meteorology and navigation, it was also used for locating enemy aircraft.

The Germans initially led in warfare technology. Like the U.S. government, the German government supported research in jet propulsion and the production of jet fighter planes. Captured tanks, planes, and rockets were examined carefully, and some of their designs were used to improve warcraft design. At the end of World War II, the United States recruited German rocket engine developer Wernher von Braun. He became the director of the George C. Marshall Space Flight Center and would be instrumental in the development of the Apollo program, which would land the first human beings on the moon in 1969.

Both military and civilian air transportation underwent profound changes during World War II. Airliners inherited the powerful piston engines developed for heavy bombers, resulting in a series of four-engine planes that could cross the Atlantic Ocean in less than twenty hours. Jet engines developed during the war were installed on military planes and later on civilian planes. The time to cross the Atlantic was then reduced to less than seven hours. Seating capacities increased and ticket prices decreased as airlines began to compete not only with one another but also with railway passenger lines. Because jet engines can develop much more thrust than can be achieved with propellers, weight became less of a problem, and large jet planes began to carry freight such as perishable foods.

Communications and Computer Technology Some of the first computers were developed as a result of military needs. American and British scientists collaborated to produce computers that could decode German military strategies. British mathematician Alan Turing led a team of scientists at the Government Code and Cipher School (GC&CS) at Bletchley Park in the development of a series of Colossus computers that could break the Enigma and Tunny codes used by German forces. Turing had become interested in ciphers while studying for his doctorate at Princeton University.

Before the United States entered World War II, the American theoretical physicist John Atanasoff and his assistant Clifford Berry began working on a computer to solve systems of linear equations. The development of the Atanasoff-Berry Computer (ABC) was postponed when both inventors were drafted for other wartime duties. Their ideas were among those later used in creating the Electronic Numerical Integrator and Computer (ENIAC), a general purpose electronic computer completed in the United States. The Automatic Sequence Controlled Calculator (ASCC), built in the United States by Harvard University and International Business Machines (IBM) was another ENIAC prototype. The ASCC and the ENIAC were originally built to calculate trajectories of projectiles for the military, but the war ended before the ENIAC was fully functional.

Computers of this period were large and slow, and they contained very little memory. The ASCC was programmed with punched tape; the ENIAC was programmed manually by setting switches and plugging in connections. As computers were improved, vacuum tubes replaced electric relays to increase calculating speed. During the postwar years, physicists who were engaged in research on semiconductors discovered transistors. The transistor replaced the vacuum tube because it was more reliable, required much less power, and produced little heat. Electronic devices containing transistors could be built compactly, yet with greater design complexity. Smaller electronic components for computers initiated a technical revolution as machines decreased in size and increased in speed and capability. Computer applications expanded from military use to include such areas as banking, civil aviation, space exploration, and petroleum exploration. During the decade after World War II ended, the Remington Rand UNIVACs, first built between 1943 and 1946, were the first electronic computers to become commercially available.

Medicines   Prior to the 1940's, improvements in public health came mainly from clean water, uncontaminated food, waste management, and increasing knowledge of relationships between germs and disease. During the 1940's, scientific research helped solve other health problems, especially those related to the war. The yellow fever vaccine saved the lives of many American soldiers sent overseas. The insecticide DDT prevented epidemics of malaria and typhus by killing mosquitoes and body lice, which carry those diseases.

Other research resulted in medical breakthroughs in antibiotics. During World War II, penicillin was needed in bulk to treat diseases and infections among soldiers. Although penicillin was clearly more potent than the sulfa drugs used earlier, it was not until war needs intensified that researchers found a way to grow the *Penicillium* mold in vats and manufacture it in large quantities. The production

of penicillin later spread to civilian use, lowering the number of deaths attributed to influenza and pneumonia.

The powerful antibiotic streptomycin became available during wartime for use against tuberculosis. Aureomycin, the first of the tetracycline antibiotics, also was made available. With such effective antibiotics and a better understanding of the transmission of infections, many diseases were nearly eradicated. Frequent use of antibiotics and sulfa drugs, however, created resistant populations of harmful bacteria. The search for new antibiotics thus continued, because bacteria resistant to one antibiotic may not be resistant to another.

By analyzing the structures of antibiotics and how they work, scientists were able to create synthetic antibiotics. Researchers also developed broad-spectrum antibiotics, which could fight many species of bacteria. A better understanding of immunology led to the development of new vaccines against viral diseases such as influenza, measles, and polio. It also led to the better understanding of immunological rejection mechanisms and the development of drugs that prevent organ rejection.

Blood transfusions were organized for military and civilian casualties. Research was done on the collection, storage, and supply of blood. Due to the discovery of the Rh factor, research also involved blood type. In his research, American surgeon Charles R. Drew found that whole blood could not be shipped safely overseas where it was needed for transfusions. Drew, with other medical researchers, established uniform procedures for procuring and processing blood and shipping the plasma. Ironically, racist segregation rules prevented the African American surgeon from donating his own blood.

Other Developments   Many scientists had to postpone their work to assume war-related research. For example, the Manhattan Project encompassed 43,000 employees, including scientists and support staffs in the United States and Canada. They were provided with financial and technical resources to develop the atomic weapon that ultimately ended the war.

During World War II, the solution of complex tactical problems requiring the collaborative efforts of many scientists led to a change in analytic methods that would later become known as operations research. Most postwar advances were thus attributed to interdisciplinary teams of experts who could present a variety of perspectives on their research. Additional reasons for the changing research methodology include the enormous expense of scientific equipment and the increasing needs of business and industrial establishments. Large companies, including General Electric, Du Pont, and Bell Telephone, established research laboratories. The corporate objective was to develop or invent new products.

Many outstanding European scientists fleeing Germany and German attacks came to the United States, providing a surge of new ideas and abilities in scientific research. German scientists with Nazi affiliations and past transgressions, along with their Japanese counterparts, were granted permission to immigrate to the United States when their scientific and technological expertise was considered vital to American national security. The United States and other Allied countries amassed the data that Axis scientists had produced, deeming it important for advancement in scientific understanding, research, and development.

The U.S. government, rather than private industry, became the major source of funding for scientific and technical research and education. As some government contracts ended, research and development for military purposes became available for civilian applications. Many companies thus needed civilian clientele to remain in business.

Noteworthy developments also occurred in various areas of science, including astronomy, biology, chemistry, and physics. After World War II ended, the Hale telescope was put into operation at Mount Palomar in California. It remained the best optical telescope in the world for nearly three decades. Biologists and chemists made advances in genetics that led to the creation of a new field, biochemistry. Research into radioactivity spurred progress in both chemistry and physics.

Biologists discovered that deoxyribonucleic acid (DNA) is the substance that transmits genetic information and later focused on how molecular encoding is accomplished. Scientists investigated the role of mutations, sudden changes in the transfer of inherited characteristics. The fruit fly, *Drosophila*, proved to be valuable in investigations of mutations. Its four chromosomes are clearly visible, and mutations such as wing shape are clearly distinguishable.

One of the most significant scientific discoveries was carbon-14, the long-lived radioactive isotope of carbon. This isotope was used in archaeology for determining the age of artifacts, and in geology for determining the age of rocks, minerals, and fossils. Carbon-14 was also used as a tracer isotope for studying photosynthesis. A radioactive iodine tracer was used to study the thyroid gland. The role of certain substances, such as enzymes and hormones produced by living organisms, became understood, and the importance of hormones to many disorders, such as diabetes, was recognized.

Further developments linked wartime with previous decades, but other ideas seemed to signify emerging eras. The understanding of the chemistry of polymers during the 1930's facilitated the systematic development of new ones during the 1940's. Many studies examined reaction mechanisms. The study of polymerization reactions led to the development of many compounds made up of macromolecules, such as artificial fibers and the first plastic materials. Such materials include polymethylmethacrylate, a transparent lightweight product later marketed as Perspex and Plexiglas, that was used to make cockpit covers for military aircraft. The chemistry of silicon, which can form complex compounds, eventually led to the development of the synthesis of silicones and resulting industrial compounds. High-cost silicone products were known for their antiadhesive properties, water repellency, and heat resistance.

The postwar period saw a change in manufacturing, from use of natural products such as wood, glass, and rubber to use of synthetic materials. For example, some clothing items were made with nylon and dacron. Plastics also began to be used.

During and after World War II, DDT was used to eliminate disease-carrying insects. Scientists discovered, however, that surviving insects continued to breed and pass along their resistance to DDT to successive generations. In response, chemists then developed new herbicides and pesticides such as chlordane, aldrin, and dieldrin. In later years, as employees involved in the manufacture of such chemicals began to exhibit illnesses, the dangers of pesticide usage were exposed.

Physics Wartime scientific research was clearly crucial, and funding for large projects in nuclear and particle physics continued. The government also recognized the economic importance of mate-

Scientists testing the effect on fish and mosquito larvae of pumping DDT into a pond in 1945. (AP/Wide World Photos)

rials science, which had produced the transistor. Technological changes thus included evolution of mechanical tools and devices to become electromechanical and eventually electronic. Automation in manufacturing allowed for some manual tasks to be done by less skilled workers. The complicated technology associated with automation, however, increasingly became the domain of a smaller, more powerful group of people.

After World War II, the discovery of the Lamb shift and its measurement by Willis Lamb in 1947 led to the solution of mathematical problems that had surfaced in the study of atoms and subatomic particles. The mathematical theory that resulted is quantum electrodynamics (QED), often called the most accurate theory in physics. QED is the blueprint for theories of particle interactions, capable of predict-

ing very tiny effects. QED describes the electromagnetic force between subatomic particles in terms of the exchange of photons. As QED was being developed, scientists studying cosmic rays discovered new subatomic particles that did not behave as predicted; they did not decay into other particles as quickly as theoretically assumed. These particles were categorized using the eightfold way, a classification scheme based on abstract mathematics.

Some of the technological developments of the 1940's made their way into ordinary households. At the start of the decade, almost no households in the United States had television sets. Construction of television transmitters and receivers was banned during the war. Phonographic records contained only a few minutes of music on each side. Radio played an important role in the dissemination of information, spreading news and ideas quickly, even among illiterate populations. By the end of the decade, television with black-and-white transmission was made commercially available; regular transmission in color began early the following decade. Radio broadcasting promoted new longer-playing high-fidelity recordings as a result of frequency modulation (FM) radio.

Cameras that could produce instant prints were made available, but other innovative ideas stalled without the appropriate technology to make them a reality. Holography stalled until the later invention of the laser. Communications via space satellites stalled until communications technology utilized advances in rocket and radar technologies.

Impact The U.S. government sponsored more research during World War II than it ever had before, and much of this research either occurred at or was managed by universities. Atomic research preceding the Manhattan Project was done at the University of Chicago. Radar systems were developed at the Massachusetts Institute of Technology's Radiation Laboratory. The University of California managed research and development of nuclear weapons at the Los Alamos Laboratory. These wartime research efforts produced such advances as the atomic bomb, high-frequency radar, and developments in the medical sciences.

Toward the end of the war, it was determined that the private sector had the principal responsibility for funding scientific and technological research and development, but industry lacked the economic incentive to support such research. The federal government continued to fund basic research as a public good. Research was to be conducted largely by universities, with the allocation of research funds determined through peer review. Many federal agencies in the United States began funding significant amounts of basic research in universities using the peer review process.

June Lundy Gastón

Further Reading

Bowler, Peter J., and Iwan Rhys Morus. *Making Modern Science: A Historical Survey.* Chicago: University of Chicago Press, 2005. Focuses on several highlights in the development of science and includes research on scientific developments during wartime periods.

Carlisle, Rodney. *Scientific American Inventions and Discoveries.* Hoboken, N.J.: John Wiley & Sons, 2004. Provides a historical overview of technological advances of worldwide importance.

Cumo, Christopher. *Science and Technology in Twentieth-Century American Life.* Westport Conn.: Greenwood Press, 2007. Discusses the impact of science and technology on selected aspects of everyday life, including the military.

Shachtman, Tom. *Terrors and Marvels: How Science and Technology Changed the Character and Outcome of World War II.* New York: William Morrow, 2002. Describes the wartime role of science, weapons that were developed but not used, and wartime tactics. Contrasts the commitment of Allied scientists with that of their Axis counterparts.

Vizard, Frank, and Bill Scott. *Twenty-first Century Soldier: The Weaponry, Gear, and Technology in the New Century.* New York: Popular Science Books, 2002. Provides a historical perspective on the development of warcraft.

Williams, Trevor, ed. *Science: A History of Discovery in the Twentieth Century.* New York: Oxford University Press, 1990. Provides a historical analysis, including charts and diagrams, of scientific and technological advances that occurred during selected time periods.

See also Aircraft design and development; Antibiotics; Atomic bomb; Computers; Manhattan Project; Medicine; Radar; Rocketry; Television; Wartime technological advances.

■ **Seeger, Pete**

Identification American folk singer, songwriter, and political activist
Born May 3, 1919; New York, New York

Seeger's work helped fuel interest in American folk music traditions throughout the twentieth century and strengthen the ties between folk music and political movements.

Pete Seeger's early influences included his father, musicologist Charles Seeger, his mother, violinist Constance Edson, and later his stepmother, the composer and folk music scholar Ruth Crawford Seeger. Huddie "Leadbelly" Ledbetter and Woody Guthrie influenced Seeger as he developed his distinctive style. He usually accompanied himself with a banjo, ukulele, or guitar, frequently using a combination of speech and melody to highlight crucial moments in a song.

During the early 1940's, Seeger sang at political and labor gatherings, with Guthrie, as a soloist, and as a founding member of the Almanac Singers. As World War II continued, the Almanac Singers' antiwar and prosocialist songs, as well as Seeger's own communist associations, became increasingly controversial, and the group lost public support. Seeger was drafted to the U.S. Army in 1942, and during furlough he married Toshi Ohta. Seeger came again to the public's attention when he participated in Henry A. Wallace's Progressive Party campaign for the 1948 presidency. In 1949, Seeger, along with Ronnie Gilbert, Lee Hays, and Fred Hellerman, formed the singing group the Weavers, whose 1950 release of Leadbelly's song "Goodnight, Irene" skyrocketed to the top of the charts, ensuring their commercial success.

Impact Through his example, mentorship, and songs, Seeger continued to influence musicians throughout the twentieth century, including Bob Dylan; Peter, Paul and Mary; Joan Baez; and Bruce Springsteen.

Joanna R. Smolko

Further Reading

Dunaway, David. *How Can I Keep From Singing: Pete Seeger.* New York: McGraw Books, 1981.

Wilkinson, Alec. *The Protest Singer: An Intimate Portrait of Pete Seeger.* New York: Alfred A. Knopf, 2009.

See also Communist Party USA; Elections in the United States: 1948; Guthrie, Woody; Music: Popular; Unionism; Wallace, Henry A.

■ Seldes, George

Identification American journalist and press critic
Born November 16, 1890; Alliance, New Jersey
Died July 2, 1995; Windsor, Vermont

A pioneer press critic and investigative journalist, Seldes who wrote newspaper articles and books and published a newsletter. In 1941, he became one of the first reporters to discuss the link between tobacco and cancer.

George Henry Seldes was still a teenager when he started working as a journalist in Pittsburgh, Pennsylvania. After taking a year off from reporting to attend Harvard University, he became a foreign correspondent for the United Press, the *Chicago Tribune*, and the *New York Post*. Over the next several decades, he interviewed scientist Albert Einstein, sang with labor activist Joe Hill, and criticized *Tribune* owner Robert R. McCormick. American politician William Jennings Bryan once threw Seldes out of a hotel after Seldes asked him a hard question; Soviet leader Joseph Stalin and Italian leader Benito Mussolini would later throw him out of their countries after he published uncensored stories about their regimes.

After World War I, Seldes defied travel restrictions and went to Germany to interview Field Marshal Paul von Hindenburg, but the interview was censored by the U.S. military. Seldes considered this censorship tragic because Hindenburg said that Germany had lost the war after the United States entered the fray, a contradiction of Nazi leader Adolf Hitler's later claim that Jews and socialists were responsible for the German defeat.

The first of Seldes's twenty-one books was *You Can't Print That! The Truth Behind the News, 1918-1928* (1929), a firsthand account of world events that he considered inadequately covered elsewhere. He also criticized the press in *Freedom of the Press* (1935) and *Lords of the Press* (1938).

During the 1940's, Seldes became an independent reporter because he thought the cost of newspaper production made journalism so expensive that only big enterprises avoiding controversy could afford to own publications. He started a four-page weekly newsletter, *In Fact*, in which he was an early proponent of consumer reporting. In 1941, he started exposing ties between tobacco and cancer based on a 1938 Johns Hopkins University study and subsequent reports. He published dozens of articles on this subject at a time when most publications suppressed the connection because cigarette companies were major advertisers.

Subscriptions by labor unions and other progressive groups caused *In Fact*'s circulation to peak at 175,000, but harassment by the Federal Bureau of Investigation (FBI) forced the newsletter to shut down in 1950.

Impact Seldes was an antiauthoritarian trailblazer for press critics, investigative reporters, and journalists exposing controversial truths, and the mainstream media eventually appreciated his work. In his book *The New Muckrackers* (1976), *Washington Post* editor Leonard Downie praised Seldes for having "exposed shocking conditions in the auto, drug, tobacco and other industries."

Bill Knight

Further Reading

Downie, Leonard. *The New Muckrakers.* New York: Simon & Schuster, 1976.

Holhut, Randolph. *The George Seldes Reader.* New York: Barricade Books, 1994.

Seldes, George. *Witness to a Century: Encounters with the Noted, the Notorious, and the Three SOBs.* New York: Ballantine Books, 1987.

See also Bourke-White, Margaret; Cancer; Censorship in the United States; Newspapers; Pyle, Ernie; Smoking and tobacco; Unionism.

Servicemen's Readjustment Act of 1944. *See* **G.I. Bill**

■ Sex and sex education

Public demand for knowledge about human sexuality increased during the 1940's. The concept of sexuality expanded beyond biological and medical aspects to social aspects. Issues included how men and women should interact on a regular basis, the physical and psychological differences between men and women, and the role sex education should play in preparing adolescents for adulthood.

During the 1940's, psychological theories of human sexuality argued that men and women were fundamentally different in ways that complemented each other mentally, emotionally, and biologically. Men were considered to be more aggressive, women relatively passive. Early twentieth century manuals on marriage and sex placed the responsibility of sexual restraint and control on men. Female satisfaction was essential to healthy marriage, and men were responsible for controlling their own sexual desires in order to delay sexual climax, satisfy their wives sexually, and refrain from immoral behaviors such as masturbation and infidelity. Female passivity was reflected in the female sex drive. Female sexual desire lay dormant until awakened by male advances. Healthy female sexual expression was always a response to healthy male sexual expression.

Sexuality and Human Behavior By the beginning of the 1940's, the link between sexuality and human behavior had long been a topic of psychological, medical, and political discussion, but the sudden and drastic shifts in gender roles precipitated by World War II complicated these portrayals of sexuality. As millions of American men left the workforce to participate in the war effort overseas, women filled traditionally "male" jobs in manufacturing and labor to meet the demands of wartime production. At the same time, anxieties over adolescent promiscuity focused on the sexual brazenness of teenage girls around "men in uniform." The association of femininity with self-reliance and personal initiative was celebrated in wartime propaganda that encouraged women to contribute to the war effort. Images of American women in films and magazines glamorized attractive, self-confident displays of femininity. However, similar assertiveness in courtship or sex was portrayed as a signature character flaw in prostitutes and "loose women." Wartime purity propaganda juxtaposed pictures of sexually provocative women with references to syphilis and gonorrhea, conveying the danger that promiscuous women posed for young men.

After World War II, women were expected to return to the domestic sphere as male veterans reintegrated into civilian peacetime society and reentered the workforce. By the end of the 1940's, the female capacity to be assertive and independent had become indisputable—even laudable for its necessary contribution to the war effort. However, rapid socioeconomic changes of postwar society, coinciding with the onset of the Cold War, contributed to a widespread perception of the contemporary world as a socially unstable place with an uncertain future. This uncertainty extended to the integrity of American families.

Hygiene and Dangers of Sexual Promiscuity Before World War II, sex education was intended primarily for adults and emphasized the tangible danger of venereal disease as a consequence of sexual promiscuity. Medical health and moral propriety were conflated in arguments for sexual restraint. Gonorrhea and syphilis punished immoral sexual behaviors not only with physical harm but also with the shame that sexual indiscretion entailed. Education about the dangers of venereal disease provided one of the few socially acceptable contexts for frank and open discussion of sex. Sex was considered an inherently salacious topic, prone to sexually excite audiences if discussed or presented too explicitly. While this made sex a delicate subject on the home front, policy makers for the U.S. military argued that sex education for American troops should not spare their sensibilities. Masculine virility and aggressiveness were considered potential advantages in war. Though medical officers encouraged sexual restraint, they did not rely on the scruples or willpower of their enlisted men to prevent the spread of disease. Physicians gave detailed lectures on sexual reproduction and distributed prophylaxis to assembled troops. Millions of condoms, the cheapest and most convenient prophylactics available, were distributed and sold to American servicemen through military commissaries.

During the war, penicillin was discovered to be an effective treatment for syphilis and gonorrhea. The mass production and distribution of penicillin undermined the threat of disease as a deterrent to promiscuity. Some physicians and policy makers worried that the widespread availability of treatment would encourage sexual immorality. Because the conduct itself was objectionable, regardless of the medical consequences, the American Social Hygiene Association (ASHA) led a transition in sex education to focus on the psychological and social consequences of sexual conduct. The resulting curricula drew on contemporary psychology to portray human sexuality within a broader context of gender roles in society. In the wake of the postwar baby boom, economic prosperity, and an increased standard of living for the middle class, the stability of the American family supplanted containment of venereal disease as the primary motivation for educating adults and young people about sex.

Sex Advice for Modern American Families   The impact of World War II on marriage and childbirth was immediate and dramatic. Beginning in 1943, the average marriage ages among men and women dropped to unprecedented lows for the twentieth century. Birth rates skyrocketed in 1946, fueling anxieties over the preparedness of women for marriage. Popular psychoanalytic theory held that women naturally desired marriage and motherhood, but that modern feminist notions of female assertiveness, dissatisfaction with home life, and aspirations for professional careers over domestic life

all reflected pathological gender confusion. In contrast to the sex manuals geared toward men during the 1920's and 1930's, wartime and postwar educational materials for adults tended to target women, shifting the burden of marital satisfaction from male performance to female receptiveness. They also shifted emphasis from the act of intimacy to its reproductive purpose: the birth and education of the next generation of Americans.

Benjamin Spock established the centrality of children to women's family life in *The Common Sense Book of Baby and Child Care* (1946), the most successful and influential instruction book on parenting of the twentieth century. Spock shared the concerns of social scientists from a variety of fields about the instability of modern society and its potential hazards to "natural" motherhood. Spock's *Baby and Child Care* advocated a return to the mother's natural maternal instincts, stressing the fragility of children and the ease with which misguided parenting could instill them with neuroses and personality problems. The book refuted traditional disciplinarian approaches toward children in favor of nurturing them and minimizing the frustrations that accompanied their growth to more advanced stages of maturity. He discouraged severe punishment and avoidable confrontation in favor of friendly guidance through life aimed at cultivating a predisposition for good behavior without the need for coercion. Written during World War II, *Baby and Child Care* juxtaposed the instability of modern society with the instability of the modern child. Spock's prescriptions were intended to ensure as stable a transition to adulthood as possible. It was this lack of stability, he argued, that led to confusion, disorder, and behavioral deviance.

Sex Education as Preparation for Adulthood   World War II prompted numerous sociological studies examining the effects of the war on American families and individuals. Sociology and psychology had begun to popularize explanations for human behavior that emphasized social influences on sexual development over the traditional assumption that biology directly influenced gender roles. In studying social problems such as juvenile delinquency in connection to World War II, American social scientists found explanations for deviant behavior in the absence of male or female role models, dysfunctional role models in the family, or other deficiencies in the individual's environment. For example, boys who lacked strong father figures might behave recklessly or engage in homosexual behavior in their attempts to define their own masculinity. The power of social influences to mold individuals implied that healthy, normal sexuality did not emerge on its own. It had to be learned.

This shift contributed to the spread of sex-education programs in public schools during the late 1940's. Family-life classes, premised on the conviction that ignorance about sexuality was a threat to public welfare, attempted to demystify sex for high school and university students. Typical lesson plans instructed teachers to foster an environment of open classroom discussion and debate. Classes were typically segregated by gender, though mixed classes became more common during the mid-twentieth century. Short films, workbooks, and other teaching aids balanced tasteful discretion with the need to satisfy curiosity and dispel myths about sex. Visceral physiological topics such as menstruation, sexual anatomy, venereal disease, and reproduction were often explained abstractly or metaphorically to avoid disturbing their audiences.

Lessons typically prescribed etiquette or moral behavior in connection to the information covered. Girls were instructed not to slouch or think of themselves as unattractive while they were menstruating, but to smile, dress attractively, and go about their day with positive attitudes. In contrast to the earlier social hygiene movements, sex- and family-life-education courses sought to curb sexual immorality by shaping students' attitudes toward sex to align with idealized conceptions of gendered adulthood.

The Significance of Heterosexuality Homosexual desire and behavior were considered criminally deviant and inherently obscene. The 1940's was consistent with earlier decades in its near-total lack of explicit references to same-sex desire. Outside psychoanalytic literature, the topic was usually described through innuendo and euphemism. Sodomy laws prohibited "unnatural" sex acts, the definition of which varied among states, but which were always interpreted to include sexual contact between men. Homosexual desire itself was generally considered a mental illness. During the 1940's, informal social networks of homosexual men began to form around bars, particularly in Southern California, which served as public refuges from the hostile political climate. These communities became precursors to

formal groups organized around homosexual identity and empowerment, such as the Mattachine Society. Postwar sex education in schools presented sexual intercourse as coitus between married adults. While sex education in the classroom stressed the importance of heterosexuality, other sexual behaviors were rarely mentioned.

Impact The changing gender dynamic during World War II and the postwar baby boom set in motion far-reaching social changes in twentieth century practices of sexual morality and sex education. The "baby boom" generation formed an age demographic that dominated much of American politics and popular culture during the latter half of the century. During the 1960's and 1970's, the so-called "second wave" of feminism attacked cultural notions of gender inequality by appropriating the same psychoanalytic theories that had defined those gender differences during the 1930's and 1940's. The statistical studies of Alfred Kinsey's *Sexual Behavior in the Human Male* (1948) and *Sexual Behavior in the Human*

Alfred Kinsey holding a copy of his best-selling book, Sexual Behavior in the Human Male, *in March, 1948.* (AP/Wide World Photos)

Female (1953) challenged the presumed correlation between human nature and human morality. Kinsey's statistics suggested that most men were bisexual, with only partial inclinations toward homosexuality or heterosexuality. Fifty percent of the men in Kinsey's statistical sample had engaged in extramarital sex. Instances of other conventionally deviant sex behaviors were alarmingly high. Though his data collection was ultimately revealed to be flawed, Kinsey's studies repudiated the sexually conservative ideology implicit in family-life courses with his evidence-based studies of sexual physiology. The shared experiences of homosexuals as a persecuted minority during the 1940's prefigured the formation of socially conscious gay-rights groups, which played a transformative role in American conceptions of sexuality and gender during the late twentieth century.

Shaun Horton

Further Reading

Berube, Allan. *Coming out Under Fire: The History of Gay Man and Women in World War Two.* New York: Free Press, 1990. Describes the experiences of gay men and women in the military, how they coped with psychiatric screening processes designed to keep them out, and how they got along with their straight comrades.

Freeman, Susan K. *Sex Goes to School: Girls and Sexual Education Before the 1960's.* Chicago: University of Illinois Press, 2008. Examines the course materials of influential sex education movements to reconstruct the values that were communicated in high school sex-education courses. Uses students' feedback and assignments to recover what the students gained from sex-education classes and how their own concerns about sex may have differed from the concerns of educators.

Moran, Jeffery P. *Teaching Sex: The Shaping of Adolescence in the Twentieth Century.* Cambridge, Mass.: Harvard University Press, 2000. Traces the social conceptions of adolescence as expressed in sex education literature from 1904 to the 1970's. Argues that American sex education has been consistently preoccupied with preserving the distinction between adolescence and adulthood rather than simply teaching factual information about sex.

Tentler, Leslie. *Catholics and Contraception: An American History.* New York: Cornell University Press, 2004. Explores the difficulties faced by American Catholics in reconciling modern family norms with the Church's prohibition of birth control. Much of the narrative is devoted to the 1930's and 1940's.

Walker, Nancy A., ed. *Women's Magazines, 1940-1960: Gender Roles and the Popular Press.* New York: Palgrave Macmillan, 1998. A collection of magazine articles on the proper role of women in society, with introduction and commentary by the editor.

See also Baby boom; Birth control; *The Common Sense Book of Baby and Child Care*; Education in the United States; G.I. Bill; Health care; Homosexuality and gay rights; Pinup girls; Pornography; Psychiatry and psychology; Sexually transmitted diseases.

■ Sexually transmitted diseases

Definition Variety of pathogens, including viruses, bacteria, fungi, and protozoa, that may result in mild infections involving the genitalia or lead to more serious problems with other organs and systems of the body

Sexually transmitted diseases, commonly known as venereal diseases until the 1990's, have plagued humankind since the beginning of recorded history. Gonorrhea and syphilis, the two most prevalent sexually transmitted diseases during the 1940's, date back to ancient times. In 1940, nearly one-half of American adults who were polled identified syphilis as their most significant health concern. Peak rates of syphilis in the United States occurred during the 1940's, with 575,600 cases reported in 1941. Before antibiotic treatment became widely available during the 1940's, insanity caused by syphilis may have accounted for as much as 10 percent of admissions to insane asylums.

Historically, sexually transmitted diseases were seen as the result of immorality and a lack of behavioral control. During the 1940's, many physicians began to view sexually transmitted diseases as a social problem. The U.S. government began monitoring syphilis in 1941 and organized a national sexually transmitted disease program aimed at military personnel that focused on education, medical treatment, case finding, contact tracing, and controlling prostitution.

The federal government attempted to eliminate

prostitution in order to protect the military, but some believed that prostitutes offered an outlet for soldiers' sexual drives and would protect society against the greater evils of homosexuality and rape. Although thousands of prostitutes were arrested by military officials, army doctors reported that these women accounted for only a small portion of the soldiers' sexual contacts. The military then turned its attention to the "victory girls," the "promiscuous" girls next door, who were eager to support the war effort by having flings with the soldiers. However, the military soon discovered it was unable to control the activities of these women, so the army stepped up its protection efforts, seemingly endorsing the sexual activities of men while criticizing the sexual activities of the "victory girl."

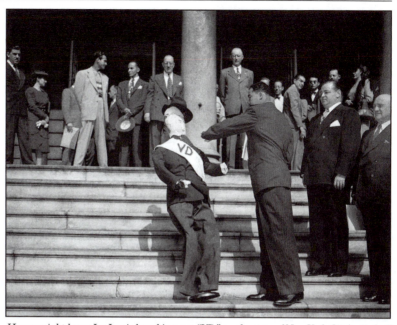

Heavyweight boxer Joe Louis knocking out "VD" on the steps of New York City's city hall during the October, 1946, campaign of the American Social Hygiene Association to raise funds to combat venereal disease. (AP/Wide World Photos)

One of the goals of sexually transmitted disease education in the military was to create "syphilophobia" among the men. However, most servicemen did not consider gonorrheal infections much more serious than common colds. When antibiotics were introduced in 1943 and syphilis and gonorrhea became treatable, the focus of the military's intervention shifted to the provision of condoms and the availability of drug treatments.

As a result of World War II, shortcuts were taken and the normal time for testing, research, production, and distribution of some promising new antibacterial drugs was reduced. By quickly employing these new antibiotics, the government may have prevented an epidemic that public health officials feared would occur when the troops were discharged. Shortly after the introduction of penicillin as a treatment, sexually transmitted disease rates began to fall dramatically. The number of recorded cases of primary and secondary syphilis peaked at 94,957 in 1946 but plummeted to 6,392 by 1956. Penicillin was seen as a wonder drug when it demonstrated how it could effectively treat both gonorrhea and syphilis, and the drug changed the approach to venereal disease control both during and after the war.

After the war, public health officials shifted their attention to identifying and treating preexisting cases of venereal disease. By 2009, the government was monitoring about twenty-five sexually transmitted diseases. The U.S. Public Health Service sponsored nationwide health campaigns in an attempt to seek out and treat sufferers. Rates of sexually transmitted diseases quickly dropped, but the new cures were short-lived. Sulfa-resistant strains of gonococci appeared, and syphilis and gonorrhea developed resistance to penicillin. By the twenty-first century, both diseases were increasing worldwide.

Impact The organization of a national sexually transmitted disease control program during the 1940's, coupled with the introduction of penicillin, almost eliminated syphilis in 1957 and provided the template for most contemporary disease prevention programs. However, there have been cyclic national epidemics every seven to ten years due to a number of factors, including prostitution, drug use, and funding cuts for sexually transmitted disease prevention programs. As a result, by 2009 the syphilis rate had returned to its highest level since the early 1950's.

Paul Finnicum

Further Reading

Brandt, Allan M. *No Magic Bullet: A Social History of Venereal Disease in the United States Since 1880.* Expanded ed. New York: Oxford University Press, 1987.

Division of STD Prevention, National Center for HIV, STD, and TB Prevention, Centers for Disease Control and Prevention. *The National Plan to Eliminate Syphilis from the United States.* Atlanta, Ga.: U.S. Department of Health and Human Services, Centers for Disease Control and Prevention, 2006.

See also Antibiotics; Bikini bathing suits; Birth control; Health care; Homosexuality and gay rights; Pornography; Sex and sex education; Sexually transmitted diseases; Tuskegee syphilis study.

■ *Shelley v. Kraemer*

The Case U.S. Supreme Court ruling upholding that racially restrictive covenants could not be enforced in state courts

Date Decided on May 3, 1948

The Supreme Court's unanimous (6-0) ruling that court enforcement of racially restrictive covenants constituted state action and therefore ran afoul of the Fourteenth Amendment's equal protection guarantees was a major victory for the Civil Rights movement.

In 1948, the Shelleys, a black family in St. Louis, Missouri, bought a house, only to learn that the property was encumbered by a covenant prohibiting African Americans and Asians from owning or living in it. Of fifty-seven parcels of land in the neighborhood, forty-seven were racially restricted. The same thing happened to the McGhee family in Detroit. In both cities, white neighbors sued to invalidate the sales, and the Supreme Courts of Missouri and Michigan upheld the rights of the neighbors to exclude the black families. Racially restrictive covenants were not uncommon at the time, so there was considerable interest nationwide when the U.S. Supreme Court agreed to hear the appeals.

The case was argued for the Shelleys and the McGhees by Thurgood Marshall, later to become the first African American justice of the U.S. Supreme Court, and by Loren Miller, a prominent civil rights attorney and later a California judge. Three justices, Robert H. Jackson, Stanley Forman Reed, and Wiley Blount Rutledge, recused themselves. Chief Justice Fred M. Vinson wrote the opinion for an otherwise unanimous Court, invalidating the enforcement by state courts of the covenants. The judgment was announced on May 3, 1948.

Marshall and Miller argued that the covenants themselves were unconstitutional, but because the covenants were private agreements, and the Fourteenth Amendment governs only state action, the Court disagreed. Attorneys for the white neighbors argued that state judges could enforce the covenants because court decisions were not state laws subject to the Fourteenth Amendment. They also argued that racial covenants were not discriminatory because they would be enforced against whites as well, making them racially neutral. The Court rejected both of these arguments. Court enforcement of the covenants was state action because a court judgment was no less a law than was a statute. Furthermore, the covenants were discriminatory: There was no evidence that racial covenants had ever restricted white ownership, and, more important, equal protection was a personal right whose violation could not be justified by saying that whites, too, can be excluded on account of race.

Impact *Shelley* was a key victory in the Civil Rights movement and the beginning of a string of legal victories leading toward fair housing. It was the first case in which the U.S. attorney general signed an amicus brief on behalf of a civil rights plaintiff. Just a year after *Shelley*, the Federal Housing Administration announced that it would no longer insure mortgages on houses with racially restrictive covenants. Five years after, in *Barrows v. Jackson* (1953), the Supreme Court broadened the scope of judicial standing to allow a white homeowner who was sued for violating a racial covenant to raise a claim that the black purchaser's rights were being violated. Twenty years after *Shelley*, in 1968, Congress finally banned private racial discrimination in housing altogether in the Fair Housing Act of 1968. Many deeds today still contain racial covenants, but since *Shelley* they have been unenforceable in court, and since the Fair Housing Act it has been unlawful to honor them privately. The Shelleys' house in St. Louis was designated a National Historic Landmark on December 14, 1990.

William V. Dunlap

Further Reading

Klarman, Michael J. *From Jim Crow to Civil Rights: The Supreme Court and the Struggle for Racial Equality.* New York: Oxford University Press, 2006.

Vosc, Clement E. *Caucasians Only: The Supreme Court, the NAACP, and the Restrictive Covenant Cases.* Berkeley: University of California Press, 1959.

See also   African Americans; *An American Dilemma: The Negro Problem and American Democracy*; Civil rights and liberties; Housing in the United States; Jim Crow laws; National Association for the Advancement of Colored People; Racial discrimination; Supreme Court, U.S.

■ Siegel, Bugsy

Identification   American gangster
Born   February 28, 1906; Brooklyn, New York
Died   June 20, 1947; Beverly Hills, California

Although Siegel was a vicious killer, he has been glamorized for his role in launching Las Vegas as the gambling mecca of the United States.

Born Benjamin Hymen Siegelbaum to a Jewish family, Bugsy Siegel became one of the most notorious American gangsters. He earned his reputation as a tumultuous member of New York's powerful Jewish syndicate and as a hit man for the infamous contract-killing squad "Murder Incorporated." By the early 1940's, Siegel resided in Beverly Hills and threw opulent parties for Hollywood celebrities. He dressed fashionably and dated Virginia Hill.

At the behest of his syndicate boss, Meyer Lansky, Siegel investigated a desert town in Nevada—Las Vegas—that was attracting gambling developers. In 1946, Siegel muscled in on the construction of the Flamingo gambling casino owned by Billy Wilkerson. Siegel was able to push the project along but also accumulated million-dollar overruns. Rumors spread that his extravagant spending angered the syndicate bosses, who also suspected him of skimming construction money off the top. On June 20, 1947, he was shot to death by an unknown assailant.

Impact   A ruthless and erratic gangster, Siegel has achieved added notoriety because of his association with the rise of Las Vegas, although his actual role in launching the city has been debated. His handsome looks and extravagant persona have made him a staple of gangster mythology, best exemplified by Warren Beatty's portrayal of him in the 1991 film *Bugsy*.

Howard Bromberg

Further Reading

Carpozi, George, Jr. *Bugsy: The Bloodthirty, Lusty Life of Benjamin "Bugsy" Siegel.* New York: Spibooks, 1992.

Papa, Paul. *It Happened in Las Vegas.* Guilford, Conn.: Globe Pequot, 2009.

Wilkerson, William. *The Man Who Invented Las Vegas.* Bellingham, Wash.: Ciro, 2000.

See also   Chandler, Raymond; Crimes and scandals; Dewey, Thomas E.; Gambling; Jews in the United States; Organized crime.

■ Sinatra, Frank

Identification   American singer and actor
Born   December 12, 1915; Hoboken, New Jersey
Died   May 14, 1998; Los Angeles, California

Sinatra was one of the most popular singers, movie stars, and radio personalities of the 1940's. He was the featured singer in the Harry James and Tommy Dorsey big bands, and he had a successful solo singing and acting career, appearing in seventeen short-length and feature films during the 1940's.

Born to Italian immigrant parents, Frank Sinatra took his musical inspiration from the singers Bing Crosby, Billie Holiday, and Mabel Mercer. He began his musical career singing in amateur talent shows, at clubs in and around Hoboken, New Jersey, and on the radio. One of his first regular jobs was singing at the Rustic Cabin in Englewood Cliffs in 1938. In 1939, trumpeter Harry James hired Sinatra, and in 1940 the trombonist and band leader Tommy Dorsey hired him as one of the band's featured singers. Dorsey's trombone technique highly influenced Sinatra, and he began to be known as "The Voice." Sinatra sang with Dorsey's band from 1940 to 1942, and they recorded eighty-three songs for RCA Records, including the number-one hit "There Are Such Things." He also sang with the band in two films, *Las Vegas Nights* (1941) and *Ship Ahoy* (1942).

In 1942, Sinatra left the Dorsey band to begin his

solo career. That year, shortly after performing at the Paramount Theater in New York City to a huge crowd of screaming teenage girls (generally referred to as bobby-soxers), Sinatra signed a recording contract with Columbia Records and a movie contract with Radio-Keith-Orpheum (RKO). His first role in which he did not appear as himself came in 1944 in *Step Lightly.* On October 11, 1944, Sinatra returned to perform at the Paramount Theater, where thirty thousand fans, mostly bobby-soxers, packed Midtown Manhattan. In 1945, he signed a movie contract with Metro-Goldwyn-Mayer (MGM) and starred with Gene Kelly in *Anchors Aweigh*, which was nominated for the Academy Award for best picture. The following year, Sinatra won an Oscar for his short antiprejudice film *The House I Live In* (1945). During this time, he also appeared on several radio shows.

Sinatra's career declined sharply in 1947. His relationship with the press and the public soured because of his several negative public comments and insults, accusations of his being a communist, and

Frank Sinatra singing at a nightclub in 1943. (Time & Life Pictures/Getty Images)

his alleged connections to the Mafia. His extramarital affair with actor Ava Gardner, whom he married in 1951, also negatively affected his public image. He made a series of movies that did not do well, and as the bobby-soxers grew up his record sales declined. By 1950, Sinatra did not have a recording or movie contract, and he reportedly attempted suicide in 1951.

Impact   Before his career stalled from 1947 to 1953, Sinatra was perhaps the biggest star in the United States during the mid-1940's. His comeback began in 1953, when he starred in *From Here to Eternity,* for which he won an Academy Award for best supporting actor. He recorded several legendary albums for Capitol Records during the mid-1950's and became the leader of the Rat Pack. Except for a brief retirement during the early 1970's, he continued to be one of the biggest and most influential entertainers. His final public performance was in 1995.

Chris Robinson

Further Reading

Freedland, Michael. *All the Way: A Biography of Frank Sinatra.* New York: St. Martin's Press, 1997.

Santopietro, Tom. *Sinatra in Hollywood.* New York: Thomas Dunne Books, 2008.

See also   Bobbysoxers; Crosby, Bing; Dorsey, Tommy; Film in the United States; Holiday, Billie; Kelly, Gene; Music: Jazz; Music: Popular.

■ *Skinner v. Oklahoma*

The Case   U.S. Supreme Court ruling on compulsory sterilization of criminal offenders
Date   Decided on June 1, 1942

The U.S. Supreme Court ruled that an Oklahoma statute mandating the forced sexual sterilization of habitual criminal offenders was unconstitutional.

In May, 1942, the Supreme Court considered the constitutionality of the Oklahoma Habitual Criminal Sterilization Act. Jack T. Skinner had been convicted of theft, and on two separate occasions he was convicted of armed robbery. Under the act, male and female offenders who had committed more than two felonies were declared habitual offenders and subject to sterilization. However, the act excluded defendants convicted of political offenses and certain white-collar offenses, such as embezzlement.

In a unanimous decision, the Supreme Court declared that the Oklahoma act was unconstitutional on the grounds that it violated the equal protection clause contained in the Fourteenth Amendment. The Court's primary argument for the unconstitutionality of the act concerned the disparate treatment of offenders—for example, grand larcenists compared to embezzlers. The Court reasoned that larceny and embezzlement involved the same basic criminal element of theft. Under Oklahoma law, grand larceny and embezzlement are both felonies and treated similarly in regard to the amount of fines and lengths of prison terms. However, those convicted of grand larceny could be eligible for sterilization, while those repeatedly convicted of embezzlement could not be despite the number of times the offender embezzled money or the amount of money embezzled. Furthermore, the justices questioned the merit of the law, as there was no evidence offered that grand larcenists needed to be sterilized in order to avoid having their children inherit undesirable genes, nor was there evidence that the same undesirable characteristics could not be passed from an embezzler to his or her children.

The Court acknowledged that the right to procreate was a fundamental right and expressed concern that forced sterilization could have insidious and long-lasting consequences, such as the decline of a certain race or ethnicity by limiting their opportunities to reproduce. The Court considered the preferential treatment of embezzlers as tantamount to racial discrimination.

Impact The issue of compulsory sterilization raised in the case of *Skinner v. Oklahoma* is derived from the larger movement of eugenics, originated by Francis Galton during the late nineteenth century and which was popular during the 1940's. After the discovery of genes and evolution, the eugenics movement advocated that a superior race of whites could be created by the breeding of those with better genes, the avoidance of interracial breeding, and the compulsory sterilization of those deemed to be social undesirables, including criminals, the feebleminded, and the mentally ill.

During the early twentieth century, more than thirty states had laws permitting forced sterilization. It was also practiced internationally. The ideology of the eugenics movement culminated in the Holocaust. Even after eugenics was discredited as based on racial stereotyping, some states continued forced sterilization into the 1970's.

Margaret E. Leigey and Christina Reese

Further Reading

Bruinius, Harry. *Better for All the World: The Secret History of Forced Sterilization and America's Quest for Racial Purity.* New York: Alfred A. Knopf, 2006.

Nourse, Victoria. *In Reckless Hands: Skinner v. Oklahoma and the Near-Triumph of American Eugenics.* New York: W. W. Norton, 2008.

See also Civil rights and liberties; Crimes and scandals; Racial discrimination; Science and technology; Supreme Court, U.S.

■ Slang, wartime

Definition   Casual language reflecting the mood and subject matter of World War II

Slang created solidarity for World War II soldiers and civilians through sharing of language, with civilians picking up terms used in the military, and also offered new ways of expressing ideas.

World War II produced a voluminous lexicon of slang, including many initials and acronyms. When things did not go quite as planned, the situation was "fubar" (fouled up beyond all recognition). Due to a "snafu" (situation normal, all fouled up, or all f——ked up), a "G.I." (an enlisted soldier, from "government issue") could go "M.I.A." (missing in action) and be "S.O.L." (sure—or something stronger—out of luck).

Slang included the adoption of foreign words. The head "honcho" (Japanese for "squad commander") could give someone "flak" (German word, *fliegerabwehrkanone*, for antiaircraft guns and their shells), and that would not be "ding how" (Chinese for "very good").

Some words were created to resemble sounds. One had to know one's "ack-ack" (antiaircraft gun) from one's "burp" gun (semiautomatic) and "coughing Clara" (heavy artillery gun). Other words evoked the subject of a proper name. For example, a "Tojo" (after Hideki Tojo, Japan's prime minister during the war) was any Japanese person. A life jacket was a

"Mae West," after the film star; an explosive mixed with flour became an "Aunt Jemima," after the pancake mix; and a "Casey Jones mission," after a famous railroad engineer, indicated an air attack against enemy railroads. To stay out of trouble, one avoided a "Dilbert" (screwball sailor) and a "Dirty Gertie of Bizerte" (a woman of loose morals).

New machines required new words. The "jeep" may have originated from a character in the *Popeye* cartoon, Eugene the Jeep, who had magical powers; the term also has been claimed to originate from "G.P.," for general-purpose vehicle. The "bazooka" was an antitank gun similar in appearance to a musical instrument with the same name. The Martin B-26, a twin-engine bomber that required skillful flying, was known as the "Flying Prostitute." A machine for mixing powdered milk and water was an "electric cow."

Humorous slang, especially for military food, lightened the mood and boosted morale. One filled a "garbage catcher" (food tray) with the "slum burner's" (cook's) "donkey dick" (cold cut sausages), "collision mats" (pancakes) with "400W" (maple syrup, named for a heavy oil), "battery acid" (coffee), and "gedunk" (ice cream).

There were euphemisms for sex, illness, and even death. A soldier might need to join the "peter parade" (venereal disease inspection) if he had been out with the "rice paddy Hatties" (Chinese prostitutes), and then take a "bayonet course" (treatment for venereal disease). If a wounded soldier did not eat a "fatal pill" (get killed), the "meat wagon" (ambulance) carried him to the "butcher shop" (hospital) where the "snow white" (nurse) helped with a "submarine" (bed pan).

Words waged war with the enemy. Terms such as "Heinie" and "ratzy" for Germans; "Nip," "rice belly," "ringtail," and "skibby" for the Japanese; and "Hit and Muss," for Adolf Hitler and Benito Mussolini, dehumanized the enemy.

"Stateside," men wore "Victory suits" (suits made to save materials) and young "Victory girls" roamed the streets looking for servicemen, who cried "hubba hubba" to express their approval for young ladies. People held "alphabet" (civilian government) jobs, with the alphabet referring to the names of agencies, abbreviated to strings of letters of major words, and served in the "cits army" (citizen's army, or National Guard). Civilians "kept 'em flying" with their contributions, and "station-wagon patriots"

volunteered for the war effort. Those who hindered or criticized the war were referred to as the "sixth column" (possibly taken from a Robert A. Heinlein story serialized in 1941 in *Astounding Science Fiction*).

Impact World War II slang developed into commonly used terms (e.g., blockbuster, bottleneck, doodle, gizmo, haywire, joyride, runaround, swing shift), and phrases such as "shoot down in flames" continue to influence language in the twenty-first century ("flaming" means "sending an angry electronic message"), adding a richness to the English language that is a far cry from "gobbledygook."

Elizabeth Marie McGhee Nelson

Further Reading

Dickson, Paul. *War Slang: American Fighting Words and Phrases from the Civil War to the Gulf War.* New York: Pocket Books, 1994.

Graeme, Donald. *Sticklers, Sideburns, and Bikinis: The Military Origins of Everyday Words and Phrases.* New York: Osprey, 2008.

See also Bikini bathing suits; Comic strips; *Sad Sack*; Tokyo Rose; World War II.

■ Slovik execution

The Event Execution of an American soldier for desertion

Date January 31, 1945

Place Near the village of Sainte-Marie-aux-Mines, France

Private Slovik was the first U.S. soldier since the Civil War to be executed for desertion. During World War II, more than twenty-one thousand servicemen were convicted of desertion and punished. Of these, forty-nine were sentenced to death, but Slovik was the only one whose sentence was not reduced to a prison term.

Born in 1920, Edward "Eddie" Donald Slovik was raised during the Great Depression by a poor and unstable Polish American family in Detroit, Michigan. At the age of twelve, he began participating in petty thefts and disorderly conduct incidents. He was imprisoned and paroled twice, in 1937-1938 and 1939-1942. Following his second parole, he worked with a plumbing company in Dearborn, Michigan, at which time he married a disabled woman, Antoinette Wisniewski, who was employed as a bookkeeper. Classified as unfit for military service because of his criminal record, he worked regularly and was perhaps on the road to becoming a responsible husband and citizen. As the demand for soldiers increased, however, he was reclassified as fit for service and then drafted into the U.S. Army in January, 1944. Following seven months of basic training in Texas, he was assigned to fight in the European theater with the Twenty-eighth Infantry Division.

When Slovik landed in northern France in August, his division was engaged in violent fighting against German soldiers who had escaped through the Falaise Gap. When he arrived at Elbeuf on August, 25, he was terrified by the loud shelling and large number of dead bodies. In the confusion, he and a friend were either unable or unwilling to report for duty, and they stayed with the Canadian army for six weeks. When the two men finally joined their unit on October 8, Slovik informed the captain that he was "too scared" to fight in the front lines, and he asked to be reassigned to a rear unit. After his request was denied, he wrote one note threatening to "run away" if sent into combat and a second note stating that he understood that his written statement would be used as evidence against him in a court-martial.

When taken into custody, Slovik was offered the opportunity to join a different regiment and to have the charges against him suspended. Believing that the maximum penalty would be a relatively short period in jail, he chose the option of a court-martial. The trial took place in Paris on November 11, and the nine officers of the court judged Slovik guilty and sentenced him to death. Although commanding officers had routinely reduced such sentences, Major General Norman Cota upheld the court's decision. Cota later said that he could not justify a lesser punishment for a deserter at the same time that he was sending thousands of soldiers to their deaths in the brutal battle of Huertgen Forest.

On December 9, Slovik wrote General Dwight D. Eisenhower a letter pleading for clemency. However, Eisenhower approved the execution, observing that it was necessary to discourage desertion, especially when thousands of American soldiers were dying at the Battle of the Bulge. Eisenhower and other officials were almost certainly influenced by Slovik's criminal record combined with his unimpressive written admission. On January 31, 1945, Slovik was executed by a firing quad near the village of Sainte-Marie-aux-Mines in eastern France. Afterward, his body was buried along with those of soldiers executed for violent felonies, such as rape and murder. Rather than publicizing Slovik's execution as an example, the military authorities chose to keep it a secret. His widow was finally informed about how and why he had died by journalist William Bradford Huie, who conducted exhaustive research into the case during the early 1950's.

Impact   Very few people had even heard of Slovik before the 1954 publication of Huie's popular book *The Execution of Private Slovik: The Hitherto Secret Story of the Only American Soldier Since 1864 to Be Shot for Desertion.* Slovik's story then attracted considerable attention, and it produced a wide variety of reactions. Some people viewed Slovik as a cowardly criminal who deserved his fate, while others considered his execution to be an unjust punishment that tarnished the reputation of Eisenhower and other officials. The incident placed a spotlight on the terrors of combat for many young draftees. In 1974, actor Martin Sheen played the role of Slovik in a television film. In 1987, a Polish American veteran persuaded President Jimmy Carter to order the return of Slovik's remains to Michigan.

Thomas Tandy Lewis

Further Reading
Ambrose, Stephen F. *Citizen Soldier.* New York: Simon & Schuster, 1998.
Huie, William Bradford. *The Execution of Private Slovik: The Hitherto Secret Story of the Only American Soldier Since 1864 to Be Shot for Desertion.* 1954. Reprint. Yardley, Pa.: Westholme, 2004.
Whiting, Charles. *Deserter: General Eisenhower and the Execution of Eddie Slovik.* York, England: Eskdale, 2005.

See also   Bulge, Battle of the; Military conscription in the United States; Psychiatry and psychology; War heroes; World War II.

■ Smith, Margaret Chase

Identification   U.S. congresswoman, 1940-1949;
     senator, 1949-1973
Born   December 14, 1897; Skowhegan, Maine
Died   May 29, 1995; Skowhegan, Maine

Smith was the first woman to be elected to both houses of Congress and the first woman to be considered for the U.S. presidency. She was nominated at the Republican Party's convention in 1964. She set the record for the longest-serving female U.S. senator.

As a young adult growing up in Maine, Margaret Chase Smith worked as a schoolteacher, a telephone operator, an executive for a textile mill, and a circulation manager for the local newspaper, the *Independent Reporter.* She attended Colby College, and she was a founder and the president of the Business and Professional Women's club in Skowhegan. She married Clyde Smith, a well-known politician in Maine, in 1930. He was elected to the U.S. House of Representatives in 1936 and in 1938.

Following the death of her husband in 1940, Smith ran for Congress to fill her husband's vacant seat. After being elected on June 3, 1940, she quickly earned a reputation as an independent voter when she supported the Selective Service Act and the Lend-Lease Act proposed by President Franklin D. Roosevelt. She stood for reelection to the House in 1942 and won. She was appointed to serve on the Naval Affairs Committee, and she also worked on other military and home-front issues, including serving as cochair of a subcommittee investigating vice in areas surrounding naval ports. In 1943, she became the first congresswoman to endorse the Equal Rights Amendment, and in 1947, she and Representative Helen Gahagan Douglas introduced an equal-pay bill for women. She devoted much of her energy in the House toward passage of the Women's Armed Services Integration Act, a law that granted women regular military status rather than auxiliary status. The act was signed into law by President Harry S. Truman on July 12, 1948.

Midway through Smith's fourth term in the House of Representatives, newspapers announced that she would run for the Senate seat of Maine's Wallace White, who was retiring. With the help of her administrative assistant, William C. Lewis, she launched her Senate campaign on January 1, 1948. She ran a tough campaign, appealing to a wide range of constituents, including women's organizations and even some Democrats. She won the primary vote by a landslide in September and 70 percent of the vote in November, and although the Republicans lost eighty-three seats in the House and the Senate, they obtained their first woman senator.

After entering the Senate, Smith was offered a seat on two important Senate committees: the Senate Republican Policy Committee and the Senate Armed Services Committee. She shared both these committee assignments with Joseph McCarthy of Wisconsin. As McCarthy began his virulent attack on so-called communists in the Truman administration, Smith found herself increasingly at odds with his behavior. On June 1, 1950,

Margaret Chase Smith being sworn in as a member of the U.S. House of Representatives on June 10, 1940, after the death of her husband left the position open. Speaker William Bankhead administers the oath as another Maine representative, James C. Oliver, looks on. (Library of Congress)

she delivered a speech in the Senate that she called her "Declaration of Conscience," clearly an indictment of McCarthy's fear tactics and abuse of Senate privilege. The speech was delivered four years before the Senate censured McCarthy.

Impact   While Smith never considered herself a feminist, she worked to promote equal opportunities for women. She supported women in the service during World War II, earning the nickname, "Mother of the WAVES." She voted for Democratic legislation when warranted, and she sometimes voted against Republican-sponsored legislation with which she did not agree. She was considered by many to be a woman of courage, especially after speaking against McCarthyism.

Yvonne J. Johnson

Further Reading

Plourde, Lynn, and David McPhail. *Margaret Chase Smith: A Woman for President—A Time Line Biography.* Watertown, Mass.: Charlesbridge, 2008.

Sherman, Janann. *No Place for a Woman: A Life of Senator Margaret Chase Smith.* New Brunswick, N.J.: Rutgers University Press, 2000.

Wallace, Patricia Ward. *Politics of Conscience: A Biography of Margaret Chase Smith.* Westport, Conn.: Praeger, 1995.

See also   Civil rights and liberties; Congress, U.S.; Conservatism in U.S. politics; Lend-Lease; Women in the U.S. military; Women's roles and rights in the United States.

■ Smith Act

The Law   Federal law making it illegal to advocate or to belong to an organization advocating the violent overthrow of the U.S. government
Also known as   Alien Registration Act of 1940
Date   Became law on June 28, 1940

The U.S. government used the Smith Act to prosecute hundreds of communists, socialists, and pro-Nazi leaders for actions such as recruiting new members or publishing books, magazines, or newspapers that advocated its overthrow.

Named for its sponsor, Congressman Howard W. Smith of Virginia, and signed into law by President Franklin D. Roosevelt, the Smith Act was the first federal sedition law since the Alien and Sedition Acts of

1798. Persons convicted of violating the Smith Act were fined and sentenced up to twenty years in prison and were ineligible to hold a government job for five years. First Amendment advocates called the Smith Act the most drastic restriction on freedom of speech ever enacted in the United States during peacetime.

Impact   The constitutionality of the Smith Act was upheld by the U.S. Supreme Court in 1951, but in 1957 the Court overturned a series of convictions under the Smith Act and restricted its use only to prosecution of active participation in or verbal encouragement of specific insurrectionary actions. The Smith Act is still in effect.

Eddith A. Dashiell

Further Reading

Belknap, Michal R. *Cold War Political Justice: The Smith Act, the Communist Party, and American Civil Liberties.* Greenwood, Conn.: Greenwood Press, 1977.

Finan, Chris. *From the Palmer Raids to the Patriot Act: A History of the Fight for Free Speech in America.* Boston: Beacon Press, 2007.

See also   Federal Bureau of Investigation; Hoover, J. Edgar; House Committee on Un-American Activities; Smith Act trials; Socialist Workers Party; Supreme Court, U.S.

■ Smith Act trials

The Events   Federal trials in which defendants were charged with violating the Smith Act of 1940, which made it illegal to advocate the overthrow of the government
Dates   December 8, 1941-October 3, 1949

Throughout the 1940's the federal government used the Smith Act to prosecute radical groups as a means of protecting national security. First Amendment advocates criticized the Smith Act trials as being a form of censorship and a violation of free speech because the defendants were being punished for their political viewpoints and not for any specific act against the government.

The Minneapolis sedition trial of 1941 was the government's first prosecution under the Smith Act of the previous year. On June 27, 1941, agents of the Federal Bureau of Investigation (FBI) raided offices of the Trotskyist Socialist Workers Party in Minneapolis and St. Paul, Minnesota, and seized large quantities of communist literature. In August, the U.S. Justice Department indicted twenty-nine members of the Socialist Party, who pleaded not guilty to charges that they were conspiring to overthrow the government and to create insubordination among the armed forces.

First Amendment advocates demanded that the government drop the charges because the defendants' speeches or publications should have been protected by the First Amendment and because they did not pose an immediate threat to national security. The government did not drop the indictments, however, and a trial began on October 27, 1941. The jury convicted eighteen of the twenty-nine defendants. Those convicted were sentenced to prison terms ranging from twelve to sixteen months. After an appeals court upheld their convictions and the U.S. Supreme Court refused to review their case, the convicted socialists began serving their prison sentences on December 31, 1943. The last prisoners were released in February, 1945. American communist leaders applauded the convictions of their rival Trotskyists. However, seven years later, they too would find themselves facing prosecution under the Smith Act.

Great Sedition Trial of 1944   The Great Sedition Trial of 1941 was a mass trial of dozens of suspected Nazi conspirators and sympathizers. The defendants, who included a former U.S. diplomat, had little in common with one another except for their shared faith in fascism and their hatred for President Franklin D. Roosevelt, Jews, and communists.

This trial began in April, 1944, and quickly evolved into circus. Despite U.S. District judge Edward Eischer's efforts to follow proper courtroom procedures, the unruly defendants frequently interrupted the proceedings with Nazi salutes, cheers, groans, and laughter. They also wore an array of costumes into the courtroom that ranged from a satin nightdress to Halloween masks. One defendant died during the trial, which lasted so long that some defendants were permitted to take vacations.

At the end of the 102d day of the trial, Judge Eischer died at home of a heart attack. A mistrial was then declared, but it was almost a full year before the government dismissed the indictments in December, 1945—four months after the end of World War II. Because Germany had been the enemy and the Soviet Union was an ally during World War II, the government had focused its attention on prosecuting pro-Nazi leaders rather than communists. That all changed after World War II ended.

Communist Party Trials   After the war ended, U.S.-Soviet relations began to deteriorate and Cold War tensions sparked fears of a possible communist takeover. President Harry S. Truman was under political pressure to take action against domestic communists in order to prove that he was not "soft on communism."

In 1948, Eugene Dennis, the general secretary of the Communist Party USA, and eleven other party leaders were arrested, charged and indicted for violating the Smith Act. They were accused of conspiring to teach and advocate the overthrow of the government by force. Their trial was held in the U.S. courthouse on Foley Square in downtown Manhattan during the same time as another celebrated trial in the same building: the perjury trial of Alger Hiss, a former U.S. State Department official accused of having spied for the Soviets. The communists' trial lasted for ten months and was marred by loud confrontations among the defendants, their lawyers, and the judge. In October, 1949, the communist defendants were found guilty, fined ten thousand dollars each and sentenced to five years in prison.

Impact   Although the U.S. Supreme Court upheld the convictions of the communist leaders in its 1951 decision, the Court later reversed itself in 1957 by ruling in a similar case that teaching anti-American ideas, no matter how objectionable it may seem, is not the same as actually implementing a plan to overthrow the government. The government eventually stopped using the Smith Act to prosecute communists and fascists, but the federal law remained on the books.

Eddith A. Dashiell

Further Reading

Belknap, Michal R. *American Political Trials: Revised, Expanded Edition.* Westport, Conn.: Greenwood Press, 1994. Examination of select trials that resulted from political persecution from the early colonial era to the late twentieth century.

_____. *Cold War Political Justice: The Smith Act, the Communist Party, and American Civil Liberties.* Westport, Conn.: Greenwood Press, 1977. Detailed history of the Smith Act and the 1949 trial of eleven leaders of the Communist Party USA who were convicted of conspiring to overthrow the U.S. government.

Finan, Chris. *From the Palmer Raids to the Patriot Act: A History of the Fight for Free Speech in America.* Boston: Beacon Press, 2007. Broad history of assaults on free speech in the United States from 1919 through 2006.

St. George, Maximilian, and Lawrence Dennis. *A Trial on Trial: The Great Sedition Trial of 1944.* Washington, D.C.: National Civil Rights Committee, 1946. A defense attorney and defendant's account of the *United States v. McWilliams* trial.

Steele, Richard W. *Free Speech in the Good War.* New York: St. Martin's Press, 1999. Analysis of the effects of foreign conflict on domestic affairs and free speech during World War II.

Stone, Geoffrey. *Perilous Times—Free Speech in Wartime: From the Sedition Act of 1798 to the War on Terrorism.* New York: W. W. Norton, 2004. Historical analysis of the tendency by the United States to compromise free speech rights in the name of national security during wartime or another national crisis.

See also   Anticommunism; Communist Party USA; Federal Bureau of Investigation; Hoover, J. Edgar; House Committee on Un-American Activities; Smith Act; Socialist Workers Party; Supreme Court, U.S.; Truman, Harry S.

■ Smith-Connally Act

The Law   Federal legislation designed to prevent labor strikes that would disrupt war production
Also known as   War Labor Disputes Act; Smith-Connally Anti-Strike Act
Date   Became law on June 25, 1943

The Smith-Connally Act helped enable the American war industry to produce twice as much as all enemy countries combined by 1944.

At the time of World War II, many American labor groups involved in war production performed jobs with tremendous risks and undesirable wages. Labor unions sought to remedy these conditions through strikes. The U.S. Congress, however, with the backing of the general population, passed the Smith-Connally Act in order to prevent strikes and to continue war production without disruption. Partly because of his ties with labor organizations and a clause in the bill that forbade union contributions to political campaigns, President Franklin D. Roosevelt vetoed the bill. For the first time during the war, Congress overrode Roosevelt's veto.

The act gave the president the power to seize and operate any private war plant that was threatened by strikes. Also, all war industry unions were forced to give thirty days notice of intent to strike or else be held financially liable for all damages. Using this executive power, President Roosevelt and his successor, Harry S. Truman, seized numerous war plants that were on the verge of strike.

Impact   Although the act expired six months after the end of the war, as designed, it had numerous lasting impacts. Most important, it helped expand the idea of executive power in times of emergency. It also was a precursor to the Taft-Hartley Act of 1947, which further regulated labor union action.

Ramses Jalalpour and Larry Grimm

Further Reading
Kersten, Andrew. *Labor's Home Front: The American Federation of Labor During World War II.* New York: New York University Press, 2006.
Mayer, Kenneth. *With the Stroke of a Pen: Executive Orders and Presidential Power.* Princeton, N.J.: Princeton University Press, 2002.

See also   Ickes, Harold; Labor strikes; Lewis, John L.; National War Labor Board; Presidential powers; Taft-Hartley Act; Unionism.

■ Smith v. Allwright

The Case   U.S. Supreme Court ruling on voting rights in relation to racial desegregation
Date   Decided on April 3, 1944

The Supreme Court's 8-1 ruling that forbade the use of all-white primary elections began a legal movement that culminated in full voting rights for African Americans.

The Fifteenth Amendment to the U.S. Constitution made it illegal to deny a citizen the right to vote based on color or race. The Texas legislature attempted to dodge the mandate by implementing all-white primary elections. Victory in the Democratic primary in Texas almost guaranteed victory in the general election; consequently, African Americans

Smith v. Allwright

The U.S. Supreme Court, in its majority opinion in Smith v. Allwright, *ruled that excluding African Americans from participation in the Democratic Party primary in Texas violated the Fifteenth Amendment.*

If the state requires a certain election procedure, prescribing a general election ballot made up of party nominees so chosen, and limits the choice of the electorate in general elections for state officers . . . to those whose names appear on such a ballot, it endorses, adopts, and enforces the discrimination against Negroes practiced by a party entrusted by Texas law with the determination of the qualifications of participants in the primary. This is state action within the meaning of the Fifteenth Amendment.

were deprived of any meaningful voter participation. When Lonnie Smith, an African American, was denied participation in Texas's Democratic primary, he sued S. E. Allwright, a Democratic Party election judge.

The Supreme Court had to decide whether the action taken by the Democratic Party was a private or state action. It was a Democratic convention that chose to prohibit black participation, and because the participants of the convention were not elected officials, the party argued that the prohibition was a private action and not subject to the Fifteenth Amendment. The Supreme Court disagreed, concluding that actions the party took in performing electoral procedures were state actions and must follow the Constitution.

Impact *Smith* did more than forbid any state from denying citizens the right to vote in primaries based on color. In *Smith*, the Court looked more at the intent of the Constitution and also the intent and effect of the action in question. This substantive approach would be similarly applied in future race-related cases, namely, *Brown v. Board of Education* (1954).

Ramses Jalalpour and Larry Grimm

Further Reading

Arlington, Karen. *Voting Rights in America.* Lanham, Md.: University Press of America, 1993.

Vile, John. "Fifteenth Amendment to the U.S. Constitution (1870)." In *Milestone Documents in American History: Exploring the Primary Sources That Shaped America,* edited by Paul Finkelman. Dallas, Tex.: Schlager Group, 2008.

See also Civil rights and liberties; National Association for the Advancement of Colored People; Racial discrimination; Stone, Harlan Fiske; Supreme Court, U.S.; Voting rights.

■ Smoking and tobacco

Spurred by combat and fueled by marketing from large manufacturers, the use of tobacco, especially in the form of cigarettes, climbed sharply after World War I, reaching the heights of acceptability in the United States during and immediately after World War II.

The seventeenth century was the pipe-smoking era. Snuff was all the rage in the eighteenth century. The nineteenth century was the age of the chaw and the cigar. Early in the twentieth century, cigarettes began to dominate as the preferred method of consuming tobacco. Introduced in hand-rolled form around the Crimean War, cigarettes began their ascent to prominence after the invention of automated rolling machinery during the late 1880's. By 1900, cigarettes challenged cigars as the smoke of choice, with annual sales of 3.5 billion cigarettes and 5 billion cigars in the United States. Per capita consumption rose steadily from 80 cigarettes in 1910 to more than 2,500 by the mid-1940's, when one-half of all adult Americans smoked.

Increasing Popularity of Cigarettes There were several reasons for the increased popularity of cigarette smoking during the 1940's. First, the cigarettes themselves had been perfected. In 1913, the R. J. Reynolds Tobacco Company launched mass-produced cigarettes, featuring blended, cured tobacco that produced smooth, flavorful smoke, easy to inhale and kept fresh in sealed, prepackaged lots of twenty. Backed by the famous "I'd walk a mile for a Camel" advertising campaign, the brand quickly grabbed more than 40 percent of the market. In self-preservation, the American Tobacco Company and Liggett & Meyers created similar products, including American Tobacco's Lucky Strike cigarettes, sold with the slogan "Lucky Strike, it's toasted." and Liggett & Myers's Chesterfield cigarettes, marketed with the phrase "Chesterfields, they satisfy." All three companies vigorously marketed their brands, making them favorites with American servicemen during World War I, when millions of young men acquired the smoking habit, thanks to cigarettes in their rations. Through a similar program that included free C-ration cigarettes, millions more soldiers, sailors, and aviators became committed smokers during World War II and afterward. At the end of the 1940's, Americans were smoking more than 300 billion domestic cigarettes per year.

A second reason for the increased popularity of smoking cigarettes was a doubling of the market. During the 1920's, when American women organized to exert their rights and independence, the Philip Morris company assisted by public relations pioneer Edward Bernays began targeting female smokers with the introduction of Marlboro cigarettes, described as "mild as May." Other manufacturers followed suit, marketing specific brands to an audience eager to demonstrate its equality in all things. By the middle of World War II, one of every three women was a confirmed smoker, following the example of First Lady Eleanor Roosevelt, who publicly lit up alongside her husband, cigarette holder-using President Franklin D. Roosevelt.

The third reason for increasing cigarette smoking was that the practice was becoming an everyday habit for many people. Regular developments in smoking technology—cigarettes by the carton; crush-proof packs; safety matches; stylish cigarette holders, cases, boxes, and ashtrays; and indestructible Zippo lighters—made the process of smoking easier, more convenient, more socially acceptable, and more aesthetically pleasing for users. In addition, smoking was relatively inexpensive, with the cost of pack of cigarettes just fifteen cents.

Finally, cigarettes garnered immense profits. The financial impact of smoking was not lost on the U.S. government. In 1930, more than $500 million was collected in federal taxes on tobacco products, with eight out of ten of these dollars coming from cigarettes. By the late 1940's, cigarettes were an even more significant contributor to the national economy.

Creating the Cigarette-Smoker's Image America has had a love-hate relationship with tobacco since the indigenous plant was first cultivated as a cash crop at the beginning of the seventeenth century. Users over millennia have enjoyed tobacco's mild narcotic effects, its use as a palliative in times of stress, and its perceived powers as a stimulant. Growers have long appreciated nicotine's physically and psychologically addictive qualities that provide a ready market for tobacco products. Nonsmoking using purists, however, have always considered tobacco use in any form sinful, like liquor or other ingested substances with the potential to adversely affect one's mind or body. Cigarettes may have offered advantages over cigars (such as mildness of taste and aroma) or chewing tobacco (by trading smoke stands for spittoons), but they still represented a vice, and thus they detracted an individual from clean living.

The two world wars helped dispel the aura of sin clinging to cigarettes, at least temporarily. Tobacco-stuffed tubes were generally seen as harmless devices to steady the nerves of military men or of civilians. Print advertising, in times of both war and peace, reinforced the impression that smoking cigarettes was a natural, ordinary, and pleasurable activity. During the 1930's and increasingly throughout the 1940's, entertainers, such as Bob Hope and Jack Benny, were sponsored on their radio shows by major cigarette brands. In 1941, Camel's renowned smoke ring-blowing billboard went up in Times Square. After the war, cigarettes made a smooth transition into television advertising.

Hollywood, aided and abetted by "big tobacco," did its part to assist the cause. Beginning in the silent film era and continuing into the 1940's, motion pictures depicted heroic soldiers, clear-thinking industrial titans, seekers of justice, romantic leads, and other admirable types holding smoldering cigarettes. Women who indulged onscreen were portrayed as bold, interesting, and self-confident characters. In cinematic plot lines, especially in such box office hits as the Academy Award-winning *Casablanca* (1942), featuring a chain-smoking Humphrey Bogart, and *Now, Voyager* (1942), in which Paul Henreid made the much copied romantic gesture of lighting two butts at once, cigarettes served many purposes. They could be icebreakers in social situations, tension relievers, or props capable of symbolizing a range of qualities, including strength, determination, and sexuality.

One of several advertisements for Chesterfield cigarettes that future U.S. president Ronald Reagan made during the 1940's. (AP/Wide World Photos)

The luster and glamour of cigarettes was heightened when actors delivered their testimonials for prominent brands. Top stars such as George Raft, Gloria Swanson, Fred Astaire, Lauren Bacall, Gary Cooper, Joan Crawford, Henry Fonda, Myrna Loy, Clark Gable, Barbara Stanwyck, Fred MacMurray, Lana Turner, Ray Milland, Carole Lombard, Spencer Tracy, and Ronald Reagan, were paid to tout cigarettes. Their collective message was plain: "You may not live the exciting life I do, but we have something in common when you smoke my brand." For the masses who perceived their lives as less exciting than those of actors, vicarious fame and fortune proved irresistible, and the public smoked in record numbers. Community conventions reflected the broad acceptance of cigarettes: During the 1940's and through most of the twentieth century, people could be seen smoking almost everywhere, including in restaurants, bars, hospitals, churches, public buildings, and airplanes.

Cigarettes and Health From their inception, cigarettes were promoted with exaggerated or specious claims of health benefits. At various times, cigarettes were endowed by their creators with the ability to cure disease, freshen breath, improve mental acuity, boost physical strength, aid digestion, or suppress appetite. Few suspected that smoking could be hazardous. It was only during the late 1930's, when cases of relatively uncommon lung cancer emerged, that Americans began to wonder if smoking was really the harmless pastime it appeared.

Despite such advances as menthol flavoring and filter tips to make cigarettes more palatable, most cigarettes smoked before the mid-1950's were unfiltered. Smokers readily acknowledged the drawbacks of the habit. Besides risking burns or fires, users typically complained of halitosis, stained teeth, raw tongues, sore throats, shortness of breath, and smoker's cough. However, for the first half of the twentieth century, and particularly during the 1940's, the possible health risks of smoking were largely unknown, ignored, or downplayed. Besides, one wondered who worried about cigarettes amid enemy fusillades or under the shadow of the atomic bomb.

Ironically, German scientists during the late 1930's had conducted a comprehensive examination of the deleterious effects of cigarette smoking on human health, and their study showed a strong correlation between smoking and lung cancer. This study came to light after World War II, when the United States shipped tons of tobacco overseas to assist in Germany's economic recovery, but the findings were discounted because its authors were unreliable Nazis. Even after similar research confirming the link between cigarettes and cancer, as well as other diseases, was conducted in the United States beginning in the early 1950's, cigarette sales continued to rise until the mid-1960's. Not surprisingly, tobacco companies hotly contested the research linking their products to cancer.

Impact The 1940's was a golden decade for cigarette smoking in America. The product was a great equalizer like its frequent companion, coffee. Cigarettes were available everywhere in many brands and were affordable to anyone for pocket change. Cigarettes could be consumed virtually anywhere, with few restrictions. They were the catalyst for a multi-billion-dollar industry and provided significant revenue for national and state budgets.

In the following decades, when health concerns were confirmed, the tobacco industry and smoking habits began to change. Domestic scientific studies of the 1950's led to the Surgeon General's report on the adverse effects of smoking during the 1960's, and these findings were responsible for a tremendous shakeup in the tobacco business. Health warnings about the adverse affects of smoking were required to appear on cigarette packs. Advertising on radio and television was prohibited. A succession of increasingly high taxes made cigarettes more costly, and legislators adopted restrictions that made it more difficult to smoke. Lawsuits against cigarette manufacturers forced companies to diversify into businesses unrelated to tobacco, and new industries sprang up that were antitobacco and aimed at helping smokers abandon their cigarette habits. Yet despite repressive measures, inflated product costs, and widespread dissemination of information about the dangers of the habit, smoking persisted into the twenty-first century. In 2009, about 21 percent of adult Americans continued to smoke, and more than a billion people around the globe regularly lit up to enjoy the special qualities found in tobacco.

Jack Ewing

Further Reading

Brandt, Allan M. *The Cigarette Century: The Rise, Fall, and Deadly Persistence of the Product That Defined America.* New York: Basic Books, 2007. An exhaustively researched study of the impact of cigarette smoking on the history, culture, and health in the United States over the last century.

Fitzgerald, James. *The Joys of Smoking Cigarettes.* New York: Harper Paperbacks, 2007. A compendium of information, trivia, and historical facts, this book examines the cigarette smoking experience from the user's perspective.

Giesenhagen, Joe. *The Collector's Guide to Vintage Cigarette Packs.* Atglen, Pa.: Schiffer, 1999. For nostalgia buffs and collectors of tobacco ephemera, this illustrated guide covers cigarette packaging art from the late nineteenth to the late twentieth centuries.

Kuntz, Kathleen. *Smoke: Cigars, Cigarettes, Pipes, and Other Combustibles.* New York: New Line Books, 2005. Profusely illustrated, this book focuses on the history and various methods of smoking tobacco.

Parker-Pope, Tara. *Cigarettes: Anatomy of an Industry from Seed to Smoke.* New York: New Press, 2002. An overview of the history of tobacco use, cigarette manufacture, marketing, and health issues.

See also Advertising in the United States; Army, U.S.; Benny, Jack; Bogart, Humphrey; Business and the economy in the United States; Cancer; *Casablanca*; Film in the United States; Films about World War II; Hope, Bob.

■ Soccer

Definition Team sport known as association football outside North America

During the 1940's, soccer was a niche sport of interest primarily to North Americans with ethnic backgrounds from European countries, where soccer was very popular. For this reason also, mainstream audiences dismissed the sport. Nevertheless, after qualifying for the 1950 World Cup competition in 1949, the U.S. national team would pull off one of the most shocking upsets in the sport's history.

With World War II raging in Europe and China in 1940, both the American Soccer League and the Canadian Soccer League finished their seasons while only Canada was directly involved in the war. In both countries soccer was a minor sport primarily associated with ethnic European Americans who, in the eyes of most North Americans, had not yet fully integrated. The fact that soccer was popular among recent immigrations helped to stigmatize it.

Ethnic Affiliation and Challenges of War Years Soccer club names in both the American and Canadian leagues often reflected pride in ethnic backgrounds. Of the six teams of the Western Division of the Canadian league, three bore ethnic suffixes such as "England United" and "Toronto Scottish." Similarly in the United States, the 1940's champion of the Metropolitan Division were the "Kearny Scots" of New Jersey, and that year's champions of the New England Division were the "Lusitania Sports Club"—a name taken from the Latin word for Portugal—followed by the "Swedish Americans." Only clubs whose names suggested Axis affiliations changed their names. For example, the "Baltimore Germans" became the "Baltimore Americans" in 1940 and the "Philadelphia German Americans" became the "Philadelphia Americans" in 1942.

Mainstream North American interest in soccer remained marginal. The Canadian Soccer League ended its activities in the summer of 1942, with Ulster United (a team with an Irish name) winning the championship. The league did not start up again until 1947.

In the United States, the New England Division folded at the end of the 1941 season, leaving the Metropolitan Division as sole professional venue. Soon after the United States entered World War II in December, 1941, many players were drafted into the military. Although the Metropolitan Division continued play throughout the war years, its officials complained that unskilled replacement players brought more roughness and brutality into the game and threatened the referees. Of the nearly two hundred American Soccer League players who served in the U.S. armed forces during World War II, six were killed in action.

Many soccer tournaments that had been held before the war were discontinued during the war years. Only the most prestigious competitions, the U.S. Open Cup Final and the U.S. National Amateur Cup Final, were held during every year of the decade. Intercollegiate soccer was also severely curtailed by 1943, only to revive after the war ended in 1945. During that year, the national association changed its name from U.S. Football Association to U.S. Soccer Football Association.

Postwar Recovery and the U.S. National Team As players returned home after the war, American clubs also drew on new immigrants and refugees from Europe who liked to play soccer. In 1946, the owner of the Chicago Maroons, Fred Weiszmann, established the new North American Soccer Football League, which included a Toronto team. However, it lasted only one and a half seasons before folding in mid-1947.

The end of the war brought revival of the prewar tradition of foreign soccer teams visiting the United States to play friendly matches. For example, Liverpool from the English leagues toured North America in mid-1946, playing one Canadian and nine teams; it won all ten of these matches. The tour drew more than 100,000 spectators and netted about $93,000—a vast sum for soccer venues in North America during the 1940's.

The success of the Liverpool tour encouraged more foreign soccer clubs to tour North America. Notable visitors included the Hapoel Football Club of Tel Aviv in 1947—the year before Israel became an independent state—and the young Israeli national team in 1948. Hapoel's first match against the New York Stars drew 43,000 spectators and was apparently the first televised soccer event in the United States

After years of wartime inactivity, the U.S. national team reassembled in 1947, only to lose against the Cuban and Mexican national teams in prerevolutionary Havana, Cuba. In 1948, the U.S. team set off to play in the 1948 London Olympics without having undergone any preliminary training. After arriving in England, the team won a friendly game against Korea, beat a Royal Air Force team, and lost to China before drawing Italy in its opening Olympics match. The team's 9-0 drubbing by the Italians was bitter. After the Olympics the team was again humiliated in an 11-0 rout by Norway and a 5-0 beating by Northern Ireland. After returning to the United States, the national team salvaged some pride by beating the visiting Israeli national team three times.

The biggest triumph for the U.S. national team came in Mexico City in September, 1949, when it qualified to play in the 1950 World Cup. The team's 6-0 loss to Mexico was offset by an important 1-1 draw against Cuba. On September 21, the United States beat Cuba 5-2 and secured a World Cup berth.

Impact Despite the ability of the American Soccer League and various amateur clubs to play soccer in America throughout the 1940's and the upswing in the fortunes of the U.S. national team, mainstream North American audiences took almost no notice of the sport. The biggest soccer audience magnets of the decade were visits by European and Israeli teams. As the decade ended, soccer remained an obscure sport favored by immigrants. The game's proponents faced an uphill struggle to popularize the game. Perhaps ironically, the U.S. national team scored what is considered one of the greatest upsets in history at the 1950 World Cup competition, when it defeated the powerful English team. Even this victory—which has remained a pinnacle of U.S. World Cup success—went largely unnoticed in the United States.

R. C. Lutz

Further Reading

Glanville, Brian. *Soccer.* New York: Crown Publishers, 1968. Discusses the U.S. national team at 1948 London Olympics and 1949 qualifiers for 1950 World Cup. Illustrated, index.

Goldblatt, David. *The Ball Is Round: A Global History of Soccer.* New York: Riverhead Books, 2008. Up-to-date, comprehensive, and entertaining history of world soccer, with considerable attention given to the game in the United States.

Markovits, Andrei, and Steven Hellerman. *Offside: Soccer and American Exceptionalism.* Princeton, N.J.: Princeton University Press, 2001. Chapter 3 looks also at the 1940's and briefly discusses best American players of that period.

Murray, Bill. *Football: A History of the World Game.* Brookfield, Vt.: Ashgate, 1994. Last chapter covers decade in America. Discusses postwar American soccer clubs with ethnic affiliations.

Szymanski, Stefan, and Andrew Zimbalist. *National Pastime: How Americans Play Baseball and the Rest of the World Plays Soccer.* Washington, D.C.: Brookings Institute, 2005. This studying comparing soccer and baseball discusses the marginal status of American soccer during the 1940's and points out how baseball team owners sought military draft exemptions for their players while soccer clubs did not.

Wangerin, David. *Soccer in a Football World.* Philadelphia: Temple University Press, 2008. Chapter 3 covers American soccer during the 1940's with a focus on postwar tours by foreign clubs, the 1948 Olympics, and the 1949 qualifiers for 1950 World Cup. Illustrated, index.

See also   Baseball; Basketball; Football; Ice hockey; Immigration to the United States; Israel, creation of; Olympic Games of 1948; Sports in Canada; Sports in the United States.

■ Social sciences

Definition   Scholarly disciplines that study human interactions and social behavior, social institutions, and culture through primarily empirical methods; examples include anthropology, economics, political science, and sociology

Social scientists engaged in various roles and activities during World War II, from price control to bombing surveys to study of enemy propaganda, and both the importance of their advice to the government and their impact on public opinion grew considerably during the 1940's. Contributions from and reactions against ideas of European émigré social thinkers who had fled Nazism played an important role in the development of the social sciences in the United States.

The social sciences during the 1940's developed ideas that had arisen during the previous two decades and prepared the way for innovations in empirical, behavioral, and quantitative social science during the 1950's and later. While continuing in their traditional roles, social scientists also took on more war-related activity.

Impact   During the 1940's, cultural anthropology predominated over biological anthropology in the United States. This cultural emphasis was strengthened with the discovery of the Nazi death camps. The camps and their use acted to discredit biological accounts of human behavior because of the horrible misuse of biology by Nazi programs of racism and cultural genocide.

Despite retiring in 1946, Alfred Kroeber continued to publish and was perhaps the leading American anthropologist. He attempted a massive synthesis of cultural and physical anthropology. His work focused on relating archaeology and culture, and he did important work in classifying Native American languages.

The "culture and personality" school was influential during the decade. During World War II, Margaret Mead became known for her work as executive secretary of the National Research Council's Committee on Food Habits, then after the war for her work as curator of ethnology at the American Museum of Natural History. Her book *And Keep Your Powder Dry* (1942) concerned the American character, and *Male and Female: A Study of the Sexes in a*

Anthropologist Margaret Mead. (Library of Congress)

Changing World (1949) expanded on her earlier work on Pacific Islander societies to draw much more extensive and explicit conclusions regarding American gender roles.

Ruth Benedict, another adherent of the "culture and personality" approach, branched out from her studies of Amerindian cultures to look at issues related to World War II. Her *Races of Mankind* (1943), coauthored by Gene Weltfish, advocated racial unity against fascism, and her 1946 *Chrysanthemum and the Sword* attempted to portray the Japanese national character.

Another figure who attempted to combine cultural anthropology with individual psychology (influenced by Freudian psychoanalysis) was Clyde Kluckhohn. Kluckhohn's major fieldwork was on the Navajo, but he became head of the Russian Research Institute at Harvard at the beginning of the Cold War.

Although Bronislaw Malinowski died unexpectedly early in 1942, his works continued to appear during the 1940's, and his version of functionalism, combined with a cross-cultural modification of Freudianism, continued to be influential. His influential books include *The Scientific Theory of Culture, and Other Essays* (1944), *Magic, Science, and Religion, and Other Essays* (1948), and *The Dynamics of Culture Change* (1945).

In contrast to the culture and personality theorists, who were often influenced by psychoanalysis and rejected earlier evolutionary views as simplistic or racist, Leslie White and Julian Steward espoused evolutionary views of anthropology. White was the more materialistic of the two. He was close to Marxism (having ties with a socialist party) and advocated a single path of evolution for all societies (unilinear evolution). Steward supported a more complex branching path of social evolution (multilinear evolution).

Claude Lévi-Strauss, an émigré from France, spent the war in the United States. He met Russian linguist Roman Jakobson while teaching in New York and learned the latter's structural linguistics. Two decades later, Levi-Strauss's work on structural anthropology greatly influenced American cultural anthropology. At the end of the 1940's, Levi-Strauss was one of the contributors to the United Nations Educational, Scientific, and Cultural Organization (UNESCO) statement "The Race Question," criticizing the notion of biological races (obviously influenced by the Holocaust, but not mentioning it).

Opposition to racism led many anthropologists to develop theories of relativism, in opposition to doctrines of white superiority. In *Myth of the Negro Past* (1941) and other works, Melville Herskovits exemplified this trend. Significantly, Herskovits in 1947 drafted the Universal Declaration on Human Rights for the United Nations, tying the issue of human rights to relativism.

Economics   Economics during the 1940's was in somewhat of an interregnum. The "years of high theory" during the 1920's and 1930's were assimilated. A number of American economists destined to be eminent in the next decade worked during the war for the Office of Price Control and for the Strategic Bombing Survey.

British economist John Maynard Keynes had published his *General Theory of Employment, Interest, and Money* in 1936. He previously had personally influenced President Franklin D. Roosevelt and his "brain trust" economic advisers. Keynes advocated government spending as a stimulus for economies in depression, as a means of lessening unemployment and restoring equilibrium. Keynes himself worked tirelessly at the 1944 Bretton Woods Conference in New Hampshire, helping to shape the world monetary system. Keynesian theory grew during the 1940's and came to be one of the dominant schools of academic economics as well as influencing government policy in the United States and elsewhere until the 1970's. Alvin Hansen at Harvard University presented a clearer and less radical version of Keynesian theory that grew in influence in American economics. Although Keynesianism was in the ascendancy, in 1948 Milton Friedman wrote an article presenting the monetarist approach to economics, claiming that control of the money supply is sufficient to prevent depressions. Monetarism competed for academic and policy influence.

Institutional economics took a more anthropological approach to economics, studying the institutions that existed in various markets. It was notably used in labor economics and the economics of development, with Clarence J. Ayers of Texas as a proponent. Many of the methods of mathematical economics were first published during the 1940's. A revised version of Paul Samuelson's dissertation came out as *Foundations of Economic Analysis* in 1947. Russian American Wassily Leontief's *The Structure of American Economy, 1919-1929* (1941) exemplified the new wave of quantitative empirical studies.

In 1942, Paul Sweezy published *The Theory of Capitalist Development*, considered by many to be the best American Marxist book in economics. Sweezy withdrew from academia, and in the late 1940's the Cold War led to a sharp decline in the influence of Marxian economic ideas in the United States.

Political Science Two trends in political science that grew during the 1940's and would dominate the following decade were behavioralism and political realism. Both opposed the idea of political theory or political science as a primarily evaluative or normative enterprise, making value judgments about political behavior. Development of these approaches was in part a reaction against the influx of pessimistic and highly evaluative political theory presented by European, primarily German, émigrés who had fled Adolf Hitler's regime and arrived in the United States during the 1930's and 1940's. On the conser-

vative side were Leo Strauss and Eric Voegelin. On the left were Frankfurt School Marxist theorists such as Herbert Marcuse. Politically opposed as these German theorists were, they agreed in condemning liberalism and empirical science, as the sources of the erosion of values that led to fascism. American political scientists, who had mainly praised and advocated American democracy and liberalism, felt a need to counter these elitist pessimists.

A number of American political scientists believed that pursuit of the scientific method and clear separation of facts from values would function to defend American democracy. Not all agreed, however, and some defended highly evaluative political science. The influence of behavioralism, which emphasized people's observable behaviors and looked for claims that could be tested empirically, grew within political science. Public opinion polling, such as that of the Gallup organization, had grown and been refined during the 1930's, offering a source of quantitative data. Two works that were important for the growth of behavioralism were Herbert Simon's *Administrative Behavior* (1947) and V. O. Key's *Southern Politics in State and Nation* (1949). In 1946, the Social Science Research Council established a Committee on Political Behavior that channeled funding toward behavioral studies.

Harold Lasswell's study of propaganda during World War I and Nazi propaganda during World War II made him especially aware of irrational aspects of politics and the power of the psychology of the unconscious, as described by psychoanalyst Sigmund Freud. Lasswell was a liberal who thought that the populace needed the guidance of elite experts who could determine the best interests of society. He contributed to political psychology, behavioralism, and a realistic conception of political power.

The second important trend in political science during the 1940's was the growth to dominance of "political realism" in the theory of international relations. Hans Morgenthau, a German-speaking Czech who came to America, criticized so-called "idealist" theorists of international relations for believing that appeals to moral principles and international law or world government could maintain international peace. He believed that the threat or exercise of power was necessary. In his *Scientific Man vs. Power Politics* (1946) and his hugely influential *Politics Among Nations* (1948), Morgenthau emphasized the balance of power as maintaining peace. The Cold War supported this view, as well as versions of it much more severe than those of Morgenthau.

Sociology Sociology during the 1940's saw the development of what would become the "grand theory" of the 1950's as well as the growth and refinement of empirical survey methods. Talcott Parsons and George C. Homans were active at Harvard University during the 1940's, but Parsons's major theoretical synthesis would appear in 1951 and Homans's in 1950. After World War II, Parsons was instrumental in bringing Eastern European anticommunist émigrés to the United States to supply intelligence on the Soviet Union.

Russian émigré Pitrim Sorokin led the sociology department at Harvard University. His sweeping, speculative theories of historical cycles of alternating "sensate" and abstract thought ended up having far less influence than the work of Parsons and Homans in succeeding decades. One student of Sorokin was Robert K. Merton, who produced classical formulations of sociological functionalism in articles published during the 1940's. Merton developed lucid explanations of social institutions in terms of the functions that they served. He also avoided both the sweep of the grand theories of people such as Sorokin and Parsons and the micro-social focus of many empiricists, with what Merton himself called "theories of the middle range."

Race relations were an important topic of sociological study as American society began an effort to integrate its black and white citizens. Economist Gunnar Myrdal also had a major impact on American sociology. His *An American Dilemma: The Negro Problem and Modern Democracy* (1944) was a major study of race relations and its impact on American society. Paul Lazarsfeld was important in bringing to the United States ideas about an empirical, quantitative social science. His ideas were quite close to those of the Vienna Circle of logical positivists.

The Frankfurt School of critical theory had some influence on American social thought, though its full impact was not felt until the 1960's. Named after its location in Germany, the school was a noncommunist Marxist group that strove to combine classical German philosophy with empirical research. With the rise of Adolf Hitler in Germany, most of the members of the Frankfurt School fled to the United States. The Institute for Social Research was transplanted to New York City. Theodor Adorno, a sociologist of music, did empirical studies of radio music for the Radio Research project in New Jersey, later at Columbia University. The empirical and quantitative Lazarsfeld oversaw Adorno's nuanced and critical work. The institute's largest project was "Studies in Prejudice," a notable product of which was the two-volume *The Authoritarian Personality* (1950), by Adorno and other authors, sponsored by the American Jewish Committee and stimulated by Nazism and fear of anti-Semitism in the United States. Extensive criticisms of the work continued through the next two decades. Only with the rise of the New Left student movement during the 1960's did the more Marxist-oriented work of the Frankfurt School gain widespread attention.

Impact The social sciences of the 1940's initiated many trends and schools of the succeeding decades. Anthropology continued in its primarily culturalist and nurture orientation for three decades. Mainstream economics continued primarily in a Keynesian mode until the simultaneous economic stagnation and inflation of the late 1970's, termed stagflation, contradicted its predictions. Monetarism and a common companion belief in free market capitalism and deregulation then acquired greater credence. Political science continued for the next two decades or more in the behavioralist mode. Sociology was dominated by structural-functional theory and empirical survey research for at least the following decade. The role of social scientists as advisers to government continued to grow.

Val Dusek

Further Reading
Blaug, Mark. *Economic Theory in Retrospect.* 5th ed. New York: Cambridge University Press, 1997. Recognized as an insightful and incisive overview of economic theory and its development, with great depth.
Harris, Marvin. *The Rise of Anthropological Theory.* Rev. ed. Lanham, Md.: AltaMira Press, 2000. Outlines the development of different theories of culture. One of the most often cited histories of anthropological theory. Develops the argument for cultural materialism.
Somit, Albert, and Joseph Tannenhaus. *The Development of American Political Science: From Burgess to Behavioralism.* Boston: Allyn & Bacon, 1967. Good survey of the development of political science.

Turner, Jonathan H. *The Structure of Sociological Theory.* 7th ed. Belmont, Calif.: Wadsworth, 2002. Detailed analyses of key theories and paradigms, with discussion of the contributions of key figures.

Weatland, Thomas. *The Frankfurt School in Exile.* Minneapolis: University of Minnesota Press, 2009. Discusses the role of the Institute for Social Research, led by scholars of the Frankfurt School, in the development of sociological theory in the United States during the 1930's and 1940's. Argues that the Frankfurt School was more influential than previously believed.

See also   *An American Dilemma: The Negro Problem and American Democracy*; Bretton Woods Conference; Cold War; Education in Canada; Education in the United States; Keynesian economics; New Deal programs; Office of Strategic Services; Psychiatry and psychology; Sex and sex education; *Studies in Social Psychology in World War II.*

■ Socialist Workers Party

Identification   Political organization
Also known as   SWP
Date   Founded on January 1, 1938

A small U.S. political group, the Socialist Workers Party has historically supported revolutionary socialism and the teachings of Leon Trotsky. The party influenced labor union politics and supported the unification of the American Federation of Labor and Congress of Industrial Organizations during the 1940's and 1950's.

The Socialist Workers Party (SWP) was an offshoot of the Socialist Party of the American partnership with the Communist League of America. The latter group split with the Communist Party USA during the 1920's over support of Leon Trotsky. Trotsky openly opposed Joseph Stalin's totalitarian communism in the Soviet Union in favor of democratically driven, worker-controlled socialism. He founded the Fourth International in Paris in 1938 to criticize capitalist economies, to challenge German National Socialism, and to support socialist revolutions around the world.

The Socialist Workers Party joined the Fourth International and prepared for the anticipated surge of workers' revolutions that would follow World War II. The war, however, left the SWP divided over whether to support the Soviet Union as a communist state or to denounce it as a failed communist dictatorship. Its response was the Proletarian Military Policy: While the party denounced the war as a struggle between imperialist powers, SWP members enlisted and promoted revolution from within the military. This policy created tensions between SWA leadership and American labor leaders throughout the 1940's.

The SWP encountered further troubles in 1941, when National Secretary James P. Cannon was sentenced to eighteen months in prison for violating the Smith Act of 1940, a law which made it a federal crime to encourage, aid, or advocate the overthrow of the U.S. government. The act was devised to control left-wing political groups; it curtailed SWP direction for the remainder of the decade.

Impact   The Socialist Workers Party championed Trotskyist, antibureaucratic socialist theory from its early development during the 1940's until the late twentieth century. Its growth, however, has been inhibited by internal ideological rifts since its formation. In 2003, the SWP drew criticism for threatening legal action against the Marxist Internet Archives for publishing essays by Trotsky. The party remains affiliated with *The Militant*, one of the nation's key left-oriented newsweeklies.

Margaret R. Jackson

Further Reading

Cherny, Robert W. *American Labor and the Cold War: Grassroots Politics and Postwar Political Culture.* New Brunswick, N.J.: Rutgers University Press, 2004.

Mandel, Ernest, and Steve Bloom, eds. *Revolutionary Marxism and Social Reality in the Twentieth Century.* Atlantic Highlands, N.J.: Humanities Press, 1994.

Myers, Constance Ashton. *The Prophet's Army: Trotskyists in America, 1928-1941.* Westport, Conn.: Greenwood Press, 1977.

See also   American Federation of Labor; Anticommunism; Communist Party USA; Congress of Industrial Organizations; House Committee on Un-American Activities; Smith Act; Smith Act trials; Unionism.

■ *South Pacific*

Identification   Broadway musical set in World
War II
Creators   Music by Richard Rodgers (1902-1979);
lyrics by Oscar Hammerstein II (1895-1960);
book by Hammerstein and Joshua Logan (1908-
1988)
Date   Premiered on April 7, 1949

*South Pacific is typically regarded as a musical comedy.
However, it is also a sensitive treatment of racial and class
prejudice, the somber nature of which is relieved by a number of comic scenes and lilting melodies. Though some critics
consider its subject matter dated, this musical has been continuously staged for decades and has been adapted as a motion picture (1958), a television production (2001), and a
concert version (2005), starring respectively Mitzi Gaynor,
Glenn Close, and Reba McEntire as the heroine, Nellie
Forbush.*

It is not only its memorable songs ("Some Enchanted Evening," "There Is Nothin' Like a Dame,"
"Bali Ha'i," "Younger than Springtime") that establish *South Pacific*'s importance. In their long collaboration, Oscar Hammerstein II would write the
book and lyrics first, then Richard Rodgers would
compose music appropriate to the plot. Hammerstein based his story upon James A. Michener's *Tales
of the South Pacific* (1947). The musical is set on two
South Pacific islands and dramatizes the reaction
of American servicemen and women to a culture
they would never have encountered but for World
War II.

South Pacific chronicles two parallel love stories.
The first is a romance between Ensign Nellie Forbush, a U.S. Navy nurse from Little Rock, Arkansas,
and Emile de Becque, an expatriate French planter.
The second is between a young Marine lieutenant,
Joe Cable of Philadelphia, and Liat, a Tonkinese
teenager. Prejudices form serious barriers for both
couples. When Nellie, reared in the segregated
South, learns that Emile lived for years with a now
dead "native" woman who bore him two mixed-race
children, she cannot imagine sharing the rest of her
life with him and the children. Joe is a Princeton
graduate whose family is well-to-do, and who has a
girl back home. Could he possibly take a young
woman of another race—who speaks not a word of
English—to Philadelphia with him after the war?
The play ends with a mixture—in the classical
sense—of comedy and tragedy. Nellie's love for
Emile and his children overcomes her racial prejudice, and they are united as a family.
Joe's affair with Liat ends abruptly
when he is wounded during a hazardous spy mission and dies three days
later.

The play was first produced on
April 7, 1949, at the Majestic Theatre
in New York City. It was published in
that same year. *South Pacific* ran until
January 16, 1954, after 1,925 performances. Mary Martin, the original
Nellie Forbush, washed her hair
on stage during every performance
while singing "I'm Gonna Wash That
Man Right Outa My Hair." Joshua Logan directed and collaborated with
Hammerstein on the libretto, although he was not originally credited. Whereas Hammerstein was a
lifelong New Yorker, Logan was born
in Texarkana, Texas, and grew up in
Shreveport, Louisiana. He was per-
fectly familiar with the southern patterns of speech appropriate to Nellie.

Mary Martin and William Tabbert in the original Broadway production of South
Pacific. *(Time & Life Pictures/Getty Images)*

Impact   *South Pacific* won the New York Drama Critics' Circle Award for best musical play of 1948-1949, nine Tony Awards, and the Pulitzer Prize in drama in 1950. It dramatized the challenges faced by so many Americans due to the dislocations of wartime and encouraged the continuing movement of the musical theater toward more serious themes. The Broadway revival of *South Pacific* on April 3, 2008, is testimony to its enduring popularity.

Patrick Adcock

Further Reading

Block, Geoffrey Holden. *Enchanted Evenings: The Broadway Musical from "Show Boat" to Sondheim.* New York: Oxford University Press, 1997.

Bloom, Ken, and Frank Vlastnik. *Broadway Musicals: The 101 Greatest Shows of All Time.* New York: Black Dog & Leventhal, 2004.

Green, Stanley, ed. *Rodgers and Hammerstein Fact Book: A Record of Their Works Together and with Other Collaborators.* New York: Lynn Farnol Group, 1980.

See also   Broadway musicals; *History of the United States Naval Operations in World War II*; Navy, U.S.; Rodgers, Richard, and Oscar Hammerstein II; Theater in the United States.

■ Spellman, Francis Joseph

Identification   Roman Catholic cardinal and archbishop of New York
Born   May 4, 1889; Whitman, Massachusetts
Died   December 2, 1967; New York, New York

A major figure in the Roman Catholic Church in the United States, Spellman was politically influential in local and national affairs and a staunch opponent of communism.

Francis Joseph Spellman was born and raised in an Irish Catholic family in a small community south of Boston. After graduating from Fordham University, he began to study for the priesthood at the Pontifical North American College in Rome. He was ordained in 1916. His linguistic and political skills brought him to the attention of the American Church hierarchy, and following World War I he was made the American attaché to the Vatican Secretariat of State. During his time in Europe, he became friends with

Archbishop Eugenio Pacelli, later to become Pope Pius XII, and was also given sensitive tasks by Pope Pius XI, which included smuggling a papal encyclical critical of Benito Mussolini out of Italy to be published abroad. On returning to the United States in 1932, he was made auxiliary bishop of Boston, and in 1939 he was appointed archbishop of New York. In 1946, Spellman was raised to the dignity of cardinal.

Spellman cultivated powerful political contacts, including Joseph P. Kennedy, Sr., and President Franklin D. Roosevelt. He was close confidant and ally of the Roosevelt administration throughout the early 1940's. Under his tenure, the archdiocese of New York instituted the annual Al Smith Dinner, a charity fund-raiser, which would remain a feature event in American political life into the twenty-first century. In 1949, Spellman had a very public dispute with former First Lady Eleanor Roosevelt over public funding for parochial schools, but the two later reconciled privately.

During the 1940's, Spellman used his influence to deepen the ties between the American Catholic Church with its blue-collar base and the Democratic Party. He also was an early and strong opponent of communism and opposed Soviet expansionist moves even before the end of World War II. Lastly, he took a very public stand against the erosion of morals that he saw stemming from the American entertainment industry. Cardinal Spellman was frequently quoted in the press excoriating movies he deemed too explicit.

Impact   Spellman's tenure as archbishop of New York marked the high point of Catholic influence within the New Deal coalition—remarkable at time when anti-Catholicism was still a major force in American life. He played an important role during the early Cold War, using his influence to encourage a more forceful response to Soviet expansionism.

John Radzilowski

Further Reading

Cooney, John. *The American Pope: The Life and Times of Francis Cardinal Spellman.* New York: Times Books, 1984.

Powers, Richard Gid. *Not Without Honor: The History of American Anticommunism.* New Haven, N.J.: Yale University Press, 1998.

See also   Cabrini canonization; New Deal programs; Religion in the United States; Roosevelt, Franklin D.

▪ Sports in Canada

Participation in Canadian sports declined during World War II, and many sports experienced shortages of players through those years. The National Hockey League, for example, shrank from ten to six teams. International competitions, such as the Olympics, canceled events in 1940 and 1944 because of the war.

Despite the traumatic impact of World War II on many sectors of Canadian life during the early 1940's, many significant sporting events still occurred. Some Canadian athletes, such as Maurice "Rocket" Richard, Gérard Côté, and Barbara-Ann Scott, rose to world-class levels. In 1943, the Canadian government passed the National Fitness Act, which provided money to provinces that promoted sport and recreational activities. Although the act garnered some criticism, it created a sports boom in Canada in the postwar years.

Significant Events in Canadian Sports   Although the Olympic Games were canceled in 1940 and 1944, Canada won three medals in the 1948 Winter Olympic Games. Canadian athletes won gold and bronze medals in figure skating and a gold medal in men's ice hockey.

In the National Hockey League (NHL), the Toronto Maple Leafs were the dominant team of the 1940's. The Maple Leafs first won the Stanley Cup in 1942 and then won it four times near the end of the decade. The 1942 Stanley Cup was especially memorable because the Maple Leafs erased a three-game deficit and won four consecutive contests to take the championship. No other team had done this prior to 1942.

In 1946, the Canadian Football League abolished a rule requiring players to reside in the cities in which the played, allowing the importation of U.S. football players. Although the Toronto Argonauts refused to sign U.S. players and won the Grey Cup three years in a row, the Calgary Stampeders, with a American coach and many American players, won the 1948 Grey Cup and created a national stir. In 1941, the Argonauts became the first team to travel by air to play a game, in Winnipeg. In 1949, the Canadian Football League mandated that all players wear helmets for the first time.

A lesser known Canadian team, the Edmonton Grads, a women's basketball team, officially ceased playing in June, 1940, because the government needed its gymnasium space for war training. The team ended its twenty-five years of league and American and European tournament play with an estimated record of 520 wins and 20 loses, including 7 wins and 2 loses against men's teams. The team played in four Olympic Games, although basketball was not an official Olympic sport at the time, and won all 25 of its games. As a result of the Grads' success, girls' sports in Canada grew dramatically during and after the 1940's.

On April 18, 1946, a significant event in American baseball history occurred that involved a Canadian team: The African American player Jackie Robinson appeared in his first professional baseball game outside the Negro Leagues after joining the Montreal Royals, a AAA minor-league team owned by the major-league Brooklyn Dodgers. Robinson played that game in front of twenty-five thousand fans in New Jersey. He had four hits, including a home run, and two stolen bases. Feeling welcomed and at home in Montreal, he went on to win the minor league's batting title and lead Montreal to the league championship. The following year, he left Montreal for the Brooklyn Dodgers.

The popularity of skiing grew dramatically during the late 1940's. Although the first ski club had started during the early twentieth century, the sport did not become big business in Canada until the 1940's. With the number of clubs climbing from four to more than two hundred during the decade, businesses began making designer ski equipment, and ski resorts and ski shops cropped up rapidly. A Canadian woman was the first in North America to finish in the top three in a European ski race. A Canadian skier named Harvey Clifford was considered the second best skier in North America in 1948.

Notable Athletes   Gérard Côté won four Boston Marathon races during the 1940's. He outpaced the rest of the world, winning the Boston Marathon in 1940, 1943, 1944, and 1948. His record of four wins stood until the 1980's when Bill Rodgers of Boston also won it four times. When Côté won his first Boston Marathon in 1940, he bested a world-class field in record time, despite the fact that he had no sponsors and no athletic trainer. His only financial backing came from his father.

Hockey player Richard, who played for the Montreal Canadiens, was the principal NHL star through

Members of the Canadian speed skating team training for the 1948 Winter Olympic Games in St. Moritz, Switzerland. (AP/Wide World Photos)

the 1940's. During the 1944-1945 season, he scored a remarkable fifty goals in fifty games—a record that stood for thirty-six years. He also scored five goals in one playoff game in 1944, also a record.

Figure skater Barbara-Ann Scott charmed the hearts of fans around the world with her blonde hair and innovative skating routines that included triple jumps. Before Scott's time, figure skating had consisted primarily of series of gliding movements across the ice. She captured Canadian championships in both junior and senior competitions between 1944 and 1948, while adding world championships in 1947 and 1948 and an Olympic gold medal in 1948. She earned honors as the Canadian athlete of the year, winning the Lou Marsh Trophy three times.

Impact   During the 1940's, sports suffered in Canada because of World War II but still included many significant events and people. Sports such as skiing came out of the war years, developing commercially during the decade. Athletes such as Scott brought figure skating into the modern era during the 1940's.

Timothy Sawicki

Further Reading

Best, Dave. *Canada: Our Century in Sport.* Markham, Ont.: Fitzhenry and Whiteside, 2002. A comprehensive look at Canadian sports in the twentieth century. Includes information about the Grey Cup and other events of the 1940's.
Howell, Colin D. *Blood, Sweat, and Cheers: Sport and*

the Making of Modern Canada. Toronto: University of Toronto Press, 2001. Focused on political, social, and historical issues that have given Canadian sports an authentic identity. Includes discussion on the impact that Scott had on figure skating.

Melancon, Benoit, and Fred A. Reed. *The Rocket: A Cultural History of Maurice Richard.* Berkeley, Calif.: Greystone Books, 2009. One of the best hockey players in history, Richard had some of his greatest moments during the 1940's.

Morrow, Don, and Mary Keyes. *A Concise History of Sport in Canada.* Toronto: Oxford University Press, 1989. Traces the development of sports culture in Canada and looks at Canadian sports during and after World War II.

See also Basketball; Ice hockey; Richard, Maurice; World War II.

■ Sports in the United States

Amateur and professional spectator sports, though altered in nature and scope, provided a diversionary experience for the United States during World War II. The country's passion for sports and athletic competition was renewed during the latter part of the 1940's as both spectator and participatory competitions drew many people to the courts and playing fields.

Fueled by the federal government's support for sports and recreation during the Great Depression, the United States entered the 1940's with a healthy appreciation and passion for organized and informal sport experiences. Large numbers of people found sport an acceptable outlet when they lacked worked or the discretionary money for other amusements. The character-shaping tradition of sport, its role in promoting a worthy use of leisure time, and its inherent appeal for men and, to a lesser extent, women, had assured its stable presence as a hallmark of American popular culture since the 1920's.

Sports During the War Years As the United States prepared for national defense, the large number of draftees inducted through the 1940 Selective Service Act were provided with sports activities and equipment by the War Department as part of their preparation for combat. Former athletes and coaches assumed positions of leadership and training, furthering sport as a vehicle for future soldiers to gain physical strength and teamwork skills. The women's branches of the service had similar athletic programs. College campuses, community facilities, and school buildings provided settings and support for social and sporting activities for members of the armed forces. In some ways, this foreshadowed the transformation that the manufacturing and automobile plants would ultimately make in their conversion to wartime production.

With the outbreak of World War II, President Franklin D. Roosevelt soon looked to the national pastime, baseball, as an example of the effort the country needed to emerge victorious while also preserving some degree of normalcy. While many high-profile athletes enlisted, Roosevelt's "green light letter" to Major League Baseball commissioner Kenesaw Mountain Landis in early 1942 allowed baseball to continue during the war, with modifications, in order to boost national pride and morale. In fact, during 1943, the professional baseball parks became collection points for rubber, scrap metal, and other materials necessary to the war effort. In addition, millions of dollars of war bonds were sold through baseball.

The All-American Girls Softball League, founded as a contingency to the possible disruption of Major League Baseball, began playing in late 1942 under the leadership of Chicago Cubs owner and chewing gum magnate Philip K. Wrigley and the renowned baseball executive Branch Rickey. Capitalizing on the established popularity of softball, which typically outdrew baseball games for spectators during the war years, the softball league eventually adopted baseball rules. Play centered in the Midwest and provided a source of entertainment for families and sports enthusiasts that addressed the growing talent pool of female players, while compensating for the manpower shortage.

In 1943, the National Football League's (NFL) Pittsburgh Steelers and Philadelphia Eagles combined franchises, resulting in the "Steagles." However, the Indianapolis 500 was suspended from 1942 until 1945 because of gas rationing, as were many United States Golf Association events and the Masters Golf Tournament, which was cancelled from 1943 until 1945. Davis Cup tennis was canceled for six years. Baseball's record book for 1944 was not published because of a paper shortage. College sports were affected to the point that many institutions disbanded teams altogether or reduced the number of games they played during the war years. The Rose Bowl game was moved from Pasadena, California, to the campus of Duke University in 1942 because of concern that the Japanese might launch another attack on the West Coast. Attendance at the 1943 Army-Navy football game was restricted to those living within a ten-mile radius of the stadium in Annapolis. A team from Randolph Field in San Antonio, Texas, tied the University of Texas 7-7 in the 1944 Cotton Bowl. Eventually, more than eleven hundred professional baseball and football players served during World War II, along with countless college athletes and sports fans. Upon conclusion, the war's legacy was one of affecting, but not dampening, the nation's obsession with sports.

Return to Normalcy As returning soldiers reclaimed their places in society after the war ended in 1945, the nation's passion for prewar activities returned, although it was influenced by the social and technological changes of the day. Desiring pleasure and fun, Americans sought refuge in sports from the horrors of the just-completed world war. Interestingly, baseball became an intentional vehicle to help restore Japanese society. Japan had banned the game during the war as a way of attacking American influence. However, General Douglas MacArthur personally ordered the restoration of the stadium that housed the Tokyo Giants, even though adaptations in the terms and customs of the game remained distinctively Japanese. As major sports returned as a welcome source of entertainment for many Americans, their celebrities and heroes often took on mythical status. In some instances, coaches became more noted than their players. The emergence of television soon augmented the interest in sport that had been sustained by radio, newspapers, and magazine advertisements for decades, and unre-

stricted travel and the elimination of gas rationing encouraged spectators to follow sports across town or across the country.

Professional Sports The late 1940's saw a challenge to the roster-depleted NFL with the All-America Football Conference competing for the best college players. Ultimately, the NFL survived and assimilated franchises in Cleveland, San Francisco, and Baltimore into the veteran league. The Cleveland franchise eventually relocated to Los Angeles, attracting a new fan base. The NFL was well positioned for the boost that expanded television coverage would provide for football during the 1950's.

The National Basketball Association was created in 1949 from a merger of the older National Basketball League and the upstart Basketball Association of America. Neither of those leagues was as popular as the Harlem Globetrotters, a travelling team that capitalized on the still-prevalent racial desegregation of postwar sport. While the Negro National and American League teams shared Major League ball-

Following a presidential tradition going back to the Taft administration, President Harry S. Truman throws out the first ball of the 1949 Major League Baseball season before a game between the Washington Senators and the Boston Red Sox. Among those looking on are the president's daughter and wife on the far left and Boston manager Joe Cronin on the far right. (Getty Images)

parks, Jackie Robinson's signing with the Brooklyn Dodgers in 1947 brought the first African American professional baseball player to the modern game. The NFL's Los Angeles Rams had acquired the services of two black athletes the year before.

In 1949, the American Bowling Congress, which oversaw the most popular participant sport of the decade, also integrated, though it would be some time before widespread breakdown of the color barrier in American sport would flourish. However, the war against Nazi racism, interracial college teams, and the migration of many African Americans to the North paved the way for greater acceptance of black athletes on the national stage. Following the death of the legendary Babe Ruth in 1948, the New York Yankees began a string of five straight World Series championships. Baseball owners opened up meetings and held discussions with players about contracts in 1946, in response to a desire for a player's union.

In horse racing, America's attention was drawn to the achievements of Assault in 1946 and Citation in 1948, with these horses becoming the third and fourth Triple Crown winners of the decade. The Thoroughbred Racing Protective Bureau was founded in 1946 and issued a professional standards code that was welcomed by states dependent on revenue from associated gambling activities. More than five million people attended harness racing events in 1948, a testimony to the sport's emergence from the smaller venues of the pre-World War II era.

Professional boxing was telecast from Madison Square Garden, which transformed Friday nights for many who had access to the broadcasts and resulted in a "golden age" for the sport. However, the retirement in 1949 of Joe Louis, who held the world heavyweight crown during World War II, led to the sport's decline shortly thereafter. Professional golf saw increased prize money and promotional exposure for men; women golfers earned competitive salaries by endorsing clothes and equipment. Men's professional tennis tended to be a series of exhibitions among top players, highlighted by Jack Kramer and Pancho Gonzales, because of the strict separation of professional and amateur competition. The Ladies Professional Golf Association was created in 1949. Babe Didrikson Zaharias built upon her previous Olympic and amateur success by becoming the top female athlete of the decade, though her achievements were more symbolic of what women could achieve than a pacesetter for change.

Amateur and Recreational Sports   The G.I. Bill enabled men beyond the traditional college age to receive higher educations and participate in intercollegiate sport. The bill's influence was primarily felt in popular sports, such as football and basketball, and greatly enhanced these sports' popularity and spectator appeal. However, these sports became particularly vulnerable to blatant abuses, and intercollegiate sport experienced a rise in the influence of the National Collegiate Athletic Association (NCAA). The NCAA's 1948 "Sanity Code" introduced scholarship awards based on financial need and a greater regulatory role for the association. College team rosters were replenished, championship competitions reinstated, and attendance revived with a euphoria unmatched during the war years. However, even college sport was not immune to gambling's influence; occasional basketball "fixes" after 1945 continued to set the stage for some of the most significant college sport sanctions during the early 1950's. The Amateur Athletic Union administered many sporting events, and an uneasy tension flared between this organization and the NCAA over which entity would be the "face" of amateur sport. The reinstatement of the Olympic Games in 1948 in London featured outstanding performances by Americans in diving, sailing, swimming, track and field, and weightlifting.

While there was a move to protect young children from the rigors of competitive athletics, youth sport programs in baseball, football, and basketball were sponsored in almost all communities. The local parks and recreation departments, the Young Men's/Women's Christian Associations, and the Jewish Community Centers offered grassroots sports education and competition. The postwar years witnessed more women participating in individual and dual sports, partly because of changing societal roles and expectations. College sport remained heavily influenced by the guidelines handed down by the American Association for Health, Physical Education, and Recreation, an organization of education professionals that oversaw extramural competition. School programs offered instruction in gymnastics and modern dance.

Following the war, swimming became a popular sport for all ages as the presence of indoor and outdoor pools was commonplace throughout the country. Badminton and handball, which flourished during the Depression, retained their presence after the war. Interest in volleyball expanded during the late

1940's, as did skiing in the Northeast and West. Well in advance of a legislative mandate, veteran's organizations, the American Athletic Association for the Deaf, and the National Wheelchair Basketball Association organized opportunities for sports participation and competition for those unable to engage in mainstream athletics.

Impact Sport in the United States mirrored the country's adaption to the events of the 1940's—worldwide war followed by the reestablishment of a postwar society. During World War II, the role of sports was to support the nation's defense through physical training and to provide an acceptable diversion from the rigors of the war effort. The middle and latter years of the decade witnessed an enthusiastic embrace of many established and new pastimes in which to channel one's participatory and spectator energies. Easily one of the most acceptable ways to witness intense competition within established rules, sport would be well positioned for the continuing societal and technical evolution that was to come during the 1950's and 1960's. Athletics also shaped the educational experience of generations of American schoolchildren. That sport not only survived the war but also thrived afterward further reinforced America's fascination and obsession with the games and their players.

P. Graham Hatcher

Further Reading

Ashe, Arthur. *A Hard Road to Glory: A History of the African-American Athlete Since 1946.* New York: Warner Books, 1988. Written by one of the greatest professional tennis players, this book chronicles the achievements of African American athletes.

Carruth, Gorton, and Eugene Ehrlich. *Facts and Dates of American Sports.* New York: Harper & Row, 1988. Anthology containing twenty-two pages of sports history from the 1940's, along with some biographies of sports legends.

Lee, Mabel. *A History of Physical Education and Sports in the U.S.A.* New York: John Wiley & Sons, 1983. Written by a leading sports historian, this book provides a broad overview of American sport. Details organizations, trends, and issues in mid-twentieth century America.

Peterson, Robert. *Cages to Jump Shots: Pro Basketball's Early Years.* New York: Oxford University Press, 1990. Summarizes the evolution of professional

basketball, with attention to the challenges and opportunities of the 1940's.

Rader, Benjamin. *American Sports: From the Age of Folk Games to the Age of Spectators.* Englewood Cliffs, N.J.: Prentice-Hall, 1983. Particularly valuable in understanding the antecedents of the nature of organized and informal sports during the 1940's.

See also Auto racing; Baseball; Basketball; Boxing; Football; Golf; Horse racing; Olympic Games of 1948; Soccer; Sports in Canada; Tennis.

Spying. *See* **Wartime espionage**

■ *Stars and Stripes*

Identification Official newspaper for members of the U.S. armed forces
Date Established on November 9, 1861

With continuous publication in Europe since 1942 and in the Pacific since 1945, Stars and Stripes *has served as the primary news source of American military personnel for generations. Although the newspaper operates from inside the Department of Defense, it is editorially separate. This independence distinguishes* Stars and Stripes *from all other sources of information distributed at U.S. military installations.*

Founded by Union troops who occupied a captured newspaper office in Bloomfield, Missouri, during the Civil War to report activities of Illinois regiments, *Stars and Stripes* has always operated as an information source for American soldiers. The original one-page paper saw only four editions, then lay dormant until the United States entered World War I. From February, 1918, until the war's end in June, 1919, *Stars and Stripes* was printed in France by the American Expeditionary Forces as an eight-page weekly distributed to U.S. troops. It attracted a staff of veteran newspapermen and young soldiers; some would later become prominent journalists, most notably *Stars and Stripes* editor Harold Ross, who founded *The New Yorker* magazine.

Following another period of dormancy, *Stars and Stripes* reemerged in London, in April, 1942. The paper changed from a full-size weekly to a daily tabloid, but the emphasis on news for G.I.'s remained constant. During World War II, dozens of editions of *Stars and Stripes* were published in various operating theaters, often close to the frontlines and sometimes in as many as twenty-five simultaneous publishing locations. By January, 1945, daily circulation exceeded 1.2 million. The Pacific edition was introduced in May, 1945, shortly after V-E Day. The paper boosted morale, kept service personnel apprised of military operations and outcomes (with forty-eight-hour delays for security), and linked soldiers to life on the home front. The irreverent cartoon featuring infantrymen Willie and Joe, created by G.I. Bill Mauldin, delighted fellow "Joes." It was syndicated by stateside newspapers and won a Pulitzer Prize. Again, the staff mixed experienced newspapermen and talented young soldiers, many of whom enjoyed long and distinguished careers after the war (most famously, Mauldin, but also including Andy Rooney, Shel Silverstein, Tom Sutton, and Louis Rukeyser).

In addition to newspaper editions that featured current news, during the 1940's *Stars and Stripes* published *G.I. Stories*, a popular series of 53 booklets, each consisting of thirty-two pages of text and a color centerfold with either a map or a photo montage. The small booklets could fit into a uniform pocket and were often mailed home. Each told the "story" of a separate division in the European theater: 28 infantry, 9 armored, 2 airborne, 7 air, and 7 support divisions.

In subsequent years, *Stars and Stripes*, which is dedicated to publishing wherever American troops are deployed, expanded to five daily newspaper editions, originating in Europe, the Middle East, Okinawa, mainland Japan, and Korea. In May, 2004, *Stars and Stripes* became available in electronic format, thus reaching a readership far broader than military service members.

Impact During the 1940's, this widely disseminated military newspaper informed, entertained, and encouraged men and women in the European and Pacific theaters. In war and peace, *Stars and Stripes* has linked American military personnel with service objectives and outcomes and with news of the greater world.

Carolyn Anderson

Further Reading

Cornebise, Alfred Emile. *Ranks and Columns: Armed Forces Newspapers in American Wars.* Westport, Conn.: Greenwood Press, 1993.
Sweeney, Michael S. *The Military and the Press: An Uneasy Truce.* Evanston, Ill.: Northwestern University Press, 2006.
Zumwalt, Ken. *The Stars and Stripes: World War II and the Early Years.* Austin, Tex.: Eakin Press, 1989.

See also Censorship in the United States; Department of Defense, U.S.; Mauldin, Bill; Newspapers; Pyle, Ernie; Slang, wartime; United Service Organizations.

■ Stein, Gertrude

Identification Expatriate American writer
Born February 3, 1874; Allegheny (now in Pittsburgh), Pennsylvania
Died July 24, 1946; Neuilly-sur-Seine, France

Stein's Parisian apartment became an important meeting place for the artists and intellectuals of early twentieth century modernism. She achieved fame in 1933 with the publication of The Autobiography of Alice B. Toklas, *written in the voice of her life partner. Following World War II, Stein often entertained and spoke to gatherings of American military personnel in liberated Paris.*

Born to Jewish American parents in Allegheny, Pennsylvania, Gertrude Stein spent the first six years of her life abroad in Europe, returning to Oakland and San Francisco in 1880. She was admitted to the Harvard Annex, a private program for the instruction of women by Harvard faculty, and studied psychology with William James. She then went on to study medicine at Johns Hopkins but never completed a degree.

In 1903, Stein moved to Paris to live with her brother, Leo, and they began to collect art. Their home at 27 rue de Fleurus was frequented by such important figures as Ernest Hemingway, Henri Matisse, and Pablo Picasso, who painted a now-famous portrait of Stein. It is often stated that Stein's experimental writing (repetitive, illogical, sparsely punctuated) reflects the influence of Picasso's visual art (abstracted, multiple, simultaneous perspectives) during the cubist period.

In 1933, Stein published *The Autobiography of Alice B. Toklas*. Unconventional in that Stein assumes the voice of her life partner, Alice B. Toklas, to tell her own life story, *The Autobiography of Alice B. Toklas* is, nonetheless, widely considered Stein's most accessible work. With its focus on the Parisian art scene during the early twentieth century, it was an immediate and surprising best seller. The following year, Stein returned to the United States on an extensive lecturing tour. According to her biographer, John Malcolm Brinnin, she achieved a celebrity of such proportions that her eminence was shared only by gangsters, baseball players, and movie stars.

With the outbreak of World War II, Stein and Toklas, both Jews, moved to a country home in France. They escaped persecution because of their friendship with Bernard Faÿ, a French historian who had previously translated some of Stein's work into French and had connections in Vichy France, a Nazi puppet state.

Following the war, Stein often spoke to and entertained American military personnel in liberated Paris, and these engagements were frequently covered in the news in America. Stein reflected on her experiences during World War II in the memoir *Wars I Have Seen* (1945). She affectionately wrote about the young American G.I.'s of World War II who gathered in her Paris apartment in *Brewsie and Willie* (1946).

Stein died in Paris from stomach cancer at the age of seventy-two. According to Toklas, when Stein was being wheeled into the operating room for surgery, she asked, "What is the answer?" When Toklas did not answer, Stein quipped, "In that case, what is the question?"

Impact American expatriate Gertrude Stein first achieved notoriety as the hostess of a famous early twentieth century modernist art salon at her 27 rue de Fleurus apartment in Paris. Stein's reputation was further bolstered by her own avant-garde writing. After the publication of the best-selling *Autobiography of Alice B. Toklas* in 1933, Stein became known for the generosity she showed toward the American G.I.'s in Paris after World War II.

Corinne Andersen

Further Reading

Dekoven, Marianne. *A Different Language: Gertrude Stein's Experimental Writing.* Madison: Univerity of Wisconsin Press, 1983.

Stein, Gertrude. *Selected Writings of Gertrude Stein.* Edited by Carl Van Vechten. New York: Vintage Books, 1945.

Stendhal, Renate, ed. *Gertrude Stein: In Words and Pictures.* Chapel Hill, N.C.: Algonquin Books, 1994.

See also Eliot, T. S.; Homosexuality and gay rights; Literature in the United States; Music: Classical; Pound, Ezra.

■ Stewart, James

Identification American film star and World War II pilot
Born May 20, 1908; Indiana, Pennsylvania
Died July 2, 1997; Beverly Hills, California

Stewart's youthful spirit, inspiring idealism, and amiability contributed to his image on the screen as an exemplar of the values and qualities that Americans liked to think were an essential aspect of the national character. Even in the darker roles he played in the latter part of his career, these aspects continued to inform his more complex performances.

Actor James Stewart (right) talking with director Frank Capra in 1946. (AP/Wide World Photos)

James Stewart was already a well-known and well-liked film star by 1940. His performance as the idealistic Jefferson Smith in Frank Capra's *Mr. Smith Goes to Washington* (1939) had established him as an icon of integrity and decency. His warm and winning relationship with Margaret Sullavan in Ernst Lubitsch's remake of a European film, *The Shop Around the Corner* (1940), further contributed to his image as a comfortable, welcome embodiment of handsome ease and approachability. Although his films credited him as James Stewart, he became known as "Jimmy," even using that name on television with *The Jimmy Stewart Show*, which aired during the 1971-1972 season. His Oscar-winning role as an endearingly sincere reporter and rival (with Cary Grant) for Katharine Hepburn's affections in *The Philadelphia Story* (1940) elevated him to major star status.

Stewart already had appeared in twenty-nine films when he was drafted into the U.S. Army in 1941. He flew twenty bombing missions over Germany from December, 1943, to June, 1944, winning the Distinguished Flying Cross for his service. The Army was reluctant to permit such a well-known person to risk his life, so it had Stewart help train B-17 crews until his desire to be treated like "Mr. Smith," an ordinary American citizen, prevailed and he became the commander of a B-24 Liberator squadron of twenty planes.

Stewart's experiences as a captain in the Army Air Corps affected him so deeply that he considered giving up acting entirely. However, Frank Capra persuaded him to take the part of George Bailey, the small-town manager of a savings and loan, in *It's a Wonderful Life* (1946). That role placed Stewart among the most memorable figures in film history, even though the film was commercially unsuccessful when it was released. The darkening of his character, without the diminution of the elements that previously had made him so accessible, encouraged directors such as Anthony Mann and Alfred Hitchcock to cast Stewart in parts that retained his unique appeal while deepening the psychological dimensions of his characters.

Following *It's a Wonderful Life*, Stewart played a pollster in William Wellman's *Magic Town* (1947) and then a crusading journalist trying to prove that a condemned man is innocent in Henry Hathaway's film noir *Call Northside 777* (1948). At the close of the decade, Stewart worked with Hitchcock for the first time in *Rope* (1948), one of Hitchcock's lesser films but one that showed Stewart depicting a man controlled by a dangerous obsession. That motif permitted Stewart to join his on-screen image of amiable accessibility (as in *The Monty Stratton Story* of 1949, a factual account of a wounded veteran who became a major-league baseball pitcher) with a contrasting impulse that created an unusual kind of tension and uncertainty.

Impact Stewart's wartime experiences and his turn at the end of the decade toward characters with darker aspects to their personalities elevated him from the youthful personification of affability on which he based his early career to a more nuanced actor who reached the highest level of film stardom in the next decade. His work in Alfred Hitchcock's *Rear Window* (1954) and *Vertigo* (1958) is regarded even more highly than when the films were released, and although the strengths of these films depend on many factors, including Hitchcock's direction, it is unlikely that they would have achieved their justifiable status as "classics" without Stewart's performances.

Leon Lewis

Further Reading

Eliot, Marc. *Jimmy Stewart: A Biography*. New York: Harmony Books, 2006.

Pickard, Roy. *Jimmy Stewart: A Life in Film*. New York: St. Martin's Press, 1992.

Von Karajan, Ellen. *Jimmy Stewart: A Life in Pictures*. New York: MetroBooks, 1999.

See also Bombers; Capra, Frank; Film in the United States; Films about World War II; Hitchcock, Alfred; *It's a Wonderful Life*; *The Philadelphia Story*.

■ Stilwell, Joseph Warren

Identification U.S. Army general
Born March 19, 1883; Palatka, Florida
Died October 12, 1946; San Francisco, California

Stilwell served as the American commander of the China-Burma-India theater and as chief of staff to Nationalist Chinese leader Chiang Kai-shek during World War II. Stilwell recognized the inherent corruption of Chiang's government and army, the significance of the threat of the Chinese communists, and the weakness of British leadership in India and South Asia.

After a distinguished, if unortho- dox, military career during World War I and the interwar period, General Joseph Warren Stilwell was especially qualified for leader- ship in Asia in the conflict with Ja- pan. Not only had Stilwell assisted in the design and execution of the St. Mihiel offensive in 1918 (for which he received the Distin- guished Service Medal), he also had served three tours in China between the wars. He was fluent in Chinese and served as the mili- tary attaché at the American Le- gation in Beijing from 1935 to 1939. He was also familiar with the progress of the Second Sino-Japa- nese War, which started in 1937, and the internal Chinese conflict between Chiang Kai-shek's Na- tionalist government and the com- munists under Mao Zedong. In 1939, Stilwell returned to the United States, where he served in the Second Infantry Division from 1939 to 1940, commanded the new Seventh Infantry Division in 1940, and was named commander of the Third Army Corps in 1941.

Lieutenant General Joseph Stilwell (right) with Chinese Nationalist leader Chiang Kai-shek and Madame Chiang Kai-shek in Burma in early 1942. (NARA)

Stilwell expected to command the American forces in the invasion of North Africa but was as- signed to the China-Burma-India theater in early 1942. From the outset of his command, he was plagued by the problems associated with the pri- macy of the wars in Europe and the South Pacific; both demanded large amounts of war materials and personnel and would continue to stifle Stilwell's op- erations during the next two years. Three additional factors impeded Stilwell's progress in South Asia: the impact of geography on supply lines, his poor re- lations with Chiang, and his disappointment with British military leadership. Of these three factors, the most significant was the reluctance of Chiang to use all the resources that had been provided to fight the Japanese. While Stilwell served as Chiang's chief of staff, much of the Lend-Lease aid was lost as a re- sult of corruption and Chiang's holding of materials for an anticipated postwar conflict with Mao. None- theless, the frustrated Stilwell began planning the invasion of northern Burma in December, 1943. A fi-

nal offensive toward Myitkyina commenced in April, 1944; with the assistance of American general Frank Merrill's famed "Marauders," Myitkyina was taken in August, and a large section of northern Burma came under Allied control. In October, 1944, Stilwell was removed from his command; he was blamed for high American casualties and for the difficult rela- tionships with Chinese and British leaders. During 1945, Stilwell commanded Army units in the attack on Okinawa.

Impact Stilwell was an effective American com- mander in South Asia during World War II. He was a demanding but supportive leader to his troops and recognized the abilities of the Chinese as effective soldiers if trained properly and provided with the basic necessities with which to fight. His reports to the U.S. government provided early warnings of the strength of Mao's communist movement and the corruption that riddled Chiang's Nationalist gov- ernment.

William T. Walker

Further Reading

Astor, Gerald. *The Jungle War: Mavericks, Marauders, and Madmen in the China-Burma-India Theater of*

World War II. Hoboken, N.J.: John Wiley & Sons, 2004.

Prefer, Nathan. *Vinegar Joe's War: Stilwell's Campaign for Burma.* Novato, Calif.: Presidio Press, 2000.

Stilwell, Joseph Warren. *The Stilwell Papers.* Edited by Theodore H. White. New York: Sloane, 1948.

Tuchman, Barbara. *Stilwell and the American Experience in China, 1911-45.* 1972. Reprint. New York: Grove Press, 2001.

See also Army, U.S.; Army Rangers; China-Burma-India theater; Doolittle bombing raid; Flying Tigers; MacArthur, Douglas; Merrill's Marauders; Nimitz, Chester W.

■ Stimson, Henry L.

Identification U.S. secretary of war, 1940-1945
Born September 21, 1867; New York, New York
Died October 20, 1950; Huntington, New York

Stimson supervised the U.S. Army effort during World War II, especially the mobilization of personnel and economic and technical resources.

Henry L. Stimson was a New York lawyer with a long and varied career in public service before 1940, capped by stints as secretary of war under William Howard Taft and as secretary of state under Herbert Hoover. He was an artillery colonel during World War I and afterward preferred to be called "colonel." During the 1930's, he opposed the aggressive Axis foreign policies. After World War II began, he advocated pro-Allied intervention. President Franklin D. Roosevelt wanted a more bipartisan administration and nominated Stimson as secretary of war on June 19, 1940.

Although the appointment had been discussed for a few weeks, it came the day after Stimson made a speech advocating such measures as repealing the Neutrality Act of 1939, repairing Allied ships in American ports, increasing war supplies to the Allies (and even convoying them with the Navy), and a draft. All became official policy within a year or so, though Stimson never got universal military service passed. Stimson's age was a major concern, so he hired a first-rate staff to assist him. His greatest reliance was on highly regarded Chief of Staff George C. Marshall (whom he knew from prior service).

Stimson worked closely with Marshall; the two kept each other fully informed of their doings. Stimson tried unsuccessfully to be sole War Department representative to the president; Roosevelt insisted (as in other departments) on communicating directly to subordinates such as Marshall. At the start, one major issue was industrial mobilization, sparked by the discovery that the United States had only forty-nine heavy bombers (Stimson was an airpower advocate) in September, 1940. This involved a large number of policy questions, with Stimson persistently urging prompt action. He pushed innovative technology such as radar and tightened up department administration despite political resistance.

Stimson strongly supported Roosevelt's interventionist initiatives, seeking to do more, and faster. The attack on Pearl Harbor in December, 1941, finally settled the question of war but was also an embarrassment of errors both locally and in Washington. Stimson had reviewed and edited the Army war warning message of November 27 and knew that General Walter Short chose to guard only against sabotage. Stimson thus bore some responsibility, though he placed the blame on Short and Admiral Husband E. Kimmel.

Stimson successfully urged an Army reorganization into ground, air, and service forces under Marshall, and he reluctantly approved interning Pacific coast Japanese Americans. He worked hard to ensure adequate manpower and supplies for the Army, while also blocking the appointment of political generals. He set up a research group at Langley Field, which helped develop centimetric radar for antisubmarine air patrols. Like Marshall, Stimson was a determined advocate of a cross-channel attack and skeptical about the Mediterranean campaign.

Though opposed to bombing attacks that targeted civilians and well aware of the difficult moral questions involved, Stimson supported using atomic bombs provided that Japan was given a warning beforehand. After the war, he successfully opposed vindictive ideas such as the Morgenthau Plan to deindustrialize Germany and proposed keeping the Japanese emperor as constitutional monarch of a demilitarized, democratized nation confined to its home islands. In 1945, he retired to write his memoirs and defend policies such as the Nuremberg Trials.

Impact   Stimson worked well with General Marshall to successfully oversee the massive expansion of the U.S. Army and its ultimately victorious campaigns in World War II.

Timothy Lane

Further Reading

Cray, Ed. *General of the Army: George C. Marshall, Soldier and Statesman.* New York: W. W. Norton, 1990.

Hodgson, Godfrey. *The Colonel: The Life and Wars of Henry Stimson, 1867-1950.* New York: Alfred A. Knopf, 1990.

Morison, Elting E. *Turmoil and Tradition: A Study of the Life and Times of Henry L. Stimson.* Boston: Houghton Mifflin, 1960.

See also   Atomic bomb; Japanese American internment; Marshall, George C.; Nuremberg Trials; Office of War Mobilization; Pearl Harbor attack; Roosevelt, Franklin D.; Truman, Harry S.; War Production Board; World War II mobilization.

■ Stone, Harlan Fiske

Identification   Twelfth chief justice of the United States, 1941-1946

Born   October 11, 1872; Chesterfield, New Hampshire

Died   April 22, 1946; Washington, D.C.

As chief justice, Stone presided over a fractious Supreme Court that was in the process of redefining itself. During his tenure, a number of important civil rights and civil liberties cases were decided. The Court also had to deal with the difficult issue of individual rights during a time of total war.

Born in New Hampshire, Harlan Fiske Stone later graduated from Amherst College and earned a law degree from Columbia Law School. He practiced law in New York City, and served as dean of his alma mater. In 1924, at the age of fifty-two, he was appointed attorney general of the United States. One year later, he became an associate justice of the U.S. Supreme Court. During his first several years on the Court, Stone often dissented in important cases, but his views became more accepted as the political makeup of the justices on the Court shifted.

In 1941, President Franklin D. Roosevelt, a Democrat, appointed Stone, a Republican, chief justice

of the United States. By that time, most of the associate justices had been appointed by Roosevelt. In addition, although his predecessor, Charles Evans Hughes, had sought to manage the Court with an eye to efficiency and consensus, Stone preferred debate and discussion. In part because of his management style and in part because of the strong personalities of his colleagues, there were more arguments among the justices than in the past—some of which became public—and an increase in nonunanimous decisions.

As an associate justice, Stone had advocated the doctrine of judicial self-restraint in the area of economic regulation, arguing that the Supreme Court should rarely overturn such legislation passed by national or state legislatures. During his chief justiceship, the majority of his colleagues agreed with this position. Thus, the power of the federal government legislative branch to regulate the American economy was enhanced during Stone's tenure as chief justice.

On the other hand, the Stone court was much more willing to invalidate statutes that impinged upon individual liberties. For instance, the Court struck down a number of laws limiting freedom of speech. In the 1943 case *West Virginia State Board of Education v. Barnette*, the Court also upheld the right of religious minorities such as Jehovah's Witnesses to refuse to engage in state-mandated pledges of allegiance. In addition, the Court supported the rights of ethnic minorities, especially African Americans, in their challenges against segregation. The Court also invalidated the infamous "white primary" system, which had been used in the South to disenfranchise black voters in *United States v. Classic* in 1941.

There were many occasions during World War II when the Court validated government actions in the alleged furtherance of war aims. For instance, the Court refused to overturn the federal government's decision to "relocate" individuals of Japanese ancestry. In *Ex parte Quirin* in 1942, the Court also acquiesced in the government's secret trial of German saboteurs who had entered the United States. Finally, it upheld the military trial and ultimate execution of a Japanese general whose "crime" had been his inability to control his troops. In effect, Stone's Court, like many others, had difficulty controlling government actions during emergency situations like war.

Impact   Although he was unable to stanch some of the bitter divisions on the Court during his tenure as chief justice, Stone was a leader in the Supreme Court's redefinition of its role, from protector of private property to protector of individual rights and liberties.

David M. Jones

Further Reading

Domnarski, William. *The Great Justices, 1941-54: Black, Douglas, Frankfurter, and Jackson in Chambers.* Ann Arbor: University of Michigan Press, 2006.

Fisher, Louis. *Nazi Saboteurs on Trial: A Military Tribunal and American Law.* Lawrence, Kansas: University Press of Kansas, 2003.

Mason, Alpheus T. *Harlan Fiske Stone: Pillar of the Law.* New York: Viking Press, 1956.

See also   Biddle, Francis; Civil rights and liberties; *Korematsu v. United States*; Presidential powers; Roosevelt, Franklin D.; *Smith v. Allwright*; Supreme Court, U.S.; *Thornhill v. Alabama*; Vinson, Fred M.; *Wickard v. Filburn*.

(Redferns/Getty Images)

■ *Stormy Weather*

Identification   All-black musical film
Director   Andrew L. Stone (1902-1999)
Date   Released on July 21, 1943

This progressive mainstream movie musical celebrated the achievements of black entertainers of the period.

Stormy Weather was created as a showcase for the most illustrious African American performers of the day. Although well intentioned, the film still managed to perpetuate racial stereotypes; nevertheless, its twenty musical numbers featured outstanding performances by such famous black artists as Fats Waller, Cab Calloway, Katherine Dunham, and the Nicholas Brothers. The story line about a returning World War I soldier is loosely based on the life of its lead, renowned dancer Bill "Bojangles" Robinson. Robinson plays Bill Williamson, whose romantic interest is a singer named Selina Rogers, played by a young Lena Horne. Her rendition of the title musical number was such that it became her signature song.

In addition to the performances commemorat-ing the accomplishments of contemporary black entertainers, *Stormy Weather* was unique at the time for its presentation of African Americans in a romantic context. Although the romance ultimately fails, both principals are presented as successful professionals in an emerging, liberal American society.

Impact   Winning high critical praise, *Stormy Weather* depicted African Americans excelling in an urban, egalitarian society of the 1940's. In 2001, the film was selected for preservation by the Library of Congress.

Margaret Boe Birns

Further Reading

Cripps, Thomas. *Making Movies Black: The Hollywood Message Movie from World War II to the Civil Rights Era.* New York: Oxford University Press, 1993.

Knight, Arthur. *Disintegrating the Musical: Black Performance and American Musical Film.* Durham, N.C.: Duke University Press, 2002.

Lamothe, Daphne. *Inventing the New Negro: Narrative,*

Culture, and Ethnography. Philadelphia: University of Pennsylvania Press, 2008.

See also   African Americans; Horne, Lena; Music: Popular; National Association for the Advancement of Colored People.

■ Strategic bombing

Definition   Use of long-range heavy bombers against enemy targets, especially urban industrial centers

World War II tested claims that a strategic bombing campaign could, by itself, defeat a foe without the need for land forces to invade the enemy's home territory. The Anglo-American air war against Germany demonstrated that strategic bombing was an indispensable component of victory but not sufficient by itself. The surrender of Japan vindicated strategic-bombing doctrine, according to its proponents.

Trying to avoid the horrendous slaughter of World War I's trench warfare, military strategists in several countries developed a new air-power doctrine. They theorized that bombers could overfly battlefields delivering war directly to the enemy's home territory. By disrupting war production and transportation systems, strategic bombings would inhibit the enemy's ability to fight back. At the same time, these air attacks would destroy morale among civilians, who then would pressure their governments to quit the war. Implementation of this doctrine during World War II brought about full-fledged war, in which entire populations, mobilized for the war effort, would also become potential war targets and victims. This challenged the long-standing international norm that civilians were not to be deliberately attacked.

Early in the war, Adolf Hitler ordered the bombing of enemy cities. In Britain, targets included London and Coventry. The outraged English demanded revenge, and their government ordered reprisal raids. For the rest of the war, the Royal Air Force (RAF) largely followed this pattern of "area" bombing, both as a matter of choice and as one dictated by the limitations of their equipment. The United States, meanwhile, adopted a different path toward realizing successful strategic bombing. American planners had serious moral qualms about area

bombing because of its indiscriminate killing of civilians. This, coupled with the American penchant for technological solutions, led the country in the direction of precision bombing. Their principled position was made more tenable by the development of the Norden bombsight, a major advance in bomb aiming.

Weak Beginnings   When war began in Europe, the United States had just started building the first aircraft actually designed for strategic bombing, the B-17. Much bigger and faster than existing bombers, capable of carrying a bigger bombload farther and equipped with rotating machine-gun turrets for self-defense, the plane was dubbed the Flying Fortress. Between 1938 and 1941, production was limited. After Pearl Harbor, production of B-17s went into high gear. Some of the bombers went to the RAF, while most of the rest were assigned to the American Eighth Air Force based at fields scattered throughout England. Though the Eighth Air Force and the RAF essentially worked side by side, there was almost as much friction as cooperation between the two units. Interweaving their command structures proved thorny, and their different targeting strategies did not always mesh. RAF's Bomber Command flew mostly nighttime area-bombing missions, while the Eighth Air Force usually flew in daylight, to better find and hit precise targets. In 1942, neither approach did much harm to the German war effort, while both the Eighth Air Force and the RAF suffered aircraft and aircrew losses at a discouraging rate.

Another Difficult Year   During the summer of 1943, a major effort was launched to destroy German aircraft production. German fighters put up a stiff defense. Without air superiority, the Allies could neither achieve effective strategic bombing nor stage the invasion of France planned for 1944. Large-scale raids, often involving hundreds of bombers, were launched from England, sometimes complemented by American B-24s based in North Africa. Regensburg and Schweinfurt were among the principal targets and, though some real damage was done, these raids did nothing to reduce German production. The raiders themselves suffered severely, losing as many as one-quarter of all the planes launched during a single raid and cumulatively sustaining an attrition rate of about 40 percent. Particular devastation was wreaked on Hamburg, where a combined Allied bombing force of more than seven hundred planes dropped both incendiary and high-explosive bombs, unleashing a firestorm of unprecedented ferocity. Many thousands were killed and many more had to flee the raging fires that destroyed much of Hamburg's housing. For all the destruction caused by the Allies, strategic bombing had not yet proved worthwhile as the war entered its fifth year.

Strategic Bombing Comes of Age The year 1944 opened with bombers continuing to attack the aircraft industry primarily. Despite greatly improved fighter escort and precision rates, German production actually reached a peak in the fall of 1944, while American casualties remained high. A dramatic change occurred when the Allies shifted their target priorities to transportation and oil production. German supplies, especially of aviation gasoline, quickly shrank. Along with German shortages of trained pilots, this technique finally gave unquestioned air superiority to the Allies; they now could carry out strategic bombing as the air-power pioneers had planned it. One example of this, soon to become

notorious, was the combined Allied bombing of Dresden early in 1945. As in Hamburg previously, a hellish firestorm was created by incendiary bombing, this time in a city already overcrowded with fleeing refugees.

Previously exempt from sustained bombing because of distance, Japan was coming under attack by air power's most advanced weapon, the B-29 Superfortress. With about double the capabilities of the B-17, the B-29 bombed Japan's home islands from China, an arduous task, and then from islands closer to Japan. Sent to do high-altitude precision bombing, the B-29s proved disappointing because of heavy cloud cover and strong crosswinds. Then, General Curtis LeMay ordered them to engage in low-level, nighttime incendiary bombing carried out by air armadas of as many as eight hundred planes. Almost immediately, scores of Japanese cities experienced what one observer called their "bath of fire." It seemed that area rather than precision bombing was the strategic means of bringing Japan to its knees. Then, on August 6, 1945, a B-29 dropped an atomic bomb directly on its aiming

B-29 Superfortresses on a bombing raid over Yokohama, Japan. (National Archives)

point in Hiroshima; Nagasaki met the same fate days later, and Japan quickly surrendered. The final chapter of air war in World War II was brought about by precision bombing after all.

Impact Because of strategic bombing, much of the urban landscape of Germany and Japan was reduced to rubble. Air Force proponents gave much of the credit for victory to strategic bombing, but their views were challenged by Army and Navy advocates. What had begun as an effort to get away from the attrition of trench warfare developed into a war of attrition against cities and their populations. In World War I, military casualties greatly outnumbered civilian. In World War II, the ratio was reversed. In 1947, champions of air power finally achieved their fondest desire: Their service became the independent U.S. Air Force. The development of jet aircraft, thermonuclear weapons, and guided missiles altered the perception of strategic bombing. In the United States, debate over the necessity of using the atomic bomb reached a crescendo in the national furor over the Smithsonian's *Enola Gay* exhibit. A few years later some German authors broke a long-standing taboo against discussing Germans as victims of strategic bombing.

Richard L. Gruber

Further Reading

Addison, Paul, and Jeremy A. Crang, eds. *Firestorm: The Bombing of Dresden, 1945.* London: Pimleco, 2006. Collection of essays examining controversial aspects of this example of strategic bombing.

Biddle, Tami Davis. *Rhetoric and Reality in Air Warfare: The Evolution of British and American Ideas About Strategic Bombing, 1914-1945.* Princeton, N.J.: Princeton University Press, 2002. Comparative examination of bombing policies and the assumptions and values on which they were based, deftly woven into an analytic narrative of bombing operations.

Budiansky, Stephen. *Air Power: The Men, Machines, and Ideas That Revolutionized War, from Kitty Hawk to Gulf War II.* New York: Viking, 2004. A well-informed and well-written overview of bombing techniques and history.

Dubin, Steven C. *Displays of Power: Controversy in the American Museum from the "Enola Gay" to "Sensation."* Chapter six is a good account of the uproar over the *Enola Gay* exhibit.

Perret, Geoffrey. *Winged Victory: The Army Air Forces in World War II.* New York: Random House, 1993. Comprehensive, reliable, and full of anecdotal details.

See also Aircraft carriers; Aircraft design and development; Atomic bomb; Balloon bombs, Japanese; Bombers; Doolittle bombing raid; Hiroshima and Nagasaki bombings; Oregon bombing.

■ *A Streetcar Named Desire*

Identification Play about a woman living with her sister and brother-in-law
Author Tennessee Williams (1911-1983)
Date Debuted on Broadway on December 3, 1947

In A Streetcar Named Desire, *playwright Tennessee Williams created a sexually daring American tragedy about the collision between the dishonest decadence of a vulnerable woman from the romantic South and the coarse vitality of a brutal man from the real industrial nation.*

Directed by Elia Kazan, *A Streetcar Named Desire* opened on December 3, 1947, in New York. Blanche DuBois (played by Jessica Tandy) arrives almost penniless from her hometown in Mississippi to stay in a dingy New Orleans apartment with her sister, Stella (Kim Hunter), and brother-in-law, Stanley Kowalski (Marlon Brando). The family plantation has been lost, and Blanche, an alcoholic, claims that she has left her teaching job because of her nerves. As for Stanley, she finds him ungentlemanly but sexually attractive. Having years earlier lost her young husband, a homosexual, to suicide, she finds Stanley's friend Harold "Mitch" Mitchell (Karl Malden) ungainly but sympathetic, and mutual affection develops. Stanley, however, has tired of Blanche's arrogance and wants privacy in the little apartment with Stella, who is pregnant. Learning of Blanche's promiscuity, Stanley ends the new romance by telling Mitch. Then, while Stella is in labor at a hospital, Stanley rapes Blanche, shattering her already cracking sanity. The play ends as a doctor escorts her to an asylum.

Impact *A Streetcar Named Desire* gained immediate acclaim, winning a Drama Critics' Circle Award and a Pulitzer Prize and enjoying a long first run. Produced on stages around the world and converted into a 1951 movie, it has transcended its era to become a classic.

Victor Lindsey

Further Reading

Kolin, Philip C. *Williams: A Streetcar Named Desire.* New York: Cambridge University Press, 2000.

———, ed. *The Tennessee Williams Encyclopedia.* Westport, Conn.: Greenwood Press, 2004.

Williams, Tennessee. *A Streetcar Named Desire.* Acting ed. New York: Dramatists Play Service, 1953.

See also Homosexuality and gay rights; Literature in the United States; Psychiatry and psychology; Sex and sex education; Theater in the United States; Williams, Tennessee.

■ Studies in Social Psychology in World War II

Identification Compilation and summary of a program of studies commissioned to explore the adjustment of citizen-soldiers to military life and to combat
Creator U.S. War Department
Dates Studies initiated and reported from 1941 to 1945; research summarized in four volumes in 1949

The research program summarized in Studies in Social Psychology in World War II *has remained the most comprehensive exploration ever undertaken of factors influencing the morale of a wartime army. Its conclusions both altered American military policy and made enduring contributions to the psychology of group dynamics.*

Aware of the importance of an army's morale in the success of military missions, General George C. Marshall commissioned Samuel A. Stouffer and his associates to study factors influencing the commitment of American soldiers in World War II. Using written questionnaires, intensive interviews, and such behavioral outcomes as the numbers of promotions and soldiers absent without leave (AWOL), Stouffer and his associates studied how morale varied with the individual soldier's background (such factors as race, education, and age), branch of the service, military assignment, length of time in the armed services, and the duration of exposure to combat. As a result of these studies, the military learned a great deal about what motivated commitment in its citizen army.

Matters of status were important with the choosy U.S. Army Air Forces, accorded a high status among military personnel, as contrasted with the infantry, often perceived as being of lower status. The researchers found that soldiers evaluated the rewards and deprivations of military life not objectively but in comparison to salient others, their "reference group." Air Force personnel, for example, were dissatisfied with their rates of promotion, which objectively were very high, because they compared themselves with other air corpsmen. In contrast, members of the military police (MPs) were satisfied with their objectively lower rate of promotion because other MPs served as their "reference group."

The researchers found that hatred of the enemy and a belief in such abstract ideals as "fighting for democracy" were relatively unimportant in sustaining military commitment, but that personal loyalty to the soldier's immediate unit had great power to sustain commitment through the rigors of battle. Above all else, soldiers did not want to "let their buddies down." The research also showed that many black servicemen were quite dissatisfied with the army's policy of segregating them into all-black units assigned subordinate, noncombat roles. When black platoons were needed to fight alongside white platoons in the crucial Battle of the Bulge, this coordinated action reportedly occurred without friction, and black soldiers were given high marks for their combat skills.

Impact When the findings of the social psychology study were reported to the military command, they had a direct influence in altering military policy. Efforts were made to raise the status of the important infantry by introducing merit awards such as sharpshooter badges. Soldiers who had endured prolonged close combat in Europe and who therefore felt "relatively deprived" were awarded extra points toward speedy discharge at the end of the war.

Some conclusions of this research led to more enduring changes in military policy. The reported success of the black servicemen integrated into combat roles was an important consideration in President Harry S. Truman's 1948 order to racially desegregate the military. Military training manuals gave new emphasis to the building of small and more cohesive military units. The demonstrated power of conformity pressures in small, cohesive groups inspired a new generation of research in social psychology that documented such pressures in other groups.

Thomas E. DeWolfe

Further Reading

Jones, Lyle V. "Some Lasting Consequences of U.S. Psychology Programs in World Wars." *Multivariate Behavioral Research* 42 (2007): 593-608.
Social Science Research Council, ed. *Studies of Social Psychology in World War II*. 4 vols. Princeton, N.J.: Princeton University Press, 1949.
Williams, Robin. "The American Soldier: An Assessment Several Wars Later." *Public Opinion Quarterly* 53 (1989): 155-174.

See also   Air Force, U.S.; Bulge, Battle of the; Casualties of World War II; Education in the United States; *The Good War: An Oral History of World War II*; "Greatest Generation"; Military conscription in the United States; Psychiatry and psychology; Social sciences; Wartime propaganda in the United States; World War II; World War II mobilization.

■ Submarine warfare

Submarines had a significant impact on naval operations during World War II and were used to sink major fleet units, especially in the Pacific, and to attack enemy commerce.

German submarine operations on the Atlantic Ocean convoy routes began as soon as Great Britain and France declared war on Germany in 1938 and continued until the end of World War II. However, after May, 1943, Germany's submarine campaign was little more than a nuisance for the Allies. In response to the Germans, the British immediately started convoying merchant ships and building a growing number of escorts, ultimately including a few hundred crewed by the Royal Canadian Navy. German submarines also sank many British warships, including two battleships and three carriers, but these numbers were too insignificant to matter greatly in the large context of naval warfare. In the fall of 1941, the United States began to support antisubmarine operations, which led to a few shoot-outs between German U-boats and American destroyers,

starting with the USS *Greer* in September, 1941, and culminating in the sinking of the destroyer USS *Reuben James* on the last day of October.

United States Against German Submarines   In January, 1942, the Germans launched Operation Drumbeat, a submarine campaign aimed at shipping activities off the East Coast of the United States. Initially, only a small number of German submarines were used, but they achieved considerable success because American commercial troops were not traveling under convoy. The Germans soon increased their forces off the East Coast, sinking large numbers of ships off Cape Hatteras and elsewhere, sometimes within sight of the shore. American admiral Ernest King began to set up escorted convoys off the East Coast, until by late 1942 there were enough escorts to provide convoys on all major routes. The Germans sent their submarines to the West Indies and the Gulf Coast, where they continued to sink large numbers of ships.

Germany eventually resumed its campaign against the North Atlantic convoy route, initially helped by its code breakers who were able to decipher the convoy codes. The Allies fought back with increased escorts; greater use of airplanes, including escort carriers, mostly American-built, that provided protection in the middle of the ocean; new weapons; and a vast array of technological equipment. In order to locate submarines, code-breaking and direction-finding devices were used on communications between the submarines and their commanders, and sonar and centimetric radar were also employed. The climax of this battle came in 1943, when the Germans won a major convoy victory in March and the Allied defenses reached critical mass and won a decisive victory in May.

Japanese Submarines   Japanese submarine warfare against the United States began at Pearl Harbor, which was attacked by midget submarines. The attack accomplished nothing except to alert antisubmarine forces. As part of the Pearl Harbor assault, Japanese submarines tried to cut off sea access to Hawaii, sinking a number of merchant ships over a two-month period, though many ships survived because of the Japanese decision to strike nonwarships with no more than one torpedo. The Japanese also struck the American carrier *Saratoga* with a torpedo in January, 1942, but the ship was repaired and returned to service.

Submarine assembly plant in Bremen in 1945. A port about forty miles up the Weser River from the North Sea, Bremen was a major shipbuilding site during World War II and was heavily bombed throughout the war. (Time & Life Pictures/Getty Images)

stroyed as it returned from Savo Island in 1942. Submarines played important roles at the Philippine Sea, where the Japanese carriers *Shokaku* and *Taiho* were sunk, and the Leyte Gulf, where two heavy cruisers were sunk and a third was destroyed while the three ships were on their way to battle. The most spectacular warship sunk by an American submarine was the Japanese supercarrier *Shinano* in November, 1944.

Despite those attacks on warships, American submarines had greater success in sinking Japanese merchant ships. By the beginning of 1945, Japanese foreign trade was virtually strangled because the nation's commercial shipping had declined by more than 60 percent. Admiral Chester W. Nimitz declared unrestricted submarine warfare as soon as he took command of the Pacific Fleet. Though problems with the Mark 14 torpedoes kept Japanese losses modest in 1942, in 1943 American submarines sank more than 1.5 million tons of shipping, and the following year this number doubled to about 3 million tons. Japanese antisubmarine efforts were hampered by the nation's technological inferiority. Submarine patrols were also stationed in the Atlantic, but they had few opportunities for combat and accomplished little.

After the assault at Pearl Harbor, Japanese submarines were primarily used to attack warships or as transportation, the latter becoming an increasingly important function as many Japanese island garrisons were otherwise cut off. The Japanese sank the carrier *Yorktown* at the close of the Battle of Midway and the carriers *Hornet* and *Wasp* off Guadalcanal. Japanese submarines also sunk the *Juneau* in November, 1942, and the cruiser *Indianapolis* in June, 1945, right after it delivered atomic bombs to Tinian.

American Submarines in the Pacific Initial problems with the Mark 14 torpedo hampered American submarine operations. These weapons accomplished little in the defense of the Philippines. Though mostly used against merchant ships, the torpedoes did sink many major Japanese warships, starting with the heavy cruiser *Kako*, which was de-

Impact German submarines inflicted modest losses on the Royal Navy and heavy losses on Anglo-American shipping until mid-1943, but these victories did not enable Germany to win the war. Japanese submarines sank a number of major warships, including enough aircraft carriers in 1942 to nearly win the Guadalcanal campaign. American submarines played the key role in strangling Japanese commerce, and the United States' sinking of Axis warships greatly aided American victories in two major naval battles in 1944.

Timothy Lane

Further Reading

Blair, Clay. *Hitler's U-Boat War.* 2 vols. New York: Random House, 1996-1998. Extensive and detailed study of German U-boat operations from 1939 to 1945.

_____. *Silent Victory.* 2 vols. Philadelphia: J. B. Lippincott, 1975. Comprehensive examination of American submarine operations against Japan from 1941 to 1945.

Burlingame, Burl. *Advance Force Pearl Harbor.* Annapolis, Md.: Naval Institute Press, 2002. Careful study of the operation of Japanese submarines, both miniature and regular, during the Pearl Harbor attack.

Gannon, Michael. *Black May.* New York: Dell, 1999. A sequel to *Operation Drumbeat*, detailing the decisive defeat of the German submarine fleet in May, 1943.

_____. *Operation Drumbeat.* New York: Harper & Sons, 1990. Detailed look of German U-boat operations off the coast of the United States in early 1942, inspired by curiosity over a sinking that the author witnessed.

Hickam, Homer. *Torpedo Junction.* New York: Dell, 1991. Examines German U-boat operations off the American coast in the first half of 1942.

Padfield, Peter. *War Beneath the Seas.* New York: John Wiley & Sons, 1995. Describes submarine operations by both the Allies and Axis Powers in the Atlantic, Mediterranean, and Pacific theaters.

See also Aircraft carriers; Atlantic, Battle of the; Code breaking; Great Marianas Turkey Shoot; *Greer* incident; Guadalcanal, Battle of; Midway, Battle of; Navy, U.S.; Nimitz, Chester W.; Pearl Harbor attack; Radar; Sullivan brothers.

The five Sullivan brothers aboard their ship in January, 1942. From left to right: Joseph, Francis, Albert, Madison, and George. In 1997, the U.S. Navy commissioned a new destroyer named The Sullivans. *(AP/Wide World Photos)*

■ Sullivan brothers

The Event Sinking of a U.S. battleship that caused the deaths of five brothers

Date November 13, 1942

Place Pacific Ocean near the island of Guadalcanal

Although the Sullivan brothers knew the risk, they asked for and received permission from the Navy to serve on the same ship. When the USS Juneau *sank, the brothers' deaths were the largest loss of life suffered by one family in a single military event.*

The five sons of Thomas and Alleta Sullivan of Waterloo, Iowa—George, Francis (Frank), Joseph (Red), Madison (Matt), and Albert—joined the Navy after one of their friends died in the bombing of Pearl Harbor in December, 1941. When they went to enlist (George and Francis reenlisted), they requested service on the same ship. Going against existing regulations that do not appear to have been enforced, the Navy approved the request.

On the night of November 13, 1942, Japanese and American ships engaged in a heavy sea battle near Guadalcanal. The USS *Juneau*, on which the Sullivan brothers served, was torpedoed. As the *Juneau* and other damaged ships were being escorted to the naval base at New Hebrides, a Japanese submarine torpedoed the *Juneau* and the ship exploded. Four of the Sullivan brothers were instantly killed. George died in a life raft.

Impact After the death of the five Sullivan brothers, the Navy enforced its policy of not allowing brothers to serve on the same ship during times of war. Brothers who were serving together immediately received different assignments.

Linda Adkins

Further Reading

Patten, Clarence Floyd, III, and Dale E. Sporleder. *124 Years Before the Navy Mast: The Patten Family.* Carmel, Ind.: Huntington, 2006.

Satterfield, John R. *We Band of Brothers: The Sullivans and World War II.* Parkersburg, Iowa: Mid-Prairie Books, 1995.

See also Guadalcanal, Battle of; *History of the United States Naval Operations in World War II*; Navy, U.S.; Pearl Harbor attack; Submarine warfare.

■ Sullivan's Travels

Identification Satirical film that deals with social conditions in the United States
Director Preston Sturges (1898-1959)
Date Released in January, 1942

One of the most important American comedies of the 1940's, Sullivan's Travels *is a stylistic masterpiece that continues to be relevant both as Hollywood satire and as social commentary.*

Starring Joel McCrea, Veronica Lake (in her breakthrough role), Robert Warwick, and William Demarest, *Sullivan's Travels* is perhaps the best in a long line of great comedies by Preston Sturges. Revered by modern filmmakers such as the Coen brothers, Joel and Ethan (who took the title *O Brother, Where Art Thou?* from this film), and writers such as Jonathan Lethem, Sturges was a writer-director who was never afraid to take chances. *Sullivan's Travels* stands as one of his biggest risks: a film that simultaneously lampoons and praises Hollywood, calling into question the significance of films in post-Depression America.

A popular Hollywood director, John L. Sullivan (played by McCrea) gets the urge to make a socially significant film. Urged instead to direct another lowbrow comedy by studio executives, Sullivan insists on making *O Brother, Where Art Thou?* and hits the road as a hobo to research his new movie. Deterred by a series of slapstick misadventures, Sullivan keeps winding up back in Hollywood. Finally, Sullivan realizes his desire to live like a "real hobo." He finds trouble, gets out of it, and, in the end, is awakened to the fact that the despairing masses find comfort in escapist Hollywood fare. Genuine and hilarious, the film sends up Hollywood but ultimately celebrates it

as a necessary and worthwhile jewel in America's thorny crown.

Impact Selected for preservation in the United States National Film Registry by the Library of Congress, *Sullivan's Travels* was ranked the sixty-first greatest movie of all time in 2007 by the American Film Institute. The film was released in a new digital transfer by The Criterion Collection in 2001, featuring an audio commentary by Noah Baumbach, Kenneth Bowser, Christopher Guest, and Michael McKean, just a few of the diverse talents influenced by Sturges's masterwork.

William Boyle

Further Reading

Chin, Daryl. "The Film That We Wanted to Live: Re-releasing Modernist Movies." *PAJ* 23, no. 3 (September, 2001): 1-12.

Curtis, James. *Between Flops: A Biography of Preston Sturges.* Lincoln, Nebr.: iUniverse, 2000.

Sturges, Preston. *Preston Sturges by Preston Sturges: His Life in His Words.* New York: Touchstone, 1990.

See also Capra, Frank; Film in the United States; Travel in the United States; Unemployment in the United States.

■ Superman

Identification Comic-book superhero
Creators Jerry Siegel (1914-1996) and Joe Shuster (1914-1992)
Date Created in 1932; first appearance in print, 1933; first appearance in a comic book, June, 1938

Superman's popularity is responsible in large part for making comic-book publishing into a profitable business and creating the American "superhero" during the 1940's. It also established a trend toward massive cross-media exploitation of pop-culture heroes that prove popular in their originating media.

A hit upon his appearance in *Action Comics* #1 in June, 1938, Superman rocketed to superstardom during the 1940's. The character was created by writer Jerry Siegel and artist Joe Shuster in 1932; he first appeared in print in "The Reign of the Super-Man," a short story in the limited-publication magazine *Science Fiction* #3 published by Siegel, and was sold to Detective Comics, Inc. (later known as DC Comics), in 1938. As the 1940's opened, Superman already had his own black-and-white daily newspaper strip and top billing in three full-color, multiple-story comic books. The character's bold design, intriguing powers, and intolerance for villainy of both fantastic and mundane social varieties quickly earned him a near-universal popularity. His popularity was enhanced by the "no kill" that the publisher insisted upon early in Superman's career; it allowed his books' entrance into homes where his more bloodthirsty pop-culture peers were not allowed. In 1940 alone, Superman comics earned the publisher nearly one million dollars. Superman pulled comics out of the unprofitable "artistic ghetto" in which they had languished and added a new character type to American mythology: the tights-wearing, public-defending, superhumanly gifted superhero.

Superman's many comic appearances soon became too widespread for his original creators to handle. To keep up with demand for the character, the publisher hired additional writers and artists to supplement Shuster's own Cleveland art studio. Superman's runaway success encouraged the publisher and creators to experiment. One early and very successful example of this experimentation, first appearing in 1945, was Superboy, the character of Superman as a youth growing up in the rural Midwest, raised by his adoptive parents, the Kents. Superboy's own comic book launched in 1949.

Superman made his first radio appearance in the syndicated program *The Adventures of Superman*, which ran from 1940 to 1951. Initially shunned by the major networks, the show soon became a ratings powerhouse and was picked up by the Mutual Network, home to legendary radio dramas such as *The Lone Ranger* and *The Shadow*. The program expanded the hero's fan base and boosted the career of Clayton "Bud" Collyer, who provided Su-

perman's radio voice. *The Adventures of Superman* is significant for adding a number of elements to the Superman mythos later adopted as canon by the comics: Superman's vulnerability to kryptonite, his ability to fly—and not merely leap—and his partnership with Batman all originated in the radio program.

In 1941, animation house Fleischer Studios, best known for its energetic Betty Boop and Popeye shorts, began producing seven-minute Superman cartoons. Beginning with *The Mad Scientist*, Fleischer produced seventeen lavishly animated Superman shorts in all, each costing around fifty thousand dollars. With their fluid, lifelike motion, they are still regarded as some of the finest examples of cel animation.

Superman's first live-action film appearance was considerably more humble than his animated debut. Sam Katzman oversaw production of the plainly titled serial *Superman* in 1948. Starring Kirk Alyn in

After starring in the fifteen-episode Superman *serial in 1948, Kirk Alyn reprised the superhero role in another serial,* Atom Man vs. Superman, *two years later.* (Getty Images)

the title role, the fifteen-part serial looked the part of its low budget. Worst of all were the crudely animated sequences of Superman flying because live-action flying scenes were too expensive to produce. Notwithstanding its flaws, the serial was so popular with younger audiences that a far more generously budgeted sequel was produced in 1950.

Impact   The father of the American superhero, Superman saw his quickest and most important growth during the 1940's. Before the decade was over, he had not only solidified into the well-known protector of justice but also acted as midwife to countless new (and later beloved) heroes, including Batman and Captain Marvel. His fame and popularity continued in comics, in the televised *Adventures of Superman* (1952-1958) starring George Reeves, feature films created decades after his emergence into popular culture, and even a Broadway musical, *It's a Bird . . . It's a Plane . . . It's Superman*, which premiered in 1966.

Abram Taylor

Further Reading

Daniels, Les. *Superman: The Complete History—The Life and Times of the Man of Steel.* San Francisco: Chronicle Books, 2004.

Fingeroth, Danny. *Superman on the Couch: What Superheroes Really Tell Us About Ourselves and Our Society.* New York: Continuum, 2004.

Grossman, Gary H. *Superman: Serial to Cereal.* New York: Popular Library, 1977.

Szasz, Ferenc M., and Issei Takechi. "Atomic Heroes and Atomic Monsters: American and Japanese Cartoonists Face the Onset of the Nuclear Age." *Historian* 69 (2007): 728-752.

See also   Animated films; Comic books; Comic strips; Film in the United States; Film serials; Radio in the United States; Wonder Woman.

■ Supreme Court, U.S.

Identification   Highest court in the U.S. judicial system, holding the power to overrule all lower court rulings and federal and state legislation

Many of the landmark decisions from the 1940's stemmed from government responses to World War II. These ranged from the forcible internment of Japanese Americans to military prosecution of German saboteurs caught out of uni- *form in the country. However, the decade also saw far-reaching decisions about other issues, such as expanding Congressional power to regulate interstate commerce.*

During the first half of the decade, membership of the U.S. Supreme Court included a number of its most famous justices, including Harlan Fiske Stone, the chief justice; former attorney general and later Nuremberg prosecutor Robert H. Jackson; former Harvard law professor Felix Frankfurter; William O. Douglas, who would later become the longest-serving justice on the Court; and civil libertarian, but former Ku Klux Klan member, Hugo L. Black. This luminary group of justices decided some of the most important cases in the Court's history, passing down rulings that have continued to color the constitutional landscape.

Japanese American Internment Cases   The most controversial Supreme Court decisions of the decade were the Japanese American curfew, exclusion, and internment cases. A few months after the devastating Japanese sneak attack on the Pearl Harbor naval base, President Franklin D. Roosevelt issued Executive Order 9066, which authorized military commanders to declare military areas off-limits. Pursuant to this executive order, Lieutenant General John L. DeWitt, the military commander for the West Coast, began issuing military orders applicable to all persons of Japanese ancestry, including American citizens, who lived within one hundred miles of the Pacific Ocean. Four cases brought by Japanese Americans subject to these military orders reached the Supreme Court.

In *Hirabayashi v. United States* (1943), the plaintiff challenged the constitutionality of an 8:00 P.M. curfew established by General DeWitt based on its discriminatory application to only persons of Japanese descent. In upholding the curfew, the Court relied upon stereotypical perceptions of Japanese Americans as isolated, insular, and still attached to Imperial Japan. Thus, although the Court stated that "[d]istinctions between citizens solely because of their ancestry are by their nature odious to a free people whose institutions are founded upon the doctrine of equality," it nevertheless concluded that military necessity justified the curfew. The companion case to *Hirabayashi* was *Yasui v. United States* (1943), which was decided on the same day. In *Yasui*, the Court upheld a former military officer's conviction for violating the curfew on the same grounds as in *Hirabayashi*.

With General DeWitt's curfew order upheld, the Court turned its attention to his subsequent orders calling for exclusion of Japanese persons from the West Coast and for forced relocation of such persons. *Korematsu v. United States* (1944) addressed the exclusion order, and *Ex parte Endo* (1944) focused on the internment. *Korematsu* was the first instance in which the Supreme Court decided that racial classifications were to be reviewed under a standard known as "rigid scrutiny"; subsequent cases called it "strict scrutiny." Under modern case law, strict scrutiny means that the government must have a compelling state interest justifying the racial classification, and the racial classification must be the least restrictive means to achieving that compelling interest. Nearly all statutes subjected to strict scrutiny have failed to survive. In *Korematsu*, despite invoking this stringent review, the Court in fact deferred to the government's claim of military necessity. Justice Black's opinion rejected Korematsu's claim that he had been singled out for exclusion because of his race, arguing instead that he "was excluded because we are at war with the Japanese Empire" and because military leaders "decided that the military urgency of the situation demanded that all citizens of Japanese ancestry be segregated from the West Coast temporarily."

Three justices dissented in *Korematsu*. Justice Frank Murphy argued that blanket exclusion of all persons of Japanese descent without regard to their citizenship and, more important, without any individual loyalty hearings, was a violation of due process. He noted that Great Britain had managed to hold expedited hearings on all the enemy aliens living there at the outset of World War II and had opted to detain only a couple thousand, with the vast majority suffering no disability at all. Justice Jackson argued that the Court should not have ruled on the case; while military necessity may require the government to act unconstitutionally, it was altogether different to have the Court validate the government's actions. However, in *Endo*, which was decided the same day as *Korematsu*, the Court rejected the forced internment of Japanese Americans who had not been shown to have been disloyal to the United States.

Although *Hirabayashi* and *Korematsu* have never been officially overturned, they are often listed with *Dred Scott v. Sanford* (1857) as among the worst decisions ever issued by the Court. At one point during the later years of the Rehnquist Court, virtually every sitting justice had indicated disapproval of the decisions. More than forty years after the end of World War II, the federal government paid each surviving detainee twenty thousand dollars. President Ronald Reagan and, subsequently, President George H. W. Bush also officially apologized for the internment. These cases have become so discredited that there was no consideration given to interning Arab Americans or Muslims after the September 11, 2001 (9/11) terrorist attacks.

Military Courts In 1942, eight German soldiers reached the East Coast, four in Florida and four in New York, with plans to blow up industrial plants and other critical targets. All eight had previously lived in the United States before World War II, and at least one of them was a dual U.S.-German citizen. Although they came ashore in uniform, they stripped down to civilian clothes, opting to bury their uniforms in the beach. However, the leader of the saboteurs decided to turn them all in to U.S. authorities. In a story line that could have come out of Hollywood, he actually had to call the Federal Bureau of Investigation (FBI) a number of times before he was taken seriously. Despite this initial misstep, the FBI soon apprehended all eight saboteurs.

On July 2, 1942, President Roosevelt issued Proclamation No. 2561, which established a military court to try the eight German soldiers for war crimes. The charges flowed from the fact that the saboteurs intended to disguise themselves as civilians and thereby fight out of uniform. Importantly, the proclamation denied military defendants access to federal courts, in effect leaving them subject to whatever procedures and substantive rules that the executive branch deemed appropriate. A week later, all eight defendants were convicted and sentenced to death. Notwithstanding the president's declaration that the federal courts would not be available to the German soldiers, the Supreme Court agreed to hear their petitions for habeas corpus. Four days later, the Court affirmed the death sentences. In a marked departure from the norm, however, the Court merely announced its judgment.

The president commuted the sentences for two of the eight to life; the other six were electrocuted on August 8, 1942. Almost three months elapsed before the Supreme Court finally issued its opinion in *Ex parte Quirin* (1942). The challenge for the Court was distinguishing a Civil War-era decision, *Ex parte Milligan* (1866), in which it had invalidated the use of a military trial against a civilian during the Civil War. According to the *Milligan* decision, the civilian courts in Indiana, where the defendant was located, were open and functioning during the time he was prosecuted; subjecting him to prosecution in a forum that denied him his Fifth and Sixth Amendment rights, therefore, was unconstitutional. Though the United States was already embroiled in World War II in 1942, civilian courts remained open for business, and *Milligan* appeared to foreclose military trials in these circumstances. In the *Quirin* case, the Court concluded, however, that the German soldiers were "unlawful combatants" who had forfeited any rights to civilian trial because of their violations of the laws of war. That one of the eight was an American citizen was of no significance, because citizenship did not relieve a belligerent of the consequences of his actions.

After many decades of relative obscurity, *Quirin* exploded into the national political and legal consciousness after the 9/11 terrorist attacks, when President George W. Bush issued an executive order authorizing the prosecution of international terrorists in military commissions. When Bush administration critics argued that the president's military commissions were unlawful, *Quirin* was offered as precedential justification.

Congress and the Commerce Clause   In addition to the wartime decisions that upheld expansive executive power, the Supreme Court expanded Congress's power under the commerce clause of the Constitution to regulate interstate commerce. Previously, the Supreme Court had invalidated various parts of the New Deal as unconstitutional, either because Congress had attempted to regulate commerce that was intrastate (as opposed to interstate) or to regulate noncommercial activities. President Roosevelt became so upset at the Court's interference that he proposed his infamous "Court-Packing" plan, by which he would have added six justices to the Supreme Court—enough to secure a majority to uphold the New Deal programs. Supposedly, this led to the "switch in time that saved the nine": Justice Owen J. Roberts began voting to uphold New Deal programs, turning 5-4 defeats into 5-4 victories for President Roosevelt.

The two key commerce cases in of the 1940's were *United States v. Darby Lumber Co.* (1941) and *Wickard v. Filburn* (1943). In *Darby*, the Supreme Court upheld parts of the Fair Labor Standards Act of 1938 that prohibited the transportation across state lines of products made in violation of the maximum-hours and minimum-wage standards of the act. The Court's decision was unexpected because twenty-three years earlier, in *Hammer v. Dagenhart* (1918), also known as the Child Labor Case, the Court had invalidated an almost identical prohibition on the interstate transportation of products made through child labor. In the Child Labor Case, the Court had concluded that Congress was attempting to regulate methods of production, rather than commerce. In *Darby*, the Court reversed course, stating that it would not review Congress' motives in legislating; thus, even if Congress really did intend to regulate the labor market, as opposed to protecting interstate commerce, the Court would not interfere.

The issue in the *Wickard* case centered on the fact that the secretary of agriculture had regulated the price of wheat by allocating specific harvesting quotas per farmer. By controlling the national wheat production, the secretary could keep wheat prices stable, without fear of overproduction and a resulting price crash. Roscoe C. Filburn was allotted 223 bushels in one year, a limit with which he complied. However, he also grew an additional 239 bushels, ostensibly for private use. For exceeding his quota, Filburn was fined $117.11.

Before the Supreme Court, Filburn argued that his own excess contribution was insignificant compared to the total amount of wheat grown in the country during that year and thus could not have had any impact on wheat prices. The Court, however, disagreed. Using a principle of aggregation, it explained that the relevant question was not whether Filburn alone affected wheat prices. Rather, the Court noted that if all farmers were to exceed their production quota, wheat prices would be affected.

Together, *Darby* and *Wickard*, along with *National Labor Relations Board v. Jones and Laughlin Steel Corporation* (1937), laid the groundwork for the next fifty years, during which the Supreme Court did not find a single federal statute that exceeded Congress' power to regulate interstate commerce. During those fifty years, Congress used the Commerce Clause to legislate in such diverse areas as civil rights in employment and access to public accommodations, environmental protection, loan-sharking, and controlled substances. Without *Darby*'s refusal to examine congressional motive and *Wickard*'s aggregation principle, many of those statutes might not have survived judicial review.

Other Key Cases Although World War II cast a long shadow on the Supreme Court's docket during the decade, the Court made significant decisions that had nothing to do with the war. Two key First Amendment decisions emerged from the early 1940's. In *Chaplinsky v. New Hampshire* (1942), the Court upheld a Jehovah's Witnesses conviction for calling someone else "an offensive or derisive name." According to the Court, the First Amendment's free speech protection did not extend to "fighting words"—which caused injury or incited violence—because such statements tended to have little or no social value. *Chaplinsky* continues to be cited, although its incitement analysis has been superseded by *Brandenburg v. Ohio* (1950).

In *West Virginia State Board of Education v. Barnette* (1943), which coincidentally also involved Jehovah's Witnesses, the Court ruled that public schools could not force schoolchildren to salute the U.S. flag. In an often-quoted passage, Justice Jackson wrote that "If there is any fixed star in our constitutional constellation, it is that no official, high or petty, can prescribe what shall be orthodox in politics, nationalism, religion, or other matters of opinion or force citizens to confess by word or act their faith therein." *Barnette* established the important principle that the First Amendment protected not only the right to speak but also the right not to speak.

Another important decision was *Shelley v. Kraemer* (1948), a case that foreshadowed the Court's increasing intolerance of state-authorized racial discrimination, which culminated six years later in the landmark decision in *Brown v. Board of Education* (1954). In *Shelley*, a Caucasian seller and an African American buyer reached a sales agreement on a house, but neighbors

---

West Virginia State Board of Education v. Barnette

Associate Justice Robert H. Jackson delivered the majority opinion, excerpted here, of the U.S. Supreme Court ruling in the case of whether students can be compelled to salute the American flag.

There is no doubt that, in connection with the pledges, the flag salute is a form of utterance. Symbolism is a primitive but effective way of communicating ideas. The use of an emblem or flag to symbolize some system, idea, institution, or personality, is a short cut from mind to mind. Causes and nations, political parties, lodges and ecclesiastical groups seek to knit the loyalty of their followings to a flag or banner, a color or design. The state announces rank, function, and authority through crowns and maces, uniforms and black robes; the church speaks through the cross, the crucifix, the altar and shrine, and clerical raiment. Symbols of state often convey political ideas just as religious symbols come to convey theological ones. Associated with many of these symbols are appropriate gestures of acceptance or respect: a salute, a bowed or bared head, a bended knee. A person gets from a symbol the meaning he puts into it, and what is one man's comfort and inspiration is another's jest and scorn. . . .

It is also to be noted that the compulsory flag salute and pledge requires affirmation of a belief and an attitude of mind. It is not clear whether the regulation contemplates that pupils forego any contrary convictions of their own and become unwilling converts to the prescribed ceremony or whether it will be acceptable if they simulate assent by words without belief and by a gesture barren of meaning. It is now a commonplace that censorship or suppression of expression of opinion is tolerated by our constitution only when the expression presents a clear and present danger of action of a kind the state is empowered to prevent and punish. It would seem that involuntary affirmation could be commanded only on even more immediate and urgent grounds than silence. But here the power of compulsion is invoked without any allegation that remaining passive during a flag salute ritual creates a clear and present danger that would justify an effort even to muffle expression. To sustain the compulsory flag salute we are required to say that a bill of rights which guards the individual's right to speak his own mind, left it open to public authorities to compel him to utter what is not in his mind.

obtained a court order blocking the sale, based on a racially restrictive covenant that forbade all home owners in the neighborhood from selling their houses to African American or Asian American buyers. Because the neighbors were private citizens, the Fourteenth Amendment's equal protection clause—which forbids most race-based state discrimination—was thought not to apply. Because a state court was involved, however, the Court concluded that "state action" was present, and as such, the home sale had to comply with the Fourteenth Amendment; because the basis for the interference was solely on the race of the buyer, the interference was unconstitutional.

Shelley fueled fears that virtually all private disputes resolved in courts could be held to constitutional standards, because a state or federal court would necessarily be involved, but subsequent cases did not extend *Shelley* to such results. The case is probably better understood as one that invoked state action because the state was blocking a transaction that otherwise would have taken place—a far different situation from typical litigation, in which the parties are at odds.

Impact   Though many of the Supreme Court's decisions during the 1940's had the specter of World War II as a backdrop, the Court made other important decisions that dealt with interstate commerce and civil rights. The decisions that the Court made during this era had lasting impacts on a wide range of issues affecting the United States.

Tung Yin

Further Reading

Abella, Alex, and Scott Gordon. *Shadow Enemies: Hitler's Secret Terrorist Plot Against the United States.* Guilford, Conn.: Lyons Press, 2002. Trade publication that covers the events leading up to and through *Ex parte Quirin*, the case of the German saboteurs.

Currie, David P. *The Constitution in the Supreme Court:*

Tom Clark (left) shakes hands with President Harry S. Truman after being sworn in as a Supreme Court justice on August 24, 1949. Looking on, left to right, are Vice President Alben W. Barkley, House Speaker Sam Rayburn, and Chief Justice Fred M. Vinson, who administered Clark's oath. (AP/Wide World Photos)

The Second Century, 1888-1986. Chicago: University of Chicago Press, 1990. Academic but readable work that covers the background and rulings of the major Supreme Court decisions during the 1940's, along with insights into the personalities of the justices.

Dorf, Michael C., ed. *Constitutional Law Stories.* New York: Foundation Press, 2004. Compilation of essays about key Supreme Court decisions, including *Wickard v. Filburn, West Virginia State Board of Education v. Barnette,* and *Korematsu v. United States.*

Fisher, Louis. *Nazi Saboteurs on Trial: A Military Tribunal and American Law.* Lawrence: University of Kansas Press, 2003. Another account of the events leading up to *Ex parte Quirin*, in a more academic tone than Abella and Gordon's book.

Schwartz, Bernard. *A History of the Supreme Court.* New York: Oxford University Press, 1993. Readable summary of major Supreme Court decisions, organized chronologically.

See also   Asian Americans; *Chaplinsky v. New Hampshire;* Civil rights and liberties; Japanese American internment; Racial discrimination; *Shelley v. Kraemer; Wickard v. Filburn.*

■ Synchrocyclotron

Definition   Form of particle accelerator with a
    higher maximum energy than a standard
    cyclotron, created by changing the frequency of
    the driving electric field

The maximum energy that could be obtained with a cyclo-
tron (a type of particle accelerator) was limited because, as
the particles approached the speed of light while rotating
in a constant magnetic field, they also gained mass and
slowed, in accordance with Alfred Einstein's theory of rela-
tivity. A synchrocyclotron has only one accelerating elec-
trode rather than the two in a standard cyclotron, and the
drive frequency is modulated to keep the pulses in phase
with the accelerating voltage.

Ernest Orlando Lawrence won the Nobel Prize in
Physics for his work on the cyclotron and built a series of the machines, but they were unable to reach
energies of 100 million electronvolts because of the
relativistic increase of mass of the particles as they
approached the speed of light. This increase in mass
caused them to get out of phase with the voltage that
drove the acceleration, falling behind the peak of
the voltage and therefore not gaining any more energy as they circled through the accelerator. Edwin
McMillan at the University of California and Berkeley, and Vladimir Veksler in Russia explained this
phenomenon and suggested that if the frequency of
the accelerating voltage was lowered as the particles
were slowed, they would remain in phase and the
particles would continue to gain energy. It was possible to obtain nearly 200 million electronvolt deuter-
ons and 400 million electronvolt alpha particles with
the first synchrocyclotron, which became operational in November of 1946.

The main disadvantage of the synchrocyclotrons
was the huge weight and cost of their magnets. This

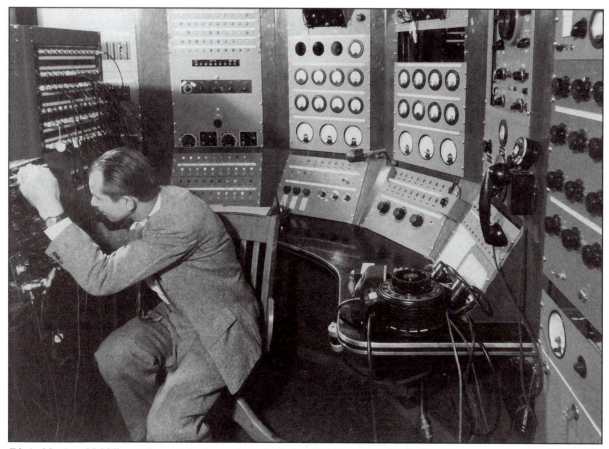

Edwin Mattison McMillan at the controls of a synchrocyclotron in 1948. (Lawrence Radiation Laboratory, Courtesy AIP Emilio
Segrè Visual Archives)

led to the next innovation in particle accelerators, keeping the particles focused in a single orbit in a circular magnet, eliminating the need for the heavy central part of the magnet. All later circular accelerators were synchrotrons of this sort.

Impact The synchrocyclotron was the highest energy particle accelerator of its time. It made possible the beginning studies of the interior of the nucleus. Mesons had been discovered in cosmic rays, but the intensities available were too small to determine their properties. The synchrocyclotron made it possible for the first time to obtain beams of pions and muons and to study their properties and interaction with atomic nuclei.

The synchrocyclotron quickly became the dominant accelerator for use in medical proton therapy. The protons were energetic enough to penetrate within the body to a tumor site, and at the end of their range they became very highly ionizing, destroying tumor cells while having only minor effects on intermediate cells.

The new field of nuclear medicine was initiated by Lawrence's 184-inch synchrocyclotron at the University of California at Berkeley. The new accelerator successfully treated acromegaly and Cushing's disease.

Raymond D. Cooper

Further Reading

Heilbron, J. L., and Robert W. Seidel. *Lawrence and His Laboratory: The History of the Lawrence Berkeley Laboratory.* Berkeley: University of California Press, 1989.

Livingston, M. Stanley. *Particle Accelerators: A Brief History.* Cambridge, Mass.: Harvard University Press, 1969.

Sessler, Andrew, and Edmund Wilson. *Engines of Discovery.* Hackensack, N.J.: World Scientific, 2007.

See also Atomic bomb; Atomic Energy Commission; Groves, Leslie Richard; Hanford Nuclear Reservation; Inventions; Medicine; Nobel Prizes; Nuclear reactors; Science and technology.

T

■ Tacoma Narrows Bridge collapse

The Event Washington State suspension bridge that collapsed under the force of strong winds only four months after it had opened

Date November 7, 1940

Place Tacoma to Gig Harbor, Washington

Although the Tacoma Narrows Bridge was designed to withstand winds of 120 miles per hour, its sudden disintegration in a forty-two-mile-per-hour gale presented an ominous warning to bridge engineers worldwide.

Intended to link Tacoma with Washington's Olympic Peninsula, the Tacoma Narrows Bridge took more than seventeen years to build. Its two-lane central span, then the third longest in the world at 2,800 feet, was only thirty-nine feet wide, narrower in proportion to its length than any other suspension bridge. Even before it was officially opened, the deck's wavelike vertical motion in light wind nauseated construction workers, and the bridge was soon dubbed "Galloping Gertie." On November 7, 1940, wind magnified Gertie's usual undulation into torsion that fed upon itself, violently twisting the deck up to twenty times per minute. Some automobiles were trapped on the failing span, but all occupants managed to crawl to safety except for a cocker spaniel that refused to leave its owner's car. The bridge collapsed shortly after 11:00 A.M.

Impact This event ultimately changed how suspension bridges were constructed. Previously, wind had not been regarded as a source of vertical movement or torsion upon the disproportionally slender Tacoma Narrows Bridge. In-

creasing the width, weight, and rigidity of such a bridge would increase its stability. To eliminate destructive twisting, slots were cut through the deck bottom to deflect the wind's force, to be replaced later by an open-grid roadway. A three-dimensional model of any bridge built with federal funds required thorough tests in a wind tunnel. Incorporating these changes, a second Tacoma Narrows Bridge was completed in 1950.

Joanne McCarthy

Further Reading

Hobbs, Richard S. *Catastrophe to Triumph: Bridges of the Tacoma Narrows.* Pullman: Washington State University Press, 2006.

Petroski, Henry. *Engineers of Dreams: Great Bridge Builders and the Spanning of America.* New York: Alfred A. Knopf, 1995.

See also Architecture; Natural disasters.

Tacoma Narrows Bridge collapsing after buckling under the pressure of strong winds. (AP/Wide World Photos)

■ Taft, Robert A.

Identification Republican leader of the U.S.
  Senate
Born September 8, 1889; Cincinnati, Ohio
Died July 31, 1953; New York, New York

*Taft's moderately conservative but partisan leadership in
the U.S. Senate earned him the sobriquet "Mr. Republican"
and made him an important legislator throughout the decade.*

Born in 1889, Robert A. Taft was the son of William
Howard Taft, who would later serve as president of
the United States (1909-1913) and as chief justice of
the U.S. Supreme Court (1921-1930). The younger
Taft became a business lawyer. Taft was counsel for
the Food Administration during World War I and
counsel for the American Relief Association after
the war. He later became a lawyer and served in the
Ohio legislature before he was elected to the U.S.
Senate from Ohio in 1938.

Even Taft's Democratic foes praised his hard
work, brilliant use of statistics, firm principles, and
integrity. However, he was also reserved, uncharis-
matic, and colorless, and these characteristics hurt

him politically. While in office, Taft was a somewhat
progressive politician, like his father and Herbert
Hoover, but all three of these men were conservative
compared to President Franklin D. Roosevelt. Taft's
political philosophy mixed moderate social liberalism with strong fiscal conservatism and strict
constitutionalism. He favored government health
care and housing, though he preferred that these
programs be administered by the states rather than
the federal government, when feasible. He supported low taxes but not at the price of budgetary
deficits, except in an emergency. Although the Congress of Industrial Organizations deemed him antiunion, Taft consistently supported basic union
rights and opposed Wall Street and monopolists, as
well as Big Labor.

In the area of foreign policy, Taft was moderately
protectionist and pacifistic because he was concerned about the costs of war and the expansion of
government, and he feared that a military victory
would make the United States a world policeman.
Therefore, he was generally isolationist, supported
stronger defense but not the draft, and opposed the
destroyers-for-bases deal and Lend-Lease until the
United States was forced to enter World War II. His
isolationism probably doomed his
chance of becoming the Republican candidate for president in
1940 because the Republican National Convention began two days
after France capitulated to Nazi
Germany. The war also contributed to his narrow reelection to
the Senate in 1944, and his opposition to farm subsidies and
slowness to mend local political
fences also cost him support.

After World War II, Taft opposed President Harry S. Truman's attempt to draft striking
steelworkers, and he supported
federal aid to education and a social safety net, which he now decided were necessary to provide
equal opportunity. He accepted
the United Nations, but he criticized the Nuremberg war crimes
trials as *ex post facto* law. After the
Republicans gained control of
Congress in the 1946 elections,

*Robert A. Taft studying a photograph of his father, former president William Howard
Taft, after announcing his candidacy for the Republican nomination for president in the
1940 election.* (Library of Congress)

Taft helped engineer enactment of the Taft-Hartley Act, which monitors the activities of labor unions. He also helped block many of Truman's domestic policy initiatives and supported the passage of a sizable tax cut. He reluctantly endorsed the Truman Doctrine, the Marshall Plan, and even the draft, and he staunchly supported Zionism.

In 1948, Taft made another attempt to be the Republican candidate for president and was supported by most party conservatives, but the nomination went to Thomas E. Dewey, who ran a superior campaign for the nomination and had a more favorable public image. When Truman reconvened Congress after the two political parties held their conventions, the partisan Taft led congressional opposition to most of Truman's proposals, and lawmakers adopted only a few banking and credit measures. After Truman was elected in November, Taft helped Congress pass a federal housing bill, but he opposed most of Truman's Fair Deal policies and the creation of the North Atlantic Treaty Organization (NATO), while he pushed for stronger resistance to communism in Asia. Taft was easily reelected to the Senate in 1950 and made a third bid for the presidential nomination in 1952, but he lost to Dwight D. Eisenhower. After the 1952 elections, he was the Senate majority leader for a few months before he died in July, 1953.

Impact   Robert A. Taft had a significant impact on congressional legislation, influencing the votes of the conservatives who would later dominate the Republican Party. However, his most enduring legacy was enactment of the Taft-Hartley Act, particularly the law's provision that allowed states to pass right-to-work laws.

Timothy Lane

Further Reading

Hayes, Michael T. "The Republican Road Not Taken." *Independent Review* 8, no. 4 (Spring, 2004): 509-525.

Merry, Robert W. "The Last Stand of Senator Robert Taft, Republicans' Guiding Voice." *Congressional Quarterly Weekly Report* 53 (March 18, 1995): 791-794.

Patterson, James T. *Mr. Republican: A Biography of Robert A. Taft.* Boston: Houghton Mifflin, 1972.

Wunderlin, Clarence E. *Robert A. Taft: Ideas, Tradition, and Party in U.S. Foreign Policy.* Lanham, Md.: S. R. Books, 2005.

See also   Congress, U.S.; Conservatism in U.S. politics; Elections in the United States: 1942 and 1946; Smith, Margaret Chase; Taft-Hartley Act; Truman, Harry S.; Willkie, Wendell.

■ Taft-Hartley Act

The Law   Federal legislation regulating labor-management relations

Also known as   Labor-Management Relations Act

Date   Passed over presidential veto on June 23, 1947; went into effect on August 22, 1947.

Twelve years after passage of the strong prolabor Wagner Act, the Taft-Hartley Act shifted the federal government's position in a more probusiness, antilabor direction.

During the Great Depression, President Franklin Delano Roosevelt expanded the federal government in order to address the growing economic calamity as well as to address several social issues. Rising unemployment and falling levels of personal income motivated Roosevelt to shape a much more active central government. Part of this effort, dubbed the New Deal, was the Wagner Act (also known as the National Labor Relations Act) of 1935. This act was important because it guaranteed the rights of workers to organize into labor unions, giving individual workers more clout in their dealings with employers. It sought to end unfair labor practices, and it set up the National Labor Relations Board (NLRB) to administer the new law.

Background in the Wagner Act   The Wagner Act specifically worked to "encourage the practice and procedure of collective bargaining" and also protected the exercise by workers of their full freedoms of association, self-organization, and designation of representatives of their choosing. Roosevelt and his successor, Harry S. Truman, were prolabor candidates. Because of the Wagner Act's prolabor position, their Democratic Party was viewed as the champion of organized workers, a position it sought to keep.

The year 1946 saw the election of the first Republican anti-New Deal Congress. Powerful business trade groups, most notably the National Association of Manufacturers (NAM) and the United States Chamber of Commerce, took advantage of this shift in the political winds. They successfully railed against the Wagner Act and pointed out its flaws.

The Wagner Act was criticized as tilting the balance between labor and management too far toward labor unions. The federal government, it was argued, had been too successful as labor's advocate and should step away from the fray. Republican congressional critics of the labor climate pointed out that some labor leaders had become too aggressive with tactics such as sit-down strikes. They also noted the often sensational antibusiness tone of major news outlets.

The Taft-Hartley Act was born out of this desire to weaken the power of labor. In the Eightieth Congress (1947-1949), which considered this legislation, the labor committees in the two houses of Congress were chaired by Representative Fred A. Hartley, Jr., and Senator Robert A. Taft, the son of William Howard Taft, who had served as U.S. president from 1909 to 1913. By the elections of 1946, it was politically popular in most congressional districts for elected officials to be antilabor. Labor and political experts at the time anticipated that the new Republican majority that was elected would pass some kind of antilabor measure. With sympathetic committees lined up in their favor, the business lobby would get what it had been lobbying for actively since the late 1930's.

President Truman vetoed the Taft-Hartley bill when he received it, arguing that it would only create more government intervention. He also pointed out that labor-ownership compromises would not come about because of a law. After Truman's veto was overridden on June 23, 1947, the Taft-Hartley Act became one of the major federal laws concerning collective bargaining and, even more broadly, the power of American workers to organize. Since its passage, it has been a source of friction between workers and the owners of capital in American workplaces. Union rhetoric often has been predicated on opposition to the bill's tenets. The most left-leaning political candidates, such as Ralph Nader, have argued vehemently against the labor environment created by Taft-Hartley.

Provisions of the Act The act retained the NLRB but expanded it from three to five members, appointed by the president and confirmed by the Senate. Detailed financial statements chronicling union activity were to be filed with the Department of Labor (DOL). Direct union contributions to political campaigns were prohibited. The DOL was seen as too biased toward labor, so federal mediation and conciliation services were moved from the DOL to a new, independent service. In these respects, Taft-Hartley was designed to sever bonds between labor and friendly political actors.

Employers could now sue unions for contract violations. Beyond this judicial intervention, union affairs were opened up by the requirement of leaders to sign noncommunist oaths. Federal employees were prohibited from going on strike, and emergency powers were developed that gave the president authority in ending strikes. The president could order laborers back to work, thus undercutting unions' weapon of last resort: the work stoppage. Truman exercised such powers several times in the late 1940's, notably in the railroad industry. Perhaps more important, discussions of picket lines were phrased more in terms of legality than in the previous sense of workplace justice.

The act was considered inflammatory, in part because the Wagner Act had established particular unfair labor practices on the part of employers. In a little-disguised frontal assault, Taft-Hartley for the first time defined unfair labor practices on the part of employees.

For workers, one portion of the act perhaps is a greater irritant than any other. Prior to passage of the act, unions could declare a workplace a "closed

Labor Rights in American Industry

Excerpt from Section 1 of the Taft-Hartley Act, also known as the Labor Management Relations Act, 1947.

Industrial strife which interferes with the normal flow of commerce and with the full production of articles and commodities for commerce, can be avoided or substantially minimized if employers, employees, and labor organizations each recognize under law one another's legitimate rights in their relations with each other, and above all recognize under law that neither party has any right in its relations with any other to engage in acts or practices which jeopardize the public health, safety, or interest.

shop," meaning that a worker had to belong to the union to be given a job. Closed shops were banned by the law. In addition, the less restrictive "union shop" environment was more heavily regulated. A union shop is a workplace at which workers must join the union soon after taking a job. The Taft-Hartley Act left it up to states whether they chose to prohibit union shops and pass other right-to-work legislation.

Impact The idea that union leaders could dominate collective bargaining through sheer force of large numbers of members was discarded. Business owners could lobby states to pass antiunion bills that made recruitment and membership drives cumbersome. This bill was the beginning of the end of the golden years of optimism for organized labor.

Some prolabor members of Congress have taken up the cause of repealing portions of the act, but with little success. There is little doubt that its passage and enactment precipitated the rapid decline in the power and membership of organized labor over the last half century. In a famous example of the act's power and importance that occurred in 1981, President Ronald Reagan ordered air traffic controllers back to work. When they refused, he worked to disband the workers' union and called for the unilateral removal of defiant strikers from their profession.

R. Matthew Beverlin

Senator Robert A. Taft leaving a speaking engagement in New York, where he was picketed by people opposed to the Taft-Hartley Act. (©Bettmann/CORBIS)

Further Reading

Beik, Mildred A. *Labor Relations.* Westport, Conn.: Greenwood Press, 2005. Walks the reader through the development of the American labor movement. Begins in the nineteenth century and moves up to Reagan's handling of the Professional Air Traffic Controllers Organization Strike. A quality place to start a research project on labor law.

Brown, Leo Cyril. *The Impact of the New Labor Law on Union-Management Relations.* St. Louis, Mo.: Institute of Social Order, St. Louis University, 1948. A treasure trove of information, written immediately after passage of the Taft-Hartley Act. Spells out provisions and implications of the law, in a question-and-answer format. Contains reprints of various forms used during the 1940's for union operation.

Cohen, Sanford. *Labor Law.* Columbus, Ohio: C. E. Merrill Books, 1964. An information-packed book that covers early American labor law through the Wagner and Taft-Hartley acts. Provides some reflection on the effects of these laws without being too far removed in time from their enactment.

Department of Labor. Bureau of Labor Standards. *Federal Labor Laws and Agencies: A Layman's Guide.* Bulletin No. 100. Washington, D.C.: Author, 1968. This government manual puts the Taft-Hartley Act into plain English, complete with simple bullet points.

Lee, R. Alton. *Truman and Taft-Hartley: A Question of Mandate.* Lexington: University of Kentucky Press, 1966. A slim volume that dives into Truman's perspective on the Taft-Hartley Act. Great insight into the wider politics of the 1940's as well.

See also American Federation of Labor; Congress, U.S.; Congress of Industrial Organizations; Labor strikes; Smith-Connally Act; Taft, Robert A.; Truman, Harry S.; Unionism.

■ Tehran Conference

The Event Meeting of leaders of the Allied Powers in Iran to formulate a strategy to defeat Germany

Date November 28-December 1, 1943

Place Soviet embassy in Tehran (now Teheran), Iran

The Tehran Conference was the first occasion on which U.S. president Franklin D. Roosevelt, British prime minister Winston Churchill, and Soviet leader Joseph Stalin met as a threesome. Despite considerable tensions, these leaders reached an agreement on a date for an Anglo-American invasion of northern France, and the shape of postwar Europe was also outlined.

By the end of the year 1943, Germany was militarily contained by the Allies. The Anglo-American invasion of southern Italy, with Italy's subsequent capitulation, and Soviet advances on the eastern front meant that an Allied victory over Germany had become probable. For these reasons, the end of 1943 was an opportune moment for the leaders of the three principal Allied Powers to come together. Iran was chosen as the site of the meeting in part because it afforded safe, though lengthy, journeys for the leaders. Each country had a large legation in Tehran, Iran's capital. Roosevelt stayed in the Soviet embassy, where the meetings were held, because the American legation was at some distance from the Soviet and British embassies.

Although Roosevelt and Churchill had previously met on a number of occasions, there were still a number of disagreements between them. Churchill wanted to continue the campaign through Italy, while Roosevelt desired a rapid invasion of northern France, the campaign code-named Operation Overlord. Roosevelt did not want himself and Churchill to appear to be pressuring Stalin, and his concerns led some commentators to suggest that Roosevelt betrayed his friendship with Churchill in order to ingratiate himself with Stalin. Several one-to-one meetings were held, but Churchill and Roosevelt both held an equal number of meetings with Stalin. Stalin's sense of the divisions in the Roosevelt-Churchill relationship encouraged him. Roosevelt also was optimistic, believing he had made a real connection with Stalin.

Soviet premier Joseph Stalin (left), U.S. president Franklin D. Roosevelt, and British prime minister Winston Churchill at the Tehran Conference—the first meeting that all three leaders attended. (AP/Wide World Photos)

The Second Front What Stalin sought from the conference, above all, was a firm commitment from Roosevelt and Churchill on opening a second front in northern France to relieve German pressure on his front line. He did not want a general commitment but insisted on negotiating specific dates for the northern France campaign; he promised that the Soviets would launch an eastern offensive on Germany if he knew the date the western offensive would begin. From the first session on November 28, Stalin made sure this issue was the first item on the agenda, even though Roosevelt was chairing all of the meetings. Stalin challenged Churchill on his reluctance, and he quickly discovered that Roosevelt would side with him against the British leader.

Churchill argued that a sea invasion was a very difficult proposition. He believed the Germans could quickly muster thirty to forty divisions to oppose an invasion of northern France. However, Stalin persisted, and eventually May, 1944, was set as the date for the northern France campaign, which would coincide with an invasion of southern France, for which the troops and landing craft were already in the Mediterranean. Meanwhile, the Allies would continue up the Italian peninsula.

German Defeat Stalin was willing to commit Soviet troops to defeat Japan as soon as Germany was defeated. However, he claimed the Soviet army was not strong enough to fight on two fronts. At the time, the Americans believed an invasion from mainland Asia would be the best way to attack Japan, and Roosevelt was relieved to receive Stalin's commitment to this action.

Churchill was keen for a decision on postwar Poland, as the Polish government-in-exile was based in London, and he felt obliged to bring it some hope for the future. The three leaders agreed that the Soviet Union was to keep the part of Poland already annexed under the Molotov-Ribbentrop Pact of 1939, but Poland would receive German territory up to the Oder River in exchange. This plan was acceptable to Roosevelt, who was facing reelection and did not want to lose the Polish vote in the United States.

Churchill also wanted Austria to be treated separately from Germany, and the other two leaders agreed. The Soviets argued that Germany should be divided into at least five parts. Although there was no clear decision on this issue, the three determined

---

Declaration of the Three Powers

After convening in Tehran, Iran, in December, 1943, Franklin Roosevelt, Winston Churchill, and Joseph Stalin, the leaders of the central Allied Powers, released a statement—an excerpt of which is reproduced below—stating the countries' collective military goals against Nazi Germany.

With our Diplomatic advisors we have surveyed the problems of the future. We shall seek the cooperation and active participation of all nations, large and small, whose peoples in heart and mind are dedicated, as are our own peoples, to the elimination of tyranny and slavery, oppression and intolerance. We will welcome them, as they may choose to come, into a world family of Democratic Nations.

No power on earth can prevent our destroying the German armies by land, their U Boats by sea, and their war plants from the air.

Our attack will be relentless and increasing.

Emerging from these cordial conferences we look with confidence to the day when all peoples of the world may live free lives, untouched by tyranny, and according to their varying desires and their own consciences.

We came here with hope and determination. We leave here, friends in fact, in spirit, and in purpose.

---

that partition of a defeated Germany would be part of the Allied victory.

The shape of a United Nations was also discussed. Stalin and Roosevelt wanted the organization to be a worldwide body, while Churchill favored regional councils. Although the Atlantic Charter of 1941 was still seen as a basis for such an organization, Stalin's intention to keep the Baltic states of Lithuania, Latvia, and Estonia was overlooked in the interests of harmony.

Impact It is difficult to assess the long-term effects of the Tehran Conference. Immediately afterward, the planning of Operation Overlord began at a meeting of the British and Americans at Cairo. However, when the invasion came, it was not met by an immediate Soviet offensive on the eastern front until two weeks later. The invasion of Italy proceeded slowly, and the landings in southern France were not simultaneous with those in the northern part of the country.

In the longer term, the United Nations was organized according to the terms desired by the Soviet Union and the United States, as was the partition of Germany. Poland and Austria were treated according to the three leaders' agreement, and the Soviets did declare war on Japan after Germany's defeat.

It is hard to determine if Roosevelt's actions at the conference encouraged Stalin in his plans for Soviet hegemony in Europe. Each leader subsequently gave rather different accounts of the interpersonal dynamics among the three meeting participants. Roosevelt seemed to be prepared to accommodate Stalin in order to obtain the Soviet Union's continued participation in the war. Roosevelt's actions may also have been a well-meant attempt to maintain world unity, but if that was the case, his efforts were a spectacular failure. It was Churchill who envisioned an "Iron Curtain" dividing a postwar Europe, and his prediction proved to be accurate.

David Barratt

Further Reading

Fenby, Jonathan. *Alliance: The Inside Story of How Roosevelt, Stalin, and Churchill Won One War and Began Another.* New York: Simon & Schuster, 2006. Devotes an entire chapter to the personal relationships that the three leaders developed at Tehran.

Foreign Relations of the United States. *Teheran Conference.* Washington, D.C.: Government Printing Office, 1944. The official U.S. report of the conference.

Gardner, Lloyd C. *Spheres of Influence: The Great Powers Partition of Europe, from Munich to Yalta.* London: John Murray, 1993. Sets the Tehran Conference's plans for postwar Europe into the wider context of self-determination and spheres of influence.

Harriman, Averell. *Special Envoy.* New York: Random House, 1975. A perspective on the conference from one of the primary American delegates.

Montefiore, Simon Sebag. *Stalin.* London: Weidenfeld & Nicholson, 2003. Gives valuable perspectives of the conference from the Soviet point of view.

See also Atlantic Charter; Cairo Conference; Casablanca Conference; Churchill, Winston; D Day; Germany, occupation of; Potsdam Conference; Roosevelt, Franklin D.; United Nations; Yalta Conference.

■ Telephone technology and service

During the 1940's, major changes occurred in the American telephone industry. The industry nearly doubled in size and also faced major antitrust challenges mounted by the U.S. Justice Department. Toward the end of the decade, the invention of the transistor would launch a technological revolution in the telephone and other electronic industries.

The telephone industry was never a true monopoly in the United States, but it came close. By 1940, the Bell Telephone System—whose corporate name was American Telephone and Telegraph (AT&T)—was by far the largest provider of telecommunications service in the country. It had grown to encompass twenty-one regional companies, which were known by such names as Illinois Bell, Mountain Bell, Pacific Bell, and Bell South. Altogether, the Bell System handled approximately 85 percent of all American telephone traffic. Much of the credit for the company's phenomenal growth can be attributed to its early twentieth century president, Theodore Newton Vail, who believed that there should be one, and only one, telephone system.

Bell Systems also owned the Western Electric Company, which manufactured telephone equipment; long-distance telephone company (AT&T Long Lines), and the premier high-tech research-and-development organization in the world, Bell Telephone Laboratories.

The Industry in 1940 Although the Bell System was huge by any measure, it was not the sole provider of telecommunications service in the United States. Then, as later, there was an independent telephone industry. At the beginning of the twentieth century, approximately 6,000 independent telephone companies were operating. Over the next four decades, that number dropped to about 1,200. Between 1940 and 1950, the complexion of the industry changed dramatically, as the number of telephones in use essentially doubled. Through these years, the role played by independent companies shrank. Nevertheless, although the vast majority of American telephones in the country were served by the Bell System, independents continued to operate in about two-thirds of the country.

The independent phone companies were of many sizes. Some served only a few dozen lines serving a few hundred square miles. Many of the smallest companies were family owned and operated. In contrast, some were large enough to serve as many as one-half million lines. General Telephone was the largest of these. Growth in the independent industry between 1940 and 1945 matched that of the Bell system. General, for example, saw the number of its telephones served increase from 547,466 in 1940 to 713,453 in 1945—an increase of more than 30 percent. Meanwhile, as the numbers of telephones in use throughout the country grew, questions arose about whether the industry was a "natural monopoly"—one that by its very nature should be controlled by a single system, as Theodore Newton Vail had believed.

The War Years Through the early years of the 1940's, telephone traffic increased dramatically but expansion of the infrastructure of the industry did not keep pace. Even regular maintenance suffered. A great deal of work had to be done to support the war effort, and because more than sixty thousand Bell System employees entered military service, few trained people were available to keep the system operating properly. All the major Bell System branches struggled to maintain their operations. AT&T Long Lines, the system's long-distance branch, was especially challenged by the greater wartime demand for long-distance communications. In 1941, the branch handled 66 million domestic long-distance telephone calls; one year later that figure jumped to 114 million calls.

Meanwhile, Western Electric, Bell System's manufacturing arm, was devoting an ever greater portion of its work to war-related needs. In 1942, about 54 percent of its production went to war work. Two years later, that figure was up to 85 percent. In 1941, the Bell System acquired the research facility that would become famous as Bell Telephone Laboratories. The following year, virtually all six thousand of the facility's employees were involved with the war effort. Much of their work was classified, and the labs' scientists and engineers were exempt from the military draft.

One of the greatest contributions that the Bell System made to the war effort was in the development of radar systems. Radar was not the invention of Bell Labs, but Bell contributed improvements and helped to produce radar units. Eventually, Western Electric would produce 57,000 radar units for ground, air, and naval use. Its work on microwave research would pay off during the postwar years, when microwave communications would become the principal means of transmitting television signals and long-distance telephone calls. Bell Labs also developed the first commercial mobile telephone service, linking moving vehicles to telephone networks by radio. The labs also developed improvements in coaxial cables that were used by radar and military radio units during the war.

Government Regulation By the mid-1930's, the U.S. Congress had decided that the entire telecommunications industry—which even then was expanding dramatically—should have some official regulation. In 1934, Congress passed the Communications Act, whose first consequence was the forma-

Super-insulated room built at the Bell Telephone Laboratories in Murray Hill, New Jersey, in 1943. Designed to absorb all but 0.02 percent of all audible sounds, the 27,000-cubic-foot "Dead Room" was used for testing sound equipment. (AP/Wide World Photos)

tion of the Federal Communications Commission (FCC). The major goal of the new law was to ensure that both wire and wireless interstate communication services would be rapid, efficient, and available to all at reasonable charges. With that goal in mind, the federal government became concerned about the possible dangers of having too much of the nation's telephone services under the control of a single entity.

During the late 1930's and early 1940's, the federal enforcement of antitrust laws remained low key. This changed, however, in 1949, when the U.S. Justice Department filed a suit against the Bell System in the U.S. District Court of Newark, New Jersey. Citing the Sherman Antitrust Act of 1890. The suit charged that the absence of effective competition in the industry had allowed the Bell System to charge higher rates for telephone service because Western Electric was charging Bell companies unreasonably high prices for its equipment. For years, government regulatory bodies had allowed the phone companies to base rates for their customers, in part, on what they paid for their equipment. In its suit, the Justice Department was, in effect, charging that Bell Systems was unfairly profiting by allowing its own equipment supplier, Western Electric, to overcharge its telephone companies, which passed the inflated charges on to their subscribers.

Among other things, the government suit asked that Western Electric be divorced entirely from AT&T and be split into three separate companies that would then compete for Bell System business. Another important demand was that the defendants be obliged to license their patents to all applicants on a nondiscriminatory and reasonable royalty basis and furnish the applicants with necessary technical assistance and know-how so that the patents might be put to use.

Little happened in the case until 1953, when many people became interested in it. In 1956, a consent decree was reached that would govern the telephone industry over the next four decades. The decree ruled that Western Electric need not be separated from AT&T, but that it must confine itself to manufacturing equipment of types bought by the Bell System, and that the company would not engage in any business other than common carrier communications. The decree also granted nonexclusive licenses and related technical information to all applicants on fair terms.

Transistors As important as the Bell Labs' advances in coaxial cables, mobile telephones, radar, and microwave communications were during the 1940's, these developments were not the mainstay of the telephone industry. More important to the telephone industry itself was the switching equipment used for connecting subscribers. The various types of devices used during the 1940's were electromechanical units employing inefficient vacuum tubes. The industry had a pressing need to find a more reliable and durable substitute for vacuum tubes.

In 1947, a single invention caused a sea change in the telephone industry. The transistor, invented by William Shockley, Walter Brattain, and John Bardeen, made its appearance, and in so doing introduced the Information Age. The transistor was the single most important invention of the twentieth century.

A solid-state substitute for glass vacuum tubes, a transistor is made up of three components: the base, the emitter, and the collector. Small electrical signals introduced at the base permit larger signals to be received at the collector. Transistors thus serve as electronic amplifying and switching devices. What makes them most remarkable is the fact that they are solid-state devices. In contrast to vacuum tubes in which electrons flow through gases or vacuums, in transistors, electrons pass through solid elements, which are usually made of germanium or silicon. They not only consume far less power than vacuum tubes, they also have almost unlimited life spans. Moreover, the original transistors were considerably smaller than vacuum tubes and over succeeding decades, they would continue to get even smaller. Eventually, transistors would make possible the extreme miniaturization of electronic equipment. Meanwhile, they launched a revolution in telephone technology by improving sound amplification and accelerating switching operations.

Impact The transistor became the genesis of the modern computer, and most certainly the telephone switching equipment of today. Laboratories around the world assembled teams of engineers who would change the world entirely. From the standpoint of the telephone industry, these changes would take place in the coming decade, as it moved from electromechanical switching to electronic switching; from amplifiers that consumed enormous amounts of power to amplifiers that could be battery-powered, and eventually to satellite and cellular communications.

Robert E. Stoffels

Further Reading

Boettinger, H. M. *The Telephone Book: Bell, Watson, Vail and American Life, 1876-1976.* Croton-on-Hudson, N.Y.: Riverwood Publishers, 1977. Pictures and text describing the telephone industry between 1876 and 1976.

Brooks, John. *Telephone: The First Hundred Years.* New York: Harper & Row, 1976. One of the most comprehensive histories of the first century of the telephone industry.

Pleasance, Charles A. *The Spirit of Independent Telephony.* Johnson City, Tenn.: Independent Telephone Books, 1989. Book dedicated to the independent telephone industry. Includes case histories of many of the independents.

Stewart, Alan, and Alan Pearce. *The U.S. Public Telecommunications Marketplace.* Cleveland: Advanstar Communications, 1993. Overview of all facets of the telephone industry throughout the twentieth century.

Stoffels, Robert E., ed. *Giants.* Palatine, Ill.: Practical Communications, 2008. Collection of articles about the people who formed, improved, and changed the telephone industry.

See also   Inventions; Radio in the United States; Science and technology; Transistors; Wartime technological advances.

■ Television

Definition   Form of electronic communication that broadcasts images and sound on a screen

Since its introduction into mainstream society, television has been one of the most widespread and important methods used to transmit information to the public. It revolutionized entertainment and eventually became a staple in households in North America and across the world. Television has also been a key part of many of the social changes that took place since the 1940's.

Television first became a reality in households during the 1940's, but the concepts that led to its invention had been developed much earlier. The first still photographic image was transmitted through wires as early as 1862, as the U.S. Civil War was still in its early stages. A decade later, scientists began experimenting with the concept that images could be placed into electronic signals. By 1887, Thomas A. Edison had patented a motion-picture camera that was used to shoot a number of short films during the early 1890's. The foundations for television had been set.

The development of the cathode ray tube by Karl Ferdinand Braun in 1897 would serve as the basis of television sets and was being used to produce television images by 1907. This began the era of electronic television. This technology developed over the following decades. The first television service in the United States began in 1928 near Washington, D.C. This initial service only showed still images. During the 1930's, developers placed attention on the device's sensitivity to light and on the clarity of the image. In 1936, the first television broadcasts were made available in London. In 1939, Radio Corporation of America (RCA) showcased a line of television receivers to be used in American households. The beginning of television thus coincided with the start of World War II, which began in Europe in September, 1939.

Developments in Television   By 1939, RCA began regularly scheduled broadcasts in New York and Los Angeles, and it televised the first sporting event on television: a baseball game between Columbia University and Princeton University. The Columbia Broadcasting System (CBS) began televising short newscasts in New York in 1941, representing the first commercial-use television in the United States. Television during the early 1940's was primitive, with vague delineations between black and white colors. These broadcasts were so blurry that the features of faces on the screen were difficult to define.

While World War II suspended the commercial use of televisions from 1942 to 1945, scientists continued to work to improve the technology. Work on tube technology advanced during the 1940's, as did a number of other technological areas. For example, scientists experimented with cable television in limited areas during the 1940's. Peter Carl Goldmark began work on the first color television system in 1946. Although only limited broadcasts in color occurred during this decade, the increased use of color films set the tone for the future of television.

High school students in Chicago watching the 1949 inauguration of President Harry S. Truman on what was then considered a moderately large television set. (AP/Wide World Photos)

Television Sets The television sets during the early years of television were simple by standards of the twenty-first century. Commonly, the face of a typical cathode ray tube was between five and seven inches in diameter; a twelve-inch set was considered large during the 1930's and 1940's. Because audio broadcasts were more common than television broadcasts, most television sets came with built-in radios. Despite the limited number of broadcasts, television sets were sold during this time. However, the decade after World War II is often considered the "Golden Age" of television. While there were only a few thousand American households with television sets during the mid-1940's, more than one-half of all American homes had sets only one decade later.

Television Broadcasts The United States was not the only country to begin television broadcasts during the 1940's. In Europe, France, Germany, and Great Britain all began experimentation with television during the 1930's, which turned into regularly scheduled broadcasts during the 1940's. Britain led the way in Europe, with regular television broadcast schedules in London between 1936 and 1939. The Soviet Union and Canada were also instrumental in the development of television, beginning

regular broadcasting in 1949 and 1952.

During the early years of television, two major broadcasting companies existed in the United States: RCA and CBS. The National Broadcasting Company (NBC) was owned by RCA, and it was split up into two broadcasting companies: NBC Blue and NBC Red. In order to assure fair competition among the networks, the Federal Communications Commission ruled that one of the NBC stations had to be sold. Thus, RCA sold NBC Blue in 1943 to Edward John Noble, who was the owner of LifeSavers candy. Noble renamed NBC Blue network the American Broadcasting Company (ABC); NBC Red was shortened to NBC. The three network stations that dominated television through the next fifty years were in place.

In 1947, a number of radio programs were adapted to television. The most popular television shows of the time included the *Howdy Doody Show* (begun in 1947), *Meet the Press* (1947), *The Ed Sullivan Show* (1948), *The Jack Benny Program* (1950), and *Amos 'n' Andy* (1951). News programs of the time were typically fifteen minutes in length and heavily reliant on news clips.

The main source of news was from newspapers and the radio. However, this changed slowly over the course of a decade. For example, in 1952, Walter Cronkite unofficially became the first anchorman at CBS, providing stability to television news. Moreover, network coverage of political conventions illustrated a key advantage of television over newspapers: live coverage.

Broadcasting companies quickly began to see profits in their early commercial broadcasts. This was aided by the number of businesses that were attracted to this forum for advertising. The success of television happened so quickly that commercial broadcasts on radio decreased rapidly, relegating the device to the broadcast of music and news.

Impact Television has had one of the greatest impacts on society of any technological development ever created. Its influence stretches across entertainment, politics, family, and culture in general. For example, television transformed the entertainment experience, bringing it into the home. Films that could only be seen in the theater were brought into the living room. Television also helped transform sports into one of the most popular forms of entertainment in the United States. Television helped turn American sports such as basketball, football, and baseball into international phenomena. Television's greatest impact may be on culture in general. It has helped amplify social issues such as civil rights, the women's rights movement, gay and lesbian rights, and international relations. Television has also helped the United States become the most influential culture in the world.

Brion Sever

Further Reading

Abramson, Albert. *The History of Television, 1942 to 2000.* Jefferson, N.C.: McFarland, 2007. Traces the technological developments that transformed television during the 1940's and beyond. Focuses mainly on developments in the United States but also takes time to review the contributions made by countries around the world.

Barnouw, Erik. *Tube of Plenty: The Evolution of American Television.* New York: Oxford University Press, 1990. Covers the history of American television and some of the factors that have shaped it over the past century. In particular, reviews the two-way relationship between culture and television, focusing on how the two have shaped each other.

Baughman, James. *Same Time, Same Station: Creating American Television, 1948-1961.* Baltimore: Johns Hopkins University Press, 2007. Study of the early corporate decisions in television that eventually shaped the nature of television shows. The author examines some of the directions that television could have taken in its early stages and the motivating factors behind the direction it did take.

Conway, Mike. *The Origins of Television News in America: The Visualizers of CBS in the 1940s.* New York: Peter Land, 2009. Traces the development of television news during the 1940's, focusing specifically on CBS.

See also   Advertising in the United States; *Amos 'n' Andy*; Censorship in the United States; *Howdy Doody Show*; Radio in the United States; Sports in the United States.

■ Tennis

Definition   Racket sport played by two players or two pairs of players on a court divided by a net

In addition to the trauma of World War II, tennis was faced with a clash between the ruling bodies that wanted players who entered sanctioned tournaments to retain their amateur status and those agencies that sought to allow professional players to participate.

By reputation, tennis was long considered a sport for those who were financially well off. The United States Lawn Tennis Association (USLTA) believed in the age-old traditions of tennis, and it adhered to the concept that only amateurs should participate in the tournaments that it sanctioned. The USLTA was a member of the International Lawn Tennis Association (ILTA). Through the ILTA, rules for tennis competition were standardized in every corner of the world. The rules set forth by USLTA and ILTA made it clear that professional tennis players were not allowed to participate in any of the tournaments that these associations organized. For this reason, independent tennis circuits were initiated for the sole purpose of allowing professional players to compete against one another.

During the 1920's, the Professional Lawn Tennis Association (PLTA) was formed by a group of professional tennis coaches. During the decades that followed, the number of professional players slowly grew. During the 1940's, professional tours were beginning to flourish. With an alteration to its charter, the USLTA even allowed one open tournament a year in which amateur and professional tennis players could compete against one another. It would not be until the late 1940's, however, that professional tennis truly began to gather fans.

The World War II Years   During the war years of the early 1940's, much of the world stopped all tennis competition. Such prestigious international tournaments as Wimbledon, the Australian National Championship, and the French National Championship were not held. Wimbledon and the French National Championship were suspended after 1939 and resumed play in 1946. The Australian National Championship ceased play after 1940 and did not start up again until 1946. However, the U.S. National Championship was held throughout the war.

During the war such amateur players as Bobby

U.S. National Tennis Championship Winners

The U.S. National Championship became the U.S. Open in 1968

Year	Men's Singles	Women's Singles	Men's Doubles	Women's Doubles
1940	Don McNeill	Alice Marble	Jack Kramer and Ted Schroeder	Sarah Palfrey Cooke and Alice Marble
1941	Bobby Riggs	Sarah Palfrey Cooke	Jack Kramer and Ted Schroeder	Sarah Palfrey Cooke and Margaret Osborne duPont
1942	Ted Schroeder	Pauline Betz Addie	Gardnar Mulloy and Bill Talbert	Louise Brough Clapp and Margaret Osborne duPont
1943	Joseph Hunt	Pauline Betz Addie	Jack Kramer and Frank Parker	Louise Brough Clapp and Margaret Osborne duPont
1944	Frank Parker	Pauline Betz Addie	Robert Falkenburg and Don McNeill	Louise Brough Clapp and Margaret Osborne duPont
1945	Frank Parker	Sarah Palfrey Cooke	Gardnar Mulloy and Bill Talbert	Louise Brough Clapp and Margaret Osborne duPont
1946	Jack Kramer	Pauline Betz Addie	Gardnar Mulloy and Bill Talbert	Louise Brough Clapp and Margaret Osborne duPont
1947	Jack Kramer	Louise Brough Clapp	Jack Kramer and Ted Schroeder	Louise Brough Clapp and Margaret Osborne duPont
1948	Pancho Gonzales	Margaret Osborne duPont	Gardnar Mulloy and Bill Talbert	Louise Brough Clapp and Margaret Osborne duPont
1949	Pancho Gonzales	Margaret Osborne duPont	John Bromwich and Bill Sidwell	Louise Brough Clapp and Margaret Osborne duPont

Riggs, Ted Schroeder, and Frank Parker won singles titles in the U.S. National Championship. Don Budge had been a remarkable tennis champion during the late 1930's. In 1938, he captured the "Grand Slam" of tennis by winning Wimbledon and the U.S., French, and Australian championships. After this extraordinary achievement, Budge decided to become a professional player. As a professional he won the 1940 and 1942 U.S. Pro Tennis Championships. With Budge's absence from the amateur ranks, it was necessary for other talented players to fill the void. The amateur players had total control of the major tennis tournaments. Similarly, the Davis Cup only allowed amateurs to play on each participating national team.

With Budge no longer an amateur, Riggs became the best American amateur tennis player in 1939, with victories at both Wimbledon and the U.S. National Championship. He won the U.S. National Championship again in 1941. At this point, Riggs

decided it was time to become a professional. His professional career, however, was interrupted by his service in the Navy during World War II. After the war he would be one of the leading American professional tennis players in the world. In 1945, Riggs captured the World Hardcourt title, and he won the U.S. Pro Tennis Championships in 1946 and 1947 by defeating Budge both years in the finals. In addition, there were many superb competitors who shined as doubles players, including such champions as Gardnar Mulloy and Bill Talbert.

During the 1940's, Althea Gibson honed her tennis skills by competing in tournaments sponsored by the American Tennis Association (ATA), which oversaw African American tennis players. In 1947, Gibson won the ATA Championship for the first time and would go on to dominate this championship through 1956. In a historic turn of events, Gibson became the first African American tennis player to play in the U.S. National Championship in 1950. During the late 1940's, American Margaret Osborne duPont was one of the most dominant female tennis players in the world. She won the French Championship in 1946 and 1949, Wimbledon in 1947, and the U.S. National Championship in 1948, 1949, and 1950.

Postwar Professionals After Budge decided it was best for him to no longer compete as an amateur, he was successful as a professional player during the early 1940's. However, he joined the Air Force after the United States entered World War II and would not compete again for five years. In 1947, Budge won the World Professional Singles Tournament. However, the war had robbed him of potential titles during what would have been some of his most competitive years, and he would never win another notable professional singles tournament. Before the war, Jack Kramer had been very successful as an amateur competitor. In 1942, he joined the Coast Guard, and he would not compete again until 1946. Kramer won the U.S. National Championship in singles in 1946 and 1947. In 1947, he won the Wimbledon title and the U.S. Indoor Championship. Kramer had conquered the amateur world and decided it was time to become a professional tennis player.

In addition to being a great champion, Kramer was an innovative promoter and started a professional tour with several younger players. He also became active in the sporting goods and sportswear businesses. His promotional skills made him a wealthy tennis player. In 1948, Kramer won the U.S. Pro Tennis Championships in singles and the doubles title with his partner Pancho Segura. Along with Frank Parker and Pancho Gonzales, Segura and Kramer became known as the "bad boys" of professional tennis during the late 1940's. As an amateur, Gonzales won the U.S. National Championship and the U.S. Clay Court Championship in both 1948 and 1949. He also was a member of the U.S. Davis Cup team that won the cup in 1949. Always a ferocious competitor, Gonzales joined the professional ranks in 1950. By the early 1950's, the professional circuit was becoming recognized as the home of superior competition, as an increasing number of great players decided to turn professional not only to earn a living but also to earn respect for the sport of tennis as a legitimate career choice.

Impact International tennis competition was nonexistent for several years because of World War II. The United States was the only country that continued to hold major tennis tournaments during wartime. Several leading players also lost some of their potentially productive years because they served in the military, but this sacrifice was commonplace during the 1940's. The tennis players of this decade learned to be tough and to look out for themselves and the sport that they loved. Because of world events and the introduction of a new breed of player that had been shaped by these events, tennis would never again be the same parochial sport. Within a few short decades, professionals would be allowed to enter all tournaments and would make the sport of tennis relevant for a growing television audience, including many people who became interested in the sport because of the great tennis players who came of age in the turbulent 1940's.

Jeffry Jensen

Don Budge (left) and Bobby Riggs in 1947. (AP/Wide World Photos)

Further Reading

Collins, Bud. *Total Tennis: The Ultimate Tennis Encyclopedia.* Toronto: Sports Media, 2003. An excellent source for all tennis facts and records.

Frayne, Trent. *Famous Tennis Players.* New York: Dodd, Mead, 1977. Includes colorful portraits of such important 1940's tennis players as Bobby Riggs, Pancho Gonzales, and Jack Kramer.

Gonzales, Pancho. *Man with a Racket: The Autobiography of Pancho Gonzales as Told to Cy Rice.* New York: Barnes, 1959. A fascinating look at the struggles Gonzales had to overcome in order to become a tennis champion.

Grimsley, Will. *Tennis: Its History, People and Events, Styles of the Greats.* Englewood Cliffs, N.J.: Prentice-Hall, 1971. Engrossing look at the world of championship tennis and the many great tennis players who have left their mark on the game.

Kramer, Jack, with Frank Deford. *The Game: My Forty Years in Tennis.* New York: Putnam, 1979. A powerful self-portrait of one of the most revolutionary figures in tennis.

Potter, Edward Clarkson. *Kings of the Court: The Story of Lawn Tennis.* Rev. ed. New York: Barnes, 1963. A solid overview of how tennis has evolved over the decades.

Riggs, Bobby. *Tennis Is My Racket.* New York: Simon and Schuster, 1949. A gripping telling of his rise to the top of the tennis world.

See also   Golf; Sports in Canada; Sports in the United States; World War II.

■ *Texaco Star Theater*

Identification   Television variety show
Date   Aired from June 8, 1948 to 1956

One of the most popular programs on early television was Texaco Star Theater, *a comedy-variety show hosted by Milton Berle, who earned the nickname "Mr. Television" for his work on the show.*

Named after the petroleum company that sponsored it, *Texaco Star Theater* originated on radio in 1938 and was hosted by Fred Allen before it moved to television in 1948. After deciding to move its show to television, Texaco engaged Milton Berle—who was already hosting another radio program that it sponsored—to be the guest host of several *Texaco*

Star Theater specials on the National Broadcasting Company's summer schedule. A natural on television, Berle was an immediate hit. In its review of the inaugural show, *Variety* said that Berle's performance "may well be remembered as a milestone in television." By the fall television season, Berle was signed on as the weekly show's permanent host.

Berle brought to the show all the comedic skills and routines he learned in vaudeville and gathered around him many of the top comedy and music stars of the time, such as Pearl Bailey, Frank Sinatra, and Eva Gabor. Berle dominated his first season on television at a level that would never be matched in the future. An estimated 80 percent of all American television sets tuned into *Texaco Star Theater* every Tuesday night, and he made the covers of both *Time* and *Newsweek* magazines in 1949. Soon, other networks were scrambling to put on similar variety shows.

As was typical of early television variety shows, *Texaco Star Theater* aggressively promoted its sponsor's name. Each show opened with a quartet of immaculately dressed Texaco service-station attendants singing,

> Oh, we're the men of Texaco
> We work from Maine to Mexico
> There's nothing like this Texaco of ours!

After intoning several verses extolling the virtues of Texaco gas stations, the quartet ushered in "television's number one star," host Milton Berle. Throughout the hour, Texaco station attendants periodically reappeared as smiling "guardian angels," performing good deeds of some kind.

Impact   *Texaco Star Theater* was a true pioneering phenomenon on television. In addition to capturing an extraordinary proportion of weekly television audiences, the show won a number of prestigious Emmy Awards. More significantly, it inspired the creation of other television variety shows and was credited with encouraging unknown thousands of people to purchase television sets, while helping American families develop their television habit.

Ursula Goldsmith

Further Reading

Bianculli, David. "Texaco Star Theater." In *Dictionary of Teleliteracy: Television's Five Hundred Biggest Hits, Misses, and Events.* New York: Continuum, 1996.

Edgerton, Gary R. *The Columbia History of American*

Television. New York: Columbia University Press, 2007.

Stark, Steven D. *Glued to the Set.* New York: Free Press, 1997.

See also Benny, Jack; Berle, Milton; Godfrey, Arthur; *Howdy Doody Show*; *Kukla, Fran, and Ollie*; Sinatra, Frank; Television.

■ Texas City disaster

The Event Cargo ship explosion that led to the deaths of 575 people
Date April 16, 1947
Place Texas City, Texas

This disaster is considered to be the worst industrial accident in U.S. history. In the aftermath, authorities reevaluated safety regulations and disaster plans, and security provisions were established for handling dangerous cargoes.

On the morning of April 16, 1947, two cargo ships, the SS *Grandcamp* and the SS *High Flyer*, were docked near each another in the harbor of the small Gulf coast town of Texas City, near Galveston. Both carried large amounts of volatile ammonium nitrate fertilizer. Near the ships stood a Monsanto Chemical Company warehouse that was also filled with ammonium nitrate fertilizer. At about 8:00 A.M., a fire broke out on the *Grandcamp*. At 9:12 A.M., the ship exploded, triggering the detonation of the warehouse and, early the next morning, the *High Flyer*. Every ship in the harbor was sunk or badly damaged, and the initial blast was heard as far as 150 miles away. Almost 600 people perished, more than 3,000 were injured, and thousands were left homeless by the fire that spread in the wake of the triple explosions. Financial losses totaled almost $33 million.

Impact In the aftermath of the disaster, victims' families filed hundreds of lawsuits against the federal government, many of which were combined into a class-action suit, *Elizabeth Dalehite, et al. v. United States*, which the plaintiffs ultimately lost in the U.S. Supreme Court. Across the country, people collected money and clothing for the survivors, and celebrities such as Frank Sinatra performed at fundraisers on their behalf.

Thomas Du Bose

Further Reading

Minutaglio, Bill. *City on Fire: The Explosion That Devastated a Texas Town and Ignited a Historic Legal Battle.* New York: HarperCollins, 2003.

Stephens, Hugh W. *The Texas City Disaster, 1947.* Austin: University of Texas Press, 1997.

See also Agriculture in the United States; Federal Tort Claims Act; Natural disasters; Port Chicago naval magazine explosion; Rhythm nightclub fire; Sinatra, Frank.

U.S. Coast Guard vessel pouring water on the Texas City dock area as the city burns. (AP/Wide World Photos)

■ Theater in Canada

During the 1940's, the pressure of wartime urgency, the growth in mass communication, especially radio, and the slow absorption of modernist techniques helped bring Canadian theater more in touch with developments elsewhere in the world and gave it a new sense of internal momentum. The 1940's also saw the inception of many theatrical institutions that would dominate Canadian drama in the second half of the twentieth century.

The development that most differentiated Canadian theater of the 1940's from previous decades was the rise of radio drama, not only comedy sketches and routine entertainment but also full-length plays that were aired on provincial and national radio programs. A key behind-the-scenes figure in this process was Andrew Allan, who was head of radio drama for the Canadian Broadcasting Corporation (CBC) from 1943 to 1955. The Scottish-born Allan was a writer himself, but he most excelled in the roles of theater coordinator and impresario.

Wartime Challenges   World War II both helped and hindered Canadian theater. It should be remembered that Canada, unlike the United States, went to war immediately after the German attack on Poland in 1939. Whereas the U.S. had almost two war-free years during the early 1940's in which the economic austerity of the Depression was easing, partially because of increased manufacturing of munitions and other goods in preparation for the war many assumed would come, Canada had to immediately direct all of its resources toward the war. Therefore, actors, theatrical producers, and audiences were quickly conscripted into the war effort, and there generally was little funding or other government assistance available for the arts.

However, the war stimulated Canadian theater in other ways. By making radio drama the only logistically feasible form of theater, the war enabled theater to be produced for a new medium, in which a new generation of talent, nurtured by Allan, would come to the fore. The writers associated with Allan, including W. O. Mitchell, Roger Lemelin, Fletcher Markle, and Gerald Noxon, were all young, most of them well under thirty, and many of them would remain prominent in Canadian arts and letters for many years to come. The list of writers associated with CBC Radio includes many of the most presti-

gious Canadian authors of the latter part of the twentieth century. Moreover, the war, by bringing Canadians into contact with foreign cultures and making Canada a far more substantial and autonomous player in the postwar world order, made Canada believe that it required cultural institutions of its own that could take their place alongside others in the world.

New Talent Emerges   For these reasons, even though more than half of the 1940's was occupied by the war, the remainder of the decade saw a great efflorescence of Canadian drama, both in terms of actual plays written and produced and in the building of institutions that would provide a foundational structure for Canadian drama for decades to come. Actor Maurice Colbourne's devastating observation in 1940 about the derivativeness and mediocrity of Canadian theater was, after some delay, decisively refuted. It is true that the war interrupted theatrical life; most of the decade's theatrical history takes place after 1945. This was in many ways a necessary hiatus, as the pause created by the war enabled new figures to emerge who provided the postwar theater with an idiom that was distinctive to that period.

A representative figure of postwar Canadian theater was Tommy Tweed, whose skill at both writing and later providing voice-overs for CBC radio productions provided a galvanizing and cheering bolt of energy. Some talents who emerged specifically in response to wartime conditions, such as writer Leonard Peterson, successfully adapted to the postwar milieu. Peterson's radio play *They're All Afraid* (1944), about family life on the Canadian home front during the war, was revised and presented several times in the late 1940's and represented the adaptability of wartime talent and themes to audiences interpreting these experiences from a longer perspective.

Regionalism in Theater   During the 1940's, Canada was very much a country of regions. The CBC, with its unmatched ability to unite the national imagination through radio, inevitably was important, especially after Allan took over the reins of CBC's radio drama division in 1943. However, without the rise of durable theater in provincial capitals and cultural centers, the theatrical community in 1940's Canada would not have been the same, regardless of what the CBC broadcast over the airwaves. The little-theater movement had begun in the United States during the 1920's in an attempt to raise the quality of theater in smaller cities, as well as to introduce modern dramatic techniques and repertoires to provincial audiences. The movement's Canadian counterpart provided ballast to this regional diversity.

In Calgary, Betty Mitchell helped stage a student production of Thornton Wilder's *Our Town* in 1942, after which some of Mitchell's students, with her encouragement, founded Workshop 14. By the mid-1940's, Workshop 14 had evolved from an improvised amateur troupe and, under Mitchell's steadfast direction, established a momentum in Calgary which gave the Alberta city an enthusiasm for theater that it maintained for decades. Mitchell was more than matched in Alberta's capital, Edmonton, by Elsie Park Gowan, whose Edmonton Little Theater produced both Gowan's plays and those of Gwen Pharis Ringwood. Both women wrote dramas about prairie life that experimented with theatrical forms. Ringwood and Gowan redefined the concept of regionalism, which had traditionally been dominated by images of men standing against an indifferent landscape; Ringwood, and to a lesser extent Gowan, sought to depict women in more intimate, if often adversarial, relations with the dry grasslands and stony plains of Alberta.

Building the Institutional Framework   The Dominion Drama Festival, a kind of a theatrical Olympics on the model of the ancient Greek drama competitions, featured productions of competing plays that rotated among several cities. The festival was suspended during the war, but it resumed afterward. The event soon took advantage of the increased quality represented by Workshop 14 and equivalent institutions in other provinces, such as the little theaters in Winnipeg, revived in 1948, and in London, Ontario.

These regional stages were not always successful; for example, after gallantly trying to cultivate a local audience, the London little theater was soon eclipsed by the larger companies in Toronto. One of these Toronto companies was the New Play Society, founded by Dora Mavor Moore in 1946. The following year, the New Play Society brought together the two strands of 1940's Canadian theater, CBC radio drama and the little-theater movement, when it produced *The Man in the Blue Moon* by Lister Sinclair, one of the CBC actors who worked for the network when Allan ran its drama division.

Playwright Harry J. Boyle's *The Inheritance*, produced in 1949, was a less challenging play than Sinclair's, and Boyle failed to achieve Sinclair's subsequent renown. However, *The Inheritance* was important in its day for being a provincially set play that was not parochial in spirit, and the drama represented the fusion between regionalism and modernism that typified 1940's Canadian theater at its most productive. Moore's sophisticated theatrical company was a catalyst for the founding of the Stratford Shakespeare Festival, which staged its first productions in 1953.

Quebec Theater   The Compagnons de Saint-Laurent had been founded in Montreal in 1937 and continued to stage plays throughout the 1940's. The themes of this company's productions were overwhelmingly religious, and the Québécois playwrights of the decade who made the most impact, such as Claude Gauvreau, sought to depict a broader range of subjects. However, the Compagnons de Saint-Laurent provided an important base against which more rebellious figures could react. Gauvreau's *Bien-être*, produced in 1947, featured elements of existentialism and challenged the Quebec establishment. Gratien Gélinas's *Tit-Coq*, produced in 1948, readily appealed to the mainstream audiences that Gauvreau had outraged and titillated, but in his own comic fashion Gélinas experimented with dramatic form.

Toward the end of the 1940's, women playwrights, such as Germaine Guèvrement, began to emerge. Roger Lemelin and Gabrielle Roy, who arguably became the leading French-Canadian writers of their generation, were also involved in the theater. Lemelin adapted his second novel, *Les Plouffe* (1948), about a typical Quebec family, for a radio production in the late 1940's; Roy worked intermittently in radio drama while writing her breakthrough novels of the 1940's. Ruth Sorel, an English-speaking Montreal Jew, in 1949 ironically produced the theatrical work that was most concerned with Quebec rural life, the dance-theater piece *La Gaspésienne*.

Impact   The influence of avant-garde drama in Canada was essentially limited to Quebec, where the cutting-edge painters Jean-Paul Riopelle and Paul-Émile Borduas cowrote the 1948 *Refus Globale* manifesto championing an unfettered, spontaneous creativity. However, there were some experimental elements in the CBC's radio dramas and in the little-theater movement in Anglo-Canada; the plays produced by the CBC and the regional companies did not follow the Aristotelian unities of action, time, and place and appealed to twentieth-century sensibilities. However, these plays did not meet the standards of theatrical productions staged in many other countries.

In 1951, the report issued by the Massey-Lévesque Commission, headed by Vincent Massey, the prominent diplomat who would later become governor-general, provided the crucial articulation of Canada's aspirations for theater as a national cultural achievement. The report called for an increased commitment to national developments in the arts and proposed the creation of an artistically independent but government-funded theater. Such a theater would be established within a generation, realizing the dreams of such pioneers of the 1940's as Gowan, Allan, and Sinclair.

Nicholas Birns

Further Reading

Benson, Eugene, and Lawrence W. Conolly. *The Oxford Companion to Canadian Theater.* Toronto: Oxford University Press, 1989. Provides basic facts, but the books by Rubin and Whittaker offer more in-depth information.

Brydon, Diana, and Irene Rima Makaryk. *Shakespeare in Canada: A World Elsewhere.* Toronto: University of Toronto Press, 2002. Theater critics often focus on plays written by Canadians but neglect to discuss Canada's important role in staging productions of works by William Shakespeare and other classic playwrights. Canadian critics Brydon and Makaryk address this omission.

Miller, Mary Jane. *Rewind and Search: Conversations with the Makers of Canadian Television Drama.* Montreal: McGill-Queen's University Press, 1996. Although devoted to television drama, this volume contains much information on the later lives and careers of many of the pioneers of 1940's radio drama.

Nothof, Anne. "Gendered Landscapes: Synergism of Place and Person in Canadian Prairie Drama." *Great Plains Quarterly* 18, no. 2 (Spring, 1998): 127-138. Addresses Gwen Pharis Ringwood's work as being subtly experimental in its revision of prairie legends to express new models of feminine empowerment.

Rubin, Don. *Canadian Theater History: Selected Readings.* Toronto: Playwrights Canada Press, 2004. The renowned York University theater historian edits an anthology of primary sources. Particularly important for the 1940's are the excerpts from the Massey-Lévesque Commission report and Herman Voaden's reflection on the growth of Canadian theater.

Whittaker, Herbert H. *Setting the Stage: Montreal Theater in the 1940s.* Montreal: McGill-Queen's University Press, 1999. Examines the theater scene in what was then Canada's largest city. Pays attention to both English- and French-speaking developments and both the literary and institutional aspects of the theater.

See also Canadian nationalism; Film in Canada; Literature in Canada; Literature in the United States; Quebec nationalism; Radio in Canada; Television; Theater in the United States.

■ Theater in the United States

Through the traditional forms of drama, comedy, and the musical, American theater during the 1940's continued the previous decade's interest in social issues, psychological explorations of character, and responses to the changes in American society as a result of the Great Depression and World War II. Although American theater continued to be dominated by New York City's Broadway productions, featuring major plays that often became Hollywood films, regional theater, stimulated by federal government sponsorship during the 1930's, remained robust and contributed important cultural developments in postwar America.

While New York City theaters continued to premier major plays by Lillian Hellman, Tennessee Williams, and Arthur Miller—the most renowned American playwrights of the 1940's—the federal government's sponsorship of regional productions expanded American theater in the late 1930's, broadening the audience to include all regions of the United States. Theater companies in major cities employed more than twelve thousand people, most of whom received public assistance. Federal funding for the theater ended in 1939. However, the ramifications of this effort to foster public support for plays and to decentralize productions so that theater flourished far beyond New York City came to fruition during the

1940's and afterward. At the same time, other traditional forms of theater production, such as summer stock, community theater, and college-sponsored drama, continued to contribute to a developing national theater.

National Impact of Broadway Musicals Arguably the Broadway musical of the 1940's achieved the broadest impact of all theater productions on American audiences throughout the United States. This was an innovative decade, both in terms of the subject matter and form of the American musical. *Cabin in the Sky* (1940), with an all African American cast and a plot centering on an angel and demon battling for a black man's soul, raised social issues that previously had been addressed only in serious dramas by playwrights such as Eugene O'Neill and Paul Green. That Hollywood would adapt the musical to a film in 1943 heralded the postwar concern with the plight of disadvantaged minorities, as well as a fascination with the mores of African Americans, Jews, and other groups that were not fully accepted into the American mainstream.

Similarly, *Pal Joey* (1940) has been cited as the first musical to focus on an antihero, a nightclub dancer and hustler, while *Lady in the Dark* (1941) introduced Broadway audiences to the role of psychoanalysis in its characters' lives. However, the musical that had the greatest impact and marked perhaps the most significant shift in subject matter and form was *Oklahoma!* (1943), in which the concerns of regional characters and the dramas of their lives were fully integrated into the play's musical score, songs, dialogue, and dances. The nearly seamless segues between speech and song electrified audiences, as did Agnes De Mille's choreography, which, like the musical score, developed the personalities of the characters rather than simply engaging in conventional, entertaining dance steps. This fresh and bracing realism injected into a form of theater that usually had been sentimental and anodyne made for a more provocative and challenging theater.

Playwright Lillian Hellman with novelist Dashiell Hammett in late 1944. (Time & Life Pictures/Getty Images)

A similar concern with contemporary events, as well as an urban sensibility, distinguished *On the Town* (1944), a collaboration between composer Leonard Bernstein and choreographer Jerome Robbins. Suddenly, the streets of New York became the stage for presenting a variety of characters and types usually associated with epic novels, such as John Dos Passos's *U.S.A.* (1937) trilogy. The film version would mute some the play's more provocative music and scenes of sailors on shore leave, but increasingly even Hollywood would endow its Broadway adaptations with a degree of realism that had its full impact during the 1950's. Musicals performed in summer stock or community theaters also introduced American audiences to characters and themes that were more complex and probing than was the case during the 1920's and 1930's, when musical theater relied on show-stopping songs and tour de force dancing only marginally related to the written script of the play.

Broadway Drama Of the three major playwrights who dominated the New York stage during the 1940's, Lillian Hellman had perhaps the most significant impact in this decade. Her play *Watch on the Rhine* (1941) focused on Kurt Muller, an antifascist visiting the Washington, D.C., home of his wife's mother, the widow of a distinguished U.S. Supreme Court justice. The play concerns Kurt's confrontation with Teck, a European nobleman who is attempting to blackmail Kurt and to therefore damage his efforts to continue his antifascist work. The play is notable for Hellman's severe criticism of American liberals and of the country's isolationist posture that made it possible for fascists to destroy much of European democracy. That Hellman could portray Kurt committing a murder on stage in the service of his cause without sacrificing the audience's empathy for him is a measure of her genius in showing how America would have to become implicated in evil in order to rid the world of the Nazis and their allies.

Nothing like Hellman's indictment of American complacency had appeared on the American stage before the 1940's, and Hellman's successful play (it also became a successful film in 1943) is in part due to her belief that her work could ultimately arouse

Lee J. Cobb as Willy Loman (center) with Arthur Kennedy (left) and Cameron Mitchell in a Broadway production of Arthur Miller's Death of a Salesman *in 1949.* (Getty Images)

American outrage at an evil world it had too long tolerated through ignorance. Thus the play ends with an American household not only condoning Kurt's crime but also abetting his escape and return to Europe in order to further the antifascist cause.

Hellman's even more complex play, *The Searching Wind* (1943), was a full-blown attack on the failure of American diplomacy to identify and then to resist the expansion of European fascism, beginning with Italian leader Benito Mussolini's march on Rome in 1922. A more diffuse play than *Watch on the Rhine*, *The Searching Wind* nevertheless heralded the postwar examination of American values that Hellman would continue in *Another Part of the Forest* (1946), a companion piece to *The Little Foxes* (1939) that resumed the saga of the Hubbard family and their venal exploitation of American capitalism. Indeed, Hellman's harsh criticism of American wealth and power in *Another Part of the Forest* perhaps accounted for the play's tepid success with audiences seeking to readjust their lives after the war by focusing on more immediate and domestic concerns, as exemplified in two plays by Williams and Miller, who were to emerge as the most important playwrights of the late 1940's and 1950's.

Tennessee Williams's *A Streetcar Named Desire* (1947) and Arthur Miller's *Death of a Salesman* (1949) heralded a new phase of American theater, one that brought a more poetic and psychologically nuanced view of individuals and society than was evident in previous drama. Greatly influenced by writer D. H. Lawrence's treatment of sexuality, Williams explored the social, psychological, and sexual tensions of characters, such as Stanley Kowalski and Blanche Dubois in *A Streetcar Named Desire*. In this confrontation between the daughter of a decadent South, driven by grim necessity to seek refuge with her sister Stella and Stella's husband Stanley, the son of Polish immigrants, Williams called into question the facile notions of America as a social melting pot. At the same time, Blanche's defense of her delicate sensibility, which relied on a code of genteel manners, remains appealing because it addresses a deep human need to idealize and elevate human aspiration. Stanley, the realist, is obviously conditioned to survive in the new postwar world, but his realism comes at the expense of a lack of imagination, a character trait that Blanche embodies. However, Williams does not sentimentalize Blanche. He depicts her as a woman who cannot cope with the harsh actuality of contemporary life that the vigorous Stanley faces head-on.

Williams's rather wistful yearning for an earlier age in *A Streetcar Named Desire* builds on his other highly successful play of the 1940's, *The Glass Menagerie* (1944), in which the hero and narrator, Tom, must turn away from the anachronistic values of a demanding mother and the pathetic yearning of his frail sister. Both plays presented audiences of the 1940's with an imperative to move on and embrace change, no matter how graceful and comforting the nostalgia of its characters could make the past appear.

Arthur Miller, who was educated during the Great Depression and dedicated to the kind of positive social, political, and economic changes initiated by the New Deal, became the progressive playwright of the 1940's and 1950's, with plays such as *All My Sons* (1947) and *Death of a Salesman* (1949). The former play is the story of an aircraft manufacturer whose shoddy production methods are responsible for the deaths of American airmen. In the course of the play, he comes to understand that his crime expresses his failure to acknowledge his connection to society. The play, still frequently performed during the early twenty-first century, accurately foreshadowed postwar concerns about a society eager to get on with making money and with individual achievement. To what extent would individuals dedicated to only their own good sabotage the good of society, and would such individuals, as in Miller's play, come to understand that their fate could not be divorced from the fate of their fellow citizens? These insistent questions would dominate Miller's work well into the 1950's and 1960's.

In *Death of a Salesman*, considered by many to be Miller's masterpiece, the playwright sought to write a modern tragedy, while drawing on techniques from the European expressionist theater. On the one hand, the main character, Willy Loman, could not be more prosaic or average—a common salesman, who is losing his grip on reality and finding it difficult to essentially sell himself by continuing to work. Willy's problem is the opposite of the aircraft manufacturer's concern in *All My Sons*, since the unsuccessful Willy thinks too much about how others regard him. He wants to be "well liked," and to have his two sons, "well liked." Consequently, Willy never

examines his own motives or the mainsprings of his character. He is a man who does not know himself. In failing the test of self-knowledge, he enacts his tragic flaw. Yet Willy's desire to achieve a kind of distinction—if not for himself than for his son, Biff—makes him a universal figure that audiences identified with deeply and expressed the hopes of 1940's America.

No one could be sure in 1949, when *Death of a Salesman* was first produced, whether the United States was headed for a new age of prosperity or would return to the depressed economy of the 1930's. Objectively, Willy's plight might not have elicited audience sympathy, except for the fact that Miller structured his play through a series of scenes that were keyed to the rhythms of Willy's psychology. Indeed, Miller's first title for the play was "The Inside of His Head." Given this eloquent access to Willy's thoughts, audiences empathized with his struggle to articulate his hopes and fears.

A Streetcar Named Desire and *Death of a Salesman* were adapted into highly creditable films, and both plays soon became staples of the American classroom, making Williams and Miller's work fixtures of the American literary canon and ensuring that their deeply probing portrayals of characters and of society extended the concerns of the 1940's well into succeeding decades.

Regional and Alternative Theater   Outside New York, various groups during the 1940's created a theater that was both innovative and traditional. Eva Le Gallienne, a celebrated actress of the 1920's and 1930's, established the American Repertory Theater, which assembled a group of actors who toured the United States performing several classic plays in rotation. Thus Hollywood film stars, such as Farley Granger, who became disenchanted with the poor quality of their roles and films, turned to the stage and created new American audiences for theater. Similarly, John Houseman, a producer who worked with Orson Welles in the Federal Theatre Project of the 1930's, continued this work with the Mercury Theatre, a select group of actors, into the early 1940's.

Another carryover from the 1930's, the American National Theatre and Academy (ANTA), continued producing drama outside the commercial market, focusing in the late 1940's and 1950's on nonprofit productions of important new contemporary plays, as well as the classics. Although ANTA, like the Mercury Theatre, was based in New York, the organization also developed several college and community theaters.

In the main, however, few theater institutions outside New York City served as training grounds for new generations of actors and playwrights. Some, such as the Hedgerow Theatre near Philadelphia, did train actors, while performing a repertoire of the dramatic works of William Shakespeare, George Bernard Shaw, Anton Chekhov, and other canonical playwrights. Similarly, the Pasadena Playhouse in Pasadena, California, not only continued its tradition of repertory that performed the classics but also became a community theater and a laboratory for experimental plays and promising new talents, such as actors Dana Andrews, Robert Preston, John Carradine, Victor Mature, Victor Jory, and Raymond Burr, who went on to significant careers in film and television beginning in the 1940's.

Other regional theaters, such as Robert Porterfield's Barter Theater in Abington, Virginia, and the Cleveland Playhouse, relied on both professional and experienced amateur actors and pursued programs related to their communities. These companies sought to create an audience for serious, even avant-garde, theater. Actors Paul Newman and Joel Grey, for example, began their early careers in Cleveland in 1940 in a company of about forty actors, which continued to expand its membership into the 1960's.

Other pioneers in regional theater include Margo Jones in Dallas, who had been trained earlier at the Pasadena Playhouse and received a grant from the Rockefeller Foundation in 1944 to develop a permanent, professional, repertory theater. By 1947, her theater in Dallas was staging works by prominent American playwrights such as Tennessee Williams, who worked on his plays there before bringing them to New York. Through Jones's efforts, later important regional theaters, such as the Guthrie Theater in Minneapolis, were able to draw on both government and community support.

Impact The 1940's was the last decade in which serious, major American playwrights were able to afford the expense of Broadway productions. Such works continued to be produced in later decades, but by the 1970's a production of an Arthur Miller or Tennessee Williams play on Broadway was a rarity.

Beginning in the early 1950's, a new generation of playwrights began to try out their work on what became known as the off-Broadway stage, small New York City theaters that did not have the high costs and rents that the larger Broadway productions required. Similarly, experimental groups, such as the Living Theater, established in 1947, premiered avant-garde European and American plays featuring casts much smaller than Broadway productions and themes that emphasized antiheroes and other characters alienated from mainstream society.

However, if theater in New York City was tending toward big-budget musicals and comedies emphasizing commercial values, the smaller theaters and regional groups just beginning their work during the 1940's would help develop arts programs and theaters in communities throughout the United States that would seek funding from season subscribers as well as local, state, and federal government grant agencies. Thus well-established institutions, such as the Arena Stage in Washington, D.C., founded in 1950, the Long Wharf Theater in New Haven, Connecticut, which began its first season in 1965, and the Mark Taper Forum, established in Los Angeles in 1967, can be seen as outgrowths of the regional, community, and little-theater movements of the 1940's.

Carl Rollyson

Further Reading

Bigsby, C. W. E. *Modern American Drama, 1945-2000.* 2d ed. New York: Cambridge University Press, 2000. Excellent overview by a noted scholar. Discussions of individual plays, playwrights, and their biographies. Includes separate chapters on Williams and Miller, and a concluding chapter, "Beyond Broadway."

Bordman, Gerald. *American Theatre: A Chronicle of Comedy and Drama, 1930-1969.* New York: Oxford University Press, 1996. Important discussions of Miller, Williams, and theater productions of the 1940's, but excludes musical theater. Includes plot synopses and discussions of theater reviews.

Cody, Gabrille H., and Evert Sprinchorn, eds. *Columbia Encyclopedia of Modern Drama.* Vol. 2. New York: Columbia University Press, 2007. Contains an excellent overview of postwar American theater, as well as individual entries on important plays and playwrights.

Hishchak, Thomas S. *The Oxford Guide to the American*

Musical: Theatre, Film, and Television. New York: Oxford University Press, 2008. Entries on the major musicals, as well as adaptations for film and television. An excellent bibliography and guide to recordings is included.

Krasner, David. *American Drama, 1945-2000: An Introduction.* New York: Wiley-Blackwell, 2006. Situates American playwrights in the context of important political, social, and economic debates. The major plays and playwrights of the period are covered, as well as their impact on American culture.

Sickels, Robert C. *The 1940s.* Westport, Conn.: Greenwood Press, 2004. Contains twelve chapters with time lines and bibliographies. Important background reading for an understanding of American theater during the 1940's.

Wertheim, Albert. *Staging the War: American Drama and World War II.* Bloomington: Indiana University Press, 2004. Especially useful for discussing the period before 1940, when the war in Europe entered American consciousness. Wertheim analyzes not only important plays, like *Watch on the Rhine* and *All My Sons,* but also more than one hundred others, many unpublished, that contributed to the growing awareness of the onset of the war and its aftermath. Includes treatments of radio dramas.

Ziegler, Joseph Wesley. *Regional Theatre: The Revolutionary Stage.* Minneapolis: University of Minnesota Press, 1973. Not a complete history of regional theater but a good survey of the beginnings of twentieth century regional theater, its growth during the 1940's, and its development in ensuing decades.

See also Broadway musicals; *Death of a Salesman; Oklahoma!;* Robbins, Jerome; Rodgers, Richard, and Oscar Hammerstein II; *South Pacific; Stormy Weather; A Streetcar Named Desire;* Welles, Orson; Williams, Tennessee.

■ Theology and theologians

The historical framework of the 1940's shaped new religious and philosophical themes in response to the changing global socioeconomic and political environment.

During the 1940's, intellectual and religious thought underwent transformations that reflected the turbulent post-Depression and World War II era. The first decades of the twentieth century had already witnessed the disruptions and trauma of one global war, rapid industrialization, and the emergence of a global economy. These rapid changes brought new ways of viewing humankind's relationship with their chosen deities and with fellow people, reflected in the writings and teachings of some of the theologians of the era.

The events of the beginning of the twentieth century in the United States prompted expression of a new theology known as the social gospel, which had spread fairly widely by the 1940's. This thought took literally the social justice issues of biblical origins and drew parallels to the modern age. The Great Depression of the preceding decade had already helped to frame a new realism, accompanied by emerging Marxist approaches to the socioeconomic climate. In philosophy, this took on the form of liberal theology, as many thinkers began to view increasing industrialization and the resulting social conditions as dehumanizing. Theologians of this era sought new answers to questions about the human condition by merging traditional Christian thought and new ideas of social analysis and responsibility.

Reinhold Niebuhr   One such liberal theologian was Reinhold Niebuhr, who was born in 1892 in Missouri as the son of a Protestant minister. Niebuhr's education in divinity studies at Yale University prepared him to become ordained by the Evangelical Synod of North America, which later became known as the United Church of Christ. While beginning a teaching career at Union Theological Seminary in New York City, Niebuhr made an unsuccessful bid for a seat in the U.S. Congress in 1930. During this time, he identified himself politically with the Socialist Party. In 1931, he married Ursula Mary Keppel-Compton.

Conditions and events of the Great Depression led Niebuhr to embrace a theology that sought a profound and introspective analysis of social power structures. In his 1932 book *Moral Man and Immoral Society,* Niebuhr challenged the traditional liberal philosophical view that viewed all history as progress, and he simultaneously interpreted the economic disaster of the Depression in purely Marxist terms. Niebuhr viewed the Depression as proof that economic wealth in the United States had become too concentrated among a small but powerful social elite, and he perceived that the logical reversal of such a position would require a dramatic realignment of wealth and resources. To this end, he argued for the application of reason, separating himself from other social gospel adherents of the era who called for radical means, including violence if necessary, to re-order society. Even with his liberal social and political outlook, Niebuhr's Christian views were traditional and orthodox.

Niebuhr remained an outspoken political activist for the remainder of his life, founding Americans for Democratic Action and the Fellowship of Socialist Christians. He died in 1971. Union Theological Seminary created an endowed professorship in his name.

Paul Tillich   A native of Brandenburg, Germany, Paul Tillich also influenced American theology of the 1940's. Born in 1886 to a Lutheran minister, Tillich showed an interest in classical philosophical study from an early age. Ordained into the Evangelical Lutheran Church in 1912, Tillich married Margaret Wever in 1914. He put his ministry career on hold when the outbreak of World War I required him to enter military service. He witnessed at first hand the reality of war, and the experience helped shape his emerging adult philosophy. Tillich emigrated to the United States in 1933 after being a vocal critic of Nazi policy.

Tillich's interest in world events from a theological perspective led to his cultivating a relationship with Niebuhr, who invited him to Union Theological Seminary as a professor of theology. Tillich's philosophical interests extended to embrace existentialism, and throughout his life he continued to develop his systematic theological ideas from that perspective. For Tillich, the object of human thought was to explain human existence, and this could be accomplished within the framework of Christian thought. From his systematic perspective, this process required examination and study of the guidance of Holy Scripture, the history of the church, and the cultural history of humankind.

Ultimately for Tillich, the analysis of human existence represented the quest for God, expressed in what he referred to as the "method of correlation." Tillich believed that all answers to human existence were to be found in the Christian message. This introspection proved to be the catalyst for Tillich's ma-

jor work, *Systematic Theology*, published in three volumes between 1951 and 1963. Tillich went on to become a professor at both Harvard Divinity School and the University of Chicago. He died in 1965.

Fundamentalism   During the 1940's in North America, another theological movement known as Fundamentalism increasingly emerged as an intellectual challenge to liberal theology. Fundamental Christianity seeks to affirm traditional Christian belief in simpler and more clearly defined doctrinal terms. Although not the religious force it would be in later decades, this school of thought nevertheless reacted against the liberal theology of Niebuhr and others who also embraced liberal political ideology as part of their understanding of God.

Among theologians who rejected both modern liberalism and Fundamentalism was Carl Henry, a New York native who founded the National Association of Evangelicals in 1942 and became the first editor of the popular magazine *Christianity Today*. Henry challenged liberal theology by asserting a strict interpretation of Holy Scripture but rejected the inerrancy doctrines of Fundamentalism. Henry emerged as one of the twentieth century's leading evangelical voices; he published his first book, *The Uneasy Conscience of Modern Fundamentalism*, in 1947. He died in 2003.

Impact   The 1940's witnessed broad expressions of theological insights in attempts to understand and interpret the dramatic events of the early twentieth century, including the human ravages of global war and economic depression. People sought answers to the crises of the times in their religions and reshaped their religions to match new needs.

Cheryl H. White

Further Reading
Carey, John J. *Paulus, Then and Now: A Study of Paul Tillich's Theological World and the Continuing Relevance of His Work*. Macon, Ga.: Mercer University Press, 2002. Provides political, social, economic, and scholarly contexts for Tillich's thought and examines how his ideas apply to contemporary problems.
Gilkey, Langdon. *On Niebuhr: A Theological Study*. Chicago: University of Chicago Press, 2001. Remarkably substantive and detailed critique of Niebuhr's political theology by an important scholar of theology and ethics. Provides close at-

tention to *The Nature and Destiny of Man.* Strong focus on Christian social ethics.

Handy, Robert T., ed. *The Social Gospel in America.* New York: Oxford University Press, 1966. Depicts the growth and development of the Social Gospel movement and provides biographical sketches and selected writings of Washington Gladden, Richard T. Ely, and Walter Rauschenbusch, three important leaders of the movement.

Lovin, Robin. Introduction to *The Nature and Destiny of Man: A Christian Interpretation,* by Reinhold Niebuhr. Louisville, Ky.: Westminster John Knox Press, 1996. Explains Christian Realism in historical, theological, and philosophical contexts.

Sifton, Elisabeth. *The Serenity Prayer: Faith and Politics in Times of Peace and War.* New York: W. W. Norton, 2003. A memoir by Niebuhr's daughter, with a focus on the 1940's as the context for Niebuhr's thought. Sifton argues for the continued relevance and importance of her father's political theology and social ethics.

West, Cornell. *The American Evasion of Philosophy: A Genealogy of Pragmatism.* Madison: University of Wisconsin Press, 1989. Places Niebuhr in the crosscurrents of American philosophical pragmatism. Special attention paid to issues of democracy and race.

White, Ronald C., and C. Howard Hopkins. *The Social Gospel.* Philadelphia: Temple University Press, 1976. Restatement of the social gospel, providing definition and history, including criticisms, personalities, and lasting effects. Examines the influence of the Social Gospel movement on issues such as human rights, social injustice, ecumenism, and social action.

See also   Auden, W. H.; Graham, Billy; Philosophy and philosophers; Religion in Canada; Religion in the United States.

■ They Were Expendable

Identification   Film about the role of PT boat crews early in World War II
Director   John Ford (1894-1973)
Date   Released on December 20, 1945

This grim portrait of duty and sacrifice was only a modest box-office success, but film historians consider it one of the

best films to come out of the war and one marked by Ford's own extensive Navy experience.

They Were Expendable was written by Frank Wead and is based on the real-life service of Lieutenant John Bulkeley (called John Brickley in the film) in the Philippines in the aftermath of the December, 1941, attack on Pearl Harbor. Brickley (Robert Montgomery) and his second-in-command lieutenant Rusty Ryan (John Wayne) are anxious to prove their small, speedy torpedo boats can be effectively used against larger warships, but they are relegated to ferrying messages and supplies around the islands. Ryan is visibly angry about this. Brickley, no less disappointed, insists that they must sacrifice personal goals and follow orders for the sake of the larger war effort. They do engage and sink some Japanese warships before the overwhelming enemy forces crush American resistance. The climax of the film occurs when they are ordered to evacuate the American commander, General Douglas MacArthur, to safety in Australia. This means leaving most of their men behind at Bataan and Corregidor and the nurses as well, one of whom (Donna Reed) has formed a strong romantic attachment to Ryan.

Impact   John Ford had personally photographed and directed combat films from Midway to D Day and knew firsthand the human costs of war. His large fee for *They Were Expendable* went entirely to support a recreation-retirement center for the veterans of the Field Photographic Unit, which he had founded. Film historians credit Ford's naval service with influencing his subsequent films in the direction of greater seriousness concerning duty and patriotism.

Richard L. Gruber

Further Reading

Basinger, Jeanine. *The World War II Combat Film: Anatomy of a Genre.* New York: Columbia University Press, 1986.

McBride, Joseph. *Searching for John Ford: A Life.* New York: St. Martin's Press, 2001.

See also   Bataan Death March; Casualties of World War II; Films about World War II; Ford, John; MacArthur, Douglas; Midway, Battle of; Navy, U.S.; Office of Strategic Services; Philippines; War heroes; World War II.

■ *Thornhill v. Alabama*

The Case U.S. Supreme Court ruling on peaceful
  labor union picketing and the First Amendment
Date Decided on April 22, 1940

*The Court extended constitutional protections of free speech
to peaceful labor picketing regarding the immediate labor
dispute while also recognizing state authority to regulate
nonexpressive aspects of labor picketing or of picketing unrelated to the immediate labor dispute.*

In 1923, the state of Alabama had enacted a comprehensive ban on all labor picketing that sought to influence others to refrain from patronizing a business
involved in a labor dispute. The ostensible purpose
of the law was to protect lawful business enterprise
from disruption, although its comprehensive nature
reflected hostility to organized labor that was prevalent in southern states.

Byron Thornhill was arrested and charged during a lawful strike against his employer, the Brown
Wood Preserving Company. Writing for the Supreme Court, Justice Frank Murphy held the Alabama statute invalid. Labor picketing intended to inform the public about the facts and circumstances of
the immediate labor dispute was speech protected
by the First Amendment to the Constitution. While
the state had a legitimate interest in regulating public order, preserving the ability of a lawful business to
continue operations, and, as later cases would confirm, preventing picketing regarding issues beyond
a particular labor dispute, these goals could be attained without a comprehensive ban on all labor
picketing. Justice James C. McReynolds dissented.

Impact The decision granted constitutional protection to labor picketing, hence to some action going beyond the use of words alone. However, states
retained the authority to preserve public order and
legitimate business practices through legislation
narrowly tailored to such purposes.

John C. Hughes

Further Reading
Hall, Kermit L. *The Oxford Companion to the Supreme
  Court.* New York: Oxford University Press, 1992.
Kalven, Harry, Jr. *A Worthy Tradition: Freedom of Speech
  in America.* New York: Harper & Row, 1988.

See also Civil rights and liberties; Labor strikes;
Supreme Court, U.S.; Unionism.

■ Three Mesquiteers

Identification Series of B-picture Westerns
Producer Republic Studios
Date Released from 1936 to 1943

*Set in contemporary times, the Three Mesquiteers films were
the most successful of the B-Westerns featuring trios of
heroes. John Wayne starred in eight of the Mesquiteers films.
The Mesquiteers battled villains from the Third Reich
and solved problems in foreign lands. Their popularity
prompted studios to create other trio Westerns, such as Republic Pictures' Range Busters series (1940-1943) and the
Producers Releasing Corporation's Texas Rangers series
(1942-1945).*

Republic Studios made fifty-one Three Mesquiteers
films. The characters originated in novels by William
Colt MacDonald. By 1940, the studio's Three Mesquiteers films had featured six different combinations of actors in the leading roles. After 1940, five
actors—Robert Livingston, Bob Steele, Rufe Davis,
Tom Tyler, and Jimmy Dodd—played the characters of Stony Brooke, Tucson Smith, and Lullaby Joslin. Duncan Renaldo played Rico and Raymond
Hatton played Rusty Joslin, replacing Tucson and
Lullaby.

Helping to endear B-Westerns to juvenile audiences, the Mesquiteers typically protected and nurtured children, and they existed in a fantasy Old
West. These capable heroes were cowboys, adminis-
trators, government agents, engineers, and survey-
ors. Their horses could outrun cars, buses, trains,
and even airplanes. They were patriots and champions of small ranchers and businessmen. Their responsible actions embodied the spirit needed to defeat both the Great Depression and aggressive
foreign powers.

Impact The Mesquiteers influenced at least five
other Western series that appeared between 1940
and 1945. A number of other series appeared with a
combination of stars such as Tex Ritter and Johnny
Mack Brown or Tex Ritter and Bill Elliott. Such Westerns served as a counterweight to the popular
singing-cowboy Westerns that featured such stars as
Roy Rogers, Gene Autry, and Eddie Dean. By 1945,
the trio Westerns had essentially run their course,
but in 1986 they were paid a reverential homage in
¡Three Amigos!, a film in which Chevy Chase, Martin
Short, and Steve Martin play a trio of down-on-their-

luck Western actors who are engaged to protect a Mexican village from bandits by villagers who think their screen exploits are real.

Roderick McGillis

Further Reading

Loy, R. Philip. *Westerns and American Culture, 1930-1955.* Jefferson, N.C.: McFarland, 2001.

McGillis, Roderick. *He Was Some Kind of a Man: Masculinities in the B Western.* Waterloo, Ont.: Wilfrid Laurier University Press, 2009.

Tuska, Jon. *The American West in Film: Critical Approaches to the Western.* Westport, Conn.: Greenwood Press, 1985.

See also   Cisco Kid; Comic strips; Cowboy films; Film in the United States; Film serials; "Maisie" films; Renaldo, Duncan; *The Treasure of the Sierra Madre.*

■ Thurmond, Strom

Identification   Governor of South Carolina, 1947-1951, and Dixiecrat presidential candidate in 1948

Born   December 5, 1902; Edgefield, South Carolina

Died   June 26, 2003; Edgefield, South Carolina

A World War II combat veteran who served in both the Atlantic and Pacific theaters, Thurmond was elected governor of South Carolina in 1946 and was an unsuccessful candidate for president in 1948 as head of the States' Rights Democratic Party, known as the Dixiecrats. He became a leader of the prosegregation forces as the South faced mounting criticism for state-mandated racial segregation.

After graduating from Clemson College (now Clemson University) in South Carolina in 1923, Strom Thurmond taught high school and later became the superintendent of education for Edgefield County. In 1930, he passed the bar exam with no formal training. He served as a South Carolina state senator from 1933 to 1938 and as a circuit court judge from 1938 to 1941. In 1942, Thurmond enlisted in the Army and became a lieutenant in the Eighty-second Airborne Division. A D-day participant, he crash-landed in a troop glider behind enemy lines, where he and his fellow soldiers found themselves surrounded. Rather than surrender, they fought desperately until finally linking up with American forces advancing from the Normandy beaches. He joined in the campaign to liberate France and participated in the Battle of the Bulge before transferring to the Pacific theater for the remainder of the war. Thurmond received five battle stars for his heroic combat service, leaving active military service in 1946.

Thurmond parlayed his wartime heroism into an electoral victory in the 1946 South Carolina gubernatorial race. Before long, Thurmond would be thrust into the national spotlight. President Harry S. Truman, in an effort to secure the loyalties of African American voters, began actively supporting civil rights. By desegregating the military, establishing a Civil Rights Commission to investigate discrimination, and placing several civil rights bills before Congress, Truman jockeyed for support in the upcoming 1948 presidential election. His actions enraged many white southerners. Southern leaders began making plans for a possible third-party challenge to the Democratic Party. At the 1948 Democratic National Convention, held in Philadelphia, a raucous crowd led by Minneapolis mayor and rising Democratic star Hubert H. Humphrey pushed a strong civil rights plank onto the party's platform. Members of the Mississippi and Alabama delegations walked out of the convention in disgust.

In July, 1948, angry southern Democrats, feeling that their party had abandoned them, nominated Thurmond as the head of the newly formed States' Rights Democratic Party, quickly dubbed the Dixiecrats by the media. An overarching conservatism informed the third party's platform, which included demands for an end to federal intrusion on state sovereignty that began with the New Deal, a return to the Constitution as "intended" by the Framers, and protections for individual citizens "threatened" by federal authority. Foremost on the minds of most in 1948 was the Dixiecrats' vow to support "segregation of the races and the racial integrity of each race." Thurmond carried four states—Louisiana, Mississippi, Alabama, and South Carolina—and won thirty-nine electoral votes, including one from Tennessee, which cast the remainder of its votes for Truman.

Many national southern leaders ultimately balked at rallying under the Dixiecrat banner because they recognized that abandoning the Democratic fold meant forfeiting the power that seniority had brought them in Congress. With segregation increasingly coming under scrutiny, many southern statesmen remained silent, even if their hearts were with Thurmond. They could ill-afford to further reduce their dwindling power in Washington. Never expecting outright victory, Thurmond and the Dixiecrats hoped that they would garner enough support so that the winner of the election would receive less than the requisite number of electoral votes, thus throwing the contest into the House of Representatives for adjudication. In order to secure victory, both major party's would then have to make concessions to the South in the form of promises that segregation would remain untouched. Truman's outright victory over the highly favored Republican Thomas E.

South Carolina governor Strom Thurmond accepting the nomination for president of the new States' Rights Democratic Party at its July, 1948, convention in Birmingham, Alabama. (AP/Wide World Photos)

Dewey undermined the Dixiecrats' plan. Despite defeat, Thurmond's personal political fortunes, at least in the South, never looked better.

Impact The Dixiecrat presence in the 1948 election marked the end of the so-called Solid South. From that point forward, southern loyalty to the national Democratic Party grew less pronounced. For Thurmond, the election only increased his reputation. Appointed to serve in the U.S. Senate from December, 1954, through January, 1955, he won his seat in his own right as a write-in candidate. He went on to serve in the Senate until he retired in 2003 at the age of one hundred. During his lengthy Senate career, he delivered the longest speech in chamber history, for twenty-four hours and eighteen minutes, against what would become the Civil Rights Act of 1957. His switch to the Republican Party in 1964 is considered by many scholars to have been instrumental in creating a viable Republican presence in the South.

Keith M. Finley

Further Reading

Bass, Jack, and Marilyn Thompson. *Strom: The Complicated Personal and Political Life of Strom Thurmond.* New York: PublicAffairs, 2006. A careful

analysis of Thurmond's political career with special emphasis on the role that race played in catapulting him into the national spotlight.

Cohodas, Nadine. *Strom Thurmond and the Politics of Southern Change.* Macon, Ga.: Mercer University Press, 1994. Even-handed, full-length biography of the South Carolina politician.

Short, R. J. Duke. *Centennial Senator: True Stories of Strom Thurmond from the People Who Knew Him Best.* Columbia: University of South Carolina Press, 2008. Reminiscences from fellow politicians and constituents. Reveals much about the senator's public and private life.

Washington-Williams, Essie Mae, and William Stadiem. *Dear Senator: A Memoir by the Daughter of Strom Thurmond.* New York: Regan Books, 2005. Important account written by Thurmond's African American daughter that reveals Thurmond's multifaceted character. Although a public defender of segregation, Thurmond did not neglect his interracial child.

See also Army, U.S.; Bulge, Battle of the; Civil rights and liberties; D Day; Desegregation of the U.S. military; Elections in the United States: 1948; Truman, Harry S.

■ Tokyo Rose

Identification Generic name for female purveyors of Japanese propaganda during World War II that is most closely associated with Iva Toguri d'Aquino

Iva Toguri d'Aquino
Born July 4, 1916; Los Angeles, California
Died September 26, 2006; Chicago, Illinois

"Tokyo Rose" was a generic name given to a number of women who were said to have broadcast anti-Allied propaganda in English over Japanese radio during World War II. The name was purely the creation of Allied military personnel serving in the Pacific. Following the war, however, it was used in connection with one individual—Iva Toguri d'Aquino—who was arrested and eventually tried for treason during the early postwar period.

Iva Ikuko Toguri grew up in the United States and Mexico, the daughter of Japanese immigrants. In July of 1941, a year after completing an undergraduate degree in zoology at the University of California, Los Angeles (UCLA), she traveled to Japan to visit an aunt who was seriously ill. Retained in Japan when World War II began, she was urged by the Japanese authorities to renounce her U.S. citizenship but refused to do so and was officially declared an enemy alien.

In November of 1943, after spending two years struggling to support herself as a typist, Toguri began working with a group of Allied prisoners of war in Tokyo who were being forced by the Japanese government to produce English-language radio programs for broadcast to Allied troops in the Pacific. She hosted a variety show called *The Zero Hour*, performing short comedy pieces and introducing music. Despite the "Tokyo Rose" legend that later grew up surrounding this work, she never actually used that name, nor did any of the other English-speaking female announcers engaged in similar activities. The content of the program itself contained no real propaganda; in fact, it has been suggested that the Allied prisoners who wrote the scripts often used military slang to create meanings quite different from what the material appeared to communicate on the surface. Also during these years, Toguri regularly engaged in secret efforts to smuggle food to Allied war prisoners and otherwise offer assistance to them. In April, 1945, Toguri married Felipe d'Aquino, a Portuguese citizen living in Japan, and took his last name.

Despite the true nature of her wartime activities, Iva Toguri d'Aquino was arrested by the occupation forces at the end of the war and served a year in prison before being released for lack of evidence. Two years later, in 1948, she was rearrested and brought to the United States to stand trial. In a highly sensational and controversial trial that took place the following year, she was found guilty of treason, fined $10,000, and sentenced to ten years in prison.

Impact The situation of d'Aquino stands as a clear example of overheated postwar emotions. A 1976 newspaper investigation, followed by a *60 Minutes* television report, demonstrated the perjured testimony and other irregularities that had taken place during her trial. On January 19, 1977, d'Aquino, who had been released from prison in 1956, was

Iva Toguri d'Aquino, better known as "Tokyo Rose," surrounded by correspondents shortly after being taken into custody by the U.S. government in September, 1945. (National Archives)

granted an official pardon by President Gerald R. Ford based on this new information, bringing her sad and tragic wartime and postwar saga to an end.

Scott Wright

Further Reading

Austin, Allan W. "Tokyo Rose." In *Americans at War: Society, Culture, and the Homefront.* Vol. 3. Detroit: Thomson Gale, 2005.

Duus, Masayo. *Tokyo Rose: Orphan of the Pacific.* Tokyo: Kodansha International, 1979.

Howe, Russell Warren. *The Hunt for "Tokyo Rose."* Lanham, Md.: Madison Books, 1990.

See also Radio in the United States; War crimes and atrocities; World War II.

■ Trans World Airlines

Identification First airline to offer commercial transatlantic service

Also known as TWA; Western Air Express; Transcontinental Air Transport; Transcontinental & Western Air

Date Established on July 13, 1925

Originally called simply TWA, Trans World Airlines grew from humble beginnings to become a world-recognized and emulated leader in the airline business. It was the first airline to establish regular transatlantic airline service from the United States to Europe and Africa.

To place the experience of TWA during the 1940's in context, it is helpful to understand the history of the airline. TWA had two corporate parents—Western Air Express, founded in 1925, and Transcontinental Air Transport, founded in 1929. Western Air Express and Transcontinental Air Transport merged in 1930 at the urging of the U.S. Post Office Department, which wanted airlines that were awarded airmail contracts to be larger. The merger created Transcontinental & Western Air (known as T&WA and TWA). TWA assumed the slogan "The Airline Run by Flyers" because Charles Lindbergh (of solo transatlantic flight fame) and William John "Jack" Frye (a renowned pilot and founder of Standard Airlines) were involved in the merger. Lindbergh served as a paid consultant, and Frye went on to become the president of TWA. The 1930's were a rocky time for TWA, marked by a 1931 crash that killed University

of Notre Dame football coach Knute Rockne, the 1934 purchase of TWA by Lehman Brothers Investment Bank and John D. Hertz (founder of the Yellow Cab Company), and purchase of more than 25 percent of TWA stock by Howard Hughes in 1938.

The 1940's saw considerable expansion of TWA. The decade began with a major fleet modernization. During the 1930's, TWA had relied upon Ford Trimotors and the Douglas DC-2 to fulfill aircraft needs. In 1940, TWA was in the process of replacing aging DC-2s with DC-3s and purchasing five Boeing 307 Stratoliners, the world's first pressurized passenger airliner. These major aircraft purchases were largely responsible for TWA posting a $200,000 loss in 1940 despite transporting more than 250,000 passengers (a 50 percent increase over 1939).

The enigmatic aviator and multimillionaire Howard Hughes continued to buy TWA stock. He would eventually own more than 75 percent of the company. As Hughes's investment grew, so did his involvement in day-to-day operations. He was eccentric and often called upon TWA to extend favors to his many friends and associates in the film industry. His disagreements with Frye led to Frye's resignation as company president in 1947.

The entry of the United States into World War II prompted the largest expansion in TWA's history. Initially, the War Department proposed federalizing all U.S. commercial airlines. This program was narrowly averted when TWA, as well as several other airlines, voluntarily relinquished dozens of aircraft to the U.S. military, including numerous aircraft that were on order from manufacturers. TWA lent the War Department its five new Boeing Stratoliners and more than forty other aircraft.

TWA also received a huge contract from the War Department, specifying that TWA transport personnel and supplies across the Atlantic to Europe and Africa. This contract resulted in TWA being the first airline to establish regular transatlantic service. Before the end of the war, TWA would conduct more than ten thousand transatlantic flights, acquiring valuable experience and credibility. Among the passengers transported on these flights were President Franklin D. Roosevelt; Generals George Patton, Omar Bradley, and George Marshall; and Chinese leader Chiang Kai-shek. The company began commercial passenger transatlantic service in 1946, using Lockheed Constellation aircraft.

Impact TWA pioneered regular transcontinental airline flights and innovated practices and procedures that were emulated by other airlines throughout the world. It took the name Trans World Airlines in 1950 and continued to innovate, notably by introducing in-flight films in 1961. The company suffered from the deregulation of the 1980's and filed for bankruptcy in 1992 and again in 1995. It flew its last flight on December 1, 2001; its assets had been acquired in April of that year by AMR Corp., the parent company of American Airlines.

Alan S. Frazier

Further Reading

Karash, Julius A., and Rick Montgomery. *TWA: Kansas City's Hometown Airline.* Kansas City, Mo.: Kansas City Star Books, 2001.

Serling, Robert. *Howard Hughes' Airline: An Informal History of TWA.* New York: St. Martin's/Marek, 1983.

See also Aircraft design and development; Hughes, Howard; Jet engines; Travel in the United States.

■ Transistors

Definition Solid-state devices designed to control electrical flow within electronic equipment

One of the most significant inventions of the twentieth century, the transistor ushered in the Information Age and would later be used in almost every type of modern technology. Although improvements in the miniaturization and speed of transistors have been continually made for more than a half-century, the fundamentals of transistors have not changed since they were invented during the late 1940's.

The invention of the transistor was the result of a decade-long search for improvements in relays and vacuum tubes in electronic devices such as telephones and radios. Although tiny, transistors are complex devices that originally were about the size of garden peas. In contrast to vastly larger vacuum tubes, transistors are solid entities without vacuum or gaseous environments. Unlike earlier electronic relay switches, they have no moving parts. Nevertheless, transistors were found to be capable of performing the same functions as both vacuum tubes and relays. A transistor can receive a signal in the form of a small voltage or current, feed it through one of its three wires, and amplify the feed to create a stronger signal that it can send out through the second of its three wires; it can also use the small signal as a trigger to activate a separate signal on another wire.

Transistors also had several other characteristics that proved to be extremely important. They consumed very much less power than vacuum tubes and could consequently be used in huge numbers without generating large amounts of heat. Transistors were also very fast, performing their designated functions in tiny fractions of a second. Modern computers would eventually take advantage of the transistor's potential for speed by developing the capability of performing millions of operations in a single second. Moreover, transistors were found to be exceptionally reliable. Indeed, an individual transistor might conceivably last almost forever. Finally, transistors were much cheaper to make than the relays and tubes that they replaced. It is rare that a single invention combines so many strong advantages, and it is rarer still that an invention with so many advantages would prove to have so many important uses.

Invention of the Transistor The transistor was invented by a team of three research scientists at Bell Telephone Laboratories, the research-and-development arm of the Bell Telephone System. The team's goal was to find a replacement for the millions of power-consuming amplifiers used in long-distance telephone networks. The researchers sought something that would be both more reliable and less expensive. Ideally, the new devices would have the potential to last indefinitely and require little or no maintenance.

The researchers had similar backgrounds in quantum mechanics and had known and worked with one another over many years. Walter H. Brattain, the oldest of the three, did his undergraduate work at Whitman College in Walla Walla, Washington. He went on to do graduate work at the University of Minnesota, where he studied quantum mechanics under John H. Van Vleck. He joined Bell Labs in 1929.

John Bardeen, who was several years younger than Brattain, had studied electrical engineering at the University of Wisconsin and worked in the engineering department of Western Electric Company

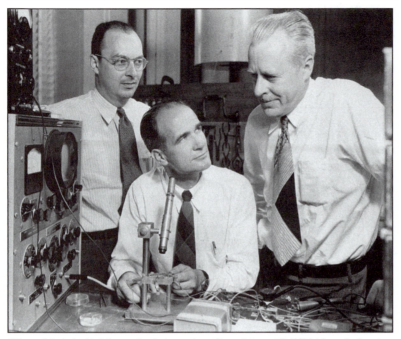

Three of the principal figures in the invention of transistors at Bell Telephone Laboratory in New Jersey in 1948: left to right, John Bardeen, William Shockley, and Walter H. Brattain. (AP/Wide World Photos)

before studying quantum mechanics with Van Vleck, when both were at Wisconsin. After earning a doctorate at Princeton University and doing postdoctoral work with Van Vleck at Harvard University, Bardeen joined the semiconductor research group at Bell Labs in 1945. While he was at Harvard, he befriended James Fisk, who would be director of research at Bell Labs by the time he went to work there. Bardeen also knew William Shockley while Shockley was a graduate student at the Massachusetts Institute of Technology (MIT), near Harvard. Shockley joined Bell Labs in 1936, immediately after receiving his doctorate from MIT. One of his fellow physics graduate students had been Fisk.

Brattain, Bardeen, and Shockley first met together in a professional capacity in July, 1945, as World War II was drawing to its end. Mervin J. Kelly, the executive vice president of Bell Labs, signed an authorization for their research. In December, 1947, the team had a working model of its first transistor ready to demonstrate.

The first device looked primitive. Bardeen had pressed two tiny strips of gold leaf, to act as contacts, onto a germanium crystal, which he then put on top of a piece of metal. This was the first transistor. It was a solid-state device, because it had neither moving parts nor a vacuum. For six months, their invention was kept secret while improvements were made and patents were drawn up.

On July 1, 1948, Bell Labs quietly reported the team's discovery. The unheralded announcement went virtually unnoticed by the general public. After an initial period of concern over the cost involved in switching production technology, the electronics industry ultimately responded.

The team's first device, a point contact transistor, was not very good, but it worked. In 1951, Shockley invented the junction transistor, which proved to be superior. During their early years, both types of transistors had limited applications and were easily damaged, unreliable, and expensive. The development of techniques to make semiconductor materials of greater purity would require time and money. Nevertheless, the essential design of the original junction transistor worked so well that it has remained in use into the twenty-first century.

Impact The development of transistors gave birth to a new era of solid-state electronics. In 1956, Brattain, Bardeen, and Shockley were rewarded for their inventions when they shared the Nobel Prize in Physics. In addition to making telephone relaying technology cheaper and more efficient, transistors would make possible a host of mass-marketed consumer electronics devices, from transistor radios to personal computers. Since the 1940's, improvements have continued to be made, as transistors and their associated components have gotten ever smaller and cheaper. By the early twenty-first century, the cost of a transistor on an integrated circuit chip would be much less than the cost of a single staple used for fastening together sheets of paper.

Robert E. Stoffels

Further Reading

Braun, Ernest, and Stuart MacDonald. *Revolution in Miniature.* 2d ed. Cambridge, Mass.: Cambridge

University Press, 1982. Excellent account of the early development of transistors.

Gregor, Arthur. *Bell Laboratories: Inside the World's Largest Communications Center.* New York: Charles Scribner's Sons, 1972. Popular illustrated history of Bell Laboratories.

Kelly, Mervin J. "The First Five Years of the Transistor." *Bell Telephone Magazine* 32 (Summer, 1993): 73-86. Explains the early types of transistor design and their applications.

Keyes, Robert W. "The Long-lived Transistor." *American Scientist* 97, no. 2 (March-April, 2009). Lengthy article recounting the history and operation of the transistor.

Orton, John. *The Story of Semiconductors.* New York: Oxford University Press, 2004. History of the impact of semiconductors upon electronics and human culture.

Riordan, Michael, and Lillian Hoddeson. *Crystal Fire: The Invention of the Transistor and the Birth of the Information Age.* New York: Norton, 1998. Account of the scientific and industrial developments behind the invention of the transistor and its subsequent applications in computing and other information-based technologies.

See also Computers; Inventions; Nobel Prizes; Radio in the United States; Science and technology; Telephone technology and service; Television.

■ Travel in the United States

The ways in which Americans traveled, as well as their reasons for traveling, changed significantly during the 1940's. Travel was both energized and hampered by World War II, and postwar prosperity helped to usher in a new era of recreational and business travel.

From wartime shortages and travel restrictions during the first half of the decade to the prosperous postwar period, the changes in the way Americans traveled and their reasons for traveling began to transform, creating patterns that would continue into the twenty-first century. Minimizing unnecessary travel and using the most efficient transportation were important concerns during wartime. However, as the postwar economy found Americans with money to spend and a shortage of goods on which to spend it, travel became a major outlet for these disposable funds. As a result, shorter vacations with more emphasis on excitement and entertainment than on rest and relaxation became a part of the American way of life. Additionally, despite wartime pressures hindering is use, by the end of the decade the personal automobile had taken its place as the centerpiece of domestic American travel.

Wartime Travel During the years between the world wars, Americans had developed the habit of using their personal cars for most of their travel, but this would change during World War II. At the beginning of the war, thirty million cars were being used in the United States, and it was estimated that on average they carried fewer than two passengers per vehicle. Those cities that had streetcar and trolley lines soon found that these systems were so lightly used that they generated insufficient income to be maintained in peak operating condition. Mass transportation in general fell into disrepair during the 1930's, but the demands and shortages of World War II would change that.

With 90 percent of the world's rubber in Japanese hands at the start of World War II, and with gasoline needed for the war effort, the federal government encouraged ride-sharing. Officials of the Office of Defense Transportation insisted that those who did not participate in shared transportation wasted rubber and petroleum and were disloyal to the war effort. Ride-sharing, a practice quickly adopted by a patriotic populace, not only helped the war effort but also enabled Americans to get the most use from their rationed gasoline and tires. Slogans such as "Share and Spare Your Car" and "Carry More to Win the War" were as common as the famous "Loose Lips Sink Ships" and "V for Victory." The ride-share program of World War II would give birth to the modern car pool.

Another change the war brought to American travel habits was a reduction in vacations far from home, whether by car or by mass transit. Travel of all types, not only automobile trips, was affected by the war. Shortages of manpower and capacity plagued the already ailing mass transportation industry. In addition to the problems caused by disuse, the industry was now faced with the loss of many of its employees to the armed forces. At the same time, however, there was a new demand for mass transit as a means of transporting servicemen and war materiel. For example, during the war more than half the railroad sleeping cars and almost one-fifth of their coach capacity were needed to transport troops. Wartime demands on the manufacturing also made the production of mass transportation equipment insufficient to meet the demand. In 1945, the Office of Defense Transportation initiated a "Vacation at Home" program that encouraged municipalities, churches, theaters, and other entities to provide local activities for home-bound vacationers. Most Americans complied and vacationed near their homes.

In an effort to avoid the imposition of travel priorities, government officials appealed to Americans to restrict their travel according to three categories:

- necessary travel—that essential to the war effort
- permissible travel—that necessary to keep the country running smoothly
- nonessential travel—that not contributing to the war effort

In 1942, the federal government imposed a national speed limit of thirty-five miles per hour. This limit was expected to double the life of tires and save gasoline, but it was also quickly determined that it also led to a significant drop in traffic accidents.

Postwar Travel The end of the war in 1945 eliminated wartime travel restrictions, but the habits of Americans continued to change. Business travel was slightly affected by a small increase in the use of airlines, although the railroads remained the most commonly used transportation for business travelers. At the same time, a more affluent and more sophisticated society considerably increased its recreational travel, and changes in transportation and attitudes altered the nature of the personal vacation.

City dwellers had traditionally defined a summer vacation as a trip that took them away from the city; extended stays at lake houses and on seashores were common. The postwar vacationer, however, was no longer simply interested in "getting away from it all." While rest and relaxation were still incentives, a search for excitement and new experiences became a more dominant motivation for vacationing. Cities were no longer a place to get away from because amusement parks, casinos, night clubs, and luxury hotels made them an attractive vacation destination. Travel restrictions had made American national parks popular vacation sites during the war, and they continued to attract vacationers when the war was over. Organized camping, which increased dramati-

cally during the war, also continued to thrive in the postwar period.

After the war, vacationing by car grew in popularity. In 1944, only 59 percent of intercity travel was by automobile; by 1949, that number had risen to 86 percent. The increasing use of cars, along with the greater number of middle-income vacationers, led to the construction of more motels. Offering little more than a roof and a bed, motels were cheaper and more convenient than the traditional urban core hotels, many of which had little or no provisions for parking. Motels attracted vacationing motorists with their flashing and sometimes gaudy neon signs, and they quickly became a part of the American landscape.

The introduction of travel-trailers during the 1930's led to the creation of trailer parks during the 1940's. A popular and cheaper alternative to hotels and motels, these increasingly livable mobile homes were dubbed house trailers, and trailer parks became a common sight.

How Americans Traveled The personal automobile had become a favorite means of intercity travel between the world wars. However, the demands of World War II affected car travel. The number of miles of intercity travel by car dropped from 89 percent in 1939 to 59 percent in 1944. The automobile's popularity returned immediately after the war, and by 1949 its share of intercity mileage had returned to its prewar level.

During the war, the railroads replaced the car as the vehicle of choice, with railroad travel mileage increasing fourfold. Railroads transported both people and war materiel, experiencing their unquestioned zenith during World War II. In 1944, for example, American railroads carried 70 percent of the freight transported in the United States, 75 percent of all commercial passengers, and 97 percent of military passengers. Rail passenger miles increased from 24 billion in 1939 to 98 billion in 1945, a 400 percent rise. Unfortunately for the railroads, this heyday ended with the war, and 1949 found the railroads' share of the travel market roughly the same as it had been in 1939, at about 8 percent.

While still a novelty, air travel enjoyed a modest increase during the 1940's, especially after the war. In 1944, less than 0.9 percent of intercity travel was by air; by 1949, that number had risen to 1.6 percent. After the war, cities purchased the airfields built by

Suburban American family packing their car for a vacation trip. (Retrofile/Getty Images)

the military and converted them to commercial airports. However, most Americans still considered airplanes more dangerous than other means of transport, and the cost was higher than travel by car or rail.

Often overlooked by travel historians, the motorized bus was an important means of intercity travel throughout the 1940's. Like the railroads, the bus lines experienced a dramatic upturn in ridership during the war, with passenger miles doubling between 1941 and 1944, and the share of the travel market climbing from a little more than 3 percent to more than 9 percent during the same period. The cheapest and slowest form of motorized travel, buses enjoyed the highest share of the travel market in their history during the 1940's. While the number of passengers decreased after the war ended, the drop was much less dramatic than that of the railroads.

Railroad market share dropped from 32 percent in 1944 to 8 percent in 1949, but the bus industry share declined from 9 percent to 5 percent during the same period.

Driving at high speeds on multilane highways was an unfamiliar idea to Americans when the decade began. The 1939-1940 New York World's Fair featured a model of the high-speed, multilane highways of the future. Ironically, the future arrived more quickly than expected when the first American superhighway, the Pennsylvania Turnpike, opened in 1940. It was followed by several turnpikes in the eastern United States, all of them precursors to the interstate highway system that began in the following decade.

International travel by Americans unconnected to the war effort was limited during the war, and it was slow to revive afterward. The bulk of overseas travel during the 1940's, whether personal or military, wartime or postwar, was by sea. In spite of a rise in commercial cooperation between Western European countries and the United States, which increased tourism and made air travel easier, Americans were still skittish about flying. Pan American World Airways had offered the first transatlantic passenger service by seaplane in 1939, but the first regularly scheduled transatlantic commercial passenger service by landplane was not introduced until October, 1945. American Export's flight from New York to Bournemouth, England, took fourteen hours for each one-way trip and included stops in Newfoundland and Ireland. A month after launching this flight, American Export merged with American Airlines to become American Overseas Airlines. Pan American followed with its own transatlantic flight in 1945, as did Trans World Airlines in 1946. In August, 1947, Pan American offered the first nonstop flight from New York to London.

Impact   Most of the changes to Americans' travel habits brought about by the exigencies of war and the exuberance of a prosperous postwar population have been enduring. Faced with limited resources and global geopolitical emergencies, Americans during the 1940's responded by changing how, where, and why they traveled, creating new habits that continued into the twenty-first century.

Wayne Shirey

Further Reading

Howes, Bill. *Travel by Pullman: A Century of Service.* St. Paul, Minn.: MBI, 2004. History of passenger trains in the United States.

Noyes, Phil, Bryan Burkhart, and Allison Arieff. *Trailer Travel: A Visual History of Mobile America.* Layton, Utah: Gibbs Smith, 2002. Illustrated history of the peculiarly American use of trailers for travel.

Rau, Dana Meachen. *Travel in American History.* Milwaukee, Wis.: Weekly Reader Early Learning Library, 2007. Eclectic survey of the various ways that Americans have traveled throughout their nation's history.

Whitman, Sylvia. *Get Up and Go: The History of American Road Travel.* Breckenridge, Colo.: Twenty-First Century Books, 1996. Lively survey of the role of automobiles in American domestic travel.

Witzel, Tim Steil. *Roadside Americana: Gas, Food, Lodging.* St. Paul, Minn.: Crestline, 2003. Well-illus-trated survey of the services and public accommodations on which automobile travelers have depended.

See also   Aircraft design and development; Automobiles and auto manufacturing; Freeways; Jet engines; Recreation; *Sullivan's Travels*; Trans World Airlines.

■ The Treasure of the Sierra Madre

Identification   Film about Americans prospecting for gold in early twentieth century Mexico
Director   John Huston (1906-1987)
Date   Released in 1948

The film won two Academy Awards for John Huston and was a notable achievement of his career.

Based on the 1927 novel of the same title by B. Traven (apparently the pseudonym of a mysterious German anarchist living in exile in Mexico), John Huston's low-budget, black-and-white film was produced by Warner Bros. Like Traven's novel, which it closely follows, the film depicts down-and-out "gringos" in early twentieth century Mexico and offers a parable about greed. Huston invited Traven to join him as an adviser to the production on location in Tampico. Traven declined the invitation and informed Huston that his literary agent, Hal Croves, would take his place. Huston discovered Croves was Traven and informed the studio of that fact. *Life* magazine featured the Traven/Croves story and helped make the movie a box-office success. However, Traven continued to deny that he was Croves.

The film's stellar cast includes Humphrey Bogart, who had also worked with Huston on *The Maltese Falcon* (1941), and Huston's father, Walter Huston, as Howard, the grizzled veteran prospector who is content to forsake wealth and live in accord with an Indian tribe. The tribe's nonmaterialistic culture embodies, in Traven's view and in John Huston's, the true treasure of the Sierra Madre. Alfonso Bedoya plays a bandit in a role that Mexican audiences found clichéd. However, Bedoya speaks some of the film's most famous lines: "Badges? We ain't got no badges! We don't need no badges! I don't have to show you any stinkin' badges!"

Impact John Huston, who appears in a cameo role as a wealthy American in Mexico, won an Academy Award as best director and another for writing the adapted screenplay. His father also won, as best supporting actor, making them the first father-son team to win Academy Awards for the same film. Stanley Kubrick included *The Treasure of the Sierra Madre* on his list of the best films ever made. Both lyrical and didactic, the film harked back to the overtly political pictures of the Depression and showed that despite the blacklist of suspected communists in the film industry, the radical 1930's cast a shadow well into the 1940's.

Jonah Raskin

Further Reading

Huston, John. *An Open Book.* New York: Alfred A. Knopf, 1980.

Raskin, Jonah. *My Search for B. Traven.* New York: Methuen, 1980.

Traven, B. *The Treasure of the Sierra Madre.* New York: Farrar, Straus and Giroux, 2010.

See also Bogart, Humphrey; *Casablanca*; Cowboy films; Film in the United States; Film noir; *The Grapes of Wrath*; Hollywood blacklisting; *The Maltese Falcon*.

■ Truman, Harry S.

Identification Thirty-third president of the United States, 1945-1953

Born May 8, 1884; Lamar, Missouri

Died December 26, 1972; Kansas City, Missouri

After President Franklin D. Roosevelt died in office, Americans were unsure of how Truman would perform as president. In fact, Truman performed solidly as commander in chief while World War II was coming to a violent close in the Pacific. He implemented domestic social programs in the vein of the New Deal, albeit with more modest results than Roosevelt's programs had achieved. Most presidential scholars consider his tenure a success.

In many ways, the prepresidential political career of Harry S. Truman, as well as his personal affairs, was decidedly ordinary. This made him simultaneously an archetypal representative of the early twentieth century Midwest and, at the same time, a unique individual to assume the esteemed office of the presidency. Truman grew up on various small farms on which his family worked. When he was a young man, he successfully courted Bess Wallace, the daughter of a local family with significantly greater material means than his own.

Prepresidential Life Upon the outbreak of World War I, the young Truman valiantly served the United States as an artillery officer. He won the respect of the soldiers in his beloved "Battery D" and got his first taste of formal leadership. After the war, Truman became the owner and operator of an unsuccessful haberdashery in downtown Kansas City. In dire financial straits, he entered local politics. Truman ran for and won office as a Jackson County judge—no law degree was required. He worked hard in this public-service role and won a reputation as a reformer, though he was helped into office by the Tom Pendergast political machine.

With Pendergast's help, Truman was elected to the U.S. Senate as a Democrat. He was derisively nicknamed the "Senator from Pendergast." His time in the Senate, 1935 to 1945, was marked by the American recovery from the Great Depression, a parallel expansion in federal government capacity, and the onset of World War II. During this period, Truman gained entry into the famed "old boy's network" of U.S. senators, marked by closed-door, whiskey meetings and party-dominated informal decision making in the political process.

Truman was thoroughly dedicated to the Democratic Party. Perhaps that explains why Roosevelt tapped the nationally unknown Truman to become his vice president in 1944. This seemed to be an improbable outcome but was no doubt aided by Truman's noteworthy Senate committee that provided aggressive oversight of the government's wartime procurement process. Just as in Jackson County, Truman had quietly earned the reputation of an honest reformer.

Commander in Chief After Roosevelt died on April 12, 1945, only a few months into his fourth term, Truman replaced the most potent president of the twentieth century. When Truman had been the vice president, Roosevelt did not engage him in the war-making process. Truman found himself alone in the storied Oval Office, with the full weight of World War II to bear. However overwhelmed Truman may have felt by his rapid political rise, he did not crack under pressure. He slept soundly from the time he came into office as president and continued to do so throughout his nearly eight years at the helm. The routine nature of Truman's day has become legend: He took a brisk morning walk each day and always ate a steak for dinner.

Because Roosevelt did not brief Truman on high-level military strategies, Truman had no knowledge of the top-secret atomic bomb before he became president. Secretary of War Henry L. Stimson was the first to tell Truman about a "new explosive of almost unbelievable destructive power." This informative message was conveyed the same day that Truman assumed the highest office in American politics. Though Truman was ultimately in charge of the vast military might of the United States, including the atom bomb, high-level strategic meetings regarding its impact and use had already been held. Truman was brought up to speed by briefings, but was the newcomer at the table.

Roosevelt had loomed large in all aspects of governance, including as an active internationalist. During World War II, Roosevelt appeared with Winston Churchill and Joseph Stalin at conferences in Tehran and Yalta. Not only had Roosevelt looked presidential, he also embodied the office in a way no American leader ever had before. Truman first met with Churchill and Stalin at the Potsdam Conference in July, 1945. This was the first time Truman had crossed the Atlantic since he had fought in World War I nearly three decades earlier.

Truman played an important role at World War II conferences he attended, setting up the international system that characterized global politics after the war. Although he did not invent the phrases "Cold War" or "Iron Curtain," his realist political actions at Potsdam helped bring them to fruition. As World War II in Europe ended, political tensions between the United States and the Soviet Union emerged. Truman's policy in this regard was defiant.

The single most controversial actions of Truman's presidency was the dropping of two powerful atomic bombs on Japan. Many have applauded Truman's actions, citing them as the "least worst" option for ending the bloody fighting in the Pacific theater. Others disagree, pointing to the barbarity inherent in the killing of hundreds of thousands of Japanese civilians. Popular opinion is that Truman made the decision to drop the bombs because he wanted to end the Pacific war and, at the same time, send a warning message to the expansionist Soviets.

Truman's decisions to drop the bombs are more poignant given his lack of international experience. Through his tough diplomatic positioning and use of the atomic bombs, Truman shaped the world of most of the latter half of the twentieth century. His implementation of the Marshall Plan to rebuild Europe was juxtaposed with defiant Cold War actions such as the Berlin blockade and airlift and the Korean War, also called "Truman's War." Cold War intrigue abounded during Truman's time in office; it was the first era of American versus Soviet spying and the beginning of strategic proxy wars.

Truman's decision to fight communist China in Korea highlighted postwar geopolitical realities. After World War II, the most destructive war in history, people of the world were not in the mood to fight another one. The Western

On April 12, 1945, after serving only eighty-two days as vice president, Harry S. Truman took the oath of office as president shortly after Franklin D. Roosevelt's death. Standing beside him in the impromptu White House ceremony are his wife, Bess, and daughter, Margaret. (Getty Images)

world adopted a strategy of containment, articulated by Truman in a speech to Congress on March 12, 1947. This firm policy of pitting the United States and the Soviet Union against each other ideologically became known as the Truman Doctrine. In both Greece and Turkey, Truman saw free nations that he could not allow to slip into the totalitarian hands of Stalin's Soviet Union. His distribution of aid to these nations set an interventionist precedent to post-World War II American foreign policy.

Chief Executive Truman is viewed not only as a strong war and foreign-policy leader but also as a successful initiator of domestic policy. No single president expanded the role of government as much as Roosevelt did. After his death, no neatly delineated blueprint existed for how his successor should carry on the work of an activist government. Though Roosevelt initiated massive New Deal social programs, such as the Work Projects Administration and Social Security, Truman had to institutionalize them. When Roosevelt died in office, many wondered if Truman would continue his policies or scale back federal growth.

In fact, Truman charged ahead with his Roosevelt's policy plans. The economy boomed under Truman, beginning a period of vitality that stretched through the 1950's. Truman presided over the world's most potent economic engine. He implemented programs to convert the old arsenal of democracy to rich peacetime uses. Factories that made tanks and fighter aircraft were encouraged by public policy to transition into making civilian airplanes and automobiles. Additionally, Truman's aggressive foreign-policy stance supported a large military after World War II ended.

The country did not experience economic growth without Truman making difficult and often unpopular decisions to realize it. He wrestled with the end of wartime commodity rationing, price controls to manage inflationary pressure, and the transition to a new cabinet and White House staff. All this happened while war hero General Dwight D. Eisenhower waited to run for the presidency. Ultimately, Truman was not opposed by Eisenhower in the 1948 election. Instead, Truman occupied a position in the center of the ideological spectrum, and he won reelection over Republican nominee Thomas E. Dewey. This election can be viewed as either the last of the Roosevelt New Deal coalition or as a shrewd win by a dedicated and underestimated politician.

In his second term, Truman had an ambivalent relationship with Congress. Truman did not have the celebrated personality or organizational skills of Roosevelt. Nonetheless, through such devices as the Hoover Commission, Truman updated the U.S. government's bureaucracy. The scale of his legislative packages and reform was not the same as with his predecessor, but he did have some accomplishments. For instance, he desegregated the armed forces and some federal housing projects. He also attained funds for the construction of federal urban housing and extended the benefits of social security to relatively younger Americans originally not covered.

Truman faced political opposition in legislative agenda. As opposed to Roosevelt, he was not a revolutionary political leader, but he was able to accomplish some important executive tasks. He took on a legislature fractured by the civil rights issue. In that hostile environment, he was able to push the nation onward from World War II in the direction mapped out by Roosevelt.

Impact Truman proved that anyone, but not everyone, could be a successful modern president. His rise from machine politics in Jackson County, Missouri, to president of the United States brought to life the principles of democratic leadership designed by the founding fathers. He was a midwesterner who followed a noted big-city easterner into office. Truman's contemporary critics considered him to be overly simple in his diplomatic view, seeing the world without shades of gray. Later historians pointed to Truman's decisiveness and firm beliefs as admirable traits in a president. While he did not achieve the soaring heights of his predecessor, he still ranks as one of the twentieth century's most successful presidents.

R. Matthew Beverlin

Further Reading

Ferrell, Robert H. *Harry S. Truman and the Modern American Presidency.* New York: Harper Collins, 1983. A short introduction to Truman by a noted Truman scholar.

McCoy, Donald R. *The Presidency of Harry S. Truman.* Lawrence: University Press of Kansas, 1984. Packed with information on his presidency.

McCullough, David. *Truman.* New York: Simon & Schuster, 1992. Major Truman biography; well-written narrative and informative historical biography.

Miscamble, Wilson D. *From Roosevelt to Truman.* New York: Cambridge University Press, 2007. This highlights the similarities and differences between Truman and Roosevelt.

Truman, Harry S. *1945: Year of Decisions. Memoirs, Volume I.* New York: Time, 1956. Significant presidential memoirs, covering how Truman felt stepping into the role of World War II commander in chief.

_____. *1946-1952: Years of Trial and Hope. Memoirs, Volume II.* New York: Time, 1956. The second volume covers the other six years of Truman's time in the White House but is the same length as the volume covering one year.

See also   Berlin blockade and airlift; Cold War; Eisenhower, Dwight D.; Elections in the United States: 1948; Fair Deal; Korea; Loyalty Program, Truman's; Marshall Plan; Roosevelt, Franklin D.; Truman Doctrine; Truman proclamations.

■ Truman Doctrine

The Event   Policy outlined by President Harry S. Truman that called for helping Greece and Turkey resist inroads that the Soviet Union was making on their sovereignty

Date   Proposed on March 12, 1947

Place   Washington, D.C.

By declaring that the United States would use its resources to assist nations resisting Soviet encroachment and to contain Soviet expansion, President Truman articulated the cornerstone of the next four decades of U.S. foreign policy.

In 1945, after the Allied forces had declared victory against their fascist opponents in World War II, the spoils and responsibilities of their victory had to be determined. The major wartime allies were the United States, Great Britain, France, and the Soviet Union. Just as the fascists had attempted to impose their way of life upon those who opposed them, the Soviets now attempted to impose communism upon the conquered areas.

The Soviets clearly were seeking to subjugate Eastern Europe, a realization that led Winston Churchill to deliver his cautionary "Iron Curtain" speech in Fulton, Missouri, in 1946. The Russians now were pressuring Turkey to share with them control of the Bosporus, the narrow strait that separates Europe from Asia, joining the Sea of Marmara with the Black Sea. Both the United States and Great Britain discouraged this bold-faced attempt at Soviet expansionism.

Truman's Proposal   Great Britain shared with the United States deep concerns about looming Soviet infringements upon the sovereignty of Greece and Turkey. The British, however, had been so devastated economically by World War II that they were unable to assume, even partially, responsibility for challenging the Russians. Great Britain was close to bankruptcy. The situation in the eastern Mediterranean at this time was grave. Greece was fighting a civil war, and Turkey could hardly resist alone the Goliath that the Soviet Union was fast becoming in the region.

President Harry S. Truman, sympathetic to the Greeks and the Turks, realized the dangers posed by Soviet expansionism. He studied the situation closely and concluded that containment of the Russian threat was imperative. He discussed the situation extensively with such statesmen as Undersecretary of State Dean Acheson, Secretary of State George C. Marshall, former secretary of state James Byrnes, and David E. Lilienthal.

Lilienthal, the head of the Atomic Energy Commission and a Truman confidant, read a draft of the speech Truman was preparing for delivery to Congress in which he requested $400 million in aid for Greece and Turkey. Lilienthal convinced Truman that if he hoped to receive congressional support and approval, he should concentrate less on rhetoric in his speech but should emphasize the communist threat the Russian incursions posed.

Truman altered his speech accordingly and gained support from twenty Republicans, most notable among them Michigan senator Arthur Hendrick Vandenberg, a recent convert to the cause of internationalism, who delivered one of the finest speeches of his career in support of Truman's proposal. Despite pockets of resistance from some members of Congress, both Democrats and Republicans, the president's recommendation was approved on April 9, 1947. The Truman Doctrine, one of the most far-reaching acts of foreign policy in the twentieth century, was officially put into effect.

Impact   At the time it was enacted, the Truman Doctrine, which has been compared in importance to the Monroe Doctrine of 1823, struck many people concerned with foreign policy as a great and unnecessary extravagance. Many Americans were isolationists, but Truman was able to gain the support of influential politicians who were gradually leaning toward international liberalism. In the long term, it became clear that the containment the Truman Doctrine assured prevented the Soviets from dominating most of Europe.

Truman was soundly criticized at the time this measure was enacted for proposing a $400 million expenditure at a time when the United States was still recovering from the financial strain of its involvement in World War II. In retrospect, however, the money the United States made available to Greece and Turkey through the Truman Doctrine was well spent and helped to save Europe from a communist takeover.

R. Baird Shuman

Further Reading

Dallek, Robert. *Harry S. Truman.* New York: Times Books, 2008. A brief but important assessment of Truman, with an accessible section on the Truman Doctrine.

Fousek, John. *To Lead the Free World: American Nationalism and the Cultural Roots of the Cold War.* Chapel Hill: University of North Carolina Press, 2000. Fousek surveys the many complex factors that resulted in the Cold War and in the standoff between the Soviet Union and the United States during the late 1940's.

Gaddis, John Lewis. *Surprise, Security, and the American Experience.* Cambridge, Mass.: Harvard University Press, 2004. A compelling account of the behind-the-scenes machinations of the Truman

---

Truman Doctrine

Excerpt from U.S. president Harry S. Truman's address to Congress on the topic of the security and autonomy of Greece and Turkey in the face of an encroaching Soviet Union in the region following World War II.

One of the primary objectives of the foreign policy of the United States is the creation of conditions in which we and other nations will be able to work out a way of life free from coercion. This was a fundamental issue in the war with Germany and Japan. Our victory was won over countries which sought to impose their will, and their way of life, upon other nations.

To ensure the peaceful development of nations, free from coercion, the United States has taken a leading part in establishing the United Nations. The United Nations is designed to make possible lasting freedom and independence for all its members. We shall not realize our objectives, however, unless we are willing to help free peoples to maintain their free institutions and their national integrity against aggressive movements that seek to impose upon them totalitarian regimes. This is no more than a frank recognition that totalitarian regimes imposed on free peoples, by direct or indirect aggression, undermine the foundations of international peace and hence the security of the United States. . . .

The seeds of totalitarian regimes are nurtured by misery and want. They spread and grow in the evil soil of poverty and strife. They reach their full growth when the hope of a people for a better life has died. We must keep that hope alive.

The free peoples of the world look to us for support in maintaining their freedoms. If we falter in our leadership, we may endanger the peace of the world—and we shall surely endanger the welfare of our own nation.

Great responsibilities have been placed upon us by the swift movement of events. I am confident that the Congress will face these responsibilities squarely.

---

administration to thwart communist expansionism following World War II.

McCullough, David. *Truman.* New York: Simon & Schuster, 1992. In this authoritative critical biography of Truman's life and presidency, McCullough provides detailed information about the evolution of the Truman Doctrine as well as the reaction of the American diplomatic community to it.

Mitrovich, Gregory. *Undermining the Kremlin: America's Strategy to Subvert the Soviet Bloc.* Ithaca, N.Y.: Cornell University Press, 2000. A well-researched and intelligently considered presentation of how Truman succeeded in maintaining close relationships with Turkey and Greece following World War II.

Offner, Arnold A. *Another Such Victory: President Truman and the Cold War, 1945-1953.* Stanford, Calif.: Stanford University Press, 2002. A thorough presentation of how the Truman Doctrine kept the Soviets from taking over much of the eastern Mediterranean following the end of World War II.

Spalding, Elizabeth Edwards. *The First Cold Warrior: Harry Truman, Containment, and the Remaking of Liberal Internationalism.* Lexington: University Press of Kentucky, 2006. Discusses the Truman Doctrine extensively, considering the reactions to it of Dean Acheson, George F. Kennan, and George C. Marshall.

See also Acheson, Dean; America First Committee; Churchill, Winston; Congress, U.S.; International trade; "Iron Curtain" speech; Isolationism; Loyalty Program, Truman's; Marshall, George C.; Truman, Harry S.; Turkey; World War II; Yalta Conference.

■ Truman proclamations

The Law Two proclamations issued by President Harry S. Truman claiming U.S. jurisdiction and control over natural resources of the seabed and subsoil of the U.S. continental shelf and asserting authority to establish conservation zones in the high seas for regulating fishing

Also known as Continental Shelf Proclamation and Coastal Fisheries Proclamation

Date Issued on September 28, 1945

These proclamations represented the first unilateral claim by a coastal state to jurisdiction over mineral resources of the continental shelf and the living resources of the coastal waters. It set off a chain reaction of maritime claims by coastal states around the world and opened a new era in the international law of the sea.

As World War II neared an end, the United States began planning for its future as a major maritime power. It was involved in several international disputes over fishery rights, and similar conflicts over

mineral rights seemed inevitable as improved technology made it possible to exploit previously inaccessible hydrocarbons and minerals beneath the seabed. On September 28, 1945, less than a month after the formal end of the war, President Harry S. Truman announced two proclamations that would radically alter the law of the sea.

U.S. Claims Change the Law At that time, nations exercised sovereignty over the three-mile territorial sea (though some had already begun claiming twelve miles), but beyond that the oceans were subject to the freedom of the high seas, for centuries a fundamental principle of international law. The United States changed that with the Truman proclamations by asserting jurisdiction over the submerged lands and subsoil of the continental shelf "in the interest of conservation and prudent development of the natural resources of the seabed," and, in the Coastal Fisheries Proclamation, the authority to establish conservation zones for regulating fishing activities. Implicit in this new "oceans enclosure movement" is the belief that states will manage and conserve resources more wisely when they have an ongoing interest in the continuing viability of the resource than when the whole world is competing for the resource in an unregulated "global commons."

Both proclamations expressly recognized the character of the surface waters above the continental shelf and within the fishery conservation zones as high seas to assure other nations that their rights of free and unimpeded navigation would be unaffected. The proclamations called for negotiations to settle disputes that might arise when two or more states shared the continental shelf or had developed competing fisheries in U.S. coastal waters.

The proclamations also recognized the rights of other states to assert comparable jurisdictional claims, and many states soon asserted claims well beyond those of the United States, such as two-hundred-mile territorial seas in which states could exercise sovereignty and restrict the traditional freedom of navigation. The international community rejected many of these claims as excessive.

Impact The startling speed with which states were asserting previously unjustifiable claims came to the attention of the United Nations, which in 1949 asked the International Law Commission to draft a treaty on the territorial sea. In 1958, the first

U.N. Conference on the Law of the Sea (UNCLOS I) adopted four conventions: on the territorial sea and the contiguous zone, the high seas, fishing and conservation of living resources of the high seas, and the continental shelf. The latter two can be seen as direct results of the two Truman proclamations. All four went into effect during the 1960's.

The proclamations have been influential in the development of international customary law as well. In 1969, in the influential North Sea Continental Shelf Case involving a dispute between Germany, Belgium, and the Netherlands, the International Court of Justice cited Truman's Continental Shelf Proclamation for its assertion of "equitable principles" as the basis for negotiating agreements between states with overlapping claims to a continental shelf.

In 1982, UNCLOS III adopted the U.N. Convention on the Law of the Sea, which continues to reflect the expanded coastal state jurisdiction begun with the Truman proclamations. The 1982 convention took effect in 1994 and has been ratified by most countries (but not the United States, as of 2009), and most of its provisions are regarded as customary international law, binding upon even those states that have not become parties. International treaties and international customary law both now recognize coastal state claims to the minerals of the continental shelf and to two-hundred-mile exclusive fishery zones.

Since the Truman proclamations in 1945, the world's view of maritime jurisdiction has radically shifted from a purely geographical one to a functional approach that recognizes a variety of legal regimes for the same region of the ocean: freedom of the high seas on the surface, fisheries regulation in the water column, and mineral claims beneath the seabed.

William V. Dunlap

Presidential Proclamation 2667

Whereas the Government of the United States of America, aware of the long range world-wide need for new sources of petroleum and other minerals, holds the view that efforts to discover and make available new supplies of these resources should be encouraged; and

Whereas its competent experts are of the opinion that such resources underlie many parts of the continental shelf off the coasts of the United States of America, and that with modern technological progress their utilization is already practicable or will become so at any early date; and

Whereas recognized jurisdiction over these resources is required in the interest of their conservation and prudent utilization when and as development is undertaken; and

Whereas it is the view of the Government of the United States that the exercise of jurisdiction over the natural resources of the subsoil and sea bed of the continental shelf by the contiguous nation is reasonable and just, since the effectiveness of measures to utilize or conserve these resources would be contingent upon cooperation and protection from shore, since the continental shelf may be regarded as an extension of the land mass of the coastal nation and thus naturally appurtenant to it, since these resources frequently form a seaward extension of a pool or deposit lying within the territory, and since self-protection compels the coastal nation to keep close watch over activities off its shores which are of their nature necessary for utilization of these resources;

Now therefore I, Harry S. Truman, President of the United States of America, do hereby proclaim the following policy of the United States of America with respect to the natural resources of the subsoil and sea bed of the continental shelf.

Having concern for the urgency of conserving and prudently utilizing its natural resources, the Government of the United States regards the natural resources of the subsoil and sea bed of the continental shelf beneath the high seas but contiguous to the coasts of the United States as appertaining to the United States, subject to its jurisdiction and control. In cases where the continental shelf extends to the shores of another State, or is shared with an adjacent State, the boundary shall be determined by the United States and the State concerned in accordance with equitable principles. The character as high seas of the waters above the continental shelf and the right to their free and unimpeded navigation are in no way thus affected.

Further Reading

Churchill, Robin, and A. Vaughan Lowe. *The Law of the Sea*. 3d ed. Manchester, England: Manchester University Press, 1999. The standard text on the law of the sea, providing a clear exposition of the development and state of the law.

Gerdes, Louise I. *Endangered Oceans: Opposing Viewpoints*. Detroit, Mich.: Greenhaven Press, 2009. One in a series of volumes presenting countervailing arguments on issues of public concern. The section on "What ocean policies are best" discusses several issues relating to the uses of the oceans.

Hardin, Garrett. "The Tragedy of the Commons." *Science* 162, no. 3859 (1968): 1243-1248. The famous, influential, and controversial essay on the dangers of leaving natural resources unregulated (such as those of the continental shelf and coastal fishery zones).

Johnston, Douglas M. *The Theory and History of Ocean Boundary-Making*. Kingston, Ontario, Canada: McGill-Queen's University Press, 1988. A clear and cogent description and history of maritime boundaries, including fishery zones and continental shelf delimitation.

Kunich, John Charles. *Killing Our Oceans: Dealing with the Mass Extinction of Marine Life*. Westport, Conn.: Praeger, 2006. A particularly useful chapter, "Law of the Sea and in the Sea," discusses law and legislation relating to living marine resources.

McCullough, David. *Truman*. New York: Simon & Schuster, 1992. This Pulitzer Prize-winning biography of President Harry S. Truman provides a highly readable and thorough history of Truman's life and administration.

Strati, Anastasia, Maria Gavouneli, and Nikolaos Skourtos, eds. *Unresolved Issues and New Challenges to the Law of the Sea: Time Before and Time After*. Boston: Martinus Nijhoff, 2006. An excellent collection of sophisticated, often technical, chapters analyzing a broad range of issues relating to maritime resources.

See also Coast Guard, U.S.; Executive orders; Foreign policy of the United States; International Court of Justice; Mexico; Natural resources; Truman, Harry S.; Truman Doctrine.

■ Tucker Torpedo

Identification Experimental car built in 1948

Although Preston Tucker's "car of tomorrow" pioneered many features that would later become standard in American automobiles, it had little chance to succeed. Bad publicity and a financial scandal doomed the car, whose production ceased after only fifty-one models had been produced.

Preston Tucker had a dream of building a car that every American could afford. He began designing and planning his new car in the aftermath of World War II, during which all production of passengers automobiles had been halted so that the automobile industry could turn its attention to manufacturing military vehicles and equipment. After the war, the American public was hungry for new cars, and the time was ripe for innovative designs.

Tucker commissioned the well-known automobile designer Alex Tremulis to design a four-door sedan and had engineers beat sheet iron to build it. The completely handmade prototype, dubbed the "Tin Goose," premiered in June of 1947. The most striking design feature of the car was a third headlight, mounted in the center of the grill, that turned with the front wheels to illuminate the new directions into which the car was about to go. The third headlight—dubbed its "Cyclops eye" by critics—was a radical design innovation, but Tucker had a greater interest in incorporating enhanced safety and performance features, such as disc brakes, padded dashboards, placement of instrument controls on the steering wheel, four-wheel independent suspension, and fuel injection. During the car's brief history, not all these features were used. Often known as the Torpedo, Tucker's sedan was officially named the Tucker '48, after the only model year in which it was produced.

Scandal and bad press doomed Tucker's car from the beginning. Not willing to give up control of his company to investors, Tucker devised a financial plan that would allow him to keep control. However, the Securities and Exchange Commission (SEC) was skeptical of his plan and twice launched a full investigation. In 1948, the second SEC investigation forced Tucker to stop production and lay off sixteen hundred workers. However, he was able to produce fifty more cars by January of 1949. Later that year, when he was accused by the SEC of fraud, Tucker faced a grand jury trial. He was ultimately found inno-

Preston Tucker unveiling his prototype Tucker Torpedo automobile in Chicago in 1947. (AP/Wide World Photos)

cent on all counts, but the trial destroyed whatever chance for success was left for Tucker and his "Torpedo."

Impact   After completion of the prototype car in 1947, Tucker's company completely assembled only fifty-one sedans. Although the car was an abject failure during the late 1940's, it later came to be regarded as a visionary classic that anticipated many design features that would later become standard in automobiles. The vast majority of the original cars have survived into the twenty-first century as highly prized and exceptionally expensive collector items.

Michael D. Cummings, Jr.

Further Reading
Egan, P. S. *Design and Destiny: The Making of the Tucker Automobile.* Orange, Calif.: On the Mark, 1989.

Willson, Q. *Classic American Cars.* New York: DK, 1997.

See also   Automobiles and auto manufacturing; Ford Motor Company; General Motors; Inventions.

■ Turkey

At the onset of the Cold War, Turkey emerged as a strategic country in America's policy of communist containment.

During the 1940's, Turkey bordered the Soviet Union, and the only way Soviet vessels could reach the Mediterranean from the Black Sea was through the Turkish-controlled Dardanelles Strait. While the Soviet Union's dissatisfaction with the international regime governing the straits led to its repeated demands for reevaluation, the United States supported Turkey's desire to retain the regime, resisting Soviet pressure from the mid-1940's into the Cold War.

For the United States, Turkey was not a particularly significant country until the end of World War II. The Soviet Union's dissatisfaction with the Montreux Convention of 1936, the regime governing the Turkish straits, resurfaced at wartime meetings of Allied leaders at Tehran, Yalta, and Postdam. Finally, Soviet leader Joseph Stalin demanded not only a new regime to regulate passage through the straits but also a Soviet military presence nearby and a rearrangement of Turkey's borders with the Soviet Union. The United States, however, wanted to contain the Soviets from threatening not only Turkey but also Greece.

The USS *Missouri*'s trip to Turkey in April, 1946, symbolized American support for Turkey. Concerned with Stalin's desire to expand the Soviet sphere of influence, President Harry S. Truman announced that the United States was committed to containing the Soviets.

Impact Both the Truman Doctrine and the Marshall Plan included aid to Turkey and provided material evidence of American support for the Middle Eastern nation. Eventually, Turkey's admission to the North Atlantic Treaty Organization (NATO) in 1952 illustrated the significance of relations between Turkey and the United States at the beginning of the Cold War, as well as Turkey's strategic importance to the United States at this time.

Baris Kesgin

Further Reading

Hale, William. *Turkish Foreign Policy, 1774-2000.* London: Frank Cass, 2000.

Howard, Harry N. *Turkey, the Straits, and U.S. Policy.* Baltimore: Johns Hopkins University Press, 1974.

Hurewitz, J. C. "Russia and the Turkish Straits: A Revaluation of the Origins of the Problem." *World Politics* 14, no. 4 (1962): 605-632.

See also Cold War; Marshall Plan; North Atlantic Treaty Organization; Potsdam Conference; Tehran Conference; Truman Doctrine; Yalta Conference.

■ Tuskegee Airmen

Identification African American Army Air Force pilots who trained at the Tuskegee Institute flying school during World War II
Date Organized in 1941
Place Tuskegee Institute, Tuskegee, Alabama

Formation of the first all-black flying unit in early 1941 brought about significant changes in racist War Department policies that had been in effect since 1925. The combat performance of these pilots altered extant beliefs that African Americans were inherently inferior to whites.

In July, 1948, U.S. president Harry S. Truman signed Executive Order 9981, which required equal treatment and opportunity for black servicemen. The order was a turning point in the history of integration of the U.S. armed services. Although the proximate causes of the president's action may have been political pressure and a need for black votes, the remote causes were threefold: the formation of an all-black fighter squadron known later as the Tuskegee Airmen (1941), the mutiny at Freeman Army Air Field (1945), and the command and leadership of Benjamin O. Davis, Jr.

The 332d Fighter Group The formation of the 332d Fighter Group, the famous "Red Tails," came about initially from the political initiatives of President Franklin D. Roosevelt. In 1939, he needed black votes for the 1940 election and insisted on allowing African Americans to serve in all branches of the armed services. Although black pilots were available from civilian training programs, no combat flying unit existed for them. The Army and its Army Air Forces (USAAF) was not quick to act, but it finally succumbed to political pressures and some legal wrangling. Tuskegee Institute in Alabama received funds to begin an Army Air Forces training program, complete with flying field, for black pilots. The group trained there, known as the Ninety-ninth Pursuit Squadron, shipped to North Africa as a fighter squadron in April, 1943. The demand for qualified pilots as the war progressed saw the formation of three more black-only squadrons, being formed into the 332d Fighter Group, activated in October, 1942.

The so-called "Tuskegee Experiment" was initiated to have a "separate but equal" flying unit for blacks—and to determine whether black pilots could meet required flying standards. The black airmen of the 332d Fighter Group overcame the racist policies of the 1925 War College Report and received top commendations from USAAF commanders due to excellent combat achievements.

The Freeman Army Air Field Mutiny Other black airmen, some experienced returnees from the Ninety-ninth or the 332d, or from various flying schools, began training as combat crews for the B-25 medium bomber. The 477th Bomber Group (Medium) was activated in January, 1944, as the only black bombardment unit. Racial tensions existed from the very beginning: The white commander promoted whites, and black officers could not be in command of white personnel. Then, in a complicated series of moves, because of local racial tensions and bad training weather, officers and crews, both trainers and trainees, were shuttled from Selfridge Field, near Detroit, Michigan, to Godman Field, near Fort Knox, Kentucky, and then again to Freeman Army Air Field, near Seymour, Indiana. These moves made over the course of a few months delayed training and lowered morale, and they were made more to calm segregationists than to further creation of a combat-ready flying unit.

Even more aggravating to the black trainees were the dual officers' clubs, established against Army regulations. Some black officers, challenging the de facto segregation, entered the white club. They were arrested. Later, 101 black officers refused to sign a newly drafted "Club Order," requiring them to accept the regulating of segregation in the officers' clubs. They were arrested, then charged subsequently with "willful disobedience" in the form of "disobeying a direct order by a superior officer in time of war." This event is known as the Freeman Field Mutiny of April 11, 1945.

With the National Association for the Advancement of Colored People (NAACP) championing their cause, the Freeman Field 101 found themselves the object of a congressional investigation. They were released, but three of them were tried in July. One was convicted and fined. (During the 1990's, all charges were dropped and reprimands were dismissed.)

Benjamin O. Davis, Jr. In May, 1945, the 477th was relocated back to Godman Field. In June, the new 477th Composite Group was placed under the command of a black officer, Benjamin O. Davis, Jr. He brought to the job his years as a black officer, as the first commander of the Ninety-ninth Pursuit Squadron, and as commander and combat pilot in the 332d Fighter Group. Part of the original Tuskegee Experiment, he endured racial discrimination and four years of silent treatment as a West Point cadet and racial prejudice within the USAAF. With his family, he lived in and around segregated and prejudiced military facilities. As a leader, he fought racial obstacles, both in combat in the Mediterranean theater and in congressional testimony before bigoted committees and groups who hoped for the failure of black pilots. By his professional efforts, his units became pride-filled examples of cooperation, yet they experienced the painful struggle toward integration, with equal rights decades away.

Impact The inroads made by the original Tuskegee Airmen and by Davis contributed to change, slow though it was, toward integration and equal rights in American society. Throughout the 1940's, segrega-

Members of the Tuskegee Airmen relaxing between missions in January, 1944. (AP/Wide World Photos)

tion and racial discrimination forced black servicemen to prove they possessed the skills and abilities to compete successfully. Truman recognized their achievement with Executive Order 9981. By 1949, the United States Air Force (USAF) had progressed further in its integration efforts than any other military service, progress that began at the Tuskegee Institute.

James F. O'Neil

Further Reading

Blackman, Douglas A. *Slavery by Another Name: The Re-enslavement of Black Americans from the Civil War to World War II.* New York: Doubleday, 2008. Provides background to issues of racism and white supremacy. This book will help readers understand the feelings of blacks at Tuskegee, and what they fought for.

Bucholtz, Chris. *332nd Fighter Group: Tuskegee Airmen.* Oxford, England: Osprey, 2007. A balanced presentation of the combat history of the all-black fighting group, this comprehensive and detailed account covers the range of military operations and achievements of the pilots.

Coggins, Patrick C. *Tuskegee Airman Fighter Pilot: A Story of an Original Tuskegee Pilot, Lt. Col. Hiram E. Mann.* Victoria, B.C.: Trafford, 2008. A testament to one Tuskegee Airman, this book documents his background, training, and achievements, providing personal insights into the pilots and the values they held.

Davis, Benjamin O., Jr. *American: An Autobiography.* Washington, D.C.: Smithsonian Institution Press, 1991. A presentation of the highs and lows of a thirty-eight-year military career. Demonstrates the courage and valor of the man who fought for the civil rights of those in his command, and for those who would come after them.

Dryden, Charles W., and Benjamin O. Davis, Jr. *A-Train: Memoirs of a Tuskegee Airman.* Tuscaloosa: University of Alabama Press, 2002. A moving personal account by one of the first Tuskegee Airmen, enumerating the obstacles he overcame in the quest to fly in World War II.

Francis, Charles E., and Adolph Caso. *The Tuskegee Airmen: The Men Who Changed a Nation.* 5th ed. Boston: Branden, 2008. A firsthand telling of the experiences undertaken and endured at Tuskegee and the significance of the experiment.

Homan, Lynn M., and Thomas Reilley. *Black Knights.*

Gretna, La.: Pelican, 2001. The authors present personal struggles, not only of the pilots but also of the crews, nurses, and others involved with the Tuskegee experience.

Scott, Lawrence P., and William M. Womack. *Double V: The Civil Rights Struggle of the Tuskegee Airmen.* East Lansing: Michigan State University Press, 1998. Devoted to the details of the suffering endured as a result of segregation on military installations. Discusses the Freeman Army Air Field 101.

Warren, James C. *The Tuskegee Airmen Mutiny at Freemen Field.* Conyers, Ga.: Conyers, 2001. A personal account of the black officers and enlisted men involved with the 477th Bomber Group and its protest at Freeman Army Air Field in 1945.

See also   African Americans; Air Force, U.S.; Civil rights and liberties; Davis, Benjamin O., Jr.; Desegregation of the U.S. military; Flying Tigers; Jim Crow laws; National Association for the Advancement of Colored People; Racial discrimination; War heroes; World War II.

■ Tuskegee syphilis study

The Event   Long-term study of the effects of
   syphilis on African American men
Date   1932-1972
Place   Macon County, Alabama

Over a period of four decades, the U.S. Public Health Service conducted research on the effects of syphilis on poor black men in one of the most outrageously unethical research programs in American medical history. Participants were allowed to think they were being treated for their conditions, but the medical personnel who saw them were interested only in observing the effects of untreated syphilis. Although the Public Health Service began prescribing penicillin to treat syphilis during the 1940's, it denied penicillin to the subjects of the Tuskegee study.

During the early 1930's, the U.S. Public Health Service determined to conduct a study of the long-term effects of untreated syphilis on men. To find ready subjects for its study, it based its program at Tuskegee Institute in Alabama. The Public Health Service then began inviting poor and generally uneducated African American men to come to the institute for free medical examinations. The provision of free meals and transportation and the prospect of free medical treatment enticed hundreds of men to volunteer. Volunteers who were diagnosed with syphilis were encouraged to make return visits for medical treatments, but they were not told they had syphilis. Moreover, the treatments they received were not effective against syphilis.

In 1940, penicillin was found to be effective in the treatment of many diseases including syphilis. By 1943, the Public Health Service was administering the antibiotic drug to syphilitic patients elsewhere, while knowingly withholding it from participants in the Tuskegee study. Their purpose was not to treat sufferers from the disease but to study its effects; they regarded infected volunteers not as "patients" but as "subjects." In the forty years the study lasted, at least twenty-eight men died from syphilis, and one hundred more died from related complications. Moreover, many of the subjects' wives were infected, and some had children who were born with congenital syphilis.

The program ended abruptly in 1972 after a former Public Health Service worker publicized what was going on in the study. A class-action suit filed against the federal government on behalf of participants in the study later the same year was settled out of court. The plaintiffs shared $10 million in cash payments and were given lifetime health and medical benefits and burial services.

Publicity surrounding the revelations of ethical improprieties in the Tuskegee study prompted the federal government to reevaluate its medical practices. In 1974, the U.S. Congress passed the National Research Act, which created the National Commission for the Protection of Human Subjects of Biomedical and Behavioral Research.

Impact   The Tuskegee syphilis study had tragic consequences on several levels. Despite the great human suffering that might have been prevented if subjects of the study had been properly treated, the information the study accumulated contributed nothing to clinical treatment of syphilis. Moreover, public exposure of the government's deliberate manipulation of black subjects engendered widespread distrust of the government in general and the Public Health Service in particular among African Americans. In later years, the effect of this distrust would be seen in the reluctance of many African Americans to heed government warnings about acquired immunodeficiency syndrome (AIDS) and the human immunodeficiency virus (HIV).

Gina Robertiello

Further Reading

Jones, J. *Bad Blood—the Tuskegee Syphilis Experiment: A Tragedy of Race and Medicine.* New York: Free Press, 1981.

MacDonald, C. J. "The Contribution of the Tuskegee Study to Medical Knowledge." *Journal of the National Medical Association* 66, no. 1 (1974): 1-7.

White, R. "Misrepresentations of the Tuskegee Study of Untreated Syphilis." *Journal of the National Medical Association* 97 (2005): 564-581.

See also   African Americans; Antibiotics; Crimes and scandals; Health care; National Association for the Advancement of Colored People; Sexually transmitted diseases; World Health Organization.

TWA. *See* **Trans World Airline**

U

■ Unconditional surrender policy

Definition   Allied insistence on the surrender without compromise or negotiation of the Axis Powers

The 1943 implementation of the policy of unconditional surrender reinforced the Allied commitment to the absolute eradication of Nazi Germany and the elimination of Imperial Japan. Critics of the policy argued that by making diplomatic negotiations with the Axis Powers impossible, it would prolong the war and later heighten postwar political tensions.

At the conclusion of the Casablanca Conference, a summit meeting of the Allied Powers, President Franklin D. Roosevelt announced the acceptance of "nothing less than the unconditional surrender of Germany, Japan and Italy" in a speech on January 24, 1943. This policy aimed to unite the Allies in achieving the unequivocal eradication of the Axis Powers and concurrently demarcate a clear line of victory at war's end.

While many people supported the policy on its fundamental moral standing and commitment to "total victory," others censured it for possibly prolonging the war and inciting an insurgence of Nazi aggression. Since the war ended, some critics have also argued that the complete annihilation of the German army at the war's conclusion created a power vacuum that complicated the oncoming Cold War. While negotiations were undertaken with the Axis-powered Italy upon the deposition of Benito Mussolini shortly after the Casablanca Conference, no such dialogue occurred with Japan. Instead, the United States chose to drop atomic bombs on Hiroshima and Nagasaki in 1945 that resulted in Japan's unconditional surrender soon thereafter.

Impact   The policy represented a commitment to an absolute military and moral victory in World War II. At the same time, it was compounded by the costly dedication to fighting toward a conclusion without diplomatic negotiation with Germany and Japan.

Eric Novod

Further Reading

Armstrong, Anne. *Unconditional Surrender: The Impact of the Casablanca Policy upon World War II.* New Brunswick, N.J.: Rutgers University Press, 1961.

Black, Conrad. *Franklin Delano Roosevelt: Champion of Freedom.* New York: PublicAffairs Books, 2003.

See also   Casablanca Conference; Casualties of World War II; Churchill, Winston; Roosevelt, Franklin D.; World War II.

General Douglas MacArthur (seated) presiding over the Japanese surrender aboard the USS Missouri *in Tokyo Bay on September 2, 1945.* (For another view of this scene, see title page of volume 2.) (National Archives)

■ Unemployment in Canada

As in the United States, Canada's involvement in World War II brought convulsive changes to the national economy that brought virtually full employment to the country. After the war ended in 1945, unemployment again increased, but expansion of the consumer-based economy kept unemployment at modest levels.

Canada's entry into World War II in late 1939 had a profound effect on the nation's rate of unemployment. Employment increased by 51 percent between the fall of 1939 and 1942. In effect, Canada enjoyed full employment throughout the first half of the 1940's. Employment dropped significantly with the ending of hostilities in 1945, but as the national economy readjusted to one that was consumer-based in the remainder of 1945 and in 1946, employment rapidly recovered. The annual increase from 1946 to 1949 was 3 percent per year.

In contrast to the wartime years, the postwar years saw numerous industrial disputes, as the Canadian labor movement regained its influence. In 1946, four major union groups dominated labor relations in Canada: the Trades and Labour Congress, patterned after the Congress of Industrial Organizations in the United States; the Canadian Congress of Labour, patterned after the American Federation of Labor in the United States; the Canadian and Catholic Confederation of Labour, which operated only in Quebec; and the Railroad Brotherhoods.

Membership in unions had grown significantly during the war, doubling between 1939 and 1945, as wartime rules made it easier to organize, though the railroads had been unionized for decades. When these laws expired, the unions were prepared to test their strength, especially in 1946, when strikes resulted in more than three times as many hours lost as in 1945.

Important legislation passed by the Dominion government had a strong influence during the 1940's. Before 1940, Canada's industrial relations had been governed by the Industrial Disputes Investigation Act of 1907, but this was replaced in 1944 by a similarly named law. This, in turn, was superseded in 1948 by another new law, the Industrial Relations and Disputes Act, which, however, governed only those industries under Dominion control, which included shipping, railroads, radio, and television. Other, more localized, industries were under the supervision of provincial governments.

During the 1940's, Canada's government, which before the war had followed a very hands-off policy with respect to the economy, began taking a much more interventionist role. In 1941, the British government had amended the British North America Act (Canada's constitutional authorization) to provide for unemployment insurance for all Canadians. This system began on July 1, 1941, and required equal contributions from employers and employees, with a modest additional contribution from the Dominion government. However, during the war years

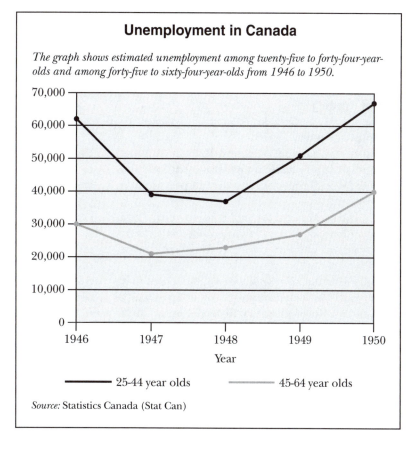

Unemployment in Canada

The graph shows estimated unemployment among twenty-five to forty-four-year-olds and among forty-five to sixty-four-year-olds from 1946 to 1950.

— 25-44 year olds   — 45-64 year olds

Source: Statistics Canada (Stat Can)

essentially full employment prevailed, making unemployment insurance unimportant. The National Selective Services program allotted labor to the military services and private employment in war-supply industries.

Where, before the war, agriculture had been Canada's biggest industry and where the majority of Canadians were employed, this distribution shifted, first during the war and then during the postwar readjustment so that manufacturing and services dominated the economy. On April 1 of 1949, 1,904,180 men were receiving unemployment insurance, and 705,990 women. The largest number of unemployed were located in Ontario, reflecting the concentration of industry in that province.

Impact   World War II brought massive changes to the Canadian economy. With only a fraction of the population of the United States, Canada played a much smaller role in the war. However, it entered the war fully two years earlier, and the role that it played had a proportionately much greater impact on its national economy. Canada's entry into the war swiftly lifted the country out of the Great Depression and brought virtually full employment. After the war, the country's robust consumer economy kept unemployment at a modest level.

Nancy M. Gordon

Further Reading

Careless, J. M. S. *Canada: A Story of Challenge.* Toronto: Macmillan, 1970.

Granatstein, J. L., and Desmond Morton. *A Nation Forged in Fire: Canadians and the Second World War, 1939-1945.* Toronto: Lester and Orpen Dennys, 1989.

Grant, Harry M., and M. H. Watkins, eds. *Canadian Economic History: Classic and Contemporary Approaches.* Ottawa: Carleton University Press, 1999.

Statistics Canada. *National Income and Expenditure Accounts: Annual Estimates, 1926-1986.* Ottawa: Canadian Government Publishing Centre, 1988.

See also   Business and the economy in Canada; Demographics of Canada; Immigration to Canada; Labor strikes; Military conscription in Canada; Unemployment in the United States; Urbanization in Canada; Women's roles and rights in Canada.

■ Unemployment in the United States

High unemployment plagued the United States at the beginning of the 1940's and remained constantly on the minds of government officials even through the years when the country's involvement in World War II led to virtually full employment. As a result, leaders took great pains to engineer the economy when the war ended to keep unemployment rates at acceptable levels.

In 1940, the United States was still recovering from the nightmare of the Great Depression. During the 1930's unemployment had risen above 25 percent, and although President Franklin D. Roosevelt's New Deal initiatives had done much to ameliorate this catastrophe, unemployment stood at an unacceptably high 14.6 percent in 1940. Nevertheless, there was a sense that government intervention had helped reverse the worst effects of the Depression. Many in the Roosevelt administration, as well as university economists, were beginning to see wisdom in the theories of British economist John Maynard Keynes. He encouraged deficit spending by governments to counterbalance reductions by the private sector in order to promote full employment and avoid recessions and depressions. Keynes's theory of active government intervention, coupled with the escalating military conflicts in Europe and East Asia, had a major influence in determining levels of unemployment in the country throughout the 1940's.

Unemployment During the War Years   Responding to requests from Great Britain in 1940, President Roosevelt authorized a number of programs to supply the Allies with war materiel. The increased business for a number of industries, coupled with the trend toward general recovery in the U.S. economy, led to a gradual improvement in unemployment, so that by 1941 the rate had fallen to 9.9 percent. As that year progressed, the federal government began issuing an increasing number of contracts for the U.S. military as well. After Japan attacked Pearl Harbor in December, 1941, and the United States entered the war, the employment picture changed dramatically. Government spending increased exponentially to pay for supplies and equipment needed by the nation's fighting forces.

Over the next three years, more than 12 million Americans entered military service. Not only were

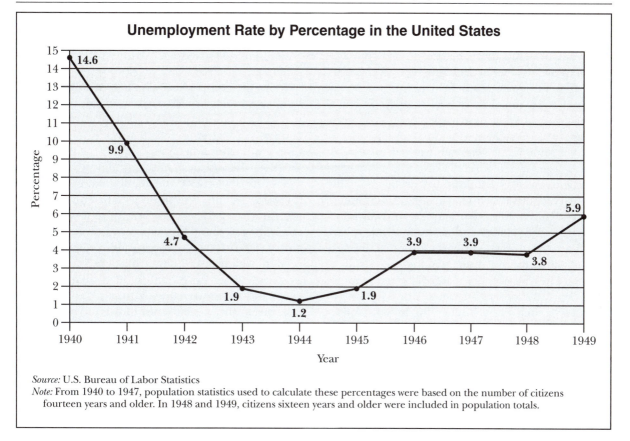

Unemployment Rate by Percentage in the United States

Source: U.S. Bureau of Labor Statistics
Note: From 1940 to 1947, population statistics used to calculate these percentages were based on the number of citizens fourteen years and older. In 1948 and 1949, citizens sixteen years and older were included in population totals.

these people employed; their departure from the civilian economy freed up positions for others to fill. So great was the demand for workers that women who would normally have stayed at home entered the workforce to replace those called to serve. As opportunities for jobs soared, unemployment levels dropped precipitously. In 1942, the rate was 4.7 percent; the following year it dropped to 1.9 percent, and in 1944 to 1.2 percent. Hostilities ended in Europe in May, 1945, and in Asia the following August, causing the federal government to cancel billions of dollars' worth of contracts. Nevertheless, the unemployment rate for that year averaged only 1.9 percent.

Planning for Postwar Employment   Even before the Axis Powers surrendered, many economists and politicians were expressing fears that the United States would fall back into a depression when the war ended. Federal officials realized that high employment during the war years was the result of billions of dollars in federal contracts for defense purposes—

work that would disappear after the war ended. Some observers were predicting that unemployment would once again rise, perhaps as high as 15 percent, idling more than 9 million Americans. Of particular concern were the millions of veterans who would be expecting to return to their jobs after their years in uniform. No one in government wanted to see a repeat of what happened after World War I, when thousands of unemployed veterans staged public protests and erected a tent city in Washington, D.C., to dramatize the poor treatment they had received.

To prevent these debacles, the Roosevelt administration set up several planning groups to determine how best to use government policy to shape the postwar economy. Politicians agreed that all Americans had the right to work; during the 1944 presidential elections both parties endorsed this idea. In 1945 some members of Congress began drafting legislation to guarantee Americans employment, directing government intervention if necessary to assure the availability of jobs. The result was a piece of legislation guaranteeing full employment and tasking the president to report annually to Congress on the plans to fulfill that promise. Although this legislation was watered down before its final passage, the Employment Act of 1946 established the principle that the government had a role to play in keeping down unemployment, using its financial resources—including deficit spending—to accomplish this goal if necessary.

At the same time, Roosevelt worked to see that some measures were taken to alleviate the impact of having millions of veterans suddenly returned to the work force. A private working group advised him to develop a comprehensive program to provide veterans a combination of extended unemployment benefits, loans to buy homes or start businesses, and substantial stipends for those wishing to enroll in school. The Servicemen's Readjustment Act of 1944, known more popularly as the G.I. Bill of Rights, provided opportunities for millions of returning veterans to wait to enter the workforce, smoothing out what could have been a substantial rise in those seeking work in the months immediately following demobilization.

Of equal concern to government officials and business leaders—those in management and labor alike—was the ability of American businesses to transform from wartime to peacetime economy. Some key industries such as automobile manufacturing had abandoned production of civilian goods in order fully to support the national war effort. Others that had maintained both civilian and military production had retooled at many factories to make specialized equipment for the war, and required similar conversions to nonmilitary production. Union leaders worried that the influx of returning veterans, coupled with reduced demand, would drive down wages and lead to a reduction in benefits.

Unemployment Trends After the War Some fears of postwar setbacks were realized, but in general the American economy underwent its conversion with a minimal impact on levels of employment. In 1946, the national unemployment rate rose to 3.9 percent and held steady at that level over the next two years. A rise in 1949 to 5.9 percent was seen by some as a troublesome trend, but this fear proved unfounded, as unemployment during the 1950's did not exceed that level until late in the decade. None of the dire predictions about double-digit unemployment were realized. Instead, a combination of factors involving

government intervention and private business practices staved off a second Great Depression and ushered in a period of extensive economic prosperity in America.

Many economists have cited three principal reasons for America's quick postwar recovery with minimal impact on employment. The first was that the country's industries were able to reconvert to peacetime production much more rapidly than expected. By 1948, the private sector was almost completely free of its dependency on the federal government for work. Second, Americans who had saved during the war when goods were scarce were suddenly able and willing to spend for consumer products. For example, by 1949, automobile sales reached or exceeded prewar levels. Other big-ticket items—such as refrigerators, stoves, and other expensive appliances and furniture items—also sold well as Americans began the move toward individual home ownership in the suburbs. A third factor particularly influencing unemployment rates was the large number of people exiting the work force voluntarily (mostly women returning to the home) or choosing not to seek work immediately (mostly veterans enrolling in school).

Not all economists agree, however, that the government's active intervention following Keynesian economic principles was responsible for the country's rapid return to prosperity and avoidance of high unemployment. Rather, it was the depression of real wages that allowed businesses to expand employment to meet consumer demand coupled with low interest rates that made it attractive for investors to put money into American businesses that spurred growth and made unemployment a non-issue.

Impact Although horrid in many ways, World War II proved a substantial stimulus for the United States economy, helping first to reduce the unemployment rate in the years immediately before and during the conflict and to sustain low levels of unemployment in those following the cessation of hostilities. Military call-ups gave work to 12 million people, and government contracts provided work for millions not enrolled in military service. At war's end the quick conversion of American industry to a peacetime economy provided jobs, thus keeping unemployment low. A robust American economy—for a time the only one in the world, as countries directly involved in the conflict struggled to rebuild their infrastructure—allowed the United States to become a world leader in production of consumer goods.

Laurence W. Mazzeno

Further Reading

Mucciaroni, Gary. *The Political Failure of Employment Policy 1945-1982*. Pittsburgh: University of Pittsburgh Press, 1990. Provides an analysis of Keynesian economic theory and its impact on the U.S. government's economic policies, including those aimed at fostering employment.

Neufeld, Charles M. *A Short History of the Unemployment Rate: Its Uses and Misuses*. Charleston, S.C.: Citadel Press, 1983. Brief analysis of the federal government's involvement in manipulating the economy to maintain acceptable levels of employment after World War II.

Severo, Richard, and Lewis Mulford. *The Wages of War: When America's Soldiers Came Home—From Valley Forge to Vietnam*. New York: Simon & Schuster, 1990. Includes a chapter describing concerns about unemployment incident to the return of U.S. military members to civilian life; discusses the Roosevelt administration's plans to dampen the impact on the economy.

Vedder, Richard K., and Lowell E. Gallaway. *Out of Work: Unemployment and Government in Twentieth-Century America*. New York: Holmes & Meier, 1993. Offers a highly critical assessment of government efforts to achieve high employment rates, and offers evidence that challenges the idea that low unemployment was always beneficial to individuals or the country as a whole.

Zieger, Robert H., and Gilbert J. Gall. *American Workers, American Unions*. 3d ed. Baltimore: Johns Hopkins University Press, 2002. Describes struggles by organized labor to maintain adequate wages and working conditions for their members during the war years and efforts to preserve jobs and improve wages and benefits in the postwar economy.

See also American Federation of Labor; Business and the economy in the United States; Congress of Industrial Organizations; Demographics of the United States; G.I. Bill; Income and wages; Labor strikes; Military conscription in the United States; Taft-Hartley Act; Unemployment in Canada; Unionism.

■ UNICEF

Identification International relief organization
Also known as International Children's Emergency Fund; United Nations International Children's Emergency Fund; United Nations Children's Fund
Date Established on December 11, 1946

In 1946, the United Nations General Assembly unanimously voted to create the International Children's Emergency Fund (ICEF), later known as UNICEF, to support the survival and the development of children worldwide. The deplorable postwar conditions, particularly in Europe, proved the immediate need for the United Nations to assist millions of children who were in danger of dying from disease and starvation.

Members of the U.S. Committee for UNICEF presenting a report on the organization's activities to President Harry S. Truman in November, 1949. From left: Undersecretary of State James Webb, Secretary of Defense Louis Johnson, Truman, committee chair Mary Lord, UNICEF delegate Katharine Lenroot, and Special Assistant to the Assistant Secretary of State for Economic Affairs Dallas Dort. (National Archives)

UNICEF increased public awareness of the plight of children and ultimately resulted in new relief sources. Maurice Pate, the first executive director of UNICEF, and his staff worked to provide emergency relief funds that would supply medicine, vaccinations, clothing, and food for suffering children. Cloth, leather, milk, and other essentials were purchased entirely from voluntary funding from individuals, groups, businesses, and governments. In 1947, the first national committee for UNICEF, the U.S. Fund, was established.

Impact Since its establishment, UNICEF has met the basic needs of millions of children around the world. In 1950, UNICEF's scope was expanded to include developmental needs of women and children. Three years later, the organization's title was changed to United Nations Children's Fund, but "UNICEF" continued to be its acronym. UNICEF's current areas of service objectives include emergency and humanitarian services, health services, safe water, sanitation, nutrition, education, and women's rights.

Cynthia J. W. Svoboda

Further Reading

Leguey-Feilleux, Jean-Robert. "UNICEF Is Established." In *Great Events from History: The Twentieth Century, 1941-1970*, edited by Robert F. Gorman. Pasadena, Calif.: Salem Press, 2008.

Smith, Roger. *UNICEF and Other Human Rights Efforts: Protecting Individuals.* Philadelphia: Mason Crest, 2007.

Spiegelman, Judith M. *We Are the Children: A Celebration of UNICEF's First Forty Years.* Boston: Atlantic Monthly Press, 1986.

See also United Nations; Wartime propaganda in Canada; World Health Organization.

■ Unionism

Definition Organization, support, and running of labor unions

By the 1940's, American labor unions were aggressively using the organizing rights and protections guaranteed them by the federal Wagner Act of 1935. During the war years unions saw significant expansion as both the American Federation of Labor and the Congress of Industrial Organi-

zations supported creation of the War Production Board to ensure that the country produced the needed military supplies. After the war ended, however, many unions became more forceful in demanding delayed wage increases, and labor unrest grew so strong the U.S. Congress passed the Taft-Hartley Act, which outlawed certain union practices and gave the president authority to impose a cooling-off period before unions could strike.

During the 1930's, the decade of the Depression, American labor unions became relatively stagnant as unemployment levels reached record highs. However, as President Franklin D. Roosevelt began launching his New Deal programs, labor conditions began to improve. In 1935, Congress passed the Wagner Act, creating the National Labor Relations Board, which was intended to ensure collective bargaining rights for unions. In addition to the rights granted by the Wagner Act, competition between the country's two great union organizations, the American Federation of Labor (AFL) and the Congress of Industrial Organizations (CIO), and the onset of World War II combined to strengthen the American union movement, which flourished through most of the decade.

Legacy of the Depression Trade unions were relatively weak during the years of the Depression. Fewer than 3 million workers were members of unions. Most of the union members were in the AFL, which represented only skill crafts workers. Workers in large industries such as steel, textiles, and automobiles were not represented by unions. In 1936, John L. Lewis, the head of the AFL's United Mine Workers union, began organizing the steel industry workers in an effort to support President Roosevelt's New Deal agenda. This put him at odds with the AFL, whose leaders looked down on efforts to organize members of an entire industry such as steel, instead of concentrating on organizing skill crafts workers. Because of this conflict, the United Mine Workers and seven other unions bolted from the AFL and formed the Congress of Industrial Organizations.

Another prolabor New Deal measure passed during the 1930's was the Fair Labor Standards Act of 1938. This law set a minimum-wage level and limited how many hours laborers could work each week. Thanks to federal legislation and the CIO's aggressive efforts to organize such industries as steel, automobiles, electrical, metal, and rubber, the numbers

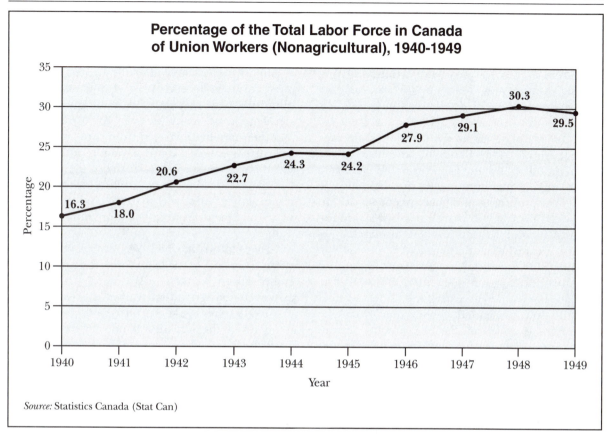

Percentage of the Total Labor Force in Canada of Union Workers (Nonagricultural), 1940-1949

Source: Statistics Canada (Stat Can)

of union members grew. By 1940, the CIO alone had 5 million members, and the AFL had slightly fewer members. Perhaps the most far reaching of all New Deal measures, the Wagner Act revitalized the labor movement and brought about a permanent change in labor-management relations. However, although the number of union members in 1940 was more than three times greater than it had been during the early 1930's, only 28 percent of all workers in the country were unionized.

World War II and the Labor Movement By the beginning of the 1940's, organized labor was in the strongest position in which it had ever been in the United States, and it was about to get even stronger. After Japan attacked the U.S. naval base at Pearl Harbor on December 7, 1941, the United States declared war on the Japanese Empire, Nazi Germany, and Fascist Italy. Over the next four years, the entire nation was absorbed in supporting the U.S. war efforts in the Pacific and in Europe. The incorporation of millions of young men into military service and a huge

expansion of wartime industries led to nearly full employment at home and gave enormous boosts to the labor movement, which wholeheartedly supported the war effort.

President Roosevelt established the War Production Board to oversee American industry transformation to wartime bases. As industries such as automobiles switching from manufacturing consumer goods to making military goods, American industry was soon able to produce more planes, tanks, ships, ammunition, and other war supplies than Germany and Japan combined. Keeping industry operating at full capacity during the war was such a high priority that unions remained on their best behavior. However, while wage increases were limited, workers earned extra pay by putting in extensive overtime hours.

Women and Minorities The removal of millions of male workers to fight in the war and the expansion of industries greatly increased opportunities for employment and union members for women and members of minority groups, particularly African Americans. Many African Americans had recently migrated from the South to the industrial areas of the Northeast, Midwest, and West, seeking the new jobs created by the war, but they still experienced racial discrimination in employment.

On the eve of American entry into the war, black labor leader A. Philip Randolph, the head of the Brotherhood of Sleeping Car Porters, threatened a march on Washington to protest discrimination in the defense industries and government service. In early 1941, President Roosevelt reached a compromise with Randolph that prevented the march by offering to create the Fair Employment Practices Commission (FEPC), which banned discrimination in war industries and government service. However, he stopped short of desegregating the armed services as Randolph demanded. Benefitting from the protections provided by the FEPC, many African Americans found work in war industries and in government agencies, and they increased their num-

bers in labor unions, primarily those representing unskilled workers in the new unions created by the CIO.

Almost immediately after the United States entered the war at the end of 1941, labor conditions for minorities began changing dramatically. Like African Americans, many Mexican American workers and their families migrated from rural areas to the industrial centers. California alone added nearly two million new residents, many of them Latinos. Union membership grew significantly among this group as they found work in the war industries where plants and factories were being organized by labor unions.

In agriculture, in which Mexican Americans constituted the bulk of the labor force, the situation was comparatively bleak. The Wagner Act had specifically excluded agricultural workers from the rights it granted to other workers. Consequently, unions did not organize the agricultural industry. Moreover, in 1942, the federal government launched the bracero program to import farmworkers from Mexico. Many

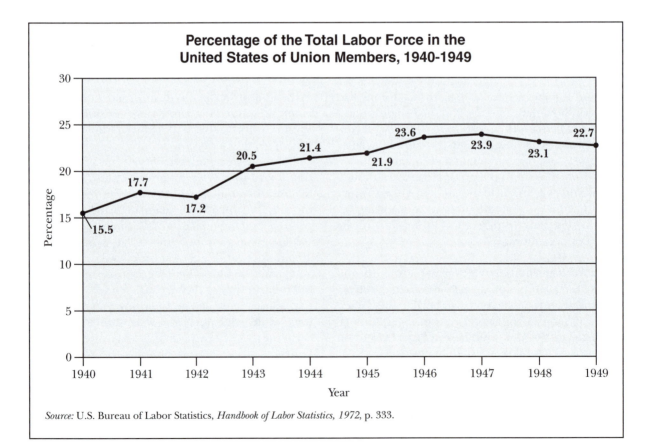

Percentage of the Total Labor Force in the United States of Union Members, 1940-1949

Source: U.S. Bureau of Labor Statistics, *Handbook of Labor Statistics, 1972,* p. 333.

Mexican Americans, both men and women, who left the fields to work in war industries became labor union members during the war years. After the war ended, however, women were sent back to their homes to become housekeepers again as returning veterans began taking over the jobs many women had successfully done during the war.

Postwar Changes Although most unions had agreed not to push for wage increases during the war years, many workers grew accustomed to big paychecks because they earned large amounts of overtime pay as wartime industries were operating beyond normal capacities. After the war ended, however, there was less overtime work, and the unions began pressing for the wage increases and better working conditions they had forsaken during the war. Labor unrest was soon stirring throughout the country, strikes began occurring in many industries. Union demands for wage increases were aggravated by postwar inflation, which was fueled by pent-up demand for consumer goods that had long been unavailable and the end of government price controls.

In 1947, labor strikes in the steel and auto industries prompted the new Republican-controlled Congress to enact the Taft-Hartley Act over President Truman's veto. Enactment of this legislation was a sign that labor unions were now being viewed as a threat to the nation's welfare, rather than as the bulwarks of patriotism they had been during the war. The Taft-Hartley Act was, in effect, an adjustment to the Wagner Act of 1935 that had given labor significant advantages. The new law authorized a number of union-busting tactics that had been used by businesses before 1935. For example, Taft-Hartley prohibited jurisdictional strikes in which unions used work stoppages to pressure employers to hire only union workers. It also prohibited secondary boycotts, in which unions supported other unions' demands by picketing or refusing to do work for businesses with which they themselves had no disputes. The law also outlawed both closed shops, which required employers to hire only union members, and union shops, in which new workers were required to join the unions. Another part of the law required unions to give sixty-day notices to businesses before undertaking strikes or other disruptive actions. Finally, and most significantly, Taft-Hartley authorized states to outlaw union security clauses by passing right-to-work laws. This played a significant role in suppressing union organizing in the Deep South and many midwestern and Rocky Mountain states, where right-to-work laws were dominant.

Impact The 1940's was probably the most significant in American labor history. The impact of the Wagner Act, which created the National Labor Relations Board and the Fair Labor Standards Act was felt most strongly during the 1940's. Competition between the AFL and CIO required their unions to make aggressive use of the union rights guaranteed under the New Deal laws. The onset of World War II also resulted in a dramatic increase in America's industrial effort after the bleak years of the Depression. Jobs were plentiful, patriotism was high, and unions played a crucial role in the nation's industrial war effort. This allowed unions to expand significantly in nearly all industries protected by the National Labor Relations Act.

Women and minorities also benefited by the job opportunities and union membership partially as a result of the creation of the Fair Employment Practices Commission as they moved from the Deep South and their barrios and rural hamlets to the industrial centers that were building planes, tanks, ships, and other war materials. During the decade unions reached a high of 35 percent of the labor force in the United States, a figure they would not see again through the rest of the century. By the end of the decade, however, there were signs and significant events such as the Congress's passage of the Taft-Hartley Act, which pointed to a decline in the strength of unions. A shift from manufacturing and heavy industries to a more global economy, which favored technology and services in the United States, also portended bleaker years for American unions.

Raymond J. Gonzales

Further Reading
Babson, Steve. *The Unfinished Struggle: Turning Points in American Labor, 1877-Present.* Lanham, Md.: Rowman & Littlefield, 1999. Concise and comprehensive history of the American labor movement.

Brooks, Thomas R. *Toil and Trouble: A History of American Labor.* 2d ed. New York: Delacorte Press, 1971. Colorful and opinionated prolabor account that is nevertheless both solid and informative.

Cutler, Jonathan. *Labor's Time: Shorter Hours, the*

UAW, and the Struggle for the American Unionism. Philadelphia: Temple University Press, 2004. Details the desires of the rank and file for a shorter work week, and the role of Reuther and the national UAW leadership in suppressing those demands.

Greene, Julie. *Pure and Simple Politics: The American Federation of Labor and Political Activism, 1881-1917.* New York: Cambridge University Press, 1998. Study of the American Federation of Labor shows the organization's attention to political activity and focuses on the dilemmas this approach posed for union members. Includes index.

Kersten, Andrew. *Labor's Home Front: The American Federation of Labor During World War II.* New York: New York University Press, 2006. Detailed examination of labor issues relating to race, gender, and work safety.

Lichtenstein, Nelson. *Labor's War at Home: The CIO in World War II.* New York: Cambridge University Press, 1982. Discusses the role and development of the Congress of Industrial Organizations, a federation of labor unions. Good summary chapters on both prewar and postwar periods.

Miller, Sally M., and Daniel A. Comford, eds. *American Labor in the Era of World War II.* San Francisco: Southwest Labor Studies Association, 1995. Collection of articles exploring the impact of World War II on the American labor movement from a variety of perspectives.

Moreno, Paul D. *Black Americans and Organized Labor: A New History.* Baton Rouge: Louisiana State University Press, 2006. History of African American employment and the relations between black workers and labor unions. Includes a chapter on the New Deal and World War II.

Wilcox, Clair. *Public Policies Toward Business.* 3d ed. Homewood, Ill.: Richard D. Irwin, 1966. Splendid analysis of the subject. Balances the interests and motives of government, business, and labor in regard to antitrust regulations. Includes table of cases.

See also American Federation of Labor; Business and the economy in the United States; Congress of Industrial Organizations; Fair Employment Practices Commission; Income and wages; Labor strikes; Taft-Hartley Act; Unemployment in the United States; *United Public Workers of America v. Mitchell*; War Production Board.

■ United Fruit Company

Identification American company with vast commercial interests in Central America
Date Established in 1899
Also known as United Brands Company (1970-1984); Chiquita Brands International (1984-   )

The United Fruit Company used its economic and political power to force concessions from the puppet governments of the developing countries in which it operated. Critics of its business practices coined the term "banana republics" to describe weak countries under the control of powerful American multinational companies.

The origins of the United Fruit Company go back to the establishment of a railway company in Costa Rica in 1871. An American businessman named Minor Keith planted banana trees along the side of the railroad tracks his company constructed and later introduced bananas to American and European consumers. Demand for bananas soared. In 1899, Keith merged his Tropical Trading and Transport Company with the Boston Fruit Company to form the United Fruit Company, which soon became the world's largest banana company. It was a vertical monopoly, controlling all the stages of producing its product and selling it to wholesalers. It eventually owned banana plantations throughout the Caribbean and Central America. Many of the plantations were adjacent to or very near the company's rail lines. These lines led to various ports where the bananas were loaded onto fleets of company-owned steamships for transport to consumer markets in the United States and Europe.

United Fruit Company's standard operating procedure was to seek out locations for banana plantations and rail lines in countries headed by dictators who were willing to grant the company extensive, long-term tax concessions and various monopolies in exchange for bribes. Thus, the United Fruit Company's executive personnel and its business interests became deeply entangled in early twentieth century political affairs in Central America. The company earned the nickname "the octopus" (*el pulpo*) because its tentacles of influence and control spread everywhere.

The United Fruit Company encouraged or forced governments to act in ways that favored the company, even at the government's own expense. On the other hand, it also provided an economic development engine, hired skilled workers at decent wages, and built medical and educational facilities for employees and their families. The company also developed research institutes to study tropical diseases that afflicted both people and bananas.

United Fruit Company faced a large, well-organized workers strike in Colombia in 1928. During the strike, the company was able to convince the government that the strike leaders were communists. The Colombian army fired upon unarmed workers, killing several thousand. Under harsh criticism, the Colombian government collapsed.

Operations in Guatemala Nowhere was the United Fruit Company more powerful than in Guatemala, where the company also had a monopoly on postal delivery for decades, owned much of the radio and telegraph system built alongside its rail lines, and controlled imports and exports at major ports. The company was exempt from paying most types of corporate income taxes and received favorable grants for huge tracts of agriculturally productive land. Land ownership in Central American countries was highly concentrated among a few wealthy families and companies, with little agriculturally productive land available for use by anyone else. Through its political and economic connections, the United Fruit Company owned thousands of acres of agriculturally productive land, some of which remained unused.

The problem of land use rights was particularly severe in Guatemala. Despite severe repression of political opposition, dictator Jorge Ubico Castañeda of Guatemala was overthrown in 1944. After a short period of rule by a military junta, Juan José Arévalo Bermej was elected president; he was succeeded by Jacobo Arbenz, who took power on March 15, 1951, after another democratic election. Both men promised widespread agrarian reform and the distribution of land to landless peasant farmers. The United Fruit Company might have lost as much as 40 percent of its holdings, but several former senior employees of the company held high positions in the U.S. State Department and convinced their colleagues that the proposed agrarian reforms were actually attempts by communists to gain popular support among poorer classes of people.

The United Fruit Company convinced the Dwight D. Eisenhower administration that the communists must be stopped, or American influence would be lost in all of Central America. The Central Intelligence Agency (CIA) orchestrated the military overthrow of President Arbenz's regime in 1954, ending democratic rule in Guatemala and setting the stage for two generations of civil war that lasted until 1996 and cost tens of thousands of lives.

Impact Although powerful companies such as the United Fruit Company provided a degree of economic development in poor countries, the level of corruption of politicians in those poor countries and the willingness of the U.S. government to disregard other countries' national sovereignty to protect American commercial interests led to abuses and conditions often unfavorable to the majority of the countries' citizens. Recognition of such problems led to more oversight and regulation of American companies, which are forbidden from offering any types of bribes or unauthorized payments when conducting business operations in foreign countries. The U.S. president cannot authorize the overthrow or invasion of other countries without explicit congressional approval, and only for demonstrated national security interests, not to protect commercial interests of American companies.

Victoria Erhart

Further reading

Bucheli, Marcelo. *Bananas and Business: The United Fruit Company in Colombia, 1899-2000.* New York: New York University Press, 2005. Covers all aspects of foreign business investment by the United Fruit Company. Concentrates primarily on the period of the 1930's and following, when labor unrest and growing nationalism throughout Central America and the Caribbean forced the United Fruit Company to change its policies and move its fields of operation.

Chapman, Peter. *Bananas: How the United Fruit Company Shaped the World.* New York: Canongate U.S., 2009. Provides a historical overview of the United Fruit Company; its political activities in countries where it did business; and its use of conspiracy, bribery, and violence to protect its own and larger U.S. interests in Central America.

Stiffler, Steve, ed. *Banana Wars: Power, Production, and History in the Americas.* Durham, N.C.: Duke University Press, 2003. Studies the banana industry with regard to Latin American and Caribbean labor and economic history. Analyzes political factors that permitted the United Fruit Company to acquire its extraordinary power.

See also Agriculture in the United States; Anticommunism; Food processing; Foreign policy of the United States; International trade; Labor strikes; Latin America; Latinos; Mexico.

■ United Nations

Identification International organization of member nations whose goals are world peace, international security, global economic development, social progress, and human rights

Date Charter ratified on October 24, 1945

Since its creation shortly after the end of World War II, the world's only globally representative international organization has worked to prevent new world wars by bringing nations together to resolve their differences peacefully. It has not achieved all its goals but has been a forum for diplomacy and for mediating and containing conflicts.

The idea of creating an international organization capable of controlling armed conflict dates back from at least the time of the Achaean League of the late fifth century B.C.E. Consequently, the immediate predecessor of the modern United Nations (U.N.), the League of Nations, which was created after World War I, was to the U.N. founders only the most recent and elaborate attempt to attain world peace. However, like its historical predecessors, the league failed in its endeavors, and the terrible costs of World War II in money, resources, and human lives made it clear that a more effective instrument for peacekeeping was needed. It is in the events during World War II, particularly in the diplomatic decisions reached by the war's eventual victors, that both the immediate origins of the United Nations and the choices that eventually handicapped its efforts to keep the peace are to be found.

Planning the United Nations The first attempt to create an international peacekeeping body occurred during formulation of the London Declaration of June 12, 1941, in which spokesmen for the countries then fighting against Nazi Germany announced their intentions to work with other free nations after the war to create a world without armed conflict. This sentiment was echoed in the Atlantic Charter of August, 1941, and expanded the following January, when representatives of twenty-six nations met in Washington, D.C., and adopted the Declaration of United Nations, in which the nations committed themselves to the creation of "a wider and permanent system of general security " after the war. The focus of that session, however, was on winning the war, and although the term "united nations" emerged in that gathering, and is credited to President Franklin D. Roosevelt, the term was clearly made in reference to those fighting against their common enemy, not as a suggestion for the name of a postwar international organization.

The shaping of such an international body began at the Moscow Conference in October, 1943, during which efforts to rebuild the League of Nations were abandoned. In its place, representatives of the United States, the Soviet Union, Great Britain, and China agreed in the Declaration of the Four Nations on General Security to establish, at the earliest practical date, a new international organization "for the maintenance of international peace and security" based on the principle of sovereign equality and open to all peace-loving states.

At the Tehran Conference of November 28-December 1, 1943, the "Big Three"—Roosevelt, British prime minister Winston Churchill, and Soviet leader Joseph Stalin—formally decided to create a new international body following the war. At the Dumbarton Oaks Conference, which convened in Washington, D.C., on August 21, 1944, delegates discussed the broad framework for the new agency. Representatives of the United States, the Soviet Union, Great Britain, and China decided that the organization would have both a General Assembly representing all member states—as had been a feature of the League of Nations—and an Executive Council charged with maintaining security, which was a part of the league. The sensitive issue of the voting system for this executive council was left to the decision of the Big Three, who were already scheduled to meet at Yalta in February, 1945.

Yalta was the last meeting of Churchill, Roosevelt, and Stalin. There, the principle of "great power unanimity" was accepted as the basis for making the Executive Council's security-related decisions. In addition, the troublesome issue of how many of the Soviet Union's supposedly autonomous republics would hold seats in the General Assembly was resolved when Stalin agreed to separate representation for only Ukraine and Belorussia. The remainder of the details and the initial drafting of the Charter of the United Nations was then left to the

Charter Members of the United Nations in 1945

Charter member nations are shaded

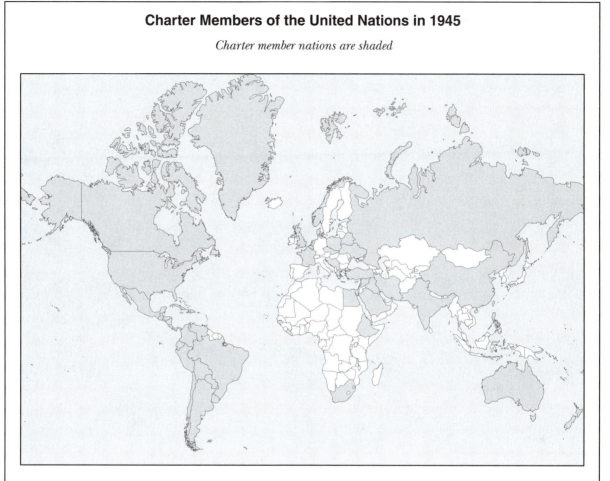

Argentina	Dominican Republic	Liberia	South Africa
Australia	Ecuador	Luxembourg	Syria
Belarus	Egypt	Mexico	Turkey
Belgium	El Salvador	Netherlands	Ukraine
Bolivia	Ethiopia	New Zealand	United States
Brazil	France	Nicaragua	United Kingdom of
Canada	Greece	Norway	Great Britain and
Chile	Guatemala	Panama	Northern Ireland
China	Haiti	Paraguay	Uruguay
Colombia	Honduras	Peru	Venezuela
Costa Rica	India	Philippines	Yugoslavia
Cuba	Iran	Poland	
Czechoslovakia	Iraq	Russia	
Denmark	Lebanon	Saudi Arabia	

Notes: Belarus, Russia, and Ukraine were all members of the Soviet Union in 1945. Czechoslovakia is a former U.N. member; Czech Republic and Slovakia, separate countries created from the dissolution of Czechoslovakia, became members in 1993. Yugoslavia is a former U.N. member. The countries formed from its dissolution—Bosnia and Herzegovina, Croatia, and Slovenia (1992); Macedonia (1993); Serbia and Montenegro (2000)—were all readmitted in the years indicated parenthetically. The Philippines was an American commonwealth in 1945, gaining independence the following year.

Workers setting the cornerstone of the United Nations Building in place on October 25, 1949, shortly before the building's formal dedication ceremony. The stone's simple inscription bears the name of the organization in the five official U.N. languages—English, French, Chinese, Russian, and Spanish. A sixth official language, Arabic, would be added in 1973. (Getty Images)

delegates scheduled to convene in San Francisco on April 25, 1945. China and France were also invited to attend as sponsoring governments.

Improving on the League of Nations   At its core, the United Nations was designed to be an effective instrument of collective security capable of deterring war by confronting member states bent on aggression with the collective response of the international community. As such, it was meant to be a second-generation improvement over the League of Nations, which President Woodrow Wilson had proposed after World War I. The U.N. founders made a studied effort to correct the defects that were widely believed to have caused the league's failure.

To most of the its critics, the primary weakness of the League of Nations had been its lack of an effec-

tive enforcement mechanism. It could only recommend that member states apply economic sanctions against aggressor states. Consequently, the compliance of member states was often weak or nonexistent. Moreover, even if members had complied wholeheartedly with league recommendations, there was little reason to believe that the threat of economic sanctions would have dissuaded Japan, Germany, or Italy from pursuing the aggressive agendas that led to World War II. Hence, it was not the U.N. General Assembly that would become the heart of the United Nations but its Security Council, which had no parallel in the league. Under the U.N. charter, the Security Council not only has the power to authorize U.N. members to militarily enforce its resolutions but also can create an international military force under its own command.

In the opinion of the U.N. founders, the League of Nations was also weakened by not having as members certain nations—most notably the United States and the Soviet Union—that played significant roles in international relations. Collective security organizations are intended to be inward-looking structures with universal membership, enforcing their mandates to maintain the peace on their member states. The League of Nations was never able to do this because some nations either failed to join or dropped out at crucial moments. The creators of the United Nations wanted to avoid this situation and were willing to pay a high price to do so. To assure their participation, the United States, Great Britain, France, the Soviet Union, and China were given permanent seats on the Security Council and the power to veto council actions that they perceived as threats to their national interests. The hope was that these countries' wartime alliance would continue in the postwar world. However, the logic here was clear: There would be no reason for these states to stay out of the United Nations and risk it being used against them when, by joining, they could prevent this from happening.

The structure of the League of Nations also failed to account adequately for the link between economic and social conditions and warfare. In a sense, the league was backward-looking, diagnosing World War I as the man-made product of poor leadership and the implementation of secret treaties of mutual assistance. Open diplomacy in the league's assembly was meant to counter that threat, but the league had no response to the effects of the Great Depression on world populations, some of which were willing to turn to radical leaders, like Adolf Hitler, to save them when unemployment rates soared into the 60 percent range. With this in mind, the architects of the United Nations created a permanent Economic and Social Council charged with the tasks of monitoring and easing socioeconomic conditions likely to lead to conflict and of calling the Security Council's attention to such conditions.

Finally, the league was seen as fatally flawed because of its identity with the outcome of World War I, and a significant effort was made to divorce the creation of the United Nations from the outcome of World War II. The league's constitution was a part of the Treaty of Versailles, which officially ended World War I, and the losers of that war were required to join the organization. Consequently, states like Germany

had little reason to view their membership as a legitimate product of their free will. The founders of the United Nations were determined not to repeat this error, which is perhaps the best explanation for why the Charter of the United Nations lacked any backup plan for effective action should the Security Council become paralyzed by vetoes, because when the San Francisco conference was scheduled, it was believed that the end of the war, at least in the Pacific, was still years in the future.

To the contrary, by the time delegates from fifty countries gathered in San Francisco on April 25, 1945, the Soviet army had already reached Berlin, and the war in Europe was all but over; it would officially end on May 8. Moreover, the United States believed it already had the capacity to construct an atomic bomb, which would quickly force Japan to accept unconditional surrender, as it did on August 14, five days after the second atomic bomb was dropped on Japan. In these rapidly changing circumstances, the delegates had to work hard to get a final draft of the charter completed on a less leisurely timetable, and the charter probably failed to contain all of the details needed to create the new organization.

Impact Less than two years after the ratification of the Charter of the United Nations in October, 1945, the wartime collaboration of the United States and the Soviet Union against the fascist regimes of Germany and Italy in World War II had evolved into a Cold War, in which U.S. foreign policy was increasingly devoted to containing further Soviet expansion. One of the first political casualties of this war was the Security Council's ability to respond effectively to many conflicts because of the competing interests of these two superpowers.

It was thus not until the end of the Cold War, and more than forty years after the founding of the United Nations, that the Security Council was able to undertake its first enforcement action; in the late summer of 1990, the United Nations authorized the use of a multinational military force under the command of a United States general to enforce United Nations resolutions demanding the withdrawal of the Iraqi army that had occupied neighboring Kuwait. However, long before that time, the United Nations had become a useful instrument in other areas of the world, where it managed conflict under the guiding hands of a series of U.N. secretary generals, who negotiated cease-fire agreements between warring parties and organized small peacekeeping forces to patrol cease-fire zones and otherwise help maintain a fragile peace. Similarly, political conflicts have often been conducted in a war of words in the Security Council or General Assembly rather than a conflict of arms on a distant battlefield, providing innumerable justifications for the existence of the United Nations, even if it has yet to become the collective security organization its founders envisioned in 1945.

Joseph R. Rudolph, Jr.

Further Reading

Forsythe, David P., and Roger A. Coat. *The United Nations and Changing World Politics.* Boulder, Colo.: Westview Press, 2001. Excellent for follow-up research on the United Nations as an instrument of collective security.

Meisler, Stanley. *United Nations: The First Fifty Years.* Eagan, Minn.: West, 1997. A useful survey analysis of the principal U.N. accomplishments and pitfalls in living up to the mandate of its charter during its first half century of existence.

Mingst, Karen A., and Margaret P. Karns. *The United Nations in the Twenty-first Century.* 3d ed. Boulder, Colo.: Westview Press, 2007. Highly recommended introductory reading on both the birth, evolution, and performance of the United Nations, measured against the visions of its creators.

Thakur, Ramesh. *The United Nations: Peace and Security from Collective Security to the Responsibility to Protect.* Cambridge, England: Cambridge University Press, 2006. Good for advanced research on how the United Nations has actually functioned since its creation as a collective security organization. Includes an excellent analysis of the current body's need for reform and of the obstacles deterring this process.

United States Delegation to the United Nations Conference on International Organization, San Francisco, 1945. *Charter of the United Nations: Report to the President on the Results of the San Francisco Conference by the Chairman of the United States Delegation, the Secretary of State.* Washington, D.C.: Government Printing Office, 1945. The official U.S. government report on the San Francisco Conference, generally available in university research libraries.

United States Department of State. *The United Nations Conference on International Organization, San Francisco, California, April 25 to June 26, 1945.* Washington, D.C.: Government Printing Office, 1946. The most readily available and perhaps the most voluminous collection of documents and speeches published at the time the United Nations was created.

See also Atlantic Charter; Cairo Conference; Foreign policy of the United States; International Court of Justice; Isolationism; North Atlantic Treaty Organization; UNICEF; Yalta Conference.

United Nations International Children's Emergency Fund. *See* **UNICEF**

United Nations Monetary and Financial Conference. *See* **Bretton Woods Conference**

■ **United Public Workers of America v. Mitchell**

The Case U.S. Supreme Court ruling on federal employees' partisan political activities
Date Decided on February 10, 1947

The Supreme Court's decision in this case upheld the constitutionality of the controversial 1939 Hatch Act, which had generally outlawed federal executive branch employees from taking part in partisan political activities.

In 1939, the U.S. Congress passed the Hatch Act in response to concerns that the political spoils system of the late nineteenth and early twentieth centuries had compromised the integrity and efficiency of the federal bureaucracy by encouraging government office holders to become mixed up with partisan politics. The Hatch Act was designed to ensure that the jobs of federal employees would depend solely upon their qualifications and performance, and not upon their partisan political connections. To that end, the act forbade executive branch officers and employees from exercising their freedom of speech by publicly endorsing candidates and engaging in political campaigning.

The plaintiff who was granted standing in *United Public Workers of America v. Mitchell* argued that the Hatch Act's restrictions violated his First Amendment rights to free speech. A plurality of the Court upheld the act by a vote of four to three. Justice Stanley F. Reed's opinion found that Congress was reasonably protecting the integrity of the executive branch and not unjustifiably stripping federal employees of their rights. He concluded that First Amendment rights may be subject to limitation because of the "elemental need for order without which the guarantees of civil rights to others would be a mockery." Several justices wrote dissents arguing that governmental efficiency and neutrality should not prevail over the constitutional rights of individual citizens who happen to be government employees.

Impact The act's restrictions continued in force, with revisions, until President Bill Clinton signed legislation in 1993 that removed much of the act's original force, except for certain senior-level officials. However, since 1947, many states have adopted their own laws restricting the involvement of government employees in partisan politics.

W. Jesse Weins

Further Reading

Gely, Rafael, and Timothy Chandler. "Restricting Public Employees' Political Activities: Good Government or Partisan Politics?" *Houston Law Review* 37, no. 3 (Fall, 2000): 775-822.

Lewis, Thomas Tandy, ed. *U.S. Court Cases*. Rev. ed. 3 vols. Pasadena, Calif.: Salem Press, 2011.

Wormuth, Francis D. "The Hatch Act Cases." *Western Political Quarterly* 1, no. 2 (1948): 165-173.

See also American Federation of Labor; Congress of Industrial Organizations; Labor strikes; Supreme Court, U.S.

■ United Service Organizations

Identification Volunteer organization founded to provide entertainment to American military personnel

Also known as USO Clubs

Date Established on February 4, 1941

Founded to help raise the morale of the expanding American armed forces, the United Service Organizations played a large role in providing service personnel with wholesome recreation and entertainment in clubs throughout the *United States and in providing high-quality entertainment to combat troops stationed around the world.*

On February 4, 1941, President Franklin D. Roosevelt announced the formation of the United Service Organizations (USO), a civilian volunteer organization created to support the morale of U.S. military personnel. With war clouds on the horizon, the mobilization of many National Guard units for one year in 1940, and the expansion of American military forces, Roosevelt and General George C. Marshall saw the need to provide wholesome, morale-sustaining activities for the armed forces. The Young Men's Christian Association (YMCA), Young Women's Christian Association (YWCA), National Catholic Community Service, National Travelers Aid Association, Salvation Army, and National Jewish Welfare Board came together to form the USO to provide "a home away from home" for the military. With a small paid staff, the USO relied on volunteer workers and public funding. By the end of World War II in 1945 it was one of the best known of all volunteer patriotic organizations in the United States.

Avoiding Past Mistakes Roosevelt and Marshall remembered the chaos and confusion that surrounded efforts to provide for the troops of World War I. There was no central volunteer organization in the United States or France on which members of the military could depend except for the Red Cross, whose traditional mission was providing wounded and convalescing soldiers with comfort items such as reading material, writing paper, cigarettes, and candy. General John J. Pershing, commander of U.S. troops in France, confused the issue when he refused to allow groups such as the YMCA to distribute comfort items free of charge. His reasoning was basically that American troops should not be the recipients of charity. Perhaps unwisely, the YMCA then agreed to sell candies, cigarettes, and cakes to the troops. After many soldiers had not been paid in months, organizations such as the YMCA and Salvation Army gave away what small stores they had, despite Pershing's directive. Meanwhile, damage had already been done to the YMCA's reputation, and many soldiers carried with them bad memories of "that damned Y." It was important that the mistakes of World War I not be repeated.

Opening of USO Centers Before the attack on Pearl Harbor in December, 1941, and American entry into World War II, USO centers opened with volunteers serving sandwiches, soft drinks, doughnuts, and coffee free to the troops. No alcoholic beverages were served, but free cigarettes were distributed. From the opening of the first USO center in Louisiana in 1941 to the end of the war in 1945, the USO maintained a reputation for wholesome entertainment, an alternative to the bars and prostitutes that infested towns near training centers.

The USO provided chaperoned dances for troops. Local young women who attended these dances were carefully screened by USO volunteers, as were the volunteer hostesses themselves. Soldiers and sailors who appeared intoxicated when they arrived at USO centers were denied entrance. The strict moral code adopted by the USO attracted many to participate in its activities. Nevertheless, problems arose that the founders of the USO had not envisioned. For example, because military units were racially segregated, most USO clubs were also racially segregated during the war. A few USO clubs tried to breach the race barrier, and African American women funded a few USO clubs for soldiers and sailors of color.

As the war grew in intensity, the number of women joining the services increased. The great question for the USO was whether these women in the uniform of their country would get the same treatment as their male counterparts. Many of the USO club directors tried to restrict their clubs to male service personnel. Their argument was basically that the young women acting as hostesses or as dancing partners were carefully screened and chaperoned. Women in uniform were not. As the role of women in the services grew more vital to the war effort service, women gained more acceptance.

The success of the USO depended on public funding. The USO could purchase many items for clubs on a tax-free basis, but it was also subject to wartime rationing. Several major fund drives for the USO were headed by famous persons such as the dynamic New York prosecutor Thomas E. Dewey and noted businessman Prescott Bush.

USO Touring Shows   When historians look at wartime letters from service personnel they find constant references to USO shows that toured the United States and the theaters of war. Many well-known Hollywood and New York entertainers joined with the USO to bring entertainment to the troops. Performers such as Bing Crosby, the Andrews Sisters, Frank Sinatra, Al Jolson, and Jack Benny traveled to every area where American troops were fighting. The largest crowds of soldiers and sailors attended the variety show hosted by famous comedian and film star Bob Hope. By the end of World War II, the USO had presented hundreds of thousands of shows. The USO had also provided entertainment in military hospitals in Europe and Asia. There was a constant flow of famous show business personalities to the hospital wards. Many of those performers recalled that these visits to the wounded were the most emotional, but rewarding experience of their service with the USO.

By 1942, the USO established its first overseas department with the objective of providing the "home away from home" for those military personnel serving in vari-

Sixteen-year-old film star Shirley Temple serving cookies to servicemen at the USO's Hollywood Canteen in August, 1944. (AP/Wide World Photos)

ous theaters of operations. By the end of the war, three thousand USO centers were operating around the world, some of the largest being in England and Australia. One and one-half million volunteers served in the USO in the United States and overseas. As American troops returned from overseas service the number of USO centers diminished, and as troops demobilized and went home the USO closed many centers in the United States.

Because the USO relied on the generosity of American donors, the end of World War II saw a decrease in contributions. The USO was not a governmental agency and therefore could not rely on funding by the Congress of the United States. In 1947 the USO was disbanded, due in great measure to the end of public funding. It had accomplished its mission of providing for American military personnel during the war. Its reputation was high, and discharged service personnel looked back favorably on their experiences with the organization.

Impact The United Service Organizations might be regarded as a nearly unqualified success in providing wholesome recreation and entertainment for American military personnel and boosting their morale. After it was disbanded, a void was soon felt in the needs of service personnel. After the Korean War began in 1950, World War II leaders such as George C. Marshall called for a revitalization of the USO to serve Army, Navy, and Air Force personnel around the world. The USO then resumed its work, which it has continued into the twenty-first century.

James J. Cooke

Further Reading

Caron, Julia. *Home Away from Home: The Story of the USO.* New York: Harper & Brothers, 1946. Sympathetic treatment of the USO written shortly after the conclusion of World War II.

Holsinger, M. Paul. *War and Popular Culture.* Westport, Conn.: Greenwood Press, 1999. Broad, thoughtful exploration of the complex interrelationships between personnel involved in military conflicts and entertainment.

Holsinger, M. Paul, and Mary Anne Scholfield. *World War II in Popular Literature and Culture.* Madison, Wis.: Popular Press, 1992. Another study of the interplay between military conflicts and popular culture, this time focusing on World War II.

Yellin, Emily. *Our Mothers' War: American Women at Home and at the Front During World War II.* New York: Free Press, 2005. Journalist's account of the diverse roles that American women played during World War II, including doing volunteer work for the USO.

See also   Andrews Sisters; Baseball; Bogart, Humphrey; Dewey, Thomas E.; Hope, Bob; Miller, Glenn; Recreation.

■ United States v. Aluminum Company of America

The Case   Federal appeals court ruling on antitrust law

Date   Decided on March 12, 1945

In this decision, the U.S. Court of Appeals for the Second Circuit ruled that Alcoa had violated the Sherman Antitrust Act, establishing the legal principle that large market share alone justified antitrust prosecution.

In *United States v. Aluminum Company of America,* a federal appeals court upheld the federal government's conviction of the Aluminum Company for violating provisions of the Sherman Antitrust Act of 1890. The U.S. Department of Justice had been mandated to investigate and pursue investigations and prosecute antitrust violations when the cases warranted suits. The Sherman Antitrust Act, which had been enacted during the late nineteenth century era of predatory robber barons, was designed to counter "willful and wanton" efforts to monopolize by combinations of legal entities that were potentially harmful to the public. The Aluminum Company of America had to prove its good intention and fealty to the law.

The company's defense attorneys argued circuitously. The company, they claimed, was the largest in its industry because it could offer more and better products at cheaper prices. Its capture of the bulk of the aluminum market was a result of its good management, not because of a conspiracy. Enforcement of the Sherman Antitrust Act is the prevention of dominance in the public sector by one business organization. The "arbitrary and artificial" raising of prices would trip the wire of investigation. The Sherman Antitrust Act's intent was to deal with unfair conduct that had the potential of destroying competition within industries. However, the language and standards are only words having a subjective interpretation even though the law attempts to set objective standards.

Governmental evidence standards required the defendant, the Aluminum Company of America, to prove its innocence by meeting several tests. The first, the "per se" violation, standard required the company to prove it did not attain its position of prominence. Because it was unable to do so, it was, by that very fact, guilty as charged. The other standard was the "rule of reason" test. This test is similar to the reasonable man test in civil cases in which defendants are required to prove what is reasonable. Because that test is also subjective and because everyone may define "reasonableness" a little differently, it may be impossible to convict on these standards. In this case, it appears that the judges may have made their judgment simply because they determined that society must be protected against monopolies of any sort. Justice Learned Hand challenged the court's majority view in his separate opinion.

Impact   Although the federal court agreed that the Aluminum Company of America had not committed predatory acts or engaged in anticompetitive practices, it nevertheless convicted the company of violating the Sherman Act on the basis of its large market share. This important ruling thereby established the principle that large market share alone justified antitrust prosecution.

Arthur Steinberg

Further Reading

Adams, Walter. "The Aluminum Case: Legal Victory—Economic Defeat." *American Economic Review* 41 (December, 1951): 915-922.

Areeda, Phillip, Louis Kaplow, and Aaron Edlin. *Antitrust Analysis: Problems, Text, Cases.* 6th ed. New York: Aspen, 2004.

Hylton, Keith N. *Antitrust Law: Economic Theory and Common Law Evolution.* New York: Cambridge University Press, 2003.

Smith, George David. *From Monopoly to Competition: The Transformation of Alcoa, 1888-1986.* New York: Cambridge University Press, 1988.

See also   Business and the economy in the United States; International Business Machines Corporation; Kaiser, Henry J.; Supreme Court, U.S.; Telephone technology and service.

■ United States v. Darby Lumber Co.

The Case   U.S. Supreme Court ruling that upheld the Fair Labor Standards Act of 1938
Date   Decided on February 3, 1941

This ruling was one of a set of favorable Supreme Court decisions issued between 1937 and 1942 on the constitutionality of President Franklin D. Roosevelt's New Deal programs. It helped establish the legal basis for expanded power of the federal government.

President Franklin D. Roosevelt and the Democrats in Congress pursued aggressive reform programs that centralized federal government control over virtually every aspect of commercial activity. The package of programs, known as the New Deal, faced stiff resistance from economic traditionalists on the Supreme Court who believed strongly in free market capitalism. During the 1930's, the Court, dominated by justices who believed that the Constitution simply did not permit the federal government to regulate private business on matters such as wages and working conditions, struck down many New Deal laws as unconstitutional. By 1941, however, Roosevelt had appointed eight justices to the Supreme Court, all of whom were sympathetic to the view that it was in the national interest that the federal government exercise greater control over economic activity. Their unanimous ruling in *United States v. Darby Lumber Co.* upheld the Fair Labor Standards Act requirements that employers abide by minimum wage and maximum hour rules set by the federal Department of Labor. Employers who defied the rules were prohibited from transporting their products across state lines.

Impact   This ruling provided the constitutional basis for Congress's power to enact wide-ranging laws to protect the health, safety, and morals of citizens in any activity that affected interstate commerce. It was one of a set of Supreme Court rulings during the 1940's that led to a significant expansion of federal authority into areas traditionally subject only to state regulation.

Philip R. Zampini

Further Reading

Rossum, Ralph A., and G. Alan Tarr. *American Constitutional Law.* Vol. 1, *The Structure of Government.* 8th ed. Belmont, Calif.: Thomson/Wadsworth, 2009.

White, G. Edward. *The Constitution and the New Deal.* Cambridge, Mass.: Harvard University Press, 2000.

See also   Congress, U.S.; Economic wartime regulations; New Deal programs; Roosevelt, Franklin D.; Supreme Court, U.S.; Unemployment in the United States; *Wickard v. Filburn.*

■ United States v. Paramount Pictures, et al.

The Case   U.S. Supreme Court case dealing with movie studio monopolies
Also known as   Hollywood Antitrust Case of 1948; *Paramount Case*
Date   Decided on May 3, 1948

In this case, the Supreme Court ordered eight major Hollywood studios to end monopolistic business practices, thereby ending the traditional studio system and changing the nature of motion-picture production. The ruling ended nearly ten years of ongoing legal action brought against Paramount Pictures by the Justice Department.

During the 1930's and 1940's, major film studios engaged in potentially anticompetitive practices such as "block booking," the practice of forcing theaters to order multiple films, and often owned entire chains of local movie theaters linked to the studios. The linkages between studios and theaters meant that certain houses could show only films produced by certain studios.

As the Great Depression wound down, President Franklin D. Roosevelt ordered the Justice Department to resume its antimonopoly proceedings against Paramount and other powerful Hollywood studios. As independent producers such as Walt Disney gained power in Hollywood, they exerted trust-busting pressure against major studios. By 1948, the case had reached the Supreme Court, where, in a 7-1 decision written by William O. Douglas, justices ordered studios to end block booking and divest themselves of ownership of linked theater chains.

Impact   The decision ended the traditional studio system and allowed independent producers such as Walt Disney more opportunity to develop and distribute their pictures. Many studios also took the opportunity to enter television production. Divestiture

meant that studios could no longer monopolize what pictures would be shown in a given town. Finally, ending block booking meant that film quality improved since studios became more selective in what movies they released for distribution.

Shawn Selby

Further Reading
Gomery, Douglas. *The Hollywood Studio System: A History.* London: British Film Institute, 2005.
Schatz, Thomas. *The Genius of the System: Hollywood Filmmaking in the Studio Era.* New York: Henry Holt, 1996.

See also   Disney films; Film in the United States; Supreme Court, U.S.; Television.

■ United States v. United Mine Workers

The Case   U.S. Supreme Court ruling on injunctions to end labor strikes
Date   Decided on March 6, 1947

The Supreme Court's ruling in this case permitted federal courts to issue injunctions to prevent strikes when the government was the employer.

As early as 1877, railroad companies obtained injunctions from federal courts to restrain their workers from striking. The use of injunctions for such a purpose was initially upheld by the Supreme Court but eventually fell into disfavor. The U.S. Congress addressed the problem by enacting the Clayton Antitrust Act in 1914 and the Norris-LaGuardia Act in 1932.

In May, 1946, the U.S. government seized control of most of the nation's coal mines when a labor strike threatened to shut down production of the vitally needed fuel. When negotiations for a new contract collapsed the following year, the miners went on strike in defiance of an injunction issued by a federal court. Both the union and John L. Lewis, the United Mine Workers (UMW) president, were held in civil and criminal contempt. Lewis was fined only $10,000, but the UMW was assessed $3.5 million—the largest fine in American history up to that time.

Because the continuation of the strike would have meant an economic breakdown and substantial hardships to the public, the Supreme Court accepted the case. A majority of its members held that the miners became employees of the federal government by virtue of the seizure of the mines and that the Norris-LaGuardia procedures did not apply to cases involving the government and its employees.

Impact In the *United States v. United Mine Workers*, the Supreme Court set a precedent for labor disputes by creating a distinction between government employees and private-industry employees. As a result, federal courts may issue injunctions to prevent strikes of government employees.

Susan Coleman

Further Reading

Cardon, R. L., R. O. Hancox, and P. F. Westbrook, Jr. "Injunction: United States v. United Mine Workers of America." *Michigan Law Review* 45, no. 4 (1947): 469-510.

Frank, John P. "United States Supreme Court: 1946-47." *Chicago Law Review* 15, no. 1 (1947): 1-50.

Levy, Leonard Williams, Kenneth L. Karst, and Adam Winkler. *Encyclopedia of the American Constitution.* 2d ed. New York: Macmillan Reference, 2000.

See also Business and the economy in the United States; Labor strikes; Lewis, John L.; Supreme Court, U.S.; Truman, Harry S.; Unionism.

■ Universal Declaration of Human Rights

The Event Ratification of the first comprehensive document of international human rights norms

Date December 10, 1948

Place New York, New York

This document was a global response to the sufferings and atrocities, such as the Holocaust, perpetrated by governments and regimes against individuals and peoples. The declaration established as fundamental the concept of human rights—that is, rights pertaining to persons as humans and not merely as citizens of a particular country—and shaped later international law and treaties on that basis.

The Universal Declaration of Human Rights (UDHR) was an immediate outcome of the creation of the United Nations. Although the UDHR was not ratified until the end of 1948, three years after the formation of the United Nations, work on this declaration began with the drafting of the Charter of the United Nations in 1945, particularly with the establishment of the U.N. Commission on Human Rights in 1946, and a mandate by the U.N. General Assembly to draft an international bill of rights. Social and political theorists had long spoken of the concept of natural rights to designate rights that individuals held simply as individuals, as opposed to the concept of legal rights that individuals held as citizens within some legal system. However, it was not until the middle of the twentieth century, following the Nuremberg and Tokyo war trials, that there was an international political push to foster and implement rights in a more global context. The language of natural rights quickly transformed into that of human rights—rights possessed by all humans regardless of their citizenship, with a corresponding assertion of the responsibility of international respect and enforcement of these rights.

The Commission on Human Rights comprised notable representatives from various nations, including the United States, Canada, Australia, the United Kingdom, the Soviet Union, Yugoslavia, France, China, India, Lebanon, Iran, Panama, Uruguay, Chile, and the Philippines. Eleanor Roosevelt, then widow of former U.S. president Franklin D. Roosevelt, was unanimously elected to chair the commission, as she had already attained world renown for her earlier work on civil rights. With particular focus on social and political matters within the United States, Roosevelt saw this advocacy for human rights as relevant to overcoming racial discrimination in her own country.

The UDHR contained thirty articles, some considered controversial. Many of the articles emphasized political rights, such as the rights of life, liberty, security, freedom from torture, and equality before the law. The final ten articles, however, emphasized social and economic rights, such as rights to education, employment, equal pay, and participation in cultural and scientific advances. Such rights were not previously enunciated by earlier rights documents, including within the United States. On December 10, 1948, the U.N. General Assembly ratified the declaration by a vote of 48 in favor, 0 against, and 8 abstentions.

Impact Following ratification of the UDHR, the U.N. General Assembly passed numerous other doc-

Universal Human Rights

The U.N. Universal Declaration of Human Rights specifically proclaimed that all persons have rights against discrimination. The U.N.'s list of rights includes the following:

- life
- liberty and security of person
- protection against slavery
- protection against torture and cruel and inhuman punishment
- recognition as a person before the law
- equal protection of the law
- access to legal remedies for violations of rights
- protection against arbitrary arrest, detention, or exile
- independent and impartial judiciary
- presumption of innocence
- protection against ex post facto laws
- protection of privacy, family, and home
- freedom of movement and residence
- asylum from persecution
- freedom from discrimination because of nationality
- marriage and family
- property
- freedom of thought, conscience, and religion
- freedom of opinion, expression, and the press
- freedom of assembly and association
- political participation
- social security
- work under favorable conditions
- free trade unions
- rest and leisure
- food, clothing, and housing
- health care and social services
- special protections for children
- education
- participation in cultural life
- social and international order needed to realize these rights

uments promoting and extending human rights, as did many other governmental and nongovernmental bodies. The UDHR itself came to be known as the first component of the International Bill of Human Rights, with later components being the International Covenant on Civil and Political Rights and the International Covenant on Economic, Social, and Cultural Rights, both passed in 1966. Later human rights declarations included the Convention on the Elimination of All Forms of Discrimination Against Women (1979), the African Charter on Human and Peoples' Rights (1981), and the Cairo Declaration on Human Rights in Islam (1990).

David Boersema

Further Reading

Glendon, Mary Ann. *A World Made New: Eleanor Roosevelt and the Universal Declaration of Human Rights.* New York: Random House, 2001.

Morsink, Johannes. *The Universal Declaration of Human Rights: Origins, Drafting, and Intent.* Philadelphia: University of Pennsylvania Press, 1999.

Streich, Michel. *Universal Declaration of Human Rights.* San Francisco: MacAdam/Cage, 2009.

See also   Civil rights and liberties; Convention on the Prevention and Punishment of the Crime of Genocide; "Four Freedoms" speech; International League for the Rights of Man; Roosevelt, Eleanor; United Nations.

■ Urbanization in Canada

Long a predominantly agricultural country, Canada was slower to urbanize than the United States. By the start of the 1940's, however, more than one-half the country's people were living in cities. The trend toward greater urbanization accelerated during the decade, prompted first by the industrial demands of World War II and later by increased mechanization of agriculture and Canada's postwar economic boom.

By 1940, more than 50 percent of all Canadians lived in cities. The process of urbanization had been gradual over the years, and it had the effect of counterbalancing the predominance of male residents in the Canadian population overall, a predominance that reflected the larger numbers of men in rural areas, where they constituted the bulk of the agricul-

Montreal Street in Montreal, Canada's largest city, in 1946. (Getty Images)

By the late 1940's, many Canadian cities had created substantial suburbs, so that Canadian statistics separated central cities from their "greater" urban areas. Montreal was already the country's largest urban center in 1941, but "metro" Montreal was the largest conurbation in the country with more than one million inhabitants. Toronto, although smaller than Montreal, was the second-largest city in Canada in 1941.

A major factor in Canada's increasing urbanization was the growing mechanization of agriculture. This process had begun before the beginning of World War II, but it proceeded at an accelerated pace after the war ended, as industrial production was freed to manufacture larger tractors and combines that took over agricultural production. As more farmers possessed these machines, they were less dependent on human workers, who then moved to the cities for employment.

Impact Although urbanization could be expected to occur in Canada's industrial centers such as Hamilton and Windsor in Ontario, it also occurred in the cities on the plains. In Manitoba, for example, the rural population still exceeded the urban population in 1941. By 1951, however, Manitoba's urban population exceeded its rural population by more than 100,000 individuals. The process of ur-

tural labor force. In contrast, women outnumbered men in urban populations.

During the 1940's, the urban predominance in Canada's overall population continued to expand. During the first half of the decade, while Canada was involved in World War II, the nation's entire focus was on expanding the production of war materials, most of which were concentrated at manufacturing plants located in the cities. The Wartime Housing Act of 1941, specifically aimed at the creation of housing needed for war workers, increased the residential facilities in the vicinity of those industries producing war material. During the second half of the decade, when Canada was busy refocusing its economy on production for consumers, the growth of cities was continued.

Urban and Rural Population in Canada, 1901-1951

Year	Total Canadian Population	Urban Population (in percent)	Rural Population (in percent)
1901	5,418,663	37	63
1911	7,221,662	45	55
1921	8,800,249	49	51
1931	10,376,379	54	46
1941	11,506,655	54	46
1951	14,009,429	62	38

Source: Statistics Canada (Stat Can).

banization moved more slowly in Saskatchewan and Alberta. In the latter province, it would not be until 1961 that the urban population exceeded the rural, and the tip-over point did not occur in Saskatchewan until 1971. However, by 1961 in the prairie provinces overall, the urban populace was greater than the rural. The process of urbanization was irresistible in the nation in the years after World War II.

Nancy M. Gordon

Further Reading

Fallick, Arthur L., and H. Peter Oberlander. *Housing a Nation: The Evolution of Canadian Housing Policy.* Ottawa: Canadian Mortgage and Housing Corporation, 1992.

Iacovetta, Franca, with Paula Draper and Robert Ventresca, eds. *A Nation of Immigrants: Readings in Canadian History, 1840s-1960s.* Toronto: University of Toronto Press, 2006.

Kalbach, W. E., and W. McVey. *The Demographic Basis of Canadian Society.* 2d ed. Toronto: McGraw-Hill Ryerson, 1979.

A National Affordable Housing Strategy. Ottawa: Federation of Canadian Municipalities, 2000.

See also Business and the economy in Canada; Canadian minority communities; Canadian regionalism; Demographics of Canada; Housing in Canada; Immigration to Canada; Unemployment in Canada; Urbanization in the United States.

■ Urbanization in the United States

The patterns of urban regional growth and movement out of the American central cities during the 1940's were direct results of limited economic recovery as the Great Depression wound down, the economic mobilization for war that followed, and demobilization following Allied victory in 1945. Deterioration of housing and other infrastructure, continued in-migration of racial minorities, and suburban development spurred unprecedented city and regional planning and the early stages of federal intervention.

American cities and urban regions suffered greatly during the decades of the Great Depression. At the same time that capital for development dried up, rural people flocked to cities in search of jobs or aid. The flight of both the relatively wealthy and jobs from the central cities to the periphery—exurban and suburban rings around most cities—began in earnest as the automobile continued to provide mobility for those who could afford it. The 1940 U.S. Census registered population losses during the last ten years for more than 20 percent of America's inner cities.

Civic leaders, both political and economic, began processes of planning to address the negative effects of these trends, counting on federal aid, the precedent for which had been amply provided for during the previous decade. The spring of 1940, however, saw the German invasion of Western Europe and the threat to England, which sparked a revival of military industries. This revival focused federal resources on military aid to America's once and future allies, revivifying factories and shipyards, which in turn soaked up much of the residual unemployment in 1940 and 1941. In 1940 alone, the federal government allocated $10 billion to defense industries, thereby creating some 80,000 new jobs in shipyards and airplane plants, most of which were located in or near larger cities.

Full Mobilization and War, 1942-1945 Shortly after the Japanese attack on Pearl Harbor on December 7, 1941, the United States formally entered World War II and established the military conscription of young men. All industries that could contribute to the war effort were expected to do so, and federal government deficit funding provided the capital. In 1942, $100 billion flowed to defense contractors. Vehicle and airplane factories, shipyards, boot camps, supply depots, training facilities, and a host of defense plants were scattered across the country along major transportation routes. Many of them were located in urban peripheries rather than central cities because of the availability and low cost of land.

On the West Coast, Seattle and San Diego specialized in aircraft construction, while shipyards in Bremerton, Washington, and Portland, Oregon, rapidly produced naval and merchant marine vessels. Between 1940 and 1943, the population of the naval center of Norfolk, Virginia, doubled to 778,000, and its Newport News Shipyard sextupled its workforce to 24,000. Once-sleepy southwestern cities such as Tucson and Phoenix hosted aircraft training facilities that took advantage of the generally cloudless skies.

Many newly employed workers and their families needed housing. As early as 1940, the federal Lanham Act funded both publicly constructed housing for workers in defense plants and private construction overseen by the Federal Housing Administration. Beginning in early 1942, the National Housing Agency acted as an umbrella agency for wartime residential construction. It designated 275 locales as "defense areas" and granted funding for development, especially housing. Between 1942 and 1945, federal funding built around 800,000 new housing units, refurbished or converted another 200,000, and provided 850,000 additional residential units, including trailers and dormitory rooms. In Wichita, Kansas, new and existing factories produced 30,000 aircraft; the city's population rose from 114,000 to 166,000, and its housing stock expanded from about 40,000 to more than 60,000 units.

During the war, around 15 million men and women entered military service, and another 9 million relocated to work in defense plants and offices. Although migration around the country during the Depression had somewhat commingled members of various ethnic and regional groups, the reorganization and mixing created by the war was on a far greater scale. Poor whites from the Deep South and Appalachia, Mexicans and Mexican Americans, rural southern African Americans, Puerto Ricans, and members of other minority groups moved into urban areas to support the war industries. Public transit allowed many to live in inner cities and commute to factories in the periphery, a factor that accelerated further changes in the inner cities, including segregation of African Americans into slum areas and deterioration of those areas.

The substandard or otherwise inadequate housing conditions angered many hard-working minorities of slender means, and even those who had accumulated wealth often were excluded by "restrictive covenants" that forbade sale of properties in upscale neighborhoods to members of racial minorities. The Supreme Court ruled in *Shelley v. Kraemer* (1948) that courts could not enforce such covenants. In cities where circumstances dictated, some slums were cleared, but rarely was affordable replacement housing built, even though that was called for in the 1937 Housing Act.

Informal racial and ethnic mixing in government housing and in other residential communities often led to discord and even violence between groups.

Longtime residents resented the appearance of, and competition for housing with, recently arrived minorities.

Postwar Demobilization The large role of government planning and spending in the economy that was developed during the Great Depression and World War II helped provide a relatively soft landing for the economy at the end of the war. By the end of 1945, 6.5 million men and women had returned to civilian life, and half that number left the armed services over the following months. Although 2 million of these demobilized people returned to rural life, the rest chose urban settings.

Demobilization meant the shutting down of many defense plants and offices as the government's needs and funding dried up. Loss of jobs put many people on the move again. The employment news was not all bad, however. Both the Depression and the war years had led to pent-up consumer demand, with consumers unable to purchase expensive and durable items either because they did not have the funds or the goods were not produced in sufficient quantities. Returning G.I.'s and factory workers now had savings and earnings, and the economy returned to a civilian orientation with this money ready to be spent.

The so-called G.I. Bill (also known as the Servicemen's Readjustment Act of 1944), which, among other things, provided funding for returning veterans to obtain education, kept many of them temporarily out of the employment pool. A large percentage of the defense industry jobs had been held by women. After the war, many of them left the workforce to marry and raise families, beginning the so-called baby boom. These factors led to a relatively smooth transition of the labor force and a relatively low rate of unemployment.

Suburbanization and Decline of Inner Cities Housing starts expanded rapidly. In 1944, there had been 142,000; in 1946, there were 1,023,000; and by 1950 there were 1,952,000. The bulk of residential development—about 60 percent—took place near but outside the central cities, in suburbia. This trend, known as decentralization, had begun early in the century, but wartime suburban industrial development and postwar demographics accelerated it.

Automobile plants immediately returned to civilian production, and by 1950 Americans owned 48.5

million cars, 50 percent more than in 1940. Wider ownership of automobiles meant that people could live farther from cities while still commuting to work in cities. Earlier suburban development occurred mostly within a ten-mile radius around city centers, but during the 1940's and 1950's this spread approximately doubled. Earlier suburban settlement had hugged lines of public transit that linked the suburbs with the central city, and the new, automobile-owning suburban settlers filled in the spaces between these spokes of the "rings" around urban centers.

Regional shopping centers concentrated dozens of consumer retail stores in pedestrian malls to serve the needs of relatively well-off and mobile families. Soon, calls were heard for expansion of limited access highways, or freeways. These would provide more direct access between the city centers and points on the periphery, yet channel auto traffic around or through the cities themselves without further congesting surface streets. Perhaps not surprisingly, Los Angeles was the first American city to plan for growth with urban freeways in mind.

All this peripheral growth meant the relative stagnation of the old urban cores of northern cities. Civic leaders and planners had identified "urban blight" as a major problem during the 1930's. By the end of World War II, much of the infrastructure was in need of repair or replacement, housing stocks had deteriorated, and many of the key businesses and industries that supported the tax base had fled to the periphery. The advance of urban poverty and concentration of racial and ethnic minorities in urban neighborhoods continued.

Between 1940 and 1948, the thirteen largest American cities had population growth of 10.6 percent, but as early as 1940 the Urban Land Institute published a report on the decline of the urban cores of 221 American cities. The black populations of many cities increased heavily between 1940 and 1950: Chicago's grew 77 percent, about the same as Cleveland's, and Detroit's doubled. The era's planners thought largely in terms of economic and physical dilapidation, but some also considered the human cost of this decline.

Urban and Rural Population in the United States, 1930-1950

Year	Total U.S. Population	Urban Population (in percent)	Rural Population (in percent)
1930	123,202,624	56.1	43.9
1940	132,164,569	56.5	43.5
1950	151,325,798	64.0	36.0

Source: United States Census Bureau (USCB).

Note: Table adapted from USCB table *Urban and Rural Populations: 1900-1990.* October, 1995.

Planning and Federal Intervention Civic leaders across the country had hoped that the federal interventions that constituted the New Deal and wartime development would continue after the hostilities and contribute to a renaissance of American cities. Cleveland pioneered civic planning committees in 1942 and produced the earliest comprehensive plan for a major city. President Franklin D. Roosevelt initially supported such efforts through the National Resources Planning Board, which sponsored plans for Corpus Christi, Texas; Salt Lake City, Utah; and Tacoma, Washington. In August, 1943, however, Congress eliminated that central agency and scattered its functions across other agencies.

Regional planning for integration of the core and periphery also began during the war, with the establishment of the Pittsburgh-area Allegheny Conference on Community Development in the fall of 1943. Similar bodies soon emerged in Detroit, Kansas City, and San Francisco/Oakland.

Postwar planning and development encountered important questions. Did cities need economic and infrastructure development or new housing? Was the lead to be taken by the public or private sector? A conservative Congress failed to pass the General Housing Bill of 1946, an important element of President Harry S. Truman's "Fair Deal" promise of "a decent standard of housing for all." To many, such measures smacked of European socialism.

In many urban peripheries, new communities rushed to incorporate themselves to ensure self-control and a modicum of self-governance. The St. Louis metropolitan area, for example, had forty-one incorporated towns in 1940 and eighty-three a decade later. Other phenomena, such as carefully plotted and prefabricated communities named Levittown in New York and Pennsylvania, highlighted the possibilities for planning even in the thriving suburbs. In 1949, the General Housing Bill passed, creating a framework for federal intervention through loans to local agencies concerned with development. These required general planning by locals, which greatly stimulated the processes. The Federal Housing Administration continued to support private provision of residences, and public housing was greatly stimulated. This set the scene for extensive slum clearance, roadway development, and relocations of urban communities.

Impact Effects of the emergency measures of the first half of the decade waned quickly, and patterns of settlement, blight, planning and renewal, and federal intervention were only in their early stages between 1945 and 1949. Americans would continue to experiment and to fine-tune their responses. The plight of inner-city minorities continued, with the problem receiving major attention in the 1960's.

Joseph P. Byrne

Further Reading

Chudacoff, Howard P., and Judith E. Smith. *The Evolution of American Urban Society.* 6th ed. New York: Prentice Hall, 2004. A standard text that balances the social, economic, and physical elements of cities. The section on the 1940's is short but meaty.

Gutfreund, Owen D. *Twentieth-Century Sprawl: Highways and the Reshaping of the American Landscape.* New York: Oxford University Press, 2004. Covers both urban and suburban effects of the postwar growth of highway and freeway networks.

Kruse, Kevin M., and Thomas Sugrue, eds. *The New Suburban History.* Chicago: University of Chicago Press, 2006. The ten essays study the interaction of suburban development with the wider American society, with discussions in most of the essays beginning in the 1940's.

Lemann, Nicholas. *The Promised Land: The Great Black Migration and How It Changed America.* New York: Alfred A. Knopf, 1991. Masterful treatment of the significant demographic trend that transformed American cities during the 1940's and surrounding decades.

Taylor, Louis, and Walter Hill. *The Historical Roots of the Urban Crisis: African Americans in the Industrial City, 1900-1950.* New York: Routledge, 2000. Classic study of the role of race and race relations in northern urban life.

Teaford, Jon C. *The Rough Road to Renaissance: Urban Revitalization in America, 1940-1985.* Baltimore, Md.: Johns Hopkins University Press, 1990. Begins with the era of wartime planning and its apparent promise of urban improvement, and examines the failure of postwar efforts to bring about quick change.

_____. *The Twentieth-Century American City.* 2d ed. Baltimore, Md.: Johns Hopkins University Press, 1993. Standard text that emphasizes social problems in urban history and the roles of conflicting interests in addressing these problems.

See also Architecture; Automobiles and auto manufacturing; Business and the economy in the United States; Freeways; Housing in the United States; Levittown; Office of War Mobilization; Racial discrimination; Unemployment in the United States; Urbanization in Canada; Wartime industries.

USO. *See* **United Service Organizations**

V

■ V-E Day and V-J Day

The Events   Dates on which Germany and Japan formally surrendered to the Allies to end World War II

Dates   May 8, 1945 (V-E Day); August 14, 1945 (V-J Day)

The end of World War II in Europe in May, 1945, and in the Pacific four months later was cause for celebrations throughout the world, with people jubilantly participating in unplanned and often unrestrained festivities. For many people, the events of these two days would be indelibly etched in their memories.

In Europe, it became obvious by April, 1945, that the fall of Nazi Germany was only days away. Soviet forces had fought their way into Berlin, while the Western Allies advanced deep into Germany. On April 30, 1945, German leader Adolf Hitler committed suicide in his Berlin bunker. His titular successor, Admiral Karl Dönitz, administered a makeshift government in the north German town of Flensburg, the sole purpose of which would be to negotiate peace with the Allies. On May 4, 1945, Dönitz brought about the first significant armistice, ending the combat operations of the units defending northwestern Germany. On May 6, German Field Marshal Alfred Jodl went to Allied headquarters at Rheims, France, to sign a general surrender. This document, signed by Jodl on May 7, called for hostilities to cease on May 8. Soviet objections to being left out of the process led to a more all-embracing surrender in Berlin on May 8, which became effective on May 9.

Proclamation and Celebrations   The official announcement of German surrender generated controversy. The news was to have been revealed on May 8 in a joint Allied proclamation of the event. However, the Associated Press news service broke the story on May 7. The term "V-E Day" (victory in Europe) appeared in the press in anticipation of the official announcements, which occurred in Washington, D.C., and London in speeches by President Harry S. Truman and Prime Minister Winston Churchill on May 8. The Soviets waited until the Berlin capitulation had been formally signed and approved by their leaders, and the Soviet Union did not proclaim victory until May 9.

All over the United States and Canada, notably in New York, Montreal, Chicago, Toronto, Los Angeles, and Ottawa, the announcement of surrender

New York subway riders joyfully responding to news of Adolf Hitler's death. The report that Hitler died in battle was incorrect, but newspaper readers were correct in surmising that his death presaged the end of the war in Europe. Germany's unconditional surrender came exactly one week later. (AP/Wide World Photos)

Germany Surrenders

INSTRUMENT OF SURRENDER of all German Forces to the Supreme Commander of the Allied Expeditionary Force, General Dwight D. Eisenhower, and to the Supreme High Command of the Red Army

Berlin, May 8, 1945

1. We the undersigned, acting by authority of the German High Command, hereby surrender unconditionally to the Supreme Commander, Allied Expeditionary Force and simultaneously to the Supreme High Command of the Red Army all forces on land, at sea, and in the air who are at this date under German control.

2. The German High Command will at once issue orders to all German military, naval and air authorities and to all forces under German control to cease active operations at 2301 hours Central European time on 8th May 1945, to remain in the positions occupied at that time and to disarm completely, handing over their weapons and equipment to the local allied commanders or officers designated by Representatives of the Allied Supreme Commands. No ship, vessel, or aircraft is to be scuttled, or any damage done to their hull, machinery or equipment, and also to machines of all kinds, armament, apparatus, and all the technical means of prosecution of war in general.

3. The German High Command will at once issue to the appropriate commanders, and ensure the carrying out of any further orders issued by the Supreme Commander, Allied Expeditionary Force and by the Supreme High Command of the Red Army.

4. This act of military surrender is without prejudice to, and will be superseded by any general instrument of surrender imposed by, or on behalf of the United Nations and applicable to GERMANY and the German armed forces as a whole.

5. In the event of the German High Command or any of the forces under their control failing to act in accordance with this Act of Surrender, the Supreme Commander, Allied Expeditionary Force and the Supreme High Command of the Red Army will take such punitive or other action as they deem appropriate.

6. This Act is drawn up in the English, Russian and German languages. The English and Russian are the only authentic texts.

was met with demonstrations of joy. In some cases, people expressed their happiness in quiet gatherings, such as special church services and prayer or thanksgiving meetings. However, many of the celebrations were more demonstrative, with conga lines forming in parks and squares in Washington, D.C., servicemen randomly kissing every woman in sight, alcohol flowing freely, and a massive victory parade in Ottawa. On occasion, violence erupted, the most serious instance of which broke out in Halifax, Nova Scotia. The Halifax V-E Day riots exploded on May 7 and 8, 1945, with combined mobs of servicemen and civilians, most of whom were intoxicated, ransacking stores and restaurants and vandalizing and destroying almost the entire business district. Three deaths occurred before order was restored.

Japan's Surrender Jubilation over victory in Europe was balanced by the realization that Japan was still very much at war. A massive invasion of Japan was planned. This campaign, code-named Operation Downfall, was expected to end the war in the fall of 1946, at a projected cost of one million Allied casualties. However, the August 6 atomic bombing of Hiroshima and the August 9 bombing of Nagasaki brought about the Japanese surrender on August 14, 1945. Many consider this date to be properly designated as "V-J Day" (victory in Japan), but this was contrary to the wishes of Truman, who insisted upon delaying his proclamation of V-J Day until the actual surrender ceremony took place on board the battleship USS *Missouri* on September 2, 1945. It was on August 14, however, that spontaneous and often highly individualized celebrations expressing joy and relief again broke loose, this time on a scale far larger than that of the previous May. In New York City's Times Square, the largest and most famous of these festivities saw the entire thoroughfare entirely blanketed with ecstatic, standing participants. In San Francisco, celebrations were marred by the worst rioting in the city's history; drunken servicemen rampaged through the downtown streets, resulting in eleven deaths, an indeterminate number of injuries and rapes, and the looting of nearly every store in the area.

Impact The positive images of millions of people openly giving vent to sheer exuberance are invariably presented in connection with the end of World War II. The best-known of these images was the snapshot taken in Times Square of a sailor and a nurse, two total strangers, who were photographed in the act of kissing by *Life* magazine photographer Alfred Eisenstaedt. This evocative scene has fascinated the world ever since. While Eisenstaedt's image and the sense of unalloyed joy and comradeship that it conveyed have endured historically to define the popular perception of both V-E and V-J Days, the uglier side of the revelry, exemplified by the riots in Halifax and San Francisco, has largely been forgotten.

Raymond Pierre Hylton

Further Reading

Axelrod, Alan. *The Real History of World War II: A New Look at the Past.* New York: Sterling, 2008. An attempt to chronicle the war from a fresh perspective. Though the account of victory celebrations is succinct, it places them in a useful perspective.

Coombs, Howard, ed. *The Insubordinate and the Noncompliant: Case Studies of Canadian Mutiny and Disobedience, 1920 to Present.* Toronto: Dundurn Press, 2008. The article by Robert H. Caldwell offers a detailed analysis of the Halifax riot.

Gilbert, Martin. *The Day the War Ended: May 8, 1945—Victory in Europe.* New York: Henry Holt, 1995. Comprehensive and readable account, which only lightly mentions the Halifax riot.

Kimber, Stephen. *Sailors, Slackers, and Blind Pigs: Halifax at War.* Toronto: Doubleday Canada, 2003. Well-researched investigative work on the nature of Halifax's wartime population and the factors behind the riot of May 7-8.

Satterfield, Archie. *The Home Front: An Oral History of the War Years in America, 1941-1945.* New York: Playboy Press, 1982. Final chapter includes some good firsthand accounts of V-J Day revelry, though it may paint too rosy a picture and only hints at the day's excesses.

See also Atomic bomb; D Day; Films about World War II; Hiroshima and Nagasaki bombings; *It's a Wonderful Life;* Manhattan Project; Okinawa, Battle of; World War II.

■ Vandenberg, Arthur Hendrick

Identification Republican senator from Michigan, 1928-1951
Born March 22, 1884; Grand Rapids, Michigan
Died April 18, 1951; Grand Rapids, Michigan

Vandenberg became an important advocate of America's internationalist foreign policy following World War II. Originally an isolationist, he embraced the need for the Marshall Plan and the United Nations, offering much-needed assistance to President Harry S. Truman.

Arthur Hendrick Vandenberg studied law at the University of Michigan before entering the newspaper industry. On March 31, 1928, he was appointed to the U.S. Senate as a member of the Republican Party, an office he retained until his death. Vandenberg early gained a reputation as a staunch opponent of President Franklin D. Roosevelt's New Deal and as a foreign policy isolationist, but American entry into World War II prompted Vandenberg to reevaluate his views on diplomacy. He soon advocated American involvement in the United Nations as well as in the North Atlantic Treaty Organization (NATO). Although fiercely anticommunist, he advocated the necessity of Soviet inclusion in the United Nations. In 1946, he was a delegate to the United Nations assembly in San Francisco, before serving as a delegate to the U.N. General Assembly. Rising to chairmanship of the Senate Foreign Relations Committee in 1947, Vandenberg played a crucial role in ensuring congressional passage of the Marshall Plan for European recovery.

Impact Vandenberg's Senate leadership opened a brief yet pivotal period of bipartisan congressional consensus following World War II in which the United States firmly embraced its role as an international power.

Keith M. Finley

Further Reading

Schlesinger, Stephen. *Act of Creation: The Founding of the United Nations.* Boulder, Colo.: Westview Press, 2003.

Tompkins, C. David. *Senator Arthur H. Vandenberg: The Evolution of a Modern Republican, 1884-1945.* East Lansing: Michigan State University Press, 1970.

See also Isolationism; Marshall Plan; New Deal programs; North Atlantic Treaty Organization; Roosevelt, Franklin D.; Taft, Robert A.; Truman, Harry S.; United Nations.

■ Vinson, Fred M.

Identification Thirteenth chief justice of the United States, 1946-1953
Born January 22, 1890; Louisa, Kentucky
Died September 8, 1953; Washington, D.C.

In addition to holding a number of positions in the federal executive branch during the 1940's, Vinson served as chief justice at a time when significant issues concerning civil rights and liberties were coming before the United States Supreme Court.

Fred M. Vinson began his political career as a member of the House of Representatives, having been first elected in 1923. In 1937, he was appointed to the U.S. Court of Appeals for the District of Columbia, a position from which he resigned in 1943 in order to serve in a number of important roles in the executive branch. In 1945, he was appointed secretary of the Treasury by President Harry S. Truman, with whom he had developed a close personal friendship. Truman admired Vinson's ability to reconcile opposing perspectives—an important attribute given that the Supreme Court was wracked by personal and ideological divisions at the time, some of which had become public. It was into this milieu that Vinson stepped, becoming chief justice in 1946.

Vinson served as chief justice during a time when the Court was still redefining its role in the American constitutional system, in particular its position with regard to civil liberties while anticommunist feelings were running high and government security cases were beginning to arise. The Vinson court tended to support the government over individual rights.

The Supreme Court also struggled with its interpretation of the Fourteenth Amendment's due process and equal protection clauses. The amendment figured prominently, for instance, in church-state cases. In a trilogy of cases, the Vinson court decided that state reimbursement of families for expenses involving transportation of students to parochial schools was constitutional (*Everson v. Board of Education of Ewing Township*, 1947), that the use of school facilities for religious instruction was unconstitutional (*Illinois ex rel. McCollum v. Board of Education*, 1948), and that released-time programs allowing students to leave school during school hours for religious instruction were constitutionally permissible (*Zorach v. Clauson*, 1952). In Fourth Amendment cases, Court decisions tended to give significant flexibility to local forces.

The Court was divided in virtually all these cases, often deciding them by one-vote margins. Thus, Truman's hopes that Vinson could bring greater unity to the Court were unfulfilled. In these cases, Vinson tended to side with the conservative justices.

The Court also faced a number of civil rights cases, and it consistently voted to strike down legislation that enforced segregation. For instance, in an opinion written by Vinson, the Court invalidated state laws enforcing segregation in interstate transportation (*Morgan v. Virginia*, 1946). Vinson was also the author of the opinion declaring unconstitutional state statutes supporting "restrictive covenants" that prohibited the selling of real estate property to African Americans (*Shelley v. Kraemer*, 1948). The Court also invalidated the state law supporting segregation in postgraduate education (*McLaurin v. Oklahoma State Regents*, 1950). Thus, during Vinson's tenure, the Court took a progressive stance against de jure segregation in the United States.

Impact While Vinson was unable to bring an end to the personal divisions among the justices, it was during his tenure that the Supreme Court began to strengthen its role in defining the meaning of civil rights and liberties in the United States.

David M. Jones

Further Reading
Domnarski, William. *The Great Justices, 1941-54: Black, Douglas, Frankfurter, and Jackson in Chambers.* Ann Arbor: University of Michigan Press, 2006.

Pritchett, C. Herman. *Civil Liberties and the Vinson Court.* Chicago: University of Chicago Press, 1954.

Urofsky, Melvin I. *Division and Discord: The Supreme Court Under Stone and Vinson, 1941-1953.* Columbia: University of South Carolina Press, 1997.

■ Voice of America

Identification   Federal communications agency
Date   Established on February 24, 1942

During World War II, Voice of America broadcasts played a central role in informing listeners in German-occupied territories and in Japan and the Pacific about the progress of the war, in a straightforward and truthful manner. During the Cold War, the system's programming shifted to a focus on countering communist propaganda and sharing information on American culture and foreign policy.

Voice of America (VOA) radio programming commenced shortly after the United States entered World War II. The organization's primary objective was to broadcast timely and factual news about the war in as unbiased a manner as possible. This was at first a burden for American programmers, as the war in 1942 consisted largely of German and Japanese victories. The U.S. government nevertheless insisted that this directive be observed in order to establish a reputation for the VOA as a reliable and truthful source of news, so that it would have greater credibility with listeners if and when the war ultimately turned in favor of the Allies.

VOA broadcasts targeted enemy soldiers, as well as foreign citizens, whether they were hostile or sympathetic to the United States. Early on, a limited production crew created broadcasts in German, French, Italian, and English on borrowed equipment in cramped studios. With the creation of the U.S. Office of War In-

formation in June, 1942, the VOA acquired new studio and work spaces in Manhattan, so it was more comfortably established by the time it covered the Allied invasion of North Africa in November, 1942. This was an important moment for the VOA because the invasion was a turning point in the war for Allied forces, and the VOA attracted attention for the remarkable efficiency it demonstrated in its reporting of the invasion.

By the end of the war, VOA had more than three thousand employees across the globe, with administrative and production centers in New York, Los Angeles, and London. It broadcasted regularly in more than forty languages. The VOA's strategy of accuracy and truthfulness, in addition to its wide broadcast range, proved to have the desired result: During debriefings and interviews of prisoners and other enemy troops after the cessation of hostilities, those soldiers attested their belief in the credibility of VOA broadcasts, resulting from the candid reporting of setbacks and challenges that Allied forces faced.

Numerous conflicts emerged throughout the war

Pianist Vladimir Horowitz (left) and Natalia Satina, the widow of the Russian-born composer and conductor Sergei Rachmaninoff, recording a Voice of America program commemorating the fourth anniversary of Rachmaninoff's death in March, 1947. The program was to be broadcast to the Soviet Union by shortwave radio. (AP/Wide World Photos)

Voice of America, the First Decade

1941: U.S. president Franklin D. Roosevelt establishes the U.S. Foreign Information Service (FIS) to begin international radio broadcasts. The FIS is headquartered in New York City and begins producing material for broadcast to Europe by the privately owned American shortwave stations.

Dec. 7, 1941: The Japanese attack on Pearl Harbor and Germany's declaration of war against the United States accelerate the growth of U.S. international broadcast efforts. John Houseman takes charge of the FIS radio operations in New York City. FIS makes its first direct broadcasts to Asia from a studio in San Francisco.

Feb. 24, 1942: FIS makes its first broadcast to Europe via BBC medium- and long-wave transmitters. Speaking from New York, Voice of America (VOA) announcer William Harlan Hale inaugurates the first broadcast.

Mar. 1942: VOA broadcasts six and one-quarter hour blocks of programming, and by April, the VOA is on the air twenty-four hours per day and adding more languages to its broadcast schedule.

June, 1942: VOA grows rapidly and has a new organizational home—the Office of War Information (OWI). Twenty-three transmitters and twenty-seven language services are on the air when the Allied summit takes place in Casablanca.

1945: As World War II draws to a close, many VOA language services are reduced or eliminated. A State Department-appointed committee of private citizens advises the U.S. government to not be "indifferent to the ways in which our society is portrayed to other countries."

1948: The Smith-Mundt Act is enacted by Congress to establish America's international informational and cultural exchange programs, a function that VOA had been carrying out for the past six years on its own.

Jan. 27, 1948: The U.S. Information and Educational Exchange Act of 1948, also known as the Smith-Mundt Act, is passed by Congress and signed into law by President Harry S. Truman, placing international overseas information activities, including VOA, under the Office of International Information at the state department.

1950: With the outbreak of the Korean War, VOA adds new language services and develops plans to construct transmitter complexes on both the East and West Coasts of the United States.

Source: Voice of America. http://www.voanews.com.

as government and military agencies fought for control over the content and focus of programming, each party with different beliefs regarding the propagandistic role that the VOA should play. As a result, the perceived partiality of the agency varied at different points throughout the course of the war.

Postwar Developments At the end of World War II, the Office of War Information was disbanded, but advocates within the U.S. State Department worked to preserve the VOA, with a new, broader mission of spreading American culture and ideology throughout the world. Assistant Secretary of State William Benton played a vital role in reorganizing the VOA and fought to maintain support and funding for the program. The U.S. Congress, however, partly at the urging of domestic and commercial press organizations that feared federally sponsored competition, did not see the need for the VOA's continued operation. By the spring of 1946, VOA personnel and broadcast hours were cut to a third of their wartime peak, and services were reduced to twenty-three languages.

Late in 1946, communist aggression saved the apparently doomed VOA. As divisions between West and East grew, communist propaganda against the United States spread, and the U.S. government felt a growing need to manage its image throughout the world. In response to attacks by communist radio programs and increasing pressure at home, the VOA deliberately shifted during the late 1940's from its original approach of impartial dissemination of facts and instead adopted an increasingly negative tone toward communism. The operations of the VOA as the United States entered the Cold War represented a balance between open dissemination of American culture and ideology versus disseminating counterpropaganda that had a more negative tone.

During both World War II and the Cold War, the VOA was forbidden from broadcasting within the United States. Two significant factors motivated this prohibition. First, it ensured that VOA resources could not be manipulated by U.S. officials to serve partisan domestic purposes, especially to build support during elections or other movements. The dangers of domestic propaganda, as demonstrated by its use within Nazi Germany, provided abundant reasons to guard against such efforts in the United States. Second, the prohibition guaranteed that commercial press services would not have to compete in a market against a federal agency with government funding.

Impact   VOA broadcasts during World War II provided factual news reports of the war and world events to listeners around the globe. The VOA explored new techniques to gain credibility with listeners who were accustomed to propaganda, some of it in the news media, that inflated or invented victories and suppressed news of defeats. Through truthful and impartial reporting, the VOA developed a reputation as a trusted source of information. Despite some policy shifts as the VOA refocused its attention on the Soviet Union after World War II, instituting broadcasts to that country, the agency retained much of that reputation during the early years of the Cold War and provided an effective counterbalance to communist propaganda during the late 1940's. In later decades, it expanded coverage and broadcast reach even farther, and in 1994 it became the first broadcast-news provider to offer continuously updated coverage on the Internet.

Paul E. Killinger

Further Reading

Cull, Nicholas J. *The Cold War and the United States Information Agency: American Propaganda and Public Diplomacy, 1945-1989*. New York: Cambridge University Press, 2008.
Elder, Robert E. *The Information Machine: The United States Information Agency and American Foreign Policy.* Syracuse, N.Y.: Syracuse University Press, 1968.
Heil, Alan L. *Voice of America: A History.* New York: Columbia University Press, 2003.
Krugler, David F. *The Voice of America and the Domestic Propaganda Battles, 1945-1953*. Columbia: University of Missouri Press, 2000.
Nelson, Michael. *War of the Black Heavens: The Battles of Western Broadcasting in the Cold War.* Syracuse, N.Y.: Syracuse University Press, 1997.

See also   Anticommunism; Cold War; Foreign policy of the United States; Radio in Canada; Radio in the United States; Wartime propaganda in the United States.

■ Voting rights

The rhetoric of democracy during World War II inspired many Americans to mount fresh challenges against discriminatory state voting laws. Such challenges brought about incomplete but nonetheless important changes, especially in African American and Native American voting rights.

In 1940, an array of state voting laws denied suffrage to paupers, felons, mental incompetents, Native Americans, African Americans, and others. African Americans constituted the largest of the actively disfranchised groups. In eleven southern states, laws barred the vast majority of blacks from voting. American entry into World War II, however, resurrected old questions about the extent of the right to vote and the role of the federal government in guarding that right. That the country was battling totalitarian forces while "Jim Crow" survived at home, made many uncomfortable and many others angry. As a result, nonwhite servicepeople, civilian activists, and sympathetic public officials began pushing for another extension of voting rights.

African Americans   In 1940, fewer than 5 percent of all African Americans of voting age were registered to vote in the eleven former Confederate states. Since the end of Reconstruction, most southern states had instituted laws to prevent black citizens from voting. Poll taxes; literacy tests, often selectively and prejudicially applied; and laws that restricted primary elections to white voters were three of the most common legal impediments to black suffrage and were the cornerstones of a larger system of racial segregation in the region.

African American voters lined up to vote at a segregated polling place in Marietta during Georgia's 1946 gubernatorial election. (AP/Wide World Photos)

After the United States entered World War II at the end of 1941, many African Americans seriously reassessed their position as second-class citizens. African Americans began to ask why they were so widely excluded from democratic government at home if the war against racist German fascism and brutal Japanese imperialism was truly a fight for democracy. Outraged by what they perceived as national hypocrisy, some African Americans resisted the draft. A few, such as writer Ralph Ellison, joined the merchant marines rather than enlist in a segregated military. The many who did serve often felt empowered to demand suffrage and other civil rights at home.

Not coincidentally, African American activists became organized as never before during the 1940's. Membership in the National Association for the Advancement of Colored People skyrocketed from 50,000 to around 400,000 during the war. Other civil rights organizations—most notably the Congress of Racial Equality—were born at this time. Energized by the same political-ideological forces, many white liberals and northern politicians from both parties who had their eyes on black votes lent support to the cause of African American voting rights.

In this climate charged with activism, important first steps were made in securing black suffrage. The first of these, the Soldier Voting Act of 1942 (amended in 1944), allowed military personnel to vote when stationed away from home and exempted them from poll taxes and registration requirements when voting in absentia, regardless of race or state laws. Many segregationists feared that this law presaged further federal meddling with state voting statutes—and these fears were not unfounded. In the landmark 1944 case of *Smith v. Allwright* the Supreme Court reversed its 1935 decision in *Grovey v. Townsend*, declaring white primaries unconstitutional.

Often fomented by whites attempting to keep black G.I.'s from voting, eruptions of racial violence in the South led President Truman to create the President's Committee on Civil Rights in 1946. Its report, *To Secure These Rights* (1947), urged the federal government to take an active role in securing the voting and other civil rights of African Americans and Native Americans. Truman, unwilling to further undermine a states-rights tradition and risk losing election in 1948, limited his own activism to desegregating the military and promising fair employment practices within the government. Congress, stalled by southern resistance, took no action for a decade.

Native Americans Though all Native Americans were granted U.S. citizenship under the Indian Citizenship Act of 1924, also known as the Snyder Act, by 1940, six states—North Carolina, Utah, Washington, Idaho, New Mexico, and Arizona—still had constitutional provisions that prevented Native Americans from voting. New Mexico and Arizona contained the largest populations of disfranchised Native Americans. Like African Americans, Native American veterans were encouraged by wartime rhetoric to push for their rights. They were joined in their efforts by missionaries and by Bureau of Indian Affairs commissioner John Collier. In two landmark federal cases, *Harrison v. Laveen* (1948) and

Trujillo v. Garley (1948), Arizona's and New Mexico's voting restrictions against Native Americans were struck down, clearing the way for consolidation of Native American voting rights during the 1950's and 1960's.

Impact   Despite the relatively limited nature of advances in black civil rights, southern resistance at the local, state, and national levels increased. Many white southerners were not willing to honor the *Smith* decision, nor any future federal innovations. Though registered African American voters quadrupled between 1940 and 1947, the majority remained hesitant to try their luck and lives at southern polls. The full realization of black voting rights did not develop until the 1950's and 1960's. Native Americans made somewhat more headway, and by the mid-1950's were organizing influential voting blocs in Western states; Native American suffrage was not yet universal, however. In short, the voting rights movements of the 1940's did not destroy racial disfranchisement in the United States. However, they did successfully lay groundwork for the movements of the 1950's and 1960's and helped set legal precedents for more far-reaching federal interventions on behalf of the disfranchised, culminating in the Voting Rights Act of 1965.

Jeremiah Taylor

Further Reading

Bernstein, Alison R. *American Indians and World War II: Toward a New Era in Indian Affairs.* Norman: University of Oklahoma Press, 1991. Offers important insights into the political-ideological atmosphere in which the Native American voting-rights movement was born.

Emmons, Caroline. "'Somebody Has Got to Do That Work': Harry T. Moore and the Struggle for African-American Voting Rights in Florida." *Journal of Negro History* 82 (1997): 232-243. State-level view of organization on behalf of black voting rights in the South during the 1940's.

Franco, Jeré. "Empowering the World War II Native American Veteran: Postwar Civil Rights." *Wicazo Ša Review* 9 (1993): 32-37. Brief but informative overview of the struggle for Native American voting rights in New Mexico and Arizona.

Keyssar, Alexander. *The Right to Vote: The Contested History of Democracy in the United States.* New York: Basic Books, 2000. Comprehensive and readable account of the right to vote in the United States; places the events of the 1940's in larger historical context.

Zelden, Charles L. *The Battle for the Black Ballot: Smith v. Allwright and the Defeat of the Texas All-White Primary.* Lawrence: University Press of Kansas, 2004. Succinct, well-contextualized account of the legal beginning of the end for the white primary.

See also   African Americans; Atlantic Charter; Civil rights and liberties; Congress of Racial Equality; Desegregation of the U.S. military; Jim Crow laws; National Association for the Advancement of Colored People; Native Americans; *Smith v. Allwright*; Supreme Court, U.S.

W

Walden Two

Identification Utopian novel about communal living
Author B. F. Skinner (1904-1990)
Date First published in 1948

Largely ignored after its initial publication, Walden Two *took on a new readership during the 1960's because of renewed popular interest in experiments in communal living. Its title is a reference to Henry David Thoreau's book* Walden *(1854).*

An attempt by its author, the noted psychologist B. F. Skinner, to demonstrate how the principles of behaviorism could be used to design a more ideal society, *Walden Two* was rejected by two publishers before it found its way into print. Over time, however, with growing popular concern about threats to the planet (such as pollution, overpopulation, and persistent armed conflict) occasioned largely by human irresponsibility, Skinner's ideas of behavioral engineering attracted greater attention.

Narrated by a psychology professor named Burris, who accepts the invitation of a former student (Rogers) and his friend (Jamnik), both World War II veterans, to investigate the utopian community established by a former graduate school classmate (T. E. Frazier), most of the book is essentially a guidebook to Walden Two, a showcase for the behaviorist theories of Frazier, Skinner's fictional surrogate. Rogers and Jamnik, aimless after the war, are searching for answers as to why people cannot live in peace with one another. With their girlfriends in tow as well as Burris and a colleague in philosophy (Castle), they undertake a three-day visit to Frazier's rural community to find out how he managed to engineer a society of one thousand happy, productive, environmentally friendly, and nonviolent inhabitants by means of a managed system of stimuli and rewards.

Impact The novel has become a lightning rod on the topic of applied psychology with some behaviorists, who regard the book as a thought-provoking guide for handling social problems, and most advocates of individual freedom and self-determination, who decry the book's emphasis on behavioral modification and social conformity.

S. Thomas Mack

Further Reading

Bjork, Daniel W. *B. F. Skinner: A Life.* New York: Basic Books, 1993.
Kuhlmann, Hilke. *Living Walden Two: B. F. Skinner's Behaviorist Utopia and Experimental Communities.* Urbana: University of Illinois Press, 2005.

See also Literature in the United States; Psychiatry and psychology; Urbanization in the United States; Women's roles and rights in the United States; World War II.

Wallace, Henry A.

Identification Vice president of the United States, 1941-1945; secretary of commerce, 1945-1946; Progressive Party candidate for president, 1948
Born October 7, 1888; Adair County, Iowa
Died November 18, 1965; Danbury, Connecticut

Drawing on his extensive experience as a farmer and a former secretary of agriculture, Wallace articulated ideas about farming and liberal views in support of world government and international control of nuclear weapons during the 1940's. He forcefully but unavailingly presented his views as the Progressive Party candidate for president in 1948. Many of his ideas, unpopular in his lifetime, became matters of intense concern in later years.

In 1940, when Henry A. Wallace was chosen by President Franklin D. Roosevelt to be the Democratic Party candidate for vice president, he stepped down as secretary of agriculture. Under his leadership, the U.S. Department of Agriculture had made sweeping economic, social, and scientific changes. Because he was strongly criticized as being a kind of wild, "mysti-

Henry A. Wallace (center right) campaigning for vice president in Iowa in 1940 with John K. Valentine, who was running for governor. (Time & Life Pictures/Getty Images)

cal" man, Wallace was not allowed to make a speech at the Democratic National Convention in 1940. However, when Roosevelt was elected to his third term that year, he gave Wallace several important positions. Wallace was appointed chairman of the Economic Defense Board and of the Supply Priorities and Allocations Board, which distributed vital resources and attempted to spur wartime production. Wallace was also made the leader of the Board of Economic Warfare, which dealt with such matters as stockpiling the natural rubber that was essential for military mobilization.

Wartime Duties   During World War II, Wallace was sent on diplomatic missions in which his work was much less successful. In a visit to Siberia and China in 1944, for example, he was seriously deceived by Soviet propaganda, and he left China after four un-

availing days of talks with Chinese leader Chiang Kai-shek. During that same year, Wallace was the voters' favorite in the vice presidential race at a time when Roosevelt had not made any clear commitment to a running mate in his fourth run for the presidency. Although Harry S. Truman was eventually nominated for vice president, Wallace came close to gaining the nomination, which would have enabled him to be president after Roosevelt died on April 12, 1945.

In 1945, Roosevelt made Wallace secretary of commerce. Wallace then set forth his goals of full employment, federal housing and health insurance, and international trade, which he described in a book called *Sixty Million Jobs* (1945). After Roosevelt died and Truman became president, Wallace disagreed with many of Truman's policies and left the administration in 1946.

The 1948 Election The year 1948 is famous for Truman's defeat of the Republican candidate, Thomas E. Dewey, but the presence of two other candidates, States' Rights Democratic Party candidate Strom Thurmond, who would obtain the votes of conservative Democrats in the South, and Wallace, the candidate of the extremely liberal Progressive Party, threatened Truman's chances for election. Wallace, who by then was serving as coeditor of the liberal *New Republic*, became a contributing editor of the magazine and continued to write a weekly column during his presidential campaign. However, his presidential bid was damaged by the support he received from Communist Party USA leaders, from whom he tried to distance himself.

Well-known liberal members of Americans for Democratic Action, such as Minneapolis Mayor Hubert H. Humphrey and the sons of Roosevelt, accused Wallace of dividing progressive thinkers and thus encouraging a revival of reactionary isolationism. Wallace was barred from speaking at several locations, including the University of Iowa in his home state, and rowdy protests took place where he did speak. In July, the publisher of *The New Republic* dismissed Wallace, who was now being viewed as a kind of wild fanatic.

The Wallace campaign made an unprecedented choice of a black lawyer and publisher from Iowa, Charles P. Howard, to deliver the keynote address at the Progressive Party nominating convention in Philadelphia. Wallace's own speech ended with a rousing call to make the American dream come true. However, he was much criticized for claiming in that speech that America's "get tough" policy was largely responsible for the Berlin blockade, which at that time necessitated the airlifting of supplies to a city divided into an eastern, Soviet-dominated sector, and a western sector. Wallace finished fourth in the presidential race, slightly behind Thurmond, and received no electoral votes. Throughout the rest of his life, he championed world government, nuclear disarmament, and expanded world trade.

Impact It can be argued that Henry A. Wallace's expertise as a scientifically oriented farmer and a businessman, and his innovations as a secretary of agriculture from 1933 to 1940, constitute his chief legacy. However, his achievements during the 1940's are also important. He was one of only three men present on October 9, 1941, when Vannevar Bush of the Office of Scientific Research and Development presented a plan for the construction of an atomic bomb to President Roosevelt.

Despite charges by his right-wing opponents, Wallace was never a member of or a spokesman for the Communist Party. However, he was convinced that an unnecessarily aggressive anti-Soviet policy by the United States was a major ingredient of the Cold War, a view that was generally rejected by other politicians and much of the public. Perhaps more than any liberal thinker, he raised a question that all students of the aftermath of World War II must confront: Whether a foreign policy could have been established that would have prevented a massive nuclear buildup and the concomitant threat to the United States and other nations of the world.

Robert P. Ellis

Further Reading
Cohen, Adam. *Nothing to Fear: FDR's Inner Circle and the Hundred Days That Created Modern America.* New York: Penguin Books, 2009. Although primarily dealing with events of the 1930's, this book describes Roosevelt's choice of Wallace as his running mate in 1940.

Culver, John C., and John Hyde. *American Dreamer: The Life and Times of Henry A. Wallace.* New York: W. W. Norton, 2000. This major biography of Wallace investigates the many strands of a complicated personality.

Wallace, Henry Agard. *The Price of Vision: The Diary of Henry A. Wallace.* Boston: Houghton Mifflin, 1973. Valuable as the work of a close witness of the decisions made by Presidents Roosevelt and Truman.

Walton, Richard J. *Henry Wallace, Harry Truman, and the Cold War.* New York: Viking, 1976. A defense of Wallace's liberal political thought after World War II.

White, Graham J., and John Maze. *Henry A. Wallace: His Search for a New World Order.* Chapel Hill: University of North Carolina, 1995. A study of Wallace's eclectic spiritualism and its influence on his social attitudes.

See also Barkley, Alben William; Communist Party USA; Elections in the United States: 1940; Elections in the United States: 1944; Elections in the

United States: 1948; Hiss, Alger; House Committee on Un-American Activities; Hull, Cordell; Ickes, Harold; Roosevelt, Franklin D.; Seeger, Pete; Stimson, Henry L.; Truman, Harry S.; Truman Doctrine.

■ War bonds

Definition   Financial instruments sold by the U.S. government during World War II to raise revenue to help pay for military operations

Successive campaigns to sell war bonds allowed the federal government to raise funds to pay for expenses incurred to support the war effort, especially between 1942 and 1945, and helped galvanize public support for the country's participation in World War II.

As early as 1940, President Franklin D. Roosevelt began planning for what he saw as the inevitable entry of the United States into armed conflict with the Axis Powers. Knowing a war would be costly, Roosevelt solicited ideas from his advisors on ways to finance wartime operations. While several advisors recommended instituting a war tax, Secretary of the Treasury Henry Morgenthau encouraged the president to sell bonds. Morgenthau argued that by doing so the president would not only raise needed money, but he could also use bond sales as a means of encouraging average citizens to take a stake in the war effort. Although Roosevelt was initially skeptical that promotion schemes might be perceived by the American public as propaganda, he agreed to Morgenthau's plan.

Government poster exhorting Americans to buy war bonds. The poster caricatures Japanese prime minister Hideki Tojo (left) and Italian prime minister Benito Mussolini (right) as the lackeys of German chancellor Adolf Hitler (center). The ground on which the three characters stand is covered with the names of places they have invaded. (Getty Images)

War Bond Drives   In the spring of 1941 the U.S. Treasury Department began offering three new series of savings bonds, including Series E bonds in denominations as low as twenty-five dollars to make it possible for ordinary citizens to purchase them. Bonds could be purchased for 75 percent of their face value, and would reach maturity—that is, their full value—in ten years. To encourage sales, the government also sold savings stamps for ten cents each, giving people who could not immediately afford to purchase bonds a program that would allow them to save up to buy them. Initially called defense bonds, war bonds were designated as "war bonds" af-

ter the Japanese bombed Pearl Harbor in December, 1941.

Initially, the Roosevelt administration intended simply to offer bonds for sale continuously without special promotional campaigns. By the spring of 1942, however, it became apparent that sales could be greatly increased by mounting special drives. These were to run for limited periods with specific financial goals and use themes designed to build support among citizens on the home front for the country's involvement in the conflict. Carefully orchestrated campaigns using posters, radio announcements, and newspaper advertising helped promote the idea that funds raised from bond sales were providing the equipment and supplies needed by America's fighting forces.

Numerous Hollywood celebrities joined in the effort to promote bond sales; even comic-book heroes and cartoon characters were used to encourage people to purchase bonds. Workers were encouraged to enroll in payroll deduction programs, and everyone was asked to pledge 10 percent of earnings toward purchase of war bonds. This initiative helped the government achieve another important objective: By reducing funds available to citizens for spending on scarce consumer goods, upward pressure on inflation was reduced during the war.

Success of War Bond Drives From 1942 until 1946, the federal government conducted eight bond drives. The first, designated the "War Loan Drive," was conducted in November and December of 1942. It had a goal of $9 billion but surprisingly raised $13 billion. The second drive, launched in spring, 1943, was even more successful, raising $18.5 billion against a $13 billion goal. The Treasury Department set a higher goal of $14.5 billion for the third drive, conducted in the fall of 1943, and managed to raise $18.9 billion. The fourth and fifth drives also exceeded expectations, bringing in $16.7 billion and $20.6 billion. The sixth drive, launched just after D Day in June, 1944, raised $21.6 billion.

An economic reality masked in the impressive sales of the drives is the fact that the majority of bonds were sold to large investors. Individual Americans were supportive but not at the levels the Roosevelt administration hoped they would be. The seventh drive, known as the "Mighty Seventh," begun just after Germany surrendered in May, 1945, had a modest $14 billion goal but generated $26.3 billion for the government. The final "Victory Loan" campaign, launched in October, 1945, and targeted at generating funds to finance America's postwar needs, brought in another $21 billion, bringing the total raised by all war bonds sales to $185 billion.

Impact The sale of war bonds was remarkably successful in raising a significant portion of the funds necessary for the U.S. government to finance military operations. While studies done in decades after World War II have revealed that not everyone in the country was enthusiastic about supporting the war effort in this way, campaigns to sell bonds had a strong, positive impact on public opinion regarding the conflict, especially during the period between American entry into the war and the Allied invasion of Europe in June 1944.

Laurence W. Mazzeno

Further Reading

Blum, John Morton. *V Was For Victory: Politics and American Culture During World War II.* New York: Harcourt, Brace, Jovanovich, 1976. Includes a brief account of the Roosevelt administration's strategy for selling war bonds and its methods for using bond sales as a means of securing public approval of the war effort.

Kimble, James J. *Mobilizing the Home Front: War Bonds and Domestic Propaganda.* College Station: Texas A&M University Press, 2006. Comprehensive analysis of each of the eight bond drives conducted by the Treasury Department, focusing on techniques used to persuade Americans to purchase bonds as a means of showing support for the war.

Morse, Jarvis. *Paying for a World War: The United States Financing of World War II.* Washington, D.C.: U.S. Savings Bond Division, 1971. Historical account of the federal government's initiative to use bond sales as a means of financing wartime operations.

Olney, Lawrence. *The War Bond Story.* Washington, D.C.: U.S. Savings Bond Division, 1971. Detailed account of the U.S. Treasury Department's program to sell war bonds, written by a key official who helped manage the effort.

O'Neill, William L. *A Democracy at War: America's Fight at Home and Abroad in World War II.* New York: Free Press, 1993. Comments on the Roosevelt administration's campaign for selling war bonds as part of a larger strategy to make the public feel they had a stake in the conflicts in Europe and the Pacific.

Samuel, Lawrence R. *Pledging Allegiance: American Identity and the Bond Drive of World War II.* Washington, D.C.: Smithsonian Institution Press, 1997. Provides an overview of the Treasury's bond program and examines in detail the responses of important subgroups of American citizens to the government's efforts to generate support for the war through the bond program.

See also Credit and debt; Economic wartime regulations; Lombard, Carole; National debt; War debt; Wartime seizures of businesses; World War II; World War II mobilization.

■ War brides

Identification   Foreign nationals who married American and Canadian service personnel during and shortly after World War II

The numerous wartime, cross-cultural marriages spurred special legislation allowing nonquota immigration of war brides and travel at government expense to their North American destinations. War brides settled all across the continent, and tried hard to fit into their new homes and communities. Their presence was a reminder of the international roles that emerged for the United States and Canada during the 1940's.

Romance and marriage was a predictable, if peripheral, result of sending large numbers of young, unmarried men overseas for training and combat during World War II. Once the wartime deployment began, soldiers from the United States and Canada spent tours in overseas English-speaking countries—Great Britain, Australia, New Zealand—before they were shipped to war zones. This caused a wave of service members wanting to marry in these countries. At first, the American government forbade such unions. When this policy proved unenforceable, the government changed regulations to allow servicemen to marry foreign nationals, but only with the permission of their commanding officers and the completion of a daunting amount of paperwork. Because most service members were sent to combat zones soon after they attained permission to marry, questions about how such couples would be reunited and what their citizen status would be were left to be settled after the end of the war.

The Wartime Setting   In English-speaking countries the Red Cross and other volunteer groups sponsored dances and canteens where servicemen could meet "respectable" young women of the host country. Most eligible young men of these areas had already been assigned to combat areas, so there was no shortage of hostesses. Other relationships started with chance meetings or because the couple worked together in military or war-related jobs. As American and Canadian troops advanced through North Africa, Italy, and northern Europe, they were greeted as liberators by most civilian populations. Although the pace of war advances and a language barrier allowed fewer formal opportunities to meet romantic partners, many servicemen did meet women during these campaigns and formed lasting ties. In these countries, civilians endured severe shortages, sometimes to the point of near-starvation. The G.I.'s had access to candy, cigarettes, and other food and sundries almost unavailable elsewhere in war-torn Europe. A gift of such items, shared with a woman's family, often quelled initial suspicions.

The only populous Pacific country where Allied servicemen arrived as liberators was the Philippines, an American territory when invaded by Japan in 1942. Although both Filipino mores and American racial attitudes tended to discourage cross-cultural relationships, close to one thousand marriages resulted between native women and American service personnel.

War-related marriages between North American soldiers and German or Japanese nationals did not occur until later in the decade. The occupation authorities in both countries at first forbade fraternization with local citizens. This policy proved impossible to enforce. Within a year or two of the end of the war, the provisions were modified, and marriages began to occur. Permission for them was more difficult to obtain, especially in Japan, where strict time limits for approval and exclusionary racial laws added to the barriers.

Characteristics of War Brides and Grooms   Older and supposedly wiser adults of all nations tended to view most wartime cross-national romances with disapproval. The typical prospective bridegroom in such matches was a young draftee in his late teens or early twenties, with little prior job experience before his military service. Their brides tended to be even younger—seventeen-year-olds were not uncommon—with little knowledge of the world beyond their hometowns. Brief courtships, promises made under the looming threat of bombardment or death in battle, or duress of pregnancies, hardly seemed promising ways to begin marriages. Add to this the uniforms' blurring of normal markers of social class and family background, and dubious military officials and parents seemed to have reason on their side.

Not all the marriages fit this profile. Noteworthy war brides included Anna Chan (later known as Anna C. Chennault), a journalist and daughter of a Chinese consul, who married Major General Claire Lee Chennault, commander of the Flying Tigers in China. Monica Dickens, a great-granddaughter of famed British novelist Charles Dickens and a writer herself, married Commander Roy Stratton of the U.S. Navy. Gloria Pablo, daughter of a prominent Filipino judge, married American Captain Mel Montesclaros in a society wedding held at an archbishop's palace.

The numbers of foreign men marrying American and Canadian women women were smaller than the numbers of foreign women marrying North American men but were not negligible. One publicized war bridegroom was Belgian resistance fighter Roger Charlier, who married an American army nurse. Their fictionalized courtship experiences were the bases of a 1949 film comedy, *I Was a Male War Bride*, which starred Cary Grant and Ann Sheridan. In real life, Charlier became a professor of oceanography after moving to the United States.

Reception in the United States Some newly minted spouses crossed the Atlantic before the end of the war, traveling on a space-available basis in returning troop transports, hospital ships, or even aircraft. This program was kept confidential. Most war brides had to remain in their home countries until hostilities ceased and legislation eased their transit to their husband's home country. On December 28, 1945, the U.S. Congress passed the War Brides Act, allowing nonquota entry for alien spouses and other dependents of any citizen who had served honorably in the armed forces during World War II. Such de-

pendents were also allowed to file papers for citizenship early, after only two years of residence in the United States. During an era when strict national-origin quotas severely limited immigration from some nations, the nonquota provision was a great boon. It especially helped brides from New Zealand, the Philippines, and China, whose annual quotas were limited to around one hundred immigrants per country. Six months later, the Fiancées Act was enacted, granting three-month visas to foreign nationals engaged to current and former U.S. armed forces members. Visa recipients were also given permanent immigrant status when their marriages took place within the three-month time frames.

Meanwhile, the U.S. and Canadian governments allocated ships to carry war brides and other dependents to their shores. Ships ranged from the luxury liner *Queen Mary* to hastily converted troop transports. Crowded conditions prevailed on the voyages, and many crossings were memorable for rough weather conditions and sick babies. The trips did provide an opportunity for meeting other war brides. Often the friendships formed on board lasted a lifetime.

When reunited, young couples often had to live with in-laws because of postwar housing shortages. Culture shock, stress from veterans' job searches, and disappointment over living conditions tested the marriages. Homesickness was another hazard, with young women suddenly thousands of miles away from parents and friends. Their reception from communities and family members varied from resentment to warm hospitality. Most people did try to welcome the war brides, whose efforts to adopt their new country's ways helped bridge the gaps.

An estimated one million foreign spouses of armed service members immigrated to the United States during World War II and the postwar years. Around forty-eight thousand European women married Canadians and went to that country during the same period. Despite dire predictions, the majority of these marriages endured and even flourished,

British wives of American servicemen boarding a ship that will carry them to the United States in 1946. (Popperfoto/Getty Images)

their existence adding a unique touch to the mosaic of these nations' cultures.

Impact Many war brides used their backgrounds and talents in careers and in family life. The larger impact of their presence was diffused by bringing an awareness of the larger world even to small, isolated North American communities.

The War Brides Act was a first crack in restrictive American immigration laws of the mid-twentieth century. The nonquota admission of Asian war brides showed officials and citizens that Asians could assimilate and become Americans. This change in sentiment ultimately made possible the Immigration and Nationality Act of 1965, which dismantled the existing race-based quota system. The Chinese American subculture was drastically changed by the War Brides Act. Prior to World War II it had been largely a bachelor society. Many Chinese American men who served in the war already had wives, some married by proxy, who could not come to the United States. The legislation gave their wives opportunities to immigrate, and a real Chinese American culture with family life evolved.

War brides formed clubs and networks, some of which endured for years. Canadian war brides were especially active in making these connections. A war bride museum in Halifax, Nova Scotia, commemorates their experiences.

Emily Alward

Further Reading

Friedman, Barbara G. *From the Battlefront to the Bridal Suite: Media Coverage of British War Brides, 1942-1946*. Columbia: University of Missouri Press, 2007. Study of media portrayal of war brides, which shifted from negative to positive within a few years. Suggests press attitudes influenced couples' behavior.

Jarratt, Melynda. *Captured Hearts: New Brunswick's War Brides*. Fredericton, N.B.: Goose Lane Editions, 2008. Exemplary survey by the foremost historian of Canadian war brides. The subjects' stories reveal successes, failures, and sometimes bewilderment in their new lives.

Shukert, Elfrieda Berthiaume, and Barbara Smith Scibetta. *War Brides of World War II*. New York: Penguin, 1989. Inclusive overview of World War II-era, cross-national marriages in all theaters of war. Contains bibliography, photos, and the text of relevant laws.

Winfield, Pamela. *Melancholy Baby*. Westport, Conn.: Bergin & Garvey, 2000. Personal accounts of "G.I. babies" of American fathers; some were raised in the United States, others were abandoned in Europe.

Zhao, Xiaojian. *Remaking Chinese America: Immigration, Family, and Community, 1940-1965*. New Brunswick, N.J.: Rutgers University Press, 2002. Scholarly but accessible account of the impact Chinese war brides had on immigration policy and on Chinese American enclaves.

See also Asian Americans; G.I. Bill; Housing in Canada; Housing in the United States; Immigration to Canada; Immigration to the United States; Philippines; Red Cross; World War II.

■ War crimes and atrocities

Definition Violations of universally recognized laws of warfare

During World War II, there were two major categories of unjustified violence relevant to American forces: mistreatment of prisoners of war (POWs) and civilians, and the use of bombing as a tool for terrorizing civilians.

The military forces of all countries participating in World War II, including the United States, committed unjustified acts of violence and violated the laws of war that were generally recognized at the time. Although historians generally agree that the conduct of the U.S. military toward prisoners of war (POWs) and enemy civilians was not as heinous as that of Germany and Japan, there are nevertheless many documented cases of Americans killing POWs, especially in the Pacific theater of war. Atrocities committed by American ground forces, however, were relatively small in comparison with the number of deaths resulting from the U.S. practice of bombing large residential areas in German and Japanese cities.

European Theater Because the United States and Germany were both signatories of the 1929 Geneva Convention Relative to the Treatment of Prisoners of War, the German military rarely killed captured Americans. Their restraint in this regard stood in striking contrast to the way they treated Jews and the Slavic peoples of Eastern Europe. The most infamous instance of Germans killing disarmed American

After Germany surrendered and the horrors of the Holocaust were fully revealed to the outside world, these German prisoners of war held on Staten Island in New York were made to watch a film graphically displaying atrocities committed by their former government. (AP/Wide World Photos)

POWs was the Malmédy Massacre of December 17, 1944. This incident came in the early phase of the Battle of the Bulge, when German lieutenant colonel Joachim Peiper's Schutzstaffel (SS) armored unit lined up and shot about eighty American prisoners. Peiper later noted that his unit was made up of "young fanatical soldiers," including many who were embittered from having lost family members to American bombing raids. Publicity about the massacre discouraged Americans from surrendering in later engagements and prompted some units to reciprocate and shoot surrendering SS troops. Following the war, Peiper and forty-three members of his unit were sentenced to death for the massacre, but they were all paroled during the mid-1950's.

Angry German civilians killed approximately two hundred American and British airmen who were shot down while conducting bombing raids on German cities. A particularly well-documented incident occurred on the North Sea island of Borkum in 1944, when a B-17 with seven U.S. crewmen was forced to crash-land. After the mayor encouraged citizens to kick and abuse the airmen, a German soldier shot each of them in the head. In addition to not punishing anyone for the crime, the German government praised the patriotism of the islanders. Following the war, the mayor and two other persons were hanged for their roles in the atrocity, and twelve other persons received prison terms.

Historian Stephen Ambrose, who interviewed at

least one thousand U.S. combat veterans, remarked that about one-third of them claimed to have witnessed the killing of German POWs. Two documented atrocities occurred on the island of Sicily, where U.S. Army captain John T. Compton ordered a firing squad to shoot about forty captured snipers, and Sergeant Horace T. West killed thirty-six prisoners with a machine gun. When court-martialed, both men referred to the stress of battle and claimed to have been influenced by the bloodthirsty rhetoric of General George S. Patton. Compton was acquitted; West was sentenced to life imprisonment, but he returned to service as a private a year later. Confident that he had no responsibility for the atrocities, Patton continued his fiery speeches.

Two major atrocities against German POWs occurred during the last year of the war. In the first, the liberation of the Dachau concentration camp, it is generally recognized that angry American soldiers summarily shot between thirty and sixty German SS guards. Allegations about the Allied mistreatment of one million German prisoners held at the Rhine Meadow Camps are on a much larger scale. Various witnesses claimed that thousands of Germans died from starvation, disease, and exposure to the cold weather. Historian James C. Bacque charges General Dwight D. Eisenhower of deliberately allowing more than one-half million POWs to die unnecessarily. Other historians, however, argue that Bacque exaggerated the numbers and failed to consider the POWs' medical problems and the food shortage in 1945-1946.

Pacific Theater The Japanese government refused to ratify the Geneva Convention on the treatment of POWs. The main reason for their decision was that Japanese military culture was profoundly influenced by the traditional Bushido code, which held surrender to be a criminal act if a soldier were able to resist. Because the Japanese regarded surrendering enemy combatants as

cowards, they often refused to take prisoners, and when they did, they were not motivated to treat them humanely. During the war, Japan held 132,756 Allied POWs, of whom more than 35,756 (about 27 percent) died in detention—a death rate nine times greater than that of POWs held by the German camps. Although claiming to liberate fellow Asians from European and American imperialism, the Japanese were even more brutal in their treatment of Chinese, Filipinos, and other Asians.

The most infamous instance of Japanese abuse of U.S. troops occurred in the Philippines after about ten thousand Americans and sixty thousand Filipinos surrendered on the Bataan Peninsula near Manila. During the resulting Bataan Death March, it is estimated that seven hundred Americans and at least seven thousand Filipinos died from starvation, disease, or intentional killing. Survivors later reported that prisoners disobeying instructions or unable to walk were summarily shot or bayoneted. In the two months after reaching Camp O'Donnell, an-

MacArthur on the Crimes of General Yamashita

U.S. general Douglas MacArthur, after the U.S. Supreme Court affirmed the conviction of Japanese general Tomoyuki Yamashita for war crimes, reviewed the case and then released a statement in February, 1946, confirming that Yamashita should indeed be hanged for his crimes.

I have reviewed the proceedings in vain search for some mitigating circumstances on his behalf. I can find none. Rarely has so cruel and wanton a record been spread to public gaze. Revolting as this may be in itself, it pales before the sinister and far reaching implication thereby attached to the profession of arms. The soldier, be he friend or foe, is charged with the protection of the weak and unarmed. It is the very essence and reason for his being. When he violates this sacred trust, he not only profanes his entire cult but threatens the very fabric of international society. The traditions of fighting men are long and honorable. They are based upon the noblest of human traits—sacrifice. This officer, of proven field merit, entrusted with high command involving authority adequate to responsibility, has failed this irrevocable standard; has failed his duty to his troops, to his country, to his enemy, to mankind; has failed utterly his soldier faith. The transgressions resulting therefrom as revealed by the trial are a blot upon the military profession, a stain upon civilization and constitute a memory of shame and dishonor that can never be forgotten.

other fifteen hundred Americans and sixteen thousand Filipinos died. Approximately four thousand emaciated Americans and perhaps twenty thousand Filipinos were still alive when Japan surrendered in August, 1945.

Although small in scale, the brutal atrocities that occurred on the Pacific island of Chichi-Jima were particularly shocking. American strategists decided not to invade the island, which served as an important center for communications, but U.S. forces attempted to disable the island's communication facilities by mounting frequent bombing raids. Japanese soldiers on Chichi-Jima, expecting to die during an anticipated invasion, either bayoneted or beheaded eight U.S. airmen who were forced to parachute or crash land on the island. In 1947, a U.S. military commission on Guam tried the Japanese officers and soldiers who participated in the Chichi-Jima executions. The commission found five officers responsible and sentenced them to death by hanging. The low-ranking soldiers who were following orders, with the threat of death for disobedience, were given prison sentences that ranged from five to seven years.

Following the attack on Pearl Harbor, most Americans despised the Japanese because of a combination of racial prejudice, cultural differences, and Japanese war practices. Journalist Ernie Pyle reported that U.S. soldiers looked on the Japanese that same way "some people feel about cockroaches or mice." Admiral William F. Halsey did not shock Americans with his slogan, "Kill Japs, kill Japs, kill more Japs."

In the classic memoir, *With the Old Breed at Peleliu and Okinawa* (1981), Eugene Sledge writes that "a passionate hatred for the Japanese burned through all the Marines I knew," and he tells how a comrade, after shooting an old Okinawan woman, dismissed her as "just an old gook woman who wanted me to put her out of her misery." Another American writer and war veteran, William Manchester, recorded in *Goodbye, Darkness: A Memoir of the Pacific War* (1980) that he observed an American soldier so enraged that he took a submarine gun and massacred a group of unarmed Japanese soldiers who had just surrendered. The March 15, 1943, issue of *Time* magazine described an incident following the Battle of the Bismarck Sea, when U.S. aircraft strafed Japanese survivors attempting to escape on lifeboats and rafts. Numerous letters to the editor applauded the conduct. In the official history of U.S. naval operations, Samuel Eliot Morison also wrote about "the

sickening business of killing survivors in boats, rafts, of wreckage," adding that it was "a grisly task, but a military necessity."

Area Bombing of Cities   Some jurists and scholars have argued that the bombing of civilian targets during World War II should be classified as a war crime. The United States was a signatory to the Hague Convention of 1907, which outlawed the bombardment of undefended towns and cities. The Hague Conference of 1923 condemned the "aerial bombardment for the purpose of terrorizing the civilian population," but the participating countries did not ratify the agreement. In 1937, nevertheless, the U.S. Department of State issued a protest against the Japanese bombing of Chinese cities as "unwarranted and contrary to the principles of war and humanity." The League of Nations Assembly proclaimed in 1938 that the intentional bombing of civilian populations was illegal. On September 1, 1939, President Franklin D. Roosevelt appealed to the nations of the world not to undertake bombardment of civilian populations and unfortified cities, upon the understanding that the same rules would be observed by their enemies.

When the U.S. Army Air Forces (USAAF) began bombing raids against Germany in January, 1943, it pursued a precision bombing strategy, in contrast to the British who were conducting area bombings at night. By early 1945, however, the USAAF began bombing large residential areas with the purpose of destroying civilian morale. On February 13-14, the joint USAAF-British bombing of Dresden produced a large firestorm that killed between 25,000 and 35,000 people. Historians estimate that when the war ended, the U.S.-British bombing of German cities had killed between 350,000 and 650,000 civilians. In Japan, moreover, the U.S. incendiary bombing of Tokyo and other cities resulted in a minimum of 200,000 deaths, and the use of atomic bombs against Hiroshima and Nagasaki killed at least another 150,000 Japanese civilians. General Curtis LeMay, who directed many of the bombings, said on several occasions that he would have been prosecuted as a war criminal if the Allies were to lose the war.

Impact   During and after World War II, countries with liberal democratic systems took war crimes and atrocities more seriously than countries with authoritarian governments. The military personnel of democratic countries, nevertheless, were often guilty of killing POWs and enemy civilians, and only rarely did they receive any punishment. As in other wars, the victorious Allies did not hesitate to exercise a double standard, which is often called "victor's justice." Whereas thousands of German and Japanese defendants were tried and punished for the mistreatment of prisoners and civilians in occupied areas, criminal acts committed against the enemy by Allied leaders and soldiers were commonly overlooked and forgotten.

No one was ever prosecuted for the civilian deaths that resulted from the bombings of large residential areas. When planning the war crimes trials at Nuremberg, the Allies initially considered filing charges against German defendants for the terror bombing of London, Warsaw, and other cities, but the Allies decided not to do so because they had conducted the same types of operations.

Thomas Tandy Lewis

Further Reading

Ambrose, Stephen, and Gunter Bischof, eds. *Eisenhower and the German POWs: Facts Against Falsehood.* Baton Rouge: Louisiana State University Press, 1992. Refutation of Bacque's allegations that Eisenhower deliberately starved more than half a million POWs.

Bacque, James C. *Crimes and Mercies: The Fate of German Civilians Under Allied Occupation, 1944-1950.* Rev. ed. Vancouver: Talonbooks, 2007. Controversial book critical of the Allies' anti-German policies, presenting evidence that 600,000 to 900,000 POWs died in U.S. and French camps.

Bauserman, John M. *The Malmédy Massacre.* Shippensburg, Pa.: White Mane, 1995. Includes both German and American versions of the event, with maps and photographs.

Bradley, James. *Flyboys: A True Story of Courage.* New York: Back Bay Books, 2003. Concentrating on eight U.S. airmen who were killed on the island of Chichi-Jima, Bradley describes atrocities committed by both the Americans and the Japanese.

Buechner, Howard. *Dachau, the Hour of the Avenger: An Eyewitness Account.* Metaire, La.: Thunderbird Press, 1986. Alleges that more than three hundred SS guards were executed when the Dachau concentration camp was liberated.

Dower, John W. *War Without Mercy: Race and Power in the Pacific War.* New York: Pantheon Books, 1986. Demonstrates that racism and cultural prejudices on both sides contributed to the brutal savagery of the war in the Pacific.

Grayling, Anthony C. *Among the Dead Cities: The History and Moral Legacy of the WWII Bombing of Civilians in Germany and Japan.* New York: Walker, 2006. Arguing that the death and destruction from area bombing resulted in disproportionate suffering in relation to its benefits, Grayling maintains that such operations constituted a "moral crime" and arguably a war crime.

Knox, Ronald. *Death March: The Survivors of Bataan.* New York: Harcourt Brace Jovanovich, 1981. Summarizes the events of the march from surrender to liberation, followed by accounts by the minority of American soldiers who survived the death march and imprisonment.

Lily, J. Robert. *Taken by Force: Rape and American Soldiers in the European Theater of Operations.* New York: Palgrave Macmillan, 2007. Finds evidence of about fourteen thousand rapes committed from 1942 to 1945 and emphasizes how the rape of British women was taken much more seriously than the rape of German women.

Weingartner, James J. "Americans, Germans, and War Crimes: Converging Narratives from the 'Good War.'" *Journal of American History* 94 (March, 2008): 1163-1183. An excellent article that compares atrocities against POWs by Germans and Americans.

See also Balloon bombs, Japanese; Bataan Death March; Bulge, Battle of the; Casualties of World War II; Convention on the Prevention and Punishment of the Crime of Genocide; Geneva Conventions; Hiroshima and Nagasaki bombings; Nuremberg Trials; Prisoners of war, North American; Strategic bombing; World War II.

■ War debt

Definition U.S. federal government debt related directly to the prosecution of World War II

The bonds and other securities issued by the U.S. Treasury committed the federal government to paying interest and redeeming the principal when due at maturity of the securities. Because tax revenue covered only about half of federal government expenditures during World War II, the national debt increased from $49 billion in mid-1941 to $269 billion in mid-1946.

Federal expenditures for national defense rose rapidly in 1940 and 1941, even before the United States entered World War II in December, 1941. Military expenditures totaled $1.8 billion in 1940, rising to $6.3 billion in 1941 and then to $22.9 billion in 1942. Although tax rates were increased and a general revival of the national economy boosted the tax base, federal spending exceeded revenues by $19 billion in 1942. The federal deficit (spending minus taxes and other income) reached its peak in fiscal year 1943, at $54 billion, then leveled off around $45 billion in 1944 and 1945.

Types of Bonds   The U.S. Treasury issued a wide variety of bonds and other securities to raise the money needed to finance expenditures. The largest component consisted of marketable long-term bonds (with maturities of more than one year), issued with a specific term to maturity and paying interest by coupon every six months. Holders of these bonds were free to buy or sell them in the open secondary market at prices that varied with supply and demand. The face value of marketable bonds increased from $31 billion in mid-1941 to $120 billion in mid-1946. Federal Reserve policy was managed so that the interest yields on these bonds did not rise above 2.5 percent per year.

United States savings bonds were created to finance World War I and had been used during the 1930's on a small scale. They became a major source of financing for World War II. This type of bond was sold at a price lower than the face value, or value at maturity. The difference between the price at issue and the price at maturity represented the interest, or return, earned on the bond. These bonds were issued in denominations as small as twenty-five dollars value at maturity. A brief time after the original issue, the holder could redeem a bond on demand, but for less than the maturity value. The redemption schedule was set so that the bonds would yield 2.9 percent per year over a ten-year period but less if the bond was redeemed before the ten-year maturity. Savings bonds were vigorously promoted during the war. The face value of savings bonds rose from $4 billion in mid-1941 to $49 billion in mid-1946. People showed no inclination to cash out large amounts of savings bonds after the war's end and instead held them to maturity.

Another major form of Treasury securities was Treasury bills. These were issued for short terms (ninety days to one year), with a new issue almost every week (to refinance the bills that were maturing). Bills were sold at a discount from the maturity value, with the discount measuring the yield to the investor. At the beginning of the war, commercial banks held substantial amounts of money as reserves (money on hand, or readily available, to meet depositors' withdrawals and to meet regulations requiring minimum reserve levels). They were willing to buy Treasury bills even at very low rates of return, largely because they did not have sufficient numbers of creditworthy customers requesting loans. In April, 1942, the Federal Reserve agreed to buy Treasury bills (from the Treasury and in the secondary market) at prices that would yield the seller 0.375 percent interest. This rate pattern was maintained until July, 1947. Because of the extremely low interest cost of this kind of borrowing, the Treasury expanded its issue of bills: The amount outstanding increased from $1.6 billion in mid-1941 to $52 billion in mid-1946.

Federal Reserve Policy   The Federal Reserve (the Fed), which as the nation's central bank supervises the nation's banks and conducts the nation's monetary policy, was faced with conflicting objectives. On one hand, it wanted to assist the Treasury in financing the war at low interest rates. It pursued this goal by purchasing Treasury securities at prices that prevented interest rates from rising (meaning that the prices were high relative to maturity value). This led to a large increase in Federal Reserve securities holdings, from $2 billion at the end of 1940 to $24 billion at the end of 1945. When the Fed purchased securities from banks, this created reserve funds for the banks, which enabled them to expand loans and thereby create more deposits.

The money supply (defined as the total amount of currency plus checking deposits) more than doubled between 1941 and 1945, contributing to inflationary pressure. This conflicted with the Federal Reserve's other primary goal, to restrain inflation. The Fed tried to combat inflation by raising reserve requirements for banks (meaning that banks had to hold more money in reserve against depositors' withdrawals, and thus had less money to lend) and by imposing direct controls on consumer credit. Regulation W of 1941 provided for minimum down payments and maximum maturities for various types of consumer credit.

When the war ended in 1945, federal expenditures were cut back rapidly, and tax revenues remained high. The national debt reached $269 billion in mid-1946, then receded to $252 million by mid-1948. With the removal of wartime price controls in 1946, prices increased rapidly. The Fed wished to bring about higher interest rates to restrain inflationary borrowing, but this conflicted with the Treasury's goal of paying low interest rates on its securities. The Fed was able to move Treasury-bill interest rates upward after 1947, and in 1950, it ceased supporting the interest rate of 2.5 percent for long-term marketable bonds.

Impact Compared to policies followed in World War I, wartime financial policies in 1941-1945 were more effective in achieving government goals. Tax rates were raised substantially, which helped restrain inflation and provided income to the government so that the federal government's deficits and increases in debt could be smaller. U.S. savings bonds provided ordinary Americans with a means of saving that had a guaranteed rate of return, could be purchased in small amounts, and was seen as contributing directly to the war effort. The inflation of the 1940's was much milder than that of 1917-1920, and the postwar economy avoided a severe recession like that of 1920-1921. Through careful conduct of policy, the Treasury was able to finance wartime borrowing without having to pay high rates of interest.

Paul B. Trescott

Further Reading

Chandler, Lester V. *Inflation in the United States, 1940-1948*. New York: Harper, 1951. Reprint. New York: Da Capo Press, 1976. Government policy related to national debt figures prominently in this comprehensive review of wartime financial policies.

Fishback, Price, et al. *Government and the American Economy: A New History*. Chicago: University of Chicago Press, 2007. Several sections deal with World War II; most relevant is chapter 14, by Robert Higgs.

Friedman, Milton, and Anna J. Schwartz. *A Monetary History of the United States, 1867-1960*. Princeton, N.J.: Princeton University Press, 1963. Chapter 10 of this classic of financial history deals with the interlocks among monetary policy, fiscal policy, and management of the national debt. Presents details of the Fed operations and analysis of policy.

Markham, Jerry W. *From J. P. Morgan to the Institutional Investor, 1900-1970*. Vol. 2 in *A Financial History of the United States*. Armonk, N.Y.: M. E. Sharpe, 2002. Chapter 5 deals with World War II and its aftermath. Succinct and comprehensive.

Murphy, Henry C. *The National Debt in War and Transition*. New York: McGraw-Hill, 1950. A definitive description and analysis of national debt policies by a longtime Treasury official.

See also Business and the economy in the United States; Credit and debt; Inflation; Keynesian economics; Lend-Lease; National debt; War bonds; World War II.

■ War heroes

Definition Individuals recognized for their personal bravery in combat or as representatives of groups that acted heroically

Stories of American heroism in battle helped boost the morale of citizens on the home front and members of the armed forces in combat zones, reinforcing the notion that the sacrifices being made by everyone who supported the Allies were worthwhile.

During World War II, the American public keenly followed events in the various theaters of operation and quickly became enamored with the exploits of its fighting forces. Both government propagandists and the media found the stories of individuals' exploits a useful way to boost the nation's morale and secure support for what President Franklin D. Roosevelt and his closest advisors realized would be a protracted conflict. Campaigns were designed to make people on the home front also feel like heroes, celebrating the sacrifices of those working to produce materials for the war, those who purchased war bonds, and even children collecting scrap materials. Although a fictional character, "Rosie the Riveter" came to symbolize the heroic actions of women joining the workforce to replace men who had gone off to fight.

Heroic Leaders The United States had its first celebrity hero just months after the country entered the war. In April, 1942, Lieutenant Colonel James "Jimmy" Doolittle led a carrier-launched bomber squadron in an attack on the Japanese mainland. Although air crew members were forced to ditch their planes or land in China, the raid boosted morale in the United States. Doolittle was honored on his return home and promoted to brigadier general. He went on to lead air units in the European theater.

Similarly, when American ground forces entered combat in 1943 in North Africa, the exploits of Major General George S. Patton in leading U.S. forces against Erwin Rommel's fabled German Afrika Korps were reported widely. Americans in the combat zone and at home began to see Patton as the type of charismatic leader who would propel the Allies to victory. Although disciplined for inappropriate behavior and held out of the D-day invasion, Patton eventually led the Third Army in the Allies' race across France and Germany to the Rhine River. One of Patton's subordinates, Brigadier General Anthony McAuliffe, became famous for his defiance of the German order to surrender his forces at Bastogne in December, 1944. However, no one achieved more iconic status than the Allies' supreme com-

mander, General Dwight D. Eisenhower, who would eventually parlay his success in war into a successful campaign for the presidency.

Common Soldiers Although not often given the same level of publicity as the prominent commanders, some lower-ranking battlefield heroes did receive national attention. Periodically the American public learned of the heroism of men such as Al Schmid, a Marine blinded by a wound on Guadalcanal who was reported to have held off a sizeable Japanese force singlehandedly, killing two hundred of the enemy.

The six men photographed raising an American flag at Iwo Jima were celebrated as representatives of the thousands of brave Marines fighting in the Pacific. The Roosevelt administration made good use of their celebrity, bringing three of them back to the United States to serve as spokespersons for the campaign to sell war bonds.

No one was more visibly lionized, however, than Army infantryman Audie Murphy, who fought in Eu-

One of the most celebrated American heroes of World War II was Marine major Gregory "Pappy" Boyington (above arrow), commander of the famed Black Sheep Squadron in the South Pacific. On January 3, 1944, he tied an American record by shooting down his twenty-sixth enemy aircraft. Ironically, he himself was shot down later the same day. After being captured by the Japanese, he never flew in combat again, and his fate was unknown until he was liberated from a prisoner camp after the war ended. He returned home a triumphant hero and lived until 1988, by which time he had seen his wartime exploits re-created in the television series Baa Baa Black Sheep *(1976-1978), in which he was portrayed by actor Robert Conrad. (AP/Wide World Photos)*

rope. The most decorated American soldier of the war, Murphy was on the cover of *Life* magazine in July, 1945. Millions of Americans learned how this undersized but overzealous warrior repeatedly returned to battle, despite multiple wounds that kept him hospitalized for months. Idolized for his heroic deeds, Murphy became the living symbol of all the brave young men who had fought, and in some cases died, to save the free world from the dangers posed by the Axis Powers. Fortuitously for Murphy, the public attention catapulted him into a film career, and he would even play himself in the 1955 film *To Hell and Back*, based on his ghostwritten memoir.

Not everyone who performed heroic deeds received public adulation. Nevertheless, the conflicts in Europe and the Pacific produced a decidedly large number of men and women recognized by the armed forces for their heroism under fire. Awards of the Combat Infantryman's Badge and Bronze Star recognized the valor of hundreds of thousands of infantrymen. The Silver Star, awarded for notable heroism, went to more than 100,000 service personnel. The Army awarded approximately five thousand Distinguished Service Crosses to ground and air forces. The Navy presented nearly four thousand Navy Crosses to sailors and marines, including one to Dorrie Miller, a crewman aboard the USS *West Virginia* at Pearl Harbor, the first African American to be so honored. The country also recognized 464 military personnel with its highest award for bravery, the Congressional Medal of Honor.

Impact The stories of America's heroes, often ordinary service personnel who had performed courageously under fire, seem to have had a significant, positive impact on Americans' morale. Soldiers, sailors, airmen, and Marines took heart from these heroes' examples and saw that the bonds forged in combat could provide every individual with the courage to fight valiantly. For the larger American public, the valor exhibited by these heroes came to symbolize not only the country's fighting spirit but also the values that the military was sent to defend in Europe and Asia.

Laurence W. Mazzeno

Further Reading

Ambrose, Stephen E. *Citizen Soldiers: The U.S. Army from the Normandy Beaches to the Bulge to the Surrender of Germany.* New York: Simon & Schuster, 1997. Contains accounts of numerous heroic acts by American soldiers fighting in the European theater during World War II.

Bergerud, Eric. *Touched with Fire: The Land War in the South Pacific.* New York: Viking, 1996. Describes the nature of the conflict on the Pacific islands, providing excellent background about conditions under which some Americans were able to perform heroic acts.

Hatfield, Ken. *Heartland Heroes: Remembering World War II.* Columbia: University of Missouri Press, 2003. Anecdotes from more than a hundred veterans of World War II provide firsthand accounts of combat operations and detail acts of bravery they witnessed personally.

Jordan, Kenneth N. *Yesterday's Heroes.* Atglen, Pa.: Schiffer, 1996. Contains the citations detailing the heroic actions of more than four hundred military service members awarded the Medal of Honor during World War II.

Whiting, Charles. *American Hero: The Life and Death of Audie Murphy.* York, England: Eskdale, 1989. Describes Murphy's exploits during the war, giving readers a glimpse of action on the battlefield and making clear why Murphy and others like him deserved to be called heroes.

See also Bulge, Battle of the; Cochran, Jacqueline; D Day; Doolittle bombing raid; Films about World War II; Iwo Jima, Battle of; Merrill's Marauders; Murphy, Audie; Patton, George S.; "Rosie the Riveter"; World War II.

∎ War Production Board

Identification   Federal agency charged with converting American industry to wartime production during World War II

Date   Established on January 16, 1942

Under the supervision of the Office of War Mobilization, the War Production Board (WPB) was responsible for procuring materials for the war effort, regulating industrial output, allocating resources to government agencies, prohibiting production of nonessential products, regulating wages and prices, and prioritizing and allocating scarce materials.

First headed by former Sears, Roebuck executive Donald Nelson, the WPB coordinated industrial production for the war effort through twelve regional offices and 120 field offices. Nelson and his successor, Julius Krug, struggled to define the WPB's broad mission while balancing the demands of private industry and the military. The WPB monitored the construction of factories that churned out airplanes, ships, tanks, and munitions. It lifted most of its production restrictions during the last months of the war. On November 3, 1945, the WPB dissolved, and the Civilian Production Administration absorbed its remaining functions and programs.

Impact The WPB directed the production of armaments and supplies totaling $185 billion. It streamlined wartime production of American industry and created networks among manufacturers that made the postwar economic and industrial reconversion much more efficient.

Aaron D. Purcell

Further Reading

Civilian Production Administration. *Program and Administration.* Vol. 1 in *Industrial Mobilization for War: History of the War Production Board and Predecessor Agencies.* Washington, D.C.: Government Printing Office, 1947.

Kennedy, David M. *Freedom from Fear: The American People in Depression and War, 1929-1945.* New York: Oxford University Press, 1999.

Koistinen, Paul A. C. *Arsenal of World War II: The Political Economy of American Warfare, 1940-1945.* Lawrence: University Press of Kansas, 2004.

Nelson, Donald M. *Arsenal of Democracy: The Story of American War Production.* New York: Harcourt, Brace, 1946.

See also Economic wartime regulations; Office of War Mobilization; Wartime industries; Wartime rationing; Wartime salvage drives; World War II; World War II mobilization.

■ War surplus

Definition Real property and materials produced for military operations that are designated as obsolete or no longer needed by the federal government

The six-year surge to build the machinery of war and equip forces of the United States and the Allies meant that, at the end of World War II, the U.S. government had significant quantities of surplus merchandise on hand. Additionally, manufacturing facilities built by the government and property requisitioned or purchased as training sites were also no longer needed. Transferring these assets in an orderly fashion to civilian entities posed a major logistical challenge to government officials.

The U.S. government has always experienced problems in disposing of materials and property no longer needed at the end of wars in which it has engaged. Charges of favoritism in selling off surplus goods were rampant after the Civil War and again after World War I. Therefore, even before the United States entered World War II, President Franklin D. Roosevelt and his advisers were sensitive to the potential impact that disposal of surplus would have on the American economy once hostilities were over. At the same time, the administration believed that, with proper planning, the return of surplus property and goods could act as a spur to the economy, which might suffer when wartime production was curtailed.

Planning for Disposal of Surplus By 1940, the Roosevelt administration realized that it would be impossible for the United States to avoid becoming embroiled in the conflict raging in Europe. With great foresight, the administration incorporated planning for disposal of surplus in its earliest plans for mobilization. Discussions were held regarding the best ways to use the leverage the government would have in disposing of military surplus when hostilities were over. Some officials hoped to use the surplus to help the economy return to a peacetime footing with greater stability than it had experienced during the decade-long Depression of the 1930's.

Specific principles for using the war surplus as a means of rejuvenating the peacetime economy were incorporated into the Surplus Property Act of 1944, which stated that every effort would be made to support small businesses when surplus property and equipment was sold off. The War Assets Administration was established to handle sales of nearly $40 billion in surplus materiel. Some assets were transferred even before the conflict ended in the summer of 1945.

Sale of Surplus Property and Goods Unfortunately, in the rush to demobilize, the government's careful planning went awry. A significant problem arose during the implementation phase of policies established by the Surplus Property Act. Under terms of the act, the government was required to conduct what amounted to distress sales, transferring property (both materials and real estate) to the highest bidder. Because larger corporations were in a much better position to bid on more expensive lots, nearly two-thirds of the surplus ended up in the hands of fewer than one hundred companies. Additionally, a number of facilities built by the government were colocated at or near major commercial enterprises such as automotive or chemical businesses, which were often the only businesses able to make use of the facilities after the war.

When it came to selling off high-dollar value goods, the government met with better success. Many of the manufacturers of aircraft, vehicles, and heavy equipment were able to buy products they had made for the government at a fraction of their original cost. Other firms purchased these items at auction in order to convert them for civilian use or, in some cases, turn them into scrap metal, a valuable commodity. Items of lesser value were attractive to another group, which took advantage of the availability of surplus equipment being sold at discount prices to establish a new kind of business: Army-Navy surplus stores. Obtaining clothing, bedding, dining ware, tools, and outdoor equipment at bargain prices, these entrepreneurs set up shops in virtually every region of the country. They found a ready market among consumers who were delighted to be able to obtain these items at reasonable prices.

Impact The impact of the Roosevelt administration's efforts to dispose of surplus property and equipment was mixed. Large corporations involved in chemical, textile, aviation, or automotive manufacturing were able to increase their assets by purchasing specialized facilities for a fraction of what it had cost the government to construct them. At the same time, the government benefited by seeing some return on its investment, and millions of individuals, especially veterans, benefited because jobs were created in these facilities. To a lesser extent, the small business community saw an increase in activity as a result of the establishment of Army-Navy surplus stores, which not only provided employment for thousands but also placed large quantities of durable and relatively inexpensive goods on the market, spurring consumption. Nevertheless, the govern-

Surplus Army trucks lined up for eventual disposal in 1948. (Time & Life Pictures/Getty Images)

ment's grand plan to use the surplus as a major means of promoting small business never really materialized.

Laurence W. Mazzeno

Further Reading

Brandes, Stuart D. *Warhogs: A History of War Profits in America.* Lexington: University Press of Kentucky, 1997. Briefly describes efforts undertaken to dispose of surplus property after World War II; explains the role of business and industry in shaping government policies.

Cain, Louis, and George Neumann. "Planning for Peace: The Surplus Property Act of 1944." *Journal of Economic History* 41, no. 1 (March, 1981): 129-135. Describes the government's plans for disposal of surplus and outlines the objectives of the law passed to set out terms for transference.

Chiles, James R. "How the Great War on War Surplus Got Won—Or Lost." *Smithsonian* 26, no. 9 (December, 1995): 52-61. Describes the types of surplus on hand in 1945, examines methods used for transferring surplus to businesses and individuals, and explores reasons for ill feelings created by public perceptions of favoritism.

Kaplan, A. D. H. *The Liquidation of War Production: Cancellation of War Contracts and Disposal of Government-Owned Plants and Surpluses.* New York: McGraw-Hill, 1944. Systematic examination of problems the United States would face at the end of hostilities, with recommendations for canceling contracts with industry and handling surplus property and equipment.

Koistinen, Paul. *Arsenal of World War II: The Political Economy of American Warfare, 1940-1945.* Lawrence: University Press of Kansas, 2004. Places the program for disposing of surplus property and equipment in the larger context of the government's strategy for managing the logistics of the war effort.

See also   Business and the economy in the United States; War Production Board; Wartime industries; Wartime rationing; World War II.

■ Warmerdam, Cornelius

Identification   Premier pole vaulter in the world throughout the 1940's

Born   July 22, 1915; Long Beach California

Died   November 13, 2001; Fresno, California

Warmerdam dominated the pole vault event during the 1940's, when he became the first person to vault higher than fifteen feet, and was one of the most outstanding track and field athletes of his era.

Cornelius "Dutch" Warmerdam learned pole vaulting by practicing in his father's peach and apricot orchard with a bamboo pole, and he developed into one of the dominant athletes of the 1940's. Before 1940, many experts thought it was impossible for humans to vault fifteen feet, but Warmerdam proved them wrong.

Unlike modern pole vaulters, who use fiberglass poles and fall on elevated, soft, cushioned mats, Warmerdam and other pole vaulters during the 1940's used rigid bamboo poles and fell on ground-level sand and sawdust pits. Warmerdam won nine National Amateur Athletic Union titles and began inching toward the magic fifteen-foot barrier. On April 6, 1940, in Berkeley, California, Warmerdam flew over the bar set at fifteen feet. He eventually raised the pole vaulting world record to 15-7¾, a record that would stand for fifteen years. He also set the world indoor record at 15-8½, and he made forty-three vaults that were higher than fifteen feet.

Impact   Despite being the greatest U.S. pole vaulter of his time, Warmerdam never competed in the Olympic Games because he had the misfortune to be at his peak during World War II, when the 1940 and 1944 games were cancelled. Warmerdam went on to a successful twenty-year head coaching career at Fresno State University.

Mark Stanbrough

Further Reading

Fimrite, Ron. "A Call to Arms." *Sports Illustrated* 75, no. 18 (Fall, 1991): 98-108.

Litsky, Frank. "Dutch Warmerdam, Pole-Vaulter,

Cornelius Warmerdam clearing the bar at the February, 1942, Millrose Games in New York City's Madison Square Garden, at which he raised the world pole vault record to 15 feet ⅞ inch. (AP/Wide World Photos)

Dies at 86." *The New York Times*, November 15, 2001, p. D10.

Wallechinsky, David, and Jaime Loucky. *The Complete Book of the Olympics: 2008 Edition*. London: Aurum Press, 2008.

Warmerdam, Cornelius. *Pole Vault Training and Technique*. Inglewood, Calif.: Gill Sporting Goods, [n.d.].

See also   Olympic Games of 1948; Sports in the United States; Zaharias, Babe Didrikson.

■ Wartime espionage

Throughout World War II, Japanese and German espionage efforts were largely inefficient. The Soviet Union was more successful and was able to effectively penetrate the Manhattan Project. Foreign efforts at intelligence gathering were combated by the Federal Bureau of Investigation, and most of the espionage operations were eventually uncovered.

During World War II, the Japanese, German, and Soviet governments all attempted to gather intelligence on the military and economic situations within the United States.

Japanese Espionage   Japanese intelligence efforts at the outset of the war were carried out mostly by members of their diplomatic corps who were based in the United States. They transmitted routine information to Japan. In 1941, a Japanese naval intelligence officer was sent to Hawaii to pass information back to Japan on the types of military hardware in Pearl Harbor. He was arrested by the Federal Bureau of Investigation (FBI) and sent to an internment camp in the United States. In addition to the naval officer, other members of the Japanese consulate in Hawaii spied on U.S. installations.

The Japanese also trained fishermen in California to report on shipping coming in and out of ports and set up a Japanese spy ring on the West Coast. Its members attempted to recruit sailors to help their espionage effort. One of the agents who was caught had a suitcase with details of antiaircraft defenses, photographs of military bases, and details of naval ships and aircraft. After early stages of the war, however, Japanese intelligence efforts in North America were so ineffective as to be virtually nonexistent.

German Espionage   The Germans concentrated their espionage efforts largely in Latin America during the war. Their agents reported on shipping and other industrial information, particularly regarding raw materials. The Germans also attempted to establish spy rings in North America. In 1939, the Abwehr, or German military intelligence, began establishing agents in the United States, who reported on military information, production levels, and shipping information. They were all eventually captured. During the week after the Japanese attacked Pearl Harbor in December, 1941, FBI agents captured thirty-three German spies in the Duquesne spy ring who were looking for industrial information and sabotage opportunities. In 1942, a German agent named Werner Janowski was landed from a U-boat on the coast of Canada. He was soon caught after leaving revealing signs of his European origins in a hotel room. In June, 1942, the Germans landed eight saboteurs on the coasts of New York's Long Island and Florida. Dressed in German uniforms, these operatives carried explosives with which to attack American industries. By the end of the month, all of them were caught before doing any actual damage.

German intelligence-gathering efforts in North America were mostly disastrous. Their agents were quickly caught and unable to operate effectively. The FBI persuaded some of the German agents to switch their allegiance and then provide the German government with false information. This effort allowed the FBI to learn more about how German intelligence operated.

Soviet Espionage   The Soviet Union had the most success with espionage in North America during World War II. Despite the wartime alliance between the United States and the Soviet Union, the Soviets maintained an active spy network in the United States. In contrast, neither the United States nor Great Britain attempted to place spies within the Soviet Union during the war. Suspicious of the United States, Soviet leader Joseph Stalin used an extensive espionage network to acquire military secrets. Much of the Soviet spying was focused on the Manhattan Project, which was developing atomic bombs.

Many persons recruited to spy for the Soviets were driven by the ideology of communism and the solidarity of an international communist movement. Some of these individuals were actually members of the Communist Party USA. Many of the early attempts by Soviet intelligence to gain assets within the Manhattan Project were foiled by U.S. counterintelligence. Nevertheless, the majority of Soviet spies were not caught until after they had already provided valuable information to the Soviet government

British national Klaus Fuchs passed information to the Soviet Union throughout the war. Early in his career, he gave the Soviets intelligence about the British atomic project. After he was reassigned to the Manhattan Project in 1944, he relayed information about the design of the atomic bomb to the Soviets. He was not caught until after the war. Theodore Hall was another spy who worked on the Manhattan Project. The information he gave the Soviets was not as extensive as that supplied by Fuchs, but it did confirm the material Fuchs was giving the Soviets. He, too, was caught after the war. Bruno Pontecorvo and Allan Nunn May also spied on the Manhattan Project. Both were stationed in Ontario, Canada. May passed along information regarding reactors to his Soviet handlers. Pontecorvo also passed along the atomic secrets he acquired during his work. He eventually defected to the Soviet Union following the arrest of Fuchs. Other Soviet agents also spied on the Manhattan Project, but their identities have remained largely unknown.

Perhaps the most famous Soviet spies were not part of the Manhattan Project. Julius and Ethel Rosenberg were involved in industrial espionage on behalf of the Soviets throughout the war. Julius Rosenberg was an engineer who provided information to the Soviets. He gave the Soviets information on military technologies, including the designs of aircraft. His brother-in-law, David Greenglass, worked as a machinist on the Manhattan Project and passed information on the atomic bomb to Julius Rosenberg. All were avowed communists and spied for ideological reasons. Eventually, Greenglass was caught and the Rosenbergs were found guilty of espionage and executed in 1953.

Elizabeth Bentley was another Soviet spy. She first passed her information to the Communist Party USA and believed that she was helping the fight against fascist Italy. However, all of the information she gave was passed along to the Soviet Union. She ultimately operated as a courier for the Silvermaster spy group, which supplied information to the Soviets, most of which had to do with Germany. Much of

the information was about troop strength, production levels in the United States, and the timetable for the Allied invasion of Europe.

Impact The espionage efforts by Nazi and Japanese agents were relatively ineffective throughout the war. The rampant fear of Japanese espionage influenced the mass internment of ethnic Japanese living in the United States and Canada. A similar fear of Nazi infiltration led to the internment of several thousand ethnic Germans as well. The espionage efforts by the Soviet Union helped to advance its own construction of an atomic bomb. The full extent of Soviet espionage in the United States was not discovered until cryptanalysts working for the British-American Venona Project figured out how to decode Soviet agents' messages. Meanwhile, the espionage charges against the Rosenbergs and the decision to execute both of them created one of the most divisive issues of the Cold War. It also gave the FBI valuable experience in counterespionage that was put to use during the Cold War.

Michael W. Cheek

Further Reading

Dobbs, Michael. *Saboteurs: The Nazi Raid on America.* New York: Alfred A. Knopf, 2004. Details the operation of the Nazi sabotage element sent to the United States.

Gimpel, Erich. *Agent 146: The True Story of a Nazi Spy in America.* New York: St. Martin's Press, 2003. Story of the Nazi saboteurs sent to the United States written by one of the saboteurs.

Haynes, John Earl, and Harvey Klehr. *Venona: Decoding Soviet Espionage in America.* New Haven, Conn.: Yale University Press, 2000. Provides an overview of the Venona decoding project that helped to expose Soviet agents operating in North America.

Matthews, Tony. *Shadow Dancing: Japanese Espionage Against the West 1939-1945.* New York: St. Martin's Press, 1994. Examines the efforts by Japanese intelligence services against the Allied forces during World War II.

Radosh, Ronald, and Joyce Milton. *The Rosenberg File.* 2d ed. New Haven, Conn.: Yale University Press, 1997. Discusses the famous case of the Rosenbergs, using numerous documents from both Soviet and U.S. sources.

Rommerstein, Herbert, and Eric Breindel. *The Venona Secrets: Exposing Soviet Espionage and America's Traitors.* Washington, D.C.: Regnery, 2001. A detailed account of the secrets revealed by Venona and the various spies operating for the Soviets.

Weinstein, Allen, and Alexander Vassiliev. *The Haunted Wood: Soviet Espionage in America—The Stalin Era.* New York: Random House, 1999. An examination of Soviet intelligence-gathering efforts in the United States during the Stalin regime.

See also   Anticommunism; Atomic bomb; Civil defense programs; Code breaking; Cold War; Federal Bureau of Investigation; Japanese American internment; Japanese Canadian internment; *Korematsu v. United States*; War crimes and atrocities; Wartime sabotage; White, Harry Dexter; World War II.

■ Wartime industries

During World War II, the United States and the Allies were heavily dependent on American industry to produce weapons, equipment, and supplies needed to fight the Axis forces. Industry's ability to convert to a wartime economy was crucial to the Allies' success in defeating Germany, Italy, and Japan.

Notwithstanding the gallantry of American troops and the brilliance of military strategists, American success in World War II was in large part attributable to the nation's industrial might. Far from the battlefields, ordinary Americans worked in steel mills, automobile factories, aircraft plants, and shipyards to produce equipment and supplies required by the armed forces. Industries' involvement in wartime production was not without controversy, however, and the nation's success in industrial mobilization was the result of a constant give-and-take among key entities involved in marshaling America's economic engine: management, labor, the armed services, and government agencies directing mobilization efforts.

Industrial Conversion, 1940-1941   Although the United States did not become a combatant in World War II until December, 1941, President Franklin D. Roosevelt realized as early as 1940 that the Allies would need help from America to defeat the Axis Powers. He also understood that war-related spending and production could help the United States emerge from the Great Depression, the effects of which still had about 15 percent of the labor force unemployed and most businesses operating below capacity. By the summer of 1941, Roosevelt had developed plans for an Army of 1.2 million men (with 800,000 reserves) and a two-ocean Navy, along with an elaborate scheme to provision America's allies.

Fearing that a massive military buildup could create even more power for the country's largest companies, New Dealers urged the president to maintain tight control over the transition to a wartime economy. Between 1940 and 1942, Roosevelt set up dozens of advisory boards, including the National Defense Advisory Council, the Office of Production Management, and the Supply Priorities and Allocations Board. Consisting of government officials, industry executives, trade association representatives, and labor union leaders, these groups assisted in allocating resources, assigning priorities for production, establishing price controls, and regulating the labor force. They were designed to serve as an important leg of a mobilization triangle consisting of civilian oversight committees, military procurement officials, and the various industries that could simultaneously meet the growing needs of the armed forces and the continuing demands of the civilian economy.

Despite the care taken to set up this arrangement, it was flawed from the beginning. The armed services already had direct ties with industry and were wary of civilian interference in the procurement process. Most large corporations, the military's preferred partners, were willing to pay lip service to oversight agencies, but many were skeptical about the shift from peacetime to wartime production and did not fully believe that this shift could end the long economic slump of the Depression. Orders for war materials appeared to be a temporary phenomenon, and manufacturers were reluctant to invest heavily in machinery and facilities to meet those orders because they believed that the production capacity would soon become unnecessary, leaving even more resources idle before they had earned a profit. Additionally, by 1940 the civilian economy was improving, and businesses did not want to forfeit opportunities to meet demands of a growing civilian market in order to fulfill government contracts.

Manufacturers of aluminum, copper, and steel initially resisted expansion of their industries because they did not want to see competitors gain advantages during wartime that might carry over into the peacetime economy. The railroads and energy producers (particularly the coal industry) also were hesitant to expand. Major chemical companies balked at accepting military contracts, fearing that they would be branded as merchants of death (as had happened during World War I) if asked to develop chemical weapons.

Several important transitional steps occurred between 1940 and 1942. In March, 1941, Congress passed the Lend-Lease Act, officially mobilizing the nation's industrial resources to begin wartime production. Lend-lease production from 1941 until the end of the war accounted for $50 billion in business, with most products going to Great Britain. Peacetime construction projects were halted to conserve lumber and steel. Automakers reduced production of private vehicles to build war machines for the Allies. Nevertheless, it was not until the Japanese attacked Pearl Harbor on December 7, 1941, that American industry became fully committed to the war effort.

Industrial Expansion After Pearl Harbor   The first six months of 1942 were a turbulent time in the United States as industries engaged in full-scale conversion to the wartime economy. Roosevelt created stronger regulatory agencies—first the War Production Board and later the War Mobilization Board—to manage production priorities. At the same time, the business community realized that its commitment to the war effort was essential to winning the war.

War-related industries expanded rapidly. The steel industry was at the center of the military buildup, with orders for steel to construct ships, tanks, and other military equipment more than making up for orders lost when the automotive industry suspended production of private vehicles. At its peak of wartime production, U.S. Steel employed 340,000 workers. Bethlehem Steel ramped up its shipbuilding operations, increasing the workforce at its shipyards from 7,000 to 180,000 over the course of the war. Eighty-one new shipyards opened after December, 1941.

During the war, the number of aircraft plants in the country doubled. The automotive industry supplemented the aircraft industry in manufacturing planes while also building military ground vehicles and various kinds of weaponry. Chrysler concentrated on building tanks, while Ford built Willys

Jeeps and B-24 bombers. Various companies pooled resources, shared patent information, and standardized procedures and equipment specifications to achieve efficient production.

Rapid growth characterized other industries as well, both in their regular product lines and in production of more war-related goods. Demand for aluminum went from 325 million pounds in 1939 to 2.3 billion pounds in 1943. Dow Chemical, which had produced modest quantities of magnesium for years, suddenly found itself flooded with orders for the light metal; the company erected a new processing plant within eight months following the attack on Pearl Harbor. The home products company Procter & Gamble made ammunition. DuPont Chemical was heavily involved in producing smokeless gunpowder and eventually was asked to help develop nuclear energy.

Labor Relations   During the buildup to American entry into the war, and even after hostilities commenced, some industries were plagued by labor unrest as unions fought to maintain the gains in wages and the improvements in working conditions they had achieved during the 1930's. Although more than 10 million Americans entered the armed forces and another 2 million joined the government in other capacities, most businesses were able to replace employees with unemployed workers (many of whom migrated to places where defense work was available) or with women who entered the workforce by the thousands beginning in 1942.

Workers avoided using labor strikes because of fears that their patriotism would be questioned and that their positions would be taken by nonunion workers. After the United States became a combatant, organized labor groups pledged not to strike and management agreed not to conduct lockouts. As inflation set in and some industries proved better than others at providing for workers, however, some work stoppages occurred. The particularly contentious activities of the United Mine Workers led to passage of the Smith-Connally Act (War Labor Disputes Act) in 1943, giving the government authority to seize manufacturing facilities affected by illegal strikes. On the whole, a spirit of sacrifice pervaded the home front. Civilians saw themselves contributing to the war effort through their performance on the job, and they were willing to make small sacrifices in furtherance of the war effort.

Scope of Wartime Production   During the buildup to war and throughout the conflict, the bulk of contracts for war-related materials went to large corporations. Although Congress and members of the Roosevelt administration tried valiantly to involve small businesses in war production, larger firms were better able to meet high-volume requirements efficiently and on time. As an example of the imbalance, of the $175 billion in contracts for national security work granted in 1944, $117 billion went to the top one hundred corporations in America, with $60 billion of that to the top thirty. Among those receiving the greatest financial benefits were General Motors, Curtiss-Wright, U.S. Steel, Bethlehem Steel, General Electric, Ford, and the Aluminum Company of America (ALCOA). The government financed two-thirds of a $26 billion expansion of manufacturing capability, sometimes using creative financing to get firms to operate plants built and owned by the Defense Plant Corporation.

Throughout the war, many larger companies managed to remain profitable or even advance their business interests. Although laws prohibited excessive profits, companies were able to reinvest a portion of their earnings in research and development, the costs of which could be deducted from profit statements. At the same time, many companies did not bill the government for research, instead retaining the rights to any new products they might develop. By contrast, smaller firms simply could not compete against larger corporations that had the staffing and relationships with the War and Navy Departments to obtain contracts for major work. Some small companies pooled assets and became creative in bidding, but many small businesses faced insurmountable losses.

Most industrial mobilization centered on existing industries; however, one fledgling industry that blossomed during the war was synthetic rubber manufacturing. Elimination of rubber imports from the Far East forced the United States to step up production of synthetic rubber: 22 million tons were produced in 1942 and 922 million tons in 1945. This change was fraught with political tensions, however. Because synthetic rubber could be made from either grain or oil, congressional representatives from oil- and grain-producing states actively demanded use of one of those raw materials over the other.

Reconversion to a Peacetime Economy   Although the wartime economy lasted through the last quarter of 1945, plans to convert back to peacetime production were well under way in 1944. Government officials and business leaders realized that planning was critical if a postwar economic crash was to be avoided, because so much of the economy had been redirected to war-related production. When wartime needs were eliminated, businesses would suddenly find themselves without customers. As indications of the scope of government purchasing, businesses received approximately $55 billion in war munitions contracts in 1942, and by 1944 purchases for national security accounted for 42 percent of the nation's gross national product (GNP). In 1944, some industries were allowed to return to producing civilian goods, as long as doing so did not affect fulfillment of military contracts. In the same year, Congress passed the Surplus Property Act to govern disposal of excess military goods and property at the

Women at Douglas Aircraft's Long Beach, California, plant assembling nose cones for A-20 attack bombers. (National Archives)

war's end. Although designed to help small businesses and veterans, the program proved most beneficial to large corporations, which were able to buy goods and property, including fully operational factories, at highly discounted prices. Furthermore, strict government controls over the economy, which had been accepted by private enterprise as necessary during wartime, were abandoned quickly when the war ended.

Impact Meeting the country's, and the Allies', wartime requirements helped America's industries overcome the economic slump of the Great Depression. Employment rose, production increased dramatically, and profits improved. American businesses provided logistical support essential to the Allies' victories in Europe and Asia. Equally important, however, was the impact of government agencies supporting industry during the conflict. Government funding to aid key industries such as steel, mining, chemical, automotive, and energy placed many firms in positions of strength when hostilities ceased, and they found themselves well positioned to meet growing consumer demands in the postwar years.

Furthermore, the close relationships that developed between the armed services and industries involved in manufacturing materials for military purposes made possible the emergence of what President Dwight D. Eisenhower later called the military-industrial complex. When elected officials and military planners discovered at the end of World War II that the Soviet Union posed a continuing threat to the United States and Western Europe, they found it easy to create an industrial sector that could sustain itself by producing weaponry and equipment for a permanent multibillion-dollar defense establishment.

Laurence W. Mazzeno

Further Reading

Atleson, James B. *Labor and the Wartime State: Labor Relations and Law During World War II*. Urbana: University of Illinois Press, 1998. Examines the interactions of government, management, and labor during the war, explaining the role each played in promoting industrial production during the period of hostilities.

Brandes, Stuart D. *Warhogs: A History of War Profits in America*. Lexington: University Press of Kentucky, 1997. Explains ways that businesses have profited from American ventures into war. Devotes several chapters to examining businesses' relationships with the government during World War II.

Janeway, Eliot. *Economics of Crisis: War, Politics, and the Dollar*. New York: Weybright and Talley, 1968. Explores the economic impact of war on the United States. Explains how Roosevelt's policies affected businesses during World War II.

Koistinen, Paul. *Arsenal of World War II: The Political Economy of American Warfare, 1940-1945*. Lawrence: University Press of Kansas, 2004. Comprehensive study of the federal government's efforts to plan and control the wartime economy. Explains relationships among regulatory agencies, the armed services, and private industry.

Vatter, Harold G. *The U.S. Economy in World War II*. New York: Columbia University Press, 1985. Surveys changes to the economy brought on by the war and provides insights into the impact of those changes on the creation of a postwar economy that featured a large defense industry.

See also Automobiles and auto manufacturing; Business and the economy in the United States; Economic wartime regulations; Labor strikes; National War Labor Board; "Rosie the Riveter"; Smith-Connally Act; War Production Board; Wartime seizures of businesses; World War II; World War II mobilization.

■ Wartime propaganda in Canada

Definition Management and dissemination of information by the Canadian government aimed at generating public support for the nation's war effort and promoting a positive image of Canada to other countries

During World War II, the Canadian government under Prime Minister William Lyon Mackenzie King established several agencies to control the flow of information about Canada both within and outside the country. These organizations were generally successful in mobilizing Canadians to support the war effort and in presenting positive images of Canada to the rest of the world. Understanding how this information was managed is crucial in shaping a clear picture of Canada's history during the war years.

The problems of managing information during World War I convinced Canadian government officials that controlling the nation's message about World War II would be critical to building and maintaining civilian support for a long battle that would have extensive human and financial costs. Thus, the government made a major commitment to organizing an effective propaganda machine that would keep Canadians informed about and committed to the war effort, ideally without misleading them. By the 1940's, Canadians obtained news through a number of media, including newspapers, radio broadcasts, films, and still photography, and wartime messages had to be delivered in all of these formats. The management of information included the creation of new materials highlighting Canada's role in the war, as well as the censorship of news arriving from the front.

Creation of Informative Materials Various agencies were given responsibility for creating new materials about Canada's war effort as the war progressed. The National Film Board (NFB) was founded in 1939 with documentary filmmaker John Grierson as its commissioner. That same year, the Bureau of Public Information (BPI) was founded under Canada's chief censor, Walter Thompson. The BPI experienced several changes in leadership before it became the Wartime Information Board (WIB) in September, 1942, under the chairmanship of Charles Vining, whose Vining Report laid out philosophies and practical approaches for effective propaganda. In October, 1942, the WIB opened offices in New York City and Washington, D.C., demonstrating the Canadian government's interest in controlling its image in the United States. In February, 1943, Grierson became general manager of the WIB, a position he held concurrently with his post as NFB commissioner.

The NFB was the most impressive arm of Canada's civilian propaganda machine. It initially had a staff of five employees, but its workforce grew to more than seven hundred by war's end. The board produced more than five hundred films on the war effort that were distributed to a large network of theaters, including almost eight hundred Famous Players theaters in Canada and more than ten thousand commercial theaters in the United States, and were also disseminated to a nontheatrical network of schools, libraries, town halls, and workplaces that reached more than 250,000 Canadians per month. The NFB also oversaw a still photography division,

which by 1945 employed seventy people and created photo stories that were sent to newspapers across Canada.

The WIB's propaganda touched on numerous war issues. For example, National Defence asked for films to help recruit and train soldiers. Munitions and Supply wanted information campaigns celebrating Canada's wartime industries. When polls showed declining support for economic controls, the Wartime Prices and Trade Board asked that Canadians receive more information about the economic realities of war. The War Finance Committee wanted the WIB to encourage Canadians to purchase Victory Bonds and war savings certificates. Controversially, a WIB campaign was undertaken that attempted to persuade Quebec of the benefits of conscription.

The WIB often organized highly integrated campaigns across different media. For example, in 1943 its Industrial Morale Committee undertook a program aimed at boosting morale in the coal mining industry, which had recently experienced increased worker absenteeism and unrest. Several steps were taken to create this program: The WIB conducted extensive research about coal mining; a series of war information films was shown in thirty-seven coal mining areas across Canada; two British films about the coal industry were revised for Canadian audiences; *Coalface, Canada*, one of the NFB's most successful films, was produced and widely released; the Canadian Broadcasting Corporation undertook a series of radio broadcasts; various photo stories ran in newspapers across the country; forty thousand rotogravure wall hangers were distributed to Canadian schools; twenty-four large photo-panel displays were exhibited in public buildings; an illustrated booklet about the importance of coal in the war economy was published; and WIB representatives met with the Department of National Revenue to suggest changes in income tax deductions for coal miners. Although the results of the campaign cannot be measured empirically, the coal mining industry enjoyed a period of peace following this multimedia campaign.

Censorship On September 3, 1939, the Canadian government used the War Measures Act to proclaim the Defence of Canada Regulations, which included the right of the federal government to censor all media in wartime. A Censorship Coordinating Committee was created in Ottawa and included representatives from the Department of National Defence, the air force, Canada Post, the Canadian Broadcasting Corporation, and the Canadian Press Association. These censors invited journalists, filmmakers, photographers, and broadcasters to share materials before publication in order to ensure their acceptability. They also punished the publication of inappropriate materials through fines or bans.

In addition, the Canadian armed forces created the post of public relations officer in January, 1940, and by war's end, the new office employed hundreds of officers, who provided press releases to newspaper and radio correspondents and censored articles and broadcasts before they were disseminated, ensuring that these news reports were free of sensitive or embarrassing information. For the most part, journalists' patriotism prevented them from trying to evade this censorship, so the military was able to effectively control its messages.

Canadian war news was usually accurate, if often incomplete. One major exception, however, was reporting on the raid of the French port of Dieppe. The raid occurred on August 19, 1942, and initial reports pronounced it a success, a claim called into question almost a month later when it was revealed that 3,367 of the 5,000 Canadian troops involved in the raid were casualties. Information management about Dieppe had been carefully orchestrated by the British Combined Operations Headquarters, which had determined that if the raid was a failure, emphasis would be placed on the bravery of the soldiers rather than the inability to attain the battle's objectives. Indeed, much of the reporting in late August and early September, 1942, focused on human interest stories and on the valor of the Canadian forces. Even after the casualty list confirmed that the raid had been a failure, most media outlets did not challenge the official version of Dieppe, and it was not until after the war that historians began to unravel the details of this battle.

Impact Easy access to newspapers, radio, and film during the 1940's meant that Canadians demanded timely and detailed news and explanations of public policy. World War II marked a major shift in the way government and military agencies provided the Canadian public with this information. In March, 1943, the cabinet gave the WIB permission to commission surveys of the Canadian people, the results of which were used to target specific demographic groups with tailored information about the government's war policy. This practice, like that of embedding reporters with troops in battle, began during World War II and has since become commonplace.

The end of the war resulted in a significant reduction in the number of Canadian information agencies. The WIB was disbanded in September, 1945, and replaced by the Canadian Information Service (CIS), which was to be responsible for disseminating information about Canada internationally, especially to the United States. In February, 1947, CIS was integrated into the Department of External Affairs, bringing a complete end to Canadian wartime propaganda. Some of the projects begun during World War II, however, have survived, notably the National Film Board of Canada, which has continued to be a highly celebrated agency providing information about Canadian culture and identity.

Pamela Bedore

Further Reading

Balzar, Timothy. "'In Case the Raid Is Unsuccessful . . .': Selling Dieppe to Canadians." *Canadian Historical Review* 87, no. 3 (2006): 409-430. Provides detailed analysis of media treatment of the 1942 Dieppe raid. Balzer's 2009 dissertation, *The Information Front*, treats wartime censorship and propaganda in Canada in more detail.

Bell, Ken. *The Way We Were.* Toronto: University of Toronto Press, 1988. Powerful picture book includes hundreds of black-and-white photographs depicting Canada's role in World War II.

Cull, Nicholas J. "Reluctant Persuaders: Canadian Propaganda in the United States, 1939-1945." *British Journal of Canadian Studies* 14, no. 2 (1999): 207-222. Covers Canada's propaganda within the United States from a historical and political perspective.

Evans, Gary. *John Grierson and the National Film Board: The Politics of Wartime Propaganda.* Toronto: University of Toronto Press, 1984. Provides a detailed account of Grierson's philosophy and accomplishments in documentary filmmaking about World War II.

Keshen, Jeffrey A. *Saints, Sinners, and Soldiers: Canada's Second World War.* Vancouver: University of British Columbia Press, 2004. The first half of this well-researched book shows how propaganda constructed World War II as a "good war" for Canada.

Thompson, Eric. "Canadian Warcos in World War II: Professionalism, Patriotism, and Propaganda." *Mosaic* 23, no. 3 (1990): 55-72. Profiles four Canadian war correspondents, providing details about their working conditions and attitudes toward information management.

Young, William R. "Academics and Social Scientists Versus the Press: The Policies of the Bureau of Public Information and the Wartime Information Board, 1939 to 1945." *Historical Papers/Communications Historiques* 13, no. 1 (1978): 217-240. Provides historical information and analysis of how Canada's wartime information apparatus used empirical methods in shaping war news. Young's many articles on wartime propaganda in Canada are all useful and well researched.

See also Canadian participation in World War II; Dieppe raid; Film in Canada; Films about World War II; Radio in Canada; Wartime propaganda in the United States; World War II.

■ Wartime propaganda in the United States

Definition Presentations in the media designed to increase homeland support for the war and to present a positive view of the United States and its allies, while denigrating the Axis Powers and their wartime achievements

The Allied victory over the Axis, accomplished through military assault, was aided by the utilization of propaganda. Prior to the Japanese bombing of Pearl Harbor in December, 1941, President Franklin D. Roosevelt understood that the United States eventually would become involved in the war and that Americans must be prepared for that eventuality. He knew that preparation must include encouraging Americans to support the war effort, but he shared with most Americans a suspicion and generally unfavorable view of propaganda.

American distrust of government propaganda was fueled by memories of hysteria stirred by public information efforts during World War I, public distrust of the advertising industry's ability to manipulate opinions, and the reluctance of Americans to be perceived as using propaganda in ways that might be viewed as similar to those of Nazi Germany. Various important individuals and groups, however, believed strongly in the need for government propaganda programs, in part because of fears of dangers to American freedoms, and sought to influence Roosevelt and the rest of the U.S. government.

The Office of War Information The American declarations of war on Japan on December 8, 1941, the day after the attack on Pearl Harbor, and on Germany and Italy three days later provoked an outcry for an information forum. Months of bickering and indecision followed, concerning the forum's shape and direction. Finally, on June 13, 1942, President Franklin D. Roosevelt signed Executive Order 9182, which combined several different government news agencies into the Office of War Information (OWI). The executive order granted OWI the power to utilize the press, radio, and motion pictures to create an "informed and intelligent understanding" of the war effort "at home and abroad." The word "propaganda" was not mentioned.

OWI was divided into domestic and overseas branches and was headed by well-known CBS newsman Elmer Davis, who, in the absence of an explicit federal policy on propaganda, pursued his own type of propaganda. OWI's mission was to present the American perspective on the war in a clear, truthful, and factual manner. Soon, OWI joined the armed forces and the Treasury Department in the task of bringing the reality of war home through mass exhibitions of posters in public places. First came a plea for Americans to participate in the increased production of planes and tanks, as the United States desperately needed to match Germany's massive production. Americans were urged to buy war bonds to help finance the war; the persuasive message often came in terms of mothers and children being threatened by European fascism.

Armed forces displays attempted to recruit more men and to remind Americans of sacrifices by American soldiers. Posters incited the public's fear of the enemy through emphasizing Nazi brutality and alerted Americans to enemy spies. Dark-colored posters of the bodies of servicemen who died because "Someone talked" stressed avoiding idle talk that could endanger troops. Other posters emphasized the alleged inhumanity of the Japanese, who were depicted as animals and undersized monsters. Women were urged to work in factories, children were informed of ways to help the brave U.S. soldiers. Other posters encouraged Americans to ration, save scrap metal, and conserve gasoline by carpooling. Representations of values most dear to America included Norman Rockwell's artwork of the "Four Freedoms" set forth by the president:

- Freedom of Speech
- Freedom of Worship
- Freedom from Want
- Freedom from Fear

Other artists donating their talents to the war effort included Thomas Hart Benton, who painted a series of works detailing the savagery of fascism.

OWI writers generated pamphlets stressing the seriousness of war to Americans: *The Unconquered People* focused on Europe's struggles, *Divide and Conquer* summarized Adolf Hitler's strategies, *How to Raise $16 Billion* proposed various ways to raise more money for the war, and *Battle Stations for All* defended rationing and urged Americans to control living costs and prevent inflation. *Negroes and the War* aimed to dispel anxieties about the American commitment to African Americans in wartime and to downplay racism. Other publications served as morale boosters by relating the war efforts of various towns and communities. Newspapers and magazines frequently featured the work of nationally known artists, such as Theodore Geisel (Dr. Seuss), whose cartoons appeared in the New York daily newspaper *PM*, and David Berger, a cartoonist for the *Saturday Evening Post* who created the comic strip *G.I. Joe*.

OWI appealed to radio broadcast chiefs, who agreed to donate airtime on various stations. One-minute messages by prominent personalities were aired regularly, as were messages following regular programs, many of which included war-related themes in their story lines. Serious discussions and dramas implored Americans to do their part. When OWI campaigned for raising and sharing food, for example, Americans responded with victory gardens.

After one year, the budget for OWI's domestic branch was slashed by an angry Congress, limiting its options. Its most significant contribution was in propaganda films. Director Frank Capra, newly commissioned as a U.S. Army major, was ordered by Chief of Staff General George C. Marshall to make a series of documented, factual films explaining to American soldiers why they were fighting and the principles for which they were fighting. Starting in 1942, Capra made seven films in the *Why We Fight* series that be-

came required viewing for military trainees and also were shown to civilians. The films also were translated into other languages and shown abroad. Employing Nazi tactics against the Nazis, Capra's "emotionalized history lessons" also used footage of animated maps and a narrator to depict the struggle between a "slave world" and a "free world." Some soldiers got their first understanding of war history through these films.

For the War Department, Capra also directed *Know Your Enemy: Japan* (1945), a film designed to acquaint soldiers and civilians with the Japanese in a more objective manner than the stereotypes seen in Hollywood propaganda films, and *The Negro Soldier* (1944), aimed toward lessening racism. Capra's character Private Snafu was featured in propaganda cartoon shorts produced by Warner Bros. Walt Disney, who created the animation for Capra's *Why We Fight* series, made films for the Navy, Army, Department of Agriculture, and Treasury Department. He also made several short anti-German and anti-Japanese animated films for soldiers and civilians, including *Der Fuehrer's Face* (1943), which won an Academy Award; *Education for Death: The Making of a Nazi* (1943); and *Commando Duck* (1944), all of which represented the Axis countries and leaders as immoral and manipulative.

OWI Abroad Working out of New York, the OWI overseas branch launched huge campaigns using radio and printed materials. OWI's principal service abroad, Voice of America, conveyed news reports with only a few transmitters. It was assisted by U.S. government control of some privately owned facilities and by the British Broadcasting Corporation (BBC) in rebroadcasting programs in more than twenty languages. The Voice of America's mission was to present war news accurately, so that Europeans would trust it, unlike the biased, propagandistic European media outlets. In time, the United States gained control of radio facilities in Tunisia in North Africa and in Palermo, Sicily, and it seized Radio Luxembourg, the second most powerful station in Europe.

Later during the war, the United States set up the American Broadcasting Station in Europe (ABSIE), operating from London, along with a transmitter in Hawaii and one on Saipan in the Pacific that reached Japanese homes. To supplement the radio programs, OWI produced leaflets, pamphlets, weekly newsletters, and parts of speeches by government leaders, all designed to circulate America's message abroad. Posters were distributed assuring the Axis of sufficient United States production of tanks and planes to defeat them, and OWI published an eighty-page magazine informing overseas civilians about America and its part in the Allied war effort. The military newspaper *Stars and Stripes* contained news of interest to servicemen and featured the cartoons of Pulitzer Prize-winning Bill Mauldin, whose Willie and Joe cartoons followed the trials of two American soldiers.

OWI produced documentaries and newsreels for foreign audiences, provided overseas goods for Allied and neutral nations, and supervised the establishment of overseas outposts for American support. Although the issue of the use of propaganda in and by a democracy had not been resolved, Roosevelt had also created in 1942 the Office of Strategic Services (OSS), a secret intelligence operation headed by William Donovan, who asserted the necessity of waging psychological warfare against the enemy.

For a branch of OSS called Morale Operations (MO), Donovan proposed the use of "black propaganda" (made to appear to have originated in enemy areas) to weaken enemy morale. His tactics were intended to promote confusion and disorder, and to employ "subversive activities against enemy governments." Working closely with the British, who relied heavily upon psychological warfare, MO refined its techniques to include a bombardment of fake leaflets, posters, magazines, newspapers, and forgeries of official documents designed to implicate enemy officials in plots against their own countries. MO also used radio broadcasts from secret transmitters to provide false directives to Nazi leaders and to disseminate rumors. On its own small scale, MO continued its covert, subversive attacks on enemy morale throughout the war, achieving a level of sophistication hitherto unused in American warfare.

In 1943, conflicts among OWI, the OSS, MO, and the U.S. Army came to a head, with the U.S. Army reluctantly agreeing to oversee the newly named Psychological Warfare Branch (PWB) and steer it more toward combat propaganda needs. Restructuring at the OWI's overseas branch facilitated its support of

Government poster reminding Americans never to reveal possibly sensitive information to anyone because "loose lips sink ships." (National Archives)

the PWB as the Allies dropped millions of leaflets in their attacks on Tunisia and Sicily. In the last stages of the war in Europe, OWI worked increasingly through military organizations. In the Normandy invasion on June 6, 1944, nine million leaflets were dropped, and as the Allies continued toward Germany, PWB units preceded them, contributing to Germany's defeat. Some PWB units moved into liberated areas and assisted with military instructions.

With the surrender of Germany in May, 1945, the new U.S. president, Harry S. Truman, began a new propaganda campaign in the Pacific. OWI followed suit with a barrage of broadcasts and an intensive leaflet program, all designed to reassure the Japanese that the American demand for "unconditional surrender" did not mean that the Japanese would be slaughtered or enslaved. Leaflets continued to be disseminated into July, 1945, warning the Japanese of impending destruction. Following the dropping of atomic bombs on the cities of Hiroshima and Nagasaki, Japan surrendered on August 15.

Impact America delayed employing propaganda during World War II primarily because of Americans' discomfort with it. Many Americans struggled with the nature of propaganda in a democratic society at war, fearing government manipulation or loss of the independence Americans valued. Fueling anxieties about propaganda was an absence of leadership from the presidential administration in interpreting the basic issues and goals of the war for Americans. Powerful individuals in the private sector with strong ideological inclinations toward affirming the value of democracy over totalitarianism, however, began to campaign for the use of propaganda.

As the only Allied country without an organized propaganda program, the United States was mired in contradiction and contention, largely between liberal views and more conservative, practical ones. Only as the U.S. Army, which had originally rejected the use of propaganda, began to recognize and prove its usefulness in military operations did the use of propaganda gain the support of Americans. The Army's objectives seemed to match those of most Americans, and propaganda seemed to mature in America and demonstrate what it could accomplish, thereby reducing Americans' fear of it. The U.S. Army went on to develop a school for psychological warfare by 1950 that consolidated the values of the Central Intelligence Agency (formerly the OSS) and continued to spread them into the Cold War and beyond. Psychological operations became an integral part of modern warfare.

Mary Hurd

Further Reading

Bernays, Edward, with an introduction by Mark Crispin Miller. *Propaganda.* Brooklyn, N.Y.: Ig, 2004. Reprint of Bernays's controversial 1928 book arguing the necessity for intelligent manipulation of public opinion in a democracy.

Horten, Gerd. *Radio Goes to War: The Cultural Politics of Propaganda During World War II.* Berkeley: University of California Press, 2002. In-depth study of the role of domestic radio propaganda in World War II and its effect on audiences. Discusses similarities between the controversy over use of pro-

paganda in World War II and current controversies involving advertising, entertainment, and propaganda.

Szanto, Andras, ed. *What Orwell Didn't Know: Propaganda and the New Face of American Politics.* New York: PublicAffairs, 2007. Essays concern recent political manipulation and information corruption, using George Orwell's essay "Propaganda and the English Language" as the starting point of discussion.

Welch, David. *The Third Reich: Politics and Propaganda.* London: Routledge, 2002. Readable, informative book about the Nazi control of the media in Germany and the role of propaganda in a totalitarian country.

See also Capra, Frank; "Four Freedoms" speech; Isolationism; Office of Strategic Services; "Rosie the Riveter"; Tokyo Rose; Voice of America; War bonds; Wartime propaganda in Canada; World War II.

■ Wartime rationing

Definition Restriction of civilian access to food and critical materials during World War II due to the needs of the armed forces and the demands of war production

Rationing changed everyday life in America, limiting dietary choices and altering lifestyle. Official restrictions concerning the use of critical materials also affected industry's ability to supply common household products to the civilian market.

During World War II, the conflicting needs of the American civilian population and its military forces and industries gave rise to various systems for apportioning goods between the two spheres. Rationing of food and critical materials began almost immediately after U.S. entry into the war in 1941, and it became one of the defining aspects of everyday life on the home front. Industries, which were as deeply affected by rationing as were individuals, sometimes discontinued the manufacture of consumer goods due to having insufficient access to needed materials. Shortages also led some businesses to embrace programs of self-rationing in order to spread their limited goods as far as possible in an equitable manner.

The task of regulating food distribution was a major concern for the federal government from the beginning, with the Food Rationing Program set into motion in the spring of 1942. The Department of Agriculture unofficially handled administrative oversight until December 5, 1942. On that date, an executive order by President Franklin D. Roosevelt reorganized the department, putting a director of food distribution in charge of all agencies dealing with food processing, storage, allocation, and distribution. The Office of Price Administration (OPA) also played an important role in the rationing of food, issuing stamp-type coupons to be used by consumers when buying officially rationed goods. Affected foods included meats and poultry, eggs, canned fish, fats and oils, coffee, and sugar.

The OPA distributed its ration stamps in a series of war ration books. Red-stamp rationing covered all meats, fats and oils, and most cheese. Blue-stamp rationing covered processed foods, including canned, bottled, and frozen fruits and vegetables, as well as dried beans. The books carried printed warnings that the violation of rationing regulations was a criminal offense. Sugar rationing took effect in May, 1943, with the distribution of sugar buying cards. The OPA also issued nonmetallic tokens for use in purchasing rationed items.

Food rationing had its positive counterpart in a public campaign to encourage the planting of gardens as a means to supplement the civilian diet with fresh vegetables. By 1945, an estimated twenty million households had established "victory gardens."

Some items of clothing, such as shoes, came under direct rationing. A far greater number, however, fell under indirect rationing as a result of strict restrictions being imposed upon manufacturers and wholesalers by the the War Production Board (WPB) program for the conservation of strategic materials. Domestic production of nylon, for instance, was entirely redirected to military use in February, 1942, with nylon stockings subsequently disappearing from the civilian marketplace. Nylon had numerous wartime uses, notably in parachutes. Similarly, the increasingly popular tennis shoes became almost impossible to obtain because of restrictions on rubber. Leather was also largely reserved for military use. Although cotton was not immediately restricted, heavy requirements by the military, the changing of cotton lands to crop production, and poor cotton crops later in the war affected the supply of even this relatively common material.

Some items that required silk, certain finishes, or kapok for their manufacture became scarce. In general, shortages of materials that had their sources in the Far East had been anticipated and sometimes even already experienced before America became directly involved in the war. Paints and lacquers came under restriction, sometimes for reasons other than heavy military demand. Chemicals used to produce certain shades of red paint had a higher priority in making explosives. Aluminum paints had already fallen under government control before the war. Such lumber items as birch veneer, heavily used in airplane manufacture, were similarly removed from the civilian sphere.

Metals naturally fell under WPB restrictions and rationing, affecting the availability of household items ranging from cutlery to Christmas tinsel. Since many goods made of steel, iron, or zinc had doubled in retail price shortly before the war, a degree of price rationing occurred even before the metals fell subject to official restrictions. Once rationing began, some metals, such as tin, were progressively removed from noncritical use in cuts of 10 percent or more at a time. Others were quickly removed from nonessential use, as was the case with copper and copper-base alloys, which were sharply cut off from many manufacturing applications on May 6, 1942.

Consumer Goods Direct rationing was imposed upon some fully manufactured consumer goods, with adult-size bicycles being one such class of item. The WPB froze their sale or transfer in April, 1942. After then releasing thousands to California aircraft plants, whose workers were experiencing intensifying transportation problems during that spring, the OPA began allotting adult bicycles to defense workers only.

The rationing of consumer goods was taken another step further on December 29, 1942, when the WPB announced Order L-219, which limited the quantities of consumer goods that retail merchants, wholesalers, and stock-carrying branches of manufacturers could keep on hand. Although a stock-reduction order, it was also designed to equalize consumer goods supplies around the country, and to help smaller outlets operate on a more even level with larger ones. The order affected some 25,000 merchants, 12,000 manufacturers, and 8,000 wholesale establishments, as well as, indirectly, all the nation's consumers. The order excluded inventories of food and petroleum.

Early 1943 government poster explaining point system used for wartime rationing. (AP/Wide World Photos)

Rubber and Gasoline Controls over rubber, which was heavily in demand by the military, were significantly tightened during the war, especially since natural rubber supplies depended on conditions in the Far East. By February, 1942, the United States had been cut off from 90 percent of its natural rubber supply.

Gasoline windshield stickers bearing letters of priority, with trucks being given a special "T" priority sticker, were issued. Most civilian automobiles carried "A" stickers, which limited the number of gallons to be used per week. Vehicles being used for higher-priority reasons were given "B" or "C" stickers. Between 1942 and 1945, a national speed limit of 35 miles per hour was imposed to conserve gasoline and rubber tires.

Restrictions on wood pulp and paper affected

magazines and newspapers across the country. By 1945, the newspaper industry was dealing with an availability of 600,000 fewer tons of newsprint than its normal yearly supply. Restrictions on wood pulp affected other manufacturing areas, since wood was used in producing many fiber products, plastics, and rayon. Cellulose sheets, including cellophane, came under restrictions early in the war.

The rationing of materials to industry had unexpected effects upon civilian life, including the virtual disappearance of low-price items from stores. Besides the imposition of pricing regulations, which made it difficult for companies to produce low-price items at a profit, manufacturers tended to reserve their small stores of scarce materials for the making of higher-ticket items.

Relaxation of Restrictions   After Japan surrendered on August 15, 1945 (known as Victory over Japan Day, or V-J Day), the secretary of agriculture, in conjunction with the price administrator, terminated rationing of meats and fish. Rationing of fats and oils also ended, although the outlook for oil production continued to be low due to reduced hog production in the United States and Canada. Sugar remained under rationing because of continuing shortages, with production being estimated to be 13 percent below prewar levels.

Even while official rationing controls were being removed, quota limitations continued to be imposed on some manufacturers and producers, including those of shortening, margarine, salad oil, and other edible oil products, so that some of the effects of food rationing continued well beyond 1945. Price controls also continued, in part because rationing's influence on price stability was being removed from the marketplace. In Canada, controls over both pricing and rationing were continued into 1946. On the whole, however, large-scale food rationing ended on June 30, 1945, when, at the request of the war food administrator, the program was returned to the oversight of the Department of Agriculture.

Self-rationing and Other Late Effects   The relaxing of rationing had immediate effects in the civilian sphere. Production of nylon for civilian goods, for instance, resumed immediately after the war, with hosiery-yarn production quickly expanding to a point above prewar levels. On the other hand, continuing short supplies of many materials made the immediate postwar months and sometimes years seem an extension of wartime restriction. While lumber requirements by the military drastically dropped after V-J Day, lumber would remain scarce or unavailable for years. Among materials still in short supply two years after the war ended were wood, paper, cardboard, steel, leather, and some textiles. Rubber also remained scarce. While controls over synthetic rubber and scrap rubber were lifted in 1945, supplies of natural rubber remained under restriction into the postwar years.

An example of widespread self-rationing occurred in the men's apparel industry. After having dealt with increasing shortages of goods through the war, in 1945 retailers faced dramatically increasing demand because of the numbers of returning sol-diers seeking to trade in their khaki for civilian clothing. Suits, shirts, and other items remained in short supply, however. To best serve the most customers, most retailers adopted a voluntary rationing plan that allowed the individual customer to buy only one of any particular type of item.

Impact   The effects of rationing varied across the country, in part because the contributions of victory gardens to local food supplies varied greatly from region to region, and in part because border populations had access to Canadian and Mexican markets, which had different and often more lax rationing programs. Since the OPA had eight regional offices, regional differences in administration and enforcement also came into play. All the same, being national in scope, the OPA and WPB programs affected the entire civilian populace. Rationing, shortages, and war ration books became a part of everyday life and culture. New recipes, new menus, and new grocery-store packaged-food favorites were some examples of this changed culture.

While some rationing programs made little or no difference to overseas military efforts, it remains a fact that the United States was able to feed, clothe, and equip its armed forces while also feeding and housing prisoners of war, and while providing food and materials to other countries in need of assistance. These successes must be regarded as having been made possible in part by the national rationing of food and materials on the home front.

Mark Rich

Further Reading

Bentley, Amy. *Eating for Victory: Food Rationing and the Politics of Domesticity.* Urbana: University of Illinois Press, 1998. Brings together social history, public policy analysis, and cultural studies in examining food rationing during the 1940's.

Hayes, Joanne Lamb. *Grandma's Wartime Kitchen: World War II and the Way We Cooked.* New York: St. Martin's Press, 2000. In addition to being a history covering government food rules, ration books, and wartime entertaining, this book collects recipes that employed common wartime commodities.

Hoopes, Roy. *Americans Remember the Home Front.* New York: Berkley Books, 2002. An oral history that focuses on the transformations of families, industries, and American society as a whole during World War II.

Lingeman, Richard R. *Don't You Know There's a War On? The American Home Front, 1941-1945.* New York: Nation Books, 2003. A widely ranging cultural history that depicts American civilian life during the war, giving coverage to work, business, and housing issues as well as domestic and social life.

Winkler, Allan M. *Home Front U.S.A.: America During World War II.* Wheeling, Ill.: Harlan Davidson, 2000. A serious and exhaustive study that details war contributions undertaken on the home front.

See also Black market; Book publishing; Coinage; Daylight saving time; Economic wartime regulations; Fashions and clothing; Food processing; Hobbies; Office of Price Administration; Office of War Mobilization; Pulp magazines; Wartime industries; Wartime salvage drives.

■ Wartime sabotage

Definition Covert military operations designed to disrupt enemy infrastructure and materials production

During World War II, certain government entities, including the Department of the Interior, the Department of Defense, and the Federal Bureau of Investigation worked together to secure facilities that were key to the stability of the nation's infrastructure and to uncover sabotage plots of German and Japanese agents.

In December, 1940, President Franklin D. Roosevelt called for the United States to mobilize the nation's industrial effort in the interests of defense. The United States had not yet entered World War II, but the president was willing to offer assistance to Great Britain by manufacturing airplanes, tanks, trucks, and weapons. This call for action significantly increased the threat of foreign espionage and sabotage on American soil. As officials in the Department of the Interior and Department of Defense discussed ways to combat possible sabotage, the Federal Bureau of Investigation (FBI) worked to increase the effectiveness of technology to test materials found at crime scenes and searched for ways to decode secret messages and to detect ways in which they were sent and received. In the end, the vigilance of the average American citizen, coupled with scientific breakthroughs in FBI crime laboratories,

helped to disrupt plots of sabotage that would have proved harmful to the operations of the infrastructure of the United States.

The Model Sabotage Prevention Act Prior to the late 1930's, the United States had never had to regard sabotage by foreign enemies as a primary concern. However, as the conflict in Europe that led to World War II developed, and the United States slowly added support to Britain and neutral countries that found themselves occupied by German forces, the U.S. government was forced to reexamine how law enforcement would handle acts of espionage and sabotage. Many individual states did not even have antisabotage laws, and some representatives of the federal government feared that prosecution of foreign saboteurs apprehended within the state would be difficult unless law-enforcement officials could find other charges to bring against the offenders.

The federal Model Sabotage Prevention Act, passed by Congress in 1940, provided alternative measures to existing laws. Its aim was to provide for the punishment of acts of sabotage already committed, facilitate in the detection of saboteurs entering unlawfully upon properties essential to national infrastructure, and make more difficult the destruction of properties essential to national defense by regulating the use of streets abutting such properties. Also, the act aided in the conviction of saboteurs by changes in the law, specifically in areas of conspiracy and the privilege against self-incrimination. This act was set to expire in 1945.

Objectives of Espionage and Sabotage During World War II, the greatest threat of sabotage to the United States came from Germany. Four days after the Japanese bombed Pearl Harbor, Adolf Hitler declared war against the United States. Hitler began ordering sabotage operations against targets inside the United States. German agents searched for any military, political, and economic information regarding the United States, intending to strike where significant damage to operations would occur. The data and blueprints on aircraft production and antisubmarine devices were sought-after classified information. Espionage groups abroad were willing to pay fantastic sums for any information about these items. However, what some German intelligence officers found was that a number of agents trained by the German Abwehr (defense) were lukewarm members of the Nazi Party. They regarded their service in the Abwehr as a way to avoid fighting on the Russian front. The level of loyalty of many of these agents to carry out the acts of sabotage against American targets was low.

Acts of sabotage by Japanese agents were feared most on the West Coast of the United States. Two months after the attack on Pearl Harbor, President Roosevelt enacted Executive Order 9066, which gave military commanders the authority to establish relocation zones for all persons living on the West Coast who were at least one-sixteenth part Japanese. Internment camps for Japanese American citizens from Washington State to California, and in parts of Arizona, were established quickly and held Japanese Americans for the duration of the war.

The internment camps did not completely alleviate fears of sabotage by the Japanese. The government was cautioned on several occasions by concerned citizens and the FBI to increase security measures for Hoover (Boulder), Grand Coulee, and Shasta dams. Increased reports of kamikaze attacks against the U.S. Navy led some to fear that similar attacks might occur on these dams. With the exception of placing a handful of additional troops at those dams, there was more talk than action where preventive measures were concerned.

The Amagansett Incident In June, 1942, after months of training, two four-man German teams landed on the beaches of Long Island, New York, with the intent of sabotage. The teams were to be brought ashore by German U-boats during two different landings. The plan was to bury their munitions crates on the beach in the dark of night where they could be dug up safely at a later time.

The first team's assignment was to destroy the hydroelectric plants at Niagara Falls; the Aluminum Company of America factories in Illinois, Tennessee, and New York; and the Philadelphia Salt Company's cryolite plant in Philadelphia. The first team was also to bomb the locks on the

Ohio River between Louisville, Kentucky, and Pittsburgh, Pennsylvania. The second team's assignment was to destroy the Pennsylvania Railroad station at Newark, New Jersey, plus the horseshoe bend section of railroad near Altoona, Pennsylvania. The attacks on the nation's railway system, the main transportation for troop movements within the United States, were to include parts of the Chesapeake and Ohio Railroad and the New York Central Railroad's Hell Gate Bridge. The lock and canal complexes at St. Louis, Missouri, and Cincinnati, Ohio, were also supposed to be attacked. The second team was instructed to plant bombs in locker rooms at major passenger railroad stations with the intent to create panic and terror.

The plans never came to fruition. After the first team landed, a U.S. Coast Guard sailor confronted the leader of the team, George Dasch, who paid the man to look the other way and thought that would be the end of any investigation. However, the sailor returned quickly to his post to alert the proper authorities. Dasch and fellow team conspirator Ernst Burger had no intention of carrying out the plot for which they had been trained and well paid. Instead, they both decided to turn themselves in to the FBI.

Four of the eight Germans captured during their abortive sabotage mission on Long Island, listening to proceedings in an improvised courtroom in Washington, D.C., in July, 1942. From left to right: Werner Thiel, alias John Thomas; Richard Quirin; an unidentified officer; Hermann Neubauer; and Edward John Kerling. (AP/Wide World Photos)

Dasch, thinking his actions would make him a hero, was the first to confess. Burger followed a week later. Of the eight men who landed in Long Island with the intent to commit sabotage on American soil, six were executed in the electric chair, and Dasch and Burger were sentenced to life sentences of hard labor in the United States, but were later deported back to Germany.

The FBI Laboratory As the threat of sabotage increased, scientists and mathematicians in FBI labs worked overtime to enhance technology created during the 1930's. Evidence of this was seen in the Amagansett incident. When the FBI recovered the boxes of supplies buried on the beach, they found boxes of matches tipped with quinine for use in sending invisible secret messages. When a message is written with this type of instrument, it can be treated with a dilute acid and read under ultraviolet light. FBI scientists had become accustomed to creating such chemical reactions in order to recover messages that could negatively impact national security.

In addition to decoding and reading secret messages, scientists were using spectrographic techniques to analyze minute fragments to detect burn patterns and the chemical compounds of their original materials. The cutting edges of foreign tools were also successfully identified and cataloged in the FBI database. This was important, as fears of attacks on hydraulic systems of fighter planes manufactured in the United States grew.

Airplane manufacturing was not the only target. The FBI's increased knowledge of metallurgy helped to bring acts of sabotage in Midwest plants that manufactured tractors, tanks, and trucks, to a halt. Fine iron granules were found in oil pans, near timing gears, in crankshafts, and on ball bearings of vehicles shipped to Melbourne, Australia. The FBI was able to analyze the samples and track down the source, preventing further sabotage attempts and ultimately keeping the soldiers and civilians who used these vehicles safe.

Impact The main goal of saboteurs during World War II was to disrupt labor interests in the United States, as well as to strike fear and terror in the hearts of a nation. With the help of the FBI and vigilant citizens, many plots to sabotage infrastructure and equipment necessary to support an Allied victory in World War II never came to fruition.

Michele Goostree

Further Reading

Ardman, Harvey. "World War II: German Saboteurs Invade America in 1942." *World War II Magazine* (February, 1997). Historical summary of the foiled sabotage attempts by German nationals on American soil.

Dobbs, Michael. *Saboteurs: The Nazi Raid on America.* New York: Knopf, 2004. Comprehensive study of the Amagansett incident, focused on the men who attempted the sabotage and their reasons for volunteering for the mission.

Hoover, John Edgar. "FBI Laboratory in Wartime." *Scientific Monthly* 60, no. 1 (January, 1945): 18-24. Highlights the innovative scientific and forensic techniques the FBI developed and used during World War II.

Pfaff, Christine. "Safeguarding Hoover Dam During World War II." *Prologue Magazine* 35, no. 2 (Summer, 2003). Discusses how Hoover dam, among other dams in the West, were considered prime targets for Japanese sneak attacks.

Rottman, Gordon L. *World War II Axis Booby Traps and Sabotage Tactics.* New York: Osprey, 2009. Mostly concentrated on the sabotage tactics used by the Nazis and the other Axis Powers on the battlefield.

Warner, Sam Bass. "The Model Sabotage Prevention Act." *Harvard Law Review* 54, no. 4 (February, 1941): 602-631. Outlines the necessity of implementing a methodology to combat and prepare for sabotage and other clandestine maneuvers.

See also Black market; Civil rights and liberties; *Korematsu v. United States*; Office of Strategic Services; Organized crime; Wartime espionage; Wartime industries; Wartime propaganda in Canada; Wartime propaganda in the United States; Wartime rationing; Wartime salvage drives; World War II.

■ Wartime salvage drives

Definition Federal government campaigns to encourage Americans to collect metals and other materials that could be recycled for wartime use

The federal government's Office of Civilian Defense, created in May, 1941, organized war drives for products such as rubber, tin, paper, and fat. These drives intensified as

World War II continued, and Americans were encouraged to conserve and salvage scrap materials in order to meet collection quotas that aided the war effort. The salvage drives provided a way for citizens to feel that they were contributing to the cause.

After the attack on Pearl Harbor on December 7, 1941, the first scrap drives were organized to ease the worries of frightened civilians, and these efforts were a means of increasing public patriotism. Communities created extensive campaigns to collect metal, cotton rags, rubber, animal fats, and newspapers, but there were questions about what to do with the tons of materials that were collected. Many of the items could not be recycled, including old newspapers, which could only be used as packing materials. Pots and pans made of aluminum were placed in the scrap heap, but only virgin aluminum could be used in the manufacturing of aircraft.

Rubber   When the Japanese took over military control of the Dutch East Indies, the United States no longer could receive supplies of natural rubber from this area. The administration of President Franklin D. Roosevelt encouraged Americans to turn in old tires, rubber raincoats, rubber shoes, bathing caps, and old garden hoses. However, there was no efficient way to recycle rubber products because of the complex chemistry involved in the process. The need to address the rubber shortage resulted in the development of synthetic rubber and rubber conservation efforts by Americans. In addition, gas rationing meant that people did not drive their vehicles over long distances, reducing the wear on their tires.

Fats and Cloth   Before the onset of World War II, the majority of glycerin, a vital ingredient in drugs and explosives, had been made from fats and oils from the Pacific Rim. During the war, women were able to salvage kitchen fats from cooking that could be used for explosives. Three pounds of fat provided enough glycerin to produce a pound of gunpowder, and 350 pounds of fat were needed to fire one shell from a naval gun. Cotton rags were shredded so the fibers could be used to make blankets or uniforms. Since cotton was in short supply and used heavily by the armed forces, women turned to clothing made

Film star Rita Hayworth promoting the government's scrap-metal drive in 1942 by posing on the trunk of her car with a sign proclaiming that she has donated the car's bumpers to the war effort. (Time & Life Pictures/ Getty Images)

of rayon. Silk and nylon were recycled for powder bags and parachutes, and by September, 1943, forty-six million pairs of hosiery had been collected nationwide. Some young women resorted to drawing lines down the back of their legs to make it appear they were wearing silk stockings, which in those days had highly visible seams.

Tin and Other Metals   The effort to salvage tin cans was one of the more successful campaigns, for several reasons. Two tin cans could be recycled into a syrette, a device that could be used to administer antiseptics and skin treatments, as well as sedatives, which helped prevent shock. A syrette was a standard part of a medic's equipment, consisting of a small tube of morphine attached with a hypodermic needle. Tin was also the only metal that could not be harmed by the corrosive elements in salt water, so it was often used to ship canned food to troops overseas. The War Production Board declared on October 19, 1942, that residents in cities with a population of more than twenty-five thousand should separate tin cans from the rest of their trash. Local newspapers ran stories on the large number of tin cans being collected by schoolchildren, and as the war continued, 100,000 pounds of tin cans were collected each month. Even the monetary system for coinage changed due to salvage drives: In 1943, pennies were made from zinc-coated steel instead of copper, which was needed for the war effort.

Impact During World War II, Americans sacrificed necessities and salvaged thousands of tons of scrap materials as the focus of the war turned to the home front and war production. Studies in the early twenty-first century contended that scrap drives were more effective in instilling patriotism and boosting morale than in recycling needed war materials. The nation's patriotism sometimes led citizens to collect relics of past wars or memorials to specific events, such as monuments, canons, church bells, and other objects of historical significance, and put them in the scrap pile.

Gayla Koerting

Further Reading

Kimble, James J. "The Militarization of the Prairie: Scrap Drives, Metaphors, and the *Omaha World Herald's* 1942 Nebraska Plan." *Great Plains Quarterly* 27, no. 2 (Spring, 2007): 83-99. Explains Nebraska scrap drives as envisioned by the publisher of the *Omaha World Herald*, Henry Doorly. The "Nebraska Plan" was very successful and became the model for other states starting salvage campaigns.

Kirk, Robert W. "Getting in the Scrap: The Mobilization of American Children in World War II." *Journal of Popular Culture* 29 (March, 2004): 223-233. Analyzes the role of young people, particularly in school and organizations such as the Boy Scouts and Girl Scouts, in scrap drives.

Lingeman, Richard R. *Don't You Know There's a War On? The American Home Front, 1941-1945.* New York: G. P. Putnam's Sons, 1970. Describes industrial production, teenage fads, Japanese American internment, and the role of women during the war years.

Rockoff, Hugh. *Keep on Scrapping: The Salvage Drives of World War II.* Cambridge, Mass.: National Bu-reau of Economic Research, 2007. Reexamines scrap drives for iron, steel, and rubber. Contends that the drives had a limited impact on the economy, but were more important for building civilian morale.

Strasser, Susan. *Waste and Want: A Social History of Trash.* New York: Metropolitan Books, 1999. A social historian explores American ideas toward refuse disposal from the colonial period to twentieth century public landfills. She chronicles how mass production, technological change, and notions of cleanliness have changed Americans' perceptions about trash over time.

See also Advertising in the United States; Civil defense programs; Coinage; "Greatest Generation"; Natural resources; Office of War Mobilization; War surplus; Wartime rationing.

■ Wartime seizures of businesses

To support the war effort and the economic aftermath, the United States government seized property and private industries before, during, and after the war. Most seizures of property occurred as a proactive strategy against labor-management disputes and to keep war production on schedule.

Prior to World War II, the U.S. government expressed concerns over disruptions to the wartime production effort. Prior to entering the war in December, 1941, the United States anticipated its own entry and also aided the opponents of Germany. Any interruption of production posed a threat to national security. Upon U.S. entry into the war, domestic production of goods accelerated and refocused even more on war-related goods. To aid wartime production, the U.S. government transferred control of private land and industries, giving them to military installations and government agencies, usually temporarily.

The first major example of government seizure of a private industry came in 1941, when the North American Aviation company came under government control. This was before the attack on Pearl Harbor, and the takeover was a tactic to end a union strike at the plant. During the war, the U.S. government seized forty-seven industrial plants, primarily as a solution to labor-management disputes.

The sectors of the American economy most directly affected were coal mining, railroads, other transportation, textile manufacturing, and retail business. Specific companies include Midwest Trucking Operators, Goodyear Tire and Rubber Co., and Montgomery Ward. Examples of government intervention for reasons beyond labor disputes focused on the manufacturing industries of wartime materials. The U.S. government took control of these industries primarily to control production and ensure prompt delivery. Even after the war, President Harry S. Truman saw the operation of railroads as vital to the nation's economy, and several times he seized railroads in the midst of labor disputes that threatened operations.

The government did not declare statutory authority to justify the World War II acquisition of property and industry, instead relying on executive orders. An executive order is a presidential directive that carries the weight of statutory law. In 1936, the U.S. Supreme Court ruled that executive orders were constitutional exercises of presidential authority, and the wartime seizures were not challenged as to their constitutionality.

One example of the use of executive orders is Executive Order 9254, which authorized government seizure of the manufacturing plants of Triumph Explosive and its affiliates in 1942. Additionally, Executive Order 9341 authorized the director of the Office of Defense Transportation to take control of the American Railroad Company in 1943. Many instances of direct government takeover were temporary, as suggested by several executive orders issued that transferred operations oversight and control back to the private sector. Executive Order 9349, for example, rescinded Executive Order 9254.

Government seizure of private enterprises during World War II became somewhat regular practice, but it did undergo some challenges. The Supreme Court stipulated in *Commissioner v. Gillette Motor Co.* (1960), a case involving seizure of a company during World War II, that the U.S. government was required to compensate private industries in an amount equal to reasonable rental value of facilities that came under direct government control for temporarily taking of business facilities during wartime.

Impact Wartime production was imperative to the American economy during the 1940's and to the overall goal of winning the war. Heavy regulation

and direct government oversight accomplished what the government intended. American industry manufactured approximately 300,000 airplanes, 400,000 pieces of artillery, 47 million tons of artillery ammunition, 44 billion rounds of small arms ammunition, nearly 87,000 warships, 86,000 tanks, and 6,500 ships, all adhering closely to production schedules. Premier Joseph Stalin of the Soviet Union, an American ally during the war, credited American production with the advancing Allied victory at the Tehran Conference of 1943.

Heather E. Yates

Further Reading
Eagleton, Thomas F. *War and Presidential Power.* New York: Liveright, 1975.
Fisher, Louis. *Presidential War Power.* Lawrence: University of Kansas Press, 1995.
Linfield, Michael. *Freedom Under Fire: U.S. Civil Liberties in Times of War.* Boston: South End Press, 1990.
Reichardt, Otto H. "Industrial Concentration and World War II: A Note on the Aircraft Industry." *The British History Review* 49 no. 4 (1975): 498-503.
Teller, Ludwig. "Government Seizure in Labor Disputes." *Harvard Law Review* 60, no. 7 (1947): 1017-1059.

See also Business and the economy in the United States; Civil rights and liberties; Economic wartime regulations; Emergency Price Control Act of 1942; Executive orders; Labor strikes; National War Labor Board; Presidential powers; Railroad seizure; *United States v. Aluminum Co. of America*; *United States v. Darby Lumber Co.*

■ Wartime technological advances

Without the major strides made in technology by the United States and its allies, the Allied victory in World War II might have been impossible.

When the Japanese bombed Pearl Harbor in December, 1941, the United States found itself poorly prepared for modern warfare. After World War I, the country had all but disbanded its military. In 1932, the U.S. military was ranked seventeenth in strength in the world. Excluding National Guard units, it had only 130,000 men in uniform. The U.S.

Army owned only 1,400 airplanes, fewer than half of which were considered modern aircraft. During the 1930's, Army Chief of Staff Douglas MacArthur declared the entire armored corps unfit for modern battle. In the meantime, Germany had become the world's leader in wartime technology, and Japan had entered a period of rapid military expansion and modernization. In response to the attack on Pearl Harbor, the United States joined its allies as well as its enemies in a race for superiority in war-related technology.

Weaponry   There is little doubt that the most significant development in the history of weaponry was the invention of the atomic bomb. In response to urging from the scientific community, particularly a letter from physicist Albert Einstein, U.S. president Franklin D. Roosevelt commissioned a panel to study the uses of uranium. After the Japanese attack on Pearl Harbor, this small committee grew rapidly into the Manhattan Project, with a presidential mandate to develop an atomic bomb. At the time of the first detonation in the desert of New Mexico on July 16, 1945, the Manhattan Project had cost the United States more than $2 billion (equivalent to approximately $25 billion in early twenty-first century currency) and employed more than 125,000 people. Less than a month later, on August 6, 1945, a working atomic bomb was dropped on Hiroshima, Japan. Nagasaki, Japan, was bombed three days later. These two attacks are credited with shortening the war by encouraging Japanese surrender.

Ballistic missiles, also developed during World War II, would later be combined with nuclear bombs to provide the world with a frightening doomsday scenario. On October 3, 1942, a group of German scientists led by Wernher von Braun launched the A-4 rocket, the world's first ballistic missile. German chancellor Adolf Hitler later called it a "vengeance weapon," and it was renamed the V-2. It was used repeatedly on Britain during the last years of the war.

Semiautomatic rifles were another important advance in weaponry. When the war began, most soldiers carried bolt-action rifles, which had to be reloaded after each shot. These weapons proved inadequate for most modern combat situations, and the semiautomatic rifle addressed this problem. The United States was the first country to make this kind of rifle general issue to its infantry troops. Its inventor, John Garand, patented the M1 Garand semiau-

tomatic rifle in 1934, but because of development issues and production delays, it was not until 1941 that the U.S. Army was fully equipped with these weapons. They gave U.S. infantry a significant firepower advantage over their German and Japanese counterparts.

Improvements to machine guns and submachine guns during the war also had a impact. The portable machine guns developed by the Germans were useful in close combat, and the submachine gun was useful to both sides. Advances in production methods made it possible for Germany to produce one million MP40 submachine guns. Near the end of the war, assault rifles were developed. They combined the advantages of rifles with those of submachine guns. They were developed too late to have a major impact on World War II, but they would later become the standard weapons of issue for most infantries.

Major advances in tank technology contributed significantly to both sides' effectiveness during the war. The small, lightly armored tanks of World War I were replaced by larger, faster, more heavily armed, and more heavily armored tanks. The American Sherman M4, the later German Panzers, and the Soviet T-34 all employed similar improvements.

Improvements in tank technology led to improvements in antitank guns. The World War I vintage antitank weaponry used by both sides proved ineffective against the improved tank armor, so both sides introduced more powerful and larger antitank guns. Their ever-increasing size made them vulnerable, however, and they were used less and less. The eventual solution to the problem of countering improved tanks was the antitank vehicle, or tank destroyer. These vehicles usually consisted of conventional tanks with their turrets removed so they could carry heavier guns.

Aircraft   World War II began with the use of biplanes and ended with jet fighters in combat. Every nation participating in the war tried desperately to keep its aircraft on at least equal footing with those of their enemies. This competition led to constant and steady improvements in technology unequaled in the history of aircraft. Aircraft were given ever larger engines, larger fuel capacities, stronger armor, and more powerful weapons throughout the war.

The United States produced the most aircraft during the war, and American planes were generally superior to those of the Axis Powers. Among the most famous American planes were the P-51 Mustang, the F4U Corsair, and the B-29 Superfortress. The Spitfires and Hurricanes of Great Britain were joined in 1944 by the Gloster Meteor, Britain's first jet aircraft. Overwhelmed by the Germans in the beginning, the Russians made improvements to the Polikarpov and Shturmovik (called the Black Death by the Germans). The improved aircraft, along with improved tactics and improved production techniques, made the Red Army Air Force a force to be reckoned with.

Germany began preparing for an air war long before its opponents. By 1939, it had almost 4,000 military aircraft. Before Great Britain and France were fully engaged in their war efforts, Germany was producing the Bf 109 E and Bf 110 fighters as well as the Ju 88, Do 17, Ju 87 Stuka, and He 111 bombers. The Germans not only started with the most aircraft, but with the exception of the British Spitfire, they had superior aircraft. Japan produced the famous Zeros and the less formidable Hayabusa. Despite being considered one of the most advanced air forces in the world prior to the war, the Royal Italian Air Force did not fare well during World War II, primarily because the superior aircraft on which its reputation has been built constituted only a tiny fraction of an air force made up mostly of obsolete and inferior aircraft.

Although helicopters never played a major role in World War II, their capabilities as military aircraft were studied and developed throughout the war. In 1943, a formerly steam-powered passenger craft, the *Governor Cobb*, was converted into the first "helicopter carrier." The helicopter's potential was finally understood near the end of the war, but it was not until the Korean War that it would make a major impact.

Ships The biggest change to ships during World War II was the ascendance of aircraft carriers over battleships. During the early days of the war, much effort was put into planning and building huge battleships. However, after a Japanese air attack sank a British battleship and battle cruiser that were under way and were firing antiaircraft weapons, it became apparent that any ship without an air escort was vulnerable to being sunk. Aircraft carriers thus replaced battleships as the most important ship in naval fleets.

As they had been in World War I, submarines were a significant weapon in World War II. Technical and electronic advances in their design were made mostly by the Germans and were partially in response to advances in radar and sonar and the increased use of aircraft. Submarines were forced to spend more time submerged, and this required the use of the slower electric engines and their short-lived storage batteries. The Germans perfected a Dutch device called a snorkel, with which they could run diesel engines and recharge batteries while just

Primitive Army radar unit on which the operator rotates around the turret along with the dish antenna. (Time & Life Pictures/Getty Images)

below the surface. The U.S. Navy also adapted the snorkel, in addition to streamlining the superstructures of its submarines and greatly improving their storage batteries. The German U-boat (submarine) was Germany's most effective naval weapon of the war. Although submarines made up less than 2 percent of U.S. naval strength, they were credited with 60 percent of all Japanese tonnage sunk during the war.

Other Advances Radar (an acronym for "*ra*dio *de*tection *and ra*nging") came of age during World War II. The Plan Position Indicator (PPI), the same sort of radar display still in use decades later, replaced the oscilloscope-type displays. It gave the operator a maplike display that was easily and intuitively understandable. In addition, the first successful fire control radars were used in World War II. Fire control radar is radar used to determine precisely the position of a target. The development of radar detectors enabled a potential target, such as a bomber or submarine, to know if a radar signal was being beamed at it. Other antiradar devices developed during the war were jammers, which saturated the target with signals, and chaff, small metal strips that are detected by radar and hide or mask the target.

Another existing technology that matured during World War II was sonar (an acronym for "*so*und *na*vigation *and ra*nging). The name "sonar" was first used during World War II. Early in the war, sonar was placed on virtually every ship in the British fleet, under the auspices of the Anti-Submarine Detection and Investigation Committee, and the technology was often referred to as ASDIC, using the initials of this committee. In 1944, the sonobuoy was developed, a device dropped from an aircraft that used sonar to detect targets and then radioed the information back to the aircraft. Refinements were made in the shape and size of the beam.

Impact Modern weapons are so far advanced from those used in World War II that it would be easy to overlook the contribution that developments during that war made to modern weaponry. The widespread use of electronics, the importance of aircraft and the aircraft carrier, and the introduction of nuclear weapons and ballistic missiles made the technological contributions to this war, and the advances in it, far more important than in any other war.

Wayne Shirey

Further Reading

Brown, Lewis. *A Radar History of World War II: Technical and Military Imperatives*. Boca Raton, Fla.: CRC Press, 1999. Offers deep insights into science and human affairs. Possibly the definitive study of the invention of radar and its use during World War II. Suitable for nonspecialist readers.

Carafano, James Jay. *GI Ingenuity: Improvisation, Technology, and Winning World War II*. Santa Barbara, Calif.: Greenwood, 2006. Clear and informative look at many of the creative solutions to the problems of modern warfare.

Pimlott, John. *B-29 Superfortress*. Englewood Cliffs, N.J.: Prentice Hall, 1993. Provides detailed information about the Superfortress aircraft. Excellent drawings and illustrations.

Shachtman, Tom. *Terrors and Marvels: How Science and Technology Changed the Character and Outcome of World War II*. New York: William Morrow, 2002. Describes the wartime role of science, weapons that were developed but not used, and wartime tactics. Contrasts the commitment of Allied scientists with that of their Axis counterparts.

Sherman, Fredrick C. *Combat Command: The American Aircraft Carriers in the Pacific War*. New York: Dutton, 1950. Addresses American air and naval operations in the Pacific during World War II. Bibliography, maps, and illustrations.

Vizard, Frank, and Bill Scott. *Twenty-first Century Soldier: The Weaponry, Gear, and Technology of the Military in the New Century*. New York: Popular Science Books, 2002. Provides a historical perspective on the development of warcraft.

Williamson, Gordon. *Wolf Pack*. Oxford, England: Osprey, 2005. Presents a detailed analysis of the complete U-boat weapons system, including boat types, operations, tactics, bases, crews, equipment, and related information. Well illustrated with numerous period photographs, drawings, and diagrams.

See also Aircraft carriers; Aircraft design and development; Atomic bomb; Inventions; Jet engines; Radar; Science and technology; Submarine warfare; Wartime industries; World War II; World War II mobilization.

Water fluoridation *See* **Fluoridation**

■ Water pollution

During the 1940's, industry and agriculture disposed of chemical, biological, and radioactive waste with minimal thought about its harm to the environment. With the growth of industry during and after World War II, many people became concerned about the potential harm of pollution to human beings.

During the 1940's, the only law to regulate dissolved constituents had been instituted by the U.S. Public Health Service in 1914 to regulate interstate water supplies. This organization could not regulate pollution within a given state. Because of water pollution resulting from toxic constituents such as arsenic, lead, mercury, radioactivity, organic carcinogens and acid waters given off by industry and because of nitrate and associated nitrogen compounds from agriculture and municipal waste, many saw a need for laws to regulate pollution during the 1940's.

Perhaps the most infamous example of groundwater pollution during this time was the Love Canal incident in Niagara Falls, New York. During the 1920's and 1930's, this area was a dump for municipal waste for Niagara Falls. From 1942 to 1952, the Hooker Electrochemical Company dumped twenty-one thousand tons of chemical wastes there and covered the waste with soil to depths of twenty-five feet. The waste included many harmful substances such as chemical solvents, such as benzene and dioxin; chlorinated hydrocarbons; and other caustic materials. The land was later sold and a school and many houses were built on the site. The site was not monitored for pollutants. Residents living over the area began to find oil and foul-smelling liquids in their yards and basements, and plants began to die. There were high rates of illnesses, including cases of cancer and mental retardation. Eventually the eight hundred families who had lived in the area were paid for their property, and this problem led to the Comprehensive Environmental Response, Compensation, and Liability Act, also known as Superfund, in which hundreds of such sites were found and cleaned up in the United States.

A second instance of water pollution occurred in the north portion of the Potomac River, which lies on the boundary between West Virginia and Maryland. Coal mining had occurred along the north branch of the river since the nineteenth century. The mines were constructed to allow water to flow out of them to the river. The problem was that pyrite, an iron-sulfide mineral, in the coal reacted with the water and oxygen to produce highly acidic waters with abundant dissolved iron and sulfate. The acid damaged concrete structures and killed many of the fish and other organisms in the river. Also, raw sewage was dumped into the river, which further degraded the quality of the waters. This problem attracted attention because the Potomac River flowed through Washington, D.C. This helped to stimulate work on the Clean Water Act.

Impact Waste problems during the 1940's stimulated other laws to control pollution in natural waters. The federal Water Pollution Control Act, or the Clean Water Act, was put into effect in 1948. The goal of the Clean Water Act was to restore and then maintain the chemical, physical, and biological integrity of waters in the United States. The act has been modified many times since 1948. The Public Health Service originally implemented the Clean Water Act, but later the control was given to the Environmental Protection Agency. This organization has the jurisdiction to implement, enforce, and finance the control of the water quality within each state.

Robert L. Cullers

Further Reading

Allen, Jeff. "The 1940s: A Change in Attitude." *Water Environment and Technology* 14, no. 12 (2002): 48.
Blum, Elizabeth D. *Love Canal Revisited.* Lawrence, Kans.: University Press of Kansas, 2008.

See also Agriculture in the United States; Air pollution; Fluoridation; Natural resources; Water pollution Control Act.

■ Water Pollution Control Act

The Law Federal legislation extending the reach of the national government to a limited degree, by establishing cooperative arrangements between it and the states for the prevention and abatement of water pollution.
Date Enacted on June 30, 1948

The Federal Water Pollution Control Act was the first major law to deal with the issue of water pollution, capping a half-century campaign of health workers, conservationists, and sportsmen to obtain legislation that would lessen the urban and industrial impacts on American lakes and rivers. Although cumbersome and ineffective in its initial formulation, the law laid the groundwork for later and more effective legislation.

During and after World War II, a burgeoning population and the rapid growth of heavy industry put unprecedented strains upon existing systems of environmental control in the United States, bolstering the arguments of conservationists that action was required at the federal level to protect the environment. Although President Harry S. Truman was opposed by the Republican-dominated Congress in his domestic initiatives, a compromise allowed the enactment of the Water Pollution Control Act of 1948.

Intended to provide a comprehensive national program for preventing and abating water pollution, the law, as it was passed, gave the federal government jurisdiction over interstate waters only. If waters entirely within a single state's boundaries became polluted, they fell outside federal control, even if they were judged to threaten public health. Moreover, the federal government's role was limited to initiating and coordinating water-protection efforts, supplying technical and research support, and awarding grants.

The law authorized the surgeon general of the United States to bring an abatement action in the case of interstate waters being polluted, but only after surmounting a series of obstacles. Even when a health issue was involved, the surgeon general had to obtain approvals from all the states involved. The law also gave the individual states practically unchecked power to override initiatives of the surgeon general.

The act effectively restricted the federal government to preparing abatement plans for remedying polluted waters, and to providing the required support for these plans. It included no prohibitions of activities that led to water pollution. It also failed to establish standards for pollutants or to enact restrictions on new pollution sources. On the other hand, the law did authorize the federal works administrator to assist states, municipalities and interstate agencies in constructing treatment plants in locations affecting interstate waters.

Impact   Little pollution abatement occurred as a direct result of the Water Pollution Control Act of 1948. In helping reduce the flow of undertreated sewage and other pollutants into interstate waters,

however, it did begin the process of mitigating a worsening water-quality situation. The 1948 measure also proved pivotal in the precedent it set. Bringing to fruition decades of effort by conservationists to enact federal protection for lakes and rivers, it provided a foundation for the more effective laws of subsequent decades, most notably the wholesale legislative overhaul that would become known as the Clean Water Act of 1973.

Mark Rich

Further Reading

Adler, Robert W., Jessica C. Landman, and Diane M. Camero. *The Clean Water Act Twenty Years Later.* Washington, D.C.: Island Press, 1993.

Francko, David A., and Robert G. Wetzel. *To Quench Our Thirst: The Present and Future Status of Freshwater Resources of the United States.* Ann Arbor: University of Michigan Press, 1983.

Vigil, Kenneth M. *Clean Water: An Introduction to Water Quality and Pollution Control.* Corvallis: Oregon State University Press, 2003.

See also   Agriculture in the United States; Air pollution; Fluoridation; Natural resources; *Our Plundered Planet*; *Walden Two*; Water pollution.

■ Welles, Orson

Identification   American film director, actor, writer, and producer
Born   May 6, 1915; Kenosha, Wisconsin
Died   October 10, 1985; Hollywood, California

During the 1940's, Orson Welles established himself as one of America's premier filmmakers, although he stood outside the typical Hollywood mold. His film Citizen Kane *is considered to be one of world cinema's most important works.*

Orson Welles arrived in Hollywood with an enviable contract with RKO Pictures that gave him the freedom to make *Citizen Kane* (1941). The film, which he directed and starred in, demonstrated a creativity and innovation that challenged the conventions of the American studio system. Welles's next film, *The Magnificent Ambersons* (1942), which he directed and narrated, appeared on track to become equally important, but the director was asked to go to Brazil to shoot a film for the U.S. Office of the Coordinator of Inter-American Affairs. That project was intended to strengthen relationships among Western Hemisphere countries and to weaken Nazi influence in South America. Although Welles shot miles of film for the project, his film titled *It's All True* was never completed. Meanwhile, during Welles's absence in South America, the studio severely changed *The Magnificent Ambersons* and released it with little fanfare.

After *The Magnificent Ambersons*, Welles acted in the modest thriller *Journey into Fear* (1943). The film's credits list Norman Foster as director, but Welles often is noted for performing some roles as codirector, and he cowrote the screenplay with Joseph Cotten. In 1946, he completed, as director, costar, and coscenarist, the melodrama *The Stranger* (1946), a film about a German war criminal hiding in an American small town. Again as both star and director, he made the film *Macbeth* (1948) for Republic Pictures, finishing it on a small budget in only twenty-one days, to prove that classic stories could be filmed cheaply and made accessible to the average filmgoer. Welles featured his wife, Rita Hayworth, in his next project, *The Lady from Shanghai* (1947), another crime film featuring the director's signature stylistics and also starring Welles himself.

During the postwar years, Welles worked at a frantic pace as an actor both on the radio and in films, directing and producing for both stage and screen, and giving speeches, making radio broadcasts, and writing editorials and newspaper columns in support of progressive political causes. He moved to Europe in 1947 and for years acted in films while seeking money to finance his independent productions. He would eventually die without ever again achieving the success of *Citizen Kane*.

Impact The Welles of the early 1940's was young, confident, and a bit arrogant. Eventually he proved to be too independent, and after initial support from RKO he ran afoul of the bosses who ran the studios. The studio system was under various stresses by the end of the 1940's, and Welles's behavior within it became increasingly self-destructive. He became a legend with *Citizen Kane*, a film that was vital in establishing an independent voice within the American studio-controlled movie industry, but his achievement was not fully realized until years after the film's

Orson Welles directing a scene in Citizen Kane. *(AP/Wide World Photos)*

release. His films contributed to the film movement later known as film noir and helped to shape its style and mood. *Citizen Kane* came at the beginning and *Touch of Evil* (1958) near the end of the classic noir period. Although most of Welles's films do not directly address World War II, his political proclivities were strongly antifascist.

Charles L. P. Silet

Further Reading

Benamou, Catherine L. *It's All True: Orson Welles's Pan-American Odyssey.* Berkeley: University of California Press, 2007.

Callow, Simon. *Orson Welles: Hello America.* London: Jonathan Cape, 2006.

Rosenbaum, Jonathan. *Discovering Orson Welles.* Berkeley: University of California Press, 2007.

See also *Citizen Kane*; Film in the United States; Film noir; Films about World War II; Flying saucers; Hayworth, Rita; Radio in the United States; Theater in the United States.

■ West Virginia State Board of Education v. Barnette

The Case   U.S. Supreme Court ruling on the First Amendment rights of students
Date   Decided on June 14, 1943

This ruling established the right of students to refuse to salute the American flag in public school.

In *Minersville School District v. Gobitis* (1940), the Supreme Court approved a school board regulation that required all teachers and pupils to salute the American flag each day. The *Minersville* ruling led to the enactment of several state laws requiring compulsory flag salutes and pledges of allegiance in public schools. Three years later, after several Jehovah's Witness students were expelled in West Virginia for refusing to salute the flag, the Court reversed its earlier ruling and overturned these state laws as violations of the First and Fourteenth Amendments. In *West Virginia State Board of Education v. Barnette*, the Court asserted the First Amendment principle that government may not coerce citizens to declare a belief nor compel them to engage in a patriotic ritual to which they have a religious or other conscientious objection.

Impact   Against the background of war and patriotic fervor in the United States, the *Barnette* ruling was a landmark defense of an individual's First Amendment right to be free of government efforts to coerce expressions of loyalty. The ruling was one of several Supreme Court cases during the 1940's involving members of the Jehovah's Witness religion that resulted in expanded protection of individual rights.

Philip R. Zampini

Further Reading

Hall, Kermit, and John J. Patrick. *The Pursuit of Justice: Supreme Court Decisions That Shaped America.* New York: Oxford University Press, 2006.

Peters, Shawn Francis. *Judging Jehovah's Witnesses: Religious Persecution and the Dawn of the Rights Revolution.* Lawrence: University Press of Kansas, 2000.

Stone, Geoffrey R. *Perilous Times: Free Speech in Wartime from the Sedition Act of 1798 to the War on Terrorism.* New York: W. W. Norton, 2004.

See also   Civil rights and liberties; Conscientious objectors; Religion in the United States; Smith Act; Smith Act trials; Supreme Court, U.S.

■ Where's Charley?

Identification   Musical comedy
Creators   Music and lyrics by Frank Loesser (1910-1969); book by George Abbott (1887-1995)
Date   Premiered on October 11, 1948

Along with South Pacific *(1949) and* Kiss Me, Kate *(1948),* Where's Charley? *was among the most memorable musicals of the late 1940's. It was one of the few hit musicals to successfully utilize farce as the basis of its plotline.*

Based on the hugely popular farce play *Charley's Aunt*, a mélange of multiple misunderstandings, *Where's Charley?* was a major hit on Broadway. Following its premiere in October, 1948, it ran almost two years for a total of 792 performances. The original play, penned by Englishman Brandon Thomas, was first performed in London in 1892 and on Broadway the following year. Wherever it was staged, it broke the record for longest-running play, and it was revived countless times. *Charley's Aunt* was adapted to film several times, including at least two American silent versions, one with Sydney Chaplin, the half brother of Charles Chaplin. Charles Ruggles and comedian Jack Benny appeared in sound productions. Given the play's widespread popularity, it was almost inevitable that it would be turned into a musical.

The musical was set in the same year as the play, 1892. Two Oxford students, Charley Wykeham and Jack Chesney, need a chaperon so that their sweethearts, Amy Spettigue and Kitty Verdun, can visit them. Although Charley's aunt is to serve that role, her visit is delayed, and Jack persuades Charley to impersonate her. When the real aunt shows up, the farcical action ensues. Cast in the leading roles of Charley Wykeham and Amy Spettigue were actor-dancer Ray Bolger and Allyn McLerie, respectively. The music and lyrics were written by the composer Frank Loesser, whose first Broadway musical this was; the director was powerhouse veteran George Abbott. Some critics felt that the forty-five-year-old Bolger was miscast as a callow university student. His costar was more than twenty years his junior. However, Bolger overcame all such objections with his peppy winning performance in the title role.

The major hit of *Where's Charley?* was the song "Once in Love with Amy," which Bolger turned into somewhat of a phenomenon by leading the audience in a sing-a-long at every performance. Another popular number to emerge from the musical was "My Darling, My Darling."

Although the musical was revived on Broadway as early as 1951, and again in 1974, it has not been frequently revived. Its relative obscurity has been attributed to the lack of an original cast album and the unavailability of the film version due to the refusal of the rights holder (Loesser's widow) to rerelease it for home viewing. The show had a successful run of more than 400 performances in London beginning in 1958.

Impact The show brought renewed life to the career of Bolger, who had been best known for his portrayal of the scarecrow in the classic 1939 film *The Wizard of Oz*. Costar Byron Palmer, who played Jack Chesney in *Where's Charley?*, won a Tony Award for best actor in 1949 for his portrayal. Bolger and McLerie reprised their roles in the 1952 motion-picture version. The musical also launched the career of Loesser, who went on to compose hit musicals such as *Guys and Dolls* (1950) and *How to Succeed in Business Without Really Trying* (1961).

Roy Liebman

Further Reading
Abbott, George. *Mr. Abbott.* New York: Random House, 1963.
Riis, Thomas L. *Frank Loesser.* New Haven, Conn.: Yale University Press, 2008.

See also Broadway musicals; *Oklahoma!*; *South Pacific*; Theater in the United States.

■ White, Harry Dexter

Identification U.S. Treasury Department officer accused of spying
Born October 9, 1892; Boston, Massachusetts
Died August 16, 1948; Fitzwilliam, New Hampshire

White was accused of espionage. One charge was that he aided the rise of the Chinese communists by delaying financial support to Chiang Kai-shek's Nationalist government. Another charge was that he handed over money-printing plates to the Soviet Union. He was also accused of prolonging the war by advocating punitive postwar policies that deterred Nazi Germany from seeking an earlier peace settlement.

The Harvard educated son of Russian immigrants, Harry Dexter White joined President Franklin D. Roosevelt's administration as an economist during the early 1930's. By all accounts, he was a brilliant man, and he was promoted quickly through the ranks, eventually becoming one of the assistant secretaries under Treasury secretary Henry Morgenthau, Jr. His specialties were foreign affairs and international finance, and he was an early advocate of détente with the Soviet Union through increased economic aid.

As a strong antifascist, White had an affinity for the Soviet Union, possibly because of his heritage, and he even studied the Russian language. His greatest contributions came during the planning for a postwar world. He was instrumental in creating the so-called Bretton Woods system after the Bretton Woods Conference of 1944. This was a program to encourage economic recovery and expanded world trade. White was also a leading figure in the establishment of the World Bank and the International Monetary Fund (IMF).

White advocated providing billions of dollars in loans to help rebuild the Soviet Union's shattered postwar economy and formed close friendships with Russian diplomats and others who later were suspected of spying. Soon after the war, Federal Bureau of Investigation chief J. Edgar Hoover suspected that White might be a spy. Despite Hoover's suspicions, and some opposition by congressional conservatives, White was named head of the IMF in 1946 by President Harry S. Truman. Although White did a commendable job, his health began to fail, possibly because of the ongoing campaign against him, and in early 1947, he resigned from his IMF position. Nevertheless, accusations of spying continued to be made, and in July, 1948, White was publicly condemned as a spy by former communists Elizabeth Bentley and Whittaker Chambers. At the time, he was the highest-ranking U.S. official to have been accused of espionage.

Called before the House Committee on Un-American Activities in 1948, White made an eloquent defense of his patriotism. He stated that he believed in all the freedoms Americans enjoyed "as living realities, and not mere words on paper." A few days later he died of a heart attack. However, his death did not end the investigations into his possible espionage. Although no hard and fast documentary evidence was found, it was later generally accepted that White had, in fact, worked for the Soviets.

Impact   The suspicion by some right-wing elements that the Truman administration was riddled with spies was heightened by the White case. These accusations hampered the Truman administration in the atmosphere of Cold War hostility. Such cases as White's eventually led directly to Senator Joseph McCarthy's witch hunt for communists in the government during the early 1950's.

Roy Liebman

Further Reading

Craig, R. Bruce. *Treasonable Doubts: The Harry Dexter White Spy Case.* Lawrence: University Press of Kansas, 2004.

Rees, David. *Harry Dexter White: A Study in Paradox.* New York: Coward, McCann & Geoghegan, 1973.

See also   Anticommunism; Bentley, Elizabeth; Bretton Woods Conference; Communist Party USA; Ford Motor Company; House Committee on Un-American Activities; Loyalty Program, Truman's; Truman, Harry S.; Wartime espionage.

■ White, Walter F.

Identification   Executive secretary of the National Association for the Advancement of Colored People, 1931-1955

Born   July 1, 1893; Atlanta, Georgia

Died   March 21, 1955; New York, New York

As executive secretary of the National Association for the Advancement of Colored People, Walter White provided leadership in the fight against segregation. He set up the NAACP's Legal Defense Fund, helped write the presidential order desegregating the military after World War II, and encouraged the efforts that led to the U.S. Supreme Court decision in Brown v. Board of Education *(1954). He was also a novelist, essayist, journalist, and an important figure in the Harlem Renaissance of the 1920's.*

Walter White was born and grew to adulthood in Atlanta, Georgia. Although he was blond, light-skinned, and blue-eyed, his family and ethnic heritage identified him as African American. One of his earliest memories was of the death and destruction he witnessed during the Atlanta race riot of 1906, when a mob threatened to burn down his family's

home. He graduated from Atlanta University in 1916, and he immediately found a position with the Standard Life Company. While working for Standard Life, he led a protest against the racist practices of the local school board and worked to organize a chapter of the National Association for the Advancement of Colored People (NAACP) in Atlanta.

In 1918, he went to New York City to work as an administrative assistant at the national headquarters of the NAACP. While employed at the NAACP, he traveled to the South to investigate lynchings and race riots, often "passing for white" in order to gain information. His home in New York became a gathering place for leaders of the Harlem Renaissance. He wrote several books during the 1920's, including two novels and a study of lynchings, *Rope and Faggot: A Biography of Judge Lynch* (1929). He became executive secretary of the NAACP in 1931, leading the struggle against lynchings, poll taxes, white primary elections, and segregation throughout the decade of the 1930's.

During the 1940's, NAACP membership grew rapidly to almost 500,000. The NAACP's influence was especially felt after the United States entered World War II, as African American soldiers served in the armed forces abroad. In 1941, with the aid of A. Philip Randolph and T. Arnold Hill, White helped persuade President Franklin D. Roosevelt to issue an executive order prohibiting racial discrimination in wartime and defense industries.

In 1944, White went to Europe and to the Pacific theater as a foreign correspondent, documenting the discrimination African American soldiers faced and publishing his findings in another book, *A Rising Wind* (1945). His book undoubtedly influenced President Harry S. Truman's decision to issue an executive order desegregating the military in 1948. That same year, White convinced Truman to establish a presidential commission on civil rights. Much of the commission's report was written into the Democratic Party's platform in 1948.

White served as executive secretary of the NAACP until his death from a heart attack in 1955. He lived to see the U.S. Supreme Court decision, *Brown v. the Board of Education* (1954), but not the flowering of the Civil Rights movement that was to follow.

Impact   Walter White was one of the most influential African Americans in the history of the United States. His decision to live in the black world, despite his appearance, revealed the doctrine of race as a social construction rather than an immutable category. He was a champion of civil rights for African Americans, fighting against segregation in education, housing, and the military. He also fought against racism in Hollywood films. He identified with the organization he led, earning the title "Mr. NAACP."

Yvonne J. Johnson

Further Reading

Janken, Kenneth Robert. *Walter White: Mr. NAACP.* Chapel Hill: University of North Carolina Press, 2003.

White, Walter. *A Man Called White: The Autobiography of Walter White.* Athens: University of Georgia Press, 1948.

See also   African Americans; Civil rights and liberties; Desegregation of the U.S. military; Executive Order 8802; Executive orders; National Association for the Advancement of Colored People; Randolph, A. Philip; Roosevelt, Franklin D.; Truman, Harry S.

■ White House renovations

The Event   Extensive structural repairs and renovations in the official home of the U.S. president
Date   1949-1952
Place   Washington, D.C.

The White House has been the home of every American president since John Adams, who moved in with his wife Abigail in 1800. After nearly 150 years of heavy use, this symbol of the United States needed renovations to extend its life and continue its usefulness.

The White House underwent renovations in 1902, 1927, and 1949, as well as a modernization in 1952. The renovations during the 1940's took place during the administration of President Harry S. Truman. The basic structure of the White House had consider-ably weakened over the years as modern conveniences were added. Walls had been cut up to accommodate gas pipes and electric wires, while indoor bathrooms and elevators also took a toll on the building.

In 1949, Truman received warnings that the White House had significant structural weaknesses that had to be immediately addressed. These problems were dramatically demonstrated when the piano played by his daughter, Margaret, started to fall through the floor on which it stood, breaking the ceiling on a state room below. The commissioner of public buildings, W. E. Reynolds, warned that the second floor was staying up only by force of habit.

The renovations took three years to complete, during which time the Trumans resided at Blair House. Workers gutted the interior in order to install a new steel reinforcing frame. They also expanded the building by excavating under the old basement. The basic four walls were not moved. When the project ended in 1952, the White House had expanded to contain 132 rooms.

Impact   In a small ceremony on the evening of March 27, 1952, Truman received a gold key to the newly renovated White House, which he used to

Workmen rebuilding the interior of the White House. After the building was gutted, little more of the original building than its exterior walls was left. The repairs eventually added 660 tons of structural steel; new electrical, heating, plumbing, and air-conditioning systems; and modern bathrooms and kitchens. (AP/Wide World Photos)

open the entrance door. Two months later, Truman conducted a guided tour of his home that was broadcast live on the three television networks. The renovations were critical to the continued use of the White House as the official home of U.S. presidents. At a time when many Americans were anxious about the spread of communism and the atomic bomb, the reconstruction project helped restore the public perception that the future of their nation, as well as the home of their president, would remain secure.

Caryn E. Neumann

Further Reading

Caroli, Betty Boyd. *Inside the White House: America's Most Famous Home, The First Two Hundred Years.* New York: Canopy Books, 1992.

Harry S. Truman Library and Museum. *The White House Revealed: Photos of the White House Renovation by Abbie Rowe.* Independence, Mo.: Author, n.d. Available at http://www.trumanlibrary.org/abierowe/whitehse.htm

See also Architecture; Presidential powers; Truman, Harry S.

WHO. *See* **World Health Organization**

■ *Wickard v. Filburn*

The Case U.S. Supreme Court ruling that expanded the definition of interstate commerce to justify federal regulations supporting much New Deal legislation.

Date Decided on November 9, 1942

The Supreme Court's unanimous ruling that the Constitution's interstate commerce clause empowered Congress to regulate the amount of wheat farmers could grow established the federal government's reach over virtually all economic activity, even if completely intrastate.

The Great Depression and World War II created upheavals in world markets for commodities. The U.S. Congress responded with the Agricultural Adjustment Act of 1938, which empowered the secretary of agriculture to limit the acreage of wheat that farmers could plant. In 1941, Roscoe Filburn, an Ohio farmer, was allotted 11.1 acres but planted 23. He was assessed a penalty of $117.11. Filburn chal-

lenged the constitutionality of the act, asserting that Congress's power to regulate interstate commerce did not extend to the production of wheat for home consumption.

The Supreme Court ruled that the federal interstate commerce power did extend to intrastate activities that, in the aggregate, could affect interstate commerce. The Court reasoned that because Filburn produced more wheat, he purchased less. If all farmers grew as much as they wanted, Congress would be powerless to achieve its aim of regulating the price and quantity of wheat sold in interstate commerce.

Impact *Filburn*'s holding was a crucial underpinning of subsequent Court decisions extending federal power over intrastate economic activities, including Congress's power to prohibit racial discrimination in local restaurants and hotels, and, in the early twenty-first century, the federal power to ban the possession of medical marijuana though allowed by state law.

Howard C. Ellis

Further Reading

Chen, Jim. "The Story of *Wickard v. Filburn*: Agriculture, Aggregation, and Congressional Power over Commerce." In *Constitutional Law Stories*, edited by Michael C. Dorf. New York: Foundation Press, 2004.

Prentice, Ezra Parmalee. *The Commerce Clause of the Federal Constitution.* Reprint. Charleston, S.C.: BiblioBazaar, 2008.

See also Agriculture in the United States; Business and the economy in the United States; Economic wartime regulations; New Deal programs; Supreme Court, U.S.; *United States v. Darby Lumber Co.*; War Production Board.

■ **Williams, Hank**

Identification American country music singer-songwriter

Born September 17, 1923; Georgiana, Alabama

Died January 1, 1953; Oak Hill, West Virginia

Williams's appearances on the Grand Ole Opry *radio program and his 1949 recording of "Lovesick Blues" marked the emergence of country music as part of main-*

stream popular music. These successes led Williams to become one of the best-known and most oft-imitated hillbilly singers of the twentieth century.

Fraught with disappointments, physical pain, addictions, and financial destitution, Hank Williams's career would drastically alter the way the world understood and conceptualized country music. Even though Williams was one of the most traditional and rural hillbilly singer-songwriters, his appeal crossed generic boundaries. Costumed in the cowboy regalia he began wearing early in his career, stooped over his microphone from perpetual back pain, and singing with versatility often unheard of in hillbilly music, Williams captured the attention of 1940's America.

Several events throughout this decade secured Williams's success and would help catapult him into the mainstream, popular media. In 1946, Williams signed on as a songwriter at Acuff-Rose, the first exclusive country music publishing company in the United States; he then secured a recording contract with Metro-Goldwyn-Mayer (MGM) in 1947. The next year, Williams joined a Saturday night radio variety show, *Louisiana Hayride*, as a headliner, while also appearing on the *Johnny Fair Syrup Hour* during the week. The exposure these shows gave him throughout the American Southwest helped secure his popularity and help him land a coveted position at the radio mecca of country music: the *Grand Ole Opry*.

Even though directors at the *Grand Ole Opry* were reticent to hire Williams, his commercial triumph with an old Tin Pan Alley song secured his spot. "Lovesick Blues," which had been previously recorded by Jack Shea and Emmett Miller, was possibly the most profitable and successful recording of his career. Williams's 1949 version was invariably unique, because he sang in the yodeling style of his fellow Alabamian Rex Griffin; Williams's distinct vocal techniques and virtuosic turns made his version outrageously popular. The song was repeatedly acclaimed, with *Billboard* making its associated album the number one country and western record of 1949, and *Cash Box* selecting it as the "Best Hillbilly Record" of the year. Staying on the country music charts for forty-two weeks, "Lovesick Blues" further

Hank Williams performing on the radio around 1948. (Michael Ochs Archives/Getty Images)

solidified country music's postwar boom period, which would ultimately end with Williams's premature death in 1953 at the age of twenty-nine.

Impact Williams influenced country music songwriters, performers, and institutions. Merging country gospel and honky-tonk, Williams created a singing style that was almost unheard of during the 1940's, and which is virtually nonexistent in the early twenty-first century. Although decidedly rural, Williams was able to begin bridging the gap between country and popular music. Moreover, his influence was grounded in his ability to communicate his story with his listeners.

April L. Prince

Further Reading

Escott, Colin. *Hank Williams: The Biography.* Boston: Little, Brown, 1994.

Koon, George William. *Hank Williams: So Lonesome.* Jackson: University Press of Mississippi, 2001.

Malone, Bill C. *Country Music, U.S.A.: A Fifty-Year History.* Rev. ed. Austin: University of Texas Press, 1985.

Waldron, Eli. "Country Music: The Death of Hank Williams." *The Reporter* 12, no. 10 (May 19, 1955): 35.

See also Cowboy films; Guthrie, Woody; Music: Popular; *Rodeo*; Seeger, Pete.

■ Williams, Ted

Identification American baseball player
Born August 30, 1918; San Diego, California
Died July 5, 2002; Inverness, Florida

Throughout the 1940's, Williams was a tremendous left-handed hitter for the Boston Red Sox. In 1941, he became the last major leaguer to hit over .400 in a season. His service in the armed forces, as with other famous ball players, was highly publicized and represented baseball's sacrifice for the war effort.

When Ted Williams arrived in the major leagues in 1939, few understood how remarkable and consistent a hitter "The Kid" would be. The summer of 1941 saw the fifty-six-game hitting streak of Joe DiMaggio of the New York Yankees, but Williams's drive for a .400 batting average also captivated fans. On the last day of the season, Williams refused to sit out a doubleheader against the Philadelphia Athletics and had six hits in eight at-bats to boost his average to .406.

Also nicknamed the "Splendid Splinter," Williams won the Triple Crown in 1942 and 1947 by leading the American League in batting average, home runs, and runs batted in. He nearly did it again in 1949. Williams remains the only American Leaguer to win the Triple Crown twice. In 1946 and 1949, he was voted the American League's most valuable player. One disappointment for the left fielder was that the Boston Red Sox lost the only World Series of his career in 1946.

Following the 1942 season, Williams joined the U.S. Marine Air Corps. He later served as a jet pilot during the Korean War.

Impact DiMaggio and Williams helped rejuvenate baseball's popularity upon their return from World War II. Intense and often contentious with the press,

Williams compiled an increasingly impressive record as DiMaggio's career wound down. Williams's career ended in 1960, and he was elected to the Baseball Hall of Fame in 1966.

M. Philip Lucas

Further Reading
Montville, Leigh. *Ted Williams: The Biography of an American Hero.* New York: Broadway Books, 2004.

Williams, Ted, and John Underwood. *My Turn at Bat: The Story of My Life.* Rev. ed. New York: Simon & Schuster, 1988.

See also All-American Girls Professional Baseball League; Baseball; DiMaggio, Joe; Gehrig, Lou; Negro Leagues; Paige, Satchel; Robinson, Jackie; Sports in the United States.

■ Williams, Tennessee

Identification American playwright
Born March 26, 1911; Columbus, Mississippi
Died February 25, 1983; New York, New York

One of the leading American playwrights of the 1940's, Williams not only was popular with theater audiences but also became an enduring figure in American drama.

Born Thomas Lanier Williams and dubbed "Tennessee" during his college years, Williams formally adopted his nickname and began writing a series of short plays, which, together with his full-length plays, would eventually total more than sixty dramatic works. Scholarly accounts vary, probably because of Williams's habit of rewriting his works and their being collected in different forms, but he also wrote two books of poetry, two novels, collections of essays, and two autobiographies/memoirs. His first professionally produced play, *Battle of Angels*, starring Miriam Hopkins, opened and closed quickly in 1940 because of poor reviews and censorship issues.

Williams's subsequent plays reflected the concerns of the 1940's and were more successful. *The Glass Menagerie* (1944) is about a woman left to care for herself and her crippled daughter after being deserted first by her husband and then by her son. The plight of Amanda, trying to uphold imagined Southern elegance in the face of a reality in which a woman needed a man to support her, is highly poignant. The play won a New York Drama Critics Circle Award for best play of the season.

Williams was similarly acclaimed for another of his most famous plays, *A Streetcar Named Desire* (1947). Once again setting his story in a world of 1940's poverty, Williams wrote the story of Blanche DuBois, a rapidly declining southern belle who comes to live with her sister Stella and brother-in-law Stanley Kowalski after the mysterious loss of the home plantation, Belle Reve, and an early dismissal from her teaching job. Conflict between the fragile Blanche, stuck in the past, and the brutish Stanley, anchored squarely in the present, leads to disaster. Williams called these works "memory plays," in which a profound and often tragic event keeps the protagonists frozen in time, forcing them to relive the conflict in dysfunctional ways until it is somehow resolved. They also fall under the heading of southern gothic. *A Streetcar Named Desire* earned for Williams the first of his Pulitzer Prizes in drama, the other coming for *Cat on a Hot Tin Roof* (1955).

Williams lived in several places over the years, notably Key West, Florida, and New Orleans, Louisiana. His personal and professional life declined over the years, as he was haunted by the lobotomy of his mentally ill sister Rose and the death of his lover Frank Merlo from cancer in 1963. He is believed to have choked to death on the cap of a medicine bottle.

Impact Williams made a name for himself in theater during the 1940's, writing two of his most famous and critically acclaimed dramas during the decade. The protagonists' dilemmas and the backgrounds reflected conditions of the United States in the post-Depression World War II era, but Williams was able to construct dramas that transcended their time period. His works are among the greatest of American theater and have been revived and revered throughout the decades. These two plays and others also earned him accolades for the film adaptations made of them. He wrote more than two dozen other major plays during the four decades following the 1940's. *The Night of the Iguana* was produced in 1961 and made into an acclaimed feature film in 1964; it is set in the 1940's in Mexico.

Charles Lewis Avinger, Jr.

Further Reading
Gross, Robert F., ed. *Tennessee Williams: A Casebook.* New York: Routledge, 2002.
Leverich, Lyle. *Tom: The Unknown Tennessee Williams.* New York: Crown, 1995.
Spoto, Donald. *The Kindness of Strangers: The Life of Tennessee Williams.* Boston: Little, Brown, 1985.
Vallela, Tony. "Tennessee Williams Revisited." *Christian Science Monitor,* July 16, 2004.
Williams, Tennessee. *Memoirs.* Garden City, N.Y.: Doubleday, 1975.

See also   Censorship in the United States; Film in the United States; Literature in the United States; Lobotomy; *A Streetcar Named Desire*; Theater in the United States.

■ Willkie, Wendell

Identification   Republican presidential candidate in 1940
Born   February 18, 1892; Elwood, Indiana
Died   October 8, 1944; New York, New York

Willkie gained fame as the 1940 Republican candidate for president of the United States, even though he had never before held elective office. Although he lost the election to Franklin D. Roosevelt, Willkie's views on democracy and fairness to minorities were his greatest contributions.

Wendell L. Willkie grew up in Indiana and graduated from law school at Indiana University. Although he was given the first name of Lewis when he was born, he was called by his middle name, Wendell. An Army error in 1917 transposed the two names and he never corrected the error. After serving as a lieutenant in World War I, Willkie moved to Akron, Ohio, where he became a corporate lawyer for Firestone Tire and Rubber Company. He became active in the Ohio Democratic Party and served as a delegate to the 1924 National Convention. In 1929, he moved to New York City, where he became a lawyer for Commonwealth & Southern Corporation, the country's largest utility holding company. By 1933, he was the company president. Willkie became a supporter of Franklin D. Roosevelt in 1932. However, Roosevelt's creation of the Tennessee Valley Authority (TVA) and other New Deal programs prompted Willkie to oppose government programs that competed with private industry. In fact, Willkie testified before Congress in 1933 against the TVA. In 1939, he switched to the Republican Party and spoke often against New Deal programs.

Wendell Willkie at a September, 1940, press conference in which he discussed the forthcoming presidential election and told the press he wanted to add a secretary of aeronautics to the president's cabinet. (AP/Wide World Photos)

There were four leading candidates for the 1940 Republican presidential nomination, Robert Taft, Arthur Hendrick Vandenberg, Herbert Hoover, and Thomas E. Dewey. Although a former Democrat and a businessman who had never run for office, Willkie was supported by a few newspapermen. A poll before the convention showed that Willkie had a 3 percent support rating. The leading candidates were all isolationists who wanted to keep America out of World War II, whereas Willkie supported aiding the British. Just before the convention, France surrendered to Nazi Germany, and there was belief that England was under threat of invasion. Suddenly, delegates to the convention were bombarded with telegrams from constituents in support of Willkie. On the first ballot, Dewey had the most votes, but far short of a majority. Taft was second and Willkie a surprising third. On the sixth ballot, Willkie received a majority of the votes.

Although Willkie lost the general election by more than 5 million votes, he garnered more support than had any previous Republican candidate. Roosevelt won the electoral vote 449 to 82, with Willkie winning ten states. Following the election, Willkie became a Roosevelt ally and traveled extensively as the president's representative. Willkie's major publication came in 1943 with _One World_, a book that advocated international peacekeeping following the war. Willkie was also an advocate of ending racism and in 1942 became one of the most noted white persons to ever address the convention of the National Association for the Advancement of Colored People (NAACP). He ranked racism as being akin to fascism. He campaigned again for the presidency in 1944 but withdrew when he finished behind Dewey and General Douglas MacArthur in the Wisconsin primary.

Impact Willkie's 1940 nomination was one of the most exciting moments in American political history. An unknown former Democrat who had found disfavor with Roosevelt's New Deal was nominated as the Republican nominee. His ideas, particularly those dealing with race relations and those expressed in his book _One World_, have survived to the present day. He is buried in Rushville, Indiana, the childhood home of his wife, Edith.

Dale L. Flesher

Further Reading

Madison, James H. _Wendell Willkie: Hoosier Internationalist._ Bloomington: Indiana University Press, 1992.

Neal, Steve. _Dark Horse: A Biography of Wendell Willkie._ Garden City, N.Y.: Doubleday, 1984.

Peters, Charles. _Five Days in Philadelphia: 1940, Wendell Willkie, and the Political Convention That Freed FDR to Win the War._ New York: PublicAffairs, 2006.

See also Dewey, Thomas E.; Elections in the United States: 1940; Elections in the United States: 1944; MacArthur, Douglas; Roosevelt, Eleanor; Roosevelt, Franklin D.; Taft, Robert A.; Vandenberg, Arthur Hendrick.

■ *Wolf v. Colorado*

The Case U.S. Supreme Court ruling on the application of the Fourth Amendment to the states

Date Decided on June 27, 1949

The Supreme Court's 6-3 ruling held that the Fourth Amendment guarantee against unreasonable searches and seizure was applicable to the states through the due process clause of the Fourteenth Amendment but that states were not required to exclude illegally obtained evidence.

Julius A. Wolf, a Colorado physician, was convicted of conspiring with others to commit abortions. He challenged the convictions on the grounds that illegally obtained evidence (Wolf's appointment book) had been admitted in his state criminal trial in violation of his Fourth Amendment rights. The Colorado Supreme Court upheld Wolf's convictions. Wolf appealed to the U.S. Supreme Court.

Prior to its decision in *Wolf v. Colorado*, the U.S. Supreme Court in *Weeks v. United States* (1914) ruled that the Fourth Amendment prohibited illegally obtained evidence in a federal criminal trial. Although the rules regarding the admissibility of illegally seized evidence were clear at the federal level, rulings on the admissibility of such evidence at the state level were inconsistent. In fact, by 1949, only sixteen states were in agreement with the *Weeks* doctrine.

In *Wolf*, the specific issue before the Supreme Court was whether states are required by the Fourth Amendment to exclude illegally seized evidence in a state criminal trial. The Court held that while the Fourth Amendment applied to the states through the Fourteenth Amendment, the exclusionary doctrine established in *Weeks* was not applicable to the states. In upholding Wolf's conviction, the Court reasoned that while the exclusion of illegally obtained evidence may serve to deter the police, other methods were equally efficient, including private remedies such as internal disciplinary proceedings.

Impact The *Wolf* decision was the first case to apply the Fourth Amendment to the states through the incorporation doctrine of the Fourteenth Amendment. Nevertheless, the private remedies espoused in *Wolf* did little to deter unlawful searches and seizures by the police. The case was overturned in *Mapp v. Ohio* in 1961, whereby the Supreme Court applied the *Weeks* exclusionary rule to the states.

LaVerne McQuiller Williams

Further Reading

Dash, Samuel. *The Intruders: Unreasonable Searches and Seizures from King John to John Ashcroft.* New Brunswick, N.J.: Rutgers University Press, 2004.

Stephens, Otis H., ed. *Unreasonable Searches and Seizures: Rights and Liberties Under the Law.* Santa Barbara, Calif.: ABC-Clio, 2006.

See also Health care; Supreme Court, U.S.

■ Women in the U.S. military

Until World War II, women had not been accepted in the U.S. military, but by the end of the decade, all four branches of service had more or less initiated comprehensive gender integration programs.

In May, 1941, the U.S. Congress worked on a bill to recruit women into low-skill Army jobs, such as laundering and cleaning. However, after the military attack on Pearl Harbor, men in these and higher positions were sent to the front lines, so Congress created the Women's Army Auxiliary Corps (WAAC) program in May, 1942. Under the initial program, the WAAC extension was controlled by the Army, which positioned servicewomen liminally between soldiers and support staff. While women's secondary status became a major handicap to recruiting efforts, the main problem was the negative and disrespectful attitudes of male soldiers toward their female colleagues, an issue that remained problematic throughout the decade. These attitudes were supported by the Army's "separate but equal" ideology concerning women: the nearly 13,000 enrolled women did not receive the same post-injury care, pay, benefits, or rank enjoyed by their male counterparts.

The Army's Women's Programs In July, 1942, 400 white women and 400 black women, who had joined out of a sense of patriotic duty, were segregated upon arrival at the Army WAAC officer-training center at Fort Des Moines. WAAC director Oveta Culp Hobby, who would eventually win the U.S. Army Distinguished Service Medal, worked closely with ambivalent male Army officers to recruit up to 63,000 additional female soldiers in two years. By then, however, the needed number had reached 1.5 million. Despite the overwhelming demand for women in the military, the Women's Army Corps (WAC) bill, which granted women equal status in the service, was not passed officially until the summer of 1943.

Margaret D. Craighill became the first woman commissioned into the Army Medical Corps at the rank of major. The Army Nurse Corps had been established under the direction of Lieutenant Colonel Florence Blanchfield, the first woman to hold a permanent commission in the Army. During the ninety-day conversion period following WAC's passing, more than 60,000 women were given the option of remaining on as soldiers or going home. By this time, women were serving both stateside and abroad, in Japan, Iran, India, and parts of Africa.

Formed in September, 1942, the Women's Auxiliary Ferrying Squadron (WAFS) became a burgeoning branch of the Army during this time partly because of efforts by pilots Jacqueline Cochran and Nancy Harkness Love. Cochran quickly established the Women's Flying Training Detachment (WFTD) in the Army Air Forces, and by November 28, the WAFS flew its first mission. Close to 400 women graduated from the program in 1943, which led Cochran to merge the WAFS and WFTD to form the Women Airforce Service Pilots in August, 1943. By the time that program disbanded in 1944, 120,000 women were serving in 401 of approximately 600 formerly off-limits military occupational specialties (MOS), as air-traffic controllers, instructors, and trainers of carrier pigeons and dogs.

After World War II, Army chief of staff Dwight D. Eisenhower supported integration through 1946 and 1947, and while full integration was granted in 1948, women remained in service in what was unofficially dubbed the "interim Army." In 1947, Lieutenant Colonel Mary A. Hallaren, a strong proponent of integration, was appointed the director of the WAC.

The Navy's WAVES   The Navy did not initially agree to allow women into its fold, but early in 1942, it recognized that it was severely understaffed and, by necessity, began admitting women. The Naval Women's Reserves was called Women Accepted for Volunteer Emergency Service (WAVES). The WAVES program took an entirely different approach to recruiting, opting for an academic route to recruit a class of potential naval officers rather than the com-

paratively uneducated group accumulated by the Army. The president of Wellesley College, Mildred McAfee, was commissioned lieutenant commander in the Naval Reserves to head the WAVES program. The Navy's recruitment goals were also more realistic that the Army's; the Navy opted to enlist 75,000 female soldiers and 12,000 female officers. These women were recruited to work in the United States; not until November, 1944, when the war had nearly ended, were WAVES deployed overseas.

By 1945, 86,000 American women were WAVES. Women made up more than one-half of all naval personnel at Navy headquarters, and this trend continued throughout top naval offices nationwide. Though it faced strict objections to retaining women past wartime, the Navy promoted war veteran Joy Bright Hancock to assistant chief of naval personnel for women in 1946 to decrease the number of women in what became a Navy-wide reduction of three million service personnel. She accomplished that mission, some say too efficiently, for the Navy soon began seeking ways to retain a dwindling naval corps. In 1948, the U.S. Senate passed a bill that created permanent jobs for women in the Navy. During the last years of the decade, the Navy secured sufficient, although low, numbers of women.

Women in the Coast Guard and the Marines   In September, 1942, the U.S. Coast Guard elected to accept women under a program titled SPAR, an acronym from its motto, "Semper Paratus—Always Ready." The Coast Guard's SPAR program followed the organization and recruitment principles established by the Navy but recruited even fewer women: 10,000 enlisted and 1,000 officers, one in four of whom served in aviation. By mid-decade, the Coast Guard had achieved this goal; by June, 1946, SPAR was demobilized.

The U.S. Marine Corps was the branch of the American armed forces most reluctant to accept women. It established the Marine Corps Women's Reserve (MCWR) in February, 1943. Both the Coast Guard and the Marines recruited women from other branches of the service to form the core of their own female programs. Nearly one-third of female Marines served in aviation; at one air station, 90 percent of the parachute workers and 80 percent of all air-traffic controllers were women. In total, there were 18,000 women Marines by mid-decade. By the end of the war, Marine Corps women held 87 percent of enlisted jobs at Marine headquarters and often up to one-half of the on-post positions. The MCWR disbanded in the years after World War II, and the Marine Corps did not integrate as quickly as the other branches of the military did.

The Women of the Air Force   After the 1948 integration legislation passed and only nine months after the Air Force fought and won independence from the Army, the Women in the Air Force (WAF) set the goal of full integration, uninterested in status as a "petticoat" corps separate from the Air Force. By summer, WAF had attracted only 168 officers and 1,433 enlisted women, well below the 2 percent ceiling the Air Force enacted to maintain low female-to-male ratios and to recruit an elite force of women that trumped the Navy's WAVES. In early 1949, the first female officers attended Officer Candidate School, the foremost coed advanced-training program in any service.

Impact   At the end of World War II, the U.S. armed forces contained 12 million service personnel, 280,000 of whom were women. More than 350,000 women had served altogether. In 1945, several top-ranking and program-founding women resigned, including Hobby, Ruth Cheney Streeter, McAfee, and Dorothy C. Stratton, ostensibly setting the pace for a rapid demobilization and disbandment of all women-in-service programs. In 1948, Congress passed the Women's Armed Services Act, which created permanent positions for women in the Army, Navy, Air Force, and Marine Corps. Although provisions were imperfect—for example, women could not surpass a certain rank or enter certain MOS positions—feminists considered it a victory for female soldiers and women's rights. The threats of the Korean War and the Cold War caused a short pause in recruitment and retention in most branches. It was women's lack of interest in the programs—not an exclusion of the gender—that caused a reduction in women's enlistment toward the end of the 1940's.

Ami R. Blue

Further Reading

Cook, Bernard A. *Women and War: A Historical Encyclopedia from Antiquity to the Present.* Santa Barbara,

Recruiting poster for the women's auxiliary branch of the U.S. Coast Guard. (National Archives)

Calif.: ABC-Clio, 2006. Broader in scope than just the 1940's, this allows for easy comparison of women's roles, attitudes, and rights among wars and cultures.

Hartmann, Susan M. *The Home Front and Beyond: American Women in the 1940's.* Boston: Twayne, 1982. Describes the educational, military, political, industrial, and legal roles of women within and outside the U.S. military during this decade.

Holm, Jeanne. *Women in the Military: An Unfinished Revolution.* Novato, Calif.: Presidio Press, 1982. Parts one and two of this informative social history contextualize women's military history in the attitudes, customs, and personalities of the era; told from an insider's perspective.

Meyer, Leisa. *Creating G.I. Jane: Sexuality and Power in the Women's Army Corps During World War II.* New York: Columbia University Press, 1998. Specifically about the WAC, examines the moral codes, racial prejudices, and societal dismissal of female soldiers, particularly black women and lesbians.

Yellin, Emily. *Our Mothers' War: American Women at Home and at the Front During World War II.* New York: Simon & Schuster, 2008. Personal account; offers a subjective perspective, conveying how women felt, thought, and interacted with their society.

See also Air Force, U.S.; Army, U.S.; Coast Guard, U.S.; Cochran, Jacqueline; G.I. Bill; Marines, U.S.; Navy, U.S.; Pearl Harbor attack; Roosevelt, Eleanor; War heroes; Women's roles and rights in the United States; World War II; World War II mobilization.

■ Women's roles and rights in Canada

In 1940, Canadian women did not enjoy the same civil rights as men and were constrained by their roles as mothers and housewives. Women received lower wages than men, and they lacked federal voting rights in Quebec. While women's opportunities increased during wartime, at the end of World War II the momentum for developing gender equity diminished.

Canada was ethnically almost completely homogenous during the 1940's. The 1941 census records approximately 11.5 million people, 98 percent of whom were of European heritage and were predominantly English and French speakers. There were small German, Ukrainian, Dutch, Jewish, Polish, and Italian communities in Canada in that year, but the women in these groups led somewhat different lives, depending on their ethnic customs or languages. In addition, Native Canadian women, including the Inuits and the Métis (people of mixed European and Indian ancestry), would have led lives marked by ethnically specific challenges, such as attending Indian boarding schools or living in impoverished conditions on reservations.

Another group that experienced poor treatment during the 1940's was the Asian Canadian population, specifically Japanese Canadians. Japanese Canadians and Japanese nationals were not differentiated by the federal government, and they were forcibly detained together in internment camps during the war years, when they lost their land,

homes, and possessions. In the postwar period, Japanese nationals were deported, and Canadians of Japanese ancestry experienced considerable hardship in finding employment and regaining their civil rights. Thus, the war was problematic for women of certain ethnic groups, resulting in a loss of freedom.

Women in Canada had obtained the right to vote federally in 1918, although the province of Quebec did not permit women to vote nationally until 1940. In a similar manner, other civil rights were distributed piecemeal across the nation, with some provinces offering greater degrees of freedom and economic security to women than others.

Effects of the War An unexpected outcome of Canada's military involvement in World War II, which lasted from September 10, 1939, through August 15, 1945, was that women were able to expand their roles in society and obtain better wages. These developments resulted in increased activism to obtain equal rights after the war was over. By 1945, more than forty-five thousand women had enlisted in the Canadian armed forces, and all three branches of the military had formed women's units, including the Canadian Women's Army Corps, the Women's Royal Canadian Navy Service, and the Women's Division in the Royal Canadian Air Force. Women served as physicians, clerks, motor transport drivers, and mechanics, but they were not permitted to pilot planes or ships or to engage in active combat.

Despite the shift by some women into nontraditional employment, for the most part Canadian women continued to perform domestic labor or were employed in the service industries. Men moving out of the labor market into military service enabled more women to take up clerical work, which was better paid than their traditional options. By 1941, white-collar women workers made up 44 percent of the female labor force. Female work opportunities continued to increase throughout the war, and by 1944, women accounted for 31.5 percent of all employed civilians.

The success of women in new occupations encouraged other women to move into less traditional roles. For example, in 1940, the Montreal Women's Symphony was founded, and within seven years these musicians had performed in New York City's Carnegie Hall, the first Canadian symphony orchestra to attain this honor. By 1941, the list of 7,920 Canadian notaries and lawyers included 129 women.

Women also excelled in athletics. Winifred "Winnie" Frances Roach-Leuszler (1926-2004) thrilled women with her win in the five-mile swim in the 1946 world swimming championships. She provided additional encouragement to young mothers by entering the competition while she was three months pregnant.

Women and Families The notion that women could be successful athletes, musicians, or lawyers and still be viewed as good mothers was contradicted by a major child-care manual available to women in the 1940's. Benjamin Spock's *Common Sense Book of Baby and Child Care* (1946) suggested that the primary job of women should be to take care of their children. Advertisements of the era provided this same message, while adding household chores to female responsibilities. At the same time, there was increased mechanization of housework; General Electric, for example, invented the automatic electric clothes washer in 1947. However, cultural expectations focused on higher degrees of household cleanliness. The combination of women's perceived roles as mothers and the emphasis on diligent housekeeping meant that housework did not actually decrease, despite the new, labor-saving devices.

By the middle of the 1940's, a national family allowance, or "baby bonus," became a regular payment to all Canadian families with children. Federal support of population growth, combined with the return of servicemen and servicewomen, resulted in a postwar baby boom. This trend also confined women to their homes, which were now often located in new suburbs constructed around the older city cores, further isolating women. By the end of the 1940's, Canada was becoming more prosperous but had rigidly defined its gender roles: Men were breadwinners who were paired with female homemakers.

Impact In some ways, the 1940's were a time of seeming advances in women's rights and an expansion of their roles in society. By the end of the decade, however, most women had returned to being mothers and homemakers, and their opportunities to broaden their horizons were more constrained than they had been during wartime.

Susan J. Wurtzburg

Further Reading

Bothwell, Robert, Ian Drummond, and John English. *Canada Since 1945.* Rev. ed. Toronto: University of Toronto Press, 2006. Social, economic, and political history of Canada covering the post World War II period.

Nelson, Adie, and Barrie W. Robinson. *Gender in Canada.* 2d ed. Toronto: Pearson Education Canada, 2002. Extensive coverage of contemporary gender issues, with some historic context.

Parr, Joy, ed. *A Diversity of Women: Women in Ontario Since 1945.* Toronto: University of Toronto Press, 1995. Wide-ranging collection of essays about women in Canada's most populated province.

Sugiman, Pamela. "Memories of Internment: Narrating Japanese Canadian Women's Life Stories." *Canadian Journal of Sociology* 29, no. 3 (2004): 359-388. Personal experiences combined with his-

Government poster promoting the sale of victory bonds by implying that one the greatest threats that war posed was to the traditional role of Canadian women as housewives and mothers. (Getty Images)

toric documents about the 1940's internment of Japanese Canadians.

See also Advertising in Canada; Baby boom; *The Common Sense Book of Baby and Child Care*; Education in Canada; Fashions and clothing; "Rosie the Riveter"; Sex and sex education; Women's roles and rights in the United States.

■ Women's roles and rights in the United States

The vital and diverse roles women played in World War II permanently changed their place in American society. Since the late 1940's, women have increased their presence in the workforce, higher education, politics, the military, athletics, and entertainment. These changes would likely have occurred eventually, but the war hastened them.

In 1940, war was raging across Europe, and the debate in the United States about whether or not to enter the war had grown intense. More women than men opposed entering the war. While most were well-intentioned pacifists, the ultraconservative confederation of groups known as the Mothers' Movement were anti-Semitic groups sympathetic to Nazism that effectively worked against U.S. involvement in the war.

World War II Before the United States entered World War II at the end of 1941, most women working outside the home were lower class and worked as maids, laundresses, nursemaids, and low-level factory employees. However, as men went off to war and as the war necessitated an expansion of certain industries, female workers were required for higher-ranking positions in the workforce.

Early in the war, employers were reluctant to hire women for jobs traditionally considered to be only for men. Furthermore, most middle-class women were not eager to leave home to work. The first women to take factory jobs were primarily minority and lower-class women already in the workforce, who left lower-paying, traditionally female jobs to take higher-paying factory jobs. The government soon realized that more workers were needed and teamed up with the media and women's organizations to launch a propaganda campaign to get middle-class women to join the labor force.

Appeals to patriotism and increases in income were used to recruit women into the labor force. Norman Rockwell painted the fictional Rosie the Riveter, a character created in a song of the same name, an image that appeared on the cover of the *Saturday Evening Post* on May 29, 1942, and afterward became iconic. The character was eventually used in a government-commissioned poster, becoming both a powerful recruiting tool and an enduring image of the female worker in World War II. Rosie is shown as a strong and competent worker, who nevertheless remains thoroughly feminine with her nail polish, curly hair, and a compact in her pocket. The campaign was highly successful; prior to the American entrance into the war, about 12 million women were in the wage-labor workforce; by the end of the war, that figure had increased to about 18 million women—a 50 percent increase. The sectors that experienced the greatest increases in female workers were manufacturing and government.

Despite the fact that women were so heavily recruited, they still faced a good deal of discrimination in obtaining traditionally male jobs. Employers, male workers, and unions did not believe women could do the work that men did. Many women experienced on-the-job harassment, humiliation, and sexual advances. Often, women themselves doubted they had the ability to perform in the workplace. Eventually they proved to employers, coworkers, and themselves that they could do the same work as men. Male and female pay rates remained unequal, however, and some discrimination in the workplace continued throughout the war.

The women who entered the workforce had difficult lives, particularly if they had children. They had to work full time (and sometimes more), care for children, and keep house. Adding to their problems was the rationing of nearly all goods. Finding good-quality childcare and getting children to and from day care before and after work were extremely difficult. The Lanham Act of 1942 provided federal aid for day care, but government day-care centers served relatively few children and were often of poor quality.

Most women who were not employed also contributed to the war effort. Millions of women volunteered in organizations such as United Service Organizations (USO) and the Red Cross. Women donated blood, grew victory gardens, collected scrap metal, and generally helped to lift the nation's morale. Nonetheless, the loneliness and stress of the war often negatively affected women and their relationships. Both divorces and the number of babies born to unmarried women increased greatly during the war.

The Women's Army Corps, the Women's Naval Reserve, the Marine Corps Women's Reserve, and the Coast Guard Women's Reserve were all established during World War II. Overall, approximately 375,000 women served in the military during the war; between 800 and 900 of these were African American women. The majority of women who served in the military during World War II held jobs traditionally associated with women, such as typists, clerks, and filers. Although not dangerous or glamorous, these jobs were essential to the war effort.

Many women in the military, particularly nurses, served in Europe, Africa, and the Pacific. Often they had to put themselves in harm's way.

Women assembling the wing of a B-17 bomber in a Seattle, Washington, aircraft plant in late 1942. (Library of Congress)

More than five hundred women in the military lost their lives serving the United States during World War II, sixteen by enemy fire. Another eighty-eight were prisoners of war. Women were awarded more than fifteen hundred medals and citations for their service during the war.

In addition to the women who formally served their country, more than one thousand women were members of the Women Airforce Service Pilots (WASP). They were the first women in the United States to fly military aircraft. Apart from combat missions, they flew every type of mission any male Army Air Force pilot flew during World War II. This freed many male pilots for combat missions. Thirty-eight of these women gave their lives for their country. In 2009, the women of the WASP were presented the Congressional Medal of Honor.

Women also worked as journalists, fighting for and getting the opportunity to cover the war at home and abroad. At least 127 American women obtained military accreditation as war correspondents. Given the chance to cover a truly important event,

they did an admirable job and paved the way for future female journalists.

With most young men in the military, women's enrollment in higher education increased greatly at both the undergraduate and the graduate levels. Because they were often employed, more women had money for higher education. Furthermore, with their sons in the military, parents had more money to spend on the education of their daughters. Also, with college-educated men less available, more businesses sought women with college educations. Increases in female enrollments were particularly large in engineering and the hard sciences.

Women also helped fill the entertainment gap left by so many men going to war. In 1943, with one-half of the professional male baseball players serving in the military, Chicago Cubs owner Philip Wrigley formed the All-American Girls Professional Baseball League that continued until 1954. Also, with many male musicians in the military, several African American and white all-female swing bands formed. They toured ballrooms, dance halls, and USO's at military bases. They helped distract people from the horrors of war while also showing that women could contribute to the country's musical legacy.

After the War In 1945, World War II ended, and millions of soldiers returned home and to the workforce. Women who had entered the workforce during the war were expected to give up their jobs. Many women were demoted, pressured to quit their jobs, or fired outright. Others were happy to leave their jobs. However, the seeds of permanent change had been planted, as many women had proved to themselves and others that they could do what had traditionally been considered "men's" work. Many women did not give up their jobs after the war, and many who did returned to the workforce a year or two later.

After the war, most women were employed in low-paying jobs, working as secretaries, waitresses, and clerks in what was called the "pink collar" workforce. Women continued to experience substantial discrimination on the job. In 1945, Congress introduced the Women's Pay Act, which called for equal pay for women for "comparable" work. It took eighteen more years, and a change in the document's phrasing from "comparable work" to "equal work," for the act to be passed by Congress.

After the trauma of the war, a national desire for normalcy and conformity settled in. Young, middle-class women were expected to get married, have babies, and be housewives. They were encouraged to be feminine without exhibiting overt sexuality in order to get a husband. From 1945 to 1950, the marriage rate soared, the divorce rate declined, the age of first marriage dropped dramatically, and couples had children at younger ages.

While the pressure to get married young and get pregnant as soon as possible was greatest for middle-class white women, the trend was evident at all levels of society. Parenting advice for mothers was strongly gender stereotypical; girls were encouraged to play with dolls and emulate their mothers, and boys were encouraged to play with trucks and guns.

The return of the soldiers from World War II, combined with the pressure to marry and have children early, fueled the baby boom. During the 1930's and early 1940's, births in the United States varied between 2.3 million and 2.8 million.

In 1946, the number jumped to 3.5 million and continued to increase until peaking at 4.3 million in 1957.

Many advances women had made in higher education during World War II were lost in the postwar 1940's. With the G.I. Bill, a large increase in men attending college occurred. Women faced discrimination in college admissions and financial aid. In 1947, the ratio of male to female undergraduates reached an all-time high of 2.3 to 1, and it remained near this ratio until the mid-1950's. Women were also systematically removed from college faculty positions, and their numbers in graduate, medical, law, and business schools declined greatly.

The Women's Armed Services Integration Act was signed into law in 1948. This act granted women permanent status in the Army and other branches of the military. However, the act also placed a cap of 2 percent on the proportion of women on active duty in each branch of the service and stated that women could not be promoted beyond lieutenant colonel. Women's compensation excluded benefits for their families. Nevertheless, this was an incremental victory for women.

Impact World War II required women to assume diverse and important roles in American society. After the war they were pressured to return to their previous submissive place in society. However, some women never left the workforce and many returned after only a few years; the percentage of working women never again fell to prewar levels. Similarly, women experienced a brief setback in their pursuit of higher education, but the proportion of women in colleges starting climbing again not long afterward.

Prior to the war, women were inhibited as much by their self-doubt as by overt discrimination. The opportunities forced upon them by the realities of World War II gave them a sense of confidence and a desire to expand their opportunities and roles in society. Many mothers, despite pressures to raise gender-stereotypical children, raised their daughters to be more self-assured, confident, and ambitious. The achievements of women in World War II and postwar American society contributed greatly to the women's movement that began during the 1960's.

Jerome L. Neapolitan

Further Reading

Anderson, Karen. *Wartime Women: Sex Roles, Family Relations, and the Status of Women During World War II.* Westport, Conn.: Greenwood Press, 1981. Examines women's wartime experiences in the defense industry centers of Baltimore, Detroit, and Seattle.

Eisenmann, Linda. *Higher Education for Women in Postwar America, 1945-1965,* Baltimore: Johns Hopkins University Press, 2007. Explains the actions of activist women in higher education and their contributions to the advancement of women's higher education.

Gluck, Sherna. *Rosie the Riveter Revisited: Women, the War, and Social Change.* Boston: Twayne, 1987. Examination of the social upheavals in gender roles caused by World War II, based on interviews with ten women who worked in the aircraft industry during the war.

Goldin, Claudia. "The Role of World War II in the Rise of Women's Employment." *American Economic Review* 81, no. 4 (1991): 741-756. Uses survey data analyses to examine the direct and indirect influences World War II had on women's employment.

Lewis, Brenda Ralph. *Women at War: The Women in World War II, at Home, at Work, on the Front Line.* New York: Readers Digest, 2002. Analysis of opportunities, pressures, and prejudices women faced in World War II.

Regis, Margaret. *When Our Mothers Went to War: An Illustrated History of Women in World War II.* Seattle, Wash.: Nav, 2008. Mixture of personal stories, factual information, and photographs, covering the wide range of roles played by women in World War II.

Weatherford, Doris. *American Women and World War II.* Victoria, B.C.: Castle Books, 2008. Interesting and easy-to-read account of the multitude of roles women played in World War II and the discrimination they often faced in work and the military.

See also African Americans; All-American Girls Professional Baseball League; Andrews Sisters; Baby boom; Bourke-White, Margaret; G.I. Bill; Roosevelt, Eleanor; Women in the U.S. military.

■ Wonder Woman

Identification   Comic book character who was one of the first superheroines
Creator   William Moulton Marston (1893-1947)
Date   First appeared in *All Star Comics* #8, in December, 1941

Comic books about Wonder Woman reflected home front propaganda, signified the paradoxical cultural expectations for white women during World War II, and mirrored a feminist ideology representative of the era, which suggested the moral superiority of women.

Created by psychologist William Moulton Marston under the pen name Charles Moulton, Wonder Woman debuted in *All Star Comics* #8 in December, 1941, and the character of Wonder Women also appeared regularly in *Sensation Comics*. Stories about Wonder Woman differed from the other books published by DC Comics, which were dominated by male superheroes, such as Superman, Batman, and Green Lantern. Although written by Marston, the comic books featured a variety of male and female illustrators.

Wonder Woman issues of the early 1940's recounted the heroine's origins as Princess Diana of Paradise Island, an isolated isle populated only by Amazonian women. When Major Steve Trevor's military plane crashed on the island, Princess Diana nursed his wounds and, relinquishing her birthright, decided to return to America with her new love interest. After arriving in the United States, Wonder Woman used her Amazonian strength, bullet-proof bracelets, invisible plane, and golden lasso that compelled honesty (a reference to Marston's invention, the polygraph) to fight Nazi and Japanese villains with primarily nonviolent force. In contrast to the brutal realities of war, the Wonder Woman comics depicted a superheroine who used violence mainly in self-defense and sought to redeem her adversaries by teaching them the error of their ways. In lieu of graphic violence, Wonder Woman often depicted its heroine binding her antagonists and deftly escaping bondage situations, perhaps symbolizing women's power to break free from the bonds of their past oppression.

The strong and self-reliant Wonder Woman character possessed the exceptional beauty of the Greek goddess of love, Aphrodite, and performed countless patriotic acts, defending her adopted country against its military foes and upholding its democratic tenets. In contrast, her alias Diana Prince worked initially as an army nurse and later as an army intelligence secretary to Trevor. As Prince, Wonder Woman replicated conventional feminine roles in her interactions with Trevor. The paradoxes embodied in her character reflect societal tensions concerning the preservation of femininity in the face of women's large-scale entrance into traditionally masculine realms, including the military and the factory, as a result of wartime mobilization.

A self-identified feminist, Marston hoped his superheroine would serve as a strong, beautiful, and wise female role model for young girls and boys. Believing in the innate moral superiority of women, an ideology rejected by later feminists as essentialist, Marston imbued Wonder Woman with the qualities of love, justice, and respect for human rights that he imagined characterized all women. Confronted with the war abroad, Marston advocated the development of a peaceful matriarchal society within the pages of Wonder Woman stories. After Marston's death in 1947, Robert Kanigher began writing Wonder Woman comics, and he later edited these books for more than twenty years. Since 1941, there have been three series of Wonder Women comic books, with the third series launched in June, 2006.

Impact Through its representation of Wonder Woman and her alter ego Diana Prince, the Wonder Woman comic books suggested the vital role of women in ending World War II and all future warfare. Portrayals of the comic-book character reflected and shaped American women's changing roles from the wartime era through the 1970's, when the superheroine was adopted as a symbol by women's liberationists, and into the twenty-first century.

Megan E. Williams

Further Reading

Daniels, Les. *Wonder Woman: The Life and Times of the Amazon Princess.* San Francisco: Chronicle Books, 2000.

Steinem, Gloria, and Phyllis Chesler. *Wonder Woman.* New York: Bonanza Books, 1972.

Wonder Woman Archives. Vols. 1-5. New York: DC Comics, 2000-2007.

See also *Brenda Starr*; Comic books; Comic strips; Psychiatry and psychology; Superman; Women's roles and rights in the United States.

World Court. *See* **International Court of Justice**

■ World Health Organization

Identification U.N. agency to promote health and fight disease worldwide
Also known as WHO
Date Established on April 7, 1948

Although the United States played a major role in addressing world health needs before 1948, it remained outside the major international structure. This changed with American entry into the new World Health Organization.

In 1902, the United States and twenty other Western nations founded the International Sanitary Bureau (ISB), headquartered in Washington, D.C., as an intergovernmental agency through which to address common medical issues related to North and South America, such as yellow fever and malaria. After World War I, the League of Nations—of which the United States was not a member—established the League of Nations Health Organization (LNHO) in 1923, to which the United States could not belong. In the same year, the ISB was reorganized as the Pan American Sanitary Bureau (PASB), and a year later it adopted the Pan American Sanitary Code. Through this new agency, the United States could actively participate in the LNHO's efforts to promote good health and limit disease across the globe. The United States had also joined the Paris-based International Office of Public Hygiene (OHIP) at its inception in 1908 and continued to participate in its disease-monitoring activities (surveillance of leprosy, tuberculosis, typhoid fever, sexually transmitted diseases, and so on) well into the 1940's.

During World War II, the LNHO greatly reduced its operations, and the U.S. Public Health Service augmented the efforts of the PASB, which received a $500,000 grant for internships and special programs. In 1943, the Allies organized the United Nations Relief and Rehabilitation Administration (UNRRA)—established prior to the United Nations—to aid postwar refugees and prevent the outbreak and spread of disease, the likes of which had plagued Europeans in 1918-1920. While victorious world leaders met in San Francisco to create the United Nations in June, 1945, there was a call for the United Nations Conference on International Organizations to hold an International Health Conference (New York, June 19-July 22, 1946) that would create an international health organization. This would replace the UNRRA, the LNHO, and the OHIP, as well as the regional PASB. A Technical Preparatory Committee of sixteen members met in Paris in March and April, 1946, to establish the conference's ground rules and agenda.

U.S. surgeon general Thomas Parran, Jr., championed the American position. He fought to retain the PASB as a regional organ of the new World Health Organization (WHO). Since his proposed general outline became the blueprint for the WHO and its constitution, the PASB remained intact as the Regional Office of the WHO for the Americas. In January, 1947, the Twelfth Pan American Sanitary Conference (PASC) met and elected American Fred L. Soper director of the PASB for a four-year term. That year, the bureau was rennamed the Pan American Sanitary Organization (later the Pan American Health Organization), which combined the functions of the PASB and the PASC, adopted a new constitution, and invited membership from all Western Hemisphere countries. Soper's energetic leadership and tour of American capitals firmly bound the organization together and saw 1947's $100,000 budget rise to $1.3 million in 1948. Clearly, this was an operation too large simply to be swallowed by the nascent WHO.

Although the WHO constitution was signed on July 22, 1946, twenty-six nations had to ratify it before the organization could formally act. The United States dithered as a House committee sat on the bill for a year and a half (Congress acting on June 14, 1948). Finally, on April 7, 1948, the last necessary ratification was recorded, and the World Health Conference met for the first time in June, electing as its first director the Yugoslav Andrija Štampar.

Impact America's fiscal and technical resources have helped the WHO meliorate and lengthen the lives of millions of people on every continent since 1948.

Joseph P. Byrne

Further Reading

Brand, Jeanne. "The United States Public Health Service and International Health, 1945-1950." *Bulletin for the History of Medicine* 63 (1989): 579-598.
Siddiqi, Javed. *World Health and World Politics: The World Health Organization and the U.N. System.* Columbia: University of South Carolina Press, 1995.
World Health Organization. *The First Ten Years of the World Health Organization.* Geneva: Author, 1958.

See also Antibiotics; Foreign policy of the United States; Medicine; Red Cross; Sexually transmitted diseases; United Nations.

■ World War II

The Event Global military conflict in which the United States and Canada fought alongside the Western Allies against the Axis Powers, led by the Japanese Empire, Nazi Germany, and Fascist Italy
Date September, 1939-August, 1945
Places Europe, North Africa, Japan, Southeast Asia, Atlantic and Pacific Oceans

Although far from being the most prolonged military conflict in world history, World War II was easily the largest-scale, most far-reaching, and most destructive conflict in history. It killed more than 50 million people—many by mass murder—and physically and psychologically wounded more than 100 million more. Vast regions of Europe and Asia were laid waste by ground, air, and naval actions. Far removed from the main combat arenas in Europe and the Far East, the United States and Canada suffered little direct damage from the war, but both nations were heavily involved in supplying combat forces, ships, planes, weapons, and other military matériel to the Allied effort. The war ended with the unconditional surrender of Germany and Japan and redefined the international balance of power.

As the storm clouds of war darkened over Europe during the late 1930's, most North Americans favored isolation from European conflicts. The United States and Canada had fought vigorously and at considerable cost in World War I, believing that the "Great War" had been a war to end all wars. Such idealism was crushed when European nationalistic interests and squabbles reemerged in the postwar era. Consequently, many disillusioned Americans chose to stand aside when World War II began in Europe with Germany's invasion of Poland in early September, 1939, which was followed by Great Britain's and France's declarations of war. Bound by its membership in the British Commonwealth, Canada soon followed Britain into the war, but not without internal conflict.

Background to the European War   The root causes of the European theater of World War II can be found in issues left unresolved by the settlement that ended World War I in November, 1918. Although the Central Powers' defeat in that war had been far from total, Germany and its allies were harshly treated by the Treaty of Versailles (1919). The postwar settlement took territories from Germany in the east and west, destroyed the Austro-Hungarian Em-

pire, humiliated Germans by including a "war guilt" clause, imposed disarmament, and demanded heavy reparation payments for war damage. Dispirited by postwar inflation and the effects of the world depression, a substantial minority of Germans voted for candidates in Adolf Hitler's extremist Nazi Party in the nation's 1933 elections. The Nazis won and Hitler legally became chancellor of Germany. Under his leadership, Germany pursued policies of economic control and rearmament. The Nazis were both anticommunist and anti-Semitic, blaming Reds and Jews for Germany's problems. Himself an Aus-

World War II: Germany and the European Theater

trian by birth, Hitler saw a need for "living space" for ethnic Germans that was to be carved from lands occupied by "inferior" Slavic peoples living to the east. To achieve his aims, he pursued an aggressive foreign policy while rearming Germany.

In violation of the Treaty of Versailles, German troops occupied the demilitarized German Rhineland in 1936, Austria in 1938, and Czechoslovakia in 1938 and 1939. Meanwhile, Great Britain and France sought to appease his regime by granting concessions in the hope that they would satisfy German ambitions. The height of their appeasement efforts came at the 1938 Munich Conference that condoned the dismemberment of Czechoslovakia. However, in the eyes of the Western democracies, concessions to Hitler appeared only to encourage more aggression. Britain and France decided to guarantee the integrity of several small states in Europe, including Poland. After Germany invaded Poland in early September, 1939, the British and French honored their pledges by declaring war on Germany. This turning point was followed by a long lull during which no major fighting occurred. This quiet phase, which became known as the "Phony War," continued through early 1940. Meanwhile, a desultory war at sea began in the Atlantic, featuring submarine sinkings and sorties by units of the German surface fleet.

Meanwhile, shortly before invading Poland, Hitler negotiated an unexpected treaty with Soviet leader Joseph Stalin. The agreement called for peaceful economic cooperation between Germany and the Soviet Union and divided Poland between them. Freed from a major military power in the east, Hitler turned his attention to the west. In the late spring of 1940, German divisions met surprisingly little resistance as they advanced through Denmark, Norway, Belgium, the Netherlands, and France.

Germany's invasion of Poland had utilized a new form of warfare featuring fast-moving armored ground advances supported by air assaults that became known as Blitzkrieg, or "lightning war" in English. Powerful columns of tanks, mobile troops, and artillery punched through soft spots in defensive lines, surrounded, and crushed defenders. The Germans employed the same tactics in their rapid advance through Western Europe. With the static trench warfare of World War I still fresh in many memories, the world marveled at the unprece-dented speed, power, and efficiency of the German army in 1940.

Great Britain and the United States After the German advance through Western Europe ended, Britain stood alone as a significant European power not under Axis domination. Most of the British troops that had tried to aid in France's defense were brought home without their equipment through a heroic evacuation from Dunkirk on the Atlantic coast of France by a flotilla of ships and boats, including many civilian craft. The next challenge to the Germans was to cross the English Channel to invade Great Britain. However, Britain's Royal Navy was too strong for Germany to move an invasion force by sea, even the short distance across the channel, so the Germans then concentrated on bombarding England by air.

The ensuing Battle of Britain was fought entirely in the air from July to November, 1940. Britain managed to survive the Nazi onslaught, thanks to its Royal Air Force, in which many Canadians and citizens of other Commonwealth countries served. Indeed, the German air force suffered such severe losses in the Battle of Britain that it eventually limited its air assaults to nighttime bombing raids, particularly against London. Britain was also threatened on the seas by a growing submarine campaign against merchant ships, which provided the imports necessary to sustain industry and feed the nation. In the Battle of the North Atlantic, which continued throughout the war, the British lost many ships, making the need for outside help ever greater. Because the Germans never achieved air superiority over Britain, a surface invasion was impossible. Britain's success in holding out against the German assault made it the paramount staging area for the Allied counterinvasion of continental Europe that would come later.

U.S. president Franklin D. Roosevelt wanted to help Britain, but because American public sentiment favored neutrality, he had to act carefully to find ways to get around international conventions that forbade neutral nations from aiding belligerent powers. One way he did this was by creating the Lend-Lease program to send money and matériel to Britain and other countries fighting Axis Powers. Anticipating that it was only a matter of time until the United States would be drawn into the war, Roosevelt oversaw a major buildup of American military forces and equipment.

Time Line of World War II: European Theater

July, 1937-February, 1938	Japanese troops invade China, beginning World War II in East Asia.
Sept. 15-29, 1938	British and German leaders meet in Munich.
August, 1939	The possibility of U.S. involvement in the war developing in Europe and East Asia prompts conversion of domestic production to meet military needs.
Sept. 1, 1939	Germany invades Poland, beginning World War II in Europe.
Sept. 3, 1939-May 4, 1945	Battle of North Atlantic: Eventual definitive victory for Allied forces.
October, 1939-Dec. 7, 1941	Polish Campaign
April 9, 1940	Germany invades Norway.
May-June, 1940	Germany occupies France.
May 10, 1940	Germany invades Luxembourg, the Netherlands, and Belgium.
June 10, 1940	Italy declares war on France and Great Britain. Italian forces enter southern France.
July 10-Oct. 31, 1940	Battle of Britain: Germany bombs Great Britain in preparation for a land invasion. Despite great losses on both sides, the British repulse German air power and avoid German occupation.
Sept. 27, 1940	Japan signs the Tripartite Pact with Germany and Italy, becoming a member of the Axis powers.
Oct. 8, 1940	Germany occupies Romania.
Oct. 28, 1940	Italy invades Greece.
Nov. 11, 1940	Battle of Taranto
Dec. 9-13, 1940	Battle of Sīdī Barrāni
1941-1942	Battle of Moscow
1941-1944	Siege of Leningrad
March 11, 1941	United States begins using the Lend-Lease program to support Great Britain's war effort while declaring official neutrality.
May 20-31, 1941	Crete campaign
Sept. 16-26, 1941	Battle of Kiev
Nov. 18, 1941-June 21, 1942	Battles of Tobruk
Dec. 8, 1941	United Stats declares war on Japan.
Dec. 11, 1941	Axis nations declare war on the United States.
1942-1943	Battles of Kharkov
June 17, 1942	President Roosevelt approves the Manhattan Project.
Aug. 19, 1942	Raid on Dieppe
Aug. 23, 1942-Feb. 2, 1943	Battle of Stalingrad
Oct. 23-Nov. 4, 1942	Battle of El Alamein
Nov. 7-8, 1942	North Africa invasion: An Allied campaign designed to drive the Germans out of North Africa. This operation provides a training ground for U.S. forces in World War II.
February, 1943	Casablanca Conference
July 5-15, 1943	Battle of Kursk

July 9-Sept. 19, 1943	Italy invasion: This campaign forces Germany to use troops and resources that might otherwise have been used in northern France.
Sept. 8, 1943	Italy surrenders unconditionally.
Sept. 9-Oct. 1, 1943	Battle of Salerno: The Allies accomplish their objective, taking the port of Naples.
November, 1943-June, 1944	Battle of Monte Cassino
Jan. 22-May 25, 1944	Battle of Anzio
June 6, 1944	D day: Operation Overlord's Normandy invasion begins.
June 22-July 11, 1944	Operation Bagration
Aug. 25, 1944	Liberation of Paris
Sept. 11, 1944	Liberation of Luxembourg
Sept. 17-26, 1944	Battle of Arnhem
Dec. 16, 1944-Jan. 25, 1945	Battle of the Bulge: German forces are routed in a desperate campaign to halt advancing Allied armies.
Feb. 4-11, 1945	Yalta Conference: This significant meeting of the "Big Three" Allied powers marks the height of Allied cooperation but also reveals conflicting agendas.
March 7-May 8, 1945	Rhine crossings
April 19-May 2, 1945	Battle of Berlin
May 7, 1945	Germany signs surrender documents.
May 8, 1945	V-E Day: President Harry S. Truman declares victory in Europe.
July 17-Aug. 2, 1945	Potsdam Conference: The third and final Big Three meeting plans a peace settlement at the end of World War II.
Aug. 6 & 9, 1945	United States drops atomic bombs on Hiroshima and Nagasaki, Japan.
Aug. 14, 1945	V-J Day: Japan accepts terms of surrender and occasion is declared "Victory in Japan" day.

New German Campaigns After occupying France in mid-1940, Germany partitioned the country. It administered the northern part of France, while allowing French collaborators to set up a fascist state, based in Vichy, in southern France under France's World War I hero General Henri-Philippe Pétain. As France was falling, Benito Mussolini's Fascist Italy came into the war on Germany's side. Another important fascist state, Spain, managed to remain neutral throughout the war, even though its leader, Francisco Franco, had been aided by the Germans when he was fighting in the Spanish Civil War of 1936-1939 that had brought him to power.

One of Italy's reasons for entering the war was to gain more territory in Africa. Italy then launched unsuccessful campaigns against British forces in North Africa in the summer of 1940 and against

Greece in October. German forces had to rescue Italian troops in both campaigns. To save the Italians, Hitler had to conquer the Balkans and send the German Afrika Corps to North Africa, led by General Erwin Rommel.

In June, 1941, after German troops had accomplished almost all that Hitler could reasonably hope for them to accomplish in western Europe, Hitler turned his attention back to the east and launched his greatest military gamble—a full-scale invasion of the Soviet Union. He had long plotted to topple Stalin's communist regime, thereby gaining vast territory and natural resources. The ensuing German campaign saw some of the most ferocious fighting and greatest human suffering of World War II. Hitler hoped for another Blitzkrieg victory, and the German invasion started well. However, Hitler had not reckoned on the terrible conditions that his army would face when they confronted the Soviet winter. By December, German troops were freezing to death on the outskirts of Moscow and Leningrad as Soviet troops began counterattacking. When weather conditions improved in the spring of 1942, the Germans renewed their advance, this time on southern Russia. However, they got only as far as Stalingrad (now Volgograd) on the Volga River.

The Pacific Theater of the War World War II actually began earlier in East Asia than it did in Europe. After a period of rapid modernization, the comparatively small island nation of Japan looked to China and other parts of Asia for resource-rich territories to conquer. By the 1930's, military leaders were dominating Japanese domestic politics and dictating a policy of ruthless military aggression that would lead their nation into a full-scale war with China. In 1931, the Japanese moved against the rich northern Chinese province of Manchuria. In 1936, Japan signed a defensive pact with Germany and Italy, with whom it would later ally to form the core of the Axis Powers. Meanwhile, the United States appeared to stand in the way of Japanese domination of East Asia, so the Japanese military made preparations to neutralize American naval power in the Pacific.

On December 7, 1941, aircraft-based planes from a large Japanese armada attacked the U.S. Pacific Fleet as it lay at anchor in Pearl Harbor. In the days that followed, the Japanese moved rapidly against the Philippines and European colonies in Southeast Asia. By attacking European possessions in Asia, Japan could claim to be liberating fellow Asians from European rule. In reality, however, the Japanese covered Southeast Asia's rich oil and rubber resources.

Despite the Japanese alliance with Germany and Italy, Japan's major contribution to the European theater of the war was to force the United States and Great Britain to commit troops, ships, planes, and equipment to the Pacific. The Japanese fought against British and American forces on their own but were fortunate to have the Soviet Union not join in the Pacific war until well into 1945.

The Japanese attack on Pearl Harbor did enough damage to the U.S. fleet to permit Japan to dominate actions in the Pacific for several months, during which Japan rapidly added to its conquests. However, while the Japanese destroyed a number of American battleships at Pearl Harbor, the vitally important American aircraft carriers were away from the harbor and thus escaped unharmed. The Japanese strategy called for the rapid conquest of Southeast Asia after crippling the U.S. fleet. U.S. forces held out in the Philippines as long as possible, but Japanese forces stormed to victory all through the area, easily conquering the British bastion of Singapore in early 1942.

Japanese expansion in the Pacific was finally checked by a brilliant American naval victory in the Battle of Midway in June, 1942, when the American aircraft carriers came fully into play, and all the Japanese carriers were put out of action. Later that same year, American forces began a slow, two-pronged advance through the Pacific, essentially fighting from island to island, starting at Guadalcanal. Navy admiral Chester W. Nimitz led one thrust toward Japan, and Army general Douglas MacArthur led the other toward the Philippines.

Turning Points in the War, 1942-1943 At the beginning of 1942, the Axis Powers reached the peak of their conquests, dominating continental Europe and the western Pacific. The Soviet Union appeared ready to collapse, and Britain was being strangled by Germany's submarine warfare. The United States was finally in the war, but it appeared unable to stop the Japanese in the Pacific. The course of the war then changed because of three dramatic turning points in the Pacific, in North Africa, and in Russia.

In the Pacific, the U.S. finally began winning significant victories over Japan in the battles of the Coral Sea (May 3-8, 1942), Midway (June 4, 1942), and Guadalcanal (August 7, 1942-February 9, 1943).

Between October 23 and November 4, 1942, the North African campaign turned against Germany and Italy when British field marshal Bernard Montgomery defeated Rommel at El Alamein in western Egypt. The most important turning point, however, was the long Battle of Stalingrad, which lasted from August 23, 1942 until February 2, 1943, when the Red Army halted the German advance on the Soviet Union and sent the badly beaten Germans limping back home, with the German reputation for invincibility shattered.

When the Germans were still advancing into Russia, Soviet dictator Joseph Stalin pressed his Western Allies to open a second front against Germany in the west to force the Germans to divert troops and equipment from the eastern front. The British and American leaders responded cautiously, however, contenting themselves with fighting Axis forces in North Africa and mounting a steadily intensifying bombing campaign against German cities. Meanwhile, the Allies' improving convoy system, increased long-range air power, and new equipment were reducing the German submarine menace in the Atlantic.

Many Allied leaders thought it would be wiser to advance on Germany from the south, rather than the west, and victory in the North African campaign put the Allies in position to advance on southern Europe in 1943. An invasion of Sicily and the Italian mainland followed, causing Italy to change sides in that year, and Benito Mussolini was captured and eventually killed by Italian partisans. By the end of the year, Axis forces were in retreat in all theaters of the war. Allied bombers continued to pound Germany and German-occupied positions in Europe. In the Pacific, carrier-borne planes raided Japanese bases and prepared islands for Marine occupation.

Allied Victories, 1944-1945   The last two years of the war featured a steady allied advance: on the plains of eastern Europe and then into eastern Germany, up the peninsula of Italy and, after the Normandy invasion of June, 1944, across France and into western Germany. Simultaneously, the Allies advanced in Asia. Mostly Anglo-Indian forces began to push the Japanese out of Burma. Meanwhile American forces got closer to the home islands of Japan by island hopping in the Pacific.

In August, 1942, Canadian troops had tested German defenses on the French coast in the ill-fated Dieppe raid. In June, 1944, the Allies returned to the French Coast in much greater force, to begin the reconquest of Europe by landing a massive invasion force at Normandy on a date remembered as D Day. In this invasion, British, Canadian, and American forces successfully stormed the Germans' formidable West Wall defenses. After bitter fighting, an American breakout under

General George C. Patton raced deep into France, while British and Canadian troops under Bernard Montgomery edged up along the coast.

Meanwhile, Soviet forces had already begun advancing toward Germany from the east. Casualties on the eastern front were enormous, accounting for three quarters of German wartime military deaths. Estimates of Soviet fatalities during the war have ranged as high as 25 million military and civilian victims.

The last gasp of German forces in the West came during the Battle of the Bulge in December of 1944. After the Western Allies counterattacked, Germany was relentlessly invaded from the west and east. After Soviet and American forces met in the center of Germany, Soviet forces turned to the costly conquest of Berlin. As they approached, Hitler committed suicide. What was left of the Nazi regime capitulated unconditionally a short time afterward.

Japan remained at war a few months longer, increasingly pounded by American planes. Costly invasions captured Iwo Jima and Okinawa, near the home islands. In these last stages the Soviet Union, which had hitherto remained neutral toward Japan, declared war and advanced on the Asian mainland. Firebombing caused the Japanese capital, Tokyo, to be devastated by a fire storm, and the United States dropped atomic bombs on Hiroshima and Nagasaki

President Harry S. Truman announcing Japan's surrender on August 14, 1945—five days after the second atomic bomb was dropped on Japan. (National Archives)

in August, 1945. Japan surrendered shortly thereafter, and what would have been a bloody and costly Allied invasion of the Japanese mainland was thus avoided.

Impact World War II was marked by horrendous murder and brutality, massive destruction and staggering loss of life. The victory of democracy over fascism was extremely costly, but it seems clear that there were no other options to rid the world of the brutal aggressors. The Nazis practiced genocide against Jews and other ethnic groups, whom they exterminated by the millions. Simultaneously, millions of Soviet prisoners were allowed to die in camps, as were German prisoners.

The United States and the Soviet Union emerged from the war as the only two significant world powers. Japan, Germany, France, and Britain lost that status as a result of the war. The wartime alliance between the Soviet Union and the Western powers fell apart after the war, and the United States and the Soviet Union would soon face off in a new contest that would become known as the Cold War.

The United States and Canada both made major contributions to the Allied war effort. As the United States had ten times as many people as Canada, its material contribution was proportionately greater. However, both nations fully mobilized to fight a total war, and their contributions clearly made the difference in the war. Huge numbers of American planes, tanks, guns, ships, and other military equipment poured off the production lines to keep the Allies supplied. This remarkable expansion of industry brought significant social changes. To meet the great need for workers in America, large numbers of women and members of minority groups were brought into the workforce to hold jobs from which they had previously been excluded. Both Canada and the United States grew more urban and less rural during the war. Patriotism united diverse peoples in a common cause. While there were some wartime shortages and consumption restrictions through rationing in North America, these deprivations were insignificant compared to the sufferings of nations directly involved in the fighting in Europe and Asia.

While Canada and the United States lost hundreds of thousands of men and women in the war, their losses were proportionately much lower than those of Continental European and East Asian nations. The total number of people who died because of the war will never be known, but most estimates have centered around 50 million, with much higher numbers of physically and mentally wounded victims of the war.

Apart from the Japanese attack on the then-U.S. territory of Hawaii and a brief Japanese occupation of the Aleutian Islands in the territory of Alaska, neither the United States nor Canada was bombed or invaded during the war. Consequently, in contrast to the massive rebuilding that European and Asian nations faced after the war, the United States and Canada were prepared to take their expanded industrial capacity into an unprecedented period of economic expansion and prosperity.

Henry Weisser

Further Reading

Boyle, David. *World War II: A Photographic History.* New York: Barnes & Noble, 1998. Lavishly illustrated history of the war with almost 600 pages of striking photographs.

Dear, Ian C. B. *The Oxford Companion to World War II.* New ed. New York: Oxford University Press, 2004. Encyclopedic work on World War II with more than seventeen hundred alphabetized entries.

Flower, Desmond, and James Reeves. *The War, 1939-1945: A Documentary History.* New York: Da Capo Press, 1997. Comprehensive history of the war with a large selection of primary documents about almost every aspect of the war.

Keegan, John. *The Second World War.* New York: Penguin Books, 1990. Keegan is widely regarded as one of the best military historians in the world, but this survey of World War II is not as easy to read as those of some of the other authors listed here.

Kennedy, David M. *Freedom from Fear: The American People in Depression and War, 1929-1945.* New York: Oxford University Press, 2005. Detailed history of everyday American life through the Great Depression and World War II.

Lyons, Michael J. *World War II: A Short History.* Saddle River, N.J.: Prentice Hall, 1999. Well-written and concise history of the war that makes a good introduction to the subject.

Stokesbury, James L. *Short History of World War II.* New York: William Morrow, 1980. Clear and useful overview of the war that has served as a very successful textbook.

Terkel, Studs. *The Good War: An Oral History of World*

War II. New York: New Press, 1984. Collection of brief, firsthand memoirs of the war by a wide variety of people representing almost every imaginable type of participant in the war—from combat soldiers to volunteers in USO canteens.

Thobaben, Robert G., ed. *For Comrade and Country: Oral Histories of World War II Veterans.* Jefferson, N.C.: McFarland, 2003. Collects first-person narratives of both the Pacific and European theaters of the war. Index.

See also   Air Force, U.S.; Army, U.S.; Canadian participation in World War II; Casualties of World War II; Films about World War II; *The Good War: An Oral History of World War II*; Historiography; Isolationism; Italian campaign; Marines, U.S.; Navy, U.S.; North African campaign; War heroes; Wartime industries; Wartime propaganda.

■ World War II mobilization

Definition   Recruitment, induction, and training of military personnel and production and distribution of their equipment

The American and Canadian efforts to mobilize for war were enormous undertakings but were remarkably successful. These efforts led not only to helping the Allies win World War II but also to advances in atomic weaponry, rocketry, synthetic rubber, sonar, radar, and other fields.

Planning for World War II might be said to have begun almost immediately after World War I ended in 1918. In 1920, the U.S. Congress passed the National Defense Act in anticipation of another war. During the 1930's, the federal government formed the Army Industrial College and the War Resources Administration. More focused mobilization plans were initiated in 1939, as it had become clear that Europe was on the threshold of a major conflict. President Franklin D. Roosevelt was particularly interested in modernizing and expanding the Army and its Air Corps. Mobilization efforts were greatly accelerated in 1942, after the United States finally entered World War II and the federal government took over industrial planning.

Mobilizing and Equipping Military Personnel   Mobilizing for the war unfolded in three broad stages. First, the Canadian and U.S. governments found people to serve in their military forces. Next, the governments trained these people in military skills. Finally, they provided the newly recruited troops and their units with such equipment as uniforms, weapons, vehicles, ships, tanks, and airplanes to fight. To procure all these materials, both Canada and the United States created war industries. At the start of the war, the Axis Powers were already several years ahead of the Allies in weapons production. To catch up, the Allies had to transform their national economies to design and build better weapons and equipment in huge numbers. In the United States, responsibility for this transformation fell to the War Production Board, which was established in June, 1942.

Only a small percentage of people who joined the military services actually saw combat. For every person involved in fighting, several others worked behind the combat zones. In the United States and Canada, hundreds more people were involved in creating materials. For example, it took only one person to fly a fighter plane, but that lone pilot depended on hundreds of direct and indirect support personnel. At air fields mechanics serviced the planes. Armorers kept the planes' machine guns working. Others specialists repaired radios, filled gas tanks, and loaded ordnance on planes. Weather forecasters told pilots when it was safe to fly (in Alaska, bad weather killed more pilots than the enemy) and when the weather would be clear enough to see targets. Cooks, truck drivers, intelligence officers, doctors, nurses, construction workers, and officers all worked behind the scenes to keep pilots in the air. A fighter squadron of only sixteen planes depended on more than 200 support personnel.

Supply Lines   Waging the war depended on worldwide supply lines. Streams of bombs, bullets, food, fuel, and equipment constantly flowed to the scattered combat fronts. Meanwhile, raw materials from all over the world were sent to North America. These materials included such exotic items as uranium from the Congo, tungsten from Spain, and rubber from Brazil. Supplies manufactured in North America had to travel more than 12,000 miles to reach fronts in India, China, and Burma. Merchant marine ships carried most of these supplies. Cargo aircraft carried much less, but offered swifter delivery.

On the home front, miners dug bauxite out of the ground to make aluminum for planes, and oil work-

A young man studying a Marine recruiting poster in early 1940.
(Retrofile/Getty Images)

als. Decisions had to be made about whether a given ship should be used to carry iron ore or tanks; whether gasoline should be allocated for industrial workers commuting, fueling bombers, or powering farm tractors. Food had to be divided among children, industrial workers, servicemen, and Allies. Construction workers needed to build airfields at the front might also be needed to build factories at home to make tanks. Shortage of equipment was a constant problem, especially as the United States and Canada were obligated to share their supplies with other Allied powers.

Generals and admirals often bickered over the distribution of personnel, equipment, and supplies. During the first years of American involvement in World War II, the bulk of U.S. forces were sent to the European theater of the war, as the Pacific theater was considered merely a holding action. Often, as a major push was made in one sector of the war, supplies would run short in the another sector. For example, the diversion of large numbers of landing craft to Normandy for D Day and to operations in the Pacific in mid-1944 left troops who had landed at Anzio in Italy marooned.

Mobilization of troops required that new personnel be trained. Infantrymen, for example, had to learn not merely how to march and use weapons but also how to behave within the military. They also had to learn such things as how to differentiate between friendly and enemy aircraft, tanks, and ships and acquire skills in tactics and strategy. Learning sanitary and health procedures was crucial to fend off medical problems, which were often more lethal than enemy bullets.

ers drilled for oil to make petroleum fuels and lubricants for vehicles. Farmers raised the food that the Allied troops ate and grew cotton to make cloth. Textile workers wove the cloth for uniforms and tents. Lumberjacks cut wood for the tent poles. Ranchers raised cattle and sheep for making boots, belts, food, and wool clothing.

As the war progressed, U.S. and Canadian manufacturing capacity grew rapidly, but as the manufacturing of war goods expanded, the production of civilian goods shrank. Many farmers had become soldiers, so maintaining agricultural production levels became a struggle. Meat, sugar, tires, and rubber goods were rationed at home. Many families grew their own vegetables. Automakers stopped making civilian cars in order to produce military trucks, tanks, and aircraft.

Bottlenecks and Training   Industry and the military competed for people, equipment, and raw materi-

Technological Advances   During the early stages of World War II, the Allies fared poorly against the better prepared Axis Powers. Eventually, the Allies caught up and surpassed the Axis Powers, and they did this with the help of advanced technology. Crash research programs were initiated, in which the military, industry, and educational research institutions worked together—forming the basis of what would come to be known as the military-industrial complex. Numerous technologies were either invented or greatly advanced during the war. For example, major advances in radar and sonar were developed to detect approaching enemy ships and aircraft.

Magnetic anomaly detection (MAD) was developed for aircraft to locate underwater submarines. Jet-assisted take off (JATO) was invented to help aircraft take off more rapidly. The first rudimentary guided missiles were developed, and one was used to sink a Japanese ship before the war ended.

Because the Japanese had captured the Allies' main sources of natural rubber in Southeast Asia, the military had to obtain rubber from Liberia and Brazil. Rubber was vitally needed for aircraft and ground vehicle tires and many other applications. To ensure that rubber supplies could never be cut off again, advances were made in the manufacture of synthetic rubber. The production of plastics grew rapidly and helped offset shortages in metal supplies. Silk, which had been a crucial component of parachutes and certain other goods, became scarce after Japan seized control of its main sources. The invention of nylon provided a versatile substitute for silk. The most complex and most dramatic technological achievement of the war, however, was the development of atomic bombs. In 1945, only six years after nuclear fission was discovered, atomic bombs were used to destroy two Japanese cities and hasten the end of World War II.

Impact The large and rapid mobilization of North American manpower and industry for wartime needs was probably without parallel in world history. Within the space of fewer than four years, the U.S. Army alone grew from 1.5 million persons on the eve of Pearl Harbor to more than 8 million at the end of the war, by which time, all the U.S. service branches had about 16 million people.

Preparing for the war and sustaining it impacted Americans and Canadians for many decades afterward politically, financially, and socially, but especially technologically. Politically, the war was won and the effort united people at home and with their allies. The U.S. government grew dramatically during the war and never reverted to its prewar size.

Jan Hall

Further Reading

Braverman, Jordan. *To Hasten the Homecoming: How Americans Fought World War II Through the Media.* New York: Madison Books, 1996. Intriguing study of the role of the entertainment, informational, and advertising industries in the home front mobilization of support for the war.

Chandler, Lester V., and Donald H. Wallace, eds. *Economic Mobilization and Stabilization: Selected Materials on the Economics of War and Defense.* New York: Henry Holt, 1951. An anthology of materials treating the problems of economic stabilization during wartime that draws heavily on the experience of the United States in World War II. Part 2 focuses on the machinery of World War II economic mobilization.

Matloff, Maurice, ed. *American Military History.* Vol. 2, *1902-1996.* New York: Da Capo Press, 1996. This second volume of a general history of American military conflicts devotes considerable space to the mobilization, organization, and deployment of the Army in World War II.

Ohl, John Kennedy. *Supplying the Troops.* DeKalb, Ill.: Northern Illinois University Press, 1994. Details the process of mobilizing and supplying U.S. forces during the war.

Polenberg, Richard. *War and Society: The United States, 1941-1945.* Philadelphia: J. B. Lippincott, 1972. An excellent survey of all aspects of the American home front during World War II. Includes a brief but perceptive treatment of the problem of industrial mobilization.

Shactman, Tom. *Terrors and Marvels.* New York: William Morrow, 2002. Describes the role of science and technology in the mobilization of U.S. forces.

Smith, Ralph Elberton. *The Army and Economic Mobilization.* Washington, D.C.: Office of Military History, U.S. Army, 1959. Balanced and judicious history of War Department planning for and involvement in World War II economic mobilization.

Stevenson, Michael D. *Canada's Greatest Wartime Muddle: National Selective Service and the Mobilization of Human Resources During World War II.* Montreal, Que.: McGill-Queen's University Press, 2001. A study of the effects of World War II-era national service on particular populations, including Native Canadians, university students, war-industry workers, coal miners, longshoremen, meatpackers, nurses, and textile workers.

See also Air Force, U.S.; Aircraft design and development; Economic wartime regulations; Lend-Lease; Liberty ships; Manhattan Project; Military conscription in Canada; Military conscription in the United States; Office of War Mobilization; War Production Board; Wartime industries; Wartime rationing; Wartime technological advances; World War II.

■ Wright, Frank Lloyd

Identification   American architect
Born   June 8, 1867; Richland Center, Wisconsin
Died   April 9, 1959; Phoenix, Arizona

A prominent architect, author, and lecturer for seven decades, Wright contributed to an innovative period in American art history, from the Arts and Crafts movement to modernism. Wright's architecture evolved from the imitation of natural forms through stylized organic architecture to experiential modern homes, churches, schools, and museums, redefining private and public spaces in North America throughout the 1940's.

Frank Lloyd Wright's architectural philosophy paved the way for modern living in America during the 1940's through the incorporation of organic materials and an open interior landscape into his de-

signs. Wright studied under the tutelage of famed Chicago architect Louis Sullivan, known for his contributions to the World's Columbian Exposition of 1893 and towering skyscrapers. Wright was associated with the Prairie School of architecture during the early twentieth century, designing structures identified by their long, low-lying profile with cantilevered porches that echoed the horizons of the midwestern prairies. Wright favored a regional style for his designs versus the Eurocentric neoclassicism that pervaded much of post-Victorian Americana.

After several decades of commissions for now-famous homes, such as Fallingwater in Bear Run, Pennsylvania, Wright set out to create an archetypal home designed to meet the needs of the everyday American. Wright dubbed his work "Usonian," a derivative of "United States of America." He con-

Frank Lloyd Wright with a model of his proposed design for the Guggenheim Museum in 1945. (AP/Wide World Photos)

structed his Usonian homes to be appropriate in size and cost for middle-income Americans; the Jacobs House, crafted in 1936, is an early example. Throughout the 1940's, Wright's affordable, Usonian homes were constructed with natural materials on slab foundations, without parlors or butler's quarters, and with an open, L-shaped floor plan that encouraged a flow of activity. He engineered the homes with sheet windows and clerestories to take advantage of surrounding vistas and natural lighting. In some instances, he even designed the furniture, dishware, and stationery for the homeowner. As designer and art educator, Wright expressed a simple message in his work: Form and function should not be separate but rather collaborative features.

Wright also designed many community structures during the 1940's, including Florida Southern College in Lakeland, Florida, and Community Christian Church in Kansas City, Missouri. The most notable public structure of Wright's career is the Solomon R. Guggenheim Museum in New York City. Commissioned for the structure in 1943, Wright started with the initial difficulty of building a sizable museum to hold Guggenheim's vast abstract art collection on a diminutive lot in a busy metropolitan area. Changing from the typical horizontal profile to a vertical thrust, Wright's design consisted of a nautilus-inspired core, narrowing in its spiral downward to meet a horizontal platform on which it was stunningly balanced. The structure was completed approximately six months after his death in 1959. Today it is one of the most popular museums in the United States.

Impact   Wright's career spanned several decades, placing him as a significant figure in both nineteenth and twentieth century architectural history. By the 1940's, Wright was thought to be at the end of his career; he had been successful in his earlier work and teaching, despite his sensationalized personal life, but had hit a plateau upon entering his seventies. However, he was more prolific from 1940 to 1959, designing more than five hundred structures, than in the whole of his career prior. The acclaim from Fallingwater and the Guggenheim Museum reintroduced Wright to a modern audience, and Wright's style continued to evolve and grow with the quickstep of modern life and industry.

Emilie Fitzhugh Sizemore

Further Reading

Huxtable, Ada Louise. *Frank Lloyd Wright: A Life*. New York: Penguin Books, 2004.

Twombly, Robert C. *Frank Lloyd Wright: His Life and His Architecture*. New York: John Wiley & Sons, 1979.

See also   Architecture; Art movements; Education in the United States; Fads; Fuller, R. Buckminster; Home furnishings; Housing in the United States; Levittown.

■ Wright, Richard

Identification   African American writer
Born   September 4, 1908; Roxie, Mississippi
Died   November 28, 1960; Paris, France

Wright was recognized by both critics and general readers as the most important African American writer of his time. He influenced both individual black writers and the tradition of African American literature.

Rising from a background of poverty in the rural South, Richard Wright left school at the age of seventeen and educated himself through extensive reading. During the 1930's, he joined the Communist Party in Chicago and went on to publish articles in socialist journals; an important essay, "Blueprint for Negro Literature" (1937), urging black writers to stop imitating white writers; and a collection of short stories, *Uncle Tom's Children* (1938). He was awarded a Guggenheim Fellowship in 1938.

The publication of *Native Son* in 1940 catapulted Wright to instant fame. The story of Bigger Thomas, a young black man who is executed after accidentally killing a white woman and then murdering his black girlfriend, was a raw, naturalistic portrayal of the rage caused by the oppression of black people in America. It became an immediate best seller and the first African American novel selected by the Book-of-the-Month Club.

In 1941, Wright published the narrative text for *Twelve Million Black Voices: A Folk History of the Negro in the United States* to accompany photographs from the rural South and the ghettos of Chicago. In 1945, he published his autobiography, *Black Boy*, the somewhat fictionalized story of his development as a writer after a brutal childhood in the South, where he suffered constant hunger, physical abuse,

Richard Wright. (Library of Congress)

the desertion of his father, and oppression by white society.

Wright's first marriage, to Dhima Meadman, ended in divorce. He next married Ellen Poplowitz (Poplar), a white woman, in 1941. They had two daughters, Julia and Rachel. Wright was a mild-mannered, soft-spoken man whose gentle demeanor often surprised those who had read his work. He generously encouraged younger black writers, including James Baldwin, Gwendolyn Brooks, and Chester Himes.

In 1944, Wright broke with the Communist Party when it attempted to interfere with his artistic free-dom. Because of his communist affiliations and his outspoken criticism of Jim Crow laws, he was investigated by the Federal Bureau of Investigation (FBI) and the Central Intelligence Agency (CIA) during the 1940's. Although he volunteered to serve in the Army during World War II, he was declared unfit to serve after his public objection to discrimination against African Americans in the military.

In 1947, Wright moved his family from New York to Paris, finding freedom from the discrimination they had experienced in America. Wright died in Paris in 1960 of a heart attack and is buried in Pere Lachaise Cemetery.

Impact Wright was the first African American writer to produce best sellers that reached a main-stream American audience. Although he continued to write and publish fiction, essays, and poetry while he lived in Paris, his best works, critics agree, are *Native Son* and *Black Boy*. Both works were originally edited for language and unacceptable subject matter but have since been reprinted with Wright's original text. Wright's place in American literature is secure; his powerful works of social protest significantly influenced black writers who would follow him. His writing raised the social consciousness of America and the world, forcing attention to the lives of African Americans who endured the evils of racism.

Marjorie Podolsky

Further Reading

Rowley, Hazel. *Richard Wright: The Life and Times.* New York: Henry Holt, 2001.

Urban, Joan. *Richard Wright.* New York: Chelsea House, 1989.

See also African Americans; Anticommunism; Civil rights and liberties; Communist Party USA; Federal Bureau of Investigation; House Committee on Un-American Activities; Jim Crow laws; Literature in the United States; *Native Son*; Racial discrimination; Stein, Gertrude.

X

■ Xerography

Definition   Patented method for document
copying

*During the 1940's document copying involved complicated
photographic methods or hand typing of stencils. Xerography, which began during the 1940's and came to full fruition during the 1960's, permitted rapid copying without
the use of liquid chemicals.*

By 1940, Chester F. Carlson had demonstrated his
method of electrostatic copying, or "electrophotography" as he called it, on a small scale. With an assistant he hired at his own expense, he developed a sort
of kit that he could use to show his process to others.
At the heart of his method was a photoconductive
layer of sulfur on a zinc plate. The sulfur layer could
be electrostatically charged by rubbing it with a silk
cloth. Seeking sponsors for further development,
Carlson contacted companies such as International
Business Machines (IBM), the Charles Bruning
Company, and several others without obtaining any
definite commitments. In 1944, Carlson contacted
the Battelle Institute in Columbus, Ohio, and made
a favorable impression with his demonstration.

Battelle Institute was an independent research facility whose scientists and engineers generally took
on specialized projects for industrial clients. In
1942, however, the institute made an agreement
with Carlson to develop electrophotography in return for a share of future royalties. At Battelle, some
fundamental improvements were soon made to
Carlson's methods. Electrostatic charging of the
photoconductive plate could be done by corona discharge, and selenium was used as the photoconductive medium. Also, advances were made in the composition of the toner powder and to the means of
transferring it to the photoconductive layer; as a result, the means of transference to paper also improved. Around this time, Carlson's work attracted
journalistic attention; Nicholas Langer wrote an article for *Radio News* magazine based on an interview

with Carlson and presented his ideas in a favorable
light. Langer's article came to the attention of management at Haloid Corporation in Rochester, New
York, a supplier of photographic paper to Eastman
Kodak. Haloid sought to diversify its business. Soon,
Battelle and Haloid had a licensing agreement, and
Carlson moved to Rochester to act as a consultant.
Research continued at Battelle, and slowly began at
Haloid, encouraged by Haloid's chairman, Joseph
Wilson.

In 1948, the term "xerography" replaced "electrophotography." The new term was suggested by a classics professor and had its origin in the Greek for "dry
writing." The occasion for the change was a meeting
of the Optical Society of America, where Battelle
and Haloid presented a joint paper on the new science. However, at this point, there was no device
to be unveiled or sold. In 1949, the Model A copier
was introduced. This was not a successful document copier, but it did well at creating multilith
masters.

Impact   The full impact of xerography was felt with
the introduction of the model 914 copier in 1959.
This model has been called the most successful
product introduction in the twentieth century. The
copiers were leased, not sold, and a fee was charged
for each copy made. Soon, millions of copies were
printed, and Carlson, as well as many other shareholders of Haloid, which had changed its name to
Xerox, became millionaires.

John R. Phillips

Further Reading

Dessauer, J. *My Years with Xerox: The Billions Nobody
Wanted.* New York: Doubleday, 1971.
Mort, J. *The Anatomy of Xerography: Its Invention and
Evolution.* Jefferson, N.C.: McFarland, 1989.
Owen, David. *Copies in Seconds.* New York: Simon &
Schuster, 2004.

See also   Book publishing; Inventions; Photography; Science and technology.

Y

Yakus v. United States

The Case   U.S. Supreme Court ruling on price
   controls
Date   Decided on March 27, 1944

*In this decision, the Supreme Court upheld the Emergency
Price Control Act of 1942, which delegated to the Office of
Price Administration the power to set maximum prices on
commodities and rents to prevent wartime inflation.*

Two Massachusetts butchers, Albert Yakus and
Benjamin Rottenberg, and the firm that employed
them were convicted of selling wholesale beef at
prices above those set by federal regulators under
the wartime price controls. The butchers were sentenced to six months' imprisonment and issued one-
thousand-dollar fines.

Yakus and Rottenberg challenged their convictions on two grounds. First, they argued that the provision of the Emergency Price Control Act that authorized the Office of Price Administration (OPA)
to set price controls provided insufficient guidance
to regulators on how to select the maximum prices.
Since the Supreme Court had struck down the National Industrial Recovery Act of 1933 on similar
grounds in *A.L.A. Schechter Poultry Corp. v. United
States* (1935), this was a credible challenge. Retreat-
ing from *Schechter*, the Court upheld the regulations
and effectively ended the courts' application of the
"nondelegation" doctrine, which states that Congress may not assign its lawmaking duties to other
branches of the government. Second, the plaintiffs
argued that the restriction of challenges to the
prices to a sixty-day period after regulations were issued and to a special court denied them due process
of law. The Court held that these restrictions were
reasonable given the need to prevent wartime
inflation.

Three members of the Court dissented. Justice
Owen J. Roberts would have overturned the act on
both grounds; Justices Wiley B. Rutledge and Frank
Murphy objected on due process grounds.

Impact   *Yakus* signaled the Supreme Court's final
retreat from an aggressive interpretation of the
nondelegation doctrine, ending one of the most potent challenges to expansion of government involvement in economic matters. While some modern legal scholars, such as David Schoenbrod, have argued
for a revival of the nondelegation doctrine, *Yakus* effectively ended such challenges.

Andrew P. Morriss

Further Reading

Harris, Seymour. *Price and Related Controls in the
   United States.* New York: McGraw-Hill, 1945.
Rockoff, Hugh. *Drastic Measures: A History of Wage
   and Price Controls in the United States.* New York:
   Cambridge University Press, 1984.
Schoenbrod, David. *Saving Our Environment from
   Washington: How Congress Grabs Power, Shirks Re-
   sponsibility, and Shortchanges People.* New Haven,
   N.J.: Yale University Press, 2006.

See also   Business and the economy in the United
States; Civil rights and liberties; Economic wartime
regulations; Emergency Price Control Act of 1942;
Labor strikes; Office of Price Administration; Supreme Court, U.S.; Wartime rationing.

Yalta Conference

The Event   Meeting of Allied leaders from the
   United States, Great Britain, and the Soviet
   Union
Date   February 4-11, 1945
Place   Yalta, Crimea, Soviet Union (now in
   Ukraine)

*The most significant of all wartime summit meetings
among Allied leaders, the Yalta Conference produced accords that publicly set forth an Allied plan for postwar Europe. Because that plan included ceding most of east-central
Europe to Soviet control, the accords became a significant
domestic political issue in the United States after the war.*

Winston Churchill (left), Franklin D. Roosevelt (center), and Joseph Stalin at the Yalta Conference. (NARA)

Although many of the most important decisions made at Yalta had already been made at the Tehran Conference in 1943, the Yalta Conference had more important consequences. The major participants in the Yalta Conference were U.S. president Franklin D. Roosevelt, British prime minister Winston Churchill, and Soviet premier Joseph Stalin. The major goal of the conference was to coordinate Allied strategy in the final phase of the war against Nazi Germany and to map out plans for postwar Europe.

The paramount Soviet aims were publicly to secure Allied support for the territorial gains they had won under the secret terms of the German-Soviet pact of 1939 and to gain de facto control over east-central Europe. These aims had been tacitly conceded by President Roosevelt at Tehran the previous year. However, before the Yalta Conference, his agreement had not been made public or even revealed to Churchill. The most significant aspect of this issue was the fate of Poland and particularly demarcation of Poland's eastern border. The Poles were providing a major contribution to the Allied war effort, but following the revelation of the graves of Polish officers murdered by Soviet government agents in 1940, relations between the Poles and the Soviets had broken down and a Polish communist puppet government had been created under Stalin's auspices. Roosevelt agreed to Stalin's demands out of a profound misunderstanding of the nature of the Soviet dictator and out of a belief that peace in a postwar world would be best kept by United States and Soviet cooperation that would arrange the rest of the world under two broad spheres of influence.

Under such a scheme, the self-determination of smaller countries would be of secondary importance. Thus, Poland was stripped of its eastern territory and given a swathe of German territory in the west instead.

A second major aim of the conference was to outline the postwar occupation of Germany and Austria in Soviet, American, British, and French zones. Berlin and Vienna were to be jointly occupied by the Allied powers. The Yalta accords and boundaries and occupation regime of Germany were further confirmed at the Potsdam Conference in the summer of 1945.

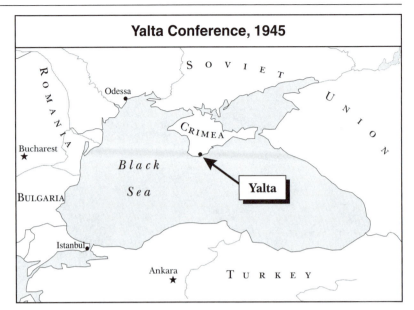

Impact The Yalta Conference had important political implications within the United States. Roman Catholic leaders and Polish Americans were highly critical of the results even before the end of the war. After Roosevelt's death in April, 1945, and the conclusion of the war in Europe the following month, this opposition grew. The Republican Party used Yalta in an attempt to pry blue-collar ethnic Catholics away from the Democratic Party. This appeared to be most successful in the 1946 midterm elections, in which significant defections in several urban enclaves with large Polish American constituencies, contributed to a significant setback for the Truman administration. The domestic backlash from Yalta was a major factor in pushing Harry S. Truman to take a harder line against Stalin in the aftermath of the 1946 elections.

John Radzilowski

Further Reading

Buhite, Russell D. *Decisions at Yalta: An Appraisal of Summit Diplomacy.* Wilmington, Del.: Scholarly Resources, 1986.

Freidel, Frank. *Franklin D. Roosevelt: A Rendezvous with Destiny.* Boston: Little, Brown, 1990.

Radzilowski, John. "Ethnic Anti-Communism in the United States." In *Anti-Communist Minorities in the U.S.: Political Activism of Ethnic Refugees,* edited by Ieva Zake. New York: Palgrave Macmillan, 2009.

Senarclens, Pierre de. *From Yalta to the Iron Curtain:* *The Great Powers and the Origins of the Cold War.* Translated by Amanda Pingree. Washington, D.C.: Berg, 1995.

See also Byrnes, James; Cairo Conference; Churchill, Winston; Cold War; Foreign policy of the United States; France and the United States; Hiss, Alger; North Atlantic Treaty Organization; Paris Peace Conference of 1946; Potsdam Conference; Quebec Conferences; Tehran Conference.

■ Yankee Doodle Dandy

Identification Biographical film about George M. Cohan

Director Michael Curtiz (1886-1962)

Date Released on June 6, 1942

This film celebrating the life of the master Broadway showman of the early twentieth century reproduced several of Cohan's rousing, flag-waving, big musical production numbers. Because it opened just six months after the attack on Pearl Harbor, its patriotic theme strongly resonated with American audiences, pushing it to the highest box-office gross of the year.

Yankee Doodle Dandy brought actor James Cagney his only Academy Award. Although he was known throughout the 1930's for his tough gangster roles, in this film he sings and dances exuberantly in the role of real-life Broadway entertainer George M. Cohan (1878-1942), performing such patriotic numbers as "Over There," "You're a Grand Old Flag," and the showstopper "Yankee Doodle Boy," as well as the New York favorite "Give My Regards to Broadway."

The film's call to patriotism is embedded in a narrative flashback review of the life of Cohan, tracing his rise to prominence from his humble vaudeville beginnings in the family act of the Four Cohans. The film suggests that with hard work, perseverance, and a positive attitude, anyone can make it in America, and that America must be protected.

Impact The great success of *Yankee Doodle Dandy* brought the film's patriotic tunes to a new generation at war. It also led to composer biopics (biographical pictures) honoring composers Irving Berlin (*This Is the Army*, 1943), George Gershwin (*Rhapsody in Blue*, 1945), and Cole Porter (*Night and Day*, 1946).

Scot M. Guenter

Further Reading

Cagney, James. *Cagney by Cagney*. 1976. Reprint. New York: Doubleday, 2005.

McLaughlin, Robert, and Sally E. Parry. *We'll Always Have the Movies: American Cinema During World War II*. Lexington: University Press of Kentucky, 2006.

See also Academy Awards; Broadway musicals; Dance; Film in the United States; Music: Popular; Roosevelt, Franklin D.; Theater in the United States; Wartime propaganda in the United States.

■ Yeager, Chuck

Identification U.S. Air Force captain and test pilot
Born February 13, 1923; Myra, West Virginia

Yeager became the first person to break the sound barrier, a remarkable and dangerous achievement that advanced aviation.

Chuck Yeager entered the U.S. Army Air Corps (later known as the Air Force) in 1941 as an airplane mechanic. He later applied for pilot training and became a flight officer by 1943, testing fighter plane propeller systems. He went to Germany, where in 1944 he became the first pilot to shoot down five German planes in one day. After World War II ended, Yeager became a test pilot at Wright Field. Then, in 1945, he was chosen to be the chief pilot for a top secret X-1 jet, a $6 million project.

The Bell Telephone Laboratories X-1 research jet was rocket-powered and specifically shaped to withstand the stress of breaking the speed of sound, or Mach 1.

Traditional airplanes experienced the cockpit controls locking up and turbulence battering the craft as it approached Mach 1, causing the plane to literally break apart. Many people believed that an aircraft could not be designed to fly faster than the speed of sound. As early as 1943, however, airplane companies realized that they needed information on high-speed flight in order to advance aircraft design. During World War II, the military in particular understood the need for high-speed aircraft that would provide a combat advantage.

The X-1 was unlike any other aircraft designed before. Shaped like a bullet, the plane was thirty-one feet long, with a twenty-seven-foot wingspan. Powered by four rocket engines with a top speed of 800 miles per hour, the plane could withstand up to eighteen times the force of gravity. Jet engines of the time were not powerful enough, so rocket propulsion had to be used. With its small size, explosive fuel, and no escape system, the test flights were extremely dangerous.

On October 14, 1947, at Muroc Air Base (later renamed Edwards Air Force Base) in California's Mojave Desert, Yeager began the ninth test of the X-1 jet. The plane was carried beneath a B-29 bomber; at 10,000 feet, Yeager climbed down a ladder from the B-29 to the X-1. At 20,000 feet, the X-1 was released. Yeager flew the plane to 40,000 feet and, at a speed of approximately 700 miles per hour, reached Mach 1.06, breaking the sound barrier. (The speed of sound is about 660 miles per hour at that altitude.) The first human-made sonic boom was heard for several miles. The entire flight lasted only fourteen minutes, and all of the fuel was used up in two and a half minutes. Yeager had to glide the plane to a landing. The Air Force officially confirmed the accomplishment to the public in June, 1948, although the magazine *Aviation Week* leaked news of the flight in December, 1947.

Impact By 1947, other airplanes were planned, with some designed to fly six times faster than the speed of sound. There were even plans to put men in space, but everything had to wait until the problems with supersonic flight were conquered. Yeager's successful flight, and the many that followed, provided invaluable information that laid the foundation for modern aviation and spaceflight. Yeager went on the break the world speed record in December, 1953, in an X-1A rocket plane, reaching a speed of Mach 2.44 (1,650 miles per hour). He also was a consultant, test pilot, and trainer of astronauts before retiring as a brigadier general in 1975.

Virginia L. Salmon

Chuck Yeager (left) with Major Gus Lundquist and Captain James Fitzgerald in front of the experimental X-1 aircraft. (Library of Congress)

Further Reading

Ethier, Bryan. "Breaking the Sound Barrier." *American History* 32, no. 4 (September/October, 1997): 24+.

Pisano, Dominick A., Robert van der Linden, and Frank H. Winter. *Chuck Yeager and the Bell X-1: Breaking the Sound Barrier.* New York: Harry N. Abrams, 2006.

Vizard, Frank. "The Last Hero Pilot." *Popular Science* 252, no. 1 (January, 1998): 70+.

Yeager, Chuck, and Leo Janos. *Yeager: An Autobiography.* New York: Bantam Books, 1985.

See also Air Force, U.S.; Aircraft design and development; Inventions; Jet engines; Rocketry; Science and technology; War heroes; Wartime technological advances.

Z

■ Zaharias, Babe Didrikson

Identification American multisport athlete
Born June 26, 1911; Port Arthur, Texas
Died September 27, 1956; Galveston, Texas

One of the greatest and most versatile athletes of the twentieth century, Zaharias was frequently in the news during the 1940s as the leading female golfer of the era.

Mildred Ella Didrikson was the sixth of seven children born to her Norwegian skating champion mother and her carpenter father. As she grew up in Beaumont, Texas, she excelled in a variety of high school sports, including volleyball, tennis, baseball, basketball, and swimming. She got the nickname "Babe"—after Major League Baseball star Babe Ruth—when she hit five home runs in a single baseball game.

While working for a Dallas insurance company in 1930, Zaharias participated in the company's sports programs. Her specialties included hurdles, high jump, broad jump, shot put, long jump, and baseball throw. At the Amateur Athletic Union meet in 1932, she entered eight events and won five, tied one, and finished fourth in another. The thirty points she amassed were eight points more than the cumulative score of the other twenty-two members of her team.

At the 1932 Olympic Games in Los Angeles, Didrikson entered three events and won gold medals in the javelin throw and hurdles and a silver medal in the high jump. The Associated Press then named her woman athlete of the year. After a controversy with the Amateur Athletic Union concerning her amateur status, she turned professional in late 1932. Throughout the 1930's, she dabbled in a wide variety of sports competitions and performed in vaudeville. By playing basketball on a barnstorming team and appearing in exhibition games during Major League Baseball's spring training and traveling with a men's baseball team, she made a good income during the 1930's. By 1935, however, her interest was shifting to golf. In 1938, she married wrestler-promoter George Zaharias, whom she made her manager.

Under her husband's direction, Zaharias began winning major golf tournaments in 1940, After the United States entered World War II in late 1941, she withdrew from professional competition for three years to regain her amateur status and concentrated on giving golf exhibitions to help sell war bonds. In 1943, the U.S. Golf Association restored her amateur standing. After the war, she emerged as the top American female golfer.

After the war, Zaharias emerged as one of the most successful and popular women golfers in his-

Babe Didrikson Zaharias holding a golf trophy she won in 1940. (Getty Images)

tory. In 1945, she played flawless golf on the amateur tour and was named woman athlete of the year by the Associated Press for the second time. More such honors would soon follow. During the 1946-1947 golf seasons, Zaharias won an unparalleled seventeen straight tournaments, including the British Women's Amateur, which she was the first American ever to win. In 1947, she again turned professional and engaged Fred Corcoran as her manager. The following year, she earned about $100,000, but most of this money came from promotions and exhibitions, not her many tournament wins. To correct this deficiency, she and Corcoran organized the Ladies Professional Golf Association (LPGA) in 1948 to help popularize women's golf and increase tournament prize money. Over the next several years, as the LPGA grew in stature, Zaharias was the LPGA tour's leading money winner.

Impact During the mid-twentieth century, when women had limited athletic opportunities, Babe Didrikson Zaharias almost single-handedly lifted women's sports to a higher level. Outstanding in virtually every sport she tried, she proved herself against the best track and field athletes in the world at the 1932 Olympic Games and against the world's top golfers during the 1940's. In addition to setting new standards for what women athletes could do, she also left a more tangible legacy by playing a major role in the creation of the Ladies Professional Golf Association.

Anita Price Davis

Further Reading

Cayleff, Susan E. *Babe: The Life and Legend of Babe Didrikson Zaharias.* Rev. ed. Urbana: University of Illinois Press, 1996.

Davis, Anita Price, and Louise Hunt. *Women on U.S. Postage Stamps.* Jefferson, N.C.: McFarland, 2008.

Johnson, William O., and Nancy P. Williamson. *Whatta-Gal! The Babe Didrikson Story.* Boston: Little, Brown, 1977.

Zaharias, Babe Didrikson, and Harry T. Paxton. *This Life I've Led: My Autobiography.* Reprint. New York: Dell, 1975.

See also All-American Girls Professional Baseball League; Baseball; Basketball; Golf; Sports in Canada; Sports in the United States; Tennis; Warmerdam, Cornelius.

■ Zoot-suit riots

The Event Street fighting between servicemen and young Latino civilians

Date Primarily June 3-9, 1943

Place Los Angeles, California

The fighting and arrests that took place during the so-called zoot-suit riots provided a poignant demonstration of the ethnic and racial tensions that existed in Los Angeles and elsewhere during the early 1940's.

In the decades before the 1940's, Los Angeles experienced an explosive growth in population. A diverse mixture of midwesterners, Mexican immigrants, African Americans, and southerners flocked to the city in search of jobs and economic opportunity. The majority of the city's white citizens harbored negative stereotypes concerning ethnic minorities. Widespread discrimination in housing and employment resulted in feelings of bitterness and alienation on the part of those minorities.

After the United States entered World War II in 1941, xenophobic prejudices became more pronounced, and some members of minority groups did not want to fight for a country that failed to give them equal rights. Most servicemen had contempt for young men who tried to avoid military service, and they resented anyone who did not show respect and deference toward men in uniform. The Los Angeles region, with its large military presence, became a tinderbox of racial and ethnic tensions.

The Zoot-Suit Subculture Zoot suits were oversized costumes with ballooned, tight-cuffed trousers and long coats with wide, padded shoulders and large lapels. Frequently the costume also featured a long watch chain and a felt hat topped by a long feather. The flamboyant attire tended to be associated with jazz music, sensual dancing, and energetic night life. African Americans in Harlem were the first to popularize the suits, which they called drapes. By the early 1940's, the zoot-suit fad had become popular among Latinos throughout the nation, and it had an especially strong appeal for rebellious young Mexican Americans who called themselves "pachucos." Although there is debate about the origin of the word "zoot," it most likely evolved from the Mexican-Spanish pronunciation of the English word "suit."

Largely because they were treated as outsiders, zoot-suiters conveyed an attitude of disdain for white middle-class values and conventions. Non-Hispanic white males, especially those in the military, resented the way the zoot-suiters proudly swaggered when they walked, and they commonly perceived the zoot subculture as a threat to the war effort. Both zoot-suiters and servicemen took their masculinity seriously, and members of each group accused the other of showing disrespect toward females of their respective cultural groups. The mainstream press tended to be hostile toward zoot-suiters, frequently portraying them as disloyal to the country, violent, and criminally delinquent. Cartoonist Al Capp helped to promote this negative stereotype in his *Li'l Abner* comic strips between April 11 and May 23, 1943. In these strips, he ascribed conspiratorial machinations to zoot-suit wearers, thereby identifying zoot-suiters as a potential threat. During a period of wartime rationing, moreover, many ordinary Americans criticized the wearing of zoot suits because of the extravagant amount of cloth required for their construction.

Growing Suspicions and Conflict An unsolved murder of a young man named José Díaz at a swimming hole called Sleepy Lagoon helped prepare the background for the zoot-suit riots. Young Latinos often went to Sleepy Lagoon, located a few miles south of Los Angeles, for parties, gang meetings, and romantic encounters. In August of 1942, after Diaz was found dead at the site, the Los Angeles Police Department (LAPD) responded with a mass arrest of about six hundred Latinos. Twenty-two members of the notorious Thirty-eighth Street Gang were prosecuted, and nineteen were found guilty in January, 1943, even though the evidence was circumstantial and weak. In reporting the trials, the majority of regional newspapers warned that criminality was rampant and growing within the Mexican American community. Most Mexican Americans, however, questioned the fairness of the verdicts, which were later overturned on procedural grounds.

During the spring of 1943, the LAPD had several violent confrontations with young Latino males, including one in which officers shot and killed an unarmed thirteen-year-old boy who was driving a stolen car. The Mexican American community usually blamed police brutality for the confrontations, whereas the mainstream press and the overwhelming majority of whites defended the LAPD. Meanwhile, Venice and other communities in the region

saw a growing number of fights between servicemen and zoot-suiters. About fifty thousand servicemen entered the city on leave each weekend, resulting in numerous opportunities for conflict. Whenever fights with zoot-suiters occurred, servicemen almost invariably claimed to have been insulted and attacked for no reason. Likewise, the zoot-suiters insisted that they were victims of unprovoked aggression.

Mobs and Riots When seaman Joe Coleman was knocked unconscious by zoot-suiters on May 30, 1943, rumors magnified the seriousness of the incident. Four days later, on June 3, about fifty Anglo sailors left the Naval Reserve Armory determined to get revenge. Storming into the Carman Theater, they clubbed at least two young zoot-suiters and then tore up their suits. That same night, in East Los Angeles, a group of eleven sailors were walking down Main Street when, according to their account, they were suddenly attacked and beaten by a gang of at least thirty-five Latinos wearing zoot suits. Although their injuries were minor, LAPD officers, calling themselves the "vengeance squad," responded by arresting about a dozen Latinos.

The next day, more than two hundred angry sailors traveled to East Los Angeles in a caravan of taxicabs and military vehicles. Whenever they saw zoot-suiters, a delegation of the sailors attacked them, hitting and kicking them and then ripping their clothing. For the next four days, hundreds of additional soldiers and Marines joined the fights. They targeted mostly Latinos, but they also attacked African Americans. Many of the victims were not wearing zoot suits. Frequently, the attackers blocked off streets to keep victims from escaping. Newspapers featured photographs of roving mobs of servicemen armed with clubs and sticks. The police generally did not intervene, although they did confiscate a few weapons. Zoot-suiters were not simply passive victims; some of them used decoys and set traps to attack small and isolated groups of servicemen.

On Monday, June 7, military officials finally issued an order restricting enlisted men from Los Angeles. Outbreaks of fighting nevertheless continued throughout the day. By then, many civilians were participating in the mob violence. That evening, a crowd of five thousand white citizens gathered downtown, and several groups from the crowd marched through minority neighborhoods in search of zoot-suiters. By Tuesday, the violence had subsided, although scattered fighting continued in the city for the next two days. By then, a total of about two hundred Mexican Americans had been arrested, and five hundred servicemen had been taken into custody temporarily by military authorities. Although dozens of people were treated for serious injuries, no deaths were reported. A few days after the riots ended, there were reports of zoot-suiters being attacked in other cities, including San Diego, Baltimore, Philadelphia, and Detroit. These disturbances foreshadowed the violent race riots that would occur in New York and Detroit later that summer.

Impact Soon after the restoration of order to Los Angeles, California's governor, Earl Warren, ordered the establishment of a citizens' council to investigate and report on the causes of the riots. Later that year, the Tenney Committee's report asserted that white racism was the central cause. Eleanor Roosevelt and other liberals expressed similar conclusions. Mayor of Los Angeles Fletcher Bowron, however, disagreed and said that the riots had simply been a clash between juvenile delinquents and a few white extremists. The city council declared its support for the police, and it came close to passing an ordinance making it a misdemeanor to wear a zoot suit. Governor Warren blamed the press for its sensational coverage and the LAPD for not taking more aggressive action to stop the riots. In the short term, the riots did not result in any major social change, but they demonstrated the potential for future violence based on racial and cultural differences.

Thomas Tandy Lewis

Further Reading

Alvarez, Luis. *The Power of the Zoot: Youth Culture and Resistance During World War II.* Berkeley: University of California Press, 2008. Interesting but one-sided account that presents zoot culture as a national movement for Latino dignity in response to racism.

Escobar, Edward. *Race, Police, and the Making of a Political Identity: Mexican Americans and the Los Angeles Police Department, 1900-1945.* Berkeley: University of California Press, 1999. Helpful study of the historical and ethnic contexts of the riots.

Macías, Anthony. *Mexican American Mojo: Dance and Urban Culture in Los Angeles, 1938-1968.* Durham, N.C.: Duke University Press, 2008. Argues that La-

tino participation in jazz, the zoot-suit phenomenon, and other cultural developments was related to a struggle for liberation and helped to transform life in Los Angeles.

Mazón, Mauricio. *The Zoot-Suit Riots: The Psychology of Symbolic Annihilation.* Austin: University of Texas Press, 1988. Good, succinct account of the riots, even though Mazón's psychoanalytic interpretations are highly speculative.

Pagán, Eduardo O. *Murder at the Sleepy Lagoon: Zoot Suits, Race, and Riot in Wartime L.A.* Chapel Hill: University of North Carolina Press, 2003. Detailed and scholarly account by a historian who supervised an excellent documentary on the topic for public television.

Ramírez, Catherine. *The Woman in the Zoot Suit: Mexican American Women, Nationalism, and the Cultural Politics of Memory.* Durham, N.C.: Duke University Press, 2009. Engaging study of *la pachuca*, the rebellious female type who was an important part of zoot culture.

Sanchez, George, and Gonzalo Sanchez. *Becoming Mexican American: Ethnicity, Culture, and Identity in Chicano Los Angeles.* New York: Oxford University Press, 1995. Study of how Mexican immigrants to Los Angeles from 1900 to 1945 modified their culture and identity to adjust to a different environment.

See also African Americans; Fads; Fashions and clothing; Immigration to the United States; Latinos; Lynching and hate crime; Mexico; Race riots; Racial discrimination; Zoot suits.

■ Zoot suits

Definition Flashy and distinctive outfits worn primarily by Mexican American youths, who were ofted called "pachucos"

The highly recognizable zoot suits were sported by members of Mexican American gangs in the Southwest and by some African Americans in big cities. During the 1940's, Latino gang members wearing zoot suits became easy prey for law-enforcement officials, many of whom regarded the outfits as manifestations of ostentatiously unpatriotic behavior during the midst of World War II.

Zoot suit outfits were built around very long coats with exaggerated shoulder pads and extra-wide la-

Actors wearing a variety of zoot suits for a Hollywood film made several months before the June, 1943, riots in Los Angeles. (AP/Wide World Photos)

pels worn over high-waisted pegged pants, typically adorned with long gold chains hanging down to the knees. Wide-brim felt hats typically completed the outfits. Although they were most popular by far among Mexican American youths, they were also worn by some young African American men in Harlem and other big cities. When the future Nation of Islam leader Malcolm X was living in Boston and New York during the 1940's, he wore a zoot suit, whose shoulders, he later said, were "padded like a lunatic's cell."

Zoot suits came into vogue as the United States was entering World War II—a coincidence that made trouble for the young men who wore them. Indeed, the U.S. War Production Board declared that the suits wasted material because of the superfluous cloth and tailoring required to produce them.

In 1942, zoot suits figured in the notorious Sleepy Lagoon murder trial. A young Mexican American named José Díaz was slain at southeast Los Angeles's Sleepy Lagoon reservoir on August 2 of that year. The ensuing investigation led to the arrest, trial, and conviction of more than twenty young Latino men. Their convictions were reversed on appeal in 1944, but the negative press coverage by the *Los Angeles Times* and the *Herald-Express* resulted in the arrest of six hundred more Latino youths in connection with the murder. Most of the arrestees were identified by the zoot suits they wore. Among the many procedural errors made during the murder trial was the judge's insistence that the defendants wear their zoot suits during all their court appearances.

The long Sleepy Lagoon murder trial's notoriety was an important contributing factor to anti-Latino violence that occurred the following year. In June of 1943, so-called zoot-suit riots took place in Los Angeles and other southwestern cities, where sailors, soldiers, and Marines attacked everyone they spotted on the streets wearing anything resembling a zoot suit. Local law-enforcement officers did little to stop the attacks until the federal government stepped in.

As early as the 1940's, Octavio Paz, one of Mexico's greatest philosophers, attempted to explain what motivated zoot-suited pachucos. In *El laberinto de la soledad: Vida y pensamiento de México* (1950), which he later enlarged and published in English as *The Labyrinth of Solitude* (1961), Paz attempted to find the essence of Mexican character. Instead, he stumbled on the essence of a "misfit" in North American society. Paz noted that having lost their entire inheritance—their language, religion, customs, and beliefs, pachucos used their clothing as a kind of disguise for protection. At the same time, the outfits both hid and pointed them out. Paz also recognized a potentially dangerous ingredient in the pachuco character. which he called an "impassive and sinister clown whose purpose is to cause terror instead of laughter." During the 1940's, pachucos carried impractical clothing to an extreme. The novelty of the outfits lay in their exaggeration, their aesthetic colors, and tattooed crosses the men had between their thumbs and index fingers. It was a sign of rebellion against authority at home, in church, and on the streets.

Impact   During the 1970's, a zoot suiter became a hero in Luis Valdez's successful play about the Sleepy Lagoon murder case, *Zoot Suit* (pr. 1978). In 1981, the play was adapted to the screen, with Edward James Olmos playing the key role of El Pachuco. By the early twenty-first century, zoot suits and the characters who wore them during the 1940's were viewed as positive images of the Mexican American past, and Latino youths often wore modernized versions of the suits at school proms, weddings, and other social celebrations.

Raymond J. Gonzales

Further Reading

Burt, Kenneth C. *The Search for a Civic Voice: California Latino Politics.* Claremont, Calif.: Regina Books, 2007.

Gonzales, Raymond J. "The Pachuco Character Searches for Identity and Recognition." *The Sacramento Bee*, February 11, 1979.

Pagán, Eduardo Obregón. *Murder at the Sleepy Lagoon: Zoot Suits, Race, and Riot in Wartime L.A.* Chapel Hill: University of North Carolina Press, 2003.

Paz, Octavio. *The Labyrinth of Solitude.* New York: Grove Press, 1985.

Redl, Fritz. "Zoot Suits: An Interpretation." *Survey Midmonthly* 73 (October, 1943): 259-262.

See also   Fads; Fashions and clothing; Latin America; Latinos; Mexico; Race riots; Zoot-suit riots.

■ Entertainment: Major Broadway Plays and Awards

This list includes all Broadway plays that ran for at least one full month between January 1, 1940, and December 31, 1949, and had total runs of at least two hundred performances. The list includes plays that opened before 1940 and ran for at least one month into the 1940's. It also includes plays with shorter runs that received major awards. Plays are listed in order of their opening dates, which are given within parentheses after the titles. An asterisk (*) next to a title or personage indicates that a full essay exists on the topic within *The Forties in America*. (Note that Richard Rodgers and Oscar Hammerstein II are covered in a single essay.)

Shows Opening Before 1940

Pins and Needles (November 27, 1937), 1,108 performances
Hellzapoppin (September 22, 1938), 1,404 performances
The Little Foxes (February 15, 1939), 410 performances
The Philadelphia Story (March 28, 1939), 417 performances
Streets of Paris (June 19, 1939), 274 performances
Yokel Boy (July 6, 1939), 208 performances
See My Lawyer (September 27, 1939), 224 performances
Skylark (October 11, 1939), 256 performances
The Man Who Came to Dinner (October 16, 1939), 739 performances
Too Many Girls (October 18, 1939), 249 performances
The Time of Your Life (October 25, 1939), 185 performances
    1940 Pulitzer Prize for Drama: William Saroyan
    1940 New York Drama Critics' Circle Award: Best American Play, Saroyan
Margin for Error (November 6, 1939), 264 performances
Life with Father (November 8, 1939), 3,224 performances
Du Barry Was a Lady (December 6, 1939), 408 performances

Shows Opening in 1940

The Male Animal (January 9, 1940), 243 performances
Separate Rooms (Mar. 23, 1940), 613 performances
There Shall Be No Night (April 29, 1940), 115 performances
    1941 Pulitzer Prize for Drama: Robert E. Sherwood
Louisiana Purchase (May 28, 1940), 444 performances

Johnny Belinda (September 18, 1940), 321 performances
It Happens on Ice (October 10, 1940), 276 performances
Panama Hattie (October 30, 1940), 501 performances
The Corn Is Green (November 26, 1940), 477 performances
    1941 New York Drama Critics' Circle Award: Best Foreign Play, Emlyn Williams
Pal Joey (December 25, 1940), 374 performances
My Sister Eileen (December 26, 1940), 864 performances

Shows Opening in 1941

Arsenic and Old Lace (January 1, 1941), 1,444 performances
Claudia (February 12, 1941), 722 performances
Watch on the Rhine (April 1, 1941), 378 performances
    1941 New York Drama Critics' Circle Award: Best American Play, Lillian Hellman
Best Foot Forward (October 1, 1941), 326 performances
Let's Face It! (October 29, 1941), 547 performances
Blithe Spirit (November 5, 1941), 657 performances
    1942 New York Drama Critics' Circle Award: Best Foreign Play, Noël Coward
Spring Again (November 10, 1941), 241 performances
Sons o' Fun (December 1, 1941), 742 performances
Angel Street (December 5, 1941), 1,295 performances

Shows Opening in 1942

Priorities of 1942 (March 12, 1942), 353 performances
Uncle Harry (May 20, 1942), 430 performances
By Jupiter (June 3, 1942), 427 performances
Star and Garter (June 24, 1942), 609 performances

Stars on Ice (July 2, 1942), 827 performances

Janie (September 10, 1942), 642 performances

Show Time (September 16, 1942), 342 performances

The Eve of St. Mark (October 7, 1942), 307 performances

Rosalinda (October 28, 1942), 611 performances

The Skin of Our Teeth (November 18, 1942), 359 performances
    1943 Pulitzer Prize for Drama: Thornton Wilder

The Doughgirls (December 30, 1942), 671 performances

Shows Opening in 1943

Something for the Boys (January 7, 1943), 422 performances

Dark Eyes (January 14, 1943), 230 performances

The Patriots (January 29, 1943), 173 performances
    1943 New York Drama Critics' Circle Award: Best American Play, Sidney Kingsley

Harriet (March 3, 1943), 377 performances

Kiss and Tell (March 17, 1943), 956 performances

*Oklahoma!** (March 31, 1943), 2,212 performances
    1944 Special Pulitzer Prize for Drama: Richard Rogers* and Oscar Hammerstein II*

Ziegfeld Follies of 1943 (April 1, 1943), 553 performances

Tomorrow the World (April 14, 1943), 500 performances

Three's a Family (May 5, 1943), 497 performances

Early to Bed (June 17, 1943), 380 performances

One Touch of Venus (October 7, 1943), 567 performances

Winged Victory (November 20, 1943), 212 performances

Carmen Jones (December 2, 1943), 503 performances

The Voice of the Turtle (December 8, 1943), 1,557 performances

Shows Opening in 1944

Over Twenty-one (January 3, 1944), 221 performances

Ramshackle Inn (January 5, 1944), 216 performances

Mexican Hayride (January 28, 1944), 481 performances

Jacobowsky and the Colonel (March 14, 1944), 417 performances
    1944 New York Drama Critics' Circle Award: Best

Foreign Play, Franz Werfel and Samuel Nathaniel Behrman

Follow the Girls (April 8, 1944), 888 performances

The Searching Wind (April 12, 1944), 318 performances

Hats Off to Ice (June 22, 1944), 889 performances

Ten Little Indians (June 27, 1944), 426 performances

School for Brides (August 1, 1944), 375 performances

The Two Mrs. Carrolls (August 14, 1944), 585 performances

Song of Norway (August 21, 1944), 860 performances

Anna Lucasta (August 30, 1944), 957 performances

Soldier's Wife (October 4, 1944), 253 performances

Bloomer Girl (October 5, 1944), 654 performances

I Remember Mama (October 19, 1944), 713 performances

Harvey (November 1, 1944), 1,775 performances
    1945 Pulitzer Prize for Drama: Mary Chase

The Late George Apley (November 23, 1944), 384 performances
    1945 Theatre World Award: Margaret Phillips

A Bell for Adano (December 6, 1944), 296 performances

Dear Ruth (December 13, 1944), 680 performances

Laffing Room Only (December 23, 1944), 232 performances

On the Town (December 28, 1944), 462 performances
    1945 Theatre World Award: Betty Comden

Shows Opening in 1945

The Hasty Heart (January 3, 1945), 204 performances
    1945 Theatre World Award: John Lund

Up in Central Park (January 27, 1945), 504 performances

Dark of the Moon (March 14, 1945), 318 performances
    1945 Theatre World Award: Richard Hart

The Glass Menagerie (March 31, 1945), 563 performances
    1945 New York Drama Critics' Circle Award: Best American Play, Tennessee Williams*

Carousel (April 19, 1945), 890 performances
    1946 New York Drama Critics' Circle Award: Best Musical, Richard Rodgers* and Oscar Hammerstein II*

1945 Theatre World Awards: Charles Lang, Bambi Linn, and John Raitt

Deep Are the Roots (September 26, 1945), 477 performances
1946 Theatre World Award: Barbara Bel Geddes

The Red Mill (October 16, 1945), 531 performances

Are You with It? (November 10, 1945), 266 performances

State of the Union (November 14, 1945), 765 performances
1946 Pulitzer Prize for Drama: Russel Crouse and Howard Lindsay

Dream Girl (December 14, 1945), 348 performances

Billion Dollar Baby (December 21, 1945), 220 performances

Shows Opening in 1946

O Mistress Mine (January 23, 1946), 482 performances

Born Yesterday (February 4, 1946), 1,642 performances
1946 Theatre World Award: Paul Douglas

Three to Make Ready (March 7, 1946), 327 performances

Call Me Mister (April 18, 1946), 734 performances
1946 Theatre World Award: Bill Callahan

Annie Get Your Gun (May 18, 1946), 1,147 performances

Icetime (June 20, 1946), 405 performances

Cyrano de Bergerac (October 8, 1946), 193 performances
1947 Tony Award: Best Actor, José Ferrer

Happy Birthday (October 31, 1946), 563 performances
1947 Tony Award: Best Actress, Helen Hayes

Joan of Lorraine (November 18, 1946), 199 performances
1947 Tony Award: Best Actress, Ingrid Bergman

Another Part of the Forest (November 20, 1946), 182 performances
1947 Tony Award: Best Featured Actress, Patricia Neal
1947 Theatre World Award: Neal

No Exit (November 26, 1946), 31 performances
1947 New York Drama Critics' Circle Award: Best Foreign Play, Jean-Paul Sartre

Years Ago (December 3, 1946), 206 performances
1947 Tony Award: Best Actor, Fredric March

Shows Opening in 1947

Finian's Rainbow (January 10, 1947), 725 performances
1947 Tony Awards: Best Featured Actor (Musical), David Wayne; Best Choreography, Michael Kidd
1947 Theatre World Award: Wayne

All My Sons (January 29, 1947), 328 performances
1947 Tony Awards: Playwright, Arthur Miller; Best Direction, Elia Kazan
1947 New York Drama Critics' Circle Award: Best American Play, Miller

John Loves Mary (February 4, 1947), 423 performances

Brigadoon (March 13, 1947), 581 performances
1947 Tony Award: Best Choreography, Agnes De Mille
1947 New York Drama Critics' Circle Award: Best Musical, Frederick Loewe and Alan Jay Lerner
1947 Theatre World Awards: Marion Bell, George Keane, and James Mitchell

The Telephone and the Medium (May 1, 1947), 212 performances

Icetime of 1948 (May 28, 1947), 422 performances

The Heiress (September 29, 1947), 410 performances

Command Decision (October 1, 1947), 409 performances
1948 Tony Awards: Outstanding Performance by a Newcomer, James Whitmore
1948 Theatre World Award: Whitmore

High Button Shoes (October 9, 1947), 727 performances
1948 Theatre World Award: Mark Dawson

Allegro (October 10, 1947), 315 performances

Medea (October 20, 1947), 214 performances
1948 Tony Award: Best Actress, Judith Anderson

The Winslow Boy (October 29, 1947), 214 performances
1948 New York Drama Critics' Circle Award: Best Foreign Play, Terence Rattigan

For Love or Money (November 9, 1947), 263 performances
1948 Tony Award: Outstanding Performance by a Newcomer, June Lockhart
1948 Theatre World Award: Lockhart

Antony and Cleopatra (November 26, 1947), 126 performances
1948 Theatre World Award: Douglass Watson

*A Streetcar Named Desire** (December 3, 1947), 855 performances

1948 Pulitzer Prize for Drama: Tennessee Williams*

1948 New York Drama Critics' Circle Award: Best American Play, Williams

Angel in the Wings (December 11, 1947), 308 performances

1948 Tony Awards: Best Actor (Musical) Paul Hartman; Best Actress (Musical), Grace Hartman

Shows Opening in 1948

Strange Bedfellows (January 14, 1948), 229 performances

Make Mine Manhattan (January 15, 1948), 429 performances

Mister Roberts (February 18, 1948), 1,157 performances

1948 Tony Awards: Best Play, Thomas Heggen and Joshua Logan; Best Actor, Henry Fonda; Best Producer, Leland Hayward; Best Authors, Heggen and Logan; Best Direction, Logan

1948 Theatre World Award: Ralph Meeker

The Happy Journey to Trenton and Camden and the Respectful Prostitute (March 16, 1948), 318 performances

1948 Theatre World Award: Meg Mundy

Inside U.S.A. (April 30, 1948), 399 performances

1948 Theatre World Awards: Valerie Bettis and Estelle Loring

Howdy, Mr. Ice (June 24, 1948), 406 performances

Edward, My Son (September 30, 1948), 260 performances

Love Life (October 1, 1948), 252 performances

1949 Tony Award: Best Actress (Musical), Nanette Fabray

Where's Charley? (October 11, 1948) 792 performances

1949 Tony Award: Best Actor (Musical), Ray Bolger

1949 Theatre World Awards: Allyn Ann McLerie and Byron Palmer

Life with Mother (October 20, 1948), 262 performances

As the Girls Go (November 13, 1948), 414 performances

1949 Tony Award: Best Conductor and Musical Director, Max Meth

Goodbye, My Fancy (November 17, 1948), 446 performances

1949 Tony Award: Best Supporting Actress, Shirley Booth

Light up the Sky (November 18, 1948), 214 performances

The Silver Whistle (November 24, 1948), 219 performances

Anne of the Thousand Days (December 8, 1948), 288 performances

1949 Tony Award: Best Actor, Rex Harrison

Lend an Ear, (December 18, 1948), 460 performances

1949 Theatre World Awards: Carol Channing, Gene Nelson, and Bob Scheerer

The Madwoman of Chaillot (December 27, 1948), 368 performances

1949 Tony Award: Best Actress, Martita Hunt

1949 New York Drama Critics' Circle Award: Best Foreign Play, Jean Giraudoux (adapted by Maurice Valency)

Kiss Me, Kate (December 30, 1948), 1,077 performances

1949 Tony Awards: Best Musical, Music and Lyrics by Cole Porter, Book by Bella and Samuel Spewack; Best Author (Musical), Bella and Samuel Spewack; Best Composer and Lyricist, Porter; Best Producer (Musical), Saint Subber and Lemuel Ayers

Shows Opening in 1949

*Death of a Salesman** (February 10, 1949), 742 performances

1949 Tony Awards: Best Play, Arthur Miller; Best Supporting Actor, Arthur Kennedy; Producer, Kermit Bloomgarden and Walter Fried; Author, Miller; Best Director, Elia Kazan

1949 Pulitzer Prize for Drama: Miller

1949 New York Drama Critics' Circle Award: Best American Play, Miller

1949 Theatre World Award: Cameron Mitchell

Detective Story (March 23, 1949), 581 performances

1950 Theatre World Award: Lydia Clarke

*South Pacific** (April 7, 1949), 1,925 performances

1950 Tony Awards: Best Musical, book by Joshua L. Logan III and Oscar Hammerstein II*; Libretto, Hammerstein; Best Original Score, Richard Rodgers*; Best Actor (Musical), Ezio Pinza; Best Actress (Musical), Mary Martin; Best Featured Actor (Musical), Myron McCormick; Best Featured Actress (Musical), Juanita Hall; Best Producer (Musical), Hammerstein, Rodgers, Leland Hayward, and Logan; Best Director, Logan

1950 Pulitzer Prize for Drama: Rogers, Hammerstein, and Logan

1949 New York Drama Critics' Circle Award: Best Musical, Rodgers and Hammerstein

Howdy, Mr. Ice of 1950 (May 26, 1949), 430 performances

Miss Liberty (July 15, 1949), 308 performances

Lost in the Stars (October 30, 1949), 273 performances

I Know My Love (November 2, 1949), 247 performances

Texas, Li'l Darlin' (November 25, 1949), 293 performances

Clutterbuck (December 3, 1949), 218 performances

Gentlemen Prefer Blondes (December 8, 1949), 740 performances

Jennie MacDonald Lewis

■ Entertainment: Academy Awards for Films

1940

Best Picture: *Rebecca*
Best Actor: James Stewart, *The Philadelphia Story*
Best Actress: Ginger Rogers, *Kitty Foyle*
Best Supporting Actor: Walter Brennan, *The Westerner*
Best Supporting Actress: Jane Darwell, *The Grapes of Wrath*
Best Director: John Ford, *The Grapes of Wrath*
Best Original Screenplay: Preston Sturges, *The Great McGinty*
Best Original Story: Benjamin Glazer and John S. Toldy, *Arise, My Love*
Best Screenplay Adaptation: Donald Ogden Stewart, *The Philadelphia Story*
Best Cinematography (B&W): George Barnes, *Rebecca*
Best Cinematography (color): Georges Périnal, *The Thief of Bagdad*
Best Art Direction (B&W): Cedric Gibbons and Paul Groesse, *Pride and Prejudice*
Best Art Direction (color): Vincent Korda, *The Thief of Bagdad*
Best Film Editing: Anne Bauchens, *North West Mounted Police*
Best Sound: Douglas Shearer, *Strike up the Band*
Best Special Effects: Lawrence Butler and Jack Whitney, *The Thief of Bagdad*

1941

Best Picture: *How Green Was My Valley*
Best Actor: Gary Cooper, *Sergeant York*
Best Actress: Joan Fontaine, *Suspicion*
Best Supporting Actor: Donald Crisp, *How Green Was My Valley*
Best Supporting Actress: Mary Astor, *The Great Lie*
Best Director: John Ford, *How Green Was My Valley*
Best Original Screenplay: Herman J. Mankiewicz and Orson Welles, *Citizen Kane*
Best Original Story: Harry Segall, *Here Comes Mr. Jordan*
Best Screenplay: Sidney Buchman and Seton I. Miller, *Here Comes Mr. Jordan*
Best Cinematography (B&W): Arthur Miller, *How Green Was My Valley*
Best Cinematography (color): Ernest Palmer and Ray Rennahan, *Blood and Sand*
Best Art Direction (B&W): Richard Day, Nathan Juran, and Thomas Little, *How Green Was My Valley*
Best Art Direction (color): Cedric Gibbons, Urie McCleary, and Edwin B. Willis, *Blossoms in the Dust*
Best Film Editing: William Holmes, *Sergeant York*
Best Sound: Jack Whitney, *That Hamilton Woman*
Best Special Effects: Farciot Edouart, Gordon Jennings, and Louis Mesenkop, *I Wanted Wings*

1942

Best Picture: *Mrs. Miniver*
Best Actor: James Cagney, *Yankee Doodle Dandy*
Best Actress: Greer Garson, *Mrs. Miniver*
Best Supporting Actor: Van Heflin, *Johnny Eager*
Best Supporting Actress: Teresa Wright, *Mrs. Miniver*
Best Director: William Wyler, *Mrs. Miniver*
Best Original Screenplay: Ring Lardner, Jr., and Michael Kanin, *Woman of the Year*
Best Original Story: Emeric Pressburger, *The Invaders*
Best Screenplay: Arthur Wimperis, George Froeschel, James Hilton, and Claudine West, *Mrs. Miniver*
Best Cinematography (B&W): Joseph Ruttenberg, *Mrs. Miniver*
Best Cinematography (color): Leon Shamroy, *The Black Swan*
Best Art Direction (B&W): Richard Day, Joseph Wright, and Thomas Little, *This Above All*
Best Art Direction (color): Richard Day, Joseph Wright, and Thomas Little, *My Gal Sal*
Best Film Editing: Daniel Mandell, *The Pride of the Yankees*
Best Sound: Nathan Levinson, *Yankee Doodle Dandy*
Best Special Effects: Gordon Jennings, Farciot Edouart, William L. Pereira, and Louis Mesenkop, *Reap the Wild Wind*

1943

Best Picture: *Casablanca*
Best Actor: Paul Lukas, *Watch on the Rhine*
Best Actress: Jennifer Jones, *The Song of Bernadette*
Best Supporting Actor: Charles Coburn, *The More the Merrier*
Best Supporting Actress: Katina Paxinou, *For Whom the Bell Tolls*

Best Director: Michael Curtiz, *Casablanca*

Best Original Story: William Saroyan, *The Human Comedy*

Best Original Screenplay: Norman Krasna, *Princess O'Rourke*

Best Screenplay: Julius J. Epstein, Philip G. Epstein, and Howard Koch, *Casablanca*

Best Cinematography (B&W): Arthur Miller, *The Song of Bernadette*

Best Cinematography (color): Hal Mohr and W. Howard Greene, *Phantom of the Opera*

Best Art Direction (B&W): James Basevi, William Darling, and Thomas Little, *The Song of Bernadette*

Best Art Direction (color): John B. Goodman, Alexander Golitzen, Russell A. Gausman, and Ira S. Webb, *Phantom of the Opera*

Best Film Editing: George Amy, *Air Force*

Best Sound: Stephen Dunn, *This Land Is Mine*

Best Special Effects: Fred Sersen, *Crash Dive*

1944

Best Picture: *Going My Way*

Best Actor: Bing Crosby, *Going My Way*

Best Actress: Ingrid Bergman, *Gaslight*

Best Supporting Actor: Barry Fitzgerald, *Going My Way*

Best Supporting Actress: Ethel Barrymore, *None but the Lonely Heart*

Best Director: Leo McCarey, *Going My Way*

Best Original Story: Leo McCarey, *Going My Way*

Best Original Screenplay: Lamar Trotti, *Wilson*

Best Screenplay: Frank Butler and Frank Cavett, *Going My Way*

Best Cinematography (B&W): Joseph LaShelle, *Laura*

Best Cinematography (color): Leon Shamroy, *Wilson*

Best Art Direction (B&W): Cedric Gibbons, William Ferrari, Edwin B. Willis, and Paul Huldschinsky, *Gaslight*

Best Art Direction (color): Wiard Ihnen and Thomas Little, *Wilson*

Best Film Editing: Barbara McLean, *Wilson*

Best Sound: E. H. Hansen, *Wilson*

Best Special Effects: A. Arnold Gillespie, Donald Jahraus, Warren Newcombe, and Douglas Shearer, *Thirty Seconds over Tokyo*

1945

Best Picture: *The Lost Weekend*

Best Actor: Ray Milland, *The Lost Weekend*

Best Actress: Joan Crawford, *Mildred Pierce*

Best Supporting Actor: James Dunn, *A Tree Grows in Brooklyn*

Best Supporting Actress: Anne Revere, *National Velvet*

Best Director: Billy Wilder, *The Lost Weekend*

Best Original Story: Charles G. Booth, *The House on Ninety-second Street*

Best Original Screenplay: Richard Schweizer, *Marie-Louise*

Best Screenplay: Charles Brackett and Billy Wilder, *The Lost Weekend*

Best Cinematography (B&W): Harry Stradling, *The Picture of Dorian Gray*

Best Cinematography (color): Leon Shamroy, *Leave Her to Heaven*

Best Art Direction (B&W): Wiard Ihnen and A. Roland Fields, *Blood on the Sun*

Best Art Direction (color): Hans Dreier, Ernst Fegte, and Sam Comer, *Frenchman's Creek*

Best Film Editing: Robert J. Kern, *National Velvet*

Best Sound: Stephen Dunn, *The Bells of St. Mary's*

Best Special Effects: John Fulton and Arthur W. Johns, *Wonder Man*

1946

Best Picture: *The Best Years of Our Lives*

Best Actor: Fredric March, *The Best Years of Our Lives*

Best Actress: Olivia de Havilland, *To Each His Own*

Best Supporting Actor: Harold Russell, *The Best Years of Our Lives*

Best Supporting Actress: Anne Baxter, *The Razor's Edge*

Best Director: William Wyler, *The Best Years of Our Lives*

Best Original Story: Clemence Dane, *Vacation from Marriage*

Best Original Screenplay: Muriel Box and Sydney Box, *The Seventh Veil*

Best Screenplay: Robert E. Sherwood, *The Best Years of Our Lives*

Best Cinematography (B&W): Arthur Miller, *Anna and the King of Siam*

Best Cinematography (color): Charles Rosher, Leonard Smith, and Arthur Arling, *The Yearling*

Best Art Direction (B&W): Lyle Wheeler, William Darling, Thomas Little, and Frank E. Hughes, *Anna and the King of Siam*

Best Art Direction (color): Cedric Gibbons, Paul Groesse, and Edwin B. Willis, *The Yearling*

Best Film Editing: Daniel Mandell, *The Best Years of Our Lives*

Best Sound: John Livadary, *The Jolson Story*

Best Special Effects: Thomas Howard, *Blithe Spirit*

1947

Best Picture: *Gentleman's Agreement*

Best Actor: Ronald Colman, *A Double Life*

Best Actress: Loretta Young, *The Farmer's Daughter*

Best Supporting Actor: Edmund Gwenn, *Miracle on Thirty-fourth Street*

Best Supporting Actress: Celeste Holm, *Gentleman's Agreement*

Best Director: Elia Kazan, *Gentleman's Agreement*

Best Story: Valentine Davies, *Miracle on Thirty-fourth Street*

Best Original Screenplay: Sidney Sheldon, *The Bachelor and the Bobby-Soxer*

Best Screenplay: George Seaton, *Miracle on Thirty-fourth Street*

Best Cinematography (B&W): Guy Green, *Great Expectations*

Best Cinematography (color): Jack Cardiff, *Black Narcissus*

Best Art Direction (B&W): John Bryan and Wilfred Shingleton, *Great Expectations*

Best Art Direction (color): Alfred Junge, *Black Narcissus*

Best Film Editing: Francis Lyon and Robert Parrish, *Body and Soul*

Best Sound: Gordon Sawyer, *The Bishop's Wife*

Best Special Effects: A. Arnold Gillespie, Warren Newcombe, Douglas Shearer, and Michael Steinore, *Green Dolphin Street*

1948

Best Picture: *Hamlet*

Best Actor: Laurence Olivier, *Hamlet*

Best Actress: Jane Wyman, *Johnny Belinda*

Best Supporting Actor: Walter Huston, *The Treasure of the Sierra Madre*

Best Supporting Actress: Claire Trevor, *Key Largo*

Best Director: John Huston, *The Treasure of the Sierra Madre*

Best Story: Richard Schweizer and David Wechsler, *The Search*

Best Screenplay: John Huston, *The Treasure of the Sierra Madre*

Best Cinematography (B&W): William Daniels, *The Naked City*

Best Cinematography (color): Joseph Valentine, William V. Skall, and Winton Hoch, *Joan of Arc*

Best Art Direction (B&W): Roger K. Furse and Carmen Dillon, *Hamlet*

Best Art Direction (color): Hein Heckroth and Arthur Lawson, *The Red Shoes*

Best Film Editing: Paul Weatherwax, *The Naked City*

Best Sound: Thomas T. Moulton, *The Snake Pit*

Best Special Effects: Paul Eagler, J. McMillan Johnson, Russell Shearman, Clarence Slifer, Charles Freeman, and James G. Stewart, *Portrait of Jennie*

1949

Best Picture: *All the King's Men*

Best Actor: Broderick Crawford, *All the King's Men*

Best Actress: Olivia de Havilland, *The Heiress*

Best Supporting Actor: Dean Jagger, *Twelve O'Clock High*

Best Supporting Actress: Mercedes McCambridge, *All the King's Men*

Best Director: Joseph L. Mankiewicz, *A Letter to Three Wives*

Best Story: Douglas Morrow, *The Stratton Story*

Best Screenplay: Joseph L. Mankiewicz, *A Letter to Three Wives*

Best Story and Screenplay: Robert Pirosh, *Battleground*

Best Cinematography (B&W): Paul C. Vogel, *Battleground*

Best Cinematography (color): Winton Hoch, *She Wore a Yellow Ribbon*

Best Art Direction (B&W): Harry Horner, John Meehan, and Emile Kuri, *The Heiress*

Best Art Direction (color): Cedric Gibbons, Paul Groesse, Edwin B. Willis, and Jack D. Moore, *Little Women*

Best Film Editing: Harry Gerstad, *Champion*

Best Sound: Thomas T. Moulton, *Twelve O'Clock High*

Best Special Effects: ARKO Productions, *Mighty Joe Young*

■ Entertainment: Major Films

The films listed here are a sampling of 1940's films now regarded as significant because of their box-office success, their Academy Award honors, or their modern critical reputations. Films whose titles are printed in SMALL CAPITAL LETTERS and directors and actors whose names are asterisked (*) are subjects of full essays in *The Forties in America*.

1940

Abe Lincoln in Illinois (RKO; dir., John Cromwell) Raymond Massey received an Academy Award for best actor for his portrayal of Abraham Lincoln, from his youth in Kentucky to his departure for the White House. James Wong Howe won an Oscar for best black-and-white cinematography. Based on a Pulitzer Prize-winning play by Robert E. Sherwood, the film was the screen debut for Ruth Gordon, as Mary Todd Lincoln.

All This and Heaven Too (Warner Bros; dir., Anatole Litvak) In this lavish costume drama set in nineteenth century France, Charles Boyer plays a duke who falls in love with the family governess, played by Bette Davis, and murders his wife (Barbara O'Neil).

The Bank Dick (Universal; dir., Edward F. Cline) Anarchic comedy starring W. C. Fields, who plays a bibulous and cantankerous security guard besieged by a shrewish wife, a censorious mother-in-law, and feral children.

FANTASIA (Walt Disney; dir., Joe Grant) Disney classic that uses inventive animation to illustrate orchestral works by many well-known composers, including Johann Sebastian Bach, Peter Ilich Tchaikovsky, Igor Stravinsky, and Franz Schubert.

Foreign Correspondent (United Artists; dir., Alfred Hitchcock*) World War II thriller nominated for six Academy Awards. Hitchcock was nominated for best director for this film but would never win the award during his long and distinguished directing career. *Foreign Correspondent* tells the story of an American journalist, played by Joel McCrea, who exposes spies in Great Britain. Released before American entry into World War II, this film aroused sympathy for the British cause.

THE GRAPES OF WRATH (Twentieth Century-Fox; dir., John Ford*) Based on the John Steinbeck novel about Okies displaced by drought and migrating to California in search of work. Henry Fonda's Tom Joad stubbornly opposes injustice.

THE GREAT DICTATOR (Charles Chaplin; dir., Chaplin) Chaplin's first all-talking film, bravely made at the height of Nazi power. Chaplin plays a comically grotesque version of Adolf Hitler, as well as a look-alike, poor Jewish barber endangered by the anti-Semitic regime of fictional Tomania.

The Great McGinty (Paramount; dir., Preston Sturges) In his directorial debut, Preston Sturges won an Oscar for his scintillating screenplay, the comic story of a tramp (played by Brian Donlevy) who becomes governor before turning honest.

His Girl Friday (Columbia; dir., Howard Hawks) In this frantically paced remake of *The Front Page*, Cary Grant plays a newspaper editor intent on keeping Rosalind Russell, his ex-wife and a reporter on his staff, on assignment and away from a wedding with Ralph Bellamy.

Kitty Foyle (RKO Radio; dir., Sam Wood) Ginger Rogers* won an Oscar for the title role, playing a fashion executive whose heart is torn between a wealthy socialite, Dennis Morgan, and a poor, idealistic doctor, James Craig.

The Long Voyage Home (Walter Wanger; dir., John Ford*) An amalgam of four one-act plays by Eugene O'Neill. The film dramatizes the experiences of crew and passengers aboard a cargo ship during its long voyage home from the West Indies to Baltimore to England during World War II.

THE PHILADELPHIA STORY (MGM; dir., George Cukor) Effervescent romantic comedy in which Katharine Hepburn plays a Philadelphia socialite whose plans to marry wealthy John Howard are disrupted by a tabloid reporter, James Stewart*, and her ex-husband, Cary Grant. Nominated for six Academy Awards, this film received two—for Donald Ogden Stewart's adapted screenplay and Stewart's performance as lead actor.

Pinocchio (RKO; dir., Ben Sharpsteen) Disney's endearing animated adaptation of the story about the wooden puppet whom a blue fairy allows to become a real boy. A moralistic story about learning the importance of bravery and honesty, it introduced the song "When You Wish upon a Star."

Rebecca (Selznick-MGM; dir., Alfred Hitchcock*) In this early Hitchcock hit, based on a popular novel by the English writer Daphne du Maurier, young Joan Fontaine finds her marriage to wealthy, enigmatic Laurence Olivier poisoned by the memory of his late first wife. Nominated for eleven Academy Awards, this film received two—for best picture and best black-and-white cinematography.

The Sea Hawk (Warner Bros.; dir., Michael Curtiz) Errol Flynn* plays an English privateer in a swashbuckling tale of high-seas adventure and court intrigue during the reign of Elizabeth I, before Philip II dispatches his Armada in an attempt to conquer England.

The Shop Around the Corner (MGM; dir., Ernst Lubitsch) The inspiration behind the 1949 musical *In the Good Old Summertime* and the 1998 film *You've Got Mail*, this romantic comedy stars James Stewart* and Margaret Sullavan as employees in a Budapest store who dislike each other but fall in love through the letters that each writes unknowingly to the other.

1941

Buck Privates (RKO; dir., Arthur Lubin) Military comedy that made stars of Bud Abbott* and Lou Costello*. They play two incompetents who reluctantly enlist in the army and inadvertently end up heroes.

CITIZEN KANE (Mercury; dir., Orson Welles*) The most celebrated of American films, this was a tour de force for young Welles as director and title character, portraying the rise and fall of a quintessential American tycoon modeled on newspaper tycoon William Randolph Hearst.

Dumbo (RKO; dir., Ben Sharpsteen) Popular Disney animated feature in which a young elephant who is scorned by other circus animals but gains respect by learning to fly by using his vastly oversized ears as wings.

How Green Was My Valley (Twentieth Century-Fox; dir., John Ford*) Nominated for ten Academy Awards and the winner of five, including best picture, this is a sentimental story of a family living and working amid the coal fields of south Wales.

The Lady Eve (Paramount; dir., Preston Sturges) Energetic screwball comedy in which Barbara Stanwyck plays a con artist out to fleece the heir to an ale fortune (Henry Fonda) on an ocean liner.

However, she falls in love with him, he dumps her, and she plots revenge.

THE MALTESE FALCON (Warner Bros.; dir., John Huston) Humphrey Bogart* plays private eye Sam Spade in John Huston's adaptation of Dashiell Hammett's novel. The death of Spade's partner and an assignment from a beautiful woman (Mary Astor) lead Spade to a string of murders connected to a gold-encrusted statue of a bird.

Sergeant York (Warner Bros.; dir., Howard Hawks) In a performance that earned him a best actor Academy Award, Gary Cooper plays Alvin York, the real-life Tennessee farmer who reluctantly went into combat against the Germans and became a hero during World War I. This was the highest-grossing film of 1941.

SULLIVAN'S TRAVELS (Paramount; dir., Preston Sturges) Sharp-edged comedy in which Joel McCrea plays a film director who, weary of his privileged life in Hollywood, sets out to discover how others live by traveling as a hobo and learns lessons that enrich his art. Veronica Lake plays a would-be actor who accompanies him on his travels.

1942

Bambi (Walt Disney; dir., David Hand) Beloved, pioneering animated feature that tells the story of a deer coping with the perils of life in the forest, along with his friends Thumper, a rabbit, and Flower, a skunk.

Casablanca (Warner Bros.; dir., Michael Curtiz) When his former lover, played by Ingrid Bergman, now married to resistance fighter Paul Henreid, walks into the cafe he runs in neutral Morocco, cynical Humphrey Bogart* is torn between hedonism and heroism. Winner of best picture Oscar.

Kings Row (Warner Bros.; dir., Sam Wood) Set in a small town at the turn of the twentieth century, this melodrama follows five children as they grow up amid cruelty and madness. One of them is played by Ronald Reagan, in his most notable Hollywood role.

The Magnificent Ambersons (RKO; dir., Orson Welles*) An adaptation of a Booth Tarkington novel, this film follows the decline of a prominent Indiana family. Joseph Cotten stars as the self-indulgent heir to an industrial fortune. A bravura display of cinematic technique, Welles's second film was removed from the director's control before the final cut.

Mrs. Miniver (MGM; dir., William Wyler) In a melodrama designed to persuade Americans to end their isolation from the troubles in Europe, Greer Garson plays an indomitable English housewife who endures the hardships of World War II. Winner of best picture Oscar.

The Pride of the Yankees (Samuel Goldwyn; dir., Sam Wood) Gary Cooper plays Lou Gehrig in an emotional biopic about a brilliant baseball career that ends prematurely, because of amytropic lateral sclerosis, with a farewell speech at Yankee Stadium.

Road to Morocco (Paramount; dir., David Butler) The third of the Bing Crosby*-Bob Hope* road comedies, this one spoofs the Arabian Nights in a tale of two smart alecks sold into slavery to a beautiful Arabian princess played by Dorothy Lamour, who appeared in most of the road films.

To Be or Not to Be (United Artists; dir., Ernst Lubitsch) A Shakespearean troupe in Warsaw, Poland, at the time of the German invasion provides the occasion for a brilliant dark comedy about the overlap of life and art. In her final screen role, Carole Lombard* plays the principal female actor in the company, while Jack Benny portrays her husband and the company's leader, a vain thespian who finds himself giving the performance of his life impersonating a high Nazi official.

YANKEE DOODLE DANDY (Warner Bros.; dir., Michael Curtiz) Vibrant musical biopic, filmed in the aftermath of Pearl Harbor and infused with patriotic fervor. James Cagney earned an Oscar for his energetic rendition of vaudeville star and impresario George M. Cohan.

1943

Cabin in the Sky (MGM; dir., Vincente Minnelli) Musical variation on the Faust theme that is notable for its entirely African American cast, which features Ethel Waters, Eddie Armstrong, Lena Horne*, Louis Armstrong, and Duke Ellington*.

For Whom the Bell Tolls (Paramount; dir., Sam Wood) The top box-office hit of 1943, this Hollywood version of the Ernest Hemingway novel set during the Spanish Civil War stars Gary Cooper and Ingrid Bergman. Though the film earned Katina Paxinou an Oscar for best supporting actress, Hemingway despised what it did to his novel.

Heaven Can Wait (Twentieth Century-Fox; dir., Ernst Lubitsch) Deft comedy in which Don Ameche, awaiting entry into hell, recounts to Satan his dissolute life in late nineteenth century New York.

Knute Rockne: All American (Warner Bros., dir. Lloyd Bacon) Now-classic biopic about the legendary University of Notre Dame football coach Knute Rockne, played by Pat O'Brien. The film is most remembered for future president Ronald Reagan's performance as George Gipp, the dying player who, according to legend, asked Rockne to tell his team to "win just one for the Gipper."

The Ox-Bow Incident (Twentieth Century-Fox; dir., William A. Wellman) Morally challenging Western based on a novel by Walter van Tilburg Clark, in which a posse impulsively lynches three men for a crime they did not commit.

Shadow of a Doubt (Skirball; dir., Alfred Hitchcock*) In this dark thriller, Teresa Wright invites her Uncle Charlie (Joseph Cotten) to visit her and her wholesome family in a small Northern California town, unaware that her charming uncle is a serial killer.

The Song of Bernadette (Twentieth Century-Fox; dir., Henry King) Reverential biopic about a nineteenth century French peasant girl who had a vision of the Virgin Mary at Lourdes, France. The film transformed Jennifer Jones, who won an Oscar for her performance as Bernadette, into a star.

Stormy Weather (Twentieth Century-Fox; dir., Andrew L. Stone) Loosely based on the life of Bill "Bojangles" Robinson, who makes an appearance, this spirited musical features memorable performances by an all-black cast, including Lena Horne*, Dooley Wilson (who also was the pianist in *Casablanca*), Cab Calloway, Katherine Dunham, Fats Waller, and the Nicholas Brothers.

Watch on the Rhine (Warner Bros; dir., Herman Shumlin) Paul Lukas received an Oscar for his performance as an antifascist German who, after seeking refuge in Washington, D.C., is pursued by Nazi agents. Based on a play by Lillian Hellman, this film was adapted for the screen by Hellman and Dashiell Hammett.

1944

Arsenic and Old Lace (Warner Bros.; dir., Frank Capra*) Dark comedy in which Cary Grant discovers that his two batty maiden aunts have been murdering lonely old men with poisoned elderberry wine and having them buried in their basement.

DOUBLE INDEMNITY (Paramount; dir., Billy Wilder) Based on a novel by James M. Cain, this is a classic film noir in which Fred MacMurray schemes with Barbara Stanwyck to collect her husband's insurance money by murdering him.

Gaslight (MGM; dir., George Cukor) Dark psychological thriller that earned Ingrid Bergman an Oscar for her performance as a woman whose cunning, homicidal husband (Charles Boyer) manipulates her into believing she is mad.

Going My Way (Paramount; dir., Leo McCarey) The highest-grossing film of 1944 and the winner of seven Academy Awards, including best picture, this film is a sentimental musical comedy about a young priest (Bing Crosby*) assigned to an impoverished New York parish who ends up charming the old pastor (Barry Fitzgerald) he has come to replace.

Hail the Conquering Hero (Paramount; dir., Preston Sturges) Mordant satire in which Eddie Bracken plays a man who, after being rejected for military service, is mistaken for a war hero by citizens of his home town.

LAURA (Twentieth Century-Fox; dir., Otto Preminger) Sophisticated murder mystery in which New York police detective Dana Andrews becomes suspicious of whether a beautiful advertising executive, Gene Tierney, has in fact, been murdered.

Lifeboat (Twentieth Century-Fox; dir., Alfred Hitchcock*) Set entirely within the claustrophobic confines of a lifeboat after a German U-boat and a passenger ship sink each other, this is a tense study in group dynamics that defied cinema's propensity toward expansiveness. The cast includes Tallulah Bankhead, William Bendix, Hume Cronyn, Canada Lee, and Walter Slezak as the only survivor of the U-boat whose strong personality puts him in command of the lifeboat.

MEET ME IN ST. LOUIS (MGM; dir., Vincente Minnelli) Nostalgic musical, starring Judy Garland* and Margaret O'Brien, focused on an affectionate midwestern family at the time of the world's fair of 1904 in St. Louis.

The Miracle of Morgan's Creek (Paramount; dir., Preston Sturges) A series of misfortunes besets Eddie Bracken when he tries to help Betty Hutton, who finds herself pregnant after a wild farewell party for a group of soldiers. An audacious screwball comedy that makes a mockery of hallowed American institutions including motherhood and politics.

National Velvet (MGM; dir., Clarence Brown) Elizabeth Taylor plays a twelve-year-old who saves a horse from slaughter and trains it for the Grand National steeplechase with the help of a jockey played by Mickey Rooney. Ann Revere received a best supporting actress Oscar for playing her mother.

None but the Lonely Heart (RKO; dir., Clifford Odets) Cary Grant plays a Cockney drifter who finds meaning in his life when he returns home to his dying mother. Ethel Barrymore received a best supporting actress Oscar for her performance as the mother.

To Have and Have Not (Warner Bros.; dir., Howard Hawks) Humphrey Bogart* plays an American charter boat captain in Martinique who gets involved with a beautiful pickpocket (Lauren Bacall) and helps Free French forces struggle against Nazi control of the Caribbean island.

Wilson (Twentieth Century-Fox; dir., Henry King) Alexander Knox plays the title role in this biographical film about the rise and fall of Woodrow Wilson, the twenty-eighth president of the United States. Although it won five Oscars and was nominated for five others, including best picture, it was a box-office dud.

1945

Anchors Aweigh (MGM; dir., George Sidney) Gene Kelly* and Frank Sinatra* play sailors on four-day leave in Los Angeles who befriend a young singer, Kathryn Grayson, and help her get an audition in Hollywood. The film is famous for a sequence in which Kelly dances with an animated mouse.

The Lost Weekend (Paramount; dir., Billy Wilder) Winner of Academy Awards for best picture, best director, and best actor for Ray Milland, for his devastating performance as an alcoholic on a four-day binge.

Mildred Pierce (Warner Bros.; dir., Michael Curtiz) Joan Crawford won an Oscar in the title role, a resolute woman who finds wealth in restaurant ownership but heartbreak in an ungrateful daughter (Ann Blyth).

THEY WERE EXPENDABLE (MGM; dir. John Ford) Dramatized recreation of the struggles of Navy PT boat crews during the early years of World War II. Drawing on the Navy experiences of director Ford, the film is regarded as one of the best combat films made during World War II. Robert Montgomery and John Wayne play torpedo boat officers anxious to avenge Japan's attack on Pearl Harbor.

A Tree Grows in Brooklyn (Twentieth Century-Fox; dir., Elia Kazan) A girl played by Peggy Ann Garner comes of age within an Irish family living in a Brooklyn tenement at the turn of the twentieth century. James Dunn won an Oscar for his performance as her alcoholic father.

1946

THE BEST YEARS OF OUR LIVES (Goldwyn-RKO; dir., William Wyler) Wrenching melodrama about the challenges of readjusting to civilian life, this film tells the intersecting stories of a soldier (Fredric March), a sailor (Harold Russell—a real veteran who lost both hands in the war), and an airman (Dana Andrews) who return from World War II to resume their lives in the same small town. Winner of best picture Oscar.

The Big Sleep (Warner Bros.; dir., Howard Hawks) Humphrey Bogart* plays Raymond Chandler's hard-boiled detective Philip Marlowe confronting a series of mysteries as well as the allure of Lauren Bacall.

IT'S A WONDERFUL LIFE (Liberty; dir., Frank Capra*) Sentimental favorite in which, during the Christmas season, suicidal businessman James Stewart* is cured of his despondency when an angel convinces him of how impoverished the world would have become without him.

The Killers (Universal; dir., Robert Siodmak) Tense melodrama about a contract killing, based on a short story by Ernest Hemingway. Burt Lancaster, in his screen debut, plays the gangster who is the target, and Edmund O'Brien sets out to solve what proves to be an unexpectedly complex case.

My Darling Clementine (Twentieth Century-Fox; dir., John Ford*) Quintessential Western, in which Henry Fonda's Wyatt Earp teams up with his brothers to clean up Tombstone by taking on the Clantons in the famous gunfight at the O.K. Corral.

Notorious (Vanguard Films; Alfred Hitchcock*) In a Hitchcock favorite, duty collides with passion when the daughter of a convicted German spy, Ingrid Bergman, is recruited by U.S. government agent Cary Grant to spy on her father's Nazi friends in Rio de Janeiro.

The Razor's Edge (Twentieth Century-Fox; dir., Edmund Goulding) An adaptation of a novel by W. Somerset Maugham, this film follows the efforts of a wealthy young man, played by Tyrone Power, to find himself and truth during the years between World War I and World War II.

Song of the South (Walt Disney; dir., Harve Foster and Wilfred Jackson) a Disney feature combining live action with animation, this film dramatizes the folksy Uncle Remus created by Joel Chandler Harris. Set in the Deep South following the Civil War, the film made the song "Zip-a-Dee-Doo-Dah" into a hit.

The Yearling (MGM; dir., Clarence Brown) Adapted from the beloved novel by Marjorie Kinnan Rawlings about a farm boy who adopts a stray deer in Florida after the Civil War. Gregory Peck plays the boy's father. The film received seven Oscar nominations and won for color cinematography and art direction.

1947

The Bachelor and the Bobby-Soxer (RKO; dir., Irving Reis) Screwball comedy in which a judge's impressionable young sister, played by a teenage Shirley Temple, develops a dangerous crush on a wayward artist, played by Cary Grant.

The Bishop's Wife (RKO; dir., Henry Koster) A debonair angel, played by Cary Grant, comes to Earth to assist a harried bishop (David Niven) in building a new cathedral but more particularly in dealing with his unhappy wife (Loretta Young).

Body and Soul (Enterprise; dir., Richard Rossen) Gritty and melodramatic account of how a young boxer, John Garfield, fights his way—in and out of the ring—to the top.

Crossfire (RKO Radio; dir., Edward Dmytryk) The first Hollywood film to take on American anti-Semitism, *Crossfire* is an expressionistic thriller in which three soldiers come under suspicion for the murder of a Jew in a hotel room in New York.

Duel in the Sun (David O. Selznick; dir., King Vidor

et al.) Lavishly produced Western, a spectacle of overwrought sensuality in which two brothers—Joseph Cotten and Gregory Peck—clash over the affections of a woman (Jennifer Jones), who is half-Indian.

The Egg and I (Universal; dir., Chester Erskine) Broadly aimed hit comedy about a young couple (Claudette Colbert and Fred MacMurray) who struggle as novice farmers. The film is best remembered for introducing Marjorie Main and Percy Kilbride as Ma and Pa Kettle—who became the central characters in a popular series of films.

The Farmer's Daughter (RKO; dir., H. C. Potter) Loretta Young won an Oscar for her portrayal of a congressman's Swedish maid who ends up outsmarting the political establishment and becoming a power in her own right.

GENTLEMAN'S AGREEMENT (Twentieth Century-Fox; dir., Elia Kazan) Like *Crossfire*, this film is a pioneering exposé of anti-Semitism in the United States. Gregory Peck plays a journalist who poses as a Jew in order to understand and write about bigotry. Winner of best picture Oscar.

The Lady from Shanghai (Columbia; dir., Orson Welles*) Elaborate noir thriller starring Welles and Rita Hayworth*. Its incoherence is due in part to the fact that Welles as director lost final control of the production. But moments of brilliance, including a shoot-out in a hall of mirrors, remain.

Lady in the Lake (MGM; dir., Robert Montgomery) Raymond Chandler murder mystery in which private eye Philip Marlowe (Montgomery) is hired to find a missing wife. What makes the film unusual is the fact that the camera is restricted solely to Marlowe's point of view.

MIRACLE ON 34TH STREET (Twentieth Century-Fox; dir., George Seaton) Classic Christmas fantasy, in which a department-store Santa Claus (Edmund Gwenn) convinces a young girl (Natalie Wood) that he is the real Santa.

Monsieur Verdoux (Charles Chaplin; dir., Chaplin) Black comedy written by Chaplin, drawing on an idea provided by Orson Welles. Chaplin plays a suave unemployed banker who marries and murders wealthy widows to support his wife and child. When he is eventually sentenced to be executed, he dismisses his murders as paltry crimes compared to the mass murders committed in wars.

The Secret Life of Walter Mitty (Samuel Goldwyn; dir. Norman Z. McLeod) Comedy adapted from a short story by James Thurber. Danny Kaye plays the title character, a feckless adventure-magazine editor whose daydreams lead to more trouble than he could have imagined.

1948

Abbott and Costello Meet Frankenstein (Universal; dir., Charles Barton) Horror spoof in which the comedy duo plays a couple of hapless railroad porters who mishandle crates containing the living bodies of three iconic horror film monsters—Dracula, the Wolf Man, and Frankenstein's monster.

Fort Apache (RKO; dir., John Ford*) Sympathetic portrayal of American Indians, in which Henry Fonda plays an arrogant, unpopular colonel who assumes command of a cavalry outpost in the Old West. John Wayne plays a veteran captain who insists on honorable treatment of the Indians but is ignored.

Johnny Belinda (Warner Bros.; dir., Jean Negulesco) Melodrama set in an insular community on remote Cape Breton Island. Jane Wyman received an Oscar for her portrayal of the young deaf woman who becomes pregnant through a rape that is blamed on a kindly doctor (Lew Ayres) who befriends her.

Key Largo (Warner Bros.; dir., John Huston) Brooding crime drama in which recently returned war veteran Humphrey Bogart* confronts a gangster played by Edward G. Robinson and wins the heart of Lauren Bacall.

Louisiana Story (Lopert Films; dir. Robert J. Flaherty) A Cajun boy with a pet raccoon watches drillers strike oil near his home in bayou country. A quasi documentary, the film is distinguished by the original music of Virgil Thomson.

The Naked City (Universal; dir., Jules Dassin) Crime thriller in which Barry Fitzgerald plays a police detective investigating the murder of a young model. Shot in black-and-white documentary style on the streets of New York, the film inspired a television series that ran from 1958 to 1963.

Red River (United Artists; dir., Howard Hawks) Epic Western set during the first cattle drive along the Chisholm Trail, from Texas to Kansas. Rancher John Wayne is the trail boss, and violent tensions develop between him and his adopted son, Montgomery Clift. In Peter Bogdanovich's 1971 film

The Last Picture Show, Red River is the film playing in the theater about to close down in a desolate Texas town.

Rope (Transatlantic; dir., Alfred Hitchcock*) Inspired by the notorious Nathan Leopold and Richard Loeb murder case of the 1920's and by the challenge of confining a feature film to one room and to ten-minute takes, this is the story of two privileged young men who attempt to conceal the fact that they have killed a friend merely for the thrill of it.

The Snake Pit (Twentieth Century-Fox; dir., Anatole Litvak) Grueling cinematic plea for sympathetic treatment of the mentally ill. After a nervous breakdown, Olivia de Havilland is institutionalized in a horrific asylum.

State of the Union (Liberty; dir., Frank Capra*) Witty political comedy about a candidate for president of the United States (Spencer Tracy) whose estranged wife (Katharine Hepburn) rejoins him for the campaign.

THE TREASURE OF THE SIERRA MADRE (Warner Bros.; dir., John Huston) Allegory based on a novel by B. Traven about greed and trust. The best-laid plans of three desperate men—Humphrey Bogart, Tim Holt, and Walter Huston—prospecting for gold in Mexico fall victim to mutual suspicions and violence. John Huston won Oscars for screenplay and direction, and his father won a best supporting actor award.

1949

Adam's Rib (MGM; dir., George Cukor) Romantic comedy in which Spencer Tracy and Katharine Hepburn play fast-talking lawyers who are married to each other but work on opposing sides of a murder case.

ALL THE KING'S MEN (Columbia; dir., Robert Rossen) This first adaptation of Robert Penn Warren's political novel received an Academy Award for best picture, and Broderick Crawford received a best actor Oscar for his performance as Willie Stark, an ambitious southern demagogue with a strong resemblance to Louisiana's Huey Long.

The Heiress (Paramount; dir., William Wyler) Film based on Henry James's 1880 novel *Washington Square*. Olivia de Havilland received an Oscar for her performance as a wealthy woman who eventually wreaks revenge on the cad (Montgomery Clift) who jilts her.

A Letter to Three Wives (Twentieth Century-Fox; dir., Joseph L. Mankiewicz) The film that elevated the status of Mankiewicz, who won Oscars for both direction and screenplay, as auteur, it is a compilation of three stories that are framed by a letter a woman sends to three friends (Linda Darnell, Ann Sothern, and Jeanne Crain), informing each that she has run off with her husband.

Little Women (MGM; dir., Mervyn LeRoy) Elizabeth Taylor, June Allyson, and Janet Leigh star in an adaptation of the classic Louisa May Alcott novel about the hardships and triumphs of a New England family in the middle of the nineteenth century.

On the Town (MGM; dir., Stanley Donen and Gene Kelly) Gene Kelly*, Frank Sinatra*, and Jules Munshin play sailors singing, dancing, and romancing during their twenty-four-hour leave in New York. Includes an exuberant musical score by Leonard Bernstein.

She Wore a Yellow Ribbon (RKO; dir., John Ford*) The second installment in Ford's trilogy of films about the U.S. cavalry, this is a visually splendid Western in which John Wayne plays a mounted officer who embarks on a final patrol before retirement.

Twelve O'Clock High (Twentieth Century-Fox; dir., Henry King) Absorbing drama, starring Gregory Peck, Hugh Marlowe, and Gary Merrill, about an American bombing crew during World War II.

White Heat (Warner Bros; dir., Raoul Walsh) In one of the most celebrated gangster films, James Cagney provides a signature performance as a violently deranged criminal who eventually gets his comeuppance.

Steven G. Kellman

■ Entertainment: Major Radio Programs

The following is a compilation of the top radio shows and radio personalities of the 1940's. Programs and personages marked with asterisks (*) are subjects of full-length essays within *The Forties in America*.

The Adventures of Ozzie and Harriet
Date: 1944-1954
Networks: 1944-1948, CBS; 1948-1949, NBC; 1949, CBS; 1949-1954, ABC

Ozzie Nelson, a bandleader, and his wife Harriet, a singer, performed on *The Red Skelton Show*, creating their own situation comedy when Skelton was drafted. Nelson portrayed a man who would take sometimes wrongheaded ideas to ridiculous lengths, and Harriet played the wife who gently controlled him. After 1949, their real sons David and future rock-star Ricky played themselves. During the 1950's, the show moved to a long and successful run on television.

The Adventures of Superman
Date: 1940-1951
Networks: 1940-1942, local; 1942-1949, Mutual; 1949-1951, ABC

Based on a comic-book character created in 1938, radio's Superman fought crime and World War II enemies, sometimes assisted by Batman and Robin. Until 1946, the identity of Superman (played by Clayton "Bud" Collyer) was concealed; he then openly campaigned against racial and religious intolerance, making the series the first to deal with such problems.

The Aldrich Family
Date: 1939-1953
Networks: 1939-1944, NBC; 1944-1946, CBS; 1946-1953, NBC

Henry Aldrich, usually played by Ezra Stone, was heard on *The Rudy Vallee Show* and *The Kate Smith Show* until audience reaction helped him gain his own weekly series. A small-town high school student, Aldrich could create chaos from any everyday situation, including inept encounters with girls.

Fred Allen
Date: 1932-1949
Networks: 1932-33, CBS; 1934-1940, NBC; 1940-1944, CBS; 1945-1949, NBC

Allen was a favorite with critics and fellow comedians. His strengths were verbal wit and political commentary; he was often censored for ridiculing corporate radio executives and sponsors. By 1942, he had developed his most successful format, a half-hour show featuring "Allen's Alley," in which he and his wife, Portland Hoffa, solicited opinions on current matters from characters who, at various times, included a pompous poet and fanatical Southern senator. The show bore several titles, including *Town Hall Tonight* and *Texaco Star Theater.*

America's Town Meeting of the Air
Date: 1935-1956
Networks: 1935-1942, NBC; 1943-1945, Blue/ABC; 1945-1956, ABC

Guest panelists discussed controversial topics of national interest from questions asked by studio audience members, who were allowed to heckle speakers; arguments among panelists also became heated. Across the country, more than one thousand local clubs were formed to continue debate.

Amos 'n' Andy*
Date: 1926-1958
Networks: 1926-1927, WGN, Chicago; 1928-1929, WMAQ, Chicago; 1929-1939, NBC; 1939-1943, CBS; 1943-1948, NBC; 1948-1960, CBS

First broadcast as *Sam 'n' Henry*, this show became *Amos 'n' Andy* in 1928, and quickly grew into the most popular radio show in the United States. White actors Freeman Gosden and Charles Correll played African American Amos Jones, Andrew H. Brown, and George "Kingfish" Stevens, originally writing their own material and playing all voices. In 1943, with falling ratings, the team revived the show's popularity with added staff, including African American and white actors. In 1954, the show was reorganized as *The Amos 'n' Andy Music Hall* with a disc-jockey format and guests.

Jack Benny*
Date: 1932-1958
Networks: 1932, NBC; 1932-33, CBS; 1933-1948, NBC; 1949-1958, CBS

Benny, whose show became a Sunday night institution, played an insensitive, jealous, but still loveable miser, who was the target of jokes by radio's strongest supporting cast: Eddie "Rochester" Anderson, Mary Livingstone, Phil Harris, Dennis Day, Frank Nelson, and Mel Blanc. The show was broadcast from many military bases during World War II and used various titles, including *The Jell-O Program* and *The Lucky Strike Program.*

Edgar Bergen and Charlie McCarthy
Date: 1937-1956
Networks: 1937-1948, NBC; 1949-1956, CBS
Ventriloquist Edgar Bergen played stern father to his dummy, Charlie McCarthy, a teenager, precociously clad in monocle and top hat, who engaged in fantasies of wealth and romance despite Bergen's nagging. Mortimer Snerd, a second dummy introduced in 1938, was a country bumpkin, whose denseness contrasted with McCarthy's subversive impudence. The show aired under several titles, including *The Chase and Sanborn Hour* and *The Edgar Bergen/Charlie McCarthy Show.*

George Burns and Gracie Allen
Date: 1929-1950
Networks: 1932-1937, CBS; 1937-1938, NBC; 1938-1940, CBS; 1940-1942, NBC; 1942-1945, CBS; 1945-1949, NBC; 1949-1950, CBS
These married former vaudeville players first appeared on radio in London in 1929 for the British Broadcast Corporation; acting on other shows before forming their own, on which Burns played stooge for the comedy created by Allen's skewed logic. By 1933, Allen was among the most famous women in the United States. The couple relied on vaudeville material until 1942, when they achieved greater success as a married couple. The program aired under several titles including *The Burns and Allen Show* and *Maxwell House Coffee Times.*

Eddie Cantor
Date: 1931-1953
Networks: 1931-1934, NBC; 1935-1939, CBS; 1940-1953, NBC
Cantor was the first major vaudeville star to succeed on radio. His energetic comedy and songs were supported by such vocalists as Dinah Shore and Thelma Carpenter, who was among the first African Americans to be hired for permanent positions on a top-ranked variety show. Cantor inadvertently drew attention to radio censorship in 1939 when, in off-air

speeches, he openly denounced Adolf Hitler's anti-Semitism and specific American anti-Semites. He briefly lost his sponsors and his show. Titles of his show included *The Chase and Sanborn Hour* and *Time to Smile.*

Captain Midnight
Date: 1939-1949
Networks: 1939-1942, Mutual; 1942-1943, NBC; 1943-1945, Blue/ABC; 1945-1949, Mutual
First run regionally, this program became a favorite children's show. Its hero flew a single-engine plane around world to thwart crime and enemy spies. Ovaltine, the sponsor, successfully marketed premiums such as badges and decoders to children who sent in a coin and proof of purchase.

Cavalcade of America
Date: 1935-1953
Networks: 1935-1939, CBS; 1940-1953, NBC
This show dramatized real but little-known episodes from American history and starred such guests as actor Clark Gable. Regarded as radio's best researched historical show, it gained heightened popularity during World War II when wartime events were dramatized.

Command Performance
Date: 1942-1949
Networks: 1942, Special Services Division of the War Department; 1943-49, Armed Forces Radio Service (AFRS); 1945-1946, CBS spin-off *Request Performances*
Produced for servicemen and women overseas, performances, production, and facilities were donated without charge and scheduled in response to mailed-in requests. Stars eagerly donated their time. One 1945 sketch starred Bing Crosby, Dinah Shore, Frank Sinatra, Bob Hope, Judy Garland, and Jimmy Durante.

Bing Crosby*
Date: 1930-1956
Networks: 1931-1935, CBS; 1936-1946, NBC; 1946-1949, ABC; 1949-1956, CBS
Early twentieth century's most important singing star, Crosby sang on various shows, including *The Bing Crosby-Woodbury Show* and *Bing Crosby-Philco Radio Time.* In 1936, Crosby replaced famed vaudeville singer Al Jolson as host of *The Kraft Music Hall.* This

marked Crosby's greatest radio success, but the network refused to allow him to prerecord his shows, and Crosby returned to his own shows. He frequently broadcast to military audiences.

Dr. I.Q.
Date: 1939-1950
Networks: 1939-1949, NBC; 1950, ABC
The most important early quiz show, *Dr. I.Q.* involved studio audiences in major cities where the traveling show broadcast from movie theaters. Announcers solicited contestants from studio audiences. When Dr. I.Q. posed questions, contestants who correctly answered within ten seconds received prizes.

Duffy's Tavern
Date: 1940-1952
Networks: 1940-1942, CBS; 1942-1944, Blue/ABC; 1944-1952, NBC
Ed Garner portrayed Archie, manager of a Manhattan tavern catering to Irish working-class patrons. Comedy arose from Archie's attempts to impress the tavern's famous guests, such as music critic Deems Taylor, and his clumsy approaches to glamorous Hollywood stars, such as Joan Bennett.

Fibber McGee and Molly
Date: 1935-1959
Network: 1935-1959, NBC
Fibber and Molly were played by married couple Marian and Jim Jordan, earlier heard in less successful radio programs. Rivaling Bob Hope's and Jack Benny's programs in popularity, the show, usually set in the couple's 79 Wistful Vista living room, generated one of radio's most famous sound effects: the sound of objects, crammed into a hall closet, cascading noisily to the floor whenever someone opened the door. Fibber was a dreamer and prevaricator; Molly was tolerant and, usually, long suffering. Situations were triggered by a series of regular guests, including Throckmorton P. Gildersleeve, who became the star of one of radio's early spin-off programs.

Gang Busters
Date: 1935-1957
Networks: 1935, NBC; 1936-1940, CBS; 1940-1942, NBC; 1943-1945, Blue/ABC; 1945-1948, ABC; 1949-1955, CBS; 1955-1957, Mutual
Originally aired as *G-Men* and loosely based on Federal Bureau of Investigation (FBI) files, *Gang Busters* reportedly offended FBI director J. Edgar Hoover with its insistence on violence instead of routine police work. The show became *Gang Busters*, based on local police files, and was best known for its sound effects—breaking glass, sirens, and submachine guns. Each show ended with an alert for a wanted criminal.

Arthur Godfrey*
Date: 1930-1955
Networks: 1930-1933, NBC; 1934-1955, CBS
First heard as a CBS staff announcer and on a number of programs, Godfrey attracted his own audience with his early morning *Arthur Godfrey's Sundial Show*, on which he read news and interviewed guests. He achieved unprecedented popularity with his daily morning variety show, *Arthur Godfrey Time*; his evening *Arthur Godfrey's Talent Scouts*, with acts judged by the studio audience; and *The Arthur Godfrey Digest* or *Arthur Godfrey's Round Table*, both of which aired taped highlights.

Grand Ole Opry
Date: 1925-
Networks: 1925-1939, WSM, Nashville; 1939-1956, NBC; 1956-   , WSM, Nashville.
The most famous of the country western shows, *Grand Ole Opry* began with the music of "Uncle" Jimmy Thompson, champion fiddle player and Civil War veteran. By the 1940's, the show was restricted to the brightest stars of country music, including Roy Acuff, Gene Autry, Patsy Cline, and Hank Williams. By 2010, it was the longest-running show in radio history.

The Great Gildersleeve
Date: 1941-1957
Network: NBC
No longer a guest on *Fibber McGee and Molly*, Throckmorton P. Gildersleeve became water commissioner of a neighboring town. The romantic, but frequently frustrated, middle-aged bachelor was guardian of orphaned niece and nephew, Marjorie and Leroy Forrester, the latter a subversive twelve-year-old.

The Green Hornet
Date: 1936-1953
Networks: 1936-1938, WXYZ, Detroit; 1938-1940, Mutual; 1940-1943, NBC; 1943-1945, Blue/ABC; 1945-1950, ABC; 1950-1953, Mutual
Developed for children by the creators of *The Lone*

Ranger, this series featured the Lone Ranger's grand-nephew, Britt Reid, who fought urban crime and corruption; the Lone Ranger's horse was replaced by a car, Black Beauty; and Tonto was replaced by an educated Asian sidekick named Kato.

The Guiding Light
Date: 1937-1956
Networks: 1937-1946, NBC; 1947-1956, CBS
When the televised version was canceled in 2009, this show was the longest-running American soap opera. Until the late 1940's, focus was on a clergyman who headed the impoverished Church of the Good Samaritan; during the 1940's, focus changed several times, eventually centering on the Bauer family.

Bob Hope*
Date: 1933-1955
Networks: 1935, NBC; 1935-36, CBS; 1937-1955, NBC
Hope's rapid-fire, topical radio comedy aired under many titles, most notably the *Pepsodent Show Starring Bob Hope.* Hope was backed by comedian Jerry Colona and such singers as Judy Garland and Frances Langford. He often broadcast from military bases, beginning five decades of entertaining troops.

I Love a Mystery
Date: 1939-1944, 1949-1952
Networks: 1939-1942, NBC; 1943-1944, CBS; 1949-1952, Mutual
Designed for young people, this show featured agents from Los Angeles's A-1 Detective Agency, who actually were rebellious soldiers of fortune traveling the world in search of adventure in such pulp-magazine-style adventures as "Temple of Vampires" and "The Thing That Cries in the Night."

Information Please
Date: 1938-1948
Networks: 1938-1945, NBC; 1946-1947, CBS; 1947-1948, Mutual
In this quiz show designed for the intelligentsia, questions were primarily excuses for witty conversation among panelists, who included sports, Latin, and Shakespeare expert John Kieran, sardonic concert pianist Oscar Levant, and various guests.

Inner Sanctum Mysteries
Date: 1941-1952
Networks: 1941-1943, NBC; 1943-1950, CBS; 1950-1951, ABC; 1952, CBS
Among the most successful horror shows, this program began each broadcast with the sound of a squeaking door. Film stars Boris Karloff and Peter Lorre frequently appeared in eerie tales, including many adapted from Edgar Allan Poe stories.

Jack Armstrong, The All American Boy
Date: 1933-1951
Networks: 1933-1936, CBS; 1936-1941, NBC; 1941-1942, Mutual; 1942-1943, NBC; 1943-1945, Blue/ABC; 1945-1951, ABC
In a show designed for young people, high school student Jack Armstrong, with Uncle Jim Fairfield and friends, traveled worldwide to right wrongs, catch spies, and thwart criminals.

Let's Pretend
Date: 1929-1954
Network: CBS
Prize-winning children's show, whose creator, Nila Mack, believed that children's stories should be told by children. Auditions were open to all children; those chosen might graduate from small to large parts. Mack emphasized dramatizations of classic children's stories and fairy tales.

The Lone Ranger
Date: 1933-1956
Networks: 1933, WXYZ, Detroit; 1933-1942, Mutual; 1942-1945, Blue/ABC; 1945-1956, ABC
A former Texas Ranger, John Reid was the only survivor of a massacre who changed his identity and dedicated his life to fighting crime, helped by his Native American friend, Tonto. Mounted on his horse Silver and, accompanied by Tonto, the Lone Ranger became radio's best-known Western hero.

Lum and Abner
Date: 1931-1950, 1953
Networks: 1931, KTHS, Hot Springs, Arkansas; 1931-1934, NBC; 1934-1935, Mutual; 1935-1938, NBC; 1938-1940, CBS; 1941-1943, NBC; 1943-1945, Blue/ABC; 1945-1947, ABC; 1947-1950, CBS; 1953, ABC
In this program, Chester Lauck and Norris Goff played owners of the Jot 'em Down Store in Pine

Ridge, Arkansas. The town was originally fictitious, but the show was so popular that the real-life town of Waters, Arkansas, changed its name to Pine Ridge. Comedy arose from situations, not from mocking "hillbillies." Columbus "Lum" Edwards (played by Lauck) and Abner Peabody (Goff) enjoyed simple pleasures around their potbellied stove in a store stocked with everything from buggywhips to lye soap.

Lux Radio Theater
Date: 1934-1955
Networks: 1934-1935, NBC; 1935-1954, CBS; 1954-1955, NBC
Hosted by famed film director Cecil B. DeMille from 1935 to 1945, this show publicized Hollywood films, airing abridged adaptations, often with the stars of the original films. The thousand-seat Los Angeles Music Box Theater filled each week; audiences wanted to see such stars as Clark Gable and Edward G. Robinson.

Ma Perkins
Date: 1933-1960
Networks: 1933, WLW, Cincinnati, Ohio; 1933-1949, NBC; 1942-1960, CBS
This was among the longest running of many, usually fifteen-minute, daytime soap operas created by Frank and Anne Hummert and their staff of writers. Ma Perkins, a widow, owned a lumberyard but took time to solve the problems of others, as did the barber hero of *Just Plain Bill* (1932-1955), another Hummert melodrama. Others dramas included *Our Gal Sunday* (1937-1959), *The Romance of Helen Trent* (1933-1960), *Stella Dallas* (1937-1955), *Lorenzo Jones* (1937-1955), and *Young Widder Brown* (1938-1956). The Hummerts also produced such prime-time shows as *Mr. Keen, Tracer of Lost Persons* (1937-1955) and *Manhattan Merry-Go-Round* (1932-1949), a fantasy nightclub tour.

One Man's Family
Date: 1933-1959
Network: NBC
Listeners followed the passing generations of Henry and Fanny Barbour's prosperous San Francisco family for twenty-seven years. The show's subjects were melodramatic, but the show was aired in prime-time and was one of only two soap operas to receive radio's prestigious Peabody Award. The other was *Against the Storm* (1939-1942, 1949, 1951-1952).

Queen for a Day
Date: 1945-1957
Network: Mutual
Each episode of *Queen for a Day* allowed several women chosen from studio audiences to compete by telling their moving or heartbreaking experiences. For example, one woman described the difficulties of raising fifteen children as a single mother. The studio audiences then selected a winner, who collected cash and valuable gifts. Like many popular radio programs of the 1940's, the show moved on to television during the 1950's.

The Quiz Kids
Date: 1940-1953
Networks: 1940-1943, NBC; 1943-1945, Blue/ABC; 1946-1951, NBC; 1952-1953, CBS
A panel of five intelligent and poised young people under sixteen answered questions that would baffle most educated adults. The three children with the highest scores were carried over to the following week, with new applicants filling the vacant seats. By late 1948, local competitions were held in thirty-five cities, and lasting panelists became celebrities.

The Shadow
Date: 1930-1954
Networks: 1930-1932, CBS; 1932-1933, NBC; 1934-1935, CBS, 1937-1954, Mutual
After airing under such titles as *The Detective Story Hour* and *The Blue Coal Radio Review*, this show was retitled *The Shadow* in 1932. Lamont Cranston was a character who learned how to make himself seem invisible and used his knowledge to track down criminals. Frank Readick, Jr., among several actors to play the Shadow, made the character famous with his sinister laugh; Orson Welles, however, was the most famous Shadow.

Sherlock Holmes
Date: 1930-1936, 1939-1950, 1955-1956
Networks: 1930-1935, NBC; 1936, Mutual; 1939-1942, NBC; 1943-1946, Mutual; 1946-1947, ABC; 1947-1949, Mutual; 1949-1950, ABC; 1955-1956, NBC
Based on Sir Arthur Conan Doyle's famous detective tales, this show featured its most celebrated cast during the 1940's, with Basil Rathbone as Holmes and Nigel Bruce as Dr. Watson in dramatizations of Doyle's work, such as *The Hound of the Baskervilles,*

and original scripts, such as "The Giant Rat of Sumatra."

Frank Sinatra*
Date: 1942-1947, 1949-1951, 1953-1955
Networks: 1942-1947, CBS; 1949-1950 NBC; 1950-1951, CBS; 1953-1955, NBC
Long before having his own regular radio shows, Sinatra broadcast his music from a New Jersey nightclub, where he attracted the attention of bandleader Harry James and, later, Tommy Dorsey, becoming a favorite of wartime teenagers. His greatest radio fame came when he starred on *Your Hit Parade* (1943-1945), which broadcast the top-ten songs of the week, but his other shows included *Songs by Sinatra, Light-Up Time*, and *Meet Frank Sinatra.*

Red Skelton
Date: 1939, 1941-1944, 1945-1949, 1951-53
Networks: 1939, NBC; 1941-1949, NBC; 1949-1952, CBS; 1952-1953, NBC
After making many guest appearances on shows during the late 1930's, Skelton became a regular on *The Raleigh Cigarette Program* and *The Red Skelton Show.* He specialized in portraying comic characters such as Junior, the Mean Widdle Kid; Clem Kadiddlehopper; Willy Lump-Lump; and J. Newton Numbskull.

Kate Smith
Date: 1931-1952, 1958
Networks: 1931, NBC; 1931-1947, CBS; 1947-1951, Mutual, ABC; 1951-1952, NBC; 1948, Mutual
Often listed as among the most influential American women of her time, Kate Smith starred on both song and talk shows. She introduced Irving Berlin's song "God Bless America" in 1938. Her identification with this song and unquestioned patriotism helped her raise more than $600 million in war-bond sales during World War II. Her shows' many titles included *Kate Smith Sings, Speaking Her Mind*, and *Kate Smith Speaks.* Smith and Jack Benny held the only radio contracts that could not be canceled except by war.

Suspense
Date: 1942-1962
Network: CBS
Among the most popular mystery shows, *Suspense* was known for off-beat casting. For example, singer Frank Sinatra portrayed a psychopath in one epi-

sode, singer Lena Horne appeared in a spy story, and comedian Lucille Ball was menaced by a killer. The best-known 1940's episode, however, was the frequently repeated 1943 show "Sorry, Wrong Number," starring Agnes Moorehead as a physically disabled woman who slowly learned through a bad telephone connection that she was about to be murdered.

Tom Mix Ralston Straight Shooters
Date: 1933-1942, 1944-1951
Networks: 1933-1942, NBC; 1944-1951, Mutual
Tom Mix, who did not act on the program, was a silent film actor. Unlike most Western stars, Mix had been a real cowboy and rodeo champion. The show was set around the Texas TM-Bar ranch, where a fictional Mix lived with his two young wards. Although intended for children, the show was known for unusually realistic depictions of pain and hardship.

Truth or Consequences
Date: 1940-1956
Networks: 1940, CBS; 1940-1950, NBC; 1950-1951, CBS; 1952-1956, NBC
Hosted by Ralph Edwards, this first stunt show demanded that members of the studio audience correctly answer listeners' mailed-in questions or pay the consequences. Consequences could include washing an elephant or howling like dogs. Elaborate stunts could last for weeks.

Johnny Wayne and Frank Shuster
Date: 1941, 1946-1955
Network: CBC
Beginning with radio's *Buckingham Blended Rhythm Show* in 1941, comedians Wayne and Shuster became famous before enlisting in the Canadian army to entertain troops abroad. They returned to immense popularity on the *RCA Victor Show*, later the *Wayne and Shuster Show.*

We, the People
Date: 1936-1951
Networks: 1936-1937, NBC; 1937-1949, CBS; 1949-1951, NBC
Delving into unusual lives for inspirational stories, this show dealt with such figures as a woman who could recall her early life in slavery, a polio victim who yearned to escape her iron lung to dance, and the widow of gangster Dutch Schultz.

The Whistler
Date: 1942-1955
Network: CBS
With its famous whistled theme music, this show featured a storyteller who knew, and dramatized, human secrets, showing how everyday life could run out of control, driving men to murder. In early episodes, the Whistler sometimes argued with the culprit, playing his conscience.

Walter Winchell
Date: 1930-1957
Networks: 1930-1932, CBS; 1932-1943, NBC; 1943-1945, Blue/ABC; 1949-1955, ABC; 1955-1957, Mutual
For many years, New York newspaperman Winchell was radio's most powerful gossip reporter. His staccato style and slang attracted listeners. His achievement was emulated by Hollywood columnists Louella Parsons, a voice of the powerful William Randolph Hearst newspaper chain, and Hedda Hopper, who was praised by FBI Director J. Edgar Hoover. Parsons and Hopper broadcast irregularly between the 1930's and the 1950's. All three used their power to make or break careers and influence political opinion.

You Are There
Date: 1947-1950
Network: CBS
Originally titled *CBS Is There*, this show pretended to transport entire newsrooms each week to present important events in world history, such as the assassination of President Abraham Lincoln, as if the newsmen were witnessing those events.

Betty Richardson

■ Legislation: Major U.S. Legislation

Laws marked with asterisks (*) are covered in full essays within *The Forties in America.*

Year	Legislation	Significance
1940	Investment Advisors Act	Required individuals and companies engaged in advising about investments to register with the Securities and Exchange Commission and to adhere to regulations pertaining to same; prohibited contracts in which investment advisors would receive a share of a client's capital gains or capital appreciation.
1940	Investment Company Act	Imbued the Securities and Exchange Commission with the authority to regulate companies that engaged in investing, reinvesting, and trading in securities; required certain companies to disclose their financial condition and investment policies to investors.
1940	Public Law 76-647	Passed over President Franklin D. Roosevelt's veto, this law provided for the alteration of certain bridges over the navigable waters of the United States and for the sharing of expenses for such repairs between the bridge owners and the federal government.
1940	Reciprocal Trade Agreement Act	Renewed the Trade Agreements Act of 1937 for an additional three years.
1940	Revenue Act	Increased corporate tax to a maximum of 19 percent; increased gift, estate, and capital stock profits taxes by 10 percent; lowered exemptions for both single persons and married couples; added a 10-percent surcharge on incomes between $6,000 and $100,000.
1940	Second Revenue Act	Increased corporate tax to 24 percent on incomes more than $25,000; imposed an excess profits tax of between 25 to 50 percent.
1940	Selective Service Act	Instituted the first peacetime draft in U.S. history; all males between the ages of twenty and thirty-six were required to register; provided for 900,000 selectees to be taken each year; length of military service was for one year.
1940	Smith Act* (Alien Registration Act)	Made promoting forceful overthrow of the U.S. government unlawful, whether it was through teaching or organizing; required all foreign nationals to register and be fingerprinted.
1941	First War Powers Act	Granted the president the authority to create, consolidate, revise, or terminate certain executive branch offices, bureaus, agencies, commissions, and corporations.
1941	Lend-Lease Act	Furnished a means by which the United States could lend goods and munitions to democratic nations in return for services and goods; provided an initial appropriation of $7 billion.
1941	Revenue Act	While increasing corporate taxes, excise taxes, surcharges on individuals, and excess profits taxes, this law likewise reduced exemptions for those filing either single or joint returns. The second part amended the Selective Service Act of 1940 to extend term of military service from twelve to eighteen months.

Year	Legislation	Significance
1941	Selective Service Extension and Selective Service Act Amendments	Instituted the first peacetime draft in U.S. history, requiring all men between the ages of twenty and thirty-six to register; provided for 900,000 selectees to be taken each year for one-year terms of military service.
1942	Economic Stabilization Act	Created the Office of Economic Stabilization; gave the president the authority to stabilize farm and nonfarm prices as well as rents, salaries, and wages.
1942	Emergency Price Control Act*	Started the Office of Price Administration in order to prevent unreasonable increases in prices and rents, though agricultural products were exempted.
1942	Revenue Act	Raised rates of personal income, corporate income, estate, excise, and excess profits taxes while lessening exemptions for single and joint tax filers.
1942	Second War Powers Act	Authorized president to allocate facilities and materials for the defense of the United States; granted additional powers to several federal agencies; permitted soldiers free postage to send mail.
1942	Teenage Draft Act	Amended Selective Service Act of 1940 to make males eighteen or nineteen subject to the draft.
1942	Women Accepted for Voluntary Emergency Service Act	Created the Women Accepted for Voluntary Emergency Service (WAVES) as a unit within the Naval Reserves.
1942	Women's Army Auxiliary Corps Act	Established the Women's Army Auxiliary Corps (WAAC) for noncombatant service with the U.S. Army; Oveta Culp Hobby was chosen as the first WAAC director.
1943	Army and Navy Female Physicians and Surgeons Act	Permitted female physicians and surgeons within the medical departments of the Army and Navy; required that those appointed under this act be commissioned in U.S. Army and Naval Reserves and receive pay and benefits equal to members of the Officers' Reserve Corps within the latter services.
1943	Chinese Exclusion Repeal Act	Repealed the Chinese Exclusion Acts of 1882, 1884, 1888, 1892, 1893, and 1898.
1943	Current Tax Payment Act	Instituted a pay-as-you-go system of withholding taxes from individual paychecks; required employers to withhold 20 percent of wages and salaries beyond exemptions; strengthened income reporting requirements for individuals and corporations.
1943	Farm Labor Supply Act	Appropriated funds for the recruitment of workers in the area of food production and distribution; provided resources and benefits for said workers; exempted foreign nationals from North and South America who were working in the agricultural area from paying taxes required under a previous immigration law.
1943	Immigration Act* (Chinese Exclusion Repeal Act; Magnuson Act)	Repealed the 1882 Chinese Exclusion Act that had prevented Chinese nationals from immigrating to the United States and seeking naturalization.

Year	Legislation	Significance
1943	Public Health Service Act	Specified that the Federal Health Service would encompass the Office of the Surgeon General, National Institutes of Health, Bureau of Health Services, and Bureau of Medical Services; delegated authority to the surgeon general to assign functions to the latter offices and to take steps necessary for the efficiency of those entities.
1943	Smith-Connally Act	Permitted the president to take control of any industry producing materials for the war effort; prohibited strikes, lockouts, and other interruptions once the government assumed possession of an industry.
1943	Women's Army Corps Bill	Created Women's Army Corps and permitted enlistments of women between ages of twenty and fifty; this law repealed most of the Women's Army Auxiliary Corps Act of 1942.
1944	Revenue Act	Regarded as the first tax bill to become law over a president's veto, this legislation made minor adjustments to corporate, income, and excise taxes; repealed the victory tax; expanded depletion allowances in extractive industries.
1944	Servicemen's Readjustment Act (G.I. Bill*)	Otherwise known as the G.I. Bill, this act furnished veterans of World War II with a variety of benefits, including tuition and expenses for education, occupational guidance, preferences in hiring for many jobs, assistance in obtaining loans, unemployment benefits, and hospitalization benefits.
1944	Soldier Vote Act	Permitted absentee voting in time of war by members of U.S. land and naval forces; established the War Ballot Commission to administer the act; prohibited the commission from violating any state voting laws pertaining to the voters covered by the act.
1944	Surplus Property Act	Created a board to supervise the disposal of surplus government property through transfer or sale; assigned preferences in acquiring such property.
1944	Veterans' Preference Act	Granted preferences to honorably discharged veterans and their wives or widows for appointments to civilian positions within the national government.
1944	War Mobilization and Reconversion Act	Established the Office of War Mobilization and Reconversion to coordinate resolution of problems arising out of the transition from war to peace; granted authority to the director of the latter office to supervise the Surplus Property Act of 1944, among other acts.
1945	Bretton Woods Agreements Act	Authorized the United States to join the International Monetary Fund and the International Bank for Reconstruction and Development.
1945	McCarran-Ferguson Act	Permitted regulation and taxation of the insurance industry by both the national government and states; reasserted the pertinence of antitrust laws as they pertained to insurance companies.

Year	Legislation	Significance
1945	United Nations Participation Act	Pursuant to ratification of the treaty for U.S. membership in the United Nations, this law authorized the appointment of representatives of the United States in units of the latter organization.
1946	Administrative Procedures Act	Required federal agencies to give notice of proposed rules, to consider written comments on these proposals, and to publish final rules in the *Federal Register;* codified existing doctrines defining judicial review of administrative action; furnished judicial recourse to individuals claiming legal injury because of any agency action.
1946	Atomic Energy Act (McMahon Act)	Established the Atomic Energy Commission (AEC) and transferred control over all aspects of atomic energy from the War Department to the AEC; created a body with responsibility for oversight of the AEC.
1946	British Loan Act	Approved loans and grants to Great Britain in settlement of lend-lease, conditional on that nation's elimination of emergency foreign exchange controls and discriminatory import restrictions.
1946	Coordination Act	Required consultation with the Fish and Wildlife Service by public and private agencies using federal permits or licenses for water projects; necessitated that water projects include conservation procedures.
1946	Employment Act	Stated that it was the policy of the federal government to promote maximum employment, production, and purchasing power; established Council of Economic Advisors within executive branch to develop economic policy; created a Joint Economic Committee within Congress to study matters related to the president's economic report.
1946	Federal Airport Act	Authorized a multiyear program of matching federal grants to cities and states for construction of airports in the continental United States as well as in Alaska and Hawaii; specified that the War and Navy Departments along with the Civil Aeronautics Administration prepare a national plan for the development of public airports.
1946	Federal Regulation of Lobbying Act	Mandated registration of lobbyists with Congress; required filing of quarterly reports by organizations soliciting or receiving money for the purpose of lobbying Congress.
1946	Federal Tort Claims Act*	Allowed private parties to sue the federal government for a number of specified torts—harmful actions or injuries—committed by individuals acting on behalf of the government.
1946	Fulbright Scholars Act	Created an international educational and cultural exchange program for American citizens to attend schools or institutions of higher learning abroad and for citizens of other nations to attend U.S. educational institutions; amended the Surplus Property Act of 1944 to enable the secretary of state to enter into executive agreements with other nations for the purpose of using currencies acquired from sales of excess property for educational purposes.
1946	Hill-Burton Hospital Survey and Construction Act	Authorized a five-year program of federal grants to states for hospital construction based on state assessments of local needs.

Year	Legislation	Significance
1946	Indian Claims Commission Act	Created the Indian Claims Commission to adjudicate claims by Native American tribes of unfair treatment in land transactions with the federal government; required that judgments favorable to tribes result in compensatory monetary awards.
1946	Legislative Reorganization Act	Reduced the number of standing committees in both the U.S. House of Representatives and the Senate; provided funds for professional committee staffs; strengthened the Legislative Reference Service as a support agency of Congress; approved creation of an annual budget to complement the president's budget; raised salaries of members of Congress to $12,500.
1946	National School Lunch Act	Furnished federal cash grants to states for nonprofit school-lunch programs in public and private schools.
1947	Foreign Relief Act	Furnished $350 million in economic assistance to several nations adversely affected by World War II and the severe winter of 1946-1947.
1947	Greek-Turkish Aid Act	Authorized $400 million in economic and military aid to Greece and Turkey, subject to withdrawal if the United Nations or the U.S. president disapproved; the act became part of what was known as the Truman Doctrine, an effort to contain the spread of communism.
1947	National Security Act*	Replaced the War and Navy Departments with the Department of Defense; created the National Security Council to coordinate security policy; established the Central Intelligence Agency to coordinate intelligence activities; started the National Security Resources Board to coordinate economic mobilization matters.
1947	Presidential Succession Act*	Revised the Presidential Succession Act of 1886 by placing the Speaker of the House of Representatives and then the president pro tempore of the Senate next in the line of succession to the presidency after the vice president; the act was later refined with the ratification of the Twenty-fifth Amendment to the U.S. Constitution.
1947	Taft-Hartley Act* (Labor-Management Relations Act)	Passed over President Harry S. Truman's veto, this law amended the Wagner Act of 1935 by reducing or eliminating labor union advantages such as the unconditional closed shop, the check-off system enabling unions to collect dues from all employed members for the purpose of contributing to political campaigns, the unlimited right to strike at any time, and immunity from employer lawsuits filed because of breach of contract or strike damage; the law empowered the attorney general to secure an injunction of eighty days in strikes affecting national health or safety.
1948	Anti-Inflation Act	Enabled the Federal Reserve System to institute curbs on installment buying.
1948	Displaced Persons Act	Permitted admission of 205,000 displaced persons to the United States, including European refugees of World War II, Czechoslovakians who fled a communist coup, and orphans under the age of sixteen.

Year	Legislation	Significance
1948	Economic Cooperation Act	Created the Economic Cooperation Administration, which is better known as the Marshall Plan; approved economic assistance to sixteen European nations, military aid to Greece and Turkey, economic and military aid to China, and a donation to a United Nations fund for children; the act resulted in $13 billion being spent on reconstruction projects in Europe over the following four years.
1948	Federal Unemployment Tax Act (Public Law 642)	Passed over President Harry S. Truman's veto, this law maintained existing provisions pertaining to certain employment taxes and social security benefits pending action by Congress on extended social security coverage.
1948	Rent Control Bill	Extended rent controls for another year; designated an Emergency Court of Appeals to decide on decontrols or increases recommended by local boards but rejected by federal housing officials.
1948	Revenue Act	Passed over President Harry S. Truman's veto, this law reduced individual income tax payments.
1948	Selective Service Act	Required registration of all men between the ages of eighteen and twenty-five; authorized draft to create an active military comprising two million persons.
1948	Vendors Bill (Public Law 492)	Passed over President Harry S. Truman's veto, this law excluded vendors of newspapers or magazines from certain provisions of the Social Security Act and the Internal Revenue Code.
1948	Water Pollution Control Act*	Extended the reach of the national government to a limited degree, by establishing cooperative arrangements between it and the states for the prevention and abatement of water pollution.
1949	Executive Reorganization Act	Following the report of the Hoover Commission on Organization of the Executive Branch of the Government, authorized the president to examine all executive branch agencies to determine what changes were necessary to promote more effective and efficient management and to eliminate duplication; required that any reorganization plan emanating from the law be submitted to Congress within four years; specified that either house of Congress could disapprove of any reorganization plan submitted by the president.
1949	Fair Labor Standards Act Amendments	Changed the Federal Fair Labor Standards Act of 1938 by raising the minimum wage to $.75 per hour; extended coverage of the minimum wage to firms affecting interstate commerce and to certain retail service firms; prohibited use of child labor under selected circumstances; directed the Secretary of Labor to administer the act's hourly wage provisions; empowered the Labor Department to sue for back wages on behalf of employees who requested the same; part of President Harry S. Truman's Fair Deal.

Year	Legislation	Significance
1949	Housing Act	Encouraged housing production and community development to remedy housing shortages; established a national housing objective; authorized loans and grants for slum clearance, community development, redevelopment programs, and low-income and farm housing; provided for a decennial census of housing; increased the authority of the housing and home administrator to study housing construction and costs; the keystone of President Harry S. Truman's domestic program known as the Fair Deal.
1949	National Security Act Amendments	Renamed and converted the National Military Defense Establishment into an executive Department of Defense, by which the departments of the Army, Navy, and Air Force were each administered by a secretary under the authority of the secretary of defense; barred the secretary of defense from consolidating, transferring, or eliminating any of the services' combat functions; provided for a deputy secretary of defense and three assistant secretaries; dropped the three service secretaries as members of the National Security Council while adding the vice president; added a nonvoting member to the Joint Chiefs of Staff; augmented the size of the joint staff.
1949	Public Law 2	Increased the salaries of the president, vice president, and Speaker of the House of Representatives; increased the president's expense account; approved an expense account for the vice president.

Samuel B. Hoff

■ Legislation: Major U.S. Supreme Court Decisions

Cases covered in full essays within *The Forties in America* are marked with asterisks (*).

Year	Case	Court's ruling
1940	*Cantwell v. Connecticut**	The First Amendment's freedom of religion clause is applicable for state governments.
1940	*Chambers v. Florida*	Coerced confessions are not admissible at trial. In this case, four confessions had been coerced out of African Americans after a week of questioning and then were used in a murder trial, resulting in four death penalty verdicts that the Court overturned as violations of due process.
1940	*Helvering v. Horst*	One is liable for the tax on income, even if that income is given away.
1940	*Minersville v. Gobitis*	Jehovah's Witnesses can be forced to salute the flag and be penalized for refusal. This ruling was reversed three years later, in *West Virginia v. Barnette*.
1940	*Thornhill v. Alabama**	Peaceful labor picketing is a protected form of free speech and states cannot ban all labor picketing.
1940	*United States v. American Trucking Associations*	Rather than relying on the face-value meaning of a law, the Court would instead try to determine what the legislature had meant by adopting the statues.
1941	*Cox v. New Hampshire*	Established the rule that states can regulate the time, place, and manner of speech as part of their police power, even though they cannot regulate the content of speech. Upheld the permit system, with restrictions and as long as the regulations were content-neutral.
1941	*Edwards v. California*	A law prohibiting the transportation of a poor person into a state is unconstitutional. The law was struck down as violating the privileges and immunities clause, as one privilege is the right to move in and out of a state. Some justices saw the question more so as one of equal protection than as one of covered under the privileges and immunities clause.
1941	*Lisenba v. California*	A confession coerced after two days of questioning without sleep, food deprivation, and physical violence is admissible. The Supreme Court did not believe this method of obtaining a confession violated due process.
1941	*Railroad Commission v. Pullman Co.*	Federal courts can choose to abstain on state-law issues in which federal constitutional issues were also raised in certain circumstances. In order to be allowed, the abstention had to permit state courts to clear up an embarrassing issue. The federal court can still take jurisdiction later if the state court decision violated the Constitution.
1941	*Sibbach v. Wilson*	In a diversity jurisdiction case, where a case is brought in federal court under state law because people of two different states are involved, federal rules of procedure apply.

Year	Case	Court's ruling
1941	*United States v. Classic*	Primary elections can, in certain cases, come under federal law. Even though political parties are private, the federal government can still regulate in cases in which a primary election has a controlling influence on the final election, as it did with some one-party states during this period.
1941	*United States v. Darby Lumber Co.**	The Fair Labor Standards Act of 1938, which set minimum wage and maximum hour provisions, is constitutional. Reversed *Hammer v. Dagenhart* and held that manufacturing and commerce are not separate designations.
1942	*Betts v. Brady*	States did not have to provide counsel for indigent defendants in all circumstances but only when denial of counsel would result in a fundamentally unfair trial and would result in a denial of due process.
1942	*Chaplinsky v. New Hampshire**	Speech deemed "fighting words" is not protected by the First Amendment.
1942	*Ex parte Quirin*	Unlawful enemy combatants can be tried in military tribunals, even though they do have access to civilian courts to try the legality of those tribunals.
1942	*Jones v. Opelika*	A law forbidding book sales is constitutional, as it regulated economic activity without regard to religion, even though religious activity was being targeted in this prosecution. Revoked the following year in *Murdock v. Pennsylvania.*
1942	*Seminole Nation v. United States*	The government's treatment of Native American affairs, trusts, and claims had to be undertaken in accordance with sound and good financial principles. Thus, the government had to manage those claims responsibly.
1942	*Skinner v. Oklahoma**	A state cannot order forced sterilization of people convicted of multiple felonies, as the state law covered only felonies that were not white-collar crimes.
1942	*Wickard v. Filburn**	The federal government can control wheat production even when that wheat is being produced for the farmer's own use.
1942	*United States v. Univis Lens Co.*	When a patented item is sold, the company's control ends there and the company cannot further fix the price at which the item is resold by a buyer.
1942	*Valentine v. Chrestensen*	Purely commercial speech, like an advertisement, is not, at the time, protected under the First Amendment. Thus, a state can regulate such speech whenever it wishes.
1943	*Burford v. Sun Oil Co.*	Federal courts can abstain from hearing cases in which state courts have more expertise and when federal issues require the use of state law anyway.
1943	*Busey v. District of Columbia*	On religious freedom grounds, a Jehovah's Witness cannot be convicted for unlicensed selling of religious publications in a public area.

Year	Case	Court's ruling
1943	*Hirabayashi v. United States*	Both the wartime curfew and the exclusion order applying to only Japanese Americans was constitutional. Allowed as a national security measure.
1943	*Jamison v. Texas*	A city ordinance forbidding the distribution of handbills was unconstitutional as applied, because the material covered and the commercial activities in the handbills were religious.
1943	*Martin v. Struthers*	An ordinance forbidding the distribution of handbills door-to-door was unconstitutional because it violated the First Amendment's freedom-of-religion clause.
1943	*Murdock v. Pennsylvania**	A city law requiring those going door-to-door to purchase a license was a violation of the First Amendment because it restricted religious liberty.
1943	*National Broadcasting Company v. United States*	The Federal Communication Commission had the right to regulate broadcasting companies and groups, even though the original legislation did not explicitly state this. Ruled that because the groups were within the scope of the original statute and since the regulations served the public interest, it would be allowed.
1943	*Taylor v. Mississippi*	A state cannot ban the dissemination of views that argue against the state in instances in which the discussion has not been shown to have been done with an evil intent. Thus, speaking against the state is permitted under proper circumstances.
1943	*West Virginia State Board of Education v. Barnette**	Under the First Amendment, no state can force a person to recite the Pledge of Allegiance, as the right of speech includes the right to remain silent in certain circumstances.
1943	*Yasui v. United States*	Another of the Japanese internment cases. This case held that the curfew ordinance was valid; and it was the first case heard at the district court level (even though the case was a Supreme Court decision). Decided the same day as *Hirabayashi v. United States* and decided on the same grounds.
1944	*Ex parte Endo*	The government cannot hold someone indefinitely who they concede to be loyal to the United States. The government wished to continue holding Mitsuye Endo even though it admitted she was loyal, claiming that wartime necessity allowed and required it. The Court ordered her release.
1944	*Falbo v. United States*	Draft-board orders must be obeyed, even if they are erroneous. The correct way to object to a draft order error is to seek administrative review, rather than to object or to seek court review.
1944	*Follett v. Town of McCormick*	Those selling religious materials should not be subject to the same licensing fees as those selling nonreligious materials.
1944	*Korematsu v. United States**	The wartime exclusion order for Japanese Americans was constitutional and the Supreme Court would not question claims of military necessity.
1944	*National Labor Relations Board v. Hearst*	For labor law purposes, the Court would not generally review an administrative board decision about who is an employee.

Year	Case	Court's ruling
1944	*Prince v. Massachusetts*	A state may prohibit a child from selling religious materials under certain circumstances, even when it cannot prohibit an adult, and the ban did not violate the First Amendment. Gave the government authority to protect children even when religious freedom is involved.
1944	*Skidmore v. Swift*	A government administrative agency should be given deference by the courts; the amount of deference depends on how persuasive and authoritative the material relied upon by the agency is.
1944	*Smith v. Allwright**	Primary elections must be open to members of all races.
1944	*United States v. Ballard*	The truth of a religious belief cannot be debated within a court of law.
1944	*United States v. South-Eastern Underwriters Association*	The Sherman Antitrust Act applied to insurance; thus the reach of the federal government in insurance was greatly expanded. This allowed Congress to regulate insurance.
1944	*Yakus v. United States**	An administrative agency can receive a large grant of administrative power and interpret rules to make this delegation of power constitutional.
1945	*Associated Press v. United States*	The Associated Press (AP) had created a monopoly by limiting access to joining the organization and prohibiting members from selling any news (provided by the AP or not) to nonmembers.
1945	*Cramer v. United States*	A conviction for treason must meet the clear standards set forth in the constitution, as provided in Article III: A person must wage war or give material assistance to the enemy. Mere association is not enough.
1945	*International Shoe Co. v. Washington*	A defendant cannot be subject to the jurisdiction of a state unless it had a sufficient minimal business presence.
1945	*Jewell Ridge Coal Corp. v. United Mine Workers*	Travel time to a work site is part of a workweek because a work site is controlled by a company for the company's benefit and required physical labor.
1945	*United States v. Aluminum Co. of America**	Federal antitrust laws did not stop at the border but instead depended on the effects of the antitrust action being regulated. Thus, federal antitrust law can govern actions taken outside the United States.
1945	*Screws v. United States*	The American justice system may prosecute state officials for violations of civil rights, but a jury must first rule that the officials meant to violate a person's civil rights.
1945	*United States v. Willow River Power Co.*	Not all decreases in economic rights from government actions are takings under the Fifth Amendment.
1946	*Anderson v. Mt. Clemens Pottery*	Nearly all time spent at a workplace is time that should be included in a calculation of how long one has worked. Thus, preparatory work should be included in the amount of hours worked.

Year	Case	Court's ruling
1946	*Ballard v. United States**	Federal law prohibited the intentional exclusion of women from serving on federal juries in states allowing women to serve on state court juries.
1946	*Commissioner v. Wilcox*	Illegally obtained income is not considered income for the purposes of the tax law.
1946	*Duncan v. Kahanamoku**	The trying of civilians by military tribunals in Hawaii is unconstitutional.
1946	*Estep v. United States*	A draft board's decisions, in the areas of classifying a Jehovah's Witness, can be scrutinized by the Courts after the draft board and its appeals have been exhausted.
1946	*Gibson v. United States*	A person may dispute his draft status without having first to be inducted into the armed forces.
1946	*Marsh v. Alabama*	A law against trespassing cannot be used to restrict religious canvassing. Because other people were permitted to use an area, so the restriction was seen as based on the ideas of the person, who was in this case a Jehovah's Witness.
1946	*Morgan v. Virginia**	Virginia's segregation of interstate buses was unconstitutional.
1946	*Pinkerton v. United States*	A conspirator can be charged with crimes in a conspiracy even if he had nothing to do specifically with those crimes but instead was part of the overall conspiracy only.
1946	*Prudential Insurance Co. v. Benjamin**	A state may impose a discriminatory tax on an out-of-state insurance company because Congress has given regulatory power over insurance companies to the states.
1946	*Tucker v. Texas*	The government cannot make it a crime to distribute religious literature in a town that is controlled by the government (in this case a town providing housing for war workers). Free exercise of religion was the reason the conviction was struck down.
1946	*United States v. Carmack*	Government has the right of eminent domain and may seize land to be used for the public good.
1946	*United States v. Causby*	A person's property rights did not extend to the airspace above it. Thus, one cannot sue to stop flights over one's land.
1947	*Adamson v. California*	The Fifth Amendment's right to avoid self-incrimination does not apply to states; some argued that the Fourteenth Amendment did create this protection. Later cases reversed this and held that the privilege against incrimination did exist in state court proceedings.
1947	*Everson v. Board of Education of Ewing Township**	The First Amendment does limit the states and there is a "wall of separation" between church and state.
1947	*Hickman v. Taylor*	Documents created by attorneys getting ready for trial are products of attorneys and thus are covered by the "work product" privilege; they do not have to be produced in discovery.
1947	*International Salt v. United States*	Companies who have a legal monopoly on an item through a patent cannot require purchasers to also buy other products over which the company does not have a legal monopoly.

Year	Case	Court's ruling
1947	*Louisiana ex rel. Francis v. Resweber**	A state's desire to try to execute someone, where the first attempt had failed, was not unconstitutional, either as a violation of double jeopardy or as an example of cruel and unusual punishment.
1947	*Securities and Exchange Commission v. Chenery*	An administrative agency can retroactively change its laws under certain circumstances and can be flexible in its administration of the laws, as long as this application is justified.
1947	*United Public Workers v. Mitchell**	Federal employees' political activity can be regulated and partisan activities may be targeted. Ninth Amendment rights concerning involvement in the political process do not prevent such controls.
1947	*United States v. United Mine Workers**	In certain circumstances the issuance of an injunction and a restraining order against a union is justified.
1948	*Goesaert v. Cleary*	A Michigan law that forbade women from being bartenders generally was not a violation of equal protection. Thus some gender discrimination is allowable.
1948	*Hirota v. MacArthur*	The U.S. Supreme Court would not review the actions of military tribunals when those tribunals were conducted overseas. This dealt with the Japanese war crimes trials. The Court refused to issue a writ of habeas corpus for one convicted by a military tribunal.
1948	*Illinois ex rel. McCollum v. Board of Education**	A program of religious education in the public schools and at their facilities, even though voluntary and not at public expense, was unconstitutional.
1948	*Oyama v. California*	California's Alien Land Law, which prohibited noncitizens from owning land, was unconstitutional as applied. The majority opinion, however, did not rule directly on whether or not the Alien Land Law itself was constitutional.
1948	*Saia v. New York*	Struck down a statute forbidding the use of amplification devices except with the permission of the police chief. Cities are thus not allowed to have total bans on such devices, as this is a violation of the freedom of speech.
1948	*Shelley v. Kraemer**	The court system may not enforce a restrictive covenant arrived at privately that forbids the selling of real estate to African Americans.
1948	*Sipuel v. Board of Regents of the University of Oklahoma*	A university's policy of excluding African Americans from the law school on the account of race violated the Fourteenth Amendment.
1948	*United States v. Congress of Industrial Organizations*	The Congress of Industrial Organizations may ask its members to vote for specific presidential candidates without violating the Federal Corrupt Practices Act.
1948	*United States v. Paramount Pictures, Inc.**	Film companies cannot own theaters, and the practice of only allowing theaters to show certain films is a violation of antitrust laws.

Year	Case	Court's ruling
1949	*Kimball Laundry Co. v. United States*	When a property is condemned through eminent domain, intangibles, such as customers, and tangibles, such as the building, must also be paid for.
1949	*Terminiello v. Chicago*	A law banning speech that stirs people to anger is unconstitutional as a violation of the First Amendment, as applied to the states through the Fourteenth Amendment.
1949	*Wolf v. Colorado**	The Fourteenth Amendment did not require states to follow the Fourth Amendment exclusionary rule and thus illegally obtained evidence can be used.

Scott A. Merriman

■ Literature: Best-Selling Books in the United States

1940 Fiction
1. *How Green Was My Valley*, Richard Llewellyn
2. *Kitty Foyle*, Christopher Morley
3. *Mrs. Miniver*, Jan Struther
4. *For Whom the Bell Tolls*, Ernest Hemingway
5. *The Nazarene*, Sholem Asch
6. *Stars on the Sea*, F. van Wyck Mason
7. *Oliver Wiswell*, Kenneth Roberts
8. *The Grapes of Wrath*, John Steinbeck
9. *Night in Bombay*, Louis Bromfield
10. *The Family*, Nina Fedorova

1940 Nonfiction
1. *I Married Adventure: The Lives and Adventures of Martin and Osa Johnson*, Osa Johnson
2. *How to Read a Book: The Art of Getting a Liberal Education*, Mortimer Adler
3. *A Smattering of Ignorance*, Oscar Levant
4. *Country Squire in the White House*, John T. Flynn
5. *Land Below the Wind*, Agnes Newton Keith
6. *American White Paper: The Story of American Diplomacy and the Second World War*, Joseph W. Alsop, Jr., and Robert Kintnor
7. *New England: Indian Summer, 1865-1915*, Van Wyck Brooks
8. *As I Remember Him: The Biography of R. S.*, Hans Zinsser
9. *Days of Our Years*, Pierre van Paassen
10. *Bet It's a Boy*, Betty B. Blunt

1941 Fiction
1. *The Keys of the Kingdom*, A. J. Cronin
2. *Random Harvest*, James Hilton
3. *This Above All*, Eric Knight
4. *The Sun Is My Undoing*, Marguerite Steen
5. *For Whom the Bell Tolls*, Ernest Hemingway
6. *Oliver Wiswell*, Kenneth Roberts
7. *H. M. Pulham, Esquire*, John P. Marquand
8. *Mr. and Mrs. Cugat: The Record of a Happy Marriage*, Isabel Scott Rorick
9. *Saratoga Trunk*, Edna Ferber
10. *Windswept*, Mary Ellen Chase

1941 Nonfiction
1. *Berlin Diary: The Journal of a Foreign Correspondent, 1934-1941*, William L. Shirer
2. *The White Cliffs*, Alice Duer Miller
3. *Out of the Night*, Jan Valtin
4. *Inside Latin America*, John Gunther
5. *Blood, Sweat, and Tears*, Winston Churchill
6. *You Can't Do Business with Hitler*, Douglas Miller
7. *Reading I've Liked: A Personal Selection Drawn from Two Decades of Reading and Reviewing*, Clifton Fadiman
8. *Reveille in Washington, 1860-1865*, Margaret Leech
9. *Exit Laughing*, Irvin S. Cobb
10. *My Sister and I: The Diary of a Dutch Boy Refugee*, Dirk van der Heide

1942 Fiction
1. *The Song of Bernadette*, Franz Werfel
2. *The Moon Is Down*, John Steinbeck
3. *Dragon Seed*, Pearl S. Buck
4. *And Now Tomorrow*, Rachel Field
5. *Drivin' Woman*, Elizabeth Pickett Chevalier
6. *Windswept*, Mary Ellen Chase
7. *The Robe*, Lloyd C. Douglas
8. *The Sun Is My Undoing*, Marguerite Steen
9. *Kings Row*, Henry Bellamann
10. *The Keys of the Kingdom*, A. J. Cronin

1942 Nonfiction
1. *See Here, Private Hargrove*, Marion Hargrove
2. *Mission to Moscow*, Joseph Edward Davies
3. *The Last Time I Saw Paris*, Elliot Paul
4. *Cross Creek*, Marjorie Kinnan Rawlings
5. *Victory Through Air Power*, Alexander P. de Seversky
6. *Past Imperfect*, Ilka Chase
7. *They Were Expendable*, William Lindsay White
8. *Flight to Arras*, Antoine de Saint-Exupéry
9. *Washington Is Like That*, Willard Monroe Kiplinger
10. *Inside Latin America*, John Gunther

1943 Fiction
1. *The Robe*, Lloyd C. Douglas
2. *The Valley of Decision*, Marcia Davenport
3. *So Little Time*, John P. Marquand
4. *A Tree Grows in Brooklyn*, Betty Smith
5. *The Human Comedy*, William Saroyan
6. *Mrs. Parkington*, Louis Bromfield
7. *The Apostle*, Sholem Asch
8. *Hungry Hill*, Daphne du Maurier
9. *The Forest and the Fort*, Hervey Allen
10. *The Song of Bernadette*, Franz Werfel

1943 Nonfiction

1. *Under Cover*, John Roy Carlson
2. *One World*, Wendell Willkie
3. *Journey Among Warriors*, Eve Curie
4. *On Being a Real Person*, Harry Emerson Fosdick
5. *Guadalcanal Diary*, Richard Tregaskis
6. *Burma Surgeon*, Gordon Stifler Seagrave
7. *Our Hearts Were Young and Gay*, Cornelia Otis Skinner and Emily Kimbrough
8. *U.S. Foreign Policy and U.S. War Aims*, Walter Lippmann
9. *Here Is Your War*, Ernie Pyle
10. *See Here, Private Hargrove*, Marion Hargrove

1944 Fiction

1. *Strange Fruit*, Lillian Smith
2. *The Robe*, Lloyd C. Douglas
3. *A Tree Grows in Brooklyn*, Betty Smith
4. *Forever Amber*, Kathleen Winsor
5. *The Razor's Edge*, W. Somerset Maugham
6. *The Green Years*, A. J. Cronin
7. *Leave Her to Heaven*, Ben Ames Williams
8. *Green Dolphin Street*, Elizabeth Goudge
9. *A Bell for Adano*, John Hersey
10. *The Apostle*, Sholem Asch

1944 Nonfiction

1. *I Never Left Home*, Bob Hope
2. *Brave Men*, Ernie Pyle
3. *Good Night, Sweet Prince: The Life and Times of John Barrymore*, Gene Fowler
4. *Under Cover*, John Roy Carlson
5. *Yankee from Olympus: Justice Holmes and His Family*, Catherine Drinker Bowen
6. *The Time for Decision*, Sumner Welles
7. *Here Is Your War*, Ernie Pyle
8. *Anna and the King of Siam*, Margaret Landon
9. *The Curtain Rises*, Quentin J. Reynolds
10. *Ten Years in Japan*, Joseph C. Grew

1945 Fiction

1. *Forever Amber*, Kathleen Winsor
2. *The Robe*, Lloyd C. Douglas
3. *The Black Rose*, Thomas B. Costain
4. *The White Tower*, James Ramsey Ullman
5. *Cass Timberlane: A Novel of Husbands and Wives*, Sinclair Lewis
6. *A Lion Is in the Streets*, Andria Locke Langley
7. *So Well Remembered*, James Hilton

8. *Captain from Castile*, Samuel Shellabarger
9. *Earth and High Heaven*, Gwethalyn Graham
10. *Immortal Wife, The Biographical Novel of Jessie Benton Fremont*, Irving Stone

1945 Nonfiction

1. *Brave Men*, Ernie Pyle
2. *Dear Sir*, Juliet Lowell
3. *Up Front*, Bill Mauldin
4. *Black Boy*, Richard Wright
5. *Try and Stop Me*, Bennett Cerf
6. *Anything Can Happen*, George Papashvily and Helen Papashvily
7. *General Marshall's Report: The Winning of the War in Europe and the Pacific*, George Marshall and the U.S. War Department General Staff
8. *The Egg and I*, Betty Bard MacDonald
9. *The Thurber Carnival*, James Thurber
10. *Pleasant Valley*, Louis Bromfield

1946 Fiction

1. *The King's General*, Daphne du Maurier
2. *This Side of Innocence*, Taylor Caldwell
3. *The River Road*, Frances Parkinson Keyes
4. *The Miracle of the Bells*, Russell Janney
5. *The Hucksters*, Frederic Wakeman
6. *The Foxes of Harrow*, Frank Yerby
7. *Arch of Triumph*, Erich Maria Remarque
8. *The Black Rose*, Thomas B. Costain
9. *B. F.'s Daughter*, John P. Marquand
10. *The Snake Pit*, Mary Jane Ward

1946 Nonfiction

1. *The Egg and I*, Betty Bard MacDonald
2. *Peace of Mind*, Joshua Loth Liebman
3. *As He Saw It*, Elliott Roosevelt
4. *The Roosevelt I Knew*, Frances Perkins
5. *Last Chapter*, Ernie Pyle
6. *Starling of the White House*, Thomas Sugrue and Edmund Starling
7. *I Chose Freedom*, Victor Kravchenko
8. *The Anatomy of Peace*, Emery Reves
9. *Top Secret*, Ralph Ingersoll
10. *A Solo in Tom-Toms*, Gene Fowler

1947 Fiction

1. *The Miracle of the Bells*, Russell Janney
2. *The Moneyman*, Thomas B. Costain
3. *Gentleman's Agreement*, Laura Z. Hobson
4. *Lydia Bailey*, Kenneth Roberts

5. *The Vixens*, Frank Yerby
6. *The Wayward Bus*, John Steinbeck
7. *House Divided*, Ben Ames Williams
8. *Kingsblood Royal*, Sinclair Lewis
9. *East Side, West Side*, Marcia Davenport
10. *Prince of Foxes*, Samuel Shellabarger

1947 Nonfiction
1. *Peace of Mind*, Joshua Loth Liebman
2. *Information Please Almanac, 1947*, John Kieran
3. *Inside U.S.A.*, John Gunther
4. *A Study of History*, Arnold Toynbee
5. *Speaking Frankly*, James Francis Byrnes
6. *Human Destiny*, Pierre Lecomte du Noüy
7. *The Egg and I*, Betty Bard MacDonald
8. *The American Past: A History of the United States from Concord to Hiroshima, 1775-1945*, Roger Butterfield
9. *The Fireside Book of Folk Songs*, Margaret B. Boni
10. *Together*, Katharine T. Marshall

1948 Fiction
1. *The Big Fisherman*, Lloyd C. Douglas
2. *The Naked and the Dead*, Norman Mailer
3. *Dinner at Antoine's*, Frances Parkinson Keyes
4. *The Bishop's Mantle*, Agnes Sligh Turnbull
5. *Tomorrow Will Be Better*, Betty Smith
6. *The Golden Hawk*, Frank Yerby
7. *Raintree County*, Ross Lockridge
8. *Shannon's Way*, A. J. Cronin
9. *Pilgrim's Inn*, Elizabeth Goudge
10. *The Young Lions*, Irwin Shaw

1948 Nonfiction
1. *Crusade in Europe*, Dwight D. Eisenhower
2. *How to Stop Worrying and Start Living*, Dale Carnegie
3. *Peace of Mind*, Joshua Loth Liebman

4. *Sexual Behavior in the Human Male*, Alfred Kinsey et al.
5. *Wine, Women, and Words*, Billy Rose
6. *The Life and Times of the Shmoo*, Al Capp
7. *The Gathering Storm*, Winston Churchill
8. *Roosevelt and Hopkins: An Intimate History*, Robert E. Sherwood
9. *A Guide to Confident Living*, Norman Vincent Peale
10. *The Plague and I*, Betty Bard MacDonald

1949 Fiction
1. *The Egyptian*, Mika Waltari
2. *The Big Fisherman*, Lloyd C. Douglas
3. *Mary*, Sholem Asch
4. *A Rage to Live*, John O'Hara
5. *Point of No Return*, John P. Marquand
6. *Dinner at Antoine's*, Frances Parkinson Keyes
7. *High Towers*, Thomas B. Costain
8. *Cutlass Empire*, F. van Wyck Mason
9. *Pride's Castle*, Frank Yerby
10. *Father of the Bride*, Edward Streeter

1949 Nonfiction
1. *White Collar Zoo*, Clare Barnes
2. *How to Win at Canasta*, Oswald Jacoby
3. *The Seven Storey Mountain*, Thomas Merton
4. *Home Sweet Zoo*, Clare Barnes
5. *Cheaper by the Dozen*, Frank B. Gilbreth, Jr., and Ernestine Gilbreth Carey
6. *The Greatest Story Ever Told*, Fulton Oursler
7. *Canasta, the Argentine Rummy Game*, Ottilie H. Reilly
8. *Canasta*, Josephine Artayeta de Viel and Ralph Michael
9. *Peace of Soul*, Fulton J. Sheen
10. *A Guide to Confident Living*, Norman Vincent Peale

■ Literature: Major Literary Awards

Nobel Prizes in Literature

Not awarded from 1940 to 1943
1944: Johannes V. Jensen
1945: Gabriela Mistral
1946: Hermann Hesse
1947: André Gide
1948: T. S. Eliot
1949: William Faulkner

Pulitzer Prizes

Until 1947 (excluding 1941 and 1946, when no award was presented), prizes were given in the "Novel" category. This category's name was afterward changed to "Fiction" for all subsequent awards.

1940

Novel: *The Grapes of Wrath*, John Steinbeck
Drama: *Time of Your Life*, William Saroyan
History: *Abraham Lincoln: The War Years*, Carl Sandburg
Biography or Autobiography: *Woodrow Wilson, Life and Letters: Volumes VII and VIII*, Ray Stannard Baker
Poetry: *Collected Poems 1922–1938*, Mark van Doren

1941

Novel: No award
Drama: *There Shall Be No Night*, Robert E. Sherwood
History: *The Atlantic Migration, 1607-1860: A History of the Continuing Settlement of the United States*, Marcus Lee Hansen
Biography or Autobiography: *Jonathan Edwards, 1703-1758: A Biography*, Ola Elizabeth Winslow
Poetry: *Sunderland Capture, and Other Poems*, Leonard Bacon

1942

Novel: *In This Our Life*, Ellen Glasgow
Drama: No award
History: *Reveille in Washington, 1860-1865*, Margaret Leech
Biography or Autobiography: *Crusader in Crinoline: The Life of Harriet Beecher Stowe*, Forrest Wilson
Poetry: *The Dust Which Is God*, William Rose Benét

1943

Novel: *Dragon's Teeth*, Upton Sinclair
Drama: *The Skin of Our Teeth*, Thornton Wilder

History: *Paul Revere and the World He Lived In*, Esther Forbes
Biography or Autobiography: *Admiral of the Ocean Sea: A Life of Christopher Columbus*, Samuel Eliot Morison
Poetry: *A Witness Tree*, Robert Frost

1944

Novel: *Journey in the Dark*, Martin Flavin
Drama: No award
History: *The Growth of American Thought*, Merle Curti
Biography or Autobiography: *The American Leonardo: The Life of Samuel F. B. Morse*, Carleton Mabee
Poetry: *Western Star*, Stephen Vincent Benét

1945

Novel: *A Bell for Adano*, John Hersey
Drama: *Harvey*, Mary Chase
History: *Unfinished Business*, Stephen Bonsal
Biography or Autobiography: *George Bancroft: Brahmin Rebel*, Russell Blaine Nye
Poetry: *V-Letter and Other Poems*, Karl Shapiro

1946

Novel: No award
Drama: *State of the Union*, Russel Crouse and Howard Lindsay
History: *The Age of Jackson*, Arthur M. Schlesinger, Jr.
Biography or Autobiography: *Son of the Wilderness: The Life of John Muir*, Linnie Marsh Wolfe
Poetry: No award

1947

Novel: *All the King's Men*, Robert Penn Warren
Drama: No award
History: *Scientists Against Time*, James Phinney Baxter III
Biography or Autobiography: *The Autobiography of William Allen White*, William Allen White
Poetry: *Lord Weary's Castle*, Robert Lowell

1948

Fiction: *Tales of the South*, James A. Michener
Drama: *A Streetcar Named Desire*, Tennessee Williams

History: *Across the Wide Missouri*, Bernard DeVoto
Biography or Autobiography: *Forgotten First Citizen: John Bigelow*, Margaret Clapp
Poetry: *The Age of Anxiety*, W. H. Auden

1949
Fiction: *Guard of Honor*, James Gould Cozzens
Drama: *Death of a Salesman*, Arthur Miller
History: *The Disruption of American Democracy*, Roy Franklin Nichols
Biography or Autobiography: *Roosevelt and Hopkins: An Intimate History*, Robert E. Sherwood
Poetry: *Terror and Decorum*, Peter Viereck

Newbery Medal for Children's Book of the Year
1940: *Daniel Boone*, James Daugherty
1941: *Call It Courage*, Armstrong Sperry
1942: *The Matchlock Gun*, Walter D. Edmonds
1943: *Adam of the Road*, Elizabeth Janet Gray
1944: *Johnny Tremain*, Esther Forbes
1945: *Rabbit Hill*, Robert Lawson
1946: *Strawberry Girl*, Lois Lenski
1947: *Miss Hickory*, Carolyn Sherwin Bailey
1948: *The Twenty-one Balloons*, William Pène du Bois
1949: *King of the Wind*, Marguerite Henry

Newbery Honor Book
1940: *The Singing Tree*, Kate Seredy
1940: *Runner of the Mountain Tops: The Life of Louis Agassiz*, Mabel Louise Robinson
1940: *The Shores of Silver Lake*, Laura Ingalls Wilder
1940: *Boy with a Pack*, Stephen W. Meader
1941: *Blue Willow*, Doris Gates
1941: *Young Mac of Fort Vancouver*, Mary Jane Carr
1941: *The Long Winter*, Laura Ingalls Wilder
1941: *Nansen*, Anna Gertrude Hall
1942: *Little Town on the Prairie*, Laura Ingalls Wilder
1942: *George Washington's World*, Genevieve Foster
1942: *Indian Captive: The Story of Mary Jemison*, Lois Lenski
1942: *Down Ryton Water*, Eva Roe Gaggin
1943: *The Middle Moffat*, Eleanor Estes
1943: *Have You Seen Tom Thumb?* Mabel Leigh Hunt
1944: *These Happy Golden Years*, Laura Ingalls Wilder
1944: *Fog Magic*, Julia L. Sauer
1944: *Rufus M.*, Eleanor Estes

1944: *Mountain Born*, Elizabeth Yates
1945: *The Hundred Dresses*, Eleanor Estes
1945: *The Silver Pencil*, Alice Dalgliesh
1945: *Abraham Lincoln's World*, Genevieve Foster
1945: *Lone Journey: The Life of Roger Williams*, Jeanette Eaton
1946: *Justin Morgan Had A Horse*, Marguerite Henry
1946: *The Moved-Outers*, Florence Crannell Means
1946: *Bhimsa, the Dancing Bear*, Christine Weston
1946: *New Found World*, Katherine B. Shippen
1947: *Wonderful Year*, Nancy Barnes
1947: *Big Tree*, Mary Buff and Conrad Buff
1947: *The Heavenly Tenants*, William Maxwell
1947: *The Avion My Uncle Flew*, Cyrus Fisher
1947: *The Hidden Treasure of Glaston*, Eleanore Myers Jewett
1948: *Pancakes-Paris*, Claire Hutchet Bishop
1948: *Li Lun, Lad of Courage*, Carolyn Treffinger
1948: *The Quaint and Curious Quest of Johnny Longfoot*, Catherine Besterman
1948: *The Cow-Tail Switch, and Other West African Stories*, Harold Courlander
1948: *Misty of Chincoteague*, Marguerite Henry
1949: *Seabird*, Holling C. Holling
1949: *Daughter of the Mountains*, Louise Rankin
1949: *My Father's Dragon*, Ruth Stiles Gannett
1949: *Story of the Negro*, Arna Bontemps

Canadian Library Association Book of the Year for Children
1947: *Starbuck Valley Winter*, Roderick Haig-Brown
1948: No award
1949: *Kristli's Trees*, Mabel Dunham

Governor General's Awards (Canada)

1940
Fiction: *Thirty Acres*, Ringuet
Poetry or Drama: *Brébeuf and His Brethren*, E. J. Pratt
Nonfiction: *Slava Bohu: The Story of the Dukhobors*, J. F. C. Wright

1941
Fiction: *Three Came to Ville Marie*, Alan Sullivan
Poetry or Drama: *Calling Adventurers*, Anne Marriott
Nonfiction: *Klee Wyck*, Emily Carr

1942

Fiction: *Little Man*, G. Herbert Sallans
Poetry or Drama: *David and Other Poems*, Earle Birney
Nonfiction: *The Unknown Country: Canada and Her People*, Bruce Hutchison; *The Unguarded Frontier: A History of American-Canadian Relations*, Edgar McInnis

1943

Fiction: *The Pied Piper of Dipper Creek*, Thomas H. Raddall
Poetry or Drama: *News of the Phoenix*, A. J. M. Smith
Nonfiction: *The Incomplete Anglers*, John D. Robins; *On Canadian Poetry*, E. K. Brown

1944

Fiction: *Earth and High Heaven*, Gwethalyn Graham
Poetry or Drama: *Day and Night*, Dorothy Livesay
Nonfiction: *Partner in Three Worlds*, Dorothy Duncan; *The War: Fourth Year*, Edgar McInnis

1945

Fiction: *Two Solitudes*, Hugh MacLennan
Poetry or Drama: *Now Is Time*, Earle Birney
Nonfiction: *We Keep a Light*, Evelyn M. Richardson; *Gauntlet to Overlord: The Story of the Canadian Army*, Ross Munro

1946

Fiction: *Keller's Continental Revue*, Winifred Bambrick
Poetry or Drama: *Poems*, Robert Finch
Nonfiction: *In Search of Myself*, Frederick Philip Grove; *Colony to Nation: A History of Canada*, Arthur R. M. Lower

1947

Fiction: *The Tin Flute*, Gabrielle Roy
Poetry or Drama: *Poems for People*, Dorothy Livesay
Nonfiction: *Haida*, William Sclater; *The Government of Canada*, Robert MacGregor Dawson

1948

Fiction: *The Precipice*, Hugh MacLennan
Poetry or Drama: *The Rocking Chair and Other Poems*, A. M. Klein
Nonfiction: *Halifax, Warden of the North*, Thomas H. Raddall; *The Canadian Army, 1939-1945: An Official Historical Summary*, C. P. Stacey

1949

Fiction: *Mr. Ames Against Time*, Philip Child
Poetry or Drama: *The Red Heart*, James Reaney
Nonfiction: *Cross-Country*, Hugh MacLennan; *Democratic Government in Canada*, Robert MacGregor Dawson

O. Henry Award (Short Story)

1940: "Freedom's a Hard-Bought Thing," Stephen Vincent Benét
1941: "Defeat," Kay Boyle
1942: "The Wide Net," Eudora Welty
1943: "Livvie is Back," Eudora Welty
1944: "Walking Wounded," Irwin Shaw
1945: "The Wind and the Snow of Winter," Walter van Tilburg Clark
1946: "Bird Song," John Mayo Goss
1947: "The White Circle," John Bell Clayton
1948: "Shut a Final Door," Truman Capote
1949: "A Courtship," William Faulkner

Caldecott Medal

1940: *Abraham Lincoln*, Ingri d'Aulaire and Edgar Parin d'Aulaire
1941: *They Were Strong and Good*, Robert Lawson
1942: *Make Way for Ducklings*, Robert McCloskey
1943: *The Little House*, Virginia Lee Burton
1944: *Many Moons*, James Thurber
1945: *Prayer for a Child*, Rachel Field
1946: *The Rooster Crows*, Maude Petersham and Miska Petersham
1947: *The Little Island*, Golden MacDonald
1948: *White Snow, Bright Snow*, Alvin Tresselt
1949: *The Big Snow*, Berta Hader and Elmer Hader

■ Music: Popular Musicians

Act	Notable Songs	Notable Facts
Almanac Singers (Woody Guthrie, Lee Hays, Millard Lampell, Pete Seeger)	"Dear Mr. President," "Which Side Are You On?"	This leftist folk group (including Woody Guthrie and Pete Seeger) promoted union organization.
Leroy Anderson	"Chicken Reel," "Sleigh Ride," "The Syncopated Clock"	Composer of light orchestral pieces and novelties, whose works were frequently played on radio and used in cartoons.
Andrews Sisters (LaVerne Andrews, Maxene Andrews, Patricia Andrews)	"Beat Me, Daddy, Eight to the Bar," "Boogie Woogie Bugle Boy," "Don't Sit Under the Apple Tree (with Anyone Else but Me)," "Don't Fence Me In," "Is You or Is You Ain't Ma Baby," "South America, Take It Away" (with Bing Crosby)	Boswell Sisters-inspired trio had many hits, recorded often with Bing Crosby, appeared in films, and entertained the Allied forces.
Louis Armstrong	"Do You Know What It Means to Miss New Orleans," "Rockin' Chair," "That Lucky Old Sun"	Jazz trumpeter and popular singer; appeared in many films during the 1940's.
Eddy Arnold	"Bouquet of Roses," "Chained to a Memory," "What a Fool I Was"	Popular country singer, songwriter, and guitarist, who became a star of the Grand Ole Opry and developed the Nashville sound.
Fred Astaire	"One for My Baby (and One More for the Road)," "So Near Yet So Far," "Steppin' out with My Baby," "This Heart of Mine"	English dancer, actor, and singer of the 1930's Astaire-Ginger Rogers motion pictures; made several songs popular in the 1940's with his unassuming and relaxed voice.
Gene Autry	"Ghost Riders in the Sky," "Here Comes Santa Claus," "Rudolph the Red-Nosed Reindeer"	The "Singing Cowboy" was also a radio, film, and television actor.
Blue Barron	"Chi-Baba, Chi-Baba," "Cruising down the River," "You Walk By"	Sweet-jazz orchestra leader.
Count Basie	"Blue Skies," "Free Eats," "I Ain't Mad at You (You Ain't Mad at Me)," "I Didn't Know About You," "One O'Clock Boogie," "Open the Door, Richard!"	African American swing and big-band leader, composer, and keyboardist; performed with leading singers of the 1940's, including Ella Fitzgerald and Billie Holiday.
Tex Beneke	"Bugle Call Rag," "Chattanooga Choo Choo," "Sunrise Serenade"	Saxophonist, singer, and bandleader; best known for his work with the Modernaires as well as his work with the Glenn Miller Orchestra.

Act	Notable Songs	Notable Facts
Les Brown, Sr.	"Brown's Little Jug," "Sentimental Journey"	Les Brown and His Band of Renown accompanied Bob Hope on radio and stage with the United Service Organizations (USO).
Cab Calloway	"Jumpin' Jive," "Minnie the Moocher"	An African American bandleader, jazz singer, and performer, who appeared in the 1943 film *Stormy Weather* (one of two major Hollywood films that year that featured a predominantly African American cast) and the 1947 film *Hi-De-Ho*.
Frankie Carle	"Beg Your Pardon," "Cruising down the River (on a Sunday Afternoon," "Roses in the Rain," "Rumors Are Flying"	A pianist, known as the "Wizard of the Keyboard," who, with his orchestra, had numerous instrumental hits.
Hoagy Carmichael	"Doctor, Lawyer, Indian Chief," "The Lamplighter's Serenade," "Rumba Jumps," "Skylark"	This popular composer was also an actor, bandleader, pianist, and singer; famous versions of his songs were recorded by Ray Charles, Nat King Cole, Glenn Miller and His Orchestra, and numerous others.
Mindy Carson	"Rumors Are Flying"	The popular singer, who appeared on radio and regularly on Guy Lombardo's television variety show, had her own television show in 1949.
Casa Loma Orchestra (Tony Briglia, Nick Denucci, Sonny Dunham, Herb Ellis, Glen Gray, Bobby Hackett, Clarence Hutchenrider, Pee Wee Hunt, Red Nichols, Frank L. Ryerson, Kenny Sargent)	"Castle of Dreams," "You've Got Me out on a Limb"	Swing then sweet jazz band that originated from Detroit and was led by saxophonist Glen Gray.
Ray Charles	"Confession Blues"	Blind African American singer and pianist whose career began in the 1940's; his vocal style was influenced by Charles Brown and Nat King Cole.
June Christy	"How High the Moon," "Shoo Fly Pie and Apple Pan Dowdy," "Tampico"	Christy's rendition of "Tampico" was the Stan Kenton Orchestra's best-selling hit.
Buddy Clark	"Linda," "Peg o' My Heart," "Where the Apple Blossoms Fall," "Love Somebody" (with Doris Day), "Baby, It's Cold Outside" (with Dinah Shore)	Popular singer on *Your Hit Parade* in the late 1930's who did not achieve another hit until the late 1940's.

Act	Notable Songs	Notable Facts
Rosemary Clooney	"Why Don't You Haul off and Love Me?"	Popular jazz and novelty singer and actress, whose career began in the late 1940's.
Nat King Cole	"The Christmas Song," "Nature Boy," "Straighten up and Fly Right"	African American singer, jazz pianist, entertainer, and actor who achieved hits in the mainstream in the 1940's; by the late 1950's, he was the first African American star of a network television show.
Perry Como	"Chi-Baba, Chi-Baba," "Some Enchanted Evening," "Till the End of Time"	Singer, as well as a radio and television personality, who had six number-one singles in the 1940's.
Eddie Condon	"A Good Man Is Hard to Find," "Having a Ball at Carnegie Hall," "Tortilla B-Flat"	Dixieland turned hot jazz guitarist and bandleader, who published the autobiography *We Called It Music* (1948).
Connee (Connie Boswell)	"Moonlight Moon," "On the Isle of May"	The former member of the Boswell Sisters had a solo career into the 1950's.
Bing Crosby`	"I Love You," "I'll Be Seeing You," "Moonlight Becomes You," "Only Forever," "San Fernando Valley," "Swing on a Star," "Along the Navajo Trail," "Don't Fence Me In," "Is You or Is You Ain't Ma Baby," "Pistol Packin' Mama," "South America, Take It Away," "Victory Polka" (with the Andrews Sisters), "Far Away Places," "Now Is the Hour" (with the Darby Choir), "Sunday, Monday, or Always," "White Christmas" (with the Darby Singers)	Crooner and actor, who recorded with prominent singers and orchestras of the 1940's.
Xavier Cugat	"Brazil," "Perfidia," "Yo Te Amo Mucho"	Catalan-Cuban bandleader who opened the doors for popular Latin music in the United States.
Vic Damone	"Again," "I Have but One Heart," "You Do," "You're Breaking My Heart"	Singer and entertainer; began by winning *Arthur Godfrey's Talent Scouts*.
Miles Davis	"Boplicity," "Moon Dreams"	By the end of the 1940's, he became best known as a trumpeter of bebop and cool jazz.

Act	Notable Songs	Notable Facts
Doris Day	"Bewitched, Bothered, and Bewildered," "You're My Thrill," "Sentimental Journey" (with Les Brown)	Singer and actress whose career began in the 1940's.
Jimmy Dorsey	"Amapola," "Bésame Mucho," "Blue Champagne," "Green Eyes," "Maria Elena," "My Sister and I," "Tangerine"	Popular jazz composer, woodwind player, big-band leader, actor, and brother of Tommy Dorsey.
Tommy Dorsey	"In the Blue Evening," "Satan Takes a Holiday," "This Love of Mine" (with Frank Sinatra), "I'll Never Smile Again" (with Sinatra, Jo Stafford, and the Pied Pipers)	Popular jazz composer, trombonist, big-band leader, actor, and brother of Jimmy Dorsey.
Ray Eberle	"At Last," "Imagination," "Polka Dots and Moonbeams," "Serenade in Blue"	Big band vocalist; sang with Glenn Miller and His Orchestra and later for the Modernaires; brother of Bob Eberly.
Bob Eberly	"Bésame Mucho," "Green Eyes"	Big band vocalist who sang with Jimmy Dorsey and His Orchestra; brother of Ray Eberle.
Billy Eckstine	"A Cottage for Sale," "My Foolish Heart," "Prisoner of Love," "Stormy Monday Blues"	African American bop and big-band leader and ballad singer.
Duke Ellington	"Carnegie Blues," "Cotton Tail," "Dusk," "I'm Beginning to See the Light," "Ko-Ko," "Moon Mist," "Take the A Train"	One of the most influential composers of jazz standards and classical music, arranger, swing bandleader, and jazz pianist, Ellington worked mainly with Billy Strayhorn in the 1940's.
Gil Evans	"Boplicity," "Donna Lee"	Canadian/American jazz composer, arranger, bandleader, and pianist.
Ella Fitzgerald	"Flying Home," "How High the Moon," "Lady Be Good"	"Lady Ella" or "The First Lady of Song" was one of the most influential singers of the 1940's; she performed with leading orchestras (jazz, big band, and bebop, among other styles).
Red Foley	"Old Shep," "Smoke on the Water"	Country music songwriter and longtime Grand Ole Opry performer.
Helen Forrest	"I Had the Craziest Dream," "Some Sunday Morning"	Jazz and big band singer; worked with Harry James.

Act	Notable Songs	Notable Facts
Stan Getz	"Early Autumn"	A popular jazz saxophonist and composer, known in the 1940's especially for his big band, swing, and bop sound; Getz worked with Stan Kenton, Lionel Hampton, and other famous bandleaders.
Dizzy Gillespie	"Groovin' High," "Manteca," "A Night in Tunisia," "Salt Peanuts"	African American bandleader, trumpeter, songwriter, and singer; interested in various kinds of jazz and Latin music.
Benny Goodman	"Clarinade," "Gotta Be This or That," "Jersey Bounce," "Mission to Moscow," "Why Don't You Do Right" (with Peggy Lee)	Famous swing and big-band leader (called the "King of Swing") and clarinetist; worked with singer Ella Fitzgerald, trumpeter Harry James, and drummer Gene Krupa, among other leading jazz musicians; appeared in numerous Hollywood films.
Woody Guthrie	"Deportee (Plane Wreck at Los Gatos)," "Pastures of Plenty," "Roll on Columbia," "This Land Is Your Land," "Worried Man's Blues"	Leftist folk and country songwriter, singer, guitarist, and radio personality.
Lionel Hampton	"Flying Home," "Stardust"	Famous African American jazz vibraphonist, bandleader, and film actor; worked with Benny Goodman, Charlie Parker, and many other prominent bandleaders and musicians.
Erskine Hawkins	"Tuxedo Junction"	Trumpeter and big-band leader.
Dick Haymes	"Laura," "Room Full of Roses," "Some Sunday Morning" (with Helen Forrest)	Argentine popular singer and actor.
Woody Herman	"Caldonia," "Laura," "Swing Shift"	Big-band leader, clarinetist, saxophonist, and singer, who worked with Dizzy Gillespie.
Billie Holiday	"Embraceable You," "God Bless the Child," "Lover Man," "Now or Never"	Leading African American blues and jazz singer and songwriter.
Lena Horne	"Stormy Weather"	African American popular singer, stage performer, entertainer, and film actress.
Eddy Howard	"To Each His Own"	Popular singer and bandleader; appeared frequently on radio.
Pee Wee Hunt	"Twelfth Street Rag"	Jazz trombonist, singer, and bandleader; helped establish the Casa Loma Orchestra.

Act	Notable Songs	Notable Facts
Ink Spots (Jerry Daniels, Charlie Fuqua, Orville Jones, Ivory Watson)	"Do I Worry," "When the Swallows Come Back from Capistrano," "Cow-Cow Boogie" (with Ella Fitzgerald)	Popular and rhythm-and-blues African American vocal group and forerunners of doo-wop.
Harry James	"Blues in the Night," "Too Marvelous for Words," "You Made Me Love You"	Swing bandleader and trumpeter; worked with many leading singers such as Frank Sinatra and Jo Stafford.
Gordon Jenkins	"Maybe You'll Be There," "My Foolish Heart," "San Fernando Valley"	Composer, arranger, and pianist who worked with the Andrews Sisters, Nat King Cole, Judy Garland, and the Weavers, among others.
Al Jolson	"Alexander's Ragtime Band," "Carolina in the Morning"	Singer, entertainer, and screen actor, who performed with the United Service Organizations and was the focus of the films *The Jolson Story* (1946) and *Jolson Sings Again* (1949).
Spike Jones	"Ghost Riders in the Sky," "All I Want for Christmas Is My Two Front Teeth" (with George Rock)	Popular drummer, bandleader, and entertainer, who also recorded novelty songs.
Stan Jones	"Ghost Riders in the Sky"	Popular and western songwriter.
Louis Jordan	"Is You or Is You Ain't My Baby," "Ration Blues"	"Ration Blues" (1943) was the first race crossover hit.
Sammy Kaye	"Daddy," "The Old Lamplighter"	Swing bandleader and songwriter; had his own radio show on NBC.
Stan Kenton	"Eager Beaver," "Laura," "The Peanut Vendor," "Tampico" (with June Christy)	Bandleader and composer of popular, jazz, and novelty songs.
King Sisters (Alyce King, Louise King, Maxine King)	"Mama Blues," "Nighty-Night"	Big band singing quartet; performed often with the Alvino Rey Orchestra and appeared on Kay Kyser's radio show.
Evelyn Knight	"Buttons and Bows," "A Little Bird Told Me" (with the Stardusters)	Popular singer who also appeared on the radio.
Gene Krupa	"Drum Boogie," "Bolero at the Savoy" (with Anita O'Day)	Jazz and big band drummer (originally worked with Benny Goodman) and bandleader.
Kay Kyser	"Ole Buttermilk Sky," "Three Little Fishes," "Strip Polka" (with Jack Martin)	Popular swing and big-band leader and radio personality whose band appeared in several films.
Frankie Laine	"Mule Train," "That Lucky Old Sun"	Popular, jazz, and western singer, songwriter, radio personality, and film actor.

Act	Notable Songs	Notable Facts
Peggy Lee	"Mañana," "Somebody Is Taking Your Place," "Why Don't You Do Right?"	Chart-topping popular and jazz singer, songwriter, and actress, who was one of the most influential singers of the decade.
Art Lund	"Mam'selle," "What'll I Do?"	A popular singer who began with Glenn Miller and Harry James.
Nellie Lutcher	"Fine Brown Frame," "He's a Real Gone Guy," "Hurry on Down"	African American singer and pianist of jazz and rhythm and blues.
Vera Lynn	"We'll Meet Again," "White Cliffs of Dover"	English popular singer; entertained troops onstage and on her own radio show.
Gordon MacRae	"Hair of Gold, Eyes of Blue," "My Darling, My Darling," "Say Something Sweet to Your Sweetheart" (with Jo Stafford)	Broadway and popular singer and actor who had some hits with Jo Stafford.
Merry Macs (Dick Baldwin, Helen Carroll, Mary Lou Cook, Clive Erard, Marjory Garland, Cheri McKay, Joe McMichael, Judd McMichael, Ted McMichael, Vern Rowe)	"Mairzy Doats," "Praise the Lord and Pass the Ammunition," "Sentimental Journey"	Popular singing quartet of changing membership known for their close harmonies and for singing with Bing Crosby.
Freddy Martin	"Tonight We Love"	Popular bandleader and saxophonist.
Tony Martin	"To Each His Own," "There's No Tomorrow"	Popular singer who also had roles in numerous films.
Johnny Mercer	"Autumn Leaves," "Blues in the Night," "Come Rain or Come Shine," "Laura," "That Old Black Magic"	Prolific popular lyricist, songwriter, and singer.
Glenn Miller	"In the Mood," "A String of Pearls," "That Old Black Magic," "Tuxedo Junction," "Chattanooga Choo Choo" (with the Modernaires)	Chart-topping songwriter, big-band leader, arranger; worked with and influenced the most prominent musicians and songwriters of the 1930's and 1940's.
Mills Brothers (Donald Mills, Harry Mills, Herbert Mills, John Mills, Jr.)	"Paper Doll," "Someday (You'll Want Me To)," "Till Then"	African American jazz and popular quartet; precursors and rivals to the Ink Spots.
The Modernaires (Ralph Brewster, Bill Conway, Hal Dickinson, Chuck Goldstein)	"There! I've Said It Again," "Chattanooga Choo Choo" (with the Glenn Miller Orchestra)	A popular trio (later quartet) that was featured on Paul Whiteman's radio show and sang with the Glenn Miller Orchestra.
Vaughn Monroe	"Let It Snow!," "There! I've Said It Again"	Popular singer, bandleader, and trumpeter.

Act	Notable Songs	Notable Facts
Art Mooney	"Baby Face," "I'm Looking over a Four Leaf Clover"	Popular singer who also had a hit in the 1950's with "Nuttin' For Christmas."
Russ Morgan	"Cruising down the River," "Forever and Ever" (with the Skylarks)	Sweet-band leader and trombonist.
Ella Mae Morse	"Shoo-Shoo Baby," "Cow-Cow Boogie" (with Freddie Slack)	Versatile singer of pop, jazz, and country standards as well as rhythm and blues.
Ray Noble	"Cherokee," "The Very Thought of You"	English bandleader, composer, arranger, and actor whose late 1930's songs were recorded by singers in the 1940's.
Helen O'Connell	"Amapola," "Green Eyes," "Tangerine," "Yours"	Popular singer, actress, and dancer, who was best known for her Latin-flavored popular standards.
Anita O'Day	"And Her Tears Flowed Like Wine," "Tabby the Cat"	Jazz and big band singer who rivaled Billie Holiday and Ella Fitzgerald.
Patti Page	"Confess," "So in Love"	Popular singer who had numerous hits.
Charlie "Bird" Parker	"Koko," "Ornithology"	Composer and virtuoso jazz saxophonist; helped popularize early bebop.
Ezio Pinza	"Some Enchanted Evening"	Popular Italian opera singer who appeared on Broadway in *South Pacific* (1949).
Pied Pipers (John Huddleston, Chuck Lowry, Jo Stafford, Billy Wilson)	"My Happiness," "I'll Never Smile Again," "These Are Such Things" (with Frank Sinatra)	Popular singing group that worked with Frank Sinatra, among others.
Alvino Rey	"Blue Rey," "My Buddy," "Nighty-Night"	Popular swing and big-band leader and pedal steel guitar player.
Tex Ritter	"I'm Wastin' My Tears on You," "Jingle, Jangle, Jingle," "Rye Whiskey"	Country, western, and popular singer, who had a film, radio, and television career.
Roy Rogers	"A Little White Cross on the Hill," "My Chickashay Girl"	Country singer and cowboy actor, who appeared in many Hollywood films.
Andy Russell	"Amor," "Bésame Mucho," "Pretending"	Singer of popular standards, songs from Broadway and film musicals, and Latin songs.
Pete Seeger	"Dear Mr. President," "Which Side Are You On?" (with The Almanac Singers), "Good Night, Irene" (with the Weavers)	Leftist folk singer who was prominent in the folk revival movement.
Artie Shaw	"Frenesi"	A popular and big-band leader, composer, and clarinetist; Shaw's Orchestra was on radio and in films and was a rival to Benny Goodman.

Act	Notable Songs	Notable Facts
Anne Shelton	"Lili Marlene"	Popular English singer; motivated the Allied forces troops on radio and onstage.
Dinah Shore	"Buttons and Bows," "Shoo Fly Pie and Apple Pan Dowdy," "You'd Be So Nice to Come Home To," "Baby, It's Cold Outside (with Buddy Clark)	A big band singer and actress, Shore was on radio and made her television debut in 1949.
Frank Sinatra	"All of Me," "Five Minutes More," "Mam'selle," "Oh! What Seemed to Be," "There Are Such Things," "Dolores," "I'll Never Smile Again" (with the Pied Pipers)	"Ol' Blue Eyes" was a prominent chart-topping popular singer, songwriter, entertainer, and Hollywood film actor by the mid 1940's, when he went solo.
Freddie Slack	"Beat Me Daddy, Eight to the Bar" (with Will Bradley), "Cow-Cow Boogie" (with Ella Mae Morse)	Swing bandleader and boogie-woogie pianist.
Ethel Smith	"Tico Tico"	Organist and entertainer.
Kate Smith	"Seems Like Old Times," "The White Cliffs of Dover," "The Woodpecker Song"	The "God Bless America" singer.
Jo Stafford	"My Happiness," "Say Something Sweet to Your Sweetheart" (with Gordon MacRae), "The Trolley Song" (with the Pied Pipers)	Singer of popular standards who sang with the Pied Pipers before her solo career.
Martha Tilton	"How Are Things in Glocca Mora," "I'll Walk Alone"	Popular singer who also sang commercial jingles.
Mel Tormé	"Careless Hands," "The Christmas Song"	"The Velvet Fog" was a singer, drummer, composer, arranger, and radio actor.
Merle Travis	"Dark as a Dungeon," "Sixteen Tons"	Country and western songwriter, singer, and versatile guitarist.
Ernest Tubb	"Blue Christmas," "Walking the Floor over You"	Country music singer and songwriter who popularized honky-tonk.
Jimmy Wakely	"Silver Bells," "Slipping Around" (with Margaret Whiting)	Country and western singer.
Fran Warren	"A Sunday Kind of Love," "I Said My Pajamas (And Put on My Pray'rs)" with Tony Martin	Jazz and popular music singer.
Fred Waring	"Battle Hymn of the Republic," "My America"	Bandleader, composer, and radio and television personality who ran choral workshops.

Act	Notable Songs	Notable Facts
Dinah Washington	"Am I Asking Too Much?," "Evil Gal Blues"	The "Queen of the Blues" was an African American blues, rhythm and blues, jazz, and popular music singer.
Ethel Waters	"Happiness Is a Thing Called Joe"	African American singer of blues, spirituals, popular music, and Broadway musicals and Academy Award nominated supporting film actress.
The Weavers (Ronnie Gilbert, Lee Hays, Fred Hellerman, Pete Seeger)	"Goodnight, Irene," "Tzena, Tzena, Tzena"	Folk music quartet that included Pete Seeger.
Ted Weems	"Heartaches," "Peg o' My Heart"	Weems directed the U.S. Merchant Marine Band during World War II.
Paul Whiteman	"My Fantasy," "Trav'lin' Light" (with Billie Holiday)	The dance band director who began in the 1920's; was featured in many films.
Margaret Whiting	"A Tree in the Meadow," "Slipping Around" (with Jimmy Wakely)	Popular-music singer and recording artist.
Hank Williams	"I'm a Long Gone Daddy," "Lovesick Blues," "Move It on Over"	The popular country singer and songwriter who developed the honky-tonk style.
Tex Williams	"Detour," "Shame on You," "Talking Boogie"	Western swing singer known for his "talking blues" style.
Bob Wills	"Smoke on the Water," "Stars and Stripes of Iwo Jima," "White Cross on Okinawa"	The "King of Western Swing" was a songwriter, bandleader, Texas fiddler, and pianist.

Ursula Goldsmith

■ Music: Top-Selling U.S. Recordings

This table lists music recordings that sold at least one million copies in the United States during the 1940's. Songs are arranged alphabetically by the years in which they first appeared on popular play charts. Listings credit the composers and recording artists. Composers' names have been displayed as they are recognized by the American Society for Composers, Authors and Publishers (ASCAP), the Society of European Stage Authors and Composers (SESAC), Broadcast Music Incorporated (BMI), and the Australian Performing Rights Association (APRA).

Date	Title	Composers	Artists
1940	"Frenesi"	Alberto Dominguez and Leonard Whitcup	Artie Shaw and His Orchestra
1940	"I'll Never Smile Again"	Ruth Lowe	Tommy Dorsey Band with Frank Sinatra and the Pied Pipers
1940	"In the Mood"	Joseph C. Garland and Andy Razaf	Glenn Miller and His Orchestra
1940	"Pennsylvania 6-5000"	William J. Finegan, Jerry Gray, and Carl Sigman	Glenn Miller and His Orchestra
1940	"Silent Night"	Josef Mohr, Franz Xaver Gruber, John Freeman Young	Bing Crosby
1940	"Tuxedo Junction"	Julian Dash, Buddy Feyne, Erskine Hawkins, and William Luther Johnson	Glenn Miller and His Orchestra with Bob Eberly and Helen O'Connell
1941	"Amapola (Pretty Little Poppy)"	Albert Gamse and Joseph Maria LaCalle	Jimmy Dorsey and His Orchestra
1941	"Chattanooga Choo Choo"	Mack Gordon, Harry Warren	Glenn Miller and His Orchestra with Tex Beneke, Marion Hutton, and the Modernaires
1941	"Dancing in the Dark"	Howard Dietz and Arthur Schwartz	Artie Shaw and His Orchestra
1941	"Green Eyes (Aquellos Ojos Verdes)"	Nilo Menendez and Adolfo Utrera Fernandez Perez	Jimmy Dorsey and His Orchestra with Bob Eberly and Helen O'Connell
1941	"Maria Elena"	Lorenzo Barcelata	Jimmy Dorsey and His Orchestra with Bob Eberly
1941	"New San Antonio Rose"	James Robert Wills	Bing Crosby with Bing Crosby Orchestra
1941	"San Antonio Rose"	James Robert Wills	Bob Wills and His Texas Playboys
1941	"Silent Night"	Josef Mohr, Franz Xaver Gruber, and John Freeman Young	Bing Crosby
1941	"Stardust"	Hoagy Carmichael and Mitchell Parish	Artie Shaw and His Orchestra

Date	Title	Composers	Artists
1941	"Summit Ridge Drive"	Artie Shaw and His Gramercy Five	Artie Shaw and His Orchestra
1941	"Tonight We Love/Piano Concerto No. 1 in B-flat minor, Op. 23"	Ray Austin, Freddy Martin, and Bobby Worth/Peter Ilich Tchaikovsky	Freddy Martin and His Orchestra with Clyde Rogers
1941	"You Made Me Love You (I Didn't Want to Do It)"	Luther Henderson, Jr. and James V. Monaco	Harry James and His Orchestra
1942	"American Patrol"	Jerry Gray	Glenn Miller and His Orchestra
1942	"Blues in the Night"	Harold Arlen and John H. Mercer	Dinah Shore
1942	"By the Light of the Silvery Moon"	Gus Edwards and Edward Madden	Ray Noble and His Orchestra with Roy Lanson
1942	"Cow-Cow Boogie"	Benny Carter, Gene De Paul, and Don Raye	Freddie Slack and His Orchestra with Ella Mae Morse
1942	"Deep in the Heart of Texas"	June Hershey and Don Swander	Horace Heidt and His Musical Knights
1942	"Der Fuehrer's Face"	Oliver G. Wallace	Spike Jones and His City Slickers
1942	"Easter Parade"	Irving Berlin	Harry James and His Orchestra
1942	"(I've Got a Gal in) Kalamazoo"	Mack Gordon and Harry Warren	Glenn Miller and His Orchestra with Tex Beneke, Marion Hutton, and the Modernaires
1942	"Jingle Jangle Jingle"	Joseph J. Lilly and Frank Loesser	Kay Kyser and His Orchestra with Harry Babbitt and Julie Carway
1942	"Praise the Lord and Pass the Ammunition!"	Frank Loesser	Kay Kyser and His Orchestra
1942	"Rose O'Day"	Al Lewis and Charles Tobias	Kate Smith
1942	"Strip Polka"	John Mercer	Kay Kyser and His Orchestra
1942	"There's a Star-Spangled Banner Waving Somewhere"	David McEnery, Bob Miller, and Paul Roberts	Elton Britt
1942	"White Christmas"	Irving Berlin	Bing Crosby with Ken Darby Singers and John Scott Trotter Orchestra
1942	"White Christmas"	Irving Berlin	Freddy Martin and His Orchestra
1942	"Who Wouldn't Love You?"	Carl Fischer and Bill Carey	Kay Kyser and His Orchestra
1943	"All or Nothing at All"	Arthur Altman and Jack Lawrence	Harry James and His Orchestra with Frank Sinatra
1943	"I Had the Craziest Dream"	Mack Gordon and Harry Warren	Harry James and His Orchestra
1943	"I'll Be Home for Christmas"	Kim Gannon, Walter Kent, and Buck Ram	Bing Crosby

Date	Title	Composers	Artists
1943	"I've Heard That Song Before"	Jule Styne and Sammy Cahn	Harry James and His Orchestra
1943	"Oklahoma!"	Oscar Hammerstein II and Richard Rogers	Original Broadway Cast (Alfred Drake, Joan Roberts, Howard Da Silva, Lee Dixon)
1943	"Paper Doll"	Johnny S. Black	Mills Brothers
1943	"Pistol Packin' Mama"	Al Dexter	Al Dexter and His Troopers
1943	"Pistol Packin' Mama"	Al Dexter	Bing Crosby and the Andrews Sisters and Vic Schoen's Orchestra
1943	"Sunday, Monday, or Always"	Johnny Burke and Jimmy Van Heusen	Bing Crosby with Ken Darby Singers
1943	"There Are Such Things"	Stanley Adams, Abel Baer, and George W. Meyer	Tommy Dorsey and His Orchestra
1943	"Why Don't You Do Right"	Joe McCoy	Benny Goodman and His Orchestra with Peggy Lee
1943	"You'll Never Know"	Mack Gordon and Harry Warren	Dick Haymes
1944	"Bésame Mucho"	Consuelo Torres Ortiz Velazquez and Sunny Skylar	Jimmy Dorsey and His Orchestra with Kitty Kellen and Bob Eberly
1944	"Boogie Woogie"	Clarence Smith	Tommy Dorsey and His Orchestra
1944	"Don't Fence Me In"	Robert H. Fletcher and Cole Porter	Bing Crosby and the Andrews Sisters with the Vic Schoen Orchestra
1944	"G.I. Jive"	John H. Mercer	Louis Jordan and His Tympany Five
1944	"Holiday for Strings"	David D. Rose	David Rose and His Orchestra
1944	"I'll Be Home for Christmas"	Kim Gannon, Walter Kent, and Buck Ram	Bing Crosby
1944	"Into Each Life a Little Rain Must Fall"	Doris Fisher and Allan Roberts	The Ink Spots and Ella Fitzgerald
1944	"Long Ago (and Far Away)"	Ira Gershwin and Jerome Kern	Guy Lombardo
1944	"Swinging on a Star"	Johnny Burke and Jimmy Van Heusen	Bing Crosby with the John Scott Trotter Orchestra
1944	"Too-Ra-Loo-Ra-Loo-Ra (That's an Irish Lullaby)"	James Royce Shannon	Bing Crosby with the Victor Young Orchestra
1944	"White Christmas"	Irving Berlin	Frank Sinatra with the Ken Lane Singers and Orchestra
1944	"You Always Hurt the One You Love"	Doris Fisher and Allan Roberts	Mills Brothers
1945	"Caldonia"	Fleecy Moore	Louis Jordan and His Tympany Five

Date	Title	Composers	Artists
1945	"Claire de Lune"	Claude Debussy	Jose Iturbi
1945	"Cocktails for Two"	Sam Coslow and Arthur Johnston	Spike Jones and His City Slickers
1945	"A Cottage for Sale"	Larry Conley and Willard Robison	Billy Eckstine and His Orchestra
1945	"Dream"	John H. Mercer	The Pied Pipers with Paul Weston's Orchestra
1945	"The Honeydripper (Parts 1 and 2)"	Joseph C. Liggins	Joe Liggins and the Honeydrippers
1945	"I Can't Begin to Tell You"	James V. Monaco and Mack Gordon	Bing Crosby and Carmen Cavallaro
1945	"I Dream of You (More than You Dream I Do)"	Marjorie Goetschius and Edna Osser	Tommy Dorsey and His Orchestra
1945	"If I Loved You"	Oscar Hammerstein II and Richard Rodgers	Perry Como with the Russ Case Orchestra
1945	"Laura"	John H. Mercer and David Raskin	Woody Herman and His Orchestra
1945	"Polonaise" (A-flat Major, Op. 53)	Frédéric Chopin	Carmen Cavallaro and His Orchestra
1945	"Polonaise" (A-flat Major, Op. 53)	Frédéric Chopin	Jose Iturbi
1945	"Rum and Coca-Cola"	Morey Amsterdam, Paul Girlando, and Jeri Kelli Sullivan	Andrews Sisters with Vic Schoen and His Orchestra
1945	"Temptation"	Nacio Herb Brown and Arthur Fred	Perry Como
1945	"There! I've Said It Again"	Redd Evans and David A. Mann	Vaughn Monroe and His Orchestra with the Norton Sisters
1945	"Till the End of Time"	Buddy Kaye and Ted Mossman	Perry Como with the Russ Case Orchestra
1945	"Sentimental Journey"	Les Brown, Bud Green, and Benjamin Homer	Les Brown and His Band of Renown with Doris Day
1945	"Tampico"	Doris Fisher and Allan Roberts	Stan Kenton and His Orchestra with June Christy
1946	"Choo Choo Ch'Boogie"	Denver Darling, Milton Gabler, and Vaughn Horton	Louis Jordan and His Tympany Five
1946	"Christmas Island"	Lyle L. Moraine	Andrews Sisters with Guy Lombardo and His Royal Canadians
1946	"The Christmas Song"	Mel Torme and Bob Wells	King Cole Trio

Date	Title	Composers	Artists
1946	"Dig You Later (A Huba-Hubba-Hubba)"	Harold Adamson and Jimmy McHugh	Perry Como with the Satisfiers
1946	"The Gypsy"	William Gordon Reid	Ink Spots
1946	"I'm Always Chasing Rainbows"	Michael Joseph McCarthy and Harry Carroll	Perry Como with the Satisfiers and Russ Case Orchestra
1946	"In a Shanty in Old Shanty Town"	Jack Little, Ira Schuster, and Joseph Young	Johnny Long and His Orchestra
1946	"McNamara's Band"	Guy Bonham, Wamp Carlson, Dwight B. Latham, Thomas Francis O'Connor, and John Stamford	Bing Crosby with the Jesters and Bob Haggart and His Orchestra
1946	"Prisoner of Love"	Russ Columbo, Clarence Gaskill, and Leo Robin	Perry Como
1946	"Prisoner of Love"	Russ Columbo, Clarence Gaskill, and Leo Robin	Billy Eckstine and His Orchestra
1946	"Shoo Fly Pie (and Apple Pan Dowdy)"	Sammy Gallop and Guy B. Wood	Stan Kenton and His Orchestra with June Christy
1946	"South America Take It Away"	Harold J. Rome	Bing Crosby and the Andrews Sisters with Vic Schoen and His Orchestra
1946	"To Each His Own"	Raymond B. Evans and Jay Livingston	Eddy Howard and His Orchestra
1946	"To Each His Own"	Raymond B. Evans and Jay Livingston	Ink Spots
1946	"To Each His Own"	Raymond B. Evans and Jay Livingston	Tony Martin
1947	"Anniversary Song from the Al Jolson Story"	Saul Chaplin and Al Jolson	Al Jolson with Morris Stoloff's Orchestra
1947	"April Showers"	B. G. DeSylva and Louis Silvers	Al Jolson with Orchestra directed by Carmen Dragon
1947	"Ballerina"	Sidney Keith Russell and Carl Sigman	Vaughn Monroe and His Band
1947	"Chi-Baba Chi-Baba (My Bambino Go to Sleep)"	Mack David, Al Hoffman, and Jerry Livingston	Perry Como
1947	"Heartaches"	Al Hoffman and John Klenner	Ted Weems Orchestra
1947	"Here Comes Santa Claus"	Gene Autry and Oakley Haldeman	Gene Autry
1947	"I Wish I Didn't Love You So"	Frank Loesser	Betty Hutton with the Joe Lilley Orchestra
1947	"Mam'selle"	Mack Gordon and Edmund Goulding	Art Lund

Date	Title	Composers	Artists
1947	"Mickey"	Harry Williams and Charles N. Daniels (as Neil Moret)	Ted Weems and His Orchestra with Bob Edwards
1947	"Move on up a Little Higher"	W. Herbert Brewster	Mahalia Jackson
1947	"Near You"	Francis Craig and Kermit Goell	Francis Craig and His Orchestra
1947	"New Jole Blonde"	Aubrey W. Mullican and Lou Wayne	Moon Mullican
1947	"Ooh! Look-a There, Ain't She Pretty"	Carmen Lombardo and Clarence E. Todd	Buddy Greco
1947	"Open the Door, Richard"	Dusty Fletcher, David Kapp, Jack MacVea, and John James Mason, Jr.	Dusty Fletcher
1947	"Peg o' My Heart"	Alfred Bryan and Fred Fisher	The Harmonicats
1947	"Smoke! Smoke! Smoke! (That Cigarette)"	Merle Travis and Sollie Paul Williams	Tex Williams and the Western Caravan
1947	"That's My Desire"	Helmy Kresa and Carroll Loveday	Frankie Laine and Mannie Klein's All-Stars
1947	"Too Fat Polka"	Ross MacLean and Arthur Richardson	Arthur Godfrey
1947	"Whiffenpoof Song"	Tod B. Galloway, Meade Minnigerode, and George S. Pomeroy	Bing Crosby with Fred Waring and the Pennsylvanians
1948	"All I Want for Christmas Is My Two Front Teeth"	Donald Yetter Gardner	Spike Jones
1948	"Anytime"	Herb Lawson	Eddy Arnold and His Tennessee Plowboys
1948	"Baby Face"	Harry Akst and Benny Davis	Art Mooney and His Orchestra
1948	"Because"	Guy D'Hardelot and Edward F. Lockton	Perry Como with the Russ Case Orchestra
1948	"Bluebird of Happiness"	Sandor Harmati, Edward Heyman, and Harry Parr Davies	Art Mooney and His Orchestra with Bud Brees
1948	"Bouquet of Roses"	Bob Hilliard and Steve Nelson	Eddy Arnold and His Tennessee Plowboys
1948	"Buttons and Bows"	Raymond B. Evans and Jay Livingston	Dinah Shore
1948	"Buttons and Bows"	Raymond B. Evans and Jay Livingston	The Dinning Sisters with the Art van Damme Orchestra

Date	Title	Composers	Artists
1948	"Cigarettes, Whisky, and Wild, Wild Women"	Tim Spencer	Red Ingle and the Natural Seven with the Might and Main Street Choral Society
1948	"I'm Looking over a Four Leaf Clover"	Mort Dixon and Harry M. Woods	Art Mooney and His Orchestra featuring Mike Pingatore
1948	"It's Magic"	Sammy Cahn and Jule Styne	Doris Day
1948	"Just a Little Lovin' (Will Go a Long Way)"	Eddy Arnold and Zeke Clements	Eddy Arnold and His Tennessee Plowboys
1948	"Little White Lies"	Walter Donaldson	Dick Haymes with Four Hits and a Miss
1948	"Love Somebody"	Alex C. Kramer and Joan Whitney	Doris Day and Buddy Clark
1948	"Mañana (Is Soon Enough for Me)"	David M. Barbour and Peggy Lee	Peggy Lee with Dave Barbour and the Brazilians
1948	"Maybe You'll Be There"	Rube Bloom and Sammy Gallop	Gordon Jenkins and His Orchestra with Charles La Vere
1948	"My Happiness"	Borney Bergantine and Betty Blasco	The Pied Pipers
1948	"My Happiness"	Borney Bergantine and Betty Blasco	Jon and Sandra Steele
1948	"Nature Boy"	Eden Ahbez	Nat King Cole
1948	"Now Is the Hour"	Maewa Kaihau, Clement Scott, and Dorothy M. R. Stewart	Bing Crosby with the Ken Darby Choir
1948	"On a Slow Boat to China"	Frank Loesser	Kay Kyser
1948	"Say Something Sweet to Your Sweetheart"	Roy C. Bennett and Sid Tepper	Jo Stafford and Gordon MacRae with the Starlighters
1948	"Shine"	Lew Brown, Ford T. Dabney, and R. C. McPherson	Frankie Laine with Carl Fischer's Orchestra
1948	"Tennessee Waltz"	Pee Wee King and Redd Stewart	Cowboy Copas
1948	"Tomorrow Night"	Sam Coslow and Wilhelm Grosz	Lonnie Johnson
1948	"A Tree in the Meadow"	William Gordon Reid	Margaret Whiting
1948	"Twelfth Street Rag"	Euday Bowman and Andy Razaf	Pee Wee Hunt and His Orchestra
1948	"Woody Woodpecker"	Ramez Idress and George F. Tibbles	Kay Kyser and His Orchestra with Gloria Wood
1948	"You Call Everybody Darling"	Sam Martin, Albert J. Trace, and Ben L. Trace	Jack Smith and the Clark Sisters

Date	Title	Composers	Artists
1948	"You Can't Be True, Dear"	J. F. Bard, Dave Dreyer, Gerhard Ebeler, Kenneth Wilson Griffin, and Hans Otten	Ken Griffin and Jerry Wayne
1949	"Again"	Dorcas Cochran and Lionel Newman	Vic Damone
1949	"Baby It's Cold Outside"	Frank Loesser	Esther Williams and Ricardo Montalban
1949	"Blue Moon"	Lorenz Hart and Richard Rogers	Billy Eckstine
1949	"Blue Skirt Waltz"	Vaclav Blaha and Mitchell Parish	Frankie Yankovich with the Marlin Sisters
1949	"Caravan"	Edward Kennedy Ellington, Irving Mills, and Juan Tizol	Billy Eckstine
1949	"Cruising down the River"	Eily Beadell and Nellie Tollerton	Blue Barron and His Orchestra
1949	"Galway Bay"	Arthur Colahan	Bing Crosby
1949	"I Never See Maggie Alone"	Horatio Nicholls (as Everett Lynton) and Henry B. Tinsley	Kenny Roberts
1949	"I Yust Go Nuts at Christmas"	Harry Stewart	Yogi Yorgesson with the John Duffy Trio
1949	"I've Got a Lovely Bunch of Coconuts"	Harold Elton Box (as Fred Heatherton), Desmond Cox, and Irwin Dash	Freddy Martin with Merv Griffin
1949	"I've Got My Love to Keep Me Warm"	Irving Berlin	Les Brown and His Band of Renown
1949	"A Little Bird Told Me"	Harvey Brooks	Evelyn Knight with the Star Dusters
1949	"Lovesick Blues"	Cliff Friend and Irving Mills	Hank Williams with His Drifting Cowboys
1949	"Mule Train"	Fred Glickman, Hy Heath, and Johnny Lange	Frankie Laine
1949	"On a Slow Boat to China"	Frank Loesser	Bennie Goodman and His Orchestra with Al Hendrickson
1949	"Riders in the Sky (a Cowboy Legend)"	Stan Jones	Vaughn Monroe and His Orchestra
1949	"Rudolph, the Red-Nosed Reindeer"	John D. Marks	Gene Autry
1949	"Saturday Night Fish Fry"	Lou Jordan and Ellis Lawrence Walsh	Louis Jordan and His Tympany Five
1949	"Slipping Around"	Floyd Tillman	Margaret Whiting and Jimmy Wakely

Date	Title	Composers	Artists
1949	"That Lucky Old Sun"	Stan Jones	Frankie Laine
1949	"Whispering Hope"	Paul Weston	Jo Stafford and Gordon MacRae with Paul Weston and His Orchestra
1949	"You're Breaking My Heart"	Pat Genaro and Sunny Skylar	Vic Damone

Gary Galván

■ Sports: Winners of Major Events

Names of personages with full-length essays within *The Forties in America* are marked with asterisks (*).

Major League Baseball

World Series
1940: Cincinnati Reds (National League) 4, Detroit Tigers (American League) 0
1941: New York Yankees (AL) 4, Brooklyn Dodgers (NL) 1
1942: St. Louis Cardinals (NL) 4, New York Yankees (AL) 1
1943: New York Yankees (AL) 4, St. Louis Cardinals (NL) 1
1944: St. Louis Cardinals (NL) 4, St. Louis Browns (AL) 2
1945: Detroit Tigers (AL) 4, Chicago Cubs (NL) 3
1946: St. Louis Cardinals (NL) 4, Boston Red Sox (AL) 3
1947: New York Yankees (AL) 4, Brooklyn Dodgers (NL) 3
1948: Cleveland Indians (AL) 4, Boston Braves (NL) 2
1949: New York Yankees (AL) 4, Brooklyn Dodgers (NL) 1

All Star Game
1940: National League 4, American League 0
1941: American League 7, National League 5
1942: American League 3, National League 1
1943: American League 5, National League 3
1944: National League 7, American League 1
1945: none (World War II)
1946: American League 12, National League 0
1947: American League 2, National League 1
1948: American League 5, National League 2
1949: American League 11, National League 7

American League Most Valuable Player
1940: Hank Greenberg, Detroit Tigers
1941: Joe DiMaggio*, New York Yankees
1942: Joe Gordon, New York Yankees
1943: Spud Chandler, New York Yankees
1944: Hal Newhouser, Detroit Tigers
1945: Hal Newhouser, Detroit Tigers
1946: Ted Williams*, Boston Red Sox
1947: Joe DiMaggio*, New York Yankees
1948: Lou Boudreau, Cleveland Indians
1949: Ted Williams*, Boston Red Sox

National League Most Valuable Player
1940: Frank McCormick, Cincinnati Reds
1941: Dolph Camilli, Brooklyn Dodgers
1942: Mort Cooper, St. Louis Cardinals
1943: Stan Musial, St. Louis Cardinals
1944: Marty Marion, St. Louis Cardinals
1945: Phil Cavarretta, Chicago Cubs
1946: Stan Musial, St. Louis Cardinals
1947: Bob Elliott, Boston Braves
1948: Stan Musial, St. Louis Cardinals
1949: Jackie Robinson*, Brooklyn Dodgers

Rookie of the Year (both leagues voted on a combined award)
1947: Jackie Robinson*, Brooklyn Dodgers
1948: Alvin Dark, Boston Braves

Rookie of the Year (each league presented its own award starting this year)
1949: (NL) Don Newcombe, Brooklyn Dodgers; (AL) Roy Seivers, St. Louis Browns

Negro League Baseball

World Series
1940: none
1941: none
1942: Kansas City Monarchs (AL) 4, Homestead Grays (NL) 0
1943: Homestead Grays (NL) 4, Birmingham Black Barons (AL) 3
1944: Homestead Grays (NL) 4, Birmingham Black Barons (AL) 1
1945: Cleveland Buckeyes (AL) 4, Homestead Grays (NL) 0
1946: Newark Eagles (NL) 4, Kansas City Monarchs (AL) 3

1947: New York Cubans (NL) 4, Cleveland
   Buckeyes (AL) 1
1948: Homestead Grays (NL) 4, Birmingham
   Black Barons (AL) 1
1949: none

All-Star Game
1940: East 11, West 0
1941: East 8, West 3

1942: East 5, West 2
1943: West 2, East 1
1944: West 7, East 4
1945: West 9, East 6
1946: East 5, West 3
1947: West 5, East 2
1948: West 3, East 0
1949: East 4, West 0

College Baseball

College World Series
1947: California 8, Yale 7

1948: Southern California 9, Yale 2
1949: Texas 10, Wake Forest 3

Professional Basketball

National Basketball Association Championship
1947: Philadelphia Warriors 4, Chicago Stags 1

1948: Baltimore Bullets 4, Philadelphia Warriors 2
1949: Minneapolis Lakers 4, Washington Capitols 2

College Basketball

NCAA Championship
1940: Indiana 60, Kansas 42
1941: Wisconsin 39, Washington State 34
1942: Stanford 53, Dartmouth 38
1943: Wyoming 46, Georgetown 34
1944: Utah 42, Dartmouth 40
1945: Oklahoma A&M 49, New York University 45
1946: Oklahoma A&M 43, North Carolina 40
1947: Holy Cross 58, Oklahoma 47
1948: Kentucky 58, Baylor 42
1949: Kentucky 46, Oklahoma A&M 36

National Invitation Tournament Championship
1940: Colorado 51, Duquesne 40
1941: Long Island 56, Ohio 42
1942: West Virginia 47, Western Kentucky 45
1943: St. John's 48, Toledo 27
1944: St. John's 47, DePaul 39
1945: DePaul 71, Bowling Green 54
1946: Kentucky 46, Rhode Island 45
1947: Utah 49, Kentucky 45
1948: St. Louis 65, New York University 52
1949: San Francisco 48, Loyola 47

Professional Football

National Football League Championship
1940: Chicago Bears 73, Washington Redskins 0
1941: Chicago Bears 37, New York Giants 9
1942: Washington Redskins 14, Chicago Bears 6
1943: Chicago Bears 41, Washington Redskins 21
1944: Green Bay Packers 14, New York Giants 7
1945: Cleveland Rams 15, Washington Redskins 14
1946: Chicago Bears 24, New York Giants 14
1947: Chicago Cardinals 28, Philadelphia
   Eagles 21

1948: Philadelphia Eagles 7, Chicago Cardinals 0
1949: Philadelphia Eagles 14, Los Angeles Rams 0

National Football League Most Valuable Player
1940: Ace Parker, Brooklyn Dodgers
1941: Don Hutson, Green Bay Packers
1942: Don Hutson, Green Bay Packers
1943: Sid Luckman, Chicago Bears
1944: Frank Sinkwich, Detroit Lions

1945: Bob Waterfield, Cleveland Rams
1946: Bill Dudley, Pittsburgh Steelers
1947: No award
1948: Pat Harder, Chicago Cardinals
1949: No award

National Football League All-Star Game
1940: Chicago Bears 28, NFL All-Stars 14
1941: Chicago Bears 35, NFL All-Stars 24
1942: NFL All-Stars 17, Washington Redskins 14
1943-1949: No games (resumed as Pro Bowl in 1950)

Canadian Football League Championship (Grey Cup)
1940: Ottawa Rough Riders 20, Toronto Balmy Beach Beachers 7
1941: Winnipeg Blue Bombers 18, Ottawa Rough Riders 6

1942: Toronto RCAF Hurricanes 8, Winnipeg RCAF Bombers 5
1943: Hamilton Flying Wildcats 23, Winnipeg RCAF Bombers 14
1944: Montreal HMCS Donnacona 7, Hamilton Flying Wildcats 6
1945: Toronto Argonauts 35, Winnipeg Blue Bombers 0
1946: Toronto Argonauts 28, Winnipeg Blue Bombers 6
1947: Toronto Argonauts 10, Winnipeg Blue Bombers 6
1948: Calgary Stampeders 12, Ottawa Rough Riders 7
1949: Montreal Alouettes 28, Calgary Stampeders 15

College Football

NCAA Champions (based on multiple title-granting entities)
1940: Minnesota, Stanford, and Tennessee
1941: Alabama, Minnesota, and Texas
1942: Georgia, Ohio State, and Wisconsin
1943: Notre Dame
1944: Army
1945: Ohio State and Army
1946: Army, Georgia, and Notre Dame
1947: Michigan and Notre Dame
1948: Michigan
1949: Notre Dame and Oklahoma

Heisman Trophy Winner
1940: Tom Harmon, Michigan
1941: Bruce Smith, Minnesota
1942: Frank Sinkwich, Georgia
1943: Angelo Bertelli, Notre Dame
1944: Les Horvath, Ohio State
1945: Doc Blanchard, Army
1946: Glenn Davis*, Army
1947: Johnny Lujack, Notre Dame
1948: Doak Walker, Southern Methodist
1949: Leon Hart, Notre Dame

Professional Hockey

National Hockey League Championship (Stanley Cup)
1940: New York Rangers 4, Toronto Maple Leafs 2
1941: Boston Bruins 4, Detroit Red Wings 0
1942: Toronto Maple Leafs 4, Detroit Red Wings 3
1943: Detroit Red Wings 4, Boston Bruins 0
1944: Montreal Canadiens 4, Chicago Black Hawks 0
1945: Toronto Maple Leafs 4, Detroit Red Wings 0
1946: Montreal Canadiens 4, Boston Bruins 1

1947: Toronto Maple Leafs 4, Montreal Canadiens 2
1948: Toronto Maple Leafs 4, Detroit Red Wings 0
1949: Toronto Maple Leafs 4, Detroit Red Wings 0

National Hockey League Most Valuable Player (Hart Memorial Trophy)
1940: Ebbie Goodfellow, Detroit Red Wings
1941: Bill Cowley, Boston Bruins
1942: Tommy Anderson, Brooklyn Americans
1943: Bill Cowley, Boston Bruins

1944: Babe Pratt, Toronto Maple Leafs
1945: Elmer Lach, Montreal Canadiens
1946: Max Bentley, Chicago Blackhawks
1947: Maurice "Rocket" Richard*, Montreal
 Canadiens
1948: Buddy O'Connor, New York Rangers
1949: Sid Abel, Detroit Red Wings

National Hockey League Rookie of the Year (Calder Memorial Trophy)
1940: Kilby MacDonald, New York Rangers
1941: Johnny Quilty, Montreal Canadiens
1942: Grant Warwick, New York Rangers

1943: Gaye Stewart, Toronto Maple Leafs
1944: Gus Bodnar, Toronto Maple Leafs
1945: Frank McCool, Toronto Maple Leafs
1946: Edgar Laprade, New York Rangers
1947: Howie Meeker, Toronto Maple Leafs
1948: Jim McFadden, Detroit Red Wings
1949: Pentti Lund, New York Rangers

National Hockey League All-Star Game
1947: All-Stars 4, Toronto Maple Leafs 3
1948: All-Stars 3, Toronto Maple Leafs 1
1949: All-Stars 3, Toronto Maple Leafs 1

Automobile Racing

Indianapolis 500 Winner
1940: Wilbur Shaw
1941: Floyd Davis/Mauri Rose (Davis started race,
 Rose finished race in same car)
1942: none (World War II)
1943: none (World War II)

1944: none (World War II)
1945: none (World War II)
1946: George Robson
1947: Mauri Rose
1948: Mauri Rose
1949: Bill Holland

Boxing

Heavyweight Champion of the World
1937-1949: Joe Louis*

1949-1951: Ezzard Charles

Running

Boston Marathon Winner
1940: Gerald Cote
1941: Leslie Pawson
1942: Joe Smith
1943: Gerald Cote
1944: Gerald Cote

1945: John Kelley
1946: Stylianos Kyriakides
1947: Suh Yun-Bok
1948: Gerald Cote
1949: Karl Leandersson

Professional Tennis

Men Singles

	Australian Open	French Open	Wimbledon	U.S. Open
1940	Adrian Quist	none (World War II)	none (WWII)	Don McNeill
1941	none (WWII)	none (WWII)	none (WWII)	Bobby Riggs
1942	none (WWII)	none (WWII)	none (WWII)	Ted Schroeder
1943	none (WWII)	none (WWII)	none (WWII)	Joseph Hunt
1944	none (WWII)	none (WWII)	none (WWII)	Frank Parker
1945	none (WWII)	none (WWII)	none (WWII)	Frank Parker
1946	John Bromwich	Marcel Bernard	Yvon Petra	Jack Kramer
1947	Dinny Pails	Jozsef Asboth	Jack Kramer	Jack Kramer
1948	Adrian Quist	Frank Parker	Bob Falkenburg	Pancho Gonzales
1949	Frank Sedgeman	Frank Parker	Ted Schroeder	Pancho Gonzales

Women Singles

	Australian Open	French Open	Wimbledon	U.S. Open
1940	none (WWII)	none (WWII)	none (WWII)	Alice Marble
1941	none (WWII)	Alice Weiwers	none (WWII)	Sarah Cooke
1942	none (WWII)	Alice Weiwers	none (WWII)	Pauline Addie
1943	none (WWII)	Simone Lefargue	none (WWII)	Pauline Addie
1944	none (WWII)	Raymonde Veber	none (WWII)	Pauline Addie
1945	none (WWII)	Lolette Payot	none (WWII)	Sarah Cooke
1946	Nancye Bolton	Margaret Osborne duPont	Pauline Addie	Pauline Addie
1947	Nancye Bolton	Patricia Todd	Margaret Osborne duPont	Louise Clapp
1948	Nancye Bolton	Nelly Landry	Louise Clapp	Margaret Osborne duPont
1949	Doris Hart	Margaret Osborne duPont	Louise Clapp	Margaret Osborne duPont

Professional Golf

Men

	U.S. Open	British Open	PGA Championship	Masters Tournament
1940	Lawson Little	none (WWII)	Byron Nelson	Jimmy Demaret
1941	Craig Wood	none (WWII)	Vic Ghezzi	Craig Wood
1942	none (WWII)	none (WWII)	Sam Snead	Byron Nelson
1943	none (WWII)	none (WWII)	none (WWII)	none (WWII)
1944	none (WWII)	none (WWII)	Bob Hamilton	none (WWII)
1945	none (WWII)	none (WWII)	Byron Nelson	none (WWII)
1946	Lloyd Mangrum	Sam Snead	Ben Hogan*	Herman Keiser
1947	Lew Worsham	Fred Daly	Jim Ferrier	Jimmy Demaret
1948	Ben Hogan*	Henry Cotton	Ben Hogan*	Claude Harmon
1949	Cary Middlecoff	Bobby Locke	Sam Snead	Sam Snead

Women

	U.S. Women's Open	Titleholders Championship	Western Open
1940	not established	Helen Hicks	Babe Didrikson Zaharias*
1941	not established	Dorothy Kirby	Patty Berg
1942	not established	Dorothy Kirby	Betty Jameson
1943	not established	none (WWII)	Patty Berg
1944	not established	none (WWII)	Babe Didrikson Zaharias*
1945	not established	none (WWII)	Babe Didrikson Zaharias*
1946	Patty Berg	Louise Suggs	Louise Suggs
1947	Betty Jameson	Babe Didrikson Zaharias*	Louise Suggs
1948	Babe Didrikson Zaharias*	Patty Berg	Patty Berg
1949	Louise Suggs	Peggy Kirk	Louise Suggs

Horse Racing

	Kentucky Derby	**Preakness Stakes**	**Belmont Stakes**	**Santa Anita Handicap**
1940	Gallahadion	Bimelech	Bimelech	Seabiscuit
1941	Whirlaway	Whirlaway	Whirlaway[3]	Bay View
1942	Shut Out	Alsab	Shut Out	none (WWII)
1943	Count Fleet	Count Fleet	Count Fleet[3]	none (WWII)
1944	Pensive	Pensive	Bounding Home	none (WWII)
1945	Hoop, Jr.	Polynesian	Pavot	Thumbs Up
1946	Assault	Assault	Assault[3]	War Knight
1947	Jet Pilot	Faultless	Phalanx	Olhaverry
1948	Citation	Citation	Citation[3]	Talon
1949	Ponder	Capot	Capot	Vulcan's Forge

[3]Triple Crown winners

Olympic Games

Summer Games

	Location	Medal Count Winner	# Of Medals
1940	None (WWII)		
1944	None (WWII)		
1948	London, England	United States	84

Winter Games

	Location	Medal Count Winner	# Of Medals
1940	None (WWII)		
1944	None (WWII)		
1948	St. Moritz, Switzerland	Switzerland	10

■ World War II: Wartime Agencies of the U.S. Government

Asterisks (*) indicate agencies for which full essays can be found in *The Forties in America*.

American Commission for the Protection and Salvage of Artistic and Historic Monuments in War Areas
Dates: August 20, 1943 to June 20, 1946
Department: Department of State
Function: This commission assisted in protecting cultural objects within war zones from damage or destruction and aided in restoring artifacts to the rightful owners. It had no operational arm; instead, it collaborated with other agencies and the armed forces to carry out its policies.

Board of Economic Warfare
Dates: December 17, 1941 to July 15, 1943
Department: Executive Office of the President
Function: Previously the Economic Defense Board, this body coordinated imports and exports critical to the war effort. It helped deny goods to enemy nations while facilitating the flow of commodities to U.S. allies. It also scheduled receipt of materials needed for manufacturing war equipment, oversaw the program whereby allies provided goods in lieu of payments for U.S. aid, and provided technical services to assess the economic impact of imports and exports for the United States and its allies. In July, 1943, its functions were transferred to the Office of Economic Warfare.

Board of War Communications
Dates: September 24, 1940 to February 27, 1947
Department: Executive Office of the President; later Office for Emergency Management
Function: Initially created as the Defense Communications Board, this group had its name changed on June 15, 1942. It was responsible for planning the most efficient use and control of radio, wire, and cable facilities under U.S. jurisdiction.

Civilian Production Administration
Dates: October 4, 1945 to April 23, 1947
Department: Office for Emergency Management
Function: Established as a successor to the War Production Board, this board promoted the conversion of industry from wartime to peacetime production. It gradually eased wartime controls and helped expand production of materials in short supply, controlled speculation, allocated scarce materials, and eventually took over efforts to dispose of surplus government property. Its activities accelerated the swift return of many civilian industries to profitability.

Committee on Fair Employment Practices
Dates: May 27, 1943 to June 30, 1946
Department: Office for Emergency Management
Function: Although originally part of other agencies, this committee became independent in 1943 and was charged with investigating discrimination in the workplace. Through its thirteen regional offices it sought out and prosecuted violators of an executive order prohibiting businesses executing government contracts from discriminating on the basis of race, creed, or national origin. Its activities were a precursor to, and a model for, those of later civil rights agencies within the Department of Justice.

Council of National Defense
Dates: May 29, 1940 to December, 1941
Department: Executive Office of the President
Function: Established by law in 1916 but inactive after 1918, this group was resurrected to coordinate mobilization and use of resources in the event of war. It was specifically charged with planning for industrial mobilization, and through subcommittees oversaw activities in industrial production, labor relations, agriculture, price stabilization, transportation, health and welfare, and consumer affairs. Most of its activities were transferred to other agencies during 1941; the council ceased operating by the end of that year.

Defense Plant Corporation
Dates: August 22, 1940 to June 30, 1945
Department: Reconstruction Finance Corporation
Function: This federally owned commercial company financed construction of plants for manufacturing arms, ammunition, military vehicles, ships, aircraft, equipment, and supplies. The government retained ownership of these facilities, leasing them to private companies, who operated them as manufacturing centers. At the end of hos-

tilities, the corporation sold many of these plants at significantly discounted prices to the companies that operated them. During its existence, the corporation invested $9 billion in approximately twenty-three hundred projects.

Defense Supplies Corporation

Dates: August 29, 1940 to June 30, 1945
Department: Reconstruction Finance Corporation
Function: This federally owned company purchased supplies and stockpiled materials deemed critical to the war effort. It bought commodities such as gasoline, alcohol, fiber, sugar, wool, tires, and rubber and resold these to civilian industries. It paid subsidies to businesses to produce agricultural products and operated oil pipelines in the country. The corporation also negotiated the purchase of key commodities from abroad.

Division of Defense Aid Reports

Dates: May 2, 1941 to October 28, 1941
Department: Office for Emergency Management
Function: This division administered the Lend-Lease Act of March 11, 1941. It oversaw lend-lease operations, maintained records of the program, and served as a clearinghouse for information regarding lend-lease activities. Its functions were transferred to the Office of Lend-Lease Administration in October, 1941.

Economic Defense Board

Dates: July 30, 1941 to December 17, 1941
Department: Executive Office of the President
Function: This board developed plans and policies to protect and strengthen U.S. international economic interests. Initially it was only an advisory board, but eventually it assumed responsibility for managing the export control program. Through its offices overseas, the board prepared economic needs assessments of foreign nations. In December, 1941, it became the Board of Economic Warfare.

Foreign Economic Administration (FEA)

Dates: September 25, 1943 to September 27, 1945
Department: Executive Office of the President
Function: This agency took over operations of Lend-Lease, the Office of Economic Warfare, and several State Department agencies. It managed export controls, lend-lease and reverse lend-lease, foreign relief, economic warfare, and economic intelligence. It bought critical raw materials from abroad, sold surplus materials, and coordinated the country's economic relations with foreign nations. The FEA also ran four corporations that procured critical commodities from foreign nations and handled international banking transactions.

Interdepartmental Committee for Coordination of Foreign and Domestic Military Purchases

Dates: December 6, 1939 to April 14, 1941
Department: Executive Office of the President
Function: This committee coordinated placement of orders for war materials by foreign nations, especially Britain and France, with companies in the United States. It also helped foreign governments negotiate contracts with American firms and helped create new facilities in the United States to produce goods for foreign allies. Its activities paved the way for establishment of the Lend-Lease Program in the spring of 1941.

Metal Reserves Company

Dates: October 28, 1940 to June 30, 1945
Department: Reconstruction Finance Corporation
Function: This federal corporation developed and managed stockpiles of critical materials such as aluminum, iron, bauxite, chrome, copper, lead, steel, tin, tungsten, and zinc. It made loans to mining companies to increase or improve their operations, and negotiated purchases of critical metals from overseas.

National Defense Mediation Board

Dates: March 19, 1941 to January 12, 1942
Department: Office for Emergency Management
Function: This board, consisting of representatives from labor, industry, and the general public, mediated labor disputes in industries considered critical to defense programs. It set up hearings on contentious cases and made nonbinding recommendations for settling those disputes. In 1942, its authority was transferred to the National War Labor Board.

National Railway Labor Panel

Dates: May 22, 1942 to August 11, 1947
Department: Executive Office of the President
Function: Operating within the framework of the

Railway Labor Act of 1934, this panel provided a means of settling labor disputes affecting common carriers. It had the authority to appoint investigators who also worked at settling controversies.

National War Labor Board*
Dates: January 12, 1942 to December 31, 1945
Department: Office for Emergency Management
Function: This twelve-person group representing labor, industry, and the general public succeeded the National Defense Mediation Board. Over its existence the board gained jurisdiction for all nongovernment labor disputes except those involving railroads and agriculture. Working chiefly through twelve regional offices, it monitored salaries and wages and turned over cases involving noncompliance with established labor laws and practices to the Office of Economic Stabilization, which could impose penalties on companies for failing to comply with the law.

Office of the Administrator of Export Control
Dates: July 2, 1940 to September 15, 1941
Department: Executive Office of the President
Function: Working with State Department officials, this office oversaw export activities involving materials essential to national defense. Through the military departments it arranged to requisition these materials for government use rather than allow them to be exported. The functions of this office were transferred to the Economic Defense Board in September, 1941.

Office of Alien Property Custodian
Dates: March 11, 1942 to October 14, 1946
Department: Office for Emergency Management
Function: This office had authority over property in the United States owned by individuals and corporations of hostile nations. While the Secretary of the Treasury handled the passive assets of these groups (cash, bank deposits, securities), the Alien Property Custodian was responsible for determining how to manage assets such as functioning businesses and copyright and trademark issues. The Custodian could decide whether to seize businesses on behalf of the United States, supervise their operations directly, or allow operations to continue under current management with some restrictions.

Office of Censorship
Dates: December 19, 1941 to November 15, 1945
Department: Executive Office of the President
Function: This office consolidated censorship efforts already begun by the Army and Navy. It had authority to censor communications between the United States and any foreign country. Postal and cable traffic was routinely screened and censored. The office also established guidelines for a voluntary censorship program within the American press. Its principal goals were to keep sensitive information out of enemy hands and to obtain sensitive information from intercepted communications. Among its most notable successes was the maintenance of secrecy surrounding the Manhattan Project, the United States' effort to develop the atomic bomb.

Office of Civilian Defense
Dates: May 20, 1941 to June 30, 1945
Department: Office for Emergency Management
Function: This office coordinated with state and local governments on matters of civil defense. It promoted civilian participation in defense programs, initially focusing on protecting citizens from air raids that might be aimed at industrial sites and population centers. It also developed programs to protect essential facilities near military centers. Eventually, it assumed responsibility for promoting blood drives, scrap-metal collections, and victory gardens. The Civil Air Patrol, later chartered by Congress, was initially created as a part of this agency.

Office of the Coordinator of Information (OCI)
Dates: July 11, 1941 to June 13, 1942
Department: Executive Office of the President
Function: This office carried out activities to collect and analyze information pertinent to national security, employing a variety of sources, including foreign nationals, to obtain information. It used these materials to prepare reports for the president and other government officials. In June, 1942, some duties of this office were transferred to the Office of War Information; the OCI then was placed under the control of the Joint Chiefs of Staff and renamed the Office of Special Services. It became the predecessor to the Central Intelligence Agency.

Office of the Coordinator of Inter-American Affairs

Dates: June 30, 1941 to April 10, 1946
Department: Office for Emergency Management
Function: This office formulated policies and programs to strengthen bonds between the United States and its neighbors in the Western Hemisphere. It conducted economic and cultural activities aimed at solidifying inter-American relationships. Gradually, however, the office lost control of many operations to other agencies and was eventually absorbed by the Department of State.

Office of Defense Health and Welfare Services

Dates: September 3, 1941 to April 29, 1943
Department: Office for Emergency Management
Function: Working closely with state and local authorities, this agency coordinated national efforts to promote physical fitness, health, and welfare. It assisted in planning health and welfare programs, especially at sites near military installations and war-related industries. It conducted educational programs promoting improved nutritional standards and good eating habits and managed federal day-care programs.

Office of Defense Transportation

Dates: December 18, 1941 to July 6, 1949
Department: Office for Emergency Management
Function: This office had limited operational authority over railroads, motor vehicles, inland waterways, pipelines, air transport, and coastal and intercoastal shipping. It determined the nation's transportation needs and initiated programs to meet them. It developed programs to minimize congestion, including backlogs of critical materials that had to be transported. The office was responsible for representing the federal government's interests with domestic carriers.

Office of the Director of Liquidation

Dates: January 4, 1946 to June 29, 1946
Department: Executive Office of the President
Function: This office served as a clearinghouse for the dismantling agencies that had been created to manage various wartime activities. It oversaw those agencies' plans to complete their affairs or transfer their functions to standing agencies of the government.

Office of Economic Stabilization

Dates: October 3, 1942 to December 12, 1946
Department: Office for Emergency Management
Function: This office was established pursuant to passage of the Economic Stabilization Act (October 10, 1942) as the mechanism for stabilizing prices in the civilian economy. It had authority to issue directives to other federal agencies, thereby exerting significant influence on costs and profits within American industries, especially as these related to salaries and manufactured goods. The office also became involved in efforts to stabilize rates for rental properties.

Office of Economic Warfare

Dates: July 15, 1943 to September 25,1943
Department: Office for Emergency Management
Function: This office assumed responsibility for all functions of the Board of Economic Warfare, as well as four former agencies of the Reconstruction Finance Corporation: the U.S. Commercial Company, Rubber Development Corporation, Petroleum Reserves Corporation, and Export-Import Bank of Washington, D.C. Within weeks, however, the office was abolished and its functions absorbed by the Foreign Economic Administration.

Office for Emergency Management (OEM)

Dates: May 25, 1940 to June 30, 1954
Department: Executive Office of the President
Function: This umbrella organization assisted the president in supervising agencies established to manage the war effort and control the civilian economy during the war. It served as a clearinghouse for information passing between the president and these organizations. Several important agencies—among them the National War Labor Board, Office of Civilian Defense, Office of Economic Stabilization, War Manpower Commission, War Production Board, and War Shipping Administration—were initially part of the OEM before becoming separate entities. By having many wartime agencies report through OEM, the president was able to monitor the nation's preparedness, mobilization, and production efforts without having too many agency heads report directly to him. Its functions were gradually transferred to other organizations within the federal government, and the office was removed from the list of active government agencies in 1954.

Office of Facts and Figures
Dates: October 24, 1941 to June 13, 1942
Department: Office for Emergency Management
Function: This office was responsible for presenting information to the public to help them understand the scope of the nation's defense efforts. It coordinated release of information from other government agencies but had no authority to clear or censor that information. The agency was incorporated into the Office of War Information in June, 1942.

Office of Lend-Lease Administration*
Dates: October 28, 1941 to September 25, 1943
Department: Office for Emergency Management
Function: This office managed the lend-lease program established by the Lend-Lease Act of March 11, 1941, replacing the Division of Defense Aid Reports. It was responsible for assuring that goods promised to other nations arrived on time and in the right places. To do so the agency coordinated routinely with other agencies, particularly the War Production Board and the armed forces. In September, 1943, it was consolidated with other agencies in the Foreign Economic Administration.

Office of the Petroleum Coordinator for National Defense
Dates: May 28, 1941 to December 2, 1942
Department: Department of the Interior
Function: This office coordinated federal programs to control the manufacture and distribution of oil and natural gas. It established priorities for allocating these commodities to the armed forces or the civilian economy. These functions were transferred to the Petroleum Administration for War in December, 1942.

Office of Price Administration*
Dates: April 11, 1941 to May 29, 1947
Department: Office for Emergency Management
Function: Originally created as the Office of Price Administration and Civilian Supply, this agency coordinated a broad range of activities concerning consumer products, rent, rationing, and agricultural pricing. It worked with industry to establish and enforce fair pricing for commodities, and had significant influence in setting rent and retail prices.

Office of Production Management
Dates: January 7, 1941 to January 24, 1942
Department: Office for Emergency Management
Function: This office was established to increase production for national defense by mobilizing the nation's industrial base. It formulated and executed plans for determining the nation's defense needs, constructing new plants, assuring the availability of raw materials, and coordinating production of material for the military. Eventually, the agency was given authority to establish priorities for ship construction and lend-lease. After the United States formally entered the war, this office was placed under the supervision of the War Production Board.

Office of Scientific Research and Development
Dates: June 28, 1941 to December 31, 1947
Department: Office for Emergency Management
Function: This office advised the president on scientific and medical research relating to national defense and helped mobilize resources to conduct such research. It developed policies and supervised research carried out by other government agencies and government contractors.

Office of Temporary Controls
Dates: December 12, 1946 to June 1, 1947
Department: Office for Emergency Management
Function: This office was organized after hostilities ended to complete the work of four wartime agencies: the Office of War Mobilization and Reconversion, Office of Economic Stabilization, Office of Price Administration, and Civilian Production Administration, the successor to the War Production Board. It oversaw the dissolution of these organizations or the transfer of functions from them to other government agencies.

Office of War Information
Dates: June 13, 1942 to September 15, 1945
Department: Executive Office of the President
Function: This agency developed programs to collect and disseminate information about the war to the general public. It developed policies for using the media in carrying out its tasks. After 1943, it was also responsible for American propaganda efforts abroad.

Office of War Mobilization*

Dates: May 27, 1943 to October 3, 1944

Department: Office for Emergency Management

Function: This office was created to bring about more effective cooperation between government agencies and American industry in mobilizing the nation's resources for war. It developed policies and programs and established priorities for using natural and industrial resources. In October, 1944, its functions were transferred to the Office of War Mobilization and Reconversion, an agency created under authority of a recently passed Congressional statute.

Office of War Mobilization and Reconversion

Dates: October 3, 1944 to July 1, 1947

Department: Executive Office of the President

Function: Assuming the responsibilities of the Office of War Mobilization, this office also was charged with formulating plans to transition the country from a wartime to a peacetime economy. Eventually it was responsible for authorizing the relaxation or removal of wartime controls on civilian production and rationing. In December, 1946, the office was transferred to the Office of Temporary Controls.

Petroleum Administration for War

Dates: December 2, 1942 to May 8, 1946

Department: Executive Office of the President

Function: Succeeding the Office of Petroleum Coordinator for War, this agency regulated the petroleum industry, developed systems for forecasting petroleum needs, and assigned priorities for production and use.

Rubber Reserves Company

Dates: June 28, 1940 to June 30, 1945

Department: Reconstruction Finance Corporation

Function: This government-owned corporation created a stockpile of rubber to meet the demands of the armed forces and serve the civilian economy. It procured rubber products from sources in the United States and abroad. It also developed and managed a program to create synthetic rubber.

Smaller War Plants Corporation

Dates: June 11, 1942 to January 28, 1946

Department: War Production Board

Function: This corporation promoted effective use of small business in producing materials for the war. Capitalized at $350 million, it made loans and leased equipment to small businesses and assisted them in competing for government contracts. In 1944, it began helping small businesses participate in programs for disposal of surplus government property.

Supply Priorities and Allocations Board

Dates: August 28, 1941 to January 16, 1942

Department: Office for Emergency Management

Function: This office drafted policies for allocating resources for military preparedness and the civilian economy. It determined total requirements for all commodities and established priorities for allocating them. The board was a policy-making agency only, however, relying on other entities such as the Office of Production Management, Office of Price Administration, various defense agencies, and the armed forces to carry out plans it developed.

United States Mission for Economic Affairs in London

Dates: October 19, 1943 to July, 1947

Department: Executive Office of the President

Function: This mission assisted the British government in solving wartime supply problems. It analyzed Britain's agricultural and industrial requirements and worked with U.S. government agencies and civilian industries to meet those needs. The mission's Petroleum Section not only monitored the needs of the Allies but also provided information used in selecting targets for bombing to disrupt the enemies' petroleum supplies and weaken their war-fighting capabilities.

War Assets Administration

Dates: March 25, 1946 to June 30, 1949

Department: Office for Emergency Management

Function: This body managed the sale or disposal of surplus government property. It determined the methods of sale, established prices, and arranged for payments to the government. Its functions were transferred to the General Services Administration in June, 1949.

War Food Administration

Dates: April 19, 1943 to August 20, 1945
Department: Department of Agriculture
Function: This body was created to consolidate a number of other agencies concerned with managing the nation's agricultural output during the war. It developed policies for regulating food production and allocating foodstuffs to military operations and the civilian economy.

War Manpower Commission

Dates: April 18, 1942 to September 19, 1945
Department: Office for Emergency Management
Function: This coordinating body formulated policies and programs for the effective mobilization and use of the nation's human resources. Representatives of more than one dozen other agencies sat on the commission. For a time, this group also oversaw the activities of the Selective Service System.

War Production Board*

Dates: January 16, 1942 to November 3, 1945
Department: Office for Emergency Management
Function: This board consolidated the activities of the Office of Production Management and Supply Priorities and Allocation Board. It became the chief agency for mobilizing the country's industries to support the war effort. It had authority to assign priorities for production to both government agencies and civilian industries.

War Relocation Authority

Dates: March 18, 1942 to June 30, 1946
Department: Office for Emergency Management
Function: This body developed programs to remove from areas near military facilities or key industrial centers any individuals designated potential security risks. Most of its efforts involved the forced relocation of Japanese living along the West Coast. The agency constructed relocation centers in fairly remote areas where individuals considered high risk were resettled for the duration of the war.

War Resources Board

Dates: August 9, 1939 to November 11, 1939
Department: Executive Office of the President
Function: This board advised the Joint Army and Navy Munitions Board on issues relating to mobilization in the event of war. It also reviewed the nation's Industrial Mobilization Plan, which had been created and periodically updated following World War I. Chief among this board's recommendations was the creation of several emergency agencies to handle key matters of mobilization and production for war. This proposal reversed the recommendation in the Industrial Mobilization Plan for a single superagency to manage the war effort.

War Shipping Administration

Dates: February 7, 1942 to September 1, 1946
Department: Office for Emergency Management
Function: This agency took over duties of the U.S. Maritime Commission for the duration of the war. It assigned shipping for use by the armed forces and other agencies, and controlled acquisition and use of all ocean-going vessels except combat ships and those engaged in coastal defense. It coordinated transportation of commodities to U.S. allies and managed a program to insure commercial shippers against losses as the result of the war.

Laurence W. Mazzeno

■ World War II Battles

To help place important aspects of World War II in a fuller historical context, this appendix offers details about selected major battles. The engagements are listed in chronological order. Battles that are covered in full essays within *The Forties in America* are marked with asterisks (*).

Battle of the Atlantic*
Date: 1939-1945
Location: Atlantic Ocean, including coasts and
  ports of the United States and Britain
The Battle of the Atlantic—so called because of the strategic warfare by German submarines and vessels against primarily British warships and commerce vessels in the Atlantic Ocean—challenged the military might of the Royal Navy and disrupted the transatlantic flow of supplies from North America that were needed by Allied ground forces in Europe. The first ship sunk during the six-year battle was a British passenger liner, *Athenia*, which went down with 112 people aboard. Twenty-eight of the dead were American citizens, thus prompting the United States to become a supplier to the British cause.

The first military vessel sunk by German submarines, the HMS *Courageous*, went down in September of 1939, taking with it more than 500 men. Shortly afterward, attacks on British naval bases followed. During the first three years of the battle for the Atlantic Ocean, German submarines (U-boats) sank more than 200 ships. Prior to American involvement in the war, German U-boats ruled the seas, as minimal escorts were available for convoy duty for either military or merchant vessels in the North Atlantic. The addition of air and sea support from Americans and Canadians helped minimize German success after 1943. The ratio of one U-boat destroyed for every fifty Allied vessels sunk changed dramatically in the later years of the war until it became a one-to-one ratio. In fact, German losses eventually became too great to continue the campaign. By the last year of the war, Allied control of the North Atlantic was nearly complete. Following German surrender however, reports showed that more than 170 German submarines had still been patrolling the coasts of the United States and its European allies.

Battle of Britain
Date: July 10-October 31, 1940
Locations: London and Plymouth, England, and
  Royal Air Force bases throughout Great Britain
Following the surrender of France in June, 1940,

German military planning in Europe concentrated on one target: Great Britain. In an effort to force Britain to negotiate a peace settlement, Germany used its larger air force to attack British cities and Royal Air Force (RAF) bases throughout Britain. Germany's air superiority was evident in the early stages of the war; also evident was an inadequate supply of well-trained and experienced British pilots. The Battle of Britain was an attempt by the Germans to gain control of the English Channel to limit the Royal Navy in blocking a possible German amphibious invasion from France.

Two things aided the British during the German air assault. First, the radar used by the British to detected incoming planes far surpassed the German ability to conceal their planes. Second, 112 Canadian pilots and a handful of American pilots (before the United States entered the war) significantly aided the outnumbered and relatively inexperienced RAF pilots against the better trained Germans. Strong rains and heavy fog also aided the British defense. By September 17, 1940, Adolf Hitler suspended daily bombings of London, Plymouth, and targets in Britain. By the time the Battle of Britain was over at the end of October, the less experienced RAF and Allied forces had shot down about 1,150 German planes, while losing only about 650 of their own. Although many cities had been seriously damaged from daily bombings and would continue to be targets throughout the war, the Battle of Britain was considered a success for Allied forces and would make a significant contribution to sustaining British morale through the rest of the war.

Pearl Harbor*
Date: December 7, 1941
Location: Pearl Harbor, Honolulu, Hawaii
In the Hawaiian Islands, December 7, 1941—a date that President Franklin D. Roosevelt said would "live in infamy"—began with a Japanese air strike at 7:48 A.M. The Japanese had succeeded in sending an attack force that included six aircraft carriers with more than 300 planes. The attack occurred prior to the formal declaration of war by the Japanese gov-

ernment. The resulting damage included the loss of the majority of the U.S. Pacific Fleet. Four battleships were sunk and four others were badly damaged, and three cruisers and three destroyers were either sunk or damaged. American casualties totaled 2,402. According to Japanese accounts, Pearl Harbor was attacked in order to give Japan a free reign over raw materials in the Pacific, most notably oil in the Philippines. The Americans were aware of a possible attack in the Philippines and the East Indies at U.S. military bases, but an attack on American territorial soil was not expected. The attack caused the opposite effect from what Japan had hoped; it angered the United States and brought the Americans into a war with Japan and its ally Germany.

Coral Sea

Date: May 4-8, 1942
Location: Coral Sea (Pacific)
The Battle of Coral Sea was the first naval campaign in which both the Japanese and Allied forces, including those of the United States and Australia, saw immediate action between rival aircraft carriers. On paper, the battle was a Japanese success because the Japanese sank more U.S. ships than they lost. However, the lasting effects of the battle became evident in the months to come. Damage suffered by several Japanese ships, including two aircraft carriers, made possible a lopsided U.S. victory in the Battle of Midway one month later. In both battles, the U.S. carriers *Yorktown* and *Enterprise* played prominent roles, and they would prove formidable foes to the Japanese Imperial Navy in the years to come.

Midway*

Date: June 3-7, 1942
Location: Midway Atoll (Pacific)
The battle of Midway Island was primarily a naval battle, although some damage was sustained by the U.S. ground forces on the Midway Atoll. The result of one of the most significant naval battles of the war was virtual parity between U.S. and Japanese naval forces. The battle cost the Japanese four carriers that were the heart of the Imperial fleet, and the loss of only one American carrier. After this battle, the Japanese had to go on the defensive in the Pacific.

El Alamein

Dates: July 1–July 27, 1942; October 23-November 4, 1942
Location: El Alamein, Egypt
The first battle of El Alamein was vital to Allied morale. The Allied forces, especially Britain, had suffered disheartening defeats by land and sea over the previous three years. If El Alamein fell to the Germans, Egypt and the Suez Canal would be next, and Allied supply routes would have to be extended to go around Southern Africa. Standing in the way of Allied forces was German field marshal Erwin Rommel. This first battle was ultimately a draw, creating a temporary stalemate that gave time to the Allies for fresh supplies to reach North Africa through the Suez Canal.

Often referred to as the first great Allied success, primarily because of British forces, the second battle of El Alamein was instrumental in both stalling the German advance in Europe and ending German plans to capture Egypt's Suez Canal and the oil fields of the Middle East.

Guadalcanal*

Date: August 7, 1942-February 9, 1943
Location: On and around Guadalcanal, Solomon Islands, South Pacific
Guadalcanal was the first major offensive for American troops in the war. The battle consisted of air, land, and sea campaigns focused primarily around the island of Guadalcanal. The first major fighting over Guadalcanal resulted in the worst surface defeat for the U.S. Navy in its history. Japanese planes and naval ships bombarded the outnumbered U.S. fleet, sinking five cruisers while enduring minimal losses themselves. The Marine landings on Guadalcanal and surrounding islands resulted in further heavy American casualties, but they provided the first major American offensive victory and consequently constituted a turning point in the war. The U.S. ended a string of victories of the previously unchallenged Japanese army. American and Australian forces successfully protected Guadalcanal's main airfield, which provided a major base on which Allied forces developed their air superiority in the Pacific.

Normandy

Date: June 6-August 25, 1944
Location: Normandy, France

The Battle of Normandy, known as D Day, is one of the most remembered land battles of the war. Twelve nations, including the United States and Canada, participated in the Normandy invasion. The initial assault on Omaha and Utah beaches resulted in the attempted landing of 130,000 Allied forces. By nightfall of the first day, nearly 10,000 Allied troops were dead or wounded. German forces were dug in, and steep cliffs overlooking the beach provided excellent cover for German machine gunners. Three nations—Great Britain, Canada, and the United States—were crucial in the D-day campaign. The outcome allowed for millions of men and tons of military might in the form of tanks, vehicles, and munitions to be delivered to Allied strongholds in Britain and France. The success of Allied forces at Normandy allowed for control of Western Europe while Russia was gaining ground in Eastern Europe. German forces were caught in between.

Philippine Sea

Date: June 19-20, 1944
Location: Near Mariana Islands

This battle was another turning point that signaled the imminent demise of the Japanese Imperial Navy. As supplies and raw materials dwindled for Japan, technological advances by the United States in plane construction and radar surpassed those of outdated Japanese aircraft. As a result, the Japanese lost three more aircraft carriers in this battle and more than 600 aircraft. Afterward, the Japanese had fewer than 100 aircraft in useable condition, and their carriers would be little use in future battles.

Leyte Gulf

Date: October 23-October 26, 1944
Location: Off the coast of Leyte, Philippine Sea

The largest naval battle in history, the Battle of Leyte Gulf was fought between the Japanese and American navies and included major engagements in the Sibuyan Sea, Surigao Strait, Cape Engaño, and Samar. The battle is known for two memorable events. First, Admiral William F. Halsey's blunder of leaving a portion of the U.S. fleet unprotected adversely affected his reputation among his sailors for a short time. Second, the battle saw the first recorded kamikaze attacks, in which Japanese pilots flew explosive-laden planes directly into American ships. Nevertheless, the Allied forces all but destroyed the remaining enemy fleet, as the Japanese were forced to retreat.

The Bulge*

Date: December 16, 1944-January 25, 1945
Location: Ardennes Region (France, Luxembourg, Belgium)

The Battle of the Bulge saw the last major offensive of Germany in the war. The battle was fought during the brutally cold winter months of December and January in the Ardennes forests of France and Luxembourg. The German attack was a surprise to U.S. forces in Belgium. German forces had immediate success in the initial days of the attack; however, the push resulted in only a small "bulge" of allied troops in retreat. The American and Allied forces quickly reassembled and regained the lost territory, resulting in a German withdrawal weeks later. Casualties on both sides were significant. The United States alone lost nearly 75,000 men. Estimates indicate the Germans lost nearly 95,000 men. The weather, bitterly cold and snowy, played the biggest role in the battle. In the initial days of the battle, the poor weather conditions hampered Allied forces' counterattack through the air, but soon after, they established air superiority. The battle also marked a first in war technology. German rocket-propelled planes were first used to bomb supply depots in the Battle of the Bulge. They were successful in their missions; however, because of unsuccessful attacks by German ground forces, the role of the planes was minimized.

Iwo Jima*

Date: February 19-March 16, 1945
Location: Iwo Jima, Ogasawara Islands, Pacific Ocean

One of the bloodiest battles of the entire war, Iwo Jima was a staging ground for U.S. and Allied superiority in the Pacific. Taking place fewer than eight hundred miles from the Japanese mainland, the battle was fiercely fought by the Japanese infantry. The battle is remembered for the record numbers of both Japanese and American casualties. Japan lost 95 percent of its fighting force, a small percentage of whom committed ritual suicide. The United States lost more than 27,000 men. The battle is also remembered because of a famous photograph taken of U.S. Marines planting an American flag on the island.

Okinawa*

Date: April 1-June 21, 1945

Location: Okinawa, Ryukyu Islands

The Battle of Okinawa was the bloodiest battle in the Pacific campaign. Allied causalities and those missing in action, primarily American, totaled more than 50,000, while Japanese numbers were 110,000. American forces initially experienced little resistance as they occupied the island. Not until American forces reached the caves of the island did Japanese forces catch them off-guard. In addition to the heavily entrenched Japanese infantry, Japanese kamikaze pilots bombarded U.S. naval support ships off the island. However, the Battle of Okinawa sealed Japan's fate. Although the United States lost 34 ships and more than 700 planes, Japan lost 16 ships from its already severely depleted fleet and more than 7,000 planes. After this battle, U.S. forces continued to leapfrog through Pacific islands, steadily increasing Allied land, air, and sea superiority in anticipation of a massive amphibious landing on mainland Japan. However, after two atomic bombs were dropped on Japan in August, Japan surrendered, and the Allies occupied Japan peacefully.

Berlin

Date: April 16-May 2, 1945

Location: Berlin, Germany

The Battle of Berlin occurred at Germany's final stronghold and signaled the last days of the Third Reich. On April 16, under agreement with the Western Allies (primarily Britain and the United States), Soviet forces advanced on the German capital. The battle lasted approximately sixteen days and provided three important historical footnotes. April 20, 1945, was the last public appearance of Adolf Hitler, who attempted a last-ditch rally of his shrinking army, which he tried to buttress with teenage and elderly conscripts. In addition, April 20 was Hitler's birthday; from the Western Allies, he received a non-stop aerial bombardment and from the Soviet Red Army on the ground, a mortar attack. Finally, on April 30, Hitler took his life. The city fell two days later to Soviet, American, and British forces. However, the Allies permitted Soviet forces to take control of the city, setting up the basis for a future conflict between the communist and noncommunist worlds.

Keith J. Bell

■ World War II: Military Leaders

This list is a selection of the top Canadian and American military leaders during World War II. Names marked with asterisks (*) are subjects of full essays in *The Forties in America*.

Arnold, General H. H. "Hap"*
Born: 1886
Died: 1950
Service branch: U.S. Army Air Force
The U.S. Army's first pilot (1911), Arnold commanded the U.S. Army Air Force in the war and is credited with creating the independent Air Force. He was named General of the Air Force (5-star) in 1949.

Barbey, Vice Admiral Daniel E.
Born: 1889
Died: 1969
Service branch: U.S. Navy
Admiral Barbey established amphibious warfare and developed the Landing Ship Tank (LST) and Landing Ship Dock (LSD). He oversaw fifty-six Pacific operations that landed a total of one million troops.

Bradley, General Omar Nelson*
Born: 1893
Died: 1981
Service branch: U.S. Army
Field commander in the North African and Italian campaigns, then commander of the First Army Group in the Normandy invasion. As the postwar chairman of the Joint Chiefs of Staff he took the Air Force's position in the "revolt of the admirals," a bitter conflict over priorities in defense. In 1950, he was named a five-star General of the Army.

Burke, Commodore Arleigh
Born: 1901
Died: 1996
Service branch: U.S. Navy
Dramatic destroyer squadron commander in the Pacific, especially at Bougainville Island, where he was known as "31-knot Burke" for his lightning attacks. In the 1950's, he was made a full admiral and Chief of Naval Operations. He lived to commission the first of many of the Arleigh Burke class of guided-missile destroyers.

Chennault, Major General Claire Lee
Born: 1890
Died: 1958
Service branch: U.S. Air Force
Founded the Flying Tigers for China against the Japanese, later incorporated into the Army as the Fourteenth Air Force. His pilots flew the "hump" over the mountains between India and China on dangerous supply runs.

Clark, General Mark
Born: 1896
Died: 1984
Service branch: U.S. Army
In 1942, he arranged the Darlan Deal, the cease-fire in North Africa that neutralized the Vichy French forces opposing the Allies. He commanded the Fifth Army in Italy, and after a near-disaster at Salerno, liberated Rome. He was named Allied High Commissioner for Austria, 1945-1947.

Clark, Rear Admiral Joseph J.
Born: 1893
Died: 1971
Service branch: U.S. Navy
Clark commanded carrier task forces in the Pacific, where he was instrumental in the Battle of the Marianas. He was the first Native American graduate of the Naval Academy and later commanded the Seventh Fleet in the Korean War.

Clay, Lieutenant General Lucius DuBignon
Born: 1897
Died: 1978
Service branch: U.S. Army
Clay brilliantly organized munitions and supplies throughout the war, then was posted to Germany, where he became famous for his 1948 Berlin Airlift, defeating the Russian siege of the city. He became a full general in 1947.

Collins, Lieutenant General J. Lawton
Born: 1896
Died: 1987
Service branch: U.S. Army
Lawton commanded the Twenty-Fifth Infantry in the Pacific at Guadalcanal and North Georgia, then the Seventh Corps at Utah Beach on D Day. He led the Seventh across France and Germany in a series of battles and liberated Cologne. After the War, he was Chief of Public Information, 1945-1947, and was made a full general in 1948 and appointed Army Chief of Staff, 1949-1953. He was instrumental in the military development of the North Atlantic Treaty Organization (NATO).

Crerar, General Henry
Born: 1888
Died: 1965
Service branch: Royal Canadian Army
Crerar was the first Canadian to lead a field army in battle as commander of the First Canadian Army in Italy (1942-1946) and the D-Day invasion. After D Day, the army struck north and took the last segment of the Siegfried Line in the Netherlands.

Darby, Colonel William O.
Born: 1911
Died: 1945
Service branch: U.S. Army
A dashing warrior who formed the First Ranger Battalion (the "Green Berets") in 1942. Fought in North Africa, Sicily, and Italy and took temporary command of the Tenth Mountain Division during the German retreat from northern Italy after its commander was taken ill. He was killed in action by a stray shot and made brigadier general posthumously.

Davis, Brigadier General Benjamin O., Sr.
Born: 1877
Died: 1970
Service branch: U.S. Army
Though Davis was named the first African American general officer in 1939, the Army was ambivalent about assigning him any commands. He was assistant Inspector-General of the Army in charge of racial issues in the European theater during the War.

Davis, Colonel Benjamin O., Jr.*
Born: 1912
Died: 2002
Service branch: U.S. Army Air Force
Davis was the son of the first African American general, and he formed and commanded the Tuskegee Airmen, an elite fighter group of all-black pilots, and later an all-black bomber group. In 1954, Davis, Jr., became the first African American general in the Air Force.

Devers, General Jacob L.
Born: 1887
Died: 1979
Service branch: U.S. Army
In 1940, Devers was appointed to choose the sites of U.S. bases in the British Caribbean in the "destroyers for bases" deal. He became the commander of the European Theater of Operations, 1943-1944, then commander of the Sixth Army Group of 750,000 men from American and French units.

Donovan, Major General William J. "Wild Bill"
Born: 1883
Died: 1959
Service branch: U.S. Army
Donovan emerged from World War I with a Medal of Honor and three Purple Hearts and then became a powerful New York attorney. In 1942, the flamboyant Donovan formed the Office of Strategic Services (OSS), bringing together scattered and rival intelligence services engaged in espionage and sabotage. At the end of the war, he was assistant prosecutor for the Nuremberg War Trials. President Harry S. Truman, who disliked Donovan, dissolved the OSS, but two years later, the Central Intelligence Agency (CIA) emerged to replace it.

Doolittle, Lieutenant General Jimmy
Born: 1896
Died: 1993
Service branch: U.S. Army Air Force
A hero for his dramatic morale-building 1942 bombing raid on Tokyo, for which he received the Congressional Medal of Honor, he held Air Force commands in North Africa and Great Britain. In 1944, as head of the Eighth Air Force, he designed carpet bombing of German cities.

Eichelberger, Lieutenant General Robert
Born: 1886
Died: 1961
Service branch: U.S. Army
Eichelberger rallied Australian troops and commanded the Thirty-second Infantry in New Guinea, where he turned back the Japanese at Buna, New Guinea, one of the first allied land victories in the Pacific. He then led the Eighth Army in the Battle of Hollandia and the liberation of the Philippines. After the war, he commanded all Allied forces in occupied Japan, 1945-1948.

Eisenhower, General of the Army Dwight D.*
Born: 1890
Died: 1969
Service branch: U.S. Army
Eisenhower headed the North African Command, then was Supreme Allied Commander, Europe, responsible for the D-Day landings. After the war, he was Supreme Allied Commander for the North Atlantic Treaty Organization (NATO) and president of the United States from 1953 to 1961.

Fredendall, Lieutenant General Lloyd R.
Born: 1883
Died: 1963
Service branch: U.S. Army
In North Africa, Fredendall commanded the Eleventh Corps, where his incompetent deployment of forces led to the American defeat at Kasserine Pass. One of the least able American commanders in the war, he was removed and made commander of a training corps.

Halsey, Fleet Admiral William F.*
Born: 1882
Died: 1959
Service branch: U.S. Navy
Halsey commanded carrier forces during the war. He was at sea on his flagship *Enterprise* when the Japanese struck Pearl Harbor, thus saving it and other carriers. He was naval commander in the South Pacific, 1942-1944, leading assaults on the Solomon and Bougainville islands. Halsey later mismanaged the Battle of Leyte Gulf, leaving a critical strait unprotected. Twice, he blundered into typhoons with loss of ships and lives and was reprimanded but never censured.

Hobby, Colonel Oveta Culp
Born: 1905
Died: 1995
Service branch: U.S. Army (Women's Army Corps)
The wife of a prominent former governor of Texas, Hobby was chosen to establish the Women's Army Corps (WAC), which she headed from 1942 to 1945. Overcoming antifemale prejudice, she grew the WAC to more than 140,000 enlisted women and officers by 1945.

Holcomb, General Thomas
Born: 1879
Died: 1965
Service branch: U.S. Marine Corps
As commandant of the Marines from 1941 to 1943, Holcomb oversaw a twelvefold increase in the corps, while defending its independence. After retiring, he was named minister to South Africa, 1944-1948.

Kimmel, Rear Admiral Husband Edward
Born: 1882
Died: 1968
Service branch: U.S. Navy
Kimmel was senior officer at Pearl Harbor at the time of the Japanese attack on December 7, 1941. He was forced to retire when he was declared guilty of dereliction of duty. A 1946 court of inquiry exonerated him but determined that he was guilty of "errors of judgment."

King, Fleet Admiral Ernest
Born: 1878
Died: 1956
Service branch: U.S. Navy
King was a gifted administrator but a touchy and hot-tempered personality who fought for Navy control of military operations in the southwest Pacific. He was Chief of Naval Operations and commander in chief of the U.S. fleet.

Kinkaid, Admiral Thomas C.
Born: 1888
Died: 1972
Service branch: U.S. Navy
Kinkaid was a carrier commander who fought in more battles than any other admiral. The list includes Midway, the eastern Solomon Islands, the Santa Cruz Islands, the Aleutian Islands, and Leyte Gulf. Following this, his fleet supported twenty-

seven amphibious assaults on the Philippines. After the war, he commanded the Eastern Sea front.

Leahy, Fleet Admiral William
Born: 1875
Died: 1959
Service branch: U.S. Navy
He retired from the Navy in 1939 and was named ambassador to Vichy, France, 1941-1942, with the goal of saving the French fleet for the Allies. Failing at that task, he returned to uniformed service to become chief of staff to President Roosevelt and chairman of the Joint Chiefs of Staff, a post he continued after the war under President Truman.

LeMay, General Curtis
Born: 1906
Died: 1990
Service branch: U.S. Army Air Force
LeMay was the U.S. bomber commander who developed shuttle bombing: striking one target, overflying to a safe base to refuel, and striking again on return. With him as commander, his Twentieth Air Force dropped 50 tons of incendiary bombs on Japan, killing 260,000 and burning 2.2 million homes to break Japanese morale. After the war, he was Air Force commander in Europe and oversaw the Berlin Airlift.

MacArthur, General of the Army Douglas*
Born: 1880
Died: 1964
Service branch: U.S. Army
After retiring from the U.S. Army, MacArthur became field marshall of the Philippine army, 1937-1941. In 1941, he was made commander of U.S. forces in the Far East, where he led the resistance to the Japanese invasion of the Philippines. MacArthur was named Supreme Allied Commander, Pacific. He directed the campaigns in New Guinea and a dramatic return to the Philippines in 1944. After accepting the Japanese surrender, he was allied governor of Japan, 1945-1951, until called to take command of all United Nations forces in the Korean War.

McAuliffe, Lieutenant General Anthony
Born: 1898
Died: 1975
Service branch: U.S. Army
As division commander of the 101st Airborne, he jumped into Normandy with his troops. In the Battle of Bastogne, seriously overmatched by German forces, he refused to surrender with the famous reply, "Nuts!" He became a symbol of American military determination against all odds.

McNaughton, Major General Andrew
Born: 1887
Died: 1966
Service branch: Royal Canadian Army
McNaughton commanded the First Canadian Army in the war, which he formed and developed in Great Britain. A scientist and engineer, during World War I, he developed the cathode-ray direction finder for artillery, a predecessor of radar. A staunch defender of Canadian military independence, he resigned in 1943 in conflict with the British over the unity of Canadian troops. He was appointed minister of defense 1944-1945 but twice failed to win a seat in Parliament, partly because of his opposition to conscription. He later served as Canadian ambassador to the United Nations, 1948-1949, and head of the U.N. Atomic Energy Commission, 1946-1948.

Marshall, General of the Army George C.*
Born: 1880
Died: 1959
Service branch: U.S. Army
As Army chief of staff from 1939 to 1945, Marshall reorganized army training for modern warfare and was called "the organizer of victory" by British prime minister Winston Churchill. He became secretary of state in 1947 and immediately introduced the Marshall Plan for the reconstruction of Europe, for which he received the Nobel Peace Prize in 1953.

Merrill, Major General Frank
Born: 1903
Died: 1955
Service branch: U.S. Army
Merrill was a romantic warrior who spoke Japanese. As a junior officer he was stranded in Burma at the start of the war. Cut off from his regular assignment, he joined General Joseph Stillwell and formed "Merrill's Maurauders," a polyglot elite jungle force of Americans, Caribbeans, Chinese, and Kachins. It grew to seven thousand men and harassed the Japanese behind their lines.

Mitscher, Admiral Marc A.
Born: 1887
Died: 1947
Service branch: U.S. Navy
A naval air commander in the Solomon Islands, he was best known for "The Great Marianas Turkey Shoot," a critical battle in which vital elements of the Japanese fleet were destroyed. After the war, Mitscher was commander of the Atlantic Fleet.

Nimitz, Fleet Admiral Chester W.*
Born: 1885
Died: 1966
Service branch: U.S. Navy
Nimitz was a submariner, but in 1941 was named commander in chief of the Pacific Fleet, and a year later, commander of all Allied forces in the Pacific Ocean area. From 1945 to 1947, he was chief of naval operations.

O'Daniel, Major General John W.
Born: 1894
Died: 1975
Service branch: U.S. National Guard
O'Daniel was an amphibious-assault specialist who developed the battle sled as a means of protecting infantry as they advanced behind tanks, significantly reducing casualties. He commanded assault landings at Algiers, Sicily, Anzio, and southern France, from where he led his troops into Germany, taking Nuremberg, Augsberg, and Munich. He later commanded the Army Infantry School, 1945-1948, and went on to command in the Korean and Vietnam wars.

Patton, Major General George S.*
Born: 1885
Died: 1945
Service branch: U.S. Army
Patton was a daring tank commander but was brash and sometimes imprudent. During the war, his forces proved critical in several major advances. After the war, he was briefly governor of Bavaria but was a lackluster administrator and was removed after an embarrassing public scene in which he lost his temper and accused a shell-shocked soldier of cowardice.

Radford, Admiral Arthur W.
Born: 1896
Died: 1973
Service branch: U.S. Navy
Radford was a carrier commander who led his task force into major battles in the Gilbert Islands, Iwo Jima, and Okinawa. After the war, he was a leader of the "revolt of the admirals," when a number of leading naval officers publicly attacked presidential policy, pitting the Air Force's insistence on superbombers against the Navy's carrier-dominated strategy.

Roosevelt, General Theodore, Jr.
Born: 1887
Died: 1944
Service branch: U.S. Army
The son of President Theodore Roosevelt, the younger Roosevelt was an infantry commander in World War I and had a prominent political career in the interwar period as assistant secretary of the Navy, governor of Puerto Rico, and governor-general of the Philippines. He returned to active duty during World War II, hiding his poor health, and was the only general to land on the beaches at D Day—for which he received the Congressional Medal of Honor. He died of a heart attack while on duty.

Simonds, General Guy
Born: 1903
Died: 1974
Service branch: Royal Canadian Army
Regarded as the finest Canadian general of the war and a soldier of remarkable tactical ability, from 1942 to 1945, Simonds shuttled among a number of commands in Italy and northwest Europe. His First Infantry Brigade in Sicily was especially successful. In 1944, his Second Canadian Corps landed at Normandy and later that year was decisive in the Battle of the Scheldt. Simonds developed the use of armored personnel carriers nicknamed "kangaroos" and innovative tank-infantry tactics. He was president of the Canadian Atomic Energy Board, 1946-1948, and in 1949, became commander of the Royal Military College, the National Defence College, and the Canadian Army Staff College.

Spatz, General Carl A. "Tooey"
Born: 1891
Died: 1974
Service branch: U.S. Army Air Force
Spatz headed the Air Force Combat Command, which became the Eighth Air Force in Britain. He became director of air operations in North Africa

and of all strategic air forces in the European invasion, then led the final air assault on Japan. In 1946, he was made commander of the Army Air Force and made the transition to the independent Air Force as first chief of staff, 1947-1948.

Spruance, Admiral Raymond A.
Born: 1886
Died: 1969
Service branch: U.S. Navy
Spruance won the critical Battle of Midway as commander of Task Force Sixteen, and from 1943 to 1945, he commanded the Fifth Fleet. He planned much of the Pacific advance, and took part in the assaults on the Gilbert and Marshall Islands, and his ships were decisive in the First Battle of the Philippine Sea. From 1946 to 1948, Spruance was president of the Naval War College.

Stilwell, General Joseph Warren*
Born: 1883
Died: 1946
Service branch: U.S. Army
Stilwell was one of the few "old China hands" in the Army at the start of the war. He was made commander of the China-Burma-India theater and chief of staff to Chiang Kai-Shek, president of China, where he fell afoul of the endless government corruption. After defeat of the Allies in Burma, Stilwell refused to leave his troops, and walked the remnant through the jungles to India.

Taylor, Major General Maxwell
Born: 1901
Died: 1987
Service branch: U.S. Army
Taylor was an airborne commander in the war, commanding the Eighty-second Airborne in Sicily and the 101st Airborne in France (where he was severely wounded) and the Netherlands. He was sent secretly to Italy when Benito Mussolini was toppled and persuaded the new government to declare war on Germany. He was made superintendant of West Point, 1945-1949, and took the Berlin Command, 1949-1951.

Vandegrift, General Alexander Archer
Born: 1887
Died: 1973
Service branch: U.S. Marine Corps
Vandegrift was the first Marine full general and the first to lead a Marine division into combat in the war. He was awarded the Congressional Medal of Honor for his heroic attack in the Solomon Islands. He was named commandant of the Marine Corps, 1944-1947, and successfully appealed to Congress against attempts by President Truman to subordinate the Marines to the Army.

Wainwright, General Jonathan
Born: 1883
Died: 1953
Service branch: U.S. Army
Wainwright replaced Douglas MacArthur as commander in the Philippines in 1942, where he led the Luzon Force in retreat to Bataan and Corregidor, for which he received the Congressional Medal of Honor. He surrendered the day the Japanese landed on Corregidor, and spent the rest of the war as a prisoner of war.

Waesche, Admiral Russell R.
Born: 1886
Died: 1946
Service branch: U.S. Coast Guard
Waesche was the longest-serving commandant of the Coast Guard, 1936-1945, and its first vice admiral and first full admiral. During the war, he oversaw the largest expansion of the Coast Guard in history and successfully defended its autonomy from the Navy.

Wedemeyer, Major General Albert C.
Born: 1897
Died: 1989
Service branch: U.S. Army
As a staff member of the War Plans Division, 1941-1943, Wedemeyer was accused of leaking top-secret plans to the press. He was exonerated but tainted and sent to Southeast Asia as aide to the British commander. He was then made commander of the China theater, regarded as a career graveyard. An outspoken critic of the corrupt Chinese Nationalists, in later years he became an icon of the far-right anti-Communist movement in the United States.

Norbert Brockman

■ Time Line

This time line provides a condensed chronology of important political, economic, military, social, and cultural events of the 1940's. Details on U.S. Supreme Court cases, major radio programs, films, and top-selling musical recordings can be found in other appendixes, as can additional details on federal legislation, best-selling books, literary awards, and Broadway plays.

1940

International: (Apr. 9-June 22) Germany attacks the Allies (Great Britain and France) through the neutral countries of Denmark, Norway, the Netherlands, Belgium, and Luxembourg; France surrenders on June 22. (June 10) Italy declares war on the Allies; U.S. president Franklin D. Roosevelt delivers the "Stab in the Back" speech, to characterize the Italian government's declaration as an act of cowardice. (July 26) Roosevelt issues executive order to freeze Japanese assets in the United States. (Aug. 18) Canadian prime minister William Lyon Mackenzie King and President Roosevelt sign the Ogdensburg Agreement, placing Canada and the United States in a common defensive alliance. (Sept. 2) In return for leases on British bases in North America, President Roosevelt announces the transfer of fifty destroyers to Britain.

Government and politics: (Mar. 26) Canadian prime minister King's ruling Liberal Party defeats Conservative coalition of Robert Manion. (Apr. 25) Women are granted the right to vote in Quebec. (June) Canadian parliament passes the National Resources Mobilization Act authorizing conscription for homeland-based military service. (June 19) Henry L. Stimson is appointed secretary of war; while Frank Knox is installed as secretary of the Navy. (June 24-28) Republican National Convention nominates New York businessman Wendell Willkie as its presidential candidate. (June 30) U.S. Fish and Wildlife Service is established. (July 15-18) Democratic National Convention nominates incumbent president Roosevelt to run for a third term. (Aug. 5) In Quebec, Canada, Montreal mayor Camillien Houde is arrested and interned for urging violation of the National Resources Mobilization Act. (Sept. 4) America First Committee is organized to lobby against U.S. intervention in European conflicts. (Sept. 14) Congress passes the Selective Service Act. (Nov. 5) Roosevelt is elected to a third presidential term. (Dec. 17) "Lend-Lease" to Britain is proposed by President Roosevelt. (Dec. 29) During a "Fireside Chat" broadcast over the radio, President Roosevelt delivers the "Arsenal of Democracy" speech.

Military: (Oct. 16) Colonel Benjamin O. Davis, Sr., is promoted and becomes the first African American general in the U. S. Army.

Society: (June 28) Smith Act designates stricter guidelines for the registration and fingerprinting of aliens and legal penalties on individuals espousing violent overthrow of the U.S. government. (July 4-Sept. 2) American Negro Exposition is held in Chicago.

Business and labor: (Aug. 22) Investment Company Act and the Investment Advisers Act of 1940 both passed into law. (Dec.) Henry J. Kaiser establishes the Richmond Shipyard in San Francisco Bay.

Science and technology: Antigravity ("G") suit invented by Canadian scientist Wilbur R. Franks. At the Berkeley Radiation Laboratory of the University of California, Edwin Mattison McMillan and Philip Abelson develop the isotope neptunium. (Feb. 27) At Berkeley, California, research chemists Samuel Rubin and Henry Kamen identify Carbon-14. (Sept. 21) First jeep vehicle is built by Bantam Car Company.

Environment: (Apr. 23) In Natchez, Mississippi, 209 die in the Rhythm Night Club fire. (Nov. 7) Tacoma Narrows Bridge over Puget Sound in Washington collapses only four months after opening for traffic. (Nov. 11-12) "Armistice Day Blizzard" covers large sections of the Midwest and causes 154 fatalities.

Arts, literature, and popular culture: Richard Wright's novel *Native Son* is published; other major published works include Paul Gallico's *The Snow Goose*, Ernest Hemingway's *For Whom the Bell Tolls*, Walter van Tilburg Clark's *The Ox-Bow Incident*, Dr. Seuss's *Horton Hatches the Egg*, and John F. Kennedy's *Why England Slept*. (Spring) *Batman Comics*, by Bob Kane and Jerry Robinson, first appears. (June 30) *Brenda Starr* comic strip debuts. (Dec. 21) Author F. Scott Fitzgerald dies of a heart attack while working on his Hollywood novel, *The Last Tycoon.* (Dec. 22) Author Nathaniel West is killed in a car crash while driving after hearing the news of Fitzgerald's death.

Sports: (Apr. 2-13) In the National Hockey League (NHL) Stanley Cup championship playoffs, the New York Rangers defeat the Toronto Maple Leafs four games to two. (Oct. 2-8) In the Major League Baseball World Series, the Cincinnati Reds defeat the Detroit Tigers four games to three. (Nov. 30-Dec. 7) In the competition for the Grey Cup Championship in Canadian football, the Ottawa Rough Riders defeat the Toronto Balmy Beach Beachers in two games, 8-2 and 12-5, to win by a combined total of 20-7. (Dec. 8) In the National Football League Championship game, the Chicago Bears beat the Washington Redskins 73 to 0.

1941

International: (June 25) President Roosevelt announces economic sanctions against Japan. (Aug. 14) Atlantic Charter of 1941 agreed to by President Roosevelt and British prime minister Winston Churchill. (Dec. 7) Japanese attack the U.S. military base at Pearl Harbor, Hawaii. Canada declares war on Japan, Romania, Finland, and Hungary. (Dec. 8) President Roosevelt delivers his "Day of Infamy" speech; United States declares war on Japan. (Dec. 11) Germany and Italy declare war on the United States. (Dec. 22, 1941-Jan. 14, 1942) At the Arcadia Conference in Washington, D.C., between Roosevelt and Churchill, officials agree that the primary Allied military effort should concentrate first on the war in North Africa and Europe.

Government and politics: (Jan. 6) President Roosevelt delivers his "Four Freedoms" speech to Congress. (Mar. 11) Lend-Lease Act, passed by Congress in Jan., comes into effect. (June 25) By means of Executive Order 8802 President Roosevelt mandates the end of discrimination in hiring, wages, benefits, and contracts in the military, and in war-related industries, establishing the Fair Employment Practices Committee to monitor compliance.

Military: (Feb. 4) United Service Organizations (USO) is established. Tuskegee Airmen begin training. (May 21) Merchant vessel SS *Robin Moor* is sunk by German submarine in neutral waters. (May 27) President Roosevelt puts U.S. armed forces on emergency status. (Sept. 4) German submarine attacks destroyer USS *Greer* en route from Greenland to Iceland. (Oct. 17) Destroyer USS *Kearney* is attacked by U-boats. (Oct. 31) Destroyer USS *Reuben James* is sunk by a German submarine.

Society: (May 1) March on Washington, D.C., called by African American labor leader A. Philip Randolph to protest racial discrimination practiced in the military and in war production contracts. (May 25) Randolph cancels the march, on learning of Roosevelt's Executive Order 8802. (Aug. 12) Canadian government mandates full registration of all Japanese, or Japanese Canadians, in the country. (Nov. 6) President Roosevelt declares fourth Thursday of each November as Thanksgiving Day.

Business and labor: (Apr.) Ford Motor Company begins construction of Willow Run Bomber Production Factory, located near Ypsilanti, Michigan.

Science and technology: (Feb. 23) Scientific team led by Glenn T. Seaborg produces plutonium at Berkeley, California. (June 28) Roosevelt administration announces formation of the Office of Scientific Research and Development to oversee all U.S. scientific wartime initiatives.

Arts, literature, and popular culture: Books published in 1941 include *My Friend Flicka* (Mary O'Hara), *Make Way For Ducklings* (Robert McCloskey), *The Keys to the Kingdom* (A. J. Cronin), *Curious George* (H. A. Rey and Margret Rey), and *The Last Tycoon* (F. Scott Fitzgerald—published posthumously). (Oct. 31) Mount Rushmore sculptures, designed and executed by Gutzon and James Lincoln Borglum, are completed. (Dec.) Bob Montana's *Archie* comic first appears in *Pep Comics 22*; Wonder Woman makes her first appearance in *All Star Comics*.

Sports: (Apr. 2-9) In the NHL Stanley Cup championship playoffs, the Boston Bruins beat the Detroit Red Wings 4 to 0. (June 2) Former New York Yankees star Lou Gehrig dies of amyotrophic lateral sclerosis (ALS), later known as Lou Gehrig's disease. (Oct. 1-6) In the World Series, the New York Yankees beat the Brooklyn Dodgers 4 to 1. (Nov. 29) In Canadian football, the Winnipeg Blue Bombers defeat the Ottawa Rough Riders 18-16 to capture the Grey Cup. (Dec. 21) In the National Football League Championship, the Chicago Bears beat the New York Giants 27 to 9.

1942

International: International League for the Rights of Man is established. (Jan. 15-28) International Conference at Rio de Janeiro establishes anti-Axis front in Latin America, with only Argentina and Chile objecting. (Feb. 24) Voice of America is established to broadcast radio programs into Axis-occupied countries.

Government and politics: (Jan. 12) National War Labor Board is established. (Jan. 16) War Production Board is set in place. (Jan. 30) Emergency Price Control Act becomes law. (Feb. 9, 1942-Sept. 30, 1945) Daylight saving time is federally mandated. (Apr. 18) War Manpower Commission is established to oversee the allocation of human resources between military and civilian needs. (Nov. 3) Midterm elections are held.

Military: (Jan. 2-May 6) Japanese invade the Philippines; Corregidor falls. (Feb. 23) Japanese submarine damages Ellwood oil production facility in California. (Feb. 24-25) "Battle of Los Angeles" occurs when antiaircraft artillery reacts to reputed sightings of Japanese planes. (Mar. 10) U.S. general Joseph Warren Stillwell assumes command in China front (China-India-Burma theater). (Apr. 10-17) Bataan Death March. (Apr. 18) Task force under the command of Lieutenant Colonel Jimmy Doolittle bombs targets in major Japanese cities. (May) Army Rangers are formed as elite commando unit. (May 7-8) In the Battle of the Coral Sea, U.S. naval and air forces stop the Japanese advance in the South Pacific. (June 3-7) In the Battle of Midway Island, U.S. naval and air forces destroy the Japanese task force attempting to attack the Hawaiian Islands. (June 3-21) Japanese forces attack the Aleutian Islands of Alaska. (Aug. 7, 1942-Feb. 9, 1943) In the Battle for Guadalcanal, U.S. forces repel a series of determined Japanese attacks. (Aug. 19) Disastrous offensive by Canadian and British forces against Dieppe in Nazi-occupied France results in losses of thirty-five hundred. (Sept. 9) Japanese plane drops incendiary bombs along Oregon coast. (Nov. 8) Operation Torch launched with U.S. troop landings near Casablanca, Morocco. (Nov. 13) Five Sullivan brothers all die when their battleship is sunk in the Pacific.

Society: (Jan. 2) Japanese Canadians are sent to internment camps. (Jan. 14) President Roosevelt's Proclamation 2537 compels all resident aliens to inform the Federal Bureau of Investigation of any change in their status. (Jan. 16) Film star Carole Lombard dies in plane crash while on a war bonds tour. (Feb. 19) Japanese Americans are ordered to internment camps by Presidential Executive Order 9906. (Apr.) James L. Farmer, Jr., and Bayard Rustin found Congress of Racial Equality (CORE). (Oct. 20) Durham Manifesto, issued by African American leaders, calls for an end to racial discrimination.

Business and labor: (Aug.) Bracero program, enabling Mexican farm workers to be temporarily employed in the United States, arises from an agreement between the Mexican and American governments.

Science and technology: Under the direction of the War Production Board, twenty-one American pharmaceutical companies undertake mass production of penicillin. (Aug. 13) Manhattan Project to develop a nuclear bomb is officially launched. (Oct. 6) Chester F. Carlson invents photo duplication technique known as "xerography." (Oct. 28) Alaska Highway is completed. (Nov.) "Bazooka" portable rocket launchers, developed by Clarence N. Hickman, are first used by United States troops in the North Africa campaign.

Environment: (Nov. 28) Boston's Cocoanut Grove nightclub goes up in flames, killing 492 people.

Arts, literature, and popular culture: Books published include *The Skin of Our Teeth* (Thornton Wilder), *Go Down, Moses* (William Faulkner), and *The Moon is Down* (John Steinbeck). (June) *The Sad Sack* comic strip is originated by Sergeant George Baker for *Yank: The Army Weekly.* (Oct. 16) Aaron Copland's ballet *Rodeo* debuts in New York. (Oct. 20) Art of This Century opens in New York City.

Sports: (Apr. 4-18) In the NHL Stanley Cup championship playoffs, the Toronto Maple Leafs beat the Detroit Red Wings four games to three. (Sept. 30-Oct. 5) In the World Series, the St. Louis Cardinals beat the New York Yankees four games to one. (Dec. 5) In Canadian football, the Toronto RCAF prevails, by the score of 8-5, over the Ottawa RCAF to win the Grey Cup. (Dec. 13) In the National Football League Championship, the Washington Redskins beat the Chicago Bears 14 to 6.

Crime: (Aug. 2) Murder of José Diaz in Los Angeles, California, later dubbed the "Sleepy Lagoon Murder," leads to the arrest of hundreds of Latino suspects, twenty-one of whom are charged with Diaz's murder.

1943

International: (Jan. 14-24) Casablanca Conference of the Allies calls for "unconditional surrender" of the Axis Powers. (Aug. 17-24) First Quebec Conference held between Franklin D. Roosevelt, Winston Churchill, and William Lyon Mackenzie King is convened. (Nov. 22-26) Cairo Conference of the Allies lays the groundwork for the postwar settlement in Asia. (Nov. 28-Dec. 1) Tehran Conference of Great Britain, United States, and Soviet Union decides upon the opening of a Western European "second front."

Government and politics: (Dec. 17) Immigration Act of 1943 (Chinese Exclusion Repeal Act) is signed into law.

Military: (Jan. 24-May 13) U.S. forces assist in sweeping Germans and Italians from North Africa. (Mar. 24-Aug. 15) Japanese are cleared from the Aleutians. (July 10, 1943-May 2, 1945) U.S. troops participate in the long and bloody Sicilian and Italian campaigns.

Society: (Apr.) General John L. DeWitt issues *Final Report: Japanese Evacuation from the West Coast-1942.* (May 31-June 7) Zoot-suit riots erupt in Los Angeles, California, as servicemen clash with Latino youths. (June 14) First Lady Eleanor Roosevelt blames the Zoot Suit Riots on racism against Mexican Americans, prompting angry rejoinders in the press denouncing Mrs. Roosevelt's remarks. (June 20) Race riot erupts in Detroit, Michigan.

Business and labor: American Enterprise Institute for Public Policy Research is established to promote free market principles. Chrysler Corporation's Chicago aircraft-engine plant is in operation. (June 25) Smith-Connally Anti-Strike Act is enacted.

Science and technology: Antihistamine diphenhydramine developed by George Rieveschl; William Sullivan and Lyle Goodhue invent the aerosol can. (Mar.) Plutonium production facility is established at Hanford Nuclear Reservation.

Environment: (Mar. 15) Jackson Hole National Monument is created. (July 26) "Black Wednesday" smog cloud pollution over Los Angeles sickens hundreds.

Arts, literature, and popular culture: Literary works published include *One World* (Wendell Willkie), *The Fountainhead* (Ayn Rand), *A Tree Grows in Brooklyn* (Betty Smith), *The Human Comedy* (William Saroyan), and *There Was an Old Woman* (Ellery Queen). Broadway musical: *Porgy and Bess.* (Jan. 15) Pentagon building, designed by George Bergstrom, is dedicated in Washington, D.C. (Mar. 31) Richard Rodgers and Oscar Hammerstein II's musical *Oklahoma!* premieres on Broadway. (Apr. 13) Jefferson Memorial, designed by the late John Russell Pope, is dedicated in Washington, D.C. (Nov. 1) *Buz Sawyer* comic strip originated by Roy Crane.

Sports: (1943-1954) All-American Girls Professional Baseball League operates through the Midwest. (Apr. 1-8) In the NHL Stanley Cup championship playoff, the Detroit Red Wings beat the Boston Bruins four games to zero. (Oct. 5-11) In the World Series, the New York Yankees beat the St. Louis Cardinals four games to one. (Nov. 27) In Canada, the Hamilton Flying Wildcats win the Grey Cup, beating Winnipeg RCAF by the score of 23 to 14. (Dec. 26) In the National Football League Championship, the Chicago Bears beat the Washington Redskins 41 to 21.

Crime: (Oct.) Murder convictions of twenty-one Sleepy Lagoon defendants are reversed in *People v. Zamora.*

1944

International: (Sept. 12-14) Second Quebec Conference between Franklin D. Roosevelt, Winston Churchill, and William Lyon Mackenzie King is convened.

Government and politics: (June 22) G.I. Bill (Servicemen's Readjustment Act of 1944) is signed into law. (June 24-28) Republican National Convention nominates New York attorney Thomas E. Dewey as its Presidential candidate. (July 15-18) Democratic convention nominates Franklin D. Roosevelt; Missouri senator Harry S. Truman is nominated as his vice-presidential running mate. (Aug. 1) Family Allowance Act passed by Canadian parliament. (Aug. 18) Former Montreal mayor Camillien Houde is released from his four-year internment and is shortly thereafter re-elected as mayor. (Oct. 8) Former presidential candidate Wendell Willkie dies. (Nov. 7) Franklin D. Roosevelt is elected to a fourth presidential term.

Military: (Mar. 25) "Great Escape" of Allied prisoners from a German prisoner-of-war camp. (June 6) Operation Overlord (D-day) landings of Allied forces, under command of U.S. general Dwight D. Eisenhower, establish a beachhead in continental Europe that the Allies exploit to drive German forces from France. (June 19-20) Great Marianas Turkey Shoot in Battle of the Philippine Sea. (July 17) Service people and civilian auxiliaries numbering 320 are killed in an ammunition explosion at the Port Chicago Naval Magazine near San Francisco, California. (Aug. 25-Nov. 16) Red Ball Express, the trucking system devised to facilitate the rapid shipment of fuel and supplies to the battle front, and primarily manned by African American drivers, is in full operation. (Oct.) Japanese begin kamikaze attacks on Allied vessels. (Nov. 3, 1944-Apr., 1945) Japanese send balloon bombs against West Coast of United States. (Nov. 24-29) Prime Minister King's decision to implement limited overseas conscription of troops leads to the Terrace (British Columbia) Mutiny, which is quickly quelled and underreported. (Dec. 16, 1944-Jan. 25, 1945) Battle of the Bulge is last major German offensive on the western front.

Business and labor: (July 1-22) Bretton Woods Conference in New Hampshire hammers together an international agreement aimed at stabilizing the world monetary systems. The International Monetary Fund (IMF) is thus established.

Science and technology: Antibiotic streptomycin developed by Selman Abraham Waksman. (Feb.) Findings of the Avery-MacLeod-McCarty experiment on DNA research are published in the *Journal of Experimental Medicine.*

Environment: (June 13) Big Bend National Park established in Texas.

Arts, literature, and popular culture: Literary works published include *An American Dilemma: The Negro Problem and Modern Democracy* (Gunnar Myrdal), *A Bell for Adano* (John Hersey—the book wins the 1945 Pulitzer Prize), *Rabbit Hill* (Robert Lawson), and *Dangling Man* (Saul Bellow). (Oct. 30) Aaron Copeland's *Appalachian Spring* ballet suite first performed in Washington, D.C. (Dec. 15) Airplane carrying noted band leader Glenn Miller disappears over the English Channel.

Sports: (Apr. 4-13) In the NHL Stanley Cup championship playoffs, the Montreal Canadiens beat the Chicago Black Hawks four games to zero. (June 4) All-America Football Conference (AAFC) founded, but will not begin organized competition until 1946 season. (Oct. 4-9) In the World Series, the St. Louis Cardinals defeat the St. Louis Browns four games to two. (Nov. 25) Montreal St. Hyacinthe-Donnacona Navy defeats the Hamilton Flying Wildcats, 7 to 6, in the Grey Cup. (Dec. 17) In the National Football League Championship, the Green Bay Packers beat the New York Giants 14 to 7.

Crime: (May) Shooting of Canadian army deserter Georges Guénette by Royal Canadian Mounted Police officers at his home near Quebec City, Quebec, sparks controversy throughout the province. (Aug. 14) Riot at Fort Lawton, Washington, results in the death of one Italian prisoner of war and in the court-martial and conviction of twenty-eight African American soldiers.

1945

International: International Court of Justice (World Court) is established; it will begin operating in 1946. CARE organization is established to deliver food packages to European civilians after the war. (Feb. 4-11) Yalta Conference meets to discuss the postwar European settlement. (Apr. 25) First meeting of the United Nations is held at San Francisco, California. (June 11) In Canada, the Liberal Party under William Lyon Mackenzie King wins its third general election. (July 16-Aug. 2) At the Potsdam Conference, Germany and Austria are divided into allied occupation zones, and the boundaries of Poland and Germany are redrawn. (Oct. 24) United Nations Charter is ratified. (Nov. 21, 1945-Oct. 1, 1946) Nuremberg Trials for crimes against humanity convenes.

Government and politics: House Committee on Un-American Activities becomes a permanent congressional committee. (Apr. 12) President Franklin D. Roosevelt dies of a stroke at Warm Springs, Georgia, and Vice President Harry S. Truman is sworn in as thirty-third president of the United States.

Military: (Jan. 9-Feb. 23) Philippines is liberated from Japan. (Jan. 31) Private Eddie Slovik is the first U.S. soldier since the Civil War executed for desertion. (Feb. 19-Mar. 17) U.S. victory over Japanese on Iwo Jima is occasion for iconic photograph of the Marines raising the flag over Mount

Suribachi. (Mar. 7) United States and Western allies push into western Germany and cross the Rhine River at the Ludendorff Bridge. (Apr. 1-June 23) Operation Iceberg: the Battle for Okinawa kills and wounds nearly forty-five thousand U.S. troops. (Apr. 18) Prize-winning war correspondent Ernie Pyle is killed by a Japanese sniper. (Apr. 30) Adolf Hitler commits suicide in his Berlin bunker. (May 8) Germany surrenders and the date becomes known as V-E Day. (Aug. 6) Atomic bomb dropped on Hiroshima kills or injures more than over 150,000 people; bomb dropped on Nagasaki three days later has similar results. (Aug. 14; V-J Day) Japan surrenders unconditionally. (Sept. 2) Formal Japanese surrender is signed aboard the USS *Missouri* in Tokyo Bay. (Dec. 21) General George S. Patton dies in Heidelberg, Germany, from injuries sustained in a traffic accident.

Business and labor: (July 25) Kaiser-Frazer Corporation (later Kaiser Motors) is launched as an auto-manufacturing company. (Sept. 21) Henry Ford retires as president of the Ford Motor Company, and his grandson, Henry Ford II, assumes the office.

Science and technology: (May 2) German rocket scientist Wernher von Braun surrenders to American forces. (May 7) "100 Ton Test" preliminary for the "Trinity" nuclear detonation is set off near Los Alamos, New Mexico. (July 16) First nuclear explosion is detonated near Los Alamos, New Mexico. (Oct. 8) First patent filed for microwave oven, by Raytheon Manufacturing Company after a design by Percy L. Spencer.

Environment: (Jan. 15-May 8) As a fuel-conservation measure, the U.S. government orders a national "dim out" of lights and electrical power. (Sept. 28) President Truman issues a proclamation claiming that the United States holds offshore jurisdiction over the seabed of the Continental Shelf.

Arts, literature, and popular culture: Children's book *Stuart Little* by E. B. White, is published, as are other literary works: *The Egg and I* (Betty McDonald), *Black Boy* (Richard Wright), *Cannery Row* (John Steinbeck), and *Tootle* (Gertrude Crampton). Cartoonist and veteran Bill Mauldin, creator of *G.I. Joe*, is awarded the Pulitzer Prize.

Sports: (Apr. 6-22) In the NHL Stanley Cup championship playoffs, the Toronto Maple Leafs beat the Detroit Red Wings four games to three. (Aug. 28) Jackie Robinson signs with the Brooklyn Dodgers, becoming the first African American in Major League Baseball, breaking the de facto "color barrier." (Oct. 3-10) In the World Series, the Detroit Tigers beat the Chicago Cubs four games to three. (Dec. 1) In the Grey Cup of Canadian football, the Toronto Argonauts beat the Winnipeg Blue Bombers 35 to 0. (Dec. 16) In the National Football League Championship, the Cleveland Rams beat the Washington Redskins 15 to 14.

1946

International: (Mar. 5) Winston Churchill delivers his "Iron Curtain" speech at Westminster College in Fulton, Missouri, acknowledging the coming of the Cold War. (July 4) Philippines gains independence from the United States. (July 29-Oct. 15) Paris Peace Conference to settle issues with German allies convenes. (Dec. 11) United Nations establishes UNICEF.

Government and politics: (Feb. 21) Truman administration sets up the Office of Economic Stabilization. (Apr. 22) Chief Justice Harlan Fiske Stone dies; President Truman names Fred M. Vinson to replace him. (July 3) Hobbs Anti-Racketeering Act becomes law. (Aug. 2) Federal Tort Claims Act of 1946 is passed as Title VI of the Legislative Reorganization Act. (Aug. 13) Indian Claims Commission begins resolving Native American legal suits. (Nov. 5) Midterm elections are held.

Society: (July 7) Mother Frances Xavier Cabrini is first American canonized by the Roman Catholic Church. (Aug. 1) Fulbright fellowship program is established.

Business and labor: (Feb. 20) Employment Act of 1946 is signed into law. (Apr. 1) United Mine Workers coal miners' strike begins; the government takes control of mining operations pending a settlement. (Dec. 7) Coal strike called off by United Mine Workers president John L. Lewis.

Science and technology: John William Mauchly and John Presper Eckert, Jr., combine to develop the Electronic Numerical Integrator and Computer (ENIAC) at the University of Pennsylvania. (Aug. 1) Atomic Energy Commission is created; will begin operating on Jan. 1, 1947. (Nov. 13) Vincent Joseph Schaefer experiments successfully with cloud seeding.

Environment: (Apr. 15) Environmentalist comic strip *Mark Trail* is originated by Ed Dodd in the *New York Post*. (July 16) Truman administration sets up the Bureau of Land Management.

Arts, literature, and popular culture: Literary works published include *The Common Sense Book of Baby and Child Care* (Benjamin Spock), *Hiroshima* (John Hersey), *The Member of the Wedding* (Carson McCullers), *All the King's Men* (Robert Penn Warren), and *The Small Rain* (Margaret L'Engle). Ballet Society is formed in New York City.

Sports (Mar. 21) National Football League's Los Angeles Rams sign the league's first African American player, Kenny Washington. (Mar. 30-Apr. 9) In the NHL Stanley Cup championship playoffs, the Montreal Canadiens beat the Boston Bruins four games to one. (June 6) Basketball Association of America is established. (Oct. 6-15) In the World Series, the St. Louis Cardinals beat the Boston Red Sox four games to three. (Nov. 30) In Canadian football's Grey Cup, the Toronto Argonauts beat the Winnipeg Blue Bombers 28 to 5. (Dec. 15) In the National Football League Championship, the Chicago Bears beat the New York Giants 24 to 14. (Dec. 22) In the All-America Football Conference Championship game, the Cleveland Browns defeat the New York Yankees 14 to 9.

1947

International: (Feb. 10) Paris Peace Treaties, confirming terms of the Paris Peace Conference of 1946, are signed. (Sept. 2) Inter-American Treaty of Reciprocal Assistance (Rio de Janeiro Pact) states that the signatory nations will join in mutual defense against an outside attacker. (Oct. 30) United States and Canada are among the signatories of the General Agreement on Tariffs and Trade (GATT) at Geneva, Switzerland.

Government and politics: Blacklisting of members of Hollywood film industry begins. (Jan. 1) Canadian Citizenship Act goes into effect, making Canadian nationality distinct from British. (Mar. 12) Truman articulates doctrine for helping Greece and Turkey resist inroads from the Soviet Union. (Mar. 21) Truman's Loyalty Program begins. (May 14) Canada's Chinese Immigration Act of 1923 is repealed. (June 23) Congress overrides President Harry S. Truman's veto to enact the Taft-Hartley Act, which cites prohibited practices by labor

unions. (July 18) Presidential Succession Act, naming the Speaker of the House as third in line to the presidency, is signed into law. (Sept. 29) Hoover Commission is established to study possible reforms of the executive branch of the federal government.

Military: (Sept. 18) Under the provisions of the National Security Act of 1947, the cabinet Departments of War and the Navy are combined into the Department of Defense, with James Vincent Forrestal as the first secretary of defense. The U.S. Air Force becomes an autonomous branch.

Society: (Apr. 9-23) Journey of Reconciliation campaign organizes racially integrated bus rides throughout the South.

Business and labor: Haloid Company (later Xerox Corporation) of Rochester, New York, buys the rights to Chester F. Carlson's photo duplication process. (Apr. 7) Henry Ford dies in Dearborn, Michigan, after suffering a stroke. (May 7) Levittown planned community building project is started in New York.

Science and technology: (Aug. 7) Harvard Mark I digital computer, designed by Howard Aiken and built by IBM, is in operation at Harvard University. (Nov. 17) At the Bell Laboratory in Berkeley Heights, New Jersey, Walter H. Brattain and John Bardeen discover the transistor principle, which William Shockley refines and develops into the first transistor. (Dec. 22) Eckert-Mauchly Computer Corporation (EMCC) is established.

Environment: (Apr. 16) Massive fertilizer chemical explosions on board the ship *Grandcamp* in Texas City, Texas, cause six hundred deaths and five thousand injuries. (July 31) Materials Act passed by Congress.

Arts, literature, and popular culture: Literary works published include *Curious George Takes a Job* (H. A. Rey and Margaret Rey), *McEligot's Pool* (Dr. Seuss), *The Pearl* (John Steinbeck), *Bend Sinister* (Vladimir Nabokov), *Tales of the South Pacific* (James A. Michener), *I. The Jury* (Mickey Spillane), and *Tarzan and the Foreign Legion* (Edgar Rice Burroughs). Samuel Eliot Morison begins publishing the multivolume *History of the United States Naval Operations in World War II*. Great Books Foundation is founded. (Jan. 13) Comic strip *Steve Canyon* is originated by Milton Caniff in the *Chicago Sun-Times*. (June 22) Charles M. Schulz's comic strip *L'il Folks*, the forerunner of *Peanuts*, appears in the *St. Paul Pioneer Press.* (Dec. 3) *A Streetcar Named Desire* by Tennessee Williams debuts on Broadway and later wins the 1947 Pulitzer Prize.

Sports: (Apr. 8-19) In the NHL Stanley Cup championship playoffs, the Toronto Maple Leafs defeat the Montreal Canadiens four games to two. (Apr. 15) After a stint in the minor leagues, Jackie Robinson plays his first game with the Brooklyn Dodgers. (Sept. 30-Oct. 6) In the World Series, the New York Yankees beat the Brooklyn Dodgers four games to three. (Nov. 29) In Canadian football's Grey Cup, the Toronto Argonauts defeat the Winnipeg Blue Bombers 10 to 9. (Dec. 14) In the All-America Football Conference Championship, the Cleveland Browns beat the New York Yankees 14 to 3. (Dec. 28) In the National Football League Championship, the Chicago Cardinals beat the Philadelphia Eagles 28 to 21.

Crime: (Jan. 15) Body of twenty-two-year-old Elizabeth Short—whom the media dub "The Black Dahlia"—is found in Los Angeles; her murder would never be solved. (June 20) Gangster "Bugsy" Siegel is shot dead in Beverly Hills, California.

1948

International: (Apr. 3) U.S. Congress passes enabling act for European Recovery Program, which will become better known as the Marshall Plan. (May 2) Organization of American States is established by the Charter of Bogota. (May 14) Independent state of Israel is proclaimed; U.S. diplomatic recognition follows. (June 24, 1948-May 12, 1949) Soviet Union places a blockade on West Berlin that will ultimately be broken by the Berlin Airlift. (Dec. 9) U.N. General Assembly approves Convention on the Prevention and Punishment of the Crime of Genocide. (Dec. 10) In Paris, the United Nations General Assembly adopts the Universal Declaration of Human Rights.

Government and politics: (June 3) In the then-British colony of Newfoundland, a voter referendum is held to determine the territory's political future. Only 14.3 percent of voters opt for continued British administration; 44.5 percent and 41.1 percent vote for independence and union with Canada, respectively. (June 21-25) In the first political convention broadcast on television, the Republican Party nominates Governor

Thomas E. Dewey of New York as its presidential candidate. (July 12) Democratic Party nominates incumbent president Harry S. Truman as its presidential candidate. (July 22) A second referendum is held in Newfoundland, with 52.9 percent voting to join Canada and 47.7 percent for independence. (Nov. 2) Truman defeats the Republican Party's Thomas E. Dewey, the new Dixiecrat Party candidate Strom Thurmond, and Progressive Party candidate Henry A. Wallace to win a full term as president. (Nov. 15) Louis St. Laurent becomes prime minister of Canada, replacing William Lyon Mackenzie King, who has retired from public office.

Military: Charles A. Beard's *President Roosevelt and the Coming of the War* offers revisionist interpretation of American entry into World War II. (July 26) President Truman's Executive Order 9981 effectively ends segregation in the military. (Sept. 28) U.S. Department of Defense is established, replacing the War Department.

Society: The first of the "Kinsey Report" books, *Sexual Behavior in the Human Male* (by Alfred Kinsey et al.) sparks an intense controversy over the propriety of the subject matter and references to pedophilia.

Business and labor: Preston Tucker introduces experimental Tucker Torpedo automobile. (Jan. 29) Twenty-eight Mexican laborers and three crew members die in a plane crash near Los Gatos Canyon, California, while being deported to Mexico; the incident is then memorialized in Woody Guthrie's protest song "Deportee (Plane Wreck at Los Gatos)."

Science and technology: (Apr. 7) World Health Organization is established at Geneva, Switzerland, under the United Nations. (June 3) Hale telescope at Mt. Palomar Observatory is dedicated.

Environment: American scientific activist Henry Fairfield Osborn, Jr., publishes pioneering environmental work: *Our Plundered Planet.* (June 30) Water Pollution Control Act is passed. (Nov. 18) Great Blizzard of 1949 begins.

Arts, literature, and popular culture: Literary works published include *The Naked and the Dead* (Norman Mailer), *The Young Lions* (Irwin Shaw), *Seraph on the Suwanee* (Zora Neale Hurston), *The Ides of March* (Thornton Wilder), *Melissa* (Taylor Caldwell), *Walden Two* (B. F. Skinner), and *Peony* (Pearl S. Buck). Comic strip *Rex Morgan, M. D.* is originated by "Dal Curtis" (Dr. Nicholas P. Dallis). (Oct. 4) Comic strip *Pogo*, by Walt Kelly, debuts in the *New York Star.*

Sports: (Apr. 7-14) In the NHL Stanley Cup championship playoffs, the Toronto Maple Leafs beat the Detroit Red Wings four games to zero. (July 29-Aug. 14) Summer Olympic Games are held in London. (Aug. 16) Baseball great Babe Ruth dies in New York City. (Oct. 6-11) In the World Series, the Cleveland Indians beat the Boston Braves four games to two. (Nov. 27) In Canadian football's Grey Cup, the Calgary Stampeders beat the Ottawa Rough Riders 12 to 7. (Dec. 19) In the National Football League Championship, the Philadelphia Eagles defeat the Chicago Cardinals 7 to 0. In the All-America Football Conference Championship, the Cleveland Browns beat the Buffalo Bills 49 to 7.

1949

International: (Apr. 4) North Atlantic Treaty Organization (NATO) is established as a deterrent to potential Soviet expansionism. (Aug. 12) International agreements known as the Geneva Conventions spell out internationally accepted laws of warfare.

Government and politics: (1949-1951) White House undergoes major renovations. (Jan. 20) Truman articulates his Fair Deal and Point Four programs. (Mar. 23) British North America Act 1949—later known as the Newfoundland Act—officially joins Newfoundland with the Dominion of Canada. (June 27) In the Canadian general election, incumbent prime minister Louis St. Laurent leads his Liberal Party to victory over George A. Drew's Progressive Conservative Party.

Society: (Apr. 8-10) Dramatic rescue attempt fails to save the life of three-year-old Kathy Fiscus after her fall down an abandoned well in California.

Business and labor: (Feb. 8) Diners Club International is founded in New York City.

Science and technology: Edward Calvin Kendall employs cortisone in the treatment of arthritis. (Jan. 26) Hale Telescope at Mt. Palomar Observatory begins operations. (Mar. 4) Willard F. Libby pub-

lishes his discovery of carbon dating. (Aug.) Binary automatic computer (BINAC) is introduced by the Eckert–Mauchly Computer Corporation for the Northrop Corporation.

Environment: Aldo Leopold publishes *A Sand County Almanac,* a book about nature and ethics.

Arts, literature, and popular culture: The play *Death of a Salesman,* by Arthur Miller, is published and first produced. Other literary works published include *Death Be Not Proud* (John Gunther), *The Dream Merchants* (Harold Robbins), *Let Love Come Last* (Taylor Caldwell), *The Angry Wife* (Pearl S. Buck), and *Shane* (Jack Schaefer). (Apr. 7) Richard Rodgers and Oscar Hammerstein II's musical *South Pacific* opens on Broadway. (Oct. 11) George Abbott's musical *Where's Charley?* opens on Broadway.

Sports: (Mar. 1) Joe Louis retires as world heavyweight boxing champion. (Apr. 8-16) In the NHL Stanley Cup championship playoffs, the Toronto Maple Leafs defeat the Detroit Red Wings four games to zero. (June 21) Ezzard Charles wins the world heavyweight boxing title by defeating "Jersey" Joe Walcott. (Aug. 3) National Basketball Association (NBA) is formed out of a merger between the Basketball Association of America and the National Basketball League. (Oct. 5-9) In the World Series, the New York Yankees defeat the Brooklyn Dodgers four games to one. (Nov. 26) In Canadian football's Grey Cup, the Montreal Alouettes defeat the Calgary Stampeders 28 to 15. (Dec. 11) In the All-America Football Conference Championship, the Cleveland Browns defeat the San Francisco Forty-Niners 21 to 7. (Dec. 18) In the NFL Championship game the Philadelphia defeat the Los Angeles Rams Eagles 14 to 0.

Crime: (Sept. 9) Canadian Pacific Airliner flying out of Quebec City is destroyed by an onboard bomb, killing all passengers and crew. Albert Guay is charged with planting the bomb in his wife's luggage with the intent of murdering her. (Guay would be convicted, and hanged on Jan. 12, 1951).

Raymond Pierre Hylton

■ Bibliography

This bibliography lists books containing substantial material about a wide variety of basic topics pertaining to the 1940's. Many additional works, and especially works on narrower subjects, can be found in the Further Readings notes at the end of each essay in *The Forties in America.*

1. Atomic Bomb

Alperovitz, Gar. *The Decision to Use the Atomic Bomb.* New York: Vintage, 1996. One of the first authors to argue that the decision to use the bomb was based on a desire to intimidate the Soviet Union rather than as a necessity for winning World War II.

Craig, Campbell, and Sergey Radchenko. *The Atomic Bomb and the Origins of the Cold War.* New Haven, Conn.: Yale University Press, 2008. Argues that the existence of the atomic bomb helped lead to the Cold War. Discusses how ideologies led to the new war, and uses Soviet documents to support its claim.

Howes, Ruth H., and Caroline C. Herzenberg. *Their Day in the Sun: Women of the Manhattan Project.* Philadelphia: Temple University Press, 1999. Documents the frequently overlooked contributions of women to the development of the atomic bomb.

Kelly, Cynthia C. *The Manhattan Project: The Birth of the Atomic Bomb in the Words of Its Creators, Eyewitnesses, and Historians.* New York: Black Dog and Leventhal, 2007. An anthology covering the history of the Manhattan Project. Includes illustrations, bibliography, time line, and index.

Kort, Michael. *The Columbia Guide to Hiroshima and the Bomb.* New York: Columbia University Press, 2007. Reference includes primary source documents from both American and Japanese archives and a summary of the issues.

Walker, J. Samuel. *Prompt and Utter Destruction: Truman and the Use of Atomic Bombs Against Japan.* Chapel Hill: University of North Carolina Press, 1997. Examines the controversy behind the use of the atomic bomb. A relatively short and readable introduction to the debate.

2. Biographies

Bird, Kai, and Martin J. Sherwin. *American Prometheus: The Triumph and Tragedy of J. Robert Oppenheimer.* New York: Vintage Books, 2005. Pulitzer Prize-winning biography of the leader of the scientific team that developed the atomic bomb.

Dallek, Robert. *Harry S. Truman.* New York: Times Books, 2008. A brief but important assessment of Truman, with an accessible section on the Truman Doctrine.

Gabler, Neal. *Walt Disney: The Triumph of the American Imagination.* New York: Alfred A. Knopf, 2006. The definitive Disney biography, focusing on his entire life and highlighting the studio strike of 1941.

Hendrickson, Kenneth E. *The Life and Presidency of Franklin Delano Roosevelt: An Annotated Bibliography.* Lanham, Md.: Scarecrow Press, 2005. With more than twelve hundred pages, this book provides a comprehensive annotated bibliography of sources about one of the central figures of the 1940's.

Jackson, Robert H. *That Man: An Insider's Portrait of Franklin D. Roosevelt.* New York: Oxford University Press, 2003. A view of Roosevelt's legacy from the vantage point of Supreme Court justice Jackson, who had been appointed to the court after serving in the New Deal administration.

Korda, Michael. *Ike: An American Hero.* New York: Harper, 2008. A long and laudatory biography focused mostly on Eisenhower before he became president. Also discusses Eisenhower's personal life, including his marriage.

McCullough, David. *Truman.* New York: Simon & Schuster, 1992. The most comprehensive biography of Truman's life and presidency. Covers both domestic issues, such as the post-World War II U.S. economy, and international issues, including Truman's decision to use nuclear weapons against Japan to end World War II.

Nolan, Brian. *King's War: Mackenzie King and the Politics of War, 1939-1945.* Toronto: Random House, 1988. Critical examination of the Canadian prime minister's role in World War II.

Tygiel, Jules. *Baseball's Great Experiment: Jackie Robinson and His Legacy.* Expanded ed. New York: Oxford University Press, 2008. The formative biography on Jackie Robinson, tracing his personal journey to the major leagues and highlighting the history of Negro League baseball.

Weintraub, Stanley. *Fifteen Stars: Eisenhower, MacArthur, Marshall: Three Generals Who Saved the American Century.* New York: Free Press, 2007. Addresses the complex relationships of three of the most prominent generals of the twentieth century and explains how they shaped World War II military strategy and Cold War policy.

3. The Cold War and Postwar United States

Belmonte, Laura A. *Selling the American Way: U.S. Propaganda and the Cold War.* Philadelphia: University of Pennsylvania Press, 2008. Examines the role of propaganda in the early Cold War and discusses the disconnect between reality and that propaganda. Details the various books, films, and other materials created to advance the idea of a perfect and already functioning American way.

Cohen, Lizabeth. *A Consumer's Republic: Mass Consumption in Postwar America.* New York: Alfred A. Knopf, 2003. Examines the growth of consumerism in the postwar period. Argues that inequality grew and divisions arose, but that people were able to fight those divisions on occasion.

Miscamble, Wilson D. *From Roosevelt to Truman: Potsdam, Hiroshima, and the Cold War.* Cambridge: Cambridge University Press, 2007. A study of the slow evolution from Roosevelt's friendly and conciliatory policies to Truman's policies of confrontation, stemming from increasing mistrust of Stalin and the Soviet Union.

Offner, Arnold A. *Another Such Victory: President Truman and the Cold War, 1945-1953.* Palo Alto, Calif.: Stanford University Press, 2002. Argues that President Truman and the United States were largely responsible for the Cold War, and that the United States viewed foreign policy through a narrow lens.

Spalding, Elizabeth E. *The First Cold Warrior: Harry Truman, Containment, and the Remaking of Liberal Internationalism.* Lexington: University Press of Kentucky, 2006. A detailed political analysis that attempts to portray Truman as the driving force behind the policy of containment.

Whitaker, Reg, and Steve Hewitt. *Canada and the Cold War.* Toronto: James Lorimer, 2003. Includes an account of how Prime Minister Louis St. Laurent helped shift Canada to postwar realities.

4. Culture

Alvarez, Luis. *The Power of the Zoot: Youth Culture and Resistance During World War II.* Berkeley: University of California Press, 2008. Presents zoot culture as a national movement for Latino dignity in response to racism.

Erenberg, Lewis A., and Susan E. Hirsch, eds. *The War in American Culture: Society and Consciousness During World War II.* Chicago: University of Chicago Press, 1996. Examines how national culture was both created and transformed by World War II.

Leder, Jane Mersky. *Thanks for the Memories: Love, Sex, and World War II.* Westport, Conn.: Praeger, 2006. Discusses how ideas and practices of love and sex changed during World War II. Notes how women became involved with the war; how women's experiences as girlfriends, lovers, and wives shaped them; and how minorities, including African Americans and lesbians, served in the armed forces.

Sarles, Ruth. *A Story of America First: The Men and Women Who Opposed U.S. Intervention in World War II.* Westport, Conn.: Praeger, 2003. Presents those who did not want the United States to go to war and details the wide range of people involved in the movement.

Shukert, Elfrieda Berthiaume, and Barbara Smith Scibetta. *War Brides of World War II.* New York: Penguin, 1989. Inclusive overview of World War II-era cross-national marriages in all theaters of war. Contains bibliography, photos, and the text of relevant laws.

Sickels, Roberts. *The 1940s.* Westport, Conn.: Greenwood, 2003. This addition to the *Daily Life Through History* series examines the many cultural shifts that occurred during the 1940's. Includes bibliographies, a time line, and cost comparisons.

5. Economic, Political, and Legal Issues

Bryce, Robert B., and Matthew Bellamy. *Canada and the Cost of World War II: The International Operations of Canada's Department of Finance, 1939-1947.* Montreal: McGill-Queens University Press, 2005. A detailed study of eight years of appropriations earmarked for expanding Canada's military capacities.

Cherny, Robert W., ed. *American Labor and the Cold War: Grassroots Politics and Postwar Political Culture.* New Brunswick, N.J.: Rutgers University Press, 2004. A collection of essays that examines the labor movement in the postwar United States, highlighting the rise of unions.

Glendon, Mary Ann. *A World Made New: Eleanor Roosevelt and the Universal Declaration of Human Rights.* New York: Random House, 2002. Reveals Roosevelt's role as the spearhead in the passage of a postwar document of global significance.

Harrison, Mark, ed. *The Economics of World War II: Six Great Powers in International Comparison.* New York: Cambridge University Press, 2000. A technical, comparative look at how the great powers handled wartime economic issues.

Heiss, Mary Ann, and S. Victor Papacosma, eds. *NATO and the Warsaw Pact: Intrabloc Conflicts.* Kent, Ohio: Kent State University Press, 2008. Examines a variety of issues related to NATO's policies toward the Warsaw Pact.

Kersten, Andrew. *Labor's Home Front: The American Federation of Labor During World War II.* New York: New York University Press, 2006. Gives detailed attention to issues such as race, gender, and work safety.

Renstrom, Peter G. *The Stone Court: Justices, Rulings, and Legacy.* Santa Barbara, Calif.: ABC-Clio, 2001. Discusses the impact and personalities of the Supreme Court under Harlan Fiske Stone, chief justice from 1941 to 1946.

Schlesinger, Stephen. *Act of Creation: The Founding of the United Nations.* Boulder, Colo.: Westview Press, 2003. Primarily focused on the 1945 conference held in San Francisco in which the organization was established.

6. Entertainment, Sports, and Fashion

Basinger, Jeanine. *The World War II Combat Film: Anatomy of a Genre.* Middletown, Conn.: Wesleyan University Press, 2003. Includes an extensive, annotated filmography. Excellent genre study of films made between 1941 and 2002.

Becker, Patti C. *Books and Libraries in American Society During World War II: Weapons in the War of Ideas.* New York: Routledge, 2004. A study of the transformation of libraries in World War II to meet new societal demands. Based on a wealth of primary and secondary sources.

Biesen, Sheri Chinen. *Blackout: World War II and the Origins of Film Noir.* Baltimore: Johns Hopkins University Press, 2005. Discusses how the political and social conditions of Hollywood during the war led to film noir.

Bony, Anne. *Furniture and Interiors of the 1940's.* Paris: Flammarion, 2003. A study of European and American interior design in this transitional period. Illustrations on every page. Includes bibliography and index.

DeVeaux, Scott. *The Birth of Bebop: A Social and Musical History.* Berkeley: University of California Press, 1997. Examines the development of bebop in both musical and cultural contexts.

Dixon, Wheeler W., ed. *American Cinema of the 1940's: Themes and Variations.* New Brunswick, N.J.: Rutgers University Press, 2006. Essays on war films, national identity, postwar recovery, Cold War politics, communist subversion, and the American family.

McClellan, Lawrence, Jr. *The Later Swing Era: 1942 to 1955.* Westport, Conn.: Greenwood Press, 2004. Documents the significant performers and works. Continues where most works on the swing era leave off.

Marshall, William. *Baseball's Pivotal Era, 1945-1951.* Lexington: University of Kentucky Press, 1999. Explores the various changes in baseball, as both a business and a sport, in the postwar years under commissioner Albert Benjamin Chandler.

Mordden, Ethan. *Beautiful Mornin': The Broadway Musical in the 1940's.* New York: Oxford University Press, 1999. The 1940's are considered by many to be the strongest decade for Broadway musicals. This books covers the groundbreaking musicals, such as *Oklahoma!* and *South Pacific,* but also concentrates on lesser-known but important, small-scale musicals.

Smith, Kathleen E. R. *God Bless America: Tin Pan Alley Goes to War.* Lexington: University of Kentucky Press, 2003. Although primarily focused on music, contains good insights into how the canteens for military personnel boosted morale with music and dance.

Walford, Jonathan. *Forties Fashion: From the Siren Suit to the New Look.* London: Thames & Hudson, 2008. Provides a worldwide look at fashion during the 1940's, including children's clothing and the postwar resurgence of French fashion.

Waller, Linda. *Knitting Fashions of the 1940's: Styles, Patterns and History.* Ramsbury, Marlborough, England: Crowood Press, 2007. Overview of knitting during the 1940's. Discusses the fact that women knitted to provide garments for not only troops but also themselves.

7. Gender and Sexuality

Goossen, Rachel Waltner. *Women Against the Good War: Conscientious Objection and Gender on the American Home Front, 1941-1947.* Chapel Hill: University of North Carolina Press, 1997. Discusses women who opposed World War II, especially those who performed alternative service during the war years rather than joining organizations such as the Women's Army Corps.

Jackson, Paul. *One of the Boys: Homosexuality in the Military During World War II.* Montreal: McGill-Queen's University Press, 2004. Detailed analysis that includes an examination of postal censorship during World War II.

Ramírez, Catherine. *The Woman in the Zoot Suit: Gender, Nationalism, and the Cultural Politics of Memory.* Durham, N.C.: Duke University Press, 2009. Engaging study of *la pachuca*, the rebellious female who was an important part of zoot culture.

Weatherford, Doris. *American Women and World War II.* Victoria, B.C.: Castle Books, 2008. Interesting and easy-to-read account of the multitude of roles women played in World War II and the discrimination they often faced at work and in the military.

Yellin, Emily. *Our Mothers' War: American Women at Home and at the Front During World War II.* New York: Free Press, 2004. Describes the experiences of women both on the home front and in the military. Relates many different individuals' stories.

8. Race and Racism

Asahina, Robert. *Just Americans: How Japanese Americans Won a War at Home and Abroad, The Story of the One Hundredth Battlion/442d Regimental Combat Team in World War II.* New York: Gotham Books, 2006. Provides a true story of the segregated Japanese American combat team in European battlefields during World War II.

Bernstein, Alison R. *American Indians and World War II: Toward a New Era in Indian Affairs.* Norman: University of Oklahoma Press, 1991. Offers important insights into the political and ideological atmosphere in which the Indian voting-rights movement was born.

Bon Tempo, Carl J. *Americans at the Gate: The United States and Refugees During the Cold War.* Princeton, N.J.: Princeton University Press, 2008. The author explores the exclusionary immigration policy of the United States and the social, political, and economic context in which American refugee policy was shaped and implemented.

Jefferson, Robert F. *Fighting for Hope: African American Troops of the Ninety-third Infantry Division in World War II and Postwar America.* Baltimore: The Johns Hopkins University Press, 2008. Uses one division's story as a lens into governmental policy during World War II. Discusses the segregation and racism faced by the troops and the lasting effect the war experiences had on these men's lives.

Kryder, Daniel. *Divided Arsenal: Race and the American State During World War II.* New York: Cambridge University Press, 2000. Looks at how Roosevelt's administration managed racial protest during World War II and at the various racial issues during the war.

Pagán, Eduardo O. *Murder at the Sleepy Lagoon: Zoot Suits, Race, and Riot in Wartime Los Angeles.* Chapel Hill: University of North Carolina, 2003. Detailed and scholarly account by the same historian who supervised an excellent documentary on the topic for public television.

Takaki, Ronald. *Double Victory: A Multicultural History of America in World War II.* New York: Back Bay Books, 2001. Examines the cultural side of World War II, noting how many minorities were fighting both racism at home and the Axis powers abroad. Argues that the war experiences set the stage for the various civil rights revolutions.

9. Science, Medicine, and Technology

Lax, Eric. *The Mold in Dr. Florey's Coat: The Story of the Penicillin Miracle.* New York: Henry Holt, 2005. The story behind the discovery and development of the most famous antibiotic. The title refers to the method of transport for penicillin from Great Britain to the United States during the war.

MacLeod, Roy M. *Science and the Pacific War: Science and Survival in the Pacific, 1939-1945.* Boston: Kluwer, 2000. Discusses scientific elements in all aspects of the Pacific war. Includes development of new technological innovations, such as landing craft, and discusses diseases. Details the involvement of many different sets of forces in the Pacific war.

Oshinsky, David. *Polio: An American Story.* New York: Oxford University Press, 2006. The story of polio, from its origins as an epidemic disease to its ultimate control. Describes the significance of John Franklin Enders's work during the 1940's.

Pursell, Carroll. *Technology in Postwar America: A History.* New York: Columbia University Press, 2007. Overview of technological advances during the postwar era. Contains some details of appliances introduced to the consumer market during the latter half of the 1940's.

Shachtman, Tom. *Terrors and Marvels, How Science and Technology Changed the Character and Outcome of World War II.* New York: Harper Collins, 2002. Describes the wartime role of science, weapons developed but unused, and wartime tactics.

10. World War II: The Home Front

Bentley, Amy. *Eating for Victory: Food Rationing and the Politics of Domesticity.* Champaign: University of Illinois Press, 1998. Brings together social history, public-policy analysis, and cultural studies in examining food rationing during the 1940's.

Goodwin, Doris Kearns. *No Ordinary Time: Franklin and Eleanor Roosevelt—The Home Front in World War II.* New York: Simon & Schuster, 1994. A Pulitzer Prize-winning book in which Goodwin presents the presidency of Roosevelt and the influence and work of First Lady Eleanor Roosevelt during World War II.

Hixson, Walter L. *The American Experience in World War II: The United States Transformed—The Lessons and Legacies of the Second World War.* New York: Taylor and Francis, 2003. A comprehensive social history of the war, with discussion of economic events.

Hoopes, Roy. *Americans Remember the Homefront.* New York: Berkley, 2002. An oral history that focuses on the transformations of families, industries, and American society in general during World War II.

Keshen, Jeffrey A. *Saints, Sinners, and Soldiers: Canada's Second World War.* Vancouver: University of British Columbia Press, 2004. The first half of this well-researched book shows how propaganda constructed World War II as a "good war" for Canada.

Lingeman, Richard R. *Don't You Know There's a War On? The American Home Front, 1941-1945.* New York: Nation Books, 2003. A wide-ranging cultural history that depicts American civilian life during the war, giving coverage to work, business, and housing issues as well as domestic and social life.

Winkler, Allan M. *Home Front U.S.A.: America During World War II.* Wheeling, Ill.: Harlan Davidson, 2000. A serious and exhaustive study that details war contributions undertaken on the home front.

11. World War II: Military History

Addison, Paul, and Jeremy A. Crang, eds. *Firestorm: The Bombing of Dresden, 1945.* London: Pimleco, 2006. Collection of essays examining controversial aspects of this example of strategic bombing and total war.

Dear, I. C. B. *The Oxford Companion to the Second World War.* New York: Oxford University Press, 1995. A straightforward discussion of the war, with more than fifteen hundred entries and nearly that many pages dealing with topics related to the war.

Gilbert, Martin. *The Second World War: A Complete History.* New York: Henry Holt, 2004. A chronological and comprehensive discussion of the events of World War II.

Miller, Donald L. *Masters of the Air: America's Bomber Boys Who Fought the Air War Against Nazi Germany.* New York: Simon & Schuster, 2006. A comprehensive look at the Eighth Air Force and its strategic bombing campaign over Germany.

Penrose, Jane. *The D-Day Companion,* Oxford: Osprey, 2004. Individual chapters provide analyses of the plans of both sides and the fighting on D Day and beyond.

Sloan, Bill. *The Ultimate Battle: Okinawa 1945—The*

Last Epic Struggle of World War II. New York: Simon & Schuster, 2007. Eyewitness accounts abound in this masterful retelling of the Okinawa campaign.

Smith, Carl. *Pearl Harbor 1941: The Day of Infamy.* Westport, Conn.: Praeger, 2004. Excellent photos, biographical vignettes, and a detailed chronology from 1936 to January, 1942.

The United States Army and World War II: An Overview. Washington, D.C.: U.S. Army Center of Military History, 2003. The U.S. Army's three-volume set surveying World War II.

Wagner, Margaret E., Linda Barrett Osborne, and Susan Reyburn. *The Library of Congress World War II Companion.* New York: Simon & Schuster, 2007. A detailed volume that examines myriad aspects of the war, including military leaders, weaponry, propaganda, war crimes, and numerous other topics.

12. World War II: Political and Humanitarian Issues

Bialystok, Franklin. *Delayed Impact: The Holocaust and the Canadian Jewish Community.* Montreal: McGill-Queen's University Press, 2000. Critical analysis of Canadian anti-Semitism, Canadian immigration policy, Jewish refugees, and Canadian Jewish community responses from the 1930's to the 1990's.

Evans, Gary. *John Grierson and the National Film Board: The Politics of Wartime Propaganda.* Toronto: University of Toronto Press, 1984. Provides detailed account of Grierson's philosophy and accomplishments in documentary filmmaking about World War II.

Fisher, Louis. *Nazi Saboteurs on Trial: A Military Tribunal and American Law.* Lawrence: University of Kansas Press, 2003. An academic account of the events leading up to *Ex Parte Quirin.*

Koistinen, Paul. *Arsenal of World War II: The Political Economy of American Warfare, 1940-1945.* Lawrence: University Press of Kansas, 2004. Comprehensive study of the federal government's efforts to plan and control the wartime economy. Explains relationships among regulatory agencies, the armed services, and private industry.

Newton, Verne W., ed. *FDR and the Holocaust.* New York: St. Martin's Press, 1996. The published proceedings on the controversial issue of President Roosevelt's actions, or lack thereof, during the Holocaust.

■ Glossary

The list is a representative collection of words and phrases that were newly coined, or that first gained prominence, in North America during the 1940's. Dates in parentheses are the earliest years in which the terms are known to have been used in the senses given here. (n. = noun; adj. = adjective; v. = verb)

A.A., ack-ack, Archie, n. Antiaircraft gun; antiaircraft. (1940-1941)

A-bomb, n. Abbreviation for atom or atomic bomb. (1945)

acronym, n. Word comprising the initial letters or syllables of the name of a concept or organization. For example: NATO for the North Atlantic Treaty Organization, or sitrep for situation report. Acronyms were first widely used during the 1940's. (1943) *See also* fubar, radar, snafu, sonar

airlift, n. Air transport of troops and/or supplies, often in response to an emergency. (1945)

alien, n., adj. A being from another planet. (1944)

alreet, adj. Period jazz slang meaning swell, good, or great.

angst, n. Overpowering yet vague sense of anxiety. The German word had been used by anglophone intellectuals for some time, but the word was formally "adopted" into English during the 1940's. (1943)

antibiotic, n. Substance derived from living organisms that destroys or inhibits the growth of microorganisms. (1944) *See also* bacitracin

atomic age, n. New epoch initiated by the use of the atomic bomb, in which public discourse, dreams, and fears would be shaped by the promise of atomic energy and the presence of nuclear weapons. As originally used, the term was full of optimism, but some early users of this neologism—including Fritz Leiber in his dystopian novel *Gather Darkness!* (1943)—also raised the specter of atomic annihilation. The term arose in 1940-1943 and came into more general use after 1945.

automation, n. Automatic control of manufacturing and other processes, resulting in the partial or total replacement of human labor by machines. (1948)

babysit, v. To look after a child while his or her parents are out, often for an evening. (1947)

bacitracin, n. Toxic, usually topical, antibiotic. (1945) *See also* antibiotic

ball-point pen/ball pen, n. Pen in which ink stored in an internal reservoir is evenly applied to writing surfaces by a minute ball in the instrument's tip. (1947)

Bamboo Curtain, n. Hypothetical barrier of silence and hostility between communist China and the noncommunist West. (1949) *See also* Cold War, Iron Curtain, West

bazooka, n. Tubular, portable antitank rocket launcher. (1943)

bebop, n. School of progressive jazz, notable for improvisation, the rejection of many musical conventions, and fast tempi. Sometimes rendered rebop and later often shortened to bop. (1945)

Big Brother, n. Ruthless, totalitarian ruler and/or state. From George Orwell's novel *Nineteen Eighty-four.* (1949)

bikini, n. Woman's two-piece bathing suit of an abbreviated cut. Named by its French creators for the Bikini Atoll in the Marshall Islands, the site of U.S. nuclear weapons tests. (1948)

biological warfare, n. Use in warfare of germs, toxins, and other biological agents harmful to living things. (1946)

bit, n. Contraction of "binary digit," a basic unit of computer information. (1948)

blender, n. Electrical kitchen appliance for chopping and pureeing food. (1948)

blockbuster, n. Especially powerful aerial bomb, capable of obliterating an entire city block. In later civilian use, a "blockbuster" is something that is phenomenally successful and popular—especially a movie, book, or play. (1944)

bobby-soxer, n. Teenage girl who follows the fads in fashion, music, and other cultural creations. Named for bobby socks/sox (1943), the rolled-down, ankle-high socks often worn by such girls. (1944)

chicken out, v. To withdraw or quit out of cowardice. (1941)

classified, adj. Regarding information made secret for purposes of national security and available only to select persons. (1944)

cleavage, n. The cleft between a woman's breasts, as revealed by a low-cut outfit. (1946)

Cold War, n. Decades-long period of intense tension and competition that existed between the United States and the Soviet Union—and their respective allies and satellites—after World War II. In more general (lowercase) terms, hostilities that stop short of an armed conflict. (1945) *See also* Bamboo Curtain, Iron Curtain, West

commando, n. Elite shock trooper; a light infantryman specially trained to conduct raids and infiltrate enemy lines. (1940)

computer, n. Electronic device that performs logical and mathematical operations at a high speed. (1945) *See also* electronic brain

cortisone, n. Steroid hormone, chiefly used as an anti-inflammatory in the treatment of arthritis, certain allergies, and medical conditions. (1949)

counseling, n. Professional help given to people with social and/or psychological problems. (1940)

counterintelligence, n. Activities intended to prevent enemies from obtaining state and/or military secrets. (1940)

crash landing, n. Emergency landing of an aircraft in which damage or further damage to said craft is unavoidable. (1942)

crew cut, n. Short haircut for men, typical of young male coiffure during the 1940's and 1950's. (1940's)

crispy, adj. A superlative or enhanced version of crisp, first used in advertising lingo. (1940)

cybernetics, n. The study of the structure of regulatory systems in animals and machines. Many researchers in the 1940's and 1950's saw in cybernetics the key to understanding and perfecting automated decision making. (1948) *See also* automation

daddy-o, n. Form of address in jazz slang, meaning fellow, guy, man. For example, "Say, daddy-o, those threads (clothes) are alreet!" (1948) *See also* alreet

data, n. Information upon which a computer performs operations. (1946)

DDT, n. Dichlorodiphenyltrichloroethane, a highly effective but controversial pesticide. (1943)

debrief, v. To question a soldier or other operative after a mission in order to determine the mission's conduct and overall effect. (1945)

disc jockey, n. Person who plays popular music recordings, usually on the radio. Sometimes informally known as a "pancake turners." (1941)

displaced person, n. Refugee driven from his or her home country by war, persecution, or other political events. Often abbreviated DP or D.P. (1944)

disposable, adj. Meant to be thrown away after a single use. Originally applied to diapers, the term was eventually used to describe a wide array of consumer items. (1943) *See also* paper towel

disposable income, n. One's earnings after the subtraction of taxes and necessary expenses. (1948)

dissident, n. Open opponent of a government or its policies—especially within a totalitarian system. (1940)

Dixiecrat, n. Common name for the States' Rights Democratic Party, a short-lived, Southern, socially conservative, and segregationist splinter from the Democratic Party. (1948)

DNA, n. Deoxyribonucleic acid, the chemical blueprint of life. (1944)

dogface, n. Ordinary enlisted man. After World War II, sometimes used to describe an ugly man.

egg in your beer, n. Unreasonable demand or too much of a good thing. "What do you want—egg in your beer?" was said to one who complained of wartime shortages.

ejector seat, n. Seat that ejects the pilot from a damaged or otherwise failing airplane. (1945)

electronic brain, n. Another name for a computer. Now obsolete. (1946) *See also* computer

existentialism, n. Philosophical doctrine that addresses the existence of individuals and posits that individuals, though alone in a seemingly meaningless world, are free agents capable of creating meaning and purpose for themselves. (1941)

fanzine, n. Specialized amateur magazine, written and published by fans for fans of a particular hobby, literary genre, or lifestyle. Both the term and the publication of fanzines originated among science-fiction fandom. (1940)

fax, n. Short for "facsimile telegraphy," the sending of a scanned image by wire or radio transmission. (1948)

flying saucer, n. Saucer-shaped objects of allegedly extraterrestrial origin; first widely appeared in the skies and imaginations of the postwar United States. (1947)

freeze-drying, n. Method of preserving food, blood

plasma, and other perishables in which freezing is followed by dehydration. (1944)

fubar, n., adj. Acronym for "f——ked up beyond all recognition." U.S. military slang for a major mistake or mishap. (1944) *See also* acronym, snafu.

futurology, n. Attempt to predict the future, based on an examination of current and past trends in human society. (1946)

G.I., adj. Abbreviation of "government issue" or "general issue" used as an informal description of all things relating to the U.S. Army. For example, a "G.I. Joe" (1942) is a common enlisted man, and many servicemen brought home G.I. brides (1945) after the war. *See also* G.I., n.

G.I., n. Enlisted man or soldier. (1943) *See also* G.I., adj.

G suit, n. Special suit designed to permit its wearer to withstand high levels of acceleration force (G's) without blacking out. (1945)

genocide, n. Systematic destruction of a race, ethnicity, or national group. (1945)

Geronimo, interj. Name of a famous turn-of-the-twentieth-century Chiricahua Apache chief, adopted as a battle cry by American paratroops. These daring parachutists were no doubt inspired by a scene in the 1939 film *Geronimo*, in which the chief yells his name before jumping from a precipice into the river below. (1944) *See also* paratroops

glamour boy, n. New draftee, still looking, thinking, and acting like a civilian. *See also* sad sack, yard bird

gobbledygook, n. Overwrought, obfuscating jargon and sloppy, overladen verbiage, often used by bureaucrats, professionals, and academics. (1944)

gremlin, n. Mischievous mythological creature, especially fond of sabotaging airplanes. The term originated among the fliers of the Royal Air Force. Many Americans probably first encountered the concept in Roald Dahl's children's book *The Gremlins* (1943) or in the Merrie Melodies short cartoon *Falling Hare* (1943).

ground zero, n. Epicenter of an explosion—especially an atomic explosion. (1946)

guided missile, n. Missile steered by remote control or onboard navigational devices. (1945)

hep to the jive, adj. Jazz slang. To be fashionable, to have inside knowledge of the latest trends. Hip is generally interchangeable with hep. Sometimes, "to the jive" is dropped altogether, and one is merely hep/hip. *See also* hipster, square

hipster, n. One who is hip/hep. (1941) *See also* hep to the jive, square

hydrogen bomb, n. Nuclear weapon of immense explosive power, based on the thermonuclear fusion of hydrogen isotopes. The first working model was tested by the United States in 1952. (1947). Also known as H-bomb.

Iron Curtain, n. Hypothetical barrier of silence and hostility separating the postwar communist Soviet bloc from the noncommunist West. First attested in 1920, but in popular usage, in reference to the Cold War, after Winston Churchill's famous 1946 "Iron Curtain" speech. *See also* Bamboo Curtain, Cold War, West

jeep, n. Small but rugged four-wheel-drive vehicle, first used by the U.S. military during World War II. Possibly named after a slurred pronunciation of its designation "G.P.." for "general purpose" or after "Eugene the Jeep," a fantastical little creature from E. C. Segar's *Thimble Theater* (Popeye) comic strip. (1941)

jet/jet plane, n. Aircraft powered by a jet engine. The first in active use was a German warplane, the Messerschmitt Me 262. (1944) *See also* jet engine

jet engine, n. Engine that achieves forward thrust by means of jet propulsion. (1943) *See also* jet/jet plane

Kilroy, n. Mythical man whose name appeared in graffiti—generally "Kilroy Was Here," sometimes accompanied by a simple caricature of an absurdly dolichocephalic person peeping over a wall—wherever U.S. soldiers served during World War II. "Kilroy" inscriptions also appeared in the United States during and after the war. (1945)

kriegie, n. Slang for an Allied prisoner of war in Germany. Short for German *Kriegsgefangener* (prisoner of war). (1944) *See also* POW

LP, n. Short for long-playing record, a long-playing $33\frac{1}{3}$-revolutions-per-minute (rpm) gramophone disc. By the mid-1950's, it had sealed the doom of the 78-rpm record. (1948)

Mae West, n. Life jacket, after the well-endowed film star Mae West because of the appearance of persons wearing the jackets. Popularized by naval personnel during World War II.

methadone, n. Synthetic painkiller, sometimes used as a substitute drug in the treatment of morphine and heroin addiction. (1947)

mug, v. To assault and rob someone, often on the street or in some other public place. (1948)

napalm, n. Highly effective incendiary substance used in bombs and flame-throwing weapons. (1942)

nerve gas, n. Chemical warfare agent that attacks the human nervous system. (1940)

never had it so good. As in the phrase, "You never had it so good." Used as a sarcastic retort when one complained about military life during World War II. Later used in a much broader—and sometimes sincere—fashion by civilians. (1946)

New Look, n. Style in women's fashion, introduced by Christian Dior in 1947. Its joyous excess of fabric was a sartorial farewell to the privations and shortages of wartime. (1947)

paper towel, n. Disposable towel, made of paper, usually available in bulk on a roll. (1943) *See also* disposable

paratroops, n. Airborne soldiers who parachute behind enemy lines. (1940) *See also* Geronimo

Phony War, n. The period between Britain and France's formal declarations of war on Germany and the commencement of real hostilities—that is, from about September 3, 1939, to the spring of 1940. Coined by U.S. senator William E. Borah, who found "something phony about this war." (1940)

POW, P.O.W., PW, n. Prisoner of war. (1944-1945) *See also* kriegie

quisling, n. Traitor, a collaborator—after the Norwegian politician and officer Vidkun Quisling, who collaborated with German occupiers. In 1940's schoolyard slang "to go quisling" was to be a teacher's pet. (1940)

Quonset hut, n. Prefabricated metal structure made of corrugated metal in the shape of a semicircular cross-section that has the appearance of one-half of a cylinder. Used extensively by the U.S. military as well as by many civilians in the postwar era. The name is taken from Quonset Point, the place in Rhode Island where the huts were first manufactured. (1942)

radar, n. Acronym for "*ra*dio *d*etection *a*nd *r*anging," a method for determining the presence of distant objects through the reflection of short radio waves. (1941) *See also* acronym, sonar

red points, n. Wartime ration coupons needed to buy animal-derived foods such as meat and butter.

robotics, n. The design, construction, and application of robots. Coined by science-fiction writer and scientist Isaac Asimov. (1941)

Rosie the Riveter, n. Idealized, muscular female factory worker who appeared in American home-front propaganda during World War II. (1942)

sad sack, n. Inept, bumbling soldier; a civilian who has trouble adapting to military life. Named for the eponymous character of George Baker's *Sad Sack* comic strip. (1942) *See also* glamour boy, yard bird

sixty-four dollar question, n. Question of particular import or difficulty. Derived from the ultimate question on the American radio quiz show *Take It or Leave It* (1941-1948). (1942)

sloppy joe, n. Heavy, oversized sweater. A teenage fashion through much of the 1940's and well into the 1950's, it was often complemented by saddle shoes and rolled-up jeans.

snafu, n. Acronym for "situation normal, all f——ked up." U.S. military slang for a typical or small mishap or mistake. (1941) *See also* acronym, fubar

soap opera, n. Melodramatic radio serial, targeted at housewives. The programs were often sponsored by soap manufacturers such Procter and Gamble and Colgate-Palmolive-Peet—hence the name. (1940)

sonar, n. Acronym for "*so*und *na*vigation *r*anging," a method for detecting submerged objects through the reflection of sound waves. (1946) *See also* acronym, radar

spaceman, n. Person who travels in space. (1942)

square, n., adj. Not hep/hip. An unfashionable person. (1944) *See also* hep to the jive, hipster

strafe, v. To fire upon ground targets from a low-flying aircraft. (1942)

superpower, n. State or nation that has a large amount of influence and/or power over the rest of the world's countries. (1944)

sweater girl, n. Young woman—especially an actor or other celebrity—who accentuates her assets by wearing a tight-fitting sweater. Lana Turner was the archetypal sweater girl. (1940)

teenager, n. Person between the ages of thirteen and nineteen. (1941)

terrorist, n. Member of an organization that seeks to overthrow or force certain concessions from a government through acts of violence against that government and/or its citizens. (1947)

Third World War, n. The hypothetical, cataclysmic—and perhaps apocalyptic—global war to follow World War II. The term World War III was not in use until the 1950's. (1945)

transistor, n. Small semiconductor device that regulates the flow of electrical current between terminals. Ultimately displaced the more unwieldy vacuum tube and made possible a revolution in computers, radios, and other electronics during the second half of the twentieth century. (1948)

TV, n. Abbreviated form of "television." (1948)

unarmed combat, n. The art of fighting with bare hands. A standard course of study for commandos. (1947) *See also* commando

V-E Day, n. May 8, 1945, the day of Germany's unconditional surrender.

V-girl/Victory girl, n. Young American woman, often a teenager, who frequently entertained, dated, and sometimes sought sexual liaisons with soldiers during World War II. Also known as "patriotutes," "goodtime Janes," and "khaki wackies"—the latter because they were obsessed with men in army khakis. (c. 1942)

V-J Day, n. August 14, 1945, the day of Japan's unconditional surrender.

voutian, n. (Pronounced VOW-shun) Variant of jazz slang, popularized by jazz musician and comedian Slim Gaillard. Made heavy use of hip rhymes, nonsense words, and superlative or superfluous suffixes such as -oreety, -reety, and -oroony. As a fad among high school and college students it was extremely short-lived. (ca. 1947)

welfare state, n. State that provides government-funded social services (such as old-age pensions and health care) to its citizens. (1941)

West, n. Geopolitical designation for those noncommunist states united in their opposition to the communist Soviet Union and its satellites. (1946) *See also* Bamboo Curtain, Cold War, Iron Curtain

whistle-stop, adj. Regarding a journey with many brief layovers—often at obscure locales—especially when taken by a politician as part of a political campaign. First used during Harry S. Truman's 1948 campaign. (1948)

xerography, n. Inkless or dry-copying process. The proprietary name Xerox (1952) is derived from this word. (1948)

yard bird, n. Raw recruit. *See also* glamour boy, sad sack

zoot suit, n. Men's suit of exaggeratedly long and generous cut, with well-padded shoulders and tight-cuffed trousers. Especially popular among black, Mexican, Italian, and Filipino American youths. (1942)

Jeremiah Taylor

■ List of Entries by Category

Subject Headings Used in List

African Americans

African Americans
American Negro Exposition
Amos 'n' Andy
*An American Dilemma: The Negro
    Problem and American Democracy*
Bunche, Ralph
Congress of Racial Equality
Davis, Benjamin O., Jr.
Davis, Miles
Demographics of the United States
Desegregation of the U.S. military
Ellington, Duke
Executive Order 8802

Fair Deal
Fair Employment Practices
    Commission
Garner, Erroll Louis
Harlem Globetrotters
Holiday, Billie
Horne, Lena
Jackson, Mahalia
Jim Crow laws
Journey of Reconciliation
Louis, Joe
Louisiana ex rel. Francis v. Resweber
Lynching and hate crime
Morgan v. Virginia

Nation of Islam
National Association for the
    Advancement of Colored People
Native Son
Negro Leagues
Paige, Satchel
Parker, Charlie
Port Chicago Naval magazine
    explosion
Race riots
Racial discrimination
Randolph, A. Philip
Rhythm nightclub fire
Robinson, Jackie

Robinson, Sugar Ray
Shelley v. Kraemer
Smith v. Allwright
Stormy Weather
Tuskegee Airmen
Tuskegee syphilis study
Voting rights
White, Walter F.
Wright, Richard

Agriculture
Agriculture in Canada
Agriculture in the United States
Bracero program
Bureau of Land Management
Cloud seeding
Food processing
Natural resources
Wallace, Henry A.
Wartime rationing
Wickard v. Filburn

Aircraft & Aviation
Aircraft design and development
Bombers
Braun, Wernher von
Byrd, Richard E.
China-Burma-India theater
Cloud seeding
Cochran, Jacqueline
Davis, Benjamin O., Jr.
Doolittle bombing raid
Enola Gay
Flying saucers
Flying Tigers
Helicopters
Hughes, Howard
Jet engines
Radar
Rocketry
Strategic bombing
Travel in the United States
Yeager, Chuck

Art & Architecture
American Negro Exposition
Animated films
Architecture
Art movements
Art of This Century
Bourke-White, Margaret
Comic books
De Kooning, Willem
Fuller, R. Buckminster

Hopper, Edward
Jackson Hole National Monument
Jefferson Memorial
Mount Rushmore National
    Memorial
Pentagon building
Photography
Pollock, Jackson
Rockwell, Norman
Wright, Frank Lloyd

Asian Americans
Asian Americans
Immigration Act of 1943
Japanese American internment
Japanese Canadian internment
Korematsu v. United States
Racial discrimination

Business & Economics
Advertising in Canada
Advertising in the United States
Agriculture in Canada
Agriculture in the United States
Automobiles and auto
    manufacturing
Ballpoint pens
Black market
Book publishing
Bretton Woods Conference
Business and the economy in
    Canada
Business and the economy in the
    United States
Coinage
Credit and debt
Demographics of the United States
Diners Club
Economic wartime regulations
Emergency Price Control Act of
    1942
Executive orders
Fashions and clothing
Food processing
Ford Motor Company
Freezing of Japanese assets
G.I. Bill
General Agreement on Tariffs and
    Trade
General Motors
Gross national product of Canada
Gross national product of the
    United States
Home appliances

Housing in Canada
Housing in the United States
Hughes, Howard
Income and wages
Inflation
International Business Machines
    Corporation
International trade
Kaiser, Henry J.
Keynesian economics
Labor strikes
Lend-Lease
Levittown
M&M candies
McCormick, Robert R.
Magazines
National debt
National War Labor Board
New Deal programs
Newspapers
Office of Price Administration
Organized crime
Sarnoff, David
Siegel, Bugsy
Taft-Hartley Act
Trans World Airlines
Unemployment in Canada
Unemployment in the United
    States
Unionism
United Fruit Company
*United States v. Aluminum Company of
    America*
United States v. Darby Lumber Co.
*United States v. Paramount Pictures,
    et al.*
War bonds
War debt
War Production Board
War surplus
Wartime industries
Wartime rationing
Wartime seizures of businesses
Wickard v. Filburn
Xerography
Yakus v. United States

Canada
Advertising in Canada
Agriculture in Canada
Business and the economy in
    Canada
Canada and Great Britain
Canadian Citizenship Act of 1946

Canadian minority communities
Canadian nationalism
Canadian participation in World
 War II
Canadian regionalism
Censorship in Canada
Demographics of Canada
Duplessis, Maurice Le Noblet
Education in Canada
Elections in Canada
Film in Canada
Foreign policy of Canada
Gross national product of
 Canada
Housing in Canada
Ice hockey
Immigration to Canada
International trade
Japanese Canadian internment
Jews in Canada
King, William Lyon Mackenzie
Literature in Canada
Maclean's
Military conscription in Canada
National parks
Natural resources
Newfoundland
Ogdensburg Agreement of 1940
Organization of American States
Quebec nationalism
Racial discrimination
Radio in Canada
Refugees in North America
Religion in Canada
Richard, Maurice
St. Laurent, Louis
Theater in Canada
Unemployment in Canada
Urbanization in Canada
V-E Day and V-J Day
Wartime propaganda in Canada
Women's roles and rights in
 Canada

Civil Rights & Liberties

Asian Americans
Censorship in the United States
Chaplinsky v. New Hampshire
Civil rights and liberties
Congress of Racial Equality
Desegregation of the U.S. military
Executive Order 8802
Executive orders
Fair Deal

Fair Employment Practices
 Commission
Homosexuality and gay rights
Indian Claims Commission
International League for the Rights
 of Man
Jews in Canada
Jim Crow laws
Journey of Reconciliation
Latinos
Louisiana ex rel. Francis v. Resweber
Murdock v. Pennsylvania
National Association for the
 Advancement of Colored People
Native Americans
Race riots
Racial discrimination
Randolph, A. Philip
Robinson, Jackie
Shelley v. Kraemer
Skinner v. Oklahoma
Smith v. Allwright
*United Public Workers of America v.
 Mitchell*
Vinson, Fred M.
Voting rights
White, Walter F.
Women's roles and rights in
 Canada
Women's roles and rights in the
 United States

Cold War

Anticommunism
Berlin blockade and airlift
Churchill, Winston
Civil defense programs
Communist Party USA
Hiss, Alger
Historiography
House Committee on Un-American
 Activities
"Iron Curtain" speech
Kennan, George F.
North Atlantic Treaty Organization
Point Four Program
Truman Doctrine
Turkey
Wallace, Henry A.
Yalta Conference

Communism

Bentley, Elizabeth
Communist Party USA

Hiss, Alger
Hollywood blacklisting
Hoover, J. Edgar
House Committee on Un-American
 Activities
"Iron Curtain" speech
Kennan, George F.
Korea
Loyalty Program, Truman's
Smith Act
Smith Act trials
Socialist Workers Party
Truman Doctrine
Voice of America
White, Harry Dexter

Courts & Court Cases

Ballard v. United States
Cantwell v. Connecticut
Chaplinsky v. New Hampshire
Duncan v. Kahanamoku
*Everson v. Board of Education of Ewing
 Township*
*Illinois ex rel. McCollum v. Board of
 Education*
International Court of Justice
Korematsu v. United States
Louisiana ex rel. Francis v. Resweber
Morgan v. Virginia
Murdock v. Pennsylvania
Nuremberg Trials
Prudential Insurance Co. v. Benjamin
Shelley v. Kraemer
Skinner v. Oklahoma
Smith Act trials
Smith v. Allwright
Stone, Harlan Fiske
Supreme Court, U.S.
Thornhill v. Alabama
*United Public Workers of America v.
 Mitchell*
*United States v. Aluminum Company of
 America*
United States v. Darby Lumber Co.
*United States v. Paramount Pictures,
 et al.*
United States v. United Mine Workers
Vinson, Fred M.
*West Virginia State Board of Education
 v. Barnette*
Wickard v. Filburn
Wolf v. Colorado
Yakus v. United States

Crime & Scandal

Black Dahlia murder
Black market
Convention on the Prevention and
    Punishment of the Crime of
    Genocide
Crimes and scandals
Federal Bureau of Investigation
Gambling
Hobbs Act
Lynching and hate crime
Nuremberg Trials
Organized crime
Siegel, Bugsy
Skinner v. Oklahoma
Smith Act trials
War crimes and atrocities
Wartime espionage
Zoot-suit riots

Dance

Appalachian Spring
Ballet Society
Bobby-soxers
Broadway musicals
Chuck and Chuckles
Coles, Honi
Dance
Fads
Jitterbug
Kelly, Gene
Miranda, Carmen
Music: Classical
Oklahoma!
Robbins, Jerome
Rodeo
Rogers, Ginger

Demographics & Immigration

African Americans
*An American Dilemma: The Negro
    Problem and American Democracy*
Asian Americans
Baby boom
Bracero program
Canadian Citizenship Act of 1946
Canadian minority communities
Demographics of Canada
Demographics of the United States
Health care
Housing in Canada
Immigration Act of 1943
Immigration to Canada
Immigration to the United States

Japanese Canadian internment
Jews in Canada
Jews in the United States
Latinos
Native Americans
Race riots
Refugees in North America
Soccer
Urbanization in Canada
Urbanization in the United States
War brides

Diplomacy & International Relations

Anticommunism
Atlantic Charter
Berlin blockade and airlift
Bracero program
Bretton Woods Conference
Bunche, Ralph
Byrnes, James
Cairo Conference
Canada and Great Britain
Casablanca Conference
China and North America
Churchill, Winston
Cold War
Foreign policy of Canada
Foreign policy of the United States
France and the United States
Fulbright fellowship program
General Agreement on Tariffs and
    Trade
Geneva Conventions
Germany, occupation of
Hiss, Alger
Hitler, Adolf
Inter-American Treaty of
    Reciprocal Assistance
International League for the Rights
    of Man
Iran
"Iron Curtain" speech
Isolationism
Israel, creation of
Japan, occupation of
Kennan, George F.
Korea
Latin America
Marshall Plan
Mexico
Nobel Prizes
North Atlantic Treaty Organization
Ogdensburg Agreement of 1940

Organization of American States
Paris Peace Conference of 1946
Philippine independence
Philippines
Point Four Program
Potsdam Conference
Quebec Conferences
Roosevelt, Eleanor
Roosevelt, Franklin D.
Tehran Conference
Truman Doctrine
Truman proclamations
Turkey
Unconditional surrender policy
United Fruit Company
United Nations
Voice of America
Wartime espionage
Yalta Conference

Disasters

Armistice Day blizzard
Cocoanut Grove nightclub fire
Fiscus rescue attempt
Great Blizzard of 1949
Natural disasters
Port Chicago Naval magazine
    explosion
Red Cross
Rhythm nightclub fire
Tacoma Narrows Bridge collapse
Texas City disaster

Education & Scholarship

Carbon dating
Curious George books
Demographics of the United States
Education in Canada
Education in the United States
*Everson v. Board of Education of Ewing
    Township*
Fulbright fellowship program
G.I. Bill
Great Books Foundation
Historiography
*Illinois ex rel. McCollum v. Board of
    Education*
Miss America pageants
Philosophhy and philosophers
Social sciences
*Studies in Social Psychology in World
    War II*
*West Virginia State Board of Education
    v. Barnette*

Engineering & Construction
Aircraft design and development
Architecture
Braun, Wernher von
Fuller, R. Buckminster
Hughes, Howard
Jefferson Memorial
Jet engines
Mount Rushmore National
   Memorial
Natural resources
Pentagon building
Rocketry
Tacoma Narrows Bridge collapse
White House renovations

Environmental Issues
Aerosol cans
Air pollution
Fish and Wildlife Service, U.S.
Fuller, R. Buckminster
National parks
Natural disasters
Natural resources
Our Plundered Planet
Sand County Almanac, A
Truman proclamations
Walden Two
Water pollution
Water Pollution Control Act

Fads & Fashions
Bikini bathing suits
Bobby-soxers
Fads
Fashions and clothing
Flying saucers
Hairstyles
Hobbies
Home furnishings
Inventions
Life
Look
Nylon stockings
Photography
Postage stamps
Slang, wartime
Zoot-suit riots
Zoot suits

Film
Academy Awards
Andy Hardy films
Animated films

The Best Years of Our Lives
Casablanca
Censorship in the United States
Cisco Kid
Citizen Kane
Cowboy films
Disney films
Double Indemnity
Fantasia
Film in Canada
Film in the United States
Film noir
Film serials
Films about World War II
For Whom the Bell Tolls
Gentleman's Agreement
The Grapes of Wrath
The Great Dictator
Hollywood blacklisting
The Human Comedy
It's a Wonderful Life
Knute Rockne: All American
Laura
"Maisie" films
Maltese Falcon, The
Meet Me in St. Louis
Miracle on 34th Street
National Velvet
Philadelphia Story, The
Pornography
Stormy Weather
Sullivan's Travels
They Were Expendable
Three Mesquiteers
Treasure of the Sierra Madre, The
United States v. Paramount Pictures,
   et al.
Yankee Doodle Dandy

Film: People
Abbott and Costello
Academy Awards
Benny, Jack
Bogart, Humphrey
Capra, Frank
Crosby, Bing
Davis, Bette
Farmer, Frances
Fields, W. C.
Flynn, Errol
Ford, John
Garland, Judy
Garson, Greer
Grable, Betty

Hayworth, Rita
Hitchcock, Alfred
Hope, Bob
Horne, Lena
Kelly, Gene
Lombard, Carole
Miranda, Carmen
Murphy, Audie
Renaldo, Duncan
Rogers, Ginger
Roland, Gilbert
Romero, César
Rooney, Mickey
Sinatra, Frank
Welles, Orson

Government Agencies & Programs
Atomic Energy Commission
Bureau of Land Management
Central Intelligence Agency
Coast Guard, U.S.
Congress, U.S.
Department of Defense, U.S.
Economic wartime regulations
Fair Deal
Fair Employment Practices
   Commission
Federal Bureau of Investigation
Fish and Wildlife Service, U.S.
Hoover Commission
Indian Claims Commission
Lend-Lease
Loyalty Program, Truman's
Manhattan Project
Marshall Plan
Medicine
National parks
National War Labor Board
New Deal programs
Office of Price Administration
Office of Strategic Services
Office of War Mobilization
Oppenheimer, J. Robert
Point Four Program
Roosevelt, Franklin D.
War brides
Wartime propaganda in Canada

Government & Politics
America First Committee
American Enterprise Institute for
   Public Policy Research
Anticommunism

Canadian nationalism
Canadian regionalism
Cold War
Communist Party USA
Congress, U.S.
Conservatism in U.S. politics
Decolonization of European
    empires
Elections in Canada
Elections in the United States: 1940
Elections in the United States: 1942
    and 1946
Elections in the United States: 1944
Elections in the United States: 1948
Executive Order 8802
Executive orders
House Committee on Un-American
    Activities
Isolationism
Korea
National Security Act of 1947
Newfoundland
North Atlantic Treaty Organization
Organization of American States
Pentagon building
Philippine independence
Philippines
Presidential powers
Presidential Succession Act of 1947
Quebec nationalism
Railroad seizure
Socialist Workers Party
Strategic bombing
Supreme Court, U.S.
Truman proclamations
Unconditional surrender policy
United Public Workers of America v.
    Mitchell
Wartime espionage
Wartime rationing
Wartime sabotage

Government & Politics:
   People
Acheson, Dean
Barkley, Alben William
Bentley, Elizabeth
Biddle, Francis
Byrnes, James
Churchill, Winston
Clifford, Clark
Dewey, Thomas E.
Duplessis, Maurice Le Noblet
Forrestal, James

Hitler, Adolf
Hull, Cordell
Ickes, Harold
Kennedy, John F.
King, William Lyon Mackenzie
La Guardia, Fiorello H.
President Roosevelt and the Coming of
    the War
Rayburn, Sam
Roosevelt, Eleanor
Roosevelt, Franklin D.
Smith, Margaret Chase
St. Laurent, Louis
Stimson, Henry L.
Stone, Harlan Fiske
Taft, Robert A.
Thurmond, Strom
Truman, Harry S.
Vandenberg, Arthur Hendrick
Wallace, Henry A.
White, Harry Dexter
Willkie, Wendell

Health & Medicine
Air pollution
Antibiotics
Birth control
Cancer
Casualties of World War II
DNA discovery
Fluoridation
Health care
Homosexuality and gay rights
Horney, Karen
Kidney dialysis
Lobotomy
Medicine
Nobel Prizes
Psychiatry and psychology
Red Cross
Sex and sex education
Sexually transmitted diseases
Smoking and tobacco
Studies in Social Psychology in World
    War II
Tuskegee syphilis study
Water pollution
Water Pollution Control Act
World Health Organization

International Trade
Agriculture in Canada
Atlantic Charter
Bretton Woods Conference

Business and the economy in
    Canada
Business and the economy in the
    United States
Canada and Great Britain
China and North America
Coast Guard, U.S.
Destroyers-for-bases deal
Food processing
France and the United States
General Agreement on Tariffs and
    Trade
Germany, occupation of
Gross national product of the
    United States
Hull, Cordell
Japan, occupation of
Latin America
Lend-Lease
United Fruit Company

Jewish Americans
Bernstein, Leonard
Einstein, Albert
Gentleman's Agreement
Israel, creation of
Jews in Canada
Jews in the United States
Racial discrimination
Refugees in North America
Robbins, Jerome
Sarnoff, David
Siegel, Bugsy
Stein, Gertrude

Journalism & Publishing
Advertising in Canada
Advertising in the United States
Book publishing
Bourke-White, Margaret
Brenda Starr
Censorship in Canada
Censorship in the United States
Comic books
Comic strips
Fiscus rescue attempt
Historiography
History of the United States Naval
    Operations in World War II
Life
Look
McCormick, Robert R.
Maclean's
Magazines

Mauldin, Bill
Murrow, Edward R.
Newspapers
Pulp magazines
Pyle, Ernie
Radio in Canada
Radio in the United States
Reader's Digest
Rockwell, Norman
Saturday Evening Post
Seldes, George
Stars and Stripes
Superman
Voice of America
Wartime propaganda in Canada
Wartime propaganda in the United
  States
Wonder Woman

Labor
Bracero program
Congress of Industrial Organizations
Fair Employment Practices
  Commission
The Grapes of Wrath
Hillman, Sidney
Hobbs Act
Income and wages
Labor strikes
Lewis, John L.
Mexico
National War Labor Board
Railroad seizure
Randolph, A. Philip
"Rosie the Riveter"
Smith-Connally Act
Socialist Workers Party
Taft, Robert A.
Taft-Hartley Act
Thornhill v. Alabama
Unemployment in Canada
Unemployment in the United States
Unionism
United Public Workers of America v.
  Mitchell
United States v. Darby Lumber Co.
United States v. United Mine Workers

Latinos
Bracero program
Cisco Kid
Latin America
Latinos
Mexico

Miranda, Carmen
Race riots
Racial discrimination
Renaldo, Duncan
Roland, Gilbert
Romero, César
United Fruit Company
Zoot-suit riots
Zoot suits

Laws & Treaties
Canadian Citizenship Act of 1946
Convention on the Prevention and
  Punishment of the Crime of
  Genocide
Emergency Price Control Act of 1942
Executive Order 8802
Federal Tort Claims Act
G.I. Bill
General Agreement on Tariffs and
  Trade
Geneva Conventions
Hobbs Act
Immigration Act of 1943
Inter-American Treaty of Reciprocal
  Assistance
Jim Crow laws
Military conscription in the United
  States
National Security Act of 1947
North Atlantic Treaty Organization
Presidential Succession Act of 1947
Smith Act
Smith-Connally Act
Taft-Hartley Act
Water Pollution Control Act

Literature
All the King's Men
Auden, W. H.
Benét, Stephen Vincent
Chandler, Raymond
Cisco Kid
Curious George books
Death of a Salesman
Eliot, T. S.
Faulkner, William
Great Books Foundation
Hiroshima
The Human Comedy
Jackson, Shirley
Literature in Canada
Literature in the United States
Naked and the Dead, The

Native Son
Nobel Prizes
Pound, Ezra
President Roosevelt and the Coming
  of the War
Pulp magazines
Rand, Ayn
Stein, Gertrude
Streetcar Named Desire, A
Williams, Tennessee
Wright, Richard

Military. *See* World War II

Music
Appalachian Spring
Broadway musicals
Fantasia
Jitterbug
Music: Classical
Music: Jazz
Music: Popular
Oklahoma!
Recording industry
Rodeo
South Pacific
Stormy Weather
Where's Charley?
Yankee Doodle Dandy

Music: People
Andrews Sisters
Bernstein, Leonard
Coles, Honi
Crosby, Bing
Davis, Miles
Dorsey, Tommy
Ellington, Duke
Fender, Leo
Garland, Judy
Garner, Erroll Louis
Godfrey, Arthur
Goodman, Benny
Guthrie, Woody
Holiday, Billie
Horne, Lena
Jackson, Mahalia
Miller, Glenn
Miranda, Carmen
Parker, Charlie
Robbins, Jerome
Rodgers, Richard, and Oscar
  Hammerstein II
Seeger, Pete

Sinatra, Frank
Williams, Hank

Native Americans
Canadian minority communities
Code talkers
Native Americans
Racial discrimination
Voting rights

Philosophy
Auden, W. H.
Education in the United States
Fuller, R. Buckminster
Great Books Foundation
Philosophy and philosophers
Rand, Ayn
Theology and theologians
Walden Two

Photography
Bourke-White, Margaret
Citizen Kane
Life
Look
Maclean's
Photography
Pinup girls
Polaroid instant cameras
Pornography
Saturday Evening Post

Popular Culture
Abbott and Costello
Andrews Sisters
Benny, Jack
The Best Years of Our Lives
Bikini bathing suits
Bobby-soxers
Bogart, Humphrey
Brenda Starr
Casablanca
Comic books
Comic strips
Fads
Fantasia
Film serials
Flying saucers
"Greatest Generation"
Hairstyles
It's a Wonderful Life
Jitterbug
Life
Look

M&M candies
Maclean's
Meet Me in St. Louis
Music: Popular
Newspapers
Photography
Pinup girls
Polaroid instant cameras
Pornography
Post, Emily
Postage stamps
Pulp magazines
Radio in the United States
Reader's Digest
Recording industry
Rockwell, Norman
Rogers, Ginger
Sad Sack
Saturday Evening Post
Slang, wartime
Sports in Canada
Sports in the United States
Superman
Television
Three Mesquiteers
Wonder Woman

Products & Inventions
Aerosol cans
Atomic clock
Ballpoint pens
Bikini bathing suits
Binary automatic computer
Computers
Diners Club
ENIAC
Fads
Fender, Leo
Fuller, R. Buckminster
General Motors
Hale telescope
Helicopters
Home appliances
Hughes, Howard
International Business Machines
   Corporation
Inventions
Jet engines
Kidney dialysis
Levittown
M&M candies
Microwave ovens
Nylon stockings
Photography

Polaroid instant cameras
Radar
Recording industry
Rocketry
Science and technology
Smoking and tobacco
Telephone technology and service
Transistors
Tucker Torpedo
Wartime technological advances
Xerography

Radio
Abbott and Costello
Advertising in Canada
Advertising in the United States
Amos 'n' Andy
Andrews Sisters
Benny, Jack
Censorship in Canada
Censorship in the United States
Cisco Kid
Godfrey, Arthur
Hope, Bob
Murrow, Edward R.
Music: Jazz
Music: Popular
Pound, Ezra
Radio in Canada
Radio in the United States
Sarnoff, David
Superman
Theater in Canada
Tokyo Rose
Voice of America
Williams, Hank

Recreation
Baseball
Book publishing
Comic books
Fads
Football
Gambling
Golf
Hobbies
Recreation
Rhythm nightclub fire
Sports in Canada
Sports in the United States
Television
Tennis
Travel in the United States
United Service Organizations

Religion & Theology

Cabrini canonization
Cantwell v. Connecticut
Chaplains in World War II
Conscientious objectors
*Everson v. Board of Education of Ewing
    Township*
Graham, Billy
*Illinois ex rel. McCollum v. Board of
    Education*
Jackson, Mahalia
Murdock v. Pennsylvania
Nation of Islam
Religion in Canada
Religion in the United States
Spellman, Francis Joseph
Theology and theologians

Science & Technology

Aerosol cans
Archaeology
Astronomy
Atomic bomb
Atomic clock
Atomic Energy Commission
Big bang theory
Binary automatic computer
Braun, Wernher von
Byrd, Richard E.
Carbon dating
Cloud seeding
Computers
DNA discovery
Einstein, Albert
ENIAC
Fermi, Enrico
Fluoridation
Gamow, George
Groves, Leslie Richard
Hale telescope
Hanford Nuclear Reservation
Hiroshima and Nagasaki bombings
Home appliances
Horney, Karen
Hughes, Howard
Kidney dialysis
Lobotomy
Manhattan Project
Medicine
Natural disasters
Nobel Prizes
Norton County meteorite
Nuclear reactors
Oppenheimer, J. Robert

Plutonium discovery
Polaroid instant cameras
Radar
Rocketry
Science and technology
*Studies in Social Psychology in World
    War II*
Synchrocyclotron
Telephone technology and service
Television
Transistors
Tuskegee syphilis study
Wartime technological advances

Social Issues

American Negro Exposition
*An American Dilemma: The Negro
    Problem and American Democracy*
Anticommunism
Asian Americans
Bentley, Elizabeth
CARE
Conscientious objectors
Demographics of Canada
Demographics of the United States
Desegregation of the U.S. military
Fair Deal
Gentleman's Agreement
Guthrie, Woody
Hollywood blacklisting
National Association for the
    Advancement of Colored People
New Deal programs
Our Plundered Planet
Philosophy and philosophers
Photography
Pornography
Port Chicago Naval magazine
    explosion
Race riots
Racial discrimination
Refugees in North America
Sand County Almanac, A
Seeger, Pete
Sexually transmitted diseases
Walden Two
White, Walter F.

Sports

All-American Girls Professional
    Baseball League
Arcaro, Eddie
Auto racing
Baseball

Basketball
Baugh, Sammy
Boxing
Davis, Glenn
DiMaggio, Joe
Football
Gambling
Gehrig, Lou
Golf
Gray, Pete
Harlem Globetrotters
Hogan, Ben
Horse racing
Ice hockey
Knute Rockne: All American
LaMotta, Jake
Louis, Joe
Mathias, Bob
National Basketball Association
Negro Leagues
Olympic Games of 1948
Paige, Satchel
Richard, Maurice
Robinson, Jackie
Robinson, Sugar Ray
Soccer
Sports in Canada
Sports in the United States
Tennis
Warmerdam, Cornelius
Williams, Ted
Zaharias, Babe Didrikson

Television

Abbott and Costello
Advertising in the United States
Benny, Jack
Berle, Milton
Cisco Kid
Fads
Fiscus rescue attempt
Godfrey, Arthur
Hope, Bob
Howdy Doody Show
Kukla, Fran, and Ollie
Sarnoff, David
Texaco Star Theater

Theater

Broadway musicals
Death of a Salesman
Fields, W. C.
Oklahoma!
Robbins, Jerome

The Forties
in America

■ Photo Index

■ Personages Index

Page numbers in **boldface** type indicate full articles devoted to the topic.

Capra, Frank, **177-178**, 361, 539-540,
901-902, 1040, 1114-1115, 1117
Cárdenas, Lázaro, 637
Cardin, Pierre-Joseph, 644
Carey, Ernestine Gilbreth, 128
Carle, Frankie, 1146
Carlson, Chester F., 1091
Carmichael, Hoagy, 1146
Carnap, Rudolf, 754
Carothers, Wallace, 716
Carpenter, Edward, 477
Carpenter, Thelma, 1119
Carr, Emily, 173, 596
Carradine, John, 946
Carrillo, Leo, 204
Carson, Johnny, 107
Carson, Mindy, 1146
Carter, Jimmy, 877
Case, Shirley Jackson, 826
Casey, Hugh, 744
Cash, Johnny, 683
Caspary, Vera, 586
Castañeda, Jorge Ubico, 985
Cerdan, Marcel, 130, 579
Chadwick, St. John, 698
Chain, Ernst, 49
Chamberlain, Neville, 160, 589
Chambers, Sidney, 249
Chambers, Whittaker, 250, 456, 487,
1059
Chan, Anna, 1017
Chandler, Albert Benjamin "Happy,"
99, 797
Chandler, Raymond, **193-194**, 290,
344, 356, 600, 1116
Chandrasekhar, Subrahmanyan, 72
Chaplin, Charles, 2, 251, 426-427,
470, 486, 1111, 1116
Chaplin, Sydney, 1058
Charbonneau, Joseph, 827
Charles, Ezzard, 130-131
Charles, Ray, 1146
Charleston, Oscar, 694
Charlier, Roger, 1018
Chase, Chevy, 950
Chávez, Denisio, 585
Chennault, Anna C., 1017
Chennault, Claire Lee, 196, 198, 369,
1017, 1182
Chiang Kai-shek, 159, 196-198, 222,
369, 496, 627, 789, 902-903, 1013;
and Cairo Conference, 158-160
Chiang Kai-shek, Madame, 903
Chireaeff, Ludmilla, 258

Chordettes, 417
Christian, Charlie, 662
Christy, June, 1146, 1150
Chrysler, Fritz, 377
Churchill, Winston, 74, 77, 158, **201-
203**, 277, 533, 769; and Arcadia
Conference, 53-54; and Atlantic
Charter, 77-78; and Cairo
Conference, 158-160; and
Casablanca Conference, 183-185;
and Dieppe raid, 280; and
Charles de Gaulle, 393; on Adolf
Hitler, 828; "Iron Curtain"
speech, 220, 533-534; and William
Lyon Mackenzie King, 568; and
Lend-Lease program, 587-589;
memoirs, 595; and North Atlantic
Treaty Organization, 709; and
Quebec Conferences, 413, 789-
790; and Stalin's propaganda
speech, 221; and Tehran
Conference, 928-930; and Yalta
Conference, 1093
Clark, Albert P., 427
Clark, Buddy, 1146, 1153
Clark, Joseph J., 1182
Clark, Lincoln, 180
Clark, Mark, 387, 538, 626, 1182
Clark, Tom C., 275, 920
Clark, Walter van Tilburg, 126, 601,
1113
Clawson, Marion, 146
Clay, Lucius, 110, 1182
Clifford, Clark, **211-212**, 319, 430,
536
Clifford, Harvey, 894
Clift, Montgomery, 1116-1117
Cline, Edward F., 1111
Cline, Patsy, 1120
Clinton, Bill, 991
Clooney, Rosemary, 1147
Coand, Henri, 552
Cobb, Lee J., 944
Cochran, Jacqueline, **214**, 1068
Cochrane, Freddy, 131
Cockcroft, John D., 78
Cohan, George M., 1094-1095, 1113
Cohen, Mickey, 250-251
Cohen, Morris Raphael, 754
Cohn, Harry, 177
Colbert, Claudette, 1116
Colbourne, Maurice, 940
Cole, Jack, 225, 258
Cole, Lester, 355

Cole, Nat King, 1146, 1147, 1150
Coles, Honi, **224**
Collier, John, 679, 1010
Collins, J. Lawton, 1183
Collyer, Clayton "Bud," 1118
Colmery, Harry W., 399
Colona, Jerry, 1121
Comden, Betty, 111
Como, Perry, 1147
Compton, John T., 1021
Comstock, Anthony, 188
Conant, James Bryant, 303
Condon, Eddie, 1147
Conn, Billy, 130
Connee, 1147
Cooper, Gary, 245, 884, 1112-1113
Cooper, Jackie, 465
Copland, Aaron, 52-53, 259, 658,
842-843
Corcoran, Fred, 1098
Cori, Carl F., 705
Cori, Gerty, 705
Correll, Charles, 1118
Costello, Bill, 802
Costello, Frank, 732
Costello, Lou, **1-2**, 245, 360, 1112,
1116
Cota, Norman, 877
Côté, Gérard, 894
Cotten, Joseph, 245, 1112-1113,
1116
Counts, George S., 300
Cowles, Gardner, Jr., 605-606
Cowles, Mike, 605
Cowley, Malcolm, 344
Cozzens, James Gould, 600
Craig, James, 1111
Craighill, Margaret D., 1068
Crain, Jeanne, 1117
Crawford, Broderick, 1117
Crawford, Joan, 3, 352, 847, 884,
1114
Crerar, H. D. G., 384, 1183
Cronin, A. J., 126
Cronin, Joe, 897
Cronkite, Walter, 934
Cronyn, Hume, 1114
Crosby, Bing, 3, **252-253**, 360, 481,
832, 1113-1114, 1145, 1147, 1151;
radio programs, 1119; USO tours,
992
Crouteau, Louis J., 189
Croves, Hal, 960
Cugat, Xavier, 1147

Roodenko, Igal, 560
Rooney, Mickey, 45-46, 122, 243, 678, **847-848**, 1114
Roosevelt, Eleanor, 311, 327, 699, **848-849**, 850, 893, 996; and civil defense, 206
Roosevelt, Franklin D., 74, 77, 96, 132, 156, 202, 277, 346, 429, 533, 543, 691, 774, **849-853**, 881, 1065; and Alaska Highway, 32; and Arcadia Conference, 53-54; "Arsenal of Democracy" speech, 65-66; and Atlantic Charter, 77-78; and atomic bomb, 78; and baseball, 98, 896; biographies of, 459, 772-773; and Cairo Conference, 158-160; and Casablanca Conference, 183-185; and Winston Churchill, 928-930; and civil defense, 206; conservatives and, 241; and daylight saving time, 264; and Thomas E. Dewey, 278; efforts to shape postwar Asia, 158; election of 1940, 386; executive orders, 328; fireside chats, 804; "Four Freedoms" speech (Roosevelt), 391, 525; funeral procession, 417; and G.I. Bill, 399; and Charles de Gaulle, 393; and health insurance, 448; and isolationism, 534; and Japanese American internment, 547; and Keynesian economics, 888; and William Lyon Mackenzie King, 384, 568, 721-722; and Lend-Lease program, 587; and Carole Lombard, 604; and Douglas MacArthur, 614; and March on Washington, 810; and Mexico, 637, 639; and military conscription, 645; and New Deal, 696-697, 994; and Office of Strategic Services, 718; and bombing of Pearl Harbor, 851; polio, 189, 849; and Quebec Conferences, 789-790; and racial segregation in the military, 12; and radio, 803, 805, 852; and saboteurs, 917; and segregation, 335; and Soviet Union, 1093; and Joseph Stalin, 928-930; and stamp collecting, 466, 768; and Supreme Court, 905; and Tehran

Conference, 928-930; U.S. agriculture and, 18; and unconditional surrender policy, 974; and United Service Organizations, 991; and war bonds, 1015; and wartime mobilization, 1033; and wartime propaganda, 1039, 1041; and Yalta Conference, 1093
Roosevelt, Theodore, 704, 734, 819
Roosevelt, Theodore, Jr., 1186
Roosevelt dime, 466
Rose, Mauri, 85
Rose, Pete, 100
Rosen, Leo, 216
Rosenberg, Alfred, 714
Rosenberg, Ethel, 1032
Rosenberg, Julius, 1032
Rosenthal, Joe, 540-541
Ross, Fred, 585
Ross, Josephine, 250
Rossen, Richard, 1115
Rossen, Robert, 1117
Rotheim, Erik, 11
Rothko, Mark, 67
Rottenberg, Benjamin, 1092
Rouverol, Aurania, 45
Rowland, Roy, 847
Rowles, Jimmy, 405
Rowlett, Frank, 216
Roxas, Manuel, 748
Roy, Gabrielle, 127, 941
Roybal, Edward R., 585
Rozen, George, 786
Rozen, Jerome, 786
Rudge, Olga, 771
Rugg, Harold, 300
Ruggles, Charles, 1058
Rundstedt, Gerd von, 143
Rupp, Adolf, 101
Russell, Andy, 1152
Russell, Harold, 4, 362, 1115
Russell, Jane, 245
Russell, Rosalind, 1111
Rustin, Bayard, 241, 556, 560
Ruth, Babe, 406
Rutherford, Ann, 46
Rutherford, Joseph, 301
Rutledge, Wiley B., 653
Ryan, Robert, 354

Saarinen, Eero, 475-476
Saddler, Sandy, 130
St. Denis, Ruth, 258

St. John, J. Allen, 786
St. Laurent, Louis, 164, **855-857**; and William Lyon Mackenzie King, 570
Salk, Jonas, 633
Samuelson, Paul, 889
Saperstein, Abe, 444, 671
Sarnoff, David, **858-859**
Saroyan, William, 127, 498, 599, 601
Sartre, Jean-Paul, 127, 754
Satina, Natalia, 1007
Satterlee, Peggy LaRue, 371
Sauckel, Fritz, 714
Schacht, Hjalmar, 714
Schaefer, Vincent Joseph, 212, 531
Schary, Dore, 847
Schechter, Steven, 458
Schirach, Baldur von, 714
Schlesinger, Arthur, Jr., 774
Schmeling, Max, 130, 607
Schmid, Al, 1026
Schneider, Ralph, 284
Schoenberg, Arnold, 656
Schoenbrod, David, 1092
Schoenbrun, David, 802
Schroeder, Ted, 936
Schulberg, Budd, 128
Schultz, Dutch, 278
Schuman, William, 658
Scott, Adrian, 4
Scott, Barbara-Ann, 894-895
Scott, F. R., 597
Scott, George C., 362
Scott, Randolph, 244
Seaborg, Glenn, 79, 760
Seaton, George, 1116
Seeger, Pete, 437, **865-866**, 1145, 1152, 1154
Segar, E. C., 1205
Segee, Robert, 249
Segura, Pancho, 937
Seldes, George, **866-867**
Selznick, David O., 245, 1115
Sessions, Roger, 658
Sevareid, Eric, 655, 802
Seymour, Edward, 11
Seyss-Inquart, Arthur, 714
Sharpless, S. L., 73
Shaw, Artie, 1152
Shaw, Irwin, 127, 600
Shaw, Wilbur, 85
Sheen, Fulton J., 832
Sheen, Martin, 877
Shelton, Anne, 1153

■ Subject Index

Page numbers in **boldface** type indicate full articles devoted to the topic.

Gaddis, John Lewis, 460
Gaines, Max, 224
Gaines, William, 224
Galivan, Kid, 130
Gallinger, Don, 251
Gambino, Carlo, 733
Gambling, 250, **402-403**, 732-734; and organized crime, 733; and sports, 251
Gamow, George, 114, **403**
Gandhi, Indira, 265
Gandhi, Mohandas K., 129, 755-756
Gang Busters (radio), 1120
Garand, John, 1052
Gardner, Erle Stanley, 786
Garfield, John, 259, 1115
Garland, Judy, 46, **403-404**, 563, 606, 635-636, 847, 1114
Garner, Ed, 1120
Garner, Erroll Louis, **404-405**
Garner, John Nance, 96
Garner, Peggy Ann, 1115
Garralaga, Martin, 204
Garson, Greer, 3, **405-406**, 1113
Gas-House McGinty (Farrell), 187
Gaslight (film), 1114
Gasoline; rationing of, 957, 1044
Gasser, Herbert Spencer, 705
Gather Darkness! (Leiber), 1203
GATT. *See* General Agreement on Tariffs and Trade
Gaulle, Charles de, 184, 392-393, 710; and Canadians, 569
Gauvreau, Claude, 941
Gay rights, 477-478
Gehrig, Lou, **406**, 1113
Geisel, Theodore, 1040
Gélinas, Gratien, 941
General Agreement on Tariffs and Trade, **407-408**, 496, 527; and Canada, 384
General Black, USS, 823
General Electric; wartime contracts, 1035
General Electric Research Laboratories, 212, 531, 863
General Land Office, 146
General Maximum Price Regulation, 150
General Motors, 86, 88-89, 154, **408-409**, 576; wartime contracts, 1035
General Telephone, 931
Genetics, 287-288

Geneva Conventions, **409-411**; and chaplains, 194; and Japan, 1021; and prisoners of war, 775, 1019
Genocide, 242-243
Gentleman's Agreement (film), 4, 354, **411**, 832, 1116
Gentlemen Prefer Blondes (musical), 224
Geodesic dome, 398
Gerald McBoing-Boing, 47
German American Bund, 38, **412-413**, 464, 588
Germany; and Allied prisoners of war, 775-777; and American jazz, 662; Berlin blockade and airlift, 109-111; emigration from, 656, 822; and Geneva Conventions, 775-776; Italian and Sicilian campaigns, 537-539; Nuremberg Trials, 713-716; occupation of, 220, **413-416**, 527, 770, 790, 929, 1094; and Olympics, 727; prisoners of war in North America, 778-780; U-boats, 74, 213, 911-913
Gernsback, Hugo, 787
"Geronimo," 1205
Gershwin, George, 661, 1095
Getz, Stan, 1149
Gibson, Althea, 936
Gibson, John, 399
Gibson, Josh, 694
Gibson, Truman K., 42
Gibson v. United States, 1136
Giesler, Jerry, 371
Gifford, Frances, 358
Gilbreth, Frank B., Jr., 128
Gilda (film), 444
Gillespie, Dizzy, 662, 1149
Gillis, Bill, 379
Gilman, Alfred, 174
Gipp, George, 571
Girl Scouts, 816
Girls Club, 816
Glass House, 59
Glass Menagerie, The (Williams), 601, 945, 1064
Glazier-Higgins-Woodward tornadoes, 685
Go West (film), 245
"Gobbledygook," 1205
"God Bless America" (Berlin), 1123
Godfrey, Arthur, 8, **417**; radio programs, 1120

God's Little Acre (Caldwell), 187
Goebbels, Joseph, 663
Goesaert v. Cleary, 1137
Goff, Bruce, 59
Goff, Norris, 1121
Goffman, Erving, 784
Going My Way (film), 3, 253, 832, 1114
Golden Age Clubs, 817
Goldman, Irving, 480
Goldmark, Peter, 531, 933
Goldwyn, Samuel, 4, 1116
Golf, **418-420**, 896, 898, 1097; Ben Hogan, 468-469; Babe Didrikson Zaharias, 1097-1098
Golos, Jacob, 108
Gompers, Samuel, 40
Gone with the Wind (film), 352, 439, 604
Gonorrhea, 867-868, 870-872
Gonzales, Pancho, 898, 937
Good Neighbor Policy, 465, 496, 581, 637, 850
Good War: An Oral History of World War II, The (Terkel), **420**
Goodhue, Lyle, 11
Goodman, Benny, **421**, 661-662, 1149-1150, 1152
Goodman, Louis S., 174
Goodman, Martin, 225
Gordo (comic strip), 228
Gordon, Caroline, 601
Gordon, Ruth, 1111
Göring, Hermann, 714-715
Gosden, Freeman, 44, 1118
Gottlieb, Adolph, 67
Gotto, Ray, 229
Goulding, Edmund, 1115
Gourmet (magazine), 330
Gouzenko, Igor, 220, 385
Governor General's Awards, 1143-1144
Gowan, Elsie Park, 941
Grable, Betty, 331, 352, 360, **422**, 439, 649, 759, 846
Graebner, Willaim, 458
Graham, Billy, **422-423**, 831
Graham, Martha, 52-53, 258, 657
Graham, Otto, 379
Grand Canyon National Park, 673-674
Grand Ole Opry, 832, 1063, 1120
Grand Teton National Park, 543
Grandcamp (ship), 939

and labor, 153, 248, 294-295, 511; wartime, 323-324, 328, 430, 1016, 1034, 1092; and wartime rationing, 120
Influenza, 862
Information Please, 802, 1121
Ink Spots, 1150
Inka Taki Trio, 730
Inner Sanctum (radio), 802, 1121
Insecticides, 11, 447
Inside U.S.A. (Gunther), 127
Instant film, 758
Insurance companies, 780-781
Interagency Archeological Salvage Program (IASP), 55
Inter-American Conference for the Maintenance of Peace, 496
Inter-American Music Bulletin, The, 731
Inter-American Treaty of Reciprocal Assistance, **519-521**, 582
Interdepartmental Committee for Coordination of Foreign and Domestic Military Purchases, 1172
International Bank for Reconstruction and Development. *See* World Bank
International Bill of Human Rights, 997
International Business Machines, 232, **521-523**, 862, 1091
International Children's Emergency Fund, 979-980
International Court of Justice, **523-524**
International League for the Rights of Man, **524-525**
International Military Tribunal at Nuremberg, 113
International Monetary Fund, 6, 137-139, 152, 220, 526; American contributions, 153; and Harry Dexter White, 1059
International Refugee Organization, 822
International Salt v. United States, 1136
International Sanitary Bureau, 1076
International Shoe Co. v. Washington, 1135
International trade, 138, **526-529**. *See also List of Entries by Category*
International Trade Organization, 407
Interstate commerce, 994-995, 1062

Intruder in the Dust (Faulkner), 127, 344, 599, 601
Inuit peoples, 165-166, 168; women, 1070
Inventions, **529-532**; aerosol cans, 11-12; bikini bathing suits, 115; general-purpose credit cards, 283-284; microwave ovens, 473; Slinky, 332. *See also List of Entries by Category under Products & Inventions*
Investment Advisors Act of 1940, 1125
Investment Company Act of 1940, 1125
Iran, 156-157; Tehran Conference, 928-930; United States and, **532-533**
Irene Morgan v. Commonwealth of Virginia, 558
IRO. *See* International Refugee Organization
"Iron Curtain," 1205
"Iron Curtain" speech (Churchill), 202, 220, **533-534**
Irvin, Monte, 695
Irwin, W. Arthur, 188, 616
Islam, Nation of, 668-669
Isle Royale National Park, 674
Isolationism, 6, 241, 277, 391, 405, 430, 502, **534-535**, 616; and art movements, 66; Canadian, 160; and conscientious objection, 240; and Lend-Lease program, 588; and Pearl Harbor, 502; and Truman Doctrine, 965; Arthur Hendrick Vandenberg, 1005-1006; and World War II, 1077
Israel, 145, 535, 556; creation of, **535-537**, 554, 556-557, 829; and Albert Einstein, 305; history of, 265; soccer teams, 886; and United Nations, 535, 557
Italian campaign, **537-539**; and Office of Strategic Services, 719; planning of, 789; prisoners, 776
Italy; and American criminals, 733; and North Atlantic Treaty Organization, 710; and Paris Peace Conference, 737; and Ezra Pound, 602, 771-772; prisoners of war in North America, 778-780
ITO. *See* International Trade Organization

It's a Wonderful Life (film), 178, **539-540**, 649, 902, 1115
It's All True (film), 1057
Iwo Jima, battle of, **540-541**, 625, 682, 703, 1026, 1180

Jack, Homer, 238
Jack Armstrong, the All-American Boy (radio), 802, 1121
Jackson, Mahalia, **542-543**, 832
Jackson, Robert H., 713, 916
Jackson, Shirley, **543**
Jackson Hole National Monument, 501, **543-544**, 675
Jacobs, Jack, 379
Jacobson, Eddie, 535
Jakobson, Roman, 888
Jam Handy Organization, 47
Jamal, Ahmad, 405
James, Harry, 873, 1123, 1148, 1149-1150, 1151
James, Richard, 332
Jameson, Betty, 419
Jamison v. Texas, 1134
Janowski, Werner, 1031
Japan; and Allied prisoners of war, 775; bombing of, 288-289, 325-326, 453-456; Cairo Declaration and, 158; invasion of China, 395-396; colonialism, 265; and Geneva Conventions, 775; occupation of, 527, **544-546**; and Olympics, 726-727; postwar land redistribution, 544; prisoners of war in North America, 778-780; submarines, 911-913; war propaganda, 953
Japanese American Citizens League, 550
Japanese American internment, 70, 113, 492, **546-550**, 572-573, 795; and Federal Bureau of Investigation, 346; and Japanese prisoners of war, 779; and Eleanor Roosevelt, 848; and Supreme Court, 905, 916-917
Japanese assets, freezing of, **395-396**
Japanese Canadian internment, **550-552**, 673, 826, 1070
Jazz, **659-663**
Jeeps, 530, 592, 1034, 1205; origin of name, 876
Jefferson, Thomas, 388, 429, 534
Jefferson Memorial, **552**
Jehovah's Witnesses, 177, 195, 241,

1006; World Health Organization, 1076-1077

United Nations Building, 988

United Nations Educational, Scientific, and Cultural Organization, 888

United Nations International Children's Emergency Fund. *See* UNICEF

United Nations Monetary and Financial Conference. *See* Bretton Woods Conference

United Nations Participation Act of 1945, 1128

United Productions of America, 47

United Public Workers of America v. Mitchell, **990-991**, 1137

United Service Organizations, 123, 261, 482, 664, 803, 815, **991-993**; baseball players, 99; and Bob Hope, 482; women in, 1072

United States, USS, 25, 28, 693

United States Golf Association, 418-420

United States Military Academy, 134, 260

United States Mission for Economic Affairs in London, 1176

United States v. Aluminum Co. of America, **993-994**, 1135

United States v. American Trucking Associations, 1132

United States v. Ballard, 1135

United States v. Carmack, 1136

United States v. Causby, 1136

United States v. Classic, 905, 1133

United States v. Congress of Industrial Organizations, 1137

United States v. Darby Lumber Co., 918, **994-995**, 1133

United States v. Local 807, 468

United States v. Paramount Pictures, et al., **995**, 1137

United States v. South-Eastern Underwriters Association, 1135

United States v. United Mine Workers, **995-996**, 1137

United States v. Univis Lens Co., 1133

United States v. Willow River Power Co., 1135

United Steelworkers of America, 237, 577

United We Stand campaign, 8

UNIVAC computer, 232-234, 435

Universal Declaration of Human Rights, 167, 888, **996-997**; and Eleanor Roosevelt, 849

Universal Studios, 358

University of Chicago, 425-426

Up Front (Mauldin), 127, 599

Uranium, 88, 114, 349, 435, 454, 529, 621-622, 689, 712, 861

Urbanization; Canadian, **997-999**; and race riots, 792-794; U.S., 299, **999-1002**

Uruguay, 582, 730

Uruguay Round, 407-408

Ushijima, Mitsuru, 722

USO. *See* United Service Organizations

Usonian houses (Wright), 59, 1088

V-2 rocket, 136, 529, 656, 839-840

"V-girl," 1207

Vacations, 957-958

Vachon, John, 756

Vail, Theodore Newton, 930

Valdez, Luis, 1102

Vale, Arnold J., 585

Valentine, John K., 1013

Valentine v. Chrestensen, 1133

Vandegrift, Alexander Archer, 1187

Vandenberg, Arthur Hendrick, 772, 964, **1005-1006**

Van Vechten, Carl, 542

Vargas, Alberto, 189

Vaudeville; Abbott and Costello, 1-2; Jack Benny, 106-107; Milton Berle, 938; Eddie Cantor, 1119; Honi Coles, 224; Correll and Gosden, 43; W. C. Fields, 350-351; Bob Hope, 481-482

V-E Day, **1003-1005**

Veeck, Bill, 99

Veksler, Vladimir Iosifovich, 921

Velcro, 532

Vendors Bill of 1948, 1130

Venezuela, 582, 730

Venona Project, 1032

Verdon, Gwen, 258

Versailles Treaty of 1919, 534

Veterans; G.I. Bill, 399-402; postwar employment, 977

Veterans Administration, 445, 493; formation of, 135; and G.I. Bill, 399; Recreation Services division, 816

Veterans' Emergency Housing Act of 1946, 493

Veterans' Preference Act of 1944, 1127

Vice Versa (magazine), 478

Vichy France, 184, 265, 387, 497; and *Casablanca*, 3, 182-183; and Japan, 396; and Québécois, 172; and United States, 392

Victory Farm Volunteers, 19

Victory gardens, 121, 331, 465-466, 1040, 1043

"Victory girls," 871, 876, 1207

Victory Through Air Power (film), 285

Vidor, King, 245

Vietnam, 222, 248

Vietnam War, 266, 276, 535; helicopters, 450; Navy Seabees, 693; prelude to, 266; war crimes, 410

Vigran, Herb, 855

Vining, Charles, 1037

Vinson, Fred M., 6, 872, 920, **1006-1007**

V-J Day, 544, 595, **1003-1005**

Vleck, John H. Van, 955

Voegelin, Eric, 889

Vogue magazine, 339

Voice of America, 852, **1007-1009**, 1040

Volksgrenadier (German army division), 143

Volleyball, 898

Vonnegut, Bernard, 531

Vonnegut, Kurt, Jr., 362

Voting rights, 881-882, **1009-1011**; Canadian, 1070

WAAC. *See* Women's Army Auxiliary Corps

Waesche, Russell R., 1187

Wagner Act of 1935, 152, 511, 925, 980-984

Wahl, Arthur C., 760

Wainwright, Jonathan, 750, 1187

Wake Island, 776

Wake Island (film), 3

Wakely, Jimmy, 244, 1153, 1154

Waksman, Selman Abraham, 49-50, 531

Walcott, Jersey Joe, 131, 479

Walden Two (Skinner), 784, **1012**

Waldorf Statement, 470

Walker, Barbara Jo, 650-651